YBM
토익

2

YBM
실전토익
LC 1000

발행인	허문호
발행처	YBM

문항 개발	백주선, Marilyn Hook
편집	노경미
디자인	김혜경, DOTS
마케팅	정연철, 박천산, 고영노, 김동진, 박찬경, 김윤하

초판발행	2018년 2월 6일
11쇄발행	2022년 9월 1일

신고일자	1964년 3월 28일
신고번호	제 300-1964-3호
주소	서울시 종로구 종로 104
전화	(02) 2000-0515 [구입문의] / (02) 2000-0429 [내용문의]
팩스	(02) 2285-1523
홈페이지	www.ybmbooks.com

ISBN 978-89-17-22913-4

토익 주관사가 만든 고난도 적중실전

YBM 실전토익 LC 1000 2를 발행하며

지난 30여 년간 우리나라에서 토익 시험을 주관하면서 토익 시장을 이끌고, 꾸준히 베스트셀러를 출간해온 YBM에서 〈YBM 실전토익 LC 1000 2〉를 출간하게 되었습니다.

YBM 토익은 이렇게 다릅니다!

YBM의 명성에 자부심을 가지고 개발했습니다!

YBM은 지난 1982년부터 우리나라의 토익 시험을 주관해온 토익 주관사로서, 지난 30여 년간 400여 권의 토익 베스트셀러를 출판해왔습니다. 그 오랜 시간 토익 문제를 분석하고 교재를 출판하면서 쌓아온 전문성과 실력으로 이번에 〈YBM 실전토익 LC 1000 2〉를 선보이게 되었습니다.

출제 예측 시스템을 기반으로 고득점 적중문제 위주로 개발했습니다!

정확한 예측 시스템을 토대로 신토익 최신 경향을 철저히 분석하여 〈YBM 실전토익 LC 1000 2〉를 개발하였습니다. 실제 시험과 가장 유사한 문제 유형을 반영하되, 고난이도 문제를 다수 포함시켜 단기간에 고득점을 달성할 수 있도록 구성했습니다.

ETS 교재를 출간한 노하우를 가지고 개발했습니다!

출제기관 ETS의 토익 교재를 독점 출간하는 YBM은 그동안 쌓아온 노하우를 바탕으로 〈YBM 실전토익 LC 1000 2〉를 개발하였습니다. 본 책에 실린 1000개의 문항은 출제자의 의도를 정확히 반영하였기 때문에 타사의 어떤 토익 교재와도 비교할 수 없는 퀄리티를 자랑합니다.

YBM의 모든 노하우가 집대성된 〈YBM 실전토익 LC 1000 2〉는 최단 시간에 최고의 점수를 수험자 여러분께 약속 드립니다.

YBM 토익연구소

토익의 구성과 수험 정보

**TOEIC은
어떤 시험인가요?**

Test of English for International Communication(국제적 의사소통을 위한 영어 시험)의 약자로서, 영어가 모국어가 아닌 사람들이 일상생활 또는 비즈니스 현장에서 꼭 필요한 실용적 영어 구사 능력을 갖추었는가를 평가하는 시험이다.

시험 구성

구성	Part	내용		문항수	시간	배점
듣기 (L/C)	1	사진 묘사		6	45분	495점
	2	질의 & 응답		25		
	3	짧은 대화		39		
	4	짧은 담화		30		
읽기 (R/C)	5	단문 빈칸 채우기(문법/어휘)		30	75분	495점
	6	장문 빈칸 채우기		16		
	7	독해	단일 지문	29		
			이중 지문	10		
			삼중 지문	15		
Total		**7 Parts**		**200문항**	**120분**	**990점**

**TOEIC 접수는
어떻게 하나요?**

TOEIC 접수는 한국 토익 위원회 사이트(www.toeic.co.kr)에서 온라인 상으로만 접수가 가능하다. 사이트에서 매월 자세한 접수 일정과 시험 일정 등의 구체적 정보 확인이 가능하니, 미리 일정을 확인하여 접수하도록 한다.

시험장에 반드시 가져가야 할 준비물은요?

신분증 규정 신분증만 가능
(주민등록증, 운전면허증, 기간 만료 전의 여권, 공무원증 등)

필기구 연필, 지우개 (볼펜이나 사인펜은 사용 금지)

시험은 어떻게 진행되나요?

09:20	입실 (09:50 이후는 입실 불가)
09:30 — 09:45	답안지 작성에 관한 오리엔테이션
09:45 — 09:50	휴식
09:50 — 10:05	신분증 확인
10:05 — 10:10	문제지 배부 및 파본 확인
10:10 — 10:55	듣기 평가 (Listening Test)
10:55 — 12:10	독해 평가 (Reading Test)

TOEIC 성적 확인은 어떻게 하죠?

시험일로부터 19일 후, 오후 3시부터 인터넷과 ARS(060-800-0515)로 성적을 확인할 수 있다. TOEIC 성적표는 우편이나 온라인으로 발급 받을 수 있다(시험 접수시, 양자 택일). 우편으로 발급 받을 경우는 성적 발표 후 대략 일주일이 소요되며, 온라인 발급을 선택하면 유효기간 내에 홈페이지에서 본인이 직접 1회에 한해 무료 출력할 수 있다. TOEIC 성적은 시험일로부터 2년간 유효하다.

TOEIC은 몇 점 만점인가요?

TOEIC 점수는 듣기 영역(LC) 점수, 읽기 영역(RC) 점수, 그리고 이 두 영역을 합계한 전체 점수 세 부분으로 구성된다. 각 부분의 점수는 5점 단위이며, 5점에서 495점에 걸쳐 주어지고, 전체 점수는 10점에서 990점까지이며, 만점은 990점이다. TOEIC 성적은 각 문제 유형의 난이도에 따른 점수 환산표에 의해 결정된다.

신토익 경향 분석

PART1 사진 묘사 Photographs 총 6문제

PART 1 최신 출제 경향

- 사람 또는 사물 중심 사진 **33**%
- 1인 등장 사진 **33**%
- 사물/배경 사진 **17**%
- 2인 이상 등장 사진 **17**%

1인 등장 사진
주어는 He/She, A man/woman, One of the men/women 등이며 주로 앞부분에 나온다.

2인 이상 등장 사진
주어는 They, Some men/women/people 등이며 주로 중간 부분에 나온다.

사물/배경 사진
주어는 A car, some chairs 등이며 주로 뒷부분에 나온다.

사람 또는 사물 중심 사진
주어가 일부는 사람, 일부는 사물이며 주로 뒷부분에 나온다.

정답의 시제와 태

- 기타 **10**%
- 단순 현재 수동태 **25**%
- 현재 진행 능동태 **65**%

현재 진행 능동태
〈is/are + 현재분사〉 형태이며 주로 사람이 주어이다.

단순 현재 수동태
〈is/are + 과거분사〉 형태이며 주로 사물이 주어이다.

기타
〈is/are + being + 과거분사〉 형태의 현재 진행 수동태, 〈has/have + been + 과거 분사〉 형태의 현재 완료 수동태, '타동사 + 목적어' 형태의 단순 현재 능동태, There is/are와 같은 단순 현재도 나온다.

PART 2 질의 & 응답 Question-Response

총 25문제

평서문
질문이 아니라 객관적인 사실이나 화자의 의견
등을 나타내는 문장이다.

명령문
동사원형이나 Please 등으로 시작한다.

의문사 의문문
각 의문사마다 1~2개씩 나온다. 의문사가 단독
으로 나오기도 하지만 What time ~?, How
long ~?, Which room ~? 등에서처럼 다른
명사나 형용사와 같이 나오기도 한다.

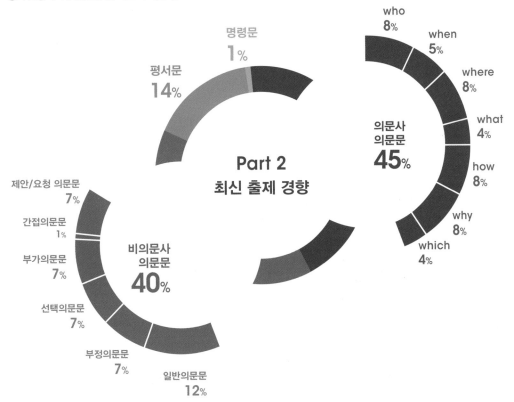

비의문사 의문문

일반(Yes/No) 의문문 적게 나올 때는 한두 개, 많이 나올 때는 서너 개씩 나오는 편이다.

부정의문문 Don't you ~?, Isn't he ~? 등으로 시작하는 문장이며 일반 긍정 의문문보다는 약간 더 적게 나온다.

선택의문문 A or B 형태로 나오며 A와 B의 형태가 단어, 구, 절일 수 있다. 구나 절일 경우 문장이 길어져서 어려워진다.

부가의문문 ~ don't you?, ~ isn't he? 등으로 끝나는 문장이며, 일반 부정 의문문과 비슷하다고 볼 수 있다.

간접의문문 의문사가 문장 처음 부분이 아니라 문장 중간에 들어 있다.

제안/요청 의문문 정보를 얻기보다는 상대방의 도움이나 동의 등을 얻기 위한 목적이 일반적이다.

PART 3 짧은 대화 Short Conversations

총 13대화문 39문제 (지문당 3문제)

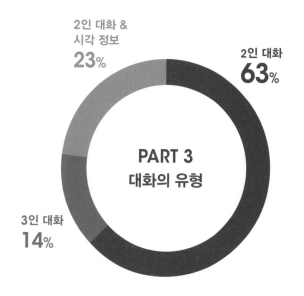

PART 3
대화의 유형

2인 대화 & 시각 정보
23%

2인 대화
63%

3인 대화
14%

- 3인 대화의 경우 남자 화자 두 명과 여자 화자 한 명 또는 남자 화자 한 명과 여자 화자 두 명이 나온다. 따라서 문제에서는 2인 대화에서와 달리 the man 이나 the woman이 아니라 the men이나 the women 또는 특정한 이름이 언급될 수 있다.

- 대화 & 시각 정보는 항상 파트의 뒷부분에 나온다.

- 시각 정보의 유형으로 chart, map, floor plan, schedule, table, weather forecast, directory, list, invoice, receipt, sign, packing slip 등 다양한 자료가 골고루 나온다.

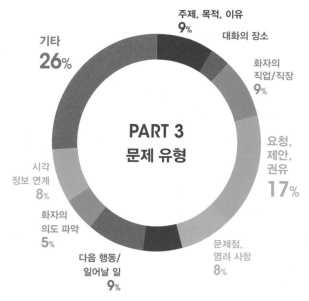

PART 3
문제 유형

주제, 목적, 이유
9%

대화의 장소

화자의 직업/직장
9%

요청, 제안, 권유
17%

기타
26%

시각 정보 연계
8%

화자의 의도 파악
5%

다음 행동/ 일어날 일
9%

문제점, 염려 사항
8%

- 주제, 목적, 이유, 대화의 장소, 화자의 직업/직장 등과 관련된 문제는 주로 대화의 첫 번째 문제로 나오며 다음 행동/일어날 일 등과 관련된 문제는 주로 대화의 세 번째 문제로 나온다.

- 화자의 의도 파악 문제는 주로 2인 대화에 나오지만, 가끔 3인 대화에 나오기도 한다. 시각 정보 연계 대화에는 나오지 않고 있다.

- Part 3 안에서 화자의 의도 파악 문제는 2개 나오고 시각 정보 연계 문제는 3개 나온다.

PART 4 짧은 담화 Short Talks

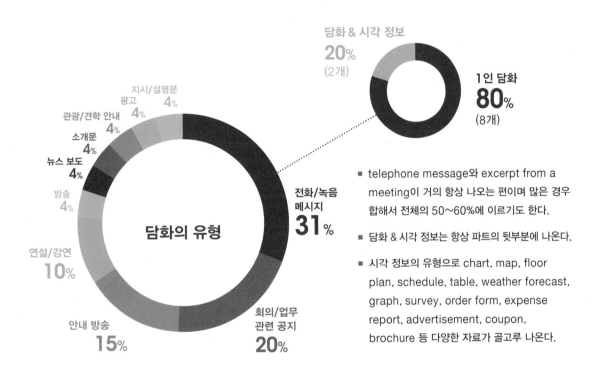

담화의 유형

- 담화 & 시각 정보 **20%** (2개)
- 1인 담화 **80%** (8개)
- 전화/녹음 메시지 **31%**
- 회의/업무 관련 공지 **20%**
- 안내 방송 **15%**
- 연설/강연 **10%**
- 방송 **4%**
- 뉴스 보도 **4%**
- 소개문 **4%**
- 관광/견학 안내 **4%**
- 광고 **4%**
- 지시/설명문 **4%**

- telephone message와 excerpt from a meeting이 거의 항상 나오는 편이며 많은 경우 합해서 전체의 50~60%에 이르기도 한다.

- 담화 & 시각 정보는 항상 파트의 뒷부분에 나온다.

- 시각 정보의 유형으로 chart, map, floor plan, schedule, table, weather forecast, graph, survey, order form, expense report, advertisement, coupon, brochure 등 다양한 자료가 골고루 나온다.

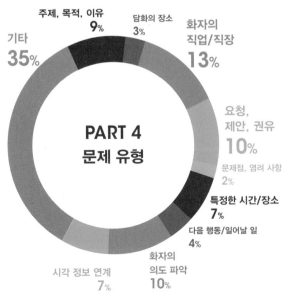

PART 4 문제 유형

- 주제, 목적, 이유 **9%**
- 담화의 장소 **3%**
- 화자의 직업/직장 **13%**
- 요청, 제안, 권유 **10%**
- 문제점, 염려 사항 **2%**
- 특정한 시간/장소 **7%**
- 다음 행동/일어날 일 **4%**
- 화자의 의도 파악 **10%**
- 시각 정보 연계 **7%**
- 기타 **35%**

- 문제 유형은 기본적으로 Part 3과 거의 비슷하다.

- 주제, 목적, 이유, 담화의 장소, 화자의 직업/직장 등과 관련된 문제는 주로 담화의 첫 번째 문제로 나오며 다음 행동/일어날 일 등과 관련된 문제는 주로 담화의 세 번째 문제로 나온다.

- Part 4 안에서 화자의 의도 파악 문제는 3개 나오고 시각 정보 연계 문제는 2개 나온다.

PART 5 단문 빈칸 채우기 Incomplete Sentences

총 30문제

문법 문제

시제와 대명사와 관련된 문법 문제가 2개씩, 한정사와 분사와 관련된 문법 문제가 1개씩 나온다. 시제 문제의 경우 능동태/수동태나 수의 일치와 연계되기도 한다. 그 밖에 한정사, 능동태/수동태, 부정사, 동명사 등과 관련된 문법 문제가 나온다.

어휘 문제

동사, 명사, 형용사, 부사와 관련된 어휘 문제가 각각 2~3개씩 골고루 나온다. 전치사 어휘 문제는 3개씩 꾸준히 나오지만, 접속사나 어구와 관련된 어휘 문제는 나오지 않을 때도 있고 3개가 나올 때도 있다.

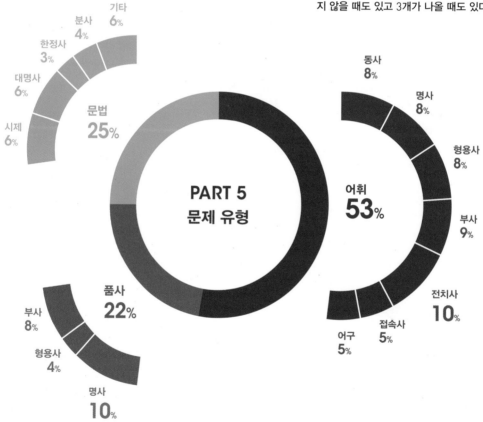

품사 문제

명사와 부사와 관련된 품사 문제가 2~3개씩 나오며, 형용사와 관련된 품사 문제가 상대적으로 적은 편이다.

PART 6 장문 빈칸 채우기 Text Completion

한 지문에 4문제가 나오며 평균적으로 어휘 문제가 2개, 품사나 문법 문제가 1개, 문맥에 맞는 문장 고르기 문제가 1개 들어간다. 문맥에 맞는 문장 고르기 문제를 제외하면 문제 유형은 기본적으로 파트 5와 거의 비슷하다.

어휘 문제

동사, 명사, 부사, 어구와 관련된 어휘 문제는 매번 1~2개씩 나온다. 부사 어휘 문제의 경우 therefore(그러므로)나 however(하지만)처럼 문맥의 흐름을 자연스럽게 연결해 주는 부사가 자주 나온다.

문맥에 맞는 문장 고르기

문맥에 맞는 문장 고르기 문제는 지문당 한 문제씩 나오는데, 나오는 위치의 확률은 4문제 중 두 번째 문제, 세 번째 문제, 네 번째 문제, 첫 번째 문제 순으로 높다.

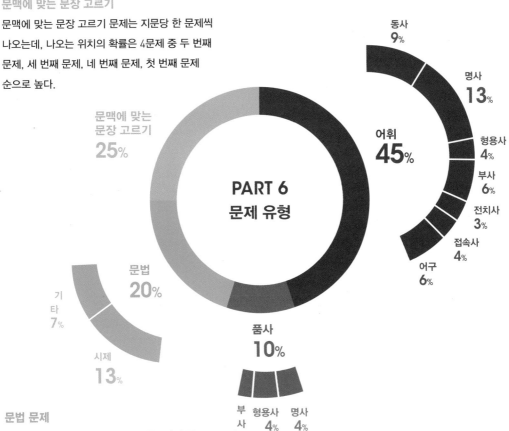

문법 문제

문맥의 흐름과 밀접하게 관련이 있는 시제 문제가 2개 정도 나오며, 능동태/수동태나 수의 일치와 연계되기도 한다. 그 밖에 대명사, 능동태/수동태, 부정사, 접속사/전치사 등과 관련된 문법 문제가 나온다.

품사 문제

명사나 형용사 문제가 부사 문제보다 좀 더 자주 나온다.

PART 7 독해 Reading Comprehension

총 15지문 54문제 (지문당 2~5문제)

지문 유형	지문당 문제 수	지문 개수	비중 %
단일 지문	2문항	4개	약 15%
	3문항	3개	약 16%
	4문항	3개	약 22%
이중 지문	5문항	2개	약 19%
삼중 지문	5문항	3개	약 28%

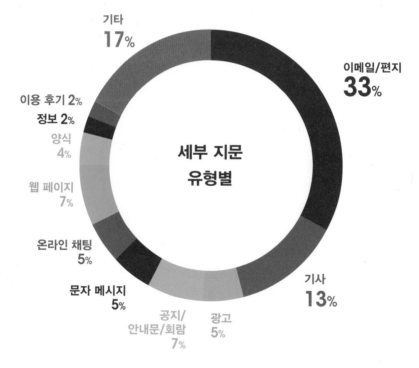

기타 **17**%
이용 후기 **2**%
정보 **2**%
양식 **4**%
웹 페이지 **7**%
온라인 채팅 **5**%
문자 메시지 **5**%
공지/안내문/회람 **7**%
광고 **5**%

세부 지문 유형별

이메일/편지 **33**%
기사 **13**%

- 이메일/편지, 기사 유형 지문은 거의 항상 나오는 편이며 많은 경우 합해서 전체의 50~60%에 이르기도 한다.

- 기타 지문 유형으로 agenda, brochure, comment card, coupon, flyer, instructions, invitation, invoice, list, menu, page from a catalog, policy statement, report, schedule, survey, voucher 등 다양한 자료가 골고루 나온다.

(이중 지문과 삼중 지문 속의 지문들을 모두 낱개로 계산함 – 총 23지문)

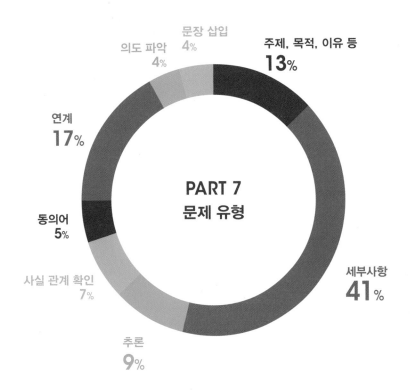

의도 파악
4%

문장 삽입
4%

주제, 목적, 이유 등
13%

연계
17%

동의어
5%

사실 관계 확인
7%

추론
9%

세부사항
41%

PART 7
문제 유형

■ 동의어 문제는 주로 이중 지문이나 삼중 지문에 나온다.

■ 연계 문제는 일반적으로 이중 지문에서 한 문제, 삼중 지문에서 두 문제가 나온다.

■ 의도 파악 문제는 문자 메시지(text-message chain)나 온라인 채팅(online chat discussion) 지문에서 출제되며 두 문제가 나온다.

■ 문장 삽입 문제는 주로 기사, 이메일, 편지, 회람 지문에서 출제되며 두 문제가 나온다.

점수 환산표

LISTENING Raw Score (맞은 개수)	LISTENING Scaled Score (환산 점수)	READING Raw Score (맞은 개수)	READING Scaled Score (환산 점수)
96–100	480–495	96–100	460–495
91–95	435–490	91–95	410–475
86–90	395–450	86–90	380–430
81–85	355–415	81–85	355–400
76–80	325–375	76–80	325–375
71–75	295–340	71–75	295–345
66–70	265–315	66–70	265–315
61–65	240–285	61–65	235–285
56–60	215–260	56–60	205–255
51–55	190–235	51–55	175–225
46–50	160–210	46–50	150–195
41–45	135–180	41–45	120–170
36–40	110–155	36–40	100–140
31–35	85–130	31–35	75–120
26–30	70–105	26–30	55–100
21–25	50–90	21–25	40–80
16–20	35–70	16–20	30–65
11–15	20–55	11–15	20–50
6–10	15–40	6–10	15–35
1–5	5–20	1–5	5–20
0	5	0	5

* 이 환산표는 본 교재에 수록된 Test용으로 개발된 것이다. 이 표를 사용하여 자신의 실제 점수를 환산 점수로 전환하도록 한다. 즉, 예를 들어 Listening Test의 실제 정답 수가 61~65개이면 환산 점수는 240점에서 285점 사이가 된다. 여기서 실제 정답 수가 61개이면 환산 점수가 240점이고, 65개이면 환산 점수가 285점임을 의미하는 것은 아니다. 본 책의 Test를 위해 작성된 이 점수 환산표가 자신의 영어 실력이 어느 정도인지 대략적으로 파악하는 데 도움이 되긴 하지만, 이 표가 실제 TOEIC 성적 산출에 그대로 사용된 적은 없다는 사실을 밝혀 둔다.

CONTENTS

TEST 1

LISTENING TEST

In the Listening test, you will be asked to demonstrate how well you understand spoken English. The entire Listening test will last approximately 45 minutes. There are four parts, and directions are given for each part. You must mark your answers on the separate answer sheet. Do not write your answers in your test book.

PART 1

Directions: For each question in this part, you will hear four statements about a picture in your test book. When you hear the statements, you must select the one statement that best describes what you see in the picture. Then find the number of the question on your answer sheet and mark your answer. The statements will not be printed in your test book and will be spoken only one time.

Statement (C), "They're sitting at a table," is the best description of the picture, so you should select answer (C) and mark it on your answer sheet.

1.

2.

GO ON TO THE NEXT PAGE →

3.

4.

5.

6.

GO ON TO THE NEXT PAGE ➔

Directions: You will hear a question or statement and three responses spoken in English. They will not be printed in your test book and will be spoken only one time. Select the best response to the question or statement and mark the letter (A), (B), or (C) on your answer sheet.

7. Mark your answer on your answer sheet.

8. Mark your answer on your answer sheet.

9. Mark your answer on your answer sheet.

10. Mark your answer on your answer sheet.

11. Mark your answer on your answer sheet.

12. Mark your answer on your answer sheet.

13. Mark your answer on your answer sheet.

14. Mark your answer on your answer sheet.

15. Mark your answer on your answer sheet.

16. Mark your answer on your answer sheet.

17. Mark your answer on your answer sheet.

18. Mark your answer on your answer sheet.

19. Mark your answer on your answer sheet.

20. Mark your answer on your answer sheet.

21. Mark your answer on your answer sheet.

22. Mark your answer on your answer sheet.

23. Mark your answer on your answer sheet.

24. Mark your answer on your answer sheet.

25. Mark your answer on your answer sheet.

26. Mark your answer on your answer sheet.

27. Mark your answer on your answer sheet.

28. Mark your answer on your answer sheet.

29. Mark your answer on your answer sheet.

30. Mark your answer on your answer sheet.

31. Mark your answer on your answer sheet.

PART 3

Directions: You will hear some conversations between two or more people. You will be asked to answer three questions about what the speakers say in each conversation. Select the best response to each question and mark the letter (A), (B), (C), or (D) on your answer sheet. The conversations will not be printed in your test book and will be spoken only one time.

32. What is the purpose of the man's call?

   (A) To inquire about a transportation service
   (B) To change a flight from Boston
   (C) To complain about a damaged bag
   (D) To follow up on a missing item

33. What does the woman ask about?

   (A) Where the man is staying
   (B) When the man will arrive
   (C) What form the man completed
   (D) Who originally helped the man

34. What does the woman remind the man to do?

   (A) Read a sign carefully
   (B) Provide a tracking number
   (C) Call the woman this afternoon
   (D) Prepare a form of identification

35. What is the purpose of the woman's call?

   (A) To make a complaint
   (B) To get some directions
   (C) To inquire about a bill
   (D) To book a hotel room

36. What does the man tell the woman about?

   (A) Inclement weather conditions
   (B) An entrance fee
   (C) A closing time
   (D) New company policies

37. What does the man suggest doing?

   (A) Walking to a site
   (B) Taking the subway
   (C) Riding a bus
   (D) Using a taxi

38. What is the purpose of the woman's call?

   (A) To change an appointment
   (B) To apply for a job opening
   (C) To inquire about business hours
   (D) To request a complimentary service

39. Why does the woman say she does not want to come on Thursday?

   (A) She has to attend a business meeting.
   (B) She prefers a haircut from a certain employee.
   (C) She plans to take a flight that day.
   (D) She lives too far from the business.

40. What does the man offer to do?

   (A) Call the woman if a customer cancels
   (B) Ask a coworker to work overtime
   (C) Print a copy of a document
   (D) Give directions to another branch

41. Where is the conversation most likely taking place?

   (A) At a sporting goods store
   (B) At an office
   (C) At a fitness facility
   (D) At a factory

42. According to the man, what does a red sticker on an item mean?

   (A) It is currently on sale.
   (B) It has been booked.
   (C) It is not working.
   (D) It is for advanced users.

43. What did the business do last month?

   (A) Received an award
   (B) Hired more workers
   (C) Moved to a better location
   (D) Conducted a survey

GO ON TO THE NEXT PAGE

44. What are the speakers discussing?

    (A) A customer complaint
    (B) A grand opening
    (C) A staff change
    (D) A restaurant inspection

45. What problem does the man mention?

    (A) A dish is not selling well.
    (B) A shipment has not arrived.
    (C) An employee is inexperienced.
    (D) An advertisement contained an error.

46. What does the man offer to do?

    (A) Proofread a menu
    (B) Contact a print shop
    (C) Call Chef Mazzi
    (D) Create a new design

47. Who most likely is the man?

    (A) A construction worker
    (B) A real estate agent
    (C) An interior designer
    (D) A homeowner

48. Why does the woman want to make some changes?

    (A) To retain employees
    (B) To follow a regulation
    (C) To save time
    (D) To increase profits

49. What is the man concerned about?

    (A) Opening an account
    (B) Upsetting a customer
    (C) Exceeding a budget
    (D) Missing a deadline

50. What kind of event are the speakers planning?

    (A) An academic lecture
    (B) A technology course
    (C) A product launch
    (D) A job fair

51. What have Oakdale Center employees been asked to do?

    (A) Confirm a booking date
    (B) Decorate a venue
    (C) Put up some signs
    (D) Keep one entrance locked

52. What does the woman say she will check?

    (A) The expected number of attendees
    (B) The ingredients in some refreshments
    (C) The cost of renting a facility
    (D) The size of some tables

53. What does the man mean when he says, "they all look the same"?

    (A) He needs help making a decision.
    (B) He is disappointed with the store's options.
    (C) He wants his devices to be the same color.
    (D) He thinks the brand does not matter.

54. What does the woman ask the man about?

    (A) The budget he has prepared for a purchase
    (B) The brands of his laptop and smartphone
    (C) The size of the area he wants to cover
    (D) The number of machines that will be used

55. What does the woman suggest about the Conway-HX?

    (A) It is not enough for the man's needs.
    (B) It is larger than the other models.
    (C) It is currently offered at a discount.
    (D) It is the most popular item.

56. Why was the woman absent last week?

    (A) She visited another branch.
    (B) She had an illness.
    (C) She went on a business trip.
    (D) She was taking a vacation.

57. Why does the man say, "Arthur Hammond is on your team"?

    (A) To thank the woman for training a coworker
    (B) To correct an error in a document sent to the woman
    (C) To explain that he cannot answer the woman's questions
    (D) To reassure the woman about an assignment

58. What does the woman suggest about Mr. Hammond?

    (A) He has a lot of experience.
    (B) He used to work at Kenner International.
    (C) He is behind schedule.
    (D) He prefers to work alone.

59. What problem are the speakers discussing?

    (A) The restaurant lacks storage space.
    (B) A delivery contained the wrong items.
    (C) Some lighting in the kitchen is not working.
    (D) The temperature of an area is too high.

60. What does the woman think the business should do?

    (A) Take out a small loan
    (B) Purchase some new equipment
    (C) Hire a repairperson
    (D) Undergo another inspection

61. What will be sent to the woman?

    (A) A shipping address
    (B) A pricing estimate
    (C) Some contact details
    (D) An application form

Aisle 1	Cleaning Supplies
Aisle 2	Meats and Fish
Aisle 3	Packaged Snacks
Aisle 4	Teas and Coffees

62. According to the man, what will happen at the store next week?

    (A) A clearance sale will take place.
    (B) An orientation session will be given.
    (C) Some new equipment will be installed.
    (D) Some safety inspectors will visit.

63. What does the woman offer to do?

    (A) Create a large sign
    (B) Update a Web site
    (C) Work an additional shift
    (D) Check on inventory levels

64. Look at the graphic. Which aisle will the man most likely go to?

    (A) Aisle 1
    (B) Aisle 2
    (C) Aisle 3
    (D) Aisle 4

GO ON TO THE NEXT PAGE

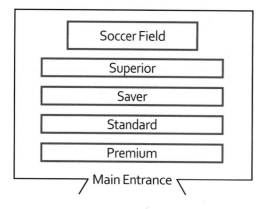

Rainbow Printing	
Customer: Marion Kimball	
Item	**Quantity**
Banner (4'X8')	15
Business card 100-count pack	25
Photo calendar	150
Trifold brochure	350

65. How did the man find out about the event?

(A) By seeing a poster
(B) By searching online
(C) By reading a newspaper
(D) By talking to a friend

66. Look at the graphic. In which section does the man want to reserve a space?

(A) Premium
(B) Standard
(C) Saver
(D) Superior

67. What does the woman tell the man about?

(A) A restriction on vehicles
(B) A parking fee
(C) A registration process
(D) A food regulation

68. What is the purpose of the man's call?

(A) To apologize for an error
(B) To request a payment
(C) To confirm a mailing address
(D) To promote a service

69. Look at the graphic. Which quantity is now incorrect?

(A) 15
(B) 25
(C) 150
(D) 350

70. What does the man say he will do?

(A) Give the woman store credit
(B) Send a discount coupon
(C) Report a problem to his manager
(D) Waive a delivery fee

PART 4

Directions: You will hear some talks given by a single speaker. You will be asked to answer three questions about what the speaker says in each talk. Select the best response to each question and mark the letter (A), (B), (C), or (D) on your answer sheet. The talks will not be printed in your test book and will be spoken only one time.

71. Who most likely are the listeners?

(A) Sales team members
(B) Product developers
(C) Company stockholders
(D) Solar panel technicians

72. What is the speaker pleased about?

(A) A contract was approved.
(B) A goal was exceeded.
(C) A product won an award.
(D) A deadline was met.

73. Why should the listeners e-mail the speaker?

(A) To confirm some figures
(B) To schedule a business trip
(C) To sign up for a group
(D) To express a preference

74. What is being advertised?

(A) An interior design studio
(B) A landscaping business
(C) A transportation company
(D) A flower shop

75. Who most likely is Spencer Shaw?

(A) An interior designer
(B) A maintenance worker
(C) A magazine journalist
(D) A television host

76. According to the speaker, what can listeners do on the Web site?

(A) View an updated price list
(B) Read customer comments
(C) Register for a free consultation
(D) Browse pictures of past projects

77. According to the speaker, what is different about the sale this year?

(A) It will be advertised in the newspaper.
(B) It will include donations from the public.
(C) It will last for more days than before.
(D) It will be held earlier in the year.

78. What are the listeners asked to do?

(A) Help set up an area
(B) Sign up for a shift
(C) Recruit some volunteers
(D) Make a financial donation

79. What does the speaker mention about the Willow Room?

(A) It is in need of some repairs.
(B) It will be used to store extra books.
(C) It is the largest room in the library.
(D) It will be the site of the next meeting.

80. What kind of business is Pyramid?

(A) A transportation company
(B) A vacation resort
(C) An accounting firm
(D) A catering service

81. What information does the speaker ask for?

(A) The departure time
(B) The billing address
(C) The number of people
(D) The event date

82. What does the speaker want the listener to do?

(A) Provide some feedback about a service
(B) Send some information by e-mail
(C) Call him at his office tomorrow
(D) Leave a message with his coworker

GO ON TO THE NEXT PAGE

83. What kind of products does Purnex Ltd. make?

(A) Beauty products
(B) Art supplies
(C) Baked goods
(D) Work uniforms

84. Why most likely does the speaker say, "the buildings are spread over a large area"?

(A) To highlight a company's business expansion
(B) To warn that a tour has a lot of walking
(C) To give a reason for starting a tour late
(D) To apologize for the large size of a tour group

85. What will the listeners most likely see next?

(A) A gift shop
(B) A production area
(C) A museum exhibit
(D) A research laboratory

86. What has Sanjay Batta recently done?

(A) Founded a university
(B) Developed a medicine
(C) Moved to another city
(D) Published a book

87. According to the speaker, what will happen in Rio de Janeiro in June?

(A) An academic lecture will be given.
(B) A medical clinic will be opened.
(C) An award will be presented.
(D) A fundraiser will be hosted.

88. What are listeners encouraged to do?

(A) Enter a prize drawing
(B) Call the radio station
(C) E-mail their questions
(D) Attend an event

89. What does the speaker tell listeners about?

(A) A training workshop
(B) An equipment installation
(C) A safety check
(D) A health examination

90. What does the speaker suggest when she says, "we don't set the schedule"?

(A) Employees can take some time off.
(B) She thinks a plan is inconvenient.
(C) Employees can work anytime.
(D) She does not mind changing a deadline.

91. According to the speaker, how can listeners get more information?

(A) By calling the speaker
(B) By visiting a Web site
(C) By attending another meeting
(D) By reading some signs

92. What will some listeners do next week?

(A) Learn how to close the store
(B) Unpack some new merchandise
(C) Give demonstrations to customers
(D) Make a list of the store's goods

93. What does the speaker imply when he says, "It took three days"?

(A) He was disappointed with a delayed shipment.
(B) He thinks a deadline for an assignment should be extended.
(C) He was impressed with how quickly a project was done.
(D) He wants to schedule another meeting later.

94. Why should listeners visit the speaker's office?

(A) To report missing items
(B) To make a suggestion
(C) To sign up for a task
(D) To check their hourly wage

Group Activities	
Safety review	Takeshi
Production floor tour	Gloria
Live demonstration	Ji-Hee
Question-and-answer session	William

Proposed Project	Projected Cost
Web site upgrades	$15,000
Landscaping changes	$25,000
Visitor center renovation	$30,000
Security upgrades	$60,000

95. What kind of goods does the speaker's company produce?

(A) Furniture
(B) Clothing
(C) Electronics
(D) Food

96. Look at the graphic. Whose activity will be longer than all the other parts?

(A) Takeshi's
(B) Gloria's
(C) Ji-Hee's
(D) William's

97. What does the speaker remind listeners to do?

(A) Select a group
(B) Avoid taking photos
(C) Stay together
(D) Carry an ID card

98. Where most likely does the speaker work?

(A) At a museum
(B) At a music venue
(C) At a hospital
(D) At a government office

99. Look at the graphic. About how much money was collected during the fundraiser?

(A) $15,000
(B) $25,000
(C) $30,000
(D) $60,000

100. What will the listeners do next?

(A) Watch a performance
(B) View some images
(C) Hear an introduction
(D) Review a document

This is the end of the Listening test.

TEST 2

LISTENING TEST

In the Listening test, you will be asked to demonstrate how well you understand spoken English. The entire Listening test will last approximately 45 minutes. There are four parts, and directions are given for each part. You must mark your answers on the separate answer sheet. Do not write your answers in your test book.

PART 1

Directions: For each question in this part, you will hear four statements about a picture in your test book. When you hear the statements, you must select the one statement that best describes what you see in the picture. Then find the number of the question on your answer sheet and mark your answer. The statements will not be printed in your test book and will be spoken only one time.

Statement (C), "They're sitting at a table," is the best description of the picture, so you should select answer (C) and mark it on your answer sheet.

1.

2.

GO ON TO THE NEXT PAGE

3.

4.

5.

6.

GO ON TO THE NEXT PAGE ➡

PART 2

Directions: You will hear a question or statement and three responses spoken in English. They will not be printed in your test book and will be spoken only one time. Select the best response to the question or statement and mark the letter (A), (B), or (C) on your answer sheet.

7. Mark your answer on your answer sheet.

8. Mark your answer on your answer sheet.

9. Mark your answer on your answer sheet.

10. Mark your answer on your answer sheet.

11. Mark your answer on your answer sheet.

12. Mark your answer on your answer sheet.

13. Mark your answer on your answer sheet.

14. Mark your answer on your answer sheet.

15. Mark your answer on your answer sheet.

16. Mark your answer on your answer sheet.

17. Mark your answer on your answer sheet.

18. Mark your answer on your answer sheet.

19. Mark your answer on your answer sheet.

20. Mark your answer on your answer sheet.

21. Mark your answer on your answer sheet.

22. Mark your answer on your answer sheet.

23. Mark your answer on your answer sheet.

24. Mark your answer on your answer sheet.

25. Mark your answer on your answer sheet.

26. Mark your answer on your answer sheet.

27. Mark your answer on your answer sheet.

28. Mark your answer on your answer sheet.

29. Mark your answer on your answer sheet.

30. Mark your answer on your answer sheet.

31. Mark your answer on your answer sheet.

PART 3

Directions: You will hear some conversations between two or more people. You will be asked to answer three questions about what the speakers say in each conversation. Select the best response to each question and mark the letter (A), (B), (C), or (D) on your answer sheet. The conversations will not be printed in your test book and will be spoken only one time.

32. Where do the speakers work?

(A) At an event planning agency
(B) At a marketing firm
(C) At a magazine publisher
(D) At a cooking equipment store

33. Who most likely is Ms. Yoon?

(A) A potential supplier
(B) A real estate agent
(C) A celebrity chef
(D) A Web site designer

34. What does the man say he will do in the afternoon?

(A) Edit a digital video
(B) Assemble a list
(C) Install a computer
(D) Lead a facility tour

35. What does the woman hope to do?

(A) Modify an online order
(B) Return a defective product
(C) Obtain a store credit card
(D) Cancel a loyalty club membership

36. What information does the man ask for?

(A) An address
(B) An error code
(C) The spelling of a name
(D) The date of a transaction

37. What does the man say the woman must do?

(A) Visit a store branch
(B) Pack an item for shipping
(C) Open a Web page
(D) Keep an invoice

38. Why does the man talk to the woman?

(A) To offer help with a development process
(B) To inform her of a financial difficulty
(C) To arrange an educational opportunity
(D) To remind her about an upcoming merger

39. What does the woman recommend doing?

(A) Hiring additional part-time staff
(B) Raising some quality standards
(C) Signing up for evening classes
(D) Showing product-testing methods

40. What does the man ask the woman to do?

(A) Clean a work area
(B) Speak with a team manager
(C) Update a software program
(D) Photocopy a report

41. What does the man want to have painted?

(A) A delivery vehicle
(B) Some store windows
(C) A warehouse floor
(D) Some furniture

42. What kind of company does the man operate?

(A) A clothing shop
(B) A catering service
(C) A laundry-cleaning business
(D) A plumbing company

43. What does the woman suggest the man do?

(A) Delay a promotional sale
(B) View some sample designs
(C) Load some packages into a van
(D) Choose a type of paint

GO ON TO THE NEXT PAGE

44. Where does the conversation most likely take place?

(A) At a nature park
(B) At an art gallery
(C) At a plant nursery
(D) At a toy store

45. What does the man say he will do tomorrow?

(A) Give a gift
(B) Decorate an office
(C) Move to a new house
(D) Go on a picnic

46. According to the man, what is most important about a product?

(A) How beautiful it is
(B) How inexpensive it is
(C) How easy it will be to maintain
(D) How soon it will be available

---

47. What is the purpose of the man's visit?

(A) To meet a client for lunch
(B) To deliver some documents
(C) To conduct a site inspection
(D) To install some equipment

48. What does the man express frustration with?

(A) A mobile app
(B) A carrying case
(C) A machine part
(D) A supervisor's instructions

49. What does the woman imply when she says, "it's really noticeable"?

(A) She is proud of a project's results.
(B) The man cannot leave an item in the lobby.
(C) A problem must be addressed quickly.
(D) A location is not difficult to find.

---

50. What is the conversation mainly about?

(A) Improving laboratory conditions
(B) Repeating an experiment
(C) Selecting student interns
(D) Publishing a scientific paper

51. What does the woman want to change?

(A) A time frame
(B) The focus of a text
(C) A method of analysis
(D) The size of a budget

52. What does the man say he will do?

(A) Buy a measuring device
(B) Register for a conference
(C) Edit some passages
(D) Schedule a meeting

---

53. What will happen in June?

(A) A recycling program will be introduced.
(B) A parking area will be upgraded.
(C) A job recruitment campaign will begin.
(D) A series of staff workshops will be held.

54. What does the woman suggest doing?

(A) Spending more money on office electronics
(B) Providing staff discounts on goods
(C) Using a new transportation link
(D) Allowing staff to work from home

55. Where will the woman share some information with others?

(A) On a bulletin board near a door
(B) At an all-staff meeting
(C) In a text message
(D) On a company Web site

---

56. Why does the man want to speak to the woman?

    (A) To order a refill of a medication
    (B) To reschedule an appointment
    (C) To complain about a treatment
    (D) To find out the results of a test

57. What will the man do next week?

    (A) Take a vacation
    (B) Appear in a performance
    (C) Increase his insurance coverage
    (D) Undergo a surgical procedure

58. What does the woman recommend?

    (A) Going to sleep earlier
    (B) Avoiding excessive sunlight
    (C) Seeing another doctor
    (D) Reducing the amount of medication used

---

59. What possibility is being discussed?

    (A) The expansion of a company
    (B) The renovation of a store
    (C) The creation of an association
    (D) The purchase of an appliance

60. What does the woman imply when she says, "It's just that business has been really good recently"?

    (A) She needs help with some work.
    (B) She is surprised by a criticism.
    (C) She is dissatisfied with a decision.
    (D) She thinks a change is unnecessary.

61. Why will the woman go to Rissville?

    (A) To conduct market research
    (B) To look into an application process
    (C) To talk to a construction contractor
    (D) To hand out promotional flyers

Sale on Reilly-brand beads!

Amount	Savings
1 box	5%
2 boxes	10%
3 boxes	15%
4 boxes	20%

62. What does the woman say about Reilly beads?

    (A) They are durable.
    (B) They are attractive.
    (C) They are cheap.
    (D) They are small.

63. Look at the graphic. Which discount does the woman qualify for?

    (A) 5%
    (B) 10%
    (C) 15%
    (D) 20%

64. What does the woman plan to do?

    (A) Take a crafting class
    (B) Make a birthday present
    (C) Compete in a costume contest
    (D) Sell handmade jewelry

GO ON TO THE NEXT PAGE

Department	Extension #
Admissions	101
Housing	102
Purchasing	103
Security	104

Duration of contract	Price per month
1 month	$60
6 months	$45
1 year	$40
2 years	$35

65. Who most likely is the man?

(A) A government researcher
(B) A science professor
(C) An educational administrator
(D) A university student

66. Look at the graphic. Which number will the woman dial?

(A) 101
(B) 102
(C) 103
(D) 104

67. According to the woman, what makes some staff able to help?

(A) Their artistic skills
(B) Their convenient schedule
(C) Their relevant training
(D) Their access to an online database

68. What most likely does the man like to watch?

(A) Music programs
(B) Travel documentaries
(C) Sports games
(D) Classic films

69. Look at the graphic. How much will the man most likely pay per month?

(A) $60
(B) $45
(C) $40
(D) $35

70. What will the woman do next?

(A) Look at a calendar
(B) Call a technician
(C) Provide a paper contract
(D) Turn on a model television

PART 4

Directions: You will hear some talks given by a single speaker. You will be asked to answer three questions about what the speaker says in each talk. Select the best response to each question and mark the letter (A), (B), (C), or (D) on your answer sheet. The talks will not be printed in your test book and will be spoken only one time.

71. Where does the speaker work?
    (A) At a manufacturing plant
    (B) At an appliance store
    (C) At a shipping center
    (D) At an industry association

72. What does the company plan to use the video for?
    (A) Organizing a celebration
    (B) Publicizing its strengths
    (C) Educating its employees
    (D) Discovering potential problems

73. What does the speaker instruct listeners to do?
    (A) Write down any questions
    (B) Leave at a certain time
    (C) Read a notice
    (D) Tidy up a space

74. Who most likely are the listeners?
    (A) Dental clinic workers
    (B) Tax accountants
    (C) Hair salon staff
    (D) Travel agents

75. What problem is the speaker discussing?
    (A) Mislabeled computer files
    (B) Undersized equipment
    (C) Unsatisfactory customer service
    (D) Misleading advertisements

76. What will happen by the end of the day?
    (A) A workshop will be announced.
    (B) A form of compensation will be determined.
    (C) Part of the workplace will be cleared out.
    (D) Some coupons will be distributed.

77. What most likely did the speaker do last Thursday?
    (A) He attended a seminar.
    (B) He trained a sales associate.
    (C) He gave a building tour.
    (D) He helped renovate an office.

78. Why does the speaker say, "you'd be among the first residents to move in"?
    (A) To highlight possible inconveniences
    (B) To express frustration with a timeline
    (C) To emphasize that an area is quiet
    (D) To recommend seizing an opportunity

79. What is the listener asked to do?
    (A) Fill out a form
    (B) Return a phone call
    (C) Look for a contact list
    (D) Check an e-mail

80. What is the speaker preparing to do?
    (A) Rehearse a performance
    (B) Photograph a concert hall
    (C) Hold auditions for a position
    (D) Make supplies for a play

81. What are the listeners asked to take from a box?
    (A) A piece of sheet music
    (B) A numbered ticket
    (C) A cleaning tool
    (D) A pencil sketch

82. What will happen after the session?
    (A) Finalists will be chosen.
    (B) Permits will be issued.
    (C) A song will be recorded.
    (D) A stage will be redecorated.

GO ON TO THE NEXT PAGE

83. What does the speaker say is opening this week?

(A) A bicycle trail
(B) A concert venue
(C) A roller coaster
(D) A water fountain

84. What did a citizens' group do to support the project?

(A) Removed trash from the park
(B) Spoke to government officials
(C) Donated necessary funds
(D) Assisted with construction

85. What will park visitors get for free on Friday?

(A) Parking
(B) Fitness instruction
(C) Beverages
(D) T-shirts

86. What is the telephone message mainly about?

(A) A written proposal
(B) A team's decision
(C) A colleague's retirement
(D) A malfunctioning machine

87. What does the speaker offer to do?

(A) Circulate a technical memo
(B) Revise a detail of a financial plan
(C) Assign a certain type of task to the listener
(D) Obtain an outside specialist's input on an idea

88. Why does the speaker say, "Not everyone can do that"?

(A) To give a compliment
(B) To oppose a recommendation
(C) To clarify his job duties
(D) To offer an apology

89. What is the speaker mainly discussing?

(A) Product demonstration procedures
(B) Strategies for negotiating contracts
(C) Nominations for staff awards
(D) Travel reimbursement policies

90. What recently happened at the speaker's company?

(A) A new client was acquired.
(B) An executive was transferred.
(C) Some departments were restructured.
(D) Some rules were changed.

91. What will the speaker give to the listeners?

(A) Corporate credit cards
(B) Hotel vouchers
(C) Reference guides
(D) Photo ID badges

92. What does the speaker suggest doing?

(A) Finding cheaper sources of office supplies
(B) Rehearsing for future sales presentations
(C) Updating a company's customer list
(D) Moving up a production deadline

93. What does the speaker say he will do in the afternoon?

(A) Drive to a research center
(B) Schedule client visits
(C) Use a messaging service
(D) Design a consumer survey

94. What does the speaker mean when he says, "use your best judgment"?

(A) There is no fixed dress code for an event.
(B) Listeners may prioritize other assignments.
(C) Listeners can decide when to go home.
(D) He will not be available all day today.

Mon.	Tues.	Wed.	Thurs.	Fri.	Sat.
12 Weekly Lecture	13	14	15 Homenway Company Picnic	16	17 Mendoza Wedding

95. What is the speaker concerned about?

(A) Inaccurate reporting
(B) Damage to plants
(C) Bad weather conditions
(D) Inconvenience to visitors

96. What will the speaker post a notice about?

(A) The opening hours of a business
(B) The requirements for obtaining a refund
(C) The presence of photographers on site
(D) The remodeling of an indoor space

97. Look at the graphic. Which day does the speaker suggest scheduling the photo shoot for?

(A) Tuesday
(B) Wednesday
(C) Thursday
(D) Friday

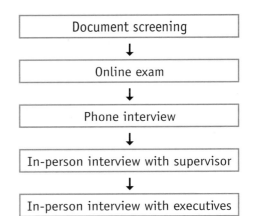

98. What department does the speaker most likely work for?

(A) Customer Service
(B) Public Relations
(C) Human Resources
(D) Information Technology

99. Look at the graphic. Which step does the speaker say was added recently?

(A) Document screening
(B) Online exam
(C) Phone interview
(D) In-person interview with executives

100. What does the speaker say about the position?

(A) It comes with excellent benefits.
(B) It is attracting many applicants.
(C) It is currently held by Yumiko.
(D) It will be temporary.

This is the end of the Listening test.

TEST 3

LISTENING TEST

In the Listening test, you will be asked to demonstrate how well you understand spoken English. The entire Listening test will last approximately 45 minutes. There are four parts, and directions are given for each part. You must mark your answers on the separate answer sheet. Do not write your answers in your test book.

PART 1

Directions: For each question in this part, you will hear four statements about a picture in your test book. When you hear the statements, you must select the one statement that best describes what you see in the picture. Then find the number of the question on your answer sheet and mark your answer. The statements will not be printed in your test book and will be spoken only one time.

Statement (C), "They're sitting at a table," is the best description of the picture, so you should select answer (C) and mark it on your answer sheet.

1.

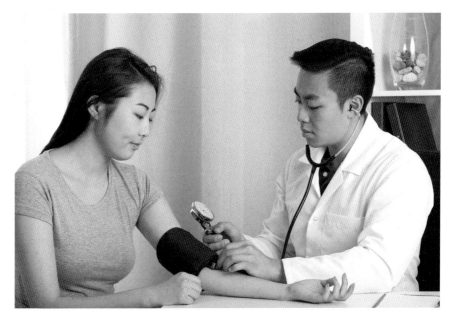

2.

GO ON TO THE NEXT PAGE ➡

3.

4.

5.

6.

GO ON TO THE NEXT PAGE ➡

Directions: You will hear a question or statement and three responses spoken in English. They will not be printed in your test book and will be spoken only one time. Select the best response to the question or statement and mark the letter (A), (B), or (C) on your answer sheet.

7. Mark your answer on your answer sheet.

8. Mark your answer on your answer sheet.

9. Mark your answer on your answer sheet.

10. Mark your answer on your answer sheet.

11. Mark your answer on your answer sheet.

12. Mark your answer on your answer sheet.

13. Mark your answer on your answer sheet.

14. Mark your answer on your answer sheet.

15. Mark your answer on your answer sheet.

16. Mark your answer on your answer sheet.

17. Mark your answer on your answer sheet.

18. Mark your answer on your answer sheet.

19. Mark your answer on your answer sheet.

20. Mark your answer on your answer sheet.

21. Mark your answer on your answer sheet.

22. Mark your answer on your answer sheet.

23. Mark your answer on your answer sheet.

24. Mark your answer on your answer sheet.

25. Mark your answer on your answer sheet.

26. Mark your answer on your answer sheet.

27. Mark your answer on your answer sheet.

28. Mark your answer on your answer sheet.

29. Mark your answer on your answer sheet.

30. Mark your answer on your answer sheet.

31. Mark your answer on your answer sheet.

PART 3

Directions: You will hear some conversations between two or more people. You will be asked to answer three questions about what the speakers say in each conversation. Select the best response to each question and mark the letter (A), (B), (C), or (D) on your answer sheet. The conversations will not be printed in your test book and will be spoken only one time.

32. What kind of item is the man shopping for?

(A) A piece of furniture
(B) A cleaning product
(C) A kitchen appliance
(D) A laundry detergent

33. What does the woman ask the man about?

(A) His schedule
(B) His business model
(C) His budget
(D) His mailing address

34. What does the woman offer to do?

(A) Give a demonstration
(B) Check another store
(C) Provide a guarantee
(D) Reduce a price

35. What is the woman's problem?

(A) Her laboratory project was canceled.
(B) She lost a parking pass.
(C) Her computer password is not working.
(D) She cannot access a room.

36. Who does the man suggest speaking with?

(A) A security guard
(B) A department manager
(C) A building owner
(D) A software technician

37. What does the man offer to do?

(A) Let the woman borrow his cell phone
(B) Take a message for a coworker
(C) Give the woman a business card
(D) Accompany the woman to the third floor

38. Why is the man calling?

(A) To follow up on an order
(B) To report being overcharged
(C) To complain about a shipping delay
(D) To inquire about installation

39. What does the woman tell the man about?

(A) A promotional sale
(B) A return policy
(C) A delivery route
(D) An additional fee

40. What does the man plan to do?

(A) Get help from a neighbor
(B) Cancel an out-of-town trip
(C) Sign a new contract
(D) Change a delivery date

41. What kind of business is the man calling?

(A) A taxi service
(B) An airline
(C) A train operator
(D) A hotel

42. What was the man concerned about?

(A) Overspending on transportation
(B) Carrying a lot of items
(C) Arriving at a site late
(D) Getting lost during a journey

43. What does the woman say the business will do?

(A) Call the man again
(B) Send a reminder
(C) Charge a credit card
(D) E-mail a receipt

GO ON TO THE NEXT PAGE

44. Why is the man calling?

(A) To cancel some weekend plans
(B) To inquire about festival tickets
(C) To offer a ride to an event
(D) To change a meeting place

45. What is the woman concerned about?

(A) A car malfunction
(B) A lack of parking
(C) A crowded bus
(D) A high admission fee

46. What does the man say he has done?

(A) Checked a neighborhood map
(B) Received a pass in advance
(C) Confirmed a booking online
(D) Requested a group discount

47. What task have the speakers been assigned?

(A) Installing a computer system
(B) Reviewing files for errors
(C) Recruiting new dental patients
(D) Adding information to a database

48. What does the man mention about Dr. Perkins?

(A) Her decision was a good one.
(B) She has no time to assist the speakers.
(C) Her business is growing steadily.
(D) She thinks the project should start today.

49. What do the speakers want to do?

(A) Work in the evening
(B) Get a larger workspace
(C) Collect files from coworkers
(D) Perform an online search

50. Who most likely is Mr. Kim?

(A) A building supply company owner
(B) An apartment rental agent
(C) A delivery driver
(D) A project manager

51. What problem does the woman mention?

(A) A shipment will be delayed.
(B) A document is missing.
(C) A measurement is incorrect.
(D) A forecast calls for bad weather.

52. What does Mr. Kim say he will most likely do later?

(A) Train some crew members
(B) Place an additional order
(C) Pay an overdue bill
(D) Approve a project

53. What is the conversation mainly about?

(A) Articles for a magazine
(B) Venues for a conference
(C) Nominees for an award
(D) Topics for a presentation

54. Why is Gregory's suggestion rejected?

(A) It will be too complex for the audience.
(B) It is not supported by evidence.
(C) It is too similar to another talk.
(D) It will take a long time to research.

55. What does the woman offer to do?

(A) Lend some publications to Jae-Young
(B) Contact an event coordinator
(C) Check Jae-Young's speech for errors
(D) Renew a magazine subscription

56. What did the woman find out about the restaurant through?

(A) A flyer in the mail
(B) A friend's recommendation
(C) An online advertisement
(D) A sign near a roadway

57. What does the woman ask about?

(A) Which entrées are the most popular
(B) When the restaurant first opened
(C) How much a meal will cost
(D) Whether food can be packed to go

58. Why does the man say, "The fish special comes with a side of vegetables"?

(A) To describe a change in the menu
(B) To suggest that an order is large enough
(C) To recommend a healthy dish
(D) To estimate a cooking time

59. Why is the man calling the woman?

(A) To request a résumé
(B) To explain a job's duties
(C) To schedule an interview
(D) To make a job offer

60. What does the woman say she will do?

(A) Provide proof of purchase
(B) E-mail the man later
(C) Speak to a supervisor
(D) Arrive at the headquarters early

61. What does the man mean when he says, "There are only three"?

(A) A group size will be small.
(B) Some time slots are filling up quickly.
(C) A task will not take very long.
(D) Some documents are still missing.

Traverse Furniture
Discount Coupon

Sofas .... $50 off
Chairs .... $25 off
Bookcases ...... $15 off
Lamps .... $10 off

Valid until June 30

62. What does the woman dislike about the Marcos product?

(A) Its color
(B) Its price
(C) Its size
(D) Its warranty

63. According to the man, what will happen next week?

(A) A new branch location will open.
(B) Some merchandise will arrive.
(C) A store's promotional sale will end.
(D) Some products will be discontinued.

64. Look at the graphic. How much will the woman save on her purchase?

(A) $50
(B) $25
(C) $15
(D) $10

GO ON TO THE NEXT PAGE

<table>
<tr><td colspan="2" align="center">Sheenan Airlines Check-In</td></tr>
<tr><td colspan="2">
First/Business Class: Counter A
Economy Class: Counter B
Group Check-in: Counter C
Bag Drop: Counter D
</td></tr>
</table>

Customer	Reported Issue
Victoria Castro	Late arrival
Motokazu Sai	Mess left behind
Chun Deng	Overcharged on bill
Rohan Baria	Unfriendly staff

65. What has the woman just finished doing?

(A) Sorting luggage
(B) Fixing a computer
(C) Taking a break
(D) Ordering dinner

66. Look at the graphic. Where will the woman most likely go next?

(A) Counter A
(B) Counter B
(C) Counter C
(D) Counter D

67. What is the woman concerned about?

(A) Missing a flight
(B) Making passengers upset
(C) Losing some luggage
(D) Using a new system

68. Who most likely are the speakers?

(A) Gardeners
(B) Taxi drivers
(C) Housekeepers
(D) Electricians

69. Look at the graphic. Whom did the woman speak to earlier today?

(A) Victoria Castro
(B) Motokazu Sai
(C) Chun Deng
(D) Rohan Baria

70. What does the man offer to do?

(A) Lead a training session
(B) Visit a customer
(C) Work on the weekend
(D) Hire more junior employees

PART 4

Directions: You will hear some talks given by a single speaker. You will be asked to answer three questions about what the speaker says in each talk. Select the best response to each question and mark the letter (A), (B), (C), or (D) on your answer sheet. The talks will not be printed in your test book and will be spoken only one time.

71. What has the listener recently done?

    (A) Received a job promotion
    (B) Purchased a home in Salem
    (C) Requested a branch transfer
    (D) Found some missing paperwork

72. What does the speaker remind the listener to do?

    (A) Read some training materials
    (B) Stay within a budget
    (C) Keep some receipts
    (D) E-mail him an update

73. What information does the speaker plan to send?

    (A) A colleague's number
    (B) An office location
    (C) A list of responsibilities
    (D) An updated schedule

74. Where is the announcement taking place?

    (A) At an annual election
    (B) At a community fundraiser
    (C) At a political debate
    (D) At a publication launch

75. How can the listeners use the card they were given?

    (A) To register for a service
    (B) To share an inquiry
    (C) To cast a vote
    (D) To make a donation

76. Who most likely is Lily Nolan?

    (A) A journalist
    (B) A city official
    (C) A business owner
    (D) An actress

77. What kind of business most likely is Lawson Incorporated?

    (A) A construction firm
    (B) A landscaping company
    (C) A catering service
    (D) A transportation firm

78. What does the speaker ask the listener about?

    (A) The billing method
    (B) The address for a service
    (C) The arrival time
    (D) The parking availability

79. When should the listener call the speaker?

    (A) By three o'clock
    (B) By five o'clock
    (C) By six o'clock
    (D) By eight o'clock

80. What does the speaker's company sell?

    (A) Camping gear
    (B) Uniforms
    (C) Footwear
    (D) Jewelry

81. What is the speaker pleased about?

    (A) A product launch had high attendance.
    (B) A new product experienced record sales.
    (C) A professional consultant approved a plan.
    (D) A celebrity will provide an endorsement.

82. What does the speaker most likely mean when she says, "We can expect major growth"?

    (A) Some competitors have left the market.
    (B) Another branch will be opened.
    (C) Many more employees will be hired.
    (D) The company's revenue will increase.

GO ON TO THE NEXT PAGE

83. According to the speaker, what is the purpose of the meeting?

(A) To introduce a loan type
(B) To announce a change in leadership
(C) To explain a hiring process
(D) To remind listeners about a policy

84. What are the listeners asked to do?

(A) Report their vacation time
(B) Memorize some information
(C) Be more friendly to customers
(D) Fill out a consent form

85. What benefit does the speaker mention?

(A) Catching up with competitors
(B) Keeping fees low
(C) Improving employee motivation
(D) Boosting productivity

---

86. What has Daily Fit Gym recently done?

(A) Expanded its building
(B) Added new exercise classes
(C) Purchased more equipment
(D) Extended its business hours

87. Who most likely is Mr. Abner?

(A) The Daily Fit Gym owner
(B) A fitness instructor
(C) A massage therapist
(D) A diet consultant

88. According to the advertisement, what can listeners do in the first week of April?

(A) Attend a welcome reception
(B) Enroll in some group classes
(C) Use the facility for free
(D) Sign up for a building tour

---

89. What is the listener preparing to do?

(A) Apply for a job
(B) Move to a new city
(C) Purchase a home
(D) Open a business

90. What does the speaker suggest when she says, "Were they from a local store"?

(A) She is trying to reduce the shipping time on some items.
(B) She wants to buy some furniture for herself.
(C) She thinks the listener should support the local economy.
(D) She hopes returning the furniture will be easy.

91. What does the speaker say she will do?

(A) Visit a site again
(B) Provide her friends' numbers
(C) Recommend a business
(D) Call the listener later

---

92. What is the report mainly about?

(A) A sports competition
(B) An awards ceremony
(C) A music festival
(D) A construction project

93. What does the speaker most likely mean when he says, "I can hardly hear myself"?

(A) The attendees are excited.
(B) Some equipment is not working.
(C) The report is getting interrupted.
(D) An area is too small.

94. What will the listeners hear next?

(A) Some music
(B) A commercial
(C) An interview
(D) A weather update

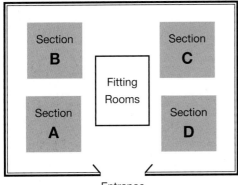

Entrance

Monthly Supply Request

Department Code: 423

Description	Quantity
Three-ring binder	12
Box of printing paper	7
Ink cartridge	4
Pack of address labels	3

95. Why is the store having a sale?

(A) To correct an ordering error
(B) To celebrate an anniversary
(C) To promote a grand opening
(D) To introduce a new brand

96. Look at the graphic. Where can listeners find discounted items?

(A) In Section A
(B) In Section B
(C) In Section C
(D) In Section D

97. When will the sale end?

(A) At the end of the day
(B) Tomorrow evening
(C) At the end of the week
(D) Next week

98. What did the speaker do in the morning?

(A) Received the wrong supplies
(B) Changed a department code
(C) Completed a PR campaign
(D) Organized a storage area

99. Look at the graphic. Which item's quantity is now incorrect?

(A) 12
(B) 7
(C) 4
(D) 3

100. What does the speaker ask the listener to do?

(A) Provide a catalog of supplies
(B) Give the items to a coworker
(C) Confirm that a change has been made
(D) Drop off another order form

This is the end of the Listening test.

TEST 4

LISTENING TEST

In the Listening test, you will be asked to demonstrate how well you understand spoken English. The entire Listening test will last approximately 45 minutes. There are four parts, and directions are given for each part. You must mark your answers on the separate answer sheet. Do not write your answers in your test book.

PART 1

Directions: For each question in this part, you will hear four statements about a picture in your test book. When you hear the statements, you must select the one statement that best describes what you see in the picture. Then find the number of the question on your answer sheet and mark your answer. The statements will not be printed in your test book and will be spoken only one time.

Statement (C), "They're sitting at a table," is the best description of the picture, so you should select answer (C) and mark it on your answer sheet.

1.

2.

GO ON TO THE NEXT PAGE

3.

4.

5.

6.

GO ON TO THE NEXT PAGE

PART 2

Directions: You will hear a question or statement and three responses spoken in English. They will not be printed in your test book and will be spoken only one time. Select the best response to the question or statement and mark the letter (A), (B), or (C) on your answer sheet.

7. Mark your answer on your answer sheet.

8. Mark your answer on your answer sheet.

9. Mark your answer on your answer sheet.

10. Mark your answer on your answer sheet.

11. Mark your answer on your answer sheet.

12. Mark your answer on your answer sheet.

13. Mark your answer on your answer sheet.

14. Mark your answer on your answer sheet.

15. Mark your answer on your answer sheet.

16. Mark your answer on your answer sheet.

17. Mark your answer on your answer sheet.

18. Mark your answer on your answer sheet.

19. Mark your answer on your answer sheet.

20. Mark your answer on your answer sheet.

21. Mark your answer on your answer sheet.

22. Mark your answer on your answer sheet.

23. Mark your answer on your answer sheet.

24. Mark your answer on your answer sheet.

25. Mark your answer on your answer sheet.

26. Mark your answer on your answer sheet.

27. Mark your answer on your answer sheet.

28. Mark your answer on your answer sheet.

29. Mark your answer on your answer sheet.

30. Mark your answer on your answer sheet.

31. Mark your answer on your answer sheet.

PART 3

Directions: You will hear some conversations between two or more people. You will be asked to answer three questions about what the speakers say in each conversation. Select the best response to each question and mark the letter (A), (B), (C), or (D) on your answer sheet. The conversations will not be printed in your test book and will be spoken only one time.

32. What is the problem?

    (A) A missing name
    (B) An outdated logo
    (C) A blurred image
    (D) A dull color

33. Why is the man concerned?

    (A) An event may be postponed.
    (B) A type of shirt may not sell well.
    (C) A sponsor may be displeased.
    (D) An event budget may be exceeded.

34. What does the woman offer to do?

    (A) Waive a production charge
    (B) Dispose of some items
    (C) Expedite a delivery
    (D) Conceal some defects

35. Where most likely are the speakers?

    (A) In a job placement agency
    (B) In an electronics store
    (C) In a bank
    (D) In a dental clinic

36. According to the man, what is a problem?

    (A) A Web site is not operating.
    (B) A promotional offer has ended.
    (C) A mobile phone has no power.
    (D) A meeting room is unavailable.

37. What does the man say he will do?

    (A) Lower a price
    (B) Supply an additional form
    (C) Find a manager
    (D) Reschedule an appointment

38. Where most likely does the woman work?

    (A) At an insurance provider
    (B) At a marketing company
    (C) At a paper manufacturer
    (D) At a customer service call center

39. What does the man say about BaxterShare?

    (A) It is difficult to use.
    (B) It has limited features.
    (C) It is available in a trial version.
    (D) It offers strong security.

40. What does the woman agree to do?

    (A) Copy some important files
    (B) Download some software
    (C) View a demonstration
    (D) Buy a notebook computer

41. What does the woman say will happen next month?

    (A) Special shipments will arrive.
    (B) A city festival will take place.
    (C) A new location will open.
    (D) Temporary employees will be hired.

42. What does the man offer to do?

    (A) Clean a sidewalk area
    (B) Print some flyers
    (C) Move a display case
    (D) Take some photographs

43. What does the woman say she will research?

    (A) The layout of a store showroom
    (B) The best place to buy some kitchen equipment
    (C) The wholesale price of a coffee drink
    (D) The costs for some online advertisements

GO ON TO THE NEXT PAGE

44. Why has the man come to the train station?

    (A) To reserve a ticket
    (B) To work in a shop
    (C) To pick up a client
    (D) To leave on a train

45. What does the woman offer to help the man do?

    (A) Carry some luggage
    (B) Understand a wall display
    (C) Locate a meeting site
    (D) Obtain an access card

46. What is the man told to do?

    (A) Make a change to a plan
    (B) Wait for an attendant
    (C) Save some printed receipts
    (D) Double-check some instructions

47. Who most likely is the woman?

    (A) A safety inspector
    (B) A new employee
    (C) A board member
    (D) A potential vendor

48. What does the woman ask about?

    (A) The need for some repair instruments
    (B) The speed of some machines
    (C) The placement of a workstation
    (D) The difficulty of hiring technicians

49. What will the woman most likely do next?

    (A) Put on a uniform
    (B) Monitor some procedures
    (C) Gather some supervisors
    (D) Make a reminder note

50. Who most likely are the speakers?

    (A) Financial consultants
    (B) School teachers
    (C) Travel photographers
    (D) Research scientists

51. What does the woman say about a workshop?

    (A) It was full.
    (B) It began late.
    (C) It was recorded.
    (D) It involved role-playing.

52. Why does the woman say, "He's wearing a green shirt"?

    (A) To complain about a person's appearance
    (B) To clarify why some lighting is unsuitable
    (C) To help the man identify a person
    (D) To indicate what the man should wear

53. What does the woman want to do?

    (A) Attend an upcoming event
    (B) Apply for a position
    (C) Place a special order
    (D) Promote her work

54. What does the man warn the woman about?

    (A) An extra fee
    (B) A new restriction
    (C) A possible delay
    (D) A dissatisfied customer

55. What does the man encourage the woman to do?

    (A) Enter a writing contest
    (B) Register for an e-mail update program
    (C) Participate in a local trade show
    (D) Visit another store location

56. What does the woman ask the man to do?

    (A) Start preparing a presentation
    (B) Proofread a section of an article
    (C) Explain a feature of a software program
    (D) Purchase some office supplies online

57. What did the man do yesterday?

    (A) Paid a utility bill
    (B) Toured a warehouse
    (C) Met a technician
    (D) Reviewed a manual

58. What does the man mean when he says "I was on my way to a meeting"?

    (A) He traveled to a site separately from others.
    (B) He was not in the area when a problem occurred.
    (C) He will not be able to make a phone call immediately.
    (D) He can make an announcement to a group of staff.

59. According to the woman, what is the problem with the fan?

    (A) It cannot be turned on.
    (B) It has stopped rotating.
    (C) It may fall off of the wall.
    (D) It is making loud noises.

60. Why is Itaru unable to assist the woman?

    (A) His work space is being used by a colleague.
    (B) He does not have the necessary skills.
    (C) He has to handle another task.
    (D) His job description does not allow it.

61. What does Adam ask about?

    (A) A building floor
    (B) A contact method
    (C) A department name
    (D) A vacation period

Inbox - Unread Messages

From	Subject
Mariana Sanchez	Estimate of expenses
Georgina Lewis	Revision to timeline
Wyatt Rayburn	Copy machine tips
Suraj Sidhu	Team outing

62. Where is the conversation most likely taking place?

    (A) In a copy room
    (B) In a break area
    (C) In a reception area
    (D) In a conference room

63. What is the woman having trouble with?

    (A) Designing new merchandise
    (B) Completing a training course
    (C) Using a filing system
    (D) Developing a sales plan

64. Look at the graphic. Who sent the e-mail that the man mentions?

    (A) Mariana Sanchez
    (B) Georgina Lewis
    (C) Wyatt Rayburn
    (D) Suraj Sidhu

GO ON TO THE NEXT PAGE

Basic package	$110.00
Evening visit surcharge	$35.00
Local taxes	$8.00
Total	**$153.00**

Sharula Hotel Pricing		
	Sea view	No sea view
With breakfast	£130	£100
Without breakfast	£115	£85

65. Look at the graphic. What amount from the invoice will be modified?

(A) $110.00
(B) $35.00
(C) $8.00
(D) $153.00

66. What service does the man's company most likely provide?

(A) Commercial moving
(B) Carpet cleaning
(C) Garden care
(D) Grocery delivery

67. What does the woman want to know about?

(A) Customized services
(B) Rewards for client referrals
(C) Appointment cancellation policies
(D) Employment opportunities

68. Why is the woman in the area?

(A) To see a performance
(B) To interview for a job
(C) To speak at a conference
(D) To spend time with a friend

69. Look at the graphic. How much will the woman most likely pay?

(A) £130
(B) £100
(C) £115
(D) £85

70. What does the man recommend doing?

(A) Arriving early for a meal
(B) Parking in front of a hotel
(C) Taking a shuttle bus downtown
(D) Getting a second room key

PART 4

Directions: You will hear some talks given by a single speaker. You will be asked to answer three questions about what the speaker says in each talk. Select the best response to each question and mark the letter (A), (B), (C), or (D) on your answer sheet. The talks will not be printed in your test book and will be spoken only one time.

71. What kind of business is being advertised?

(A) An ocean cruise provider
(B) A sportswear store
(C) A seaside café
(D) A boat repair shop

72. What does the speaker emphasize about the business?

(A) Its numerous branches
(B) Its famous customers
(C) Its advanced technology
(D) Its relaxed atmosphere

73. How can listeners get a free gift?

(A) By mentioning an advertisement
(B) By signing up for a loyalty card
(C) By visiting on a certain day
(D) By referring a friend

74. Who most likely is making the announcement?

(A) A public official
(B) An event coordinator
(C) A bank manager
(D) A radio program host

75. What will Mr. Jensen speak about at the event?

(A) A regional economy
(B) A negotiation method
(C) Business management
(D) Personal finance

76. What is mentioned about the event?

(A) Its attendees will be given handouts.
(B) It will be followed by a reception.
(C) Its date has been moved.
(D) It is predicted to sell out.

77. What is the speaker calling about?

(A) A furniture order
(B) A broken appliance
(C) A rental contract
(D) A delivery van

78. What does the speaker imply when he says, "don't get your hopes up"?

(A) An item may not arrive on time.
(B) A phone number may not be correct.
(C) A space may be too small for a vehicle.
(D) An item may be damaged in transit.

79. What does the speaker request that the listener do?

(A) Leave a message on a door
(B) Speak to his coworker
(C) Look for some records
(D) Take some measurements

80. What is the purpose of the talk?

(A) To persuade the listeners to purchase some items
(B) To educate listeners about a manufacturing process
(C) To report on the progress of a design project
(D) To introduce the new head of a department

81. What does the speaker's company make?

(A) Portable electronic devices
(B) Skin care goods
(C) Food packaging
(D) Stationery products

82. What does the speaker show on a screen?

(A) A sales chart
(B) A regional map
(C) Pictures of an event
(D) Results from a survey

GO ON TO THE NEXT PAGE

83. What will take place at the end of the year?

    (A) The launch of a product line
    (B) A retirement ceremony
    (C) The renovation of a store
    (D) A holiday banquet

84. What are the listeners asked to do?

    (A) Forward an e-mail to some contacts
    (B) Stay later than usual today
    (C) Outline some goals
    (D) Participate in a vote

85. What does the speaker imply when she says, "That was really something"?

    (A) She hopes to avoid repeating a mistake.
    (B) Customers appreciated a special service.
    (C) An achievement was impressive.
    (D) A proposal was too impractical.

86. What is the main topic of the broadcast?

    (A) A video game
    (B) A television series
    (C) A classic novel
    (D) A recent film

87. According to the speaker, what did Mr. Tarver do last year?

    (A) He starred in a commercial.
    (B) He met a politician.
    (C) He wrote a play.
    (D) He traveled abroad.

88. What will the speaker do next?

    (A) Bring out a guest
    (B) Give a Web site address
    (C) Describe a story's contents
    (D) Read letters from viewers

89. What is mentioned about the train?

    (A) It does not go above ground.
    (B) It offers wireless Internet service.
    (C) It crosses a national border.
    (D) It does not stop at all stations.

90. What information does the speaker announce?

    (A) The number of passengers on board
    (B) The time of an arrival
    (C) The location of a dining car
    (D) The charge for transferring to a bus

91. What does the speaker encourage listeners to do?

    (A) Browse around some stores
    (B) Buy special transport passes
    (C) Use a short-term storage facility
    (D) Install a new mobile app

92. What has caused a problem?

    (A) Shortages of special ingredients
    (B) New city regulations for restaurants
    (C) Improvements to another neighborhood
    (D) Negative customer reviews posted online

93. What does the speaker intend to do?

    (A) Build some parking garages
    (B) Extend some opening hours
    (C) Schedule a press conference
    (D) Reconsider a hiring requirement

94. Why does the speaker say, "it will be a temporary situation"?

    (A) To give a reason for a decision
    (B) To express frustration with an agreement
    (C) To suggest postponing an announcement
    (D) To reassure the listeners about a change

Expense Report
Section: Magazines

Title	Cost per year
Celebrity Gossip	£96
Wise Consumer	£55
Games for Children	£48
Earth in Photographs	£27

Tuesday	Wednesday	Thursday	Friday
☁️🌤️	☁️🌧️	☁️🌤️	☀️

95. Who most likely are the listeners?

(A) Medical clinic staff
(B) Magazine designers
(C) Librarians
(D) Journalism students

96. Look at the graphic. Which title did the speaker read recently?

(A) *Celebrity Gossip*
(B) *Wise Consumer*
(C) *Games for Children*
(D) *Earth in Photographs*

97. What will most likely be discussed next?

(A) Who will take on an assignment
(B) Whether to renew a subscription
(C) How to arrange a magazine rack
(D) Why some expenses have increased

98. Look at the graphic. On what day was a meeting scheduled?

(A) Tuesday
(B) Wednesday
(C) Thursday
(D) Friday

99. What is the speaker offering to provide for an event?

(A) The transportation
(B) The refreshments
(C) The venue
(D) The decorations

100. Why should the listener visit a Web site?

(A) To obtain a coupon
(B) To watch a video
(C) To join a mailing list
(D) To make a tour reservation

This is the end of the Listening test.

TEST 5

LISTENING TEST

In the Listening test, you will be asked to demonstrate how well you understand spoken English. The entire Listening test will last approximately 45 minutes. There are four parts, and directions are given for each part. You must mark your answers on the separate answer sheet. Do not write your answers in your test book.

PART 1

Directions: For each question in this part, you will hear four statements about a picture in your test book. When you hear the statements, you must select the one statement that best describes what you see in the picture. Then find the number of the question on your answer sheet and mark your answer. The statements will not be printed in your test book and will be spoken only one time.

Statement (C), "They're sitting at a table," is the best description of the picture, so you should select answer (C) and mark it on your answer sheet.

1.

2.

GO ON TO THE NEXT PAGE ➤

3.

4.

5.

6.

GO ON TO THE NEXT PAGE ➡

PART 2

Directions: You will hear a question or statement and three responses spoken in English. They will not be printed in your test book and will be spoken only one time. Select the best response to the question or statement and mark the letter (A), (B), or (C) on your answer sheet.

7. Mark your answer on your answer sheet.

8. Mark your answer on your answer sheet.

9. Mark your answer on your answer sheet.

10. Mark your answer on your answer sheet.

11. Mark your answer on your answer sheet.

12. Mark your answer on your answer sheet.

13. Mark your answer on your answer sheet.

14. Mark your answer on your answer sheet.

15. Mark your answer on your answer sheet.

16. Mark your answer on your answer sheet.

17. Mark your answer on your answer sheet.

18. Mark your answer on your answer sheet.

19. Mark your answer on your answer sheet.

20. Mark your answer on your answer sheet.

21. Mark your answer on your answer sheet.

22. Mark your answer on your answer sheet.

23. Mark your answer on your answer sheet.

24. Mark your answer on your answer sheet.

25. Mark your answer on your answer sheet.

26. Mark your answer on your answer sheet.

27. Mark your answer on your answer sheet.

28. Mark your answer on your answer sheet.

29. Mark your answer on your answer sheet.

30. Mark your answer on your answer sheet.

31. Mark your answer on your answer sheet.

Directions: You will hear some conversations between two or more people. You will be asked to answer three questions about what the speakers say in each conversation. Select the best response to each question and mark the letter (A), (B), (C), or (D) on your answer sheet. The conversations will not be printed in your test book and will be spoken only one time.

32. What does the woman want the man to do?

(A) View an instructional video
(B) Watch a demonstration
(C) Try a sample of coffee
(D) Provide customer feedback

33. Why does the man want to leave quickly?

(A) He will meet up with someone.
(B) He needs to catch a bus.
(C) He parked in a restricted area.
(D) He has to start a work shift.

34. What does the woman offer to do?

(A) Give the man some product information
(B) Mail a brochure to the man's address
(C) Add the man to a waiting list
(D) Start an activity earlier than usual

35. Where does the conversation take place?

(A) At an art museum
(B) At a library
(C) At an electronics store
(D) At a hotel

36. Why is the woman unable to help the man?

(A) A service has been discontinued.
(B) The business closes in fifteen minutes.
(C) A system has not been upgraded.
(D) Some equipment is in use.

37. What does the woman suggest doing?

(A) Waiting on another floor
(B) Coming back later
(C) Calling for an update
(D) Verifying a time online

38. What is the man trying to do?

(A) Arrange some advertising
(B) Volunteer for a fundraiser
(C) Register for a race
(D) Sign up for a community picnic

39. What does the woman tell the man about?

(A) A meeting place
(B) An enrollment fee
(C) A Web site upgrade
(D) A deadline change

40. What does the man plan to do tomorrow?

(A) Submit a form
(B) Call the woman again
(C) Go out of town
(D) Send a payment

41. What has changed about the meeting?

(A) Its location
(B) Its start time
(C) Its duration
(D) Its guest list

42. Why is the man concerned about the change?

(A) He believes people cannot be informed on short notice.
(B) He does not know how to use the sound system.
(C) He worries that it will cause confusion among guests.
(D) He thinks there will not be enough space.

43. According to the woman, what will Mr. Padilla do?

(A) Handle the first presentation to investors
(B) Remove a piece of furniture
(C) Set up some electrical equipment
(D) Call visitors to inform them

GO ON TO THE NEXT PAGE

Test 5

44. What does the man say he has done?

(A) Created a customer questionnaire
(B) Analyzed some sales techniques
(C) Reviewed feedback from patrons
(D) Contacted some regular customers

45. What did the speakers' company do last month?

(A) Discontinued unpopular items
(B) Changed to a new supplier
(C) Added a shipping fee
(D) Increased its product prices

46. What does the woman plan to do?

(A) Research information about new suppliers
(B) Have a discussion with some coworkers
(C) Prepare an application for financial assistance
(D) Publish some information about a trend

47. Why did the woman call the man?

(A) To request insurance information
(B) To introduce a new service
(C) To explain a clinic's policy
(D) To reschedule an appointment

48. What does the man inquire about?

(A) The duration of some procedures
(B) The expertise of some employees
(C) Confidentiality rights
(D) Payment methods

49. What does the woman recommend doing?

(A) Arriving early to complete a form
(B) Checking a schedule online
(C) Reviewing some rates in advance
(D) Settling a service fee by mail

50. What does the man want to change about his reservation?

(A) The type of vehicle
(B) The pick-up time
(C) The duration of a service
(D) The drop-off destination

51. Why does the man say, "Is that the only way"?

(A) To suggest another driving route
(B) To accept a suggestion
(C) To express disappointment
(D) To point out an error

52. What does the woman offer to do?

(A) Credit the man's account
(B) Reduce the price of a service
(C) Issue a partial refund
(D) Send a discount coupon

53. Where most likely are the speakers?

(A) At a fundraising dinner
(B) At a coworker's birthday party
(C) At an awards banquet
(D) At a new staff orientation

54. What does the man say he is nervous about?

(A) Sending a copy of some notes
(B) Meeting the company's president
(C) Speaking in front of others
(D) Making a formal complaint

55. What will the speakers most likely do next?

(A) Make a meal selection
(B) Put on some name tags
(C) Greet the company's president
(D) Find a place to sit

56. What problem does the woman mention about the recruitment process?

(A) The number of responses to the posting was low.
(B) Many candidates do not want to commute to the university.
(C) The applicants lack the necessary qualifications.
(D) Some information on the job posting was incorrect.

57. How does the man know Mr. Gomez?

(A) They met at a fundraising event.
(B) They are former coworkers.
(C) They had university classes together.
(D) They live in the same building.

58. What does the woman ask the man to do?

(A) E-mail Mr. Gomez a link to the job posting
(B) Give her e-mail address to Mr. Gomez
(C) Send a copy of Mr. Gomez's résumé
(D) Ask Mr. Gomez to call her office

59. According to the woman, what is a problem with a room?

(A) It is too large.
(B) It has been double-booked.
(C) It is missing some equipment.
(D) It is being cleaned.

60. Why most likely does Randy say, "I just started a new project today"?

(A) To explain a deadline
(B) To seek extra help
(C) To show excitement
(D) To decline an invitation

61. What will the woman probably do next?

(A) Update a Web site
(B) Edit an e-mail message
(C) Move some furniture
(D) Take a meal break

Heating Instructions	
Microwave Wattage	Cooking Time
650	6 minutes
800	4 minutes
900	3 minutes
1,000	2.5 minutes

62. Where is the conversation most likely taking place?

(A) In a food production facility
(B) In an office break room
(C) In a grocery store
(D) In an electronics store

63. What does the man indicate about Swift-Cup?

(A) It contains healthy ingredients.
(B) It does not need to be refrigerated.
(C) It was distributed as a free sample.
(D) It is available in different flavors.

64. Look at the graphic. For how long should the man run the microwave?

(A) 6 minutes
(B) 4 minutes
(C) 3 minutes
(D) 2.5 minutes

GO ON TO THE NEXT PAGE

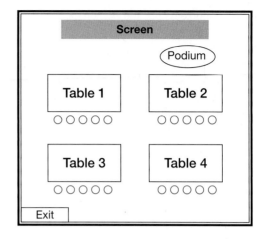

Val's Accessories
Discount Coupon

15% off
any Evans brand watch

Minimum purchase: $60
Expiration Date: July 31

65. What does the man mention that he likes about the item?

(A) Its warranty
(B) Its appearance
(C) Its price
(D) Its technology

66. What does the woman ask the man about?

(A) What he intends to do with the item
(B) Which wrapping paper he prefers
(C) How he will pay for the merchandise
(D) Whether he is a rewards club member

67. Look at the graphic. Why is the man most likely unable to use the coupon?

(A) It cannot be used for a clearance item.
(B) It has passed its expiration date.
(C) His total purchase is not large enough.
(D) He is purchasing the wrong brand.

68. What is the purpose of Thursday's meeting?

(A) To demonstrate a service
(B) To secure funding
(C) To introduce new employees
(D) To develop a product

69. What has the speakers' company recently done?

(A) Renovated some rooms
(B) Merged with a competitor
(C) Moved to a new building
(D) Expanded a meeting space

70. Look at the graphic. Where should the representatives from Tully Incorporated sit?

(A) Table 1
(B) Table 2
(C) Table 3
(D) Table 4

PART 4

Directions: You will hear some talks given by a single speaker. You will be asked to answer three questions about what the speaker says in each talk. Select the best response to each question and mark the letter (A), (B), (C), or (D) on your answer sheet. The talks will not be printed in your test book and will be spoken only one time.

71. What is being advertised?

(A) A volunteer program
(B) A travel agency
(C) A cooking institute
(D) A language school

72. What does the business offer to customers?

(A) A first-time discount
(B) Assurance of achievement
(C) A money-back guarantee
(D) A free trial period

73. According to the speaker, what can listeners do online?

(A) Take a test
(B) View a schedule
(C) Request a brochure
(D) Check availability

74. Where most likely are the listeners?

(A) At a construction site
(B) At a furniture store
(C) At a production facility
(D) At a textile warehouse

75. What does the speaker suggest about the Bolton-360?

(A) It was recently released on the market.
(B) It has an impressive safety record.
(C) It is the company's best-seller.
(D) It is made from recycled materials.

76. Who most likely is Mr. Spinelli?

(A) A government inspector
(B) A tour guide
(C) A raw materials supplier
(D) A business's owner

77. What is the main purpose of the broadcast?

(A) To advertise a community event
(B) To provide a weather update
(C) To report on traffic conditions
(D) To explain a new city regulation

78. What is happening downtown this evening?

(A) A community parade
(B) A political debate
(C) A sporting event
(D) A theater show

79. According to the speaker, why should listeners visit a Web site?

(A) To review the hours of operation
(B) To view a broadcasting schedule
(C) To send questions to the speaker
(D) To get road closure information

80. What is the broadcast mainly about?

(A) A film
(B) A musical
(C) A comedy show
(D) A theater performance

81. What does the speaker suggest when he says, "but Marcus Dorsett rarely performs live"?

(A) Mr. Dorsett is inexperienced.
(B) An event's tickets are sold out.
(C) Mr. Dorsett plans to retire soon.
(D) An experience is worth the cost.

82. According to the speaker, how can listeners get more information?

(A) By visiting a Web site
(B) By reading a review in a newspaper
(C) By contacting a venue directly
(D) By calling the radio station

GO ON TO THE NEXT PAGE

83. Where is the speech most likely taking place?

(A) At an employee orientation
(B) At an awards banquet
(C) At a store's grand opening
(D) At a groundbreaking ceremony

84. What does the speaker imply when he says, "It was the one"?

(A) He was impressed with a product.
(B) He thought a site was perfect.
(C) He found the cause of an achievement.
(D) He was pleased to find a corporate partner.

85. Who will speak next?

(A) A graphic designer
(B) An architect
(C) A city official
(D) A store manager

___

86. What will the listeners learn about?

(A) Fire prevention methods
(B) Evacuation procedures
(C) Customer service skills
(D) Volunteer opportunities

87. What is indicated about the listeners?

(A) They work on different floors of the building.
(B) They were recommended by their supervisors.
(C) They will be financially compensated for their time.
(D) They must pass a test at the end of the session.

88. What will the speaker do next?

(A) Assign people to groups
(B) Respond to questions
(C) Distribute a map
(D) Examine the corridors

___

89. Where does the speaker work?

(A) At a luxury hotel
(B) At a regional airport
(C) At an insurance company
(D) At a car rental firm

90. What problem does the speaker mention?

(A) A payment is still owed.
(B) A request was not processed.
(C) A price has recently increased.
(D) A service has been canceled.

91. What is the listener asked to do?

(A) Provide a form of ID
(B) Pay a deposit
(C) Approve a change
(D) Sign a form

___

92. According to the speaker, what is the purpose of the change?

(A) To recognize an upcoming holiday
(B) To make a good impression on clients
(C) To respond to customer requests
(D) To make employees easier to recognize

93. What does the speaker mean when he says, "It's up to you"?

(A) The start date of the change could be postponed.
(B) Staff members should vote on their preferences.
(C) The listeners do not need attire approved in advance.
(D) Employees are not required to dress casually.

94. What does the speaker ask the listeners to do?

(A) View some examples
(B) Share their opinions
(C) Attend a brief meeting
(D) Confirm their participation

___

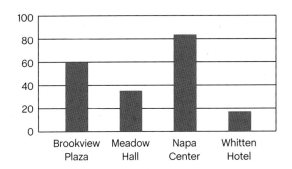

Inventory List	
Product	**Quantity**
Carpet Cleaner	12 boxes
Deodorizing Spray	7 bottles
Glass Cleaner	3 bottles
Bleach	9 bottles

95. What is the speaker in charge of doing?

(A) Organizing a product launch
(B) Selecting a site for a new branch
(C) Planning an employee retreat
(D) Holding a recruitment event

96. Look at the graphic. Which venue will the speaker contact today?

(A) Brookview Plaza
(B) Meadow Hall
(C) Napa Center
(D) Whitten Hotel

97. What will the listeners most likely do next?

(A) Have a workout
(B) Sign up for an event
(C) Review a report
(D) Suggest some activities

98. Why did the speaker do a task early?

(A) He needs to train some coworkers.
(B) His other project was canceled.
(C) He plans to go out of town.
(D) His manager requested it.

99. Look at the graphic. Which amount is incorrect?

(A) 12
(B) 7
(C) 3
(D) 9

100. When will Ms. Edwards place the next order?

(A) Today
(B) Tomorrow
(C) On the weekend
(D) Next week

This is the end of the Listening test.

TEST 6

LISTENING TEST

In the Listening test, you will be asked to demonstrate how well you understand spoken English. The entire Listening test will last approximately 45 minutes. There are four parts, and directions are given for each part. You must mark your answers on the separate answer sheet. Do not write your answers in your test book.

PART 1

Directions: For each question in this part, you will hear four statements about a picture in your test book. When you hear the statements, you must select the one statement that best describes what you see in the picture. Then find the number of the question on your answer sheet and mark your answer. The statements will not be printed in your test book and will be spoken only one time.

Statement (C), "They're sitting at a table," is the best description of the picture, so you should select answer (C) and mark it on your answer sheet.

1.

2.

GO ON TO THE NEXT PAGE

3.

4.

5.

6.

GO ON TO THE NEXT PAGE

PART 2

Directions: You will hear a question or statement and three responses spoken in English. They will not be printed in your test book and will be spoken only one time. Select the best response to the question or statement and mark the letter (A), (B), or (C) on your answer sheet.

7. Mark your answer on your answer sheet.

8. Mark your answer on your answer sheet.

9. Mark your answer on your answer sheet.

10. Mark your answer on your answer sheet.

11. Mark your answer on your answer sheet.

12. Mark your answer on your answer sheet.

13. Mark your answer on your answer sheet.

14. Mark your answer on your answer sheet.

15. Mark your answer on your answer sheet.

16. Mark your answer on your answer sheet.

17. Mark your answer on your answer sheet.

18. Mark your answer on your answer sheet.

19. Mark your answer on your answer sheet.

20. Mark your answer on your answer sheet.

21. Mark your answer on your answer sheet.

22. Mark your answer on your answer sheet.

23. Mark your answer on your answer sheet.

24. Mark your answer on your answer sheet.

25. Mark your answer on your answer sheet.

26. Mark your answer on your answer sheet.

27. Mark your answer on your answer sheet.

28. Mark your answer on your answer sheet.

29. Mark your answer on your answer sheet.

30. Mark your answer on your answer sheet.

31. Mark your answer on your answer sheet.

PART 3

Directions: You will hear some conversations between two or more people. You will be asked to answer three questions about what the speakers say in each conversation. Select the best response to each question and mark the letter (A), (B), (C), or (D) on your answer sheet. The conversations will not be printed in your test book and will be spoken only one time.

32. Why is the man calling?
    (A) To confirm a treatment technique
    (B) To find out some business hours
    (C) To order some prescriptions
    (D) To give an authorization

33. What problem does the woman mention?
    (A) A pharmacist has not yet arrived.
    (B) A pharmacy is closed on weekends.
    (C) A handwritten message is unclear.
    (D) A product is not in stock.

34. What does the woman recommend?
    (A) Trying a direct shipping service
    (B) Reading the back of a box
    (C) Communicating by e-mail
    (D) Taking another medication

35. What does the woman imply when she says, "What is it"?
    (A) She needs assistance with a task.
    (B) She is curious about a machine.
    (C) She has time to listen to the man.
    (D) She thinks an error has been made.

36. Where most likely does the conversation take place?
    (A) At a clothing store
    (B) At a stadium
    (C) At an airport
    (D) At a supermarket

37. What does the man suggest changing?
    (A) A dress code
    (B) A heating method
    (C) An inventory procedure
    (D) A rest break policy

38. Where does the woman most likely work?
    (A) At a car dealership
    (B) At a moving company
    (C) At an interior design firm
    (D) At a furniture store

39. What problem does the man have?
    (A) He does not have a vehicle.
    (B) He did not order an item.
    (C) He is currently not at home.
    (D) He did not receive an invoice.

40. What does the man agree to do?
    (A) Give driving directions
    (B) Wait for a few days
    (C) Pay an extra fee
    (D) Visit the woman's office

41. What is the purpose of the telephone call?
    (A) To cancel a plan
    (B) To correct a misunderstanding
    (C) To ask the man to head a committee
    (D) To suggest a type of transport

42. What does the woman say she has already done?
    (A) Chosen an entertainer
    (B) Checked a fuel level
    (C) Notified an organizer
    (D) Looked up a location

43. What will the man bring to the woman?
    (A) A guest list
    (B) A sign-up sheet
    (C) An expense report
    (D) A thank-you gift

GO ON TO THE NEXT PAGE

44. What are the speakers mainly discussing?

(A) A problem with some landscaping
(B) A new team member starting work
(C) A strategy for a team-building seminar
(D) A delivery date for some furnishings

45. What does the woman say she did yesterday?

(A) Began preparing a slide show
(B) Completed some request forms
(C) Introduced herself to colleagues
(D) Studied some project materials

46. What does Richard ask for help with?

(A) Presenting a budget
(B) Selecting some plants
(C) Investigating flooring options
(D) Distributing a memo

47. What is the man unable to do?

(A) Join a rewards program
(B) Update an address
(C) View a balance
(D) Transfer some money

48. What does the woman say caused the problem?

(A) A promotional period has ended.
(B) An account has been closed.
(C) A message was deleted.
(D) A Web browser is out-of-date.

49. What does the woman offer to do for the man?

(A) Provide a Web page link
(B) Explain a registration process
(C) Put his information into a system
(D) Reduce a service charge

50. What did the woman recently do?

(A) She built a recreational facility.
(B) She accepted a promotion.
(C) She conducted an interview.
(D) She played on a sports team.

51. What does the man ask the woman about?

(A) Her other skills
(B) Her reading habits
(C) Her next assignment
(D) Her food preferences

52. What does the man mean when he says, "I saw a café around the corner"?

(A) He hopes the woman can talk now.
(B) He would like to have a snack before an event.
(C) A photo needs a better background.
(D) It is too cold to wait outdoors.

53. Who most likely are the speakers?

(A) Auto mechanics
(B) Electronics vendors
(C) Warehouse clerks
(D) Construction supervisors

54. What does the man like about the product?

(A) It passed a special safety test.
(B) It uses energy efficiently.
(C) It is powerful.
(D) It is lightweight.

55. What does the woman propose?

(A) Making a comparative chart
(B) Placing an advance order
(C) Negotiating a lower price
(D) Consulting a technical expert

56. Who most likely is Mr. Kawakami?

(A) A hiring manager at an organization
(B) An admissions officer for a graduate program
(C) A reporter for a business journal
(D) A participant in an open forum

57. What does the woman say she hopes to do?

(A) Oversee a large group of people
(B) Take advantage of new technology
(C) Experience a casual office culture
(D) Work in service of a certain cause

58. What does the woman say is her strong point?

(A) Attention to detail
(B) Flexibility
(C) Creativity
(D) Trustworthiness

59. What are the speakers discussing?

(A) The focus of an advertisement
(B) The cover of a pamphlet
(C) A claim in a blog post
(D) A listing on an online map

60. What does the woman confirm has changed about a dry cleaner?

(A) Its operating status
(B) Its phone number
(C) Its specialty
(D) Its owner

61. What does the man say he will do?

(A) Remove a section from a text
(B) Make the size of some words larger
(C) Add a note to some contents
(D) Rearrange the layout of a page

Notice
New earlier shuttle departures!

Route	Destination Building	First departure
One	Martell	6:30 A.M.
Two	Spinatak	6:45 A.M.
Three	Bayareth	6:00 A.M.
Four	Rossmore	6:15 A.M.

62. According to the man, what is difficult?

(A) Logging on to a staff e-mail program
(B) Obtaining an employee access card
(C) Finding nearby parking spaces
(D) Using a renovated office building

63. Look at the graphic. Which building does the man most likely work in?

(A) Martell
(B) Spinatak
(C) Bayareth
(D) Rossmore

64. What does the woman say shuttle bus passengers can do?

(A) Enjoy views of the city
(B) Connect to the Internet
(C) Charge electronic devices
(D) Read local newsletters

GO ON TO THE NEXT PAGE

Item to Be Cleaned	Vinegar to Use Per Gallon of Water
Solid Flooring	1/2 cup
Refrigerators	1 cup
Windows	2 cups
Food Jars	1 gallon

Bus Line Map

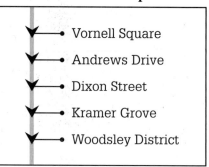

65. Why does the woman want to clean with vinegar?

   (A) It costs less than other products.
   (B) It is environmentally-friendly.
   (C) It is widely available.
   (D) It can be used on various surfaces.

66. Look at the graphic. How much vinegar should the woman mix with a gallon of water?

   (A) 1/2 cup
   (B) 1 cup
   (C) 2 cups
   (D) 1 gallon

67. What does the woman decide to buy in addition to vinegar?

   (A) Some cleaning sponges
   (B) Some rubber gloves
   (C) A dishtowel
   (D) A measuring cup

68. What will the speakers do at their destination?

   (A) Eat a meal
   (B) Shop for a party
   (C) Hand out flyers
   (D) Attend a workshop

69. According to the woman, what did the speakers' company do?

   (A) Launched a publicity campaign
   (B) Relocated to a different area
   (C) Restructured its intern training course
   (D) Announced a corporate merger

70. Look at the graphic. Which stop will the speakers get off at?

   (A) Vornell Square
   (B) Andrews Drive
   (C) Kramer Grove
   (D) Woodsley District

PART 4

Directions: You will hear some talks given by a single speaker. You will be asked to answer three questions about what the speaker says in each talk. Select the best response to each question and mark the letter (A), (B), (C), or (D) on your answer sheet. The talks will not be printed in your test book and will be spoken only one time.

71. Who most likely is Ms. Boyce?

    (A) A soccer coach
    (B) A sportswriter
    (C) A school principal
    (D) A city politician

72. What are some listeners encouraged to do?

    (A) Watch a sports competition
    (B) Write letters to a newspaper
    (C) Donate to a building project
    (D) Vote on an educational initiative

73. According to the speaker, what will be broadcast next?

    (A) Some song rankings
    (B) Some traffic updates
    (C) A news debate
    (D) An advertisement

74. What are the listeners about to do?

    (A) Take an employment exam
    (B) Participate in a focus group
    (C) Observe a graphic design class
    (D) Attend a television show taping

75. What will the speaker distribute?

    (A) Pencils
    (B) Headphones
    (C) Tablet computers
    (D) Survey forms

76. What are the listeners instructed to do?

    (A) Remain quiet
    (B) Double-check their work
    (C) Raise their hands to ask questions
    (D) Turn off their mobile phones

77. What department does the listener most likely work for?

    (A) Legal
    (B) Administration
    (C) Information Technology
    (D) Public Relations

78. What does the speaker imply when she says, "the program was made for the Andeskie system"?

    (A) She intends to uninstall a program.
    (B) She is surprised that Andeskie created a program.
    (C) She cannot answer a technical question.
    (D) She uses a different operating system.

79. What is the listener asked to do?

    (A) Locate a software manual
    (B) Move a project deadline
    (C) Return a phone call
    (D) Lead a training session

80. Where is the announcement taking place?

    (A) In a hotel
    (B) At a museum
    (C) On a boat
    (D) In a restaurant

81. What is the purpose of the event?

    (A) To present an award
    (B) To open a conference
    (C) To welcome a new director
    (D) To raise money for a charity

82. What are the listeners urged to do?

    (A) Save a purchase receipt
    (B) Put on an identification badge
    (C) Examine an informative brochure
    (D) Form an orderly line

GO ON TO THE NEXT PAGE

83. What have the listeners been concerned about?

(A) The range of some choices
(B) The elimination of some requirements
(C) The format of a document
(D) The distance to a venue

84. Why does the speaker say, "They're really busy these days"?

(A) To encourage listeners to handle tasks by themselves
(B) To explain a delayed response to an inquiry
(C) To congratulate a team on an achievement
(D) To suggest offering support to a committee

85. According to the speaker, where is some information available?

(A) In a meeting agenda
(B) On a projection screen
(C) In an event invitation
(D) On a posted notice

86. What type of business does DRC Resources provide consulting services for?

(A) Savings banks
(B) Convenience stores
(C) Fitness centers
(D) Medical clinics

87. According to the speaker, what can DRC Resources help a business do?

(A) Adjust to market trends
(B) Enlarge its client base
(C) Improve employee morale
(D) Decrease its operating costs

88. What will happen in July?

(A) A new service will become available.
(B) A Web site will offer a discount.
(C) A discussion will be broadcast.
(D) A trade show will be held.

89. Who most likely is the speaker?

(A) A film producer
(B) An event photographer
(C) A publishing executive
(D) A tourism official

90. What does the speaker mean when she says, "We've got to get back to him right away"?

(A) A mistake must be fixed immediately.
(B) She is impressed with a résumé.
(C) She wants to accept a proposal.
(D) A company may choose another firm.

91. What does the speaker ask the listener to do?

(A) Revise a production budget
(B) Meet with her later in the day
(C) Forward a confirmation e-mail
(D) Contact a branch office

92. What is being announced?

(A) A change to a tax law
(B) The release of a publication
(C) The expansion of a business
(D) A rise in an exchange rate

93. What are listeners advised to do?

(A) Exercise more patience
(B) Look for digital coupons
(C) Invest in new industries
(D) Use a mobile app

94. What does the speaker say can be found in a newspaper?

(A) A press interview
(B) A book review
(C) Some job descriptions
(D) Some editorials

Room	1 P.M.–2 P.M.	2 P.M.–3 P.M.
Seminar Room A		Reserved (Bruce)
Seminar Room B		
Seminar Room C	Reserved (Elisha)	
Seminar Room D	Reserved (David)	

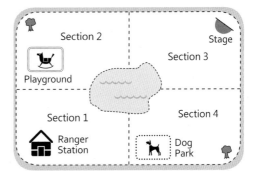

95. What will the speaker discuss at a meeting?

(A) A funding shortage
(B) Some software upgrades
(C) Some staff benefits
(D) A travel itinerary

96. Look at the graphic. Which room will the speaker try to reserve for a 2 P.M. meeting?

(A) Seminar Room A
(B) Seminar Room B
(C) Seminar Room C
(D) Seminar Room D

97. What does the speaker say he will do before lunch?

(A) Photocopy some instructions
(B) Finalize an estimate
(C) Unpack a shipment
(D) Send some notifications

98. Why have the listeners come to the park?

(A) To assist with cleaning it
(B) To take part in a festival
(C) To decorate it for a holiday
(D) To go on a guided tour

99. Look at the graphic. Which section is partially closed?

(A) Section 1
(B) Section 2
(C) Section 3
(D) Section 4

100. What can listeners do at a table?

(A) Look at a park map
(B) Enter a prize drawing
(C) Get some special gear
(D) Throw away some waste

This is the end of the Listening test.

TEST 7

LISTENING TEST

In the Listening test, you will be asked to demonstrate how well you understand spoken English. The entire Listening test will last approximately 45 minutes. There are four parts, and directions are given for each part. You must mark your answers on the separate answer sheet. Do not write your answers in your test book.

PART 1

Directions: For each question in this part, you will hear four statements about a picture in your test book. When you hear the statements, you must select the one statement that best describes what you see in the picture. Then find the number of the question on your answer sheet and mark your answer. The statements will not be printed in your test book and will be spoken only one time.

Statement (C), "They're sitting at a table," is the best description of the picture, so you should select answer (C) and mark it on your answer sheet.

1.

2.

GO ON TO THE NEXT PAGE

3.

4.

5.

6.

GO ON TO THE NEXT PAGE

PART 2

Directions: You will hear a question or statement and three responses spoken in English. They will not be printed in your test book and will be spoken only one time. Select the best response to the question or statement and mark the letter (A), (B), or (C) on your answer sheet.

7. Mark your answer on your answer sheet.

8. Mark your answer on your answer sheet.

9. Mark your answer on your answer sheet.

10. Mark your answer on your answer sheet.

11. Mark your answer on your answer sheet.

12. Mark your answer on your answer sheet.

13. Mark your answer on your answer sheet.

14. Mark your answer on your answer sheet.

15. Mark your answer on your answer sheet.

16. Mark your answer on your answer sheet.

17. Mark your answer on your answer sheet.

18. Mark your answer on your answer sheet.

19. Mark your answer on your answer sheet.

20. Mark your answer on your answer sheet.

21. Mark your answer on your answer sheet.

22. Mark your answer on your answer sheet.

23. Mark your answer on your answer sheet.

24. Mark your answer on your answer sheet.

25. Mark your answer on your answer sheet.

26. Mark your answer on your answer sheet.

27. Mark your answer on your answer sheet.

28. Mark your answer on your answer sheet.

29. Mark your answer on your answer sheet.

30. Mark your answer on your answer sheet.

31. Mark your answer on your answer sheet.

Directions: You will hear some conversations between two or more people. You will be asked to answer three questions about what the speakers say in each conversation. Select the best response to each question and mark the letter (A), (B), (C), or (D) on your answer sheet. The conversations will not be printed in your test book and will be spoken only one time.

32. What problem does the woman mention?

(A) A product has been discontinued.
(B) A coupon has expired.
(C) An item is out of stock.
(D) A sale period has ended.

33. Where most likely are the speakers?

(A) At a hardware store
(B) At a pharmacy
(C) At a clothing shop
(D) At a bookstore

34. What will the woman most likely do next?

(A) Show the man some merchandise
(B) Contact a supervisor
(C) Give the man a receipt
(D) Authorize a discount

35. What is the conversation mainly about?

(A) A company relocation
(B) A product launch
(C) A change in policy
(D) A decline in sales

36. What does the woman mention about Ms. Beck?

(A) She completed a project quickly.
(B) She has compiled a report.
(C) She joined the team last quarter.
(D) She has expertise in the field.

37. What does the woman say she will do?

(A) Reserve a meeting space
(B) Update some figures
(C) Recruit group members
(D) Congratulate some volunteers

38. What is the man's problem?

(A) He missed a registration deadline.
(B) He does not have an admission pass.
(C) He could not get a Web site to load.
(D) He lost his welcome packet.

39. What does the man inquire about?

(A) Signing up for a different talk
(B) Getting a partial refund
(C) Making a last-minute payment
(D) Entering a session late

40. What will the woman most likely do next?

(A) Verify the man's address
(B) Confirm some details
(C) Reserve a seat near the back
(D) Print out a registration form

41. What does the woman mean when she says, "It's one night only"?

(A) A deadline for a task is too short.
(B) She cannot work in the man's place.
(C) A payment will not be large enough.
(D) She plans to take a short vacation.

42. Why does the man ask for the woman's help?

(A) He has tickets to a music festival.
(B) He would like to get training at an industry event.
(C) He is preparing himself for a job promotion.
(D) He wants to attend a celebratory event.

43. What does the woman offer to do?

(A) Give the man a confirmation number
(B) Provide some contact information
(C) Work more hours than usual
(D) Call Gary about the situation

GO ON TO THE NEXT PAGE

Test 7

44. What has the speaker's company recently done?

(A) Hired a new executive
(B) Developed a unique product
(C) Undergone an inspection
(D) Obtained board certification

45. What does the woman suggest when she says, "My former company did the same thing"?

(A) She is not planning to take part in a course.
(B) She wants the company to remain competitive.
(C) She thinks a proposal is a good idea.
(D) She will ask an old employer for information.

46. What will the man show the woman?

(A) Some alternative suggestions
(B) Some instructional materials
(C) A training schedule
(D) A copy of a certificate

47. What is the woman concerned about doing?

(A) Making a bad impression
(B) Delaying a delivery of supplies
(C) Completing repairs in a lobby
(D) Investing in the wrong company

48. What does the man say about Adam?

(A) He ordered the wrong supplies.
(B) He is taking a lunch break.
(C) He arrived to work late.
(D) He is a new employee.

49. What will Adam be asked to do?

(A) Move some containers
(B) Set up some equipment
(C) Clean a conference room
(D) Organize a storage room

50. Who most likely is Ms. Volker?

(A) An event planner
(B) A job applicant
(C) A venue owner
(D) A private caterer

51. What does the woman want to do?

(A) Move the deadline of a project
(B) Add people to a guest list
(C) Update information on an invitation
(D) Change the location of a party

52. What does Mr. Irwin ask the woman to do?

(A) Call back when Ms. Volker is available
(B) Give information about dietary restrictions
(C) Wait on the phone line for a moment
(D) Select some entrées for a meal

53. Why does the woman congratulate the man?

(A) He secured a major client.
(B) He found an error in a contract.
(C) He was offered a promotion.
(D) He will transfer to an overseas office.

54. What does the man suggest about Haven Finance?

(A) It will be a useful corporate partner.
(B) It is currently expanding its workforce.
(C) It is his company's largest competitor.
(D) It recently changed its owner.

55. What does the woman recommend doing?

(A) Reviewing budget details
(B) Hiring another employee
(C) Attending a board meeting
(D) Holding a staff celebration

56. Why is the woman calling?

(A) To book a cruise
(B) To check ID requirements
(C) To update a reservation
(D) To renew a passport

57. What does the man recommend doing?

(A) Saving a receipt
(B) Visiting a Web site
(C) Using an express service
(D) Reviewing a list

58. What information does the man ask for?

(A) A license number
(B) A mailing address
(C) A preferred date
(D) A confirmation code

59. What kind of business do the speakers most likely work for?

(A) A catering company
(B) A commercial bank
(C) A package delivery service
(D) A job placement agency

60. What is mentioned about Oscar?

(A) He will help open a branch office.
(B) He is a newly hired employee.
(C) He received a gift from a customer.
(D) He is invited to speak at a conference.

61. What does the woman ask Fumio to do?

(A) Phone a client
(B) Clean out a storage area
(C) Print out a document
(D) Revise a training manual

Subscription Fees	
3 Months	$22.99
6 Months	$41.99
1 Year	$79.99
2 Years	$139.99

62. What is the purpose of the call?

(A) To promote a renewal
(B) To request a late payment
(C) To confirm contact details
(D) To sign up a new customer

63. What does the woman plan to do in July?

(A) Upgrade a service
(B) Start a new job
(C) Cancel her subscription
(D) Move to a new home

64. Look at the graphic. How much will the woman pay today?

(A) $22.99
(B) $41.99
(C) $79.99
(D) $139.99

GO ON TO THE NEXT PAGE

Book Signing Events: Proposed Schedule	
Date	**Author**
May 2	Greta Tretiakov
May 9	Linda Holmes
May 16	Cai Quan
May 23	Spencer Clarke

Brand: Haynes

R590   R210   R667   R45

153cm

65. Who did the woman speak to in the morning?

(A) A prospective publisher
(B) A famous author
(C) A bookstore manager
(D) A literary agent

66. Look at the graphic. Who will the woman contact?

(A) Greta Tretiakov
(B) Linda Holmes
(C) Cai Quan
(D) Spencer Clarke

67. Why is the man relieved?

(A) Some information has not been posted online.
(B) A schedule was approved by his boss.
(C) The turnout at an event was high.
(D) A book received a favorable review.

68. What kind of business is the woman most likely calling?

(A) A delivery service
(B) A department store
(C) A Web design company
(D) A manufacturing facility

69. Look at the graphic. Which item was the woman sent?

(A) R590
(B) R210
(C) R667
(D) R45

70. What does the man recommend doing?

(A) Visiting a business in person
(B) Waiting for the next delivery
(C) Calling back another day
(D) Checking an order's status online

PART 4

Directions: You will hear some talks given by a single speaker. You will be asked to answer three questions about what the speaker says in each talk. Select the best response to each question and mark the letter (A), (B), (C), or (D) on your answer sheet. The talks will not be printed in your test book and will be spoken only one time.

71. Where does the speaker work?
(A) At a fitness facility
(B) At a medical clinic
(C) At a pharmacy
(D) At a hair salon

72. According to the speaker, what has caused a problem?
(A) A double-booking
(B) An absent employee
(C) A technical issue
(D) A lost document

73. What should the listener do by Friday?
(A) Update contact information
(B) Renew a membership
(C) Make a payment
(D) Rebook an appointment

74. Who most likely is Helen Anderson?
(A) A gallery owner
(B) A painting instructor
(C) A museum tour guide
(D) A professional photographer

75. According to the speaker, what has Helen Anderson recently done?
(A) Launched a Web site
(B) Started a class
(C) Won an award
(D) Published a book

76. What will most likely happen next?
(A) The listeners will watch a video.
(B) Ms. Anderson will respond to questions.
(C) The speaker will check the attendance.
(D) The listeners will take a break.

77. Why will the listener travel to Atlanta?
(A) To inspect a hotel
(B) To attend a conference
(C) To open a business
(D) To visit family members

78. What problem does the speaker mention?
(A) The hotel is fully booked for the requested date.
(B) The listener was given an incorrect price quote.
(C) The reserved rooms are not next to each other.
(D) A reservation was canceled accidentally.

79. What does the speaker say he will do?
(A) Contact another branch
(B) Provide discount vouchers
(C) Issue a refund of a deposit
(D) Offer a free room upgrade

80. What will happen on November 20?
(A) A community parade
(B) A local election
(C) A food festival
(D) A musical performance

81. According to the speaker, what can listeners do on the Web site?
(A) Download a calendar
(B) Order some tickets
(C) View a planned route
(D) Share their opinions

82. What project will be supported by the event?
(A) Improving an animal shelter
(B) Renovating a city building
(C) Running a future event
(D) Maintaining a public park

83. What does the company plan to change?

(A) A dress code policy
(B) The hours of operation
(C) A benefits package
(D) The vacation request process

84. What does the speaker mean when he says, "Be sure to get the right one"?

(A) He wants listeners to make a decision.
(B) Listeners should know that the data is personalized.
(C) Each department has to use a different form.
(D) He is concerned about errors in a report.

85. What should listeners do if they have questions?

(A) Stay after the meeting
(B) E-mail them to the speaker
(C) Complete a survey
(D) Meet with their team leader

86. Who most likely is the speaker?

(A) A delivery person
(B) A travel agent
(C) A caterer
(D) A hotel manager

87. What is the listener asked to do?

(A) Bring some equipment
(B) Recruit more employees
(C) Contact a client
(D) Work an extra shift

88. What does the speaker suggest when she says, "I'm the only one here right now"?

(A) She decided to work after hours.
(B) She made an error with the schedule.
(B) She is upset about a late employee.
(D) She does not want to leave a site.

89. What is the broadcast mainly about?

(A) A jazz festival
(B) A building permit
(C) A reading program
(D) A library expansion

90. What will begin from September 1?

(A) Some construction work
(B) A fundraising event
(C) Computer classes
(D) A recruitment drive

91. What was Mr. Cervantes pleased about?

(A) How popular a new program is
(B) How high some donations were
(C) How quickly a project was completed
(D) How inexpensive some work was

92. What kind of business is the listener most likely calling?

(A) A construction company
(B) A utility company
(C) An electronics store
(D) An Internet provider

93. What does the speaker suggest when he says, "we recommend visiting the Web site"?

(A) Online customers can get a discount.
(B) Some new information has been posted.
(C) A process will be faster online.
(D) There is a charge for phone inquiries.

94. Why should the listeners press the star key?

(A) To pay a bill
(B) To leave a message
(C) To repeat the recording
(D) To access a staff directory

Top Seller

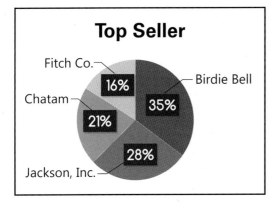

Station Café	
Sandwich	£3.49
Hot coffee	£2.99
Hot tea	£2.59
Iced tea	£2.29

95. What kind of goods does the speaker's company produce?

(A) Telephones
(B) Furniture
(C) Cosmetics
(D) Clothing

96. Look at the graphic. Where do the listeners work?

(A) Birdie Bell
(B) Jackson Inc.
(C) Chatam
(D) Fitch Co.

97. What will Ms. Foster's team be in charge of doing?

(A) Running an advertising campaign
(B) Planning an outdoor activity
(C) Finding new suppliers
(D) Developing some new products

98. Why does the speaker apologize?

(A) A train car was overbooked.
(B) A journey has been canceled.
(C) A station will close early.
(D) A train has been delayed.

99. Look at the graphic. Which price will not be changed?

(A) £3.49
(B) £2.99
(C) £2.59
(D) £2.29

100. What are the listeners reminded to do?

(A) Listen for announcements
(B) Wait at the platform
(C) Exchange their tickets
(D) Keep their luggage with them

This is the end of the Listening test.

TEST 8

LISTENING TEST

In the Listening test, you will be asked to demonstrate how well you understand spoken English. The entire Listening test will last approximately 45 minutes. There are four parts, and directions are given for each part. You must mark your answers on the separate answer sheet. Do not write your answers in your test book.

PART 1

Directions: For each question in this part, you will hear four statements about a picture in your test book. When you hear the statements, you must select the one statement that best describes what you see in the picture. Then find the number of the question on your answer sheet and mark your answer. The statements will not be printed in your test book and will be spoken only one time.

Statement (C), "They're sitting at a table," is the best description of the picture, so you should select answer (C) and mark it on your answer sheet.

1.

2.

GO ON TO THE NEXT PAGE

3.

4.

5.

6.

GO ON TO THE NEXT PAGE ➤

Test 8

PART 2

Directions: You will hear a question or statement and three responses spoken in English. They will not be printed in your test book and will be spoken only one time. Select the best response to the question or statement and mark the letter (A), (B), or (C) on your answer sheet.

7. Mark your answer on your answer sheet.

8. Mark your answer on your answer sheet.

9. Mark your answer on your answer sheet.

10. Mark your answer on your answer sheet.

11. Mark your answer on your answer sheet.

12. Mark your answer on your answer sheet.

13. Mark your answer on your answer sheet.

14. Mark your answer on your answer sheet.

15. Mark your answer on your answer sheet.

16. Mark your answer on your answer sheet.

17. Mark your answer on your answer sheet.

18. Mark your answer on your answer sheet.

19. Mark your answer on your answer sheet.

20. Mark your answer on your answer sheet.

21. Mark your answer on your answer sheet.

22. Mark your answer on your answer sheet.

23. Mark your answer on your answer sheet.

24. Mark your answer on your answer sheet.

25. Mark your answer on your answer sheet.

26. Mark your answer on your answer sheet.

27. Mark your answer on your answer sheet.

28. Mark your answer on your answer sheet.

29. Mark your answer on your answer sheet.

30. Mark your answer on your answer sheet.

31. Mark your answer on your answer sheet.

PART 3

Directions: You will hear some conversations between two or more people. You will be asked to answer three questions about what the speakers say in each conversation. Select the best response to each question and mark the letter (A), (B), (C), or (D) on your answer sheet. The conversations will not be printed in your test book and will be spoken only one time.

32. Where most likely do the speakers work?

   (A) At a university
   (B) At a rental car agency
   (C) At a staffing service
   (D) At a post office

33. What does the woman want to do?

   (A) Correct a billing error
   (B) Apply for a promotion
   (C) Obtain a parking permit
   (D) Remodel an office space

34. What does the man recommend doing?

   (A) Using an expense account
   (B) Going through a process online
   (C) Contacting a former coworker
   (D) Scanning a set of documents

35. Where most likely are the speakers?

   (A) At a fitness center
   (B) At an art gallery
   (C) At a pharmacy
   (D) At a hotel

36. What is out of order?

   (A) An electronic lock
   (B) A water dispenser
   (C) A desktop computer
   (D) An elevator door

37. Why should the repair be done quickly?

   (A) Some complaints were received.
   (B) Many visitors are expected.
   (C) A warranty will expire.
   (D) A security issue may arise.

38. What is the conversation mainly about?

   (A) A trade fair
   (B) A staff uniform
   (C) A prize drawing
   (D) A company logo

39. What does the woman offer to do?

   (A) Arrange a brainstorming session
   (B) Order some promotional items
   (C) Collect some packing boxes
   (D) Notify a graphic designer

40. What does the man request?

   (A) A purchase receipt
   (B) A floor plan
   (C) Contact details
   (D) Product specifications

41. What has a client done?

   (A) Reported a problem
   (B) Missed a deadline
   (C) Arrived at a building
   (D) Filled out an online form

42. What does Klaus mean when he says, "Brandon, aren't you taking night classes in Web development"?

   (A) Brandon is probably not interested in an opportunity.
   (B) Brandon can describe an educational program.
   (C) Brandon will not be able to work overtime.
   (D) Brandon might know how to fix a technical issue.

43. What does the woman guess that Lorna is doing?

   (A) Running some errands
   (B) Attending to an illness
   (C) Leading a technology workshop
   (D) Playing a winter sport

GO ON TO THE NEXT PAGE

44. Why does the woman speak to the man?

(A) To suggest collaborating on a book
(B) To ask for his opinion on an advertisement
(C) To invite him to a negotiation meeting
(D) To inform him of a business deal

45. What does the woman say about Jadley Publishing?

(A) It won an industry award.
(B) Its headquarters are nearby.
(C) Some of its branches were founded a year ago.
(D) Some of its books are aimed at a certain age range.

46. What does the woman say she will do?

(A) Set up a conference call
(B) Sign up for a newsletter
(C) Browse a catalog
(D) Create a display

47. What are the speakers mainly discussing?

(A) A vacation policy
(B) A booking procedure
(C) A trip itinerary
(D) A workshop venue

48. What does the man say he did?

(A) Checked an account balance
(B) Listened to a traffic report
(C) Used a route-planning service
(D) Edited a travel brochure

49. What does the woman mention about a resort?

(A) It has many rooms.
(B) It received good reviews.
(C) It recently closed.
(D) It is far away.

50. What is the man doing?

(A) Training a technician
(B) Inspecting a factory
(C) Promoting a product
(D) Installing a machine

51. What does the woman ask about?

(A) Benefits for employees
(B) The cause of a loud noise
(C) The procedure for requesting a repair
(D) A protective covering for a device

52. What does the man say is explained in a booklet?

(A) How to understand the information on a screen
(B) How often a test should be performed
(C) How to operate an electric vehicle
(D) How many levels a course has

53. Who most likely are the women?

(A) Magazine editors
(B) Research scientists
(C) Medical care providers
(D) Academic librarians

54. Why are the women being introduced?

(A) They will appear on television together.
(B) They will travel to a convention together.
(C) They went to the same school.
(D) They live in the same area.

55. What will the women talk about later?

(A) Their typical work schedules
(B) Their preferred contact methods
(C) The topics they are interested in
(D) The places they want to visit

56. What is the woman responsible for?

(A) Making a costume
(B) Choosing some lighting
(C) Decorating a ballroom
(D) Rewriting some scripts

57. Why does the man say, "We need to begin filming the scene tomorrow morning"?

(A) To indicate that filming may take a long time
(B) To explain why he cannot provide help
(C) To remind the woman to arrive early
(D) To urge the woman to work quickly

58. What does the man decide to do?

(A) Speak with an actor
(B) Try out a camera filter
(C) Lend the woman his car
(D) Pack up an outfit

59. What is the topic of the conversation?

(A) Aircraft layouts
(B) Ticketing machines
(C) A baggage requirement
(D) A mileage program

60. What does the man say is the benefit of a change?

(A) Reduced wait times for passengers
(B) Fairer distribution of staff workloads
(C) Better communication between staff
(D) More types of savings for passengers

61. What will most likely happen in February?

(A) A mobile app will be released.
(B) A decision will be announced.
(C) A law will go into effect.
(D) A new terminal will open.

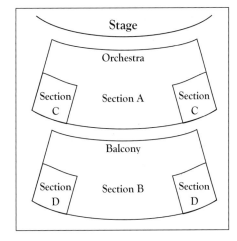

62. What does the woman want to know?

(A) The price of a ticket
(B) The size of a theater
(C) The length of a performance
(D) The popularity of a play

63. Look at the graphic. Which area will the speakers most likely sit in?

(A) Section A
(B) Section B
(C) Section C
(D) Section D

64. What does the woman suggest doing?

(A) Checking a seating chart
(B) Visiting a souvenir shop
(C) Taking some pictures
(D) Buying some snacks

Test 8

GO ON TO THE NEXT PAGE

Invoice

Order no. 36433

Item	Quantity	Total price
Drinking glass	4	$24
Scented candle	8	$32
Toaster	1	$45
Small chair	2	$56

65. What is the problem with the woman's shipment?

(A) It was delayed in transit.
(B) It was not gift-wrapped.
(C) It contains damaged goods.
(D) It is missing a tracking number.

66. What does the man say about some tableware?

(A) It is no longer manufactured.
(B) It has beautiful products.
(C) It is inexpensive.
(D) It is imported from overseas.

67. Look at the graphic. What refund amount will the woman most likely receive?

(A) $24
(B) $32
(C) $45
(D) $56

68. What is the purpose of the man's visit?

(A) To find a lost item
(B) To register for a course
(C) To attend a job interview
(D) To repair a piece of equipment

69. Look at the graphic. Which room does the woman direct the man to?

(A) Classroom 1
(B) Classroom 2
(C) The Student Lounge
(D) The Staff Room

70. What does the man ask for?

(A) A business card
(B) A writing tool
(C) A connecting cable
(D) A network password

PART 4

Directions: You will hear some talks given by a single speaker. You will be asked to answer three questions about what the speaker says in each talk. Select the best response to each question and mark the letter (A), (B), (C), or (D) on your answer sheet. The talks will not be printed in your test book and will be spoken only one time.

71. What does the store mainly sell?

(A) Children's toys
(B) Groceries
(C) Clothing
(D) Gardening supplies

72. According to the announcement, what is new at the store?

(A) Monthly classes
(B) Spaces for relaxation
(C) Discounts on large purchases
(D) Home delivery options

73. What can customers do at the front of the store?

(A) Obtain a coupon
(B) Have refreshments
(C) See new merchandise
(D) Buy a gift certificate

74. What will the listener do for a conference?

(A) Write a news article
(B) Design an advertisement
(C) Provide housing for a visitor
(D) Lead a discussion

75. What does the speaker say Ms. Reed might do?

(A) Cancel an appearance
(B) Bring a colleague
(C) Take a later flight
(D) Call the listener

76. What is the speaker preparing?

(A) A conference program
(B) A profile of a participant
(C) A set of questions
(D) An expense estimate

77. Who will visit the speaker's workplace?

(A) An athlete
(B) A diplomat
(C) A musician
(D) A journalist

78. What are listeners asked to do?

(A) Plan a lunch
(B) Read a notice
(C) Tidy a work area
(D) Put up decorations

79. What does the speaker imply when she says, "I won't forget it"?

(A) The listeners will be rewarded for some work.
(B) The listeners do not need to handle a task.
(C) She was impressed by a previous event.
(D) She has memorized some information.

80. Where most likely does the speaker work?

(A) At a bank
(B) At a real estate agency
(C) At a utility company
(D) At a law office

81. What potential problem does the speaker mention?

(A) The listener may not need a service.
(B) The listener may be charged extra.
(C) A contract may not be renewed.
(D) A government regulation may change.

82. What is the listener asked to do?

(A) Withdraw an application
(B) Confirm an account number
(C) Read an e-mail message
(D) Find a postal address

GO ON TO THE NEXT PAGE

83. What are listeners encouraged to do on a Web site?

(A) Leave comments
(B) Watch instructional videos
(C) Vote in a contest
(D) Download recipes

84. What will be discussed on the broadcast?

(A) A cookbook
(B) Some restaurant locations
(C) Some packaged food
(D) A kitchen appliance

85. What does the speaker say Mr. Huber will do?

(A) Conduct a taste test
(B) Describe a manufacturing process
(C) Display a collection of accessories
(D) Announce a career change

86. What is the workshop about?

(A) Becoming a more effective manager
(B) Designing customer surveys
(C) Maintaining company Web sites
(D) Giving better sales presentations

87. What will the workshop include?

(A) An acting task
(B) A painting exercise
(C) A question-and-answer period
(D) A physical competition

88. What does the speaker mean when he says, "there's no room for that"?

(A) An item must be moved to a storage area.
(B) It is important for listeners to avoid careless mistakes.
(C) The listeners must overcome their discomfort.
(D) A planned activity cannot take place.

89. Who most likely are the listeners?

(A) Waitstaff
(B) Cooks
(C) Cashiers
(D) Dishwashers

90. Why does the speaker say they will not visit the kitchen?

(A) It is poorly lit.
(B) It is under renovation.
(C) Its doors are locked.
(D) Its flooring is being cleaned.

91. Why does the speaker say, "the dishware was just delivered"?

(A) To assign a responsibility
(B) To make an excuse
(C) To show relief
(D) To emphasize a policy

92. What kind of business is being advertised?

(A) A disposal service
(B) A moving company
(C) A groundskeeping company
(D) An environmental advising firm

93. What does the speaker mention is now offered?

(A) A free consultation session
(B) An extra-large container
(C) Landscaping machinery rentals
(D) Transport of dangerous materials

94. What are listeners encouraged to do?

(A) Sign up on a Web site
(B) Visit a local branch
(C) Look at some reviews
(D) Compare some offers

Arden's Amusement Complex

20% Off

entrance to the main park

– Valid July 1 to July 31
– For groups of 30 or more people

Date	Seminar Name
January 8	Our Brand Identity
February 5	Dealing with Customer Objections
March 4	Sharing Success Stories
April 9	Voicemail Practices

95. What most likely is being celebrated?

   (A) A company's anniversary
   (B) The end of a business year
   (C) The completion of a project
   (D) Improved sales results

96. Look at the graphic. What will prevent the speaker from using the coupon?

   (A) The time of the group's arrival
   (B) The number of attendees
   (C) The date of the outing
   (D) The location of the venue

97. What does the speaker say about the outing?

   (A) The participants will share transportation.
   (B) It will include an overnight stay.
   (C) Employees' family members are welcome.
   (D) A supervisor's permission is required to attend.

98. Look at the graphic. Which seminar has been postponed?

   (A) Our Brand Identity
   (B) Dealing with Customer Objections
   (C) Sharing Success Stories
   (D) Voicemail Practices

99. What will the speaker's company do next week?

   (A) Revise a manual
   (B) Release new software
   (C) Determine a seminar date
   (D) Request feedback from the listeners

100. What will the listeners most likely do next?

   (A) View a television commercial
   (B) Read over a handout
   (C) Form some small groups
   (D) Count some product samples

This is the end of the Listening test.

TEST 9

LISTENING TEST

In the Listening test, you will be asked to demonstrate how well you understand spoken English. The entire Listening test will last approximately 45 minutes. There are four parts, and directions are given for each part. You must mark your answers on the separate answer sheet. Do not write your answers in your test book.

PART 1

Directions: For each question in this part, you will hear four statements about a picture in your test book. When you hear the statements, you must select the one statement that best describes what you see in the picture. Then find the number of the question on your answer sheet and mark your answer. The statements will not be printed in your test book and will be spoken only one time.

Statement (C), "They're sitting at a table," is the best description of the picture, so you should select answer (C) and mark it on your answer sheet.

1.

2.

GO ON TO THE NEXT PAGE ➡

Test 9

3.

4.

5.

6.

GO ON TO THE NEXT PAGE ➤

Test 9

PART 2

Directions: You will hear a question or statement and three responses spoken in English. They will not be printed in your test book and will be spoken only one time. Select the best response to the question or statement and mark the letter (A), (B), or (C) on your answer sheet.

7. Mark your answer on your answer sheet.

8. Mark your answer on your answer sheet.

9. Mark your answer on your answer sheet.

10. Mark your answer on your answer sheet.

11. Mark your answer on your answer sheet.

12. Mark your answer on your answer sheet.

13. Mark your answer on your answer sheet.

14. Mark your answer on your answer sheet.

15. Mark your answer on your answer sheet.

16. Mark your answer on your answer sheet.

17. Mark your answer on your answer sheet.

18. Mark your answer on your answer sheet.

19. Mark your answer on your answer sheet.

20. Mark your answer on your answer sheet.

21. Mark your answer on your answer sheet.

22. Mark your answer on your answer sheet.

23. Mark your answer on your answer sheet.

24. Mark your answer on your answer sheet.

25. Mark your answer on your answer sheet.

26. Mark your answer on your answer sheet.

27. Mark your answer on your answer sheet.

28. Mark your answer on your answer sheet.

29. Mark your answer on your answer sheet.

30. Mark your answer on your answer sheet.

31. Mark your answer on your answer sheet.

PART 3

Directions: You will hear some conversations between two or more people. You will be asked to answer three questions about what the speakers say in each conversation. Select the best response to each question and mark the letter (A), (B), (C), or (D) on your answer sheet. The conversations will not be printed in your test book and will be spoken only one time.

32. Why did the woman visit the building?

(A) To conduct a survey
(B) To deliver some goods
(C) To attend an interview
(D) To perform an inspection

33. What does the woman say about Ms. Monroe's office?

(A) It is difficult to find.
(B) It is near the elevators.
(C) It is being renovated.
(D) It is on the highest floor.

34. What does the man recommend doing?

(A) Coming back later
(B) Waiting in the lobby
(C) Calling Ms. Monroe directly
(D) Checking a building map

35. How did the woman find out about the business?

(A) By watching a commercial
(B) By visiting a Web site
(C) By receiving an advertising leaflet
(D) By talking to a friend

36. Why is the woman disappointed?

(A) The store is out of stock on some products.
(B) The discount does not apply to the item she wants.
(C) The delivery fee is higher than she expected.
(D) The store's promotional sale has ended.

37. What does the man tell the woman about?

(A) A product catalog
(B) A payment option
(C) A membership program
(D) A monthly sale

38. What does the woman mention about Florenti?

(A) It received excellent reviews.
(B) It is near the speakers' office.
(C) It takes phone reservations.
(D) It serves a variety of dishes.

39. Why does the man say, "someone dropped out"?

(A) To show disappointment
(B) To request some assistance
(C) To explain an error
(D) To extend an invitation

40. What does the man offer to do on Friday?

(A) Introduce the woman to his colleagues
(B) Let the woman leave early
(C) Make a menu recommendation
(D) Give the woman a ride

41. What is the purpose of the man's call?

(A) To inquire about a tour
(B) To schedule a newspaper interview
(C) To purchase a ticket
(D) To check the museum's hours

42. What is the man concerned about?

(A) A security issue
(B) An increase in price
(C) A minimum group size
(D) An upcoming holiday closure

43. What does the woman offer to do?

(A) Book an appointment
(B) Offer a discount voucher
(C) Speak to a manager
(D) Provide additional information

GO ON TO THE NEXT PAGE

44. What is the purpose of the meeting?

    (A) To explain a policy
    (B) To demonstrate a product
    (C) To negotiate a contract
    (D) To welcome new employees

45. Why is the woman concerned about the meeting?

    (A) Some attendees will be late.
    (B) The agenda is not ready yet.
    (C) Some guests might be uncomfortable.
    (D) A conference room is too small.

46. Who most likely is Mr. Aguilar?

    (A) A furniture designer
    (B) A potential client
    (C) A moving company owner
    (D) A maintenance worker

47. What are the speakers mainly discussing?

    (A) A job interview
    (B) A product demonstration
    (C) A national conference
    (D) A company policy

48. What problem does the woman mention?

    (A) A room is too small.
    (B) Some guests have canceled.
    (C) An activity is expensive.
    (D) The wrong copies were made.

49. Why does the woman suggest that the man visit her office?

    (A) To obtain a parking pass
    (B) To sign up for a carpool
    (C) To pick up a subway map
    (D) To ask for driving directions

50. Why is the man calling?

    (A) He had a loss of service.
    (B) He wants to sign up as a customer.
    (C) He was overcharged on his bill.
    (D) He intends to cancel a contract.

51. Where do the women most likely work?

    (A) At a power company
    (B) At an Internet provider
    (C) At a telephone company
    (D) At a courier company

52. What is the man asked to do?

    (A) Provide a customer number
    (B) Wait for a new document
    (C) Hold the line
    (D) Verify his residential address

53. What does the woman say she has done?

    (A) Updated an employee handbook
    (B) Posted informational signs
    (C) Trained some new employees
    (D) Worked as a guide for guests

54. Why does the man praise the woman?

    (A) She saved the company money.
    (B) She completed a task early.
    (C) She provided useful graphics.
    (D) She worked extra hours.

55. What does the man suggest doing?

    (A) Printing a document in color
    (B) Requesting an express service
    (C) Asking for a bulk discount
    (D) Using long-lasting materials

56. Where do the speakers work?

(A) At an accounting firm
(B) At a financial institution
(C) At a recruitment agency
(D) At a job training center

57. What does the woman mean when she says, "The last day was Friday"?

(A) A deadline has passed.
(B) A decision has been made.
(C) A meeting was held.
(D) A position has been filled.

58. What does the woman tell the man to do?

(A) Check a résumé for errors
(B) Share her contact details with a friend
(C) E-mail her a job description
(D) Provide a list of job candidates

59. What is the conversation mainly about?

(A) An industry award
(B) An inspection result
(C) A business proposal
(D) A workforce expansion

60. According to the man, what did Mr. McCroy do?

(A) Held training sessions
(B) Issued a line of credit
(C) Purchased new equipment
(D) Hired some experts

61. What will the woman most likely do next?

(A) Contact a news agency
(B) Post information online
(C) Make an announcement
(D) Review some applications

DLT Bike Rentals

Our rental rates are:	
3 hours	$12
6 hours	$20
1 day	$30
2 days	$45

62. What does the woman say about DLT Bike Rentals?

(A) It has more than one rental office.
(B) It is in its first month of business.
(C) It also purchases used bicycles.
(D) It does not accept reservations.

63. Look at the graphic. How much will the man probably pay for a rental?

(A) $12
(B) $20
(C) $30
(D) $45

64. What does the woman give the man?

(A) A bicycle lock
(B) A loyalty card
(C) A guide map
(D) A parking voucher

GO ON TO THE NEXT PAGE

Test 9

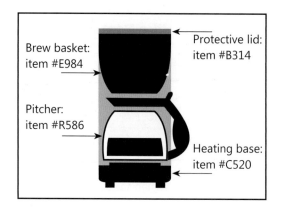

Brew basket: item #E984

Protective lid: item #B314

Pitcher: item #R586

Heating base: item #C520

Current Writing Assignments

Jerry Mitchell	"Fashion Trends for Professionals"
Misa Kure	"Proposed Immigration Changes"
Keesha Gibbs	"Domestic Transportation Safety"
Pavit Chanda	"The Power of Manners"

65. When was the device delivered to the woman?

(A) This morning
(B) Yesterday
(C) A few days ago
(D) Two weeks ago

66. Look at the graphic. What component did the woman have a problem with?

(A) B314
(B) E984
(C) R586
(D) C520

67. What does the man say he will do?

(A) Send a replacement part
(B) Give the woman a refund
(C) Exchange the entire item
(D) Contact a local store

68. What kind of event is taking place in March?

(A) A company's grand opening
(B) A political debate
(C) An environmental conference
(D) A career fair

69. Look at the graphic. Which article has been canceled?

(A) "Fashion Trends for Professionals"
(B) "Proposed Immigration Changes"
(C) "Domestic Transportation Safety"
(D) "The Power of Manners"

70. What will the woman do tomorrow morning?

(A) Meet with a colleague
(B) Scan an itinerary
(C) Book a flight
(D) Send a file

PART 4

Directions: You will hear some talks given by a single speaker. You will be asked to answer three questions about what the speaker says in each talk. Select the best response to each question and mark the letter (A), (B), (C), or (D) on your answer sheet. The talks will not be printed in your test book and will be spoken only one time.

71. Who most likely is Ms. Walpole?
    (A) A professor
    (B) A medical patient
    (C) A pet owner
    (D) A veterinarian

72. What does the speaker tell Ms. Walpole about?
    (A) An increase in fees
    (B) An appointment cancellation
    (C) A change in policy
    (D) A business relocation

73. What does the speaker suggest doing?
    (A) Calling back another day
    (B) Visiting a different site
    (C) Using a side entrance
    (D) Checking information online

74. What is the broadcast about?
    (A) A community picnic
    (B) A garden festival
    (C) A local election
    (D) A building repair project

75. According to the speaker, what can listeners do on the Web site?
    (A) Check a schedule
    (B) Purchase a ticket
    (C) Make a donation
    (D) View some photos

76. Who will the speaker interview next?
    (A) A city official
    (B) A landscape architect
    (C) A financial expert
    (D) An award winner

77. Where does the speaker most likely work?
    (A) At a repair shop
    (B) At a courier service
    (C) At an appliance store
    (D) At a clothing shop

78. When does the business close on weekdays?
    (A) At 7 P.M.
    (B) At 8 P.M.
    (C) At 9 P.M.
    (D) At 10 P.M.

79. According to the speaker, what will happen tomorrow?
    (A) A service will be free.
    (B) A discount promotion will begin.
    (C) A delivery will be made.
    (D) A new brand will be introduced.

80. Who most likely are the listeners?
    (A) Potential clients
    (B) New employees
    (C) Medical professionals
    (D) Community volunteers

81. What are the listeners reminded to do?
    (A) Provide their mailing information
    (B) Sign up for a seminar
    (C) Greet some special guests
    (D) Vote for a prize winner

82. What will the speaker do next?
    (A) Introduce a company
    (B) Show a video
    (C) Present an award
    (D) Answer audience questions

GO ON TO THE NEXT PAGE

Test 9

83. According to the man, why didn't he read a memo?

(A) His assistant lost it.
(B) He was away on business.
(C) He had a busy month.
(D) His computer malfunctioned.

84. What does the man mean when he says, "they'll be here first thing in the morning"?

(A) He will come to work earlier than usual.
(B) A meeting time should be changed.
(C) He is unable to move some furniture.
(D) A delivery will be made to the office.

85. What does the man plan to do?

(A) Approve overtime work
(B) Call one of his coworkers
(C) Leave a room unlocked
(D) Make a formal complaint

86. Who most likely is the speaker addressing?

(A) Computer programmers
(B) Sales clerks
(C) Accountants
(D) Department managers

87. Why does the woman say, "The Forestlane location had about a hundred"?

(A) To update an inventory list
(B) To correct a misunderstanding
(C) To emphasize an achievement
(D) To compare recruitment drives

88. What can the listeners do at 5 P.M.?

(A) Collect a bonus check
(B) Leave work early
(C) Have some refreshments
(D) Visit the speaker's office

89. What has recently been opened in Romano Valley?

(A) An art museum
(B) An amusement park
(C) A sports facility
(D) A music institute

90. What benefit of the site does the speaker mention?

(A) It will offer educational opportunities.
(B) It will increase public funds.
(C) It will attract out-of-town tourists.
(D) It will improve the city's image.

91. What are the listeners encouraged to do?

(A) E-mail the speaker
(B) Attend a special event
(C) Call their supervisor
(D) Share their opinions

92. What is mentioned about the workshop?

(A) It is sponsored by an art gallery.
(B) It is designed for beginners.
(C) It is being offered free of charge.
(D) It was rescheduled from a previous date.

93. What does the speaker remind the listeners to do?

(A) Register for upcoming classes
(B) Pick up parking vouchers
(C) Display their name tags
(D) Post feedback on a Web site

94. What does the speaker imply when she says, "another group used this room before us"?

(A) She is disappointed by the number of participants.
(B) A facility does not have many rooms.
(C) A room schedule was incorrect.
(D) Some supplies are unorganized.

Carolina Hardware: Equipment Rental	
Device	**Brand**
Circular Saw	Scharf
Floor Sander	Tikko
Nail Gun	Ashford
Paint Sprayer	Viera

Grand Isle Railways

One-Way Ticket
Adult: 1
Destination: Manchester
Departure Time: 1 P.M.

95. What does the speaker say about Carolina Hardware?

(A) It has the area's widest selection.
(B) It has recently introduced a new brand.
(C) It has been open for a long time.
(D) It has regular demonstrations for customers.

96. Look at the graphic. Which brand is not available for rental?

(A) Scharf
(B) Tikko
(C) Ashford
(D) Viera

97. According to the speaker, where can shoppers get discount coupons?

(A) From a Web site
(B) From the customer service desk
(C) From the checkout area
(D) From a display stand

98. Why does the speaker apologize?

(A) Seats cannot be reserved.
(B) Beverages are not available.
(C) A train departed late.
(D) A restroom is off limits.

99. What does the speaker encourage listeners to do?

(A) Stay seated during the journey
(B) Keep their personal belongings with them
(C) Have their tickets ready to present
(D) Read some safety information

100. Look at the graphic. What time is the train expected to arrive at Manchester?

(A) At around one o'clock
(B) At around two o'clock
(C) At around three o'clock
(D) At around four o'clock

This is the end of the Listening test.

TEST 10

LISTENING TEST

In the Listening test, you will be asked to demonstrate how well you understand spoken English. The entire Listening test will last approximately 45 minutes. There are four parts, and directions are given for each part. You must mark your answers on the separate answer sheet. Do not write your answers in your test book.

PART 1

Directions: For each question in this part, you will hear four statements about a picture in your test book. When you hear the statements, you must select the one statement that best describes what you see in the picture. Then find the number of the question on your answer sheet and mark your answer. The statements will not be printed in your test book and will be spoken only one time.

Statement (C), "They're sitting at a table," is the best description of the picture, so you should select answer (C) and mark it on your answer sheet.

1.

2.

GO ON TO THE NEXT PAGE →

Test 10

3.

4.

5.

6.

GO ON TO THE NEXT PAGE ➤

Test 10

PART 2

Directions: You will hear a question or statement and three responses spoken in English. They will not be printed in your test book and will be spoken only one time. Select the best response to the question or statement and mark the letter (A), (B), or (C) on your answer sheet.

7. Mark your answer on your answer sheet.

8. Mark your answer on your answer sheet.

9. Mark your answer on your answer sheet.

10. Mark your answer on your answer sheet.

11. Mark your answer on your answer sheet.

12. Mark your answer on your answer sheet.

13. Mark your answer on your answer sheet.

14. Mark your answer on your answer sheet.

15. Mark your answer on your answer sheet.

16. Mark your answer on your answer sheet.

17. Mark your answer on your answer sheet.

18. Mark your answer on your answer sheet.

19. Mark your answer on your answer sheet.

20. Mark your answer on your answer sheet.

21. Mark your answer on your answer sheet.

22. Mark your answer on your answer sheet.

23. Mark your answer on your answer sheet.

24. Mark your answer on your answer sheet.

25. Mark your answer on your answer sheet.

26. Mark your answer on your answer sheet.

27. Mark your answer on your answer sheet.

28. Mark your answer on your answer sheet.

29. Mark your answer on your answer sheet.

30. Mark your answer on your answer sheet.

31. Mark your answer on your answer sheet.

PART 3

Directions: You will hear some conversations between two or more people. You will be asked to answer three questions about what the speakers say in each conversation. Select the best response to each question and mark the letter (A), (B), (C), or (D) on your answer sheet. The conversations will not be printed in your test book and will be spoken only one time.

32. Why is the woman calling?

(A) To inquire about a procedure
(B) To pay a late fee
(C) To book some plane tickets
(D) To report a lost passport

33. Why will the woman travel to Singapore?

(A) To inspect a facility
(B) To receive an award
(C) To sign a contract
(D) To take a vacation

34. What does the woman plan to do?

(A) Call back later
(B) Use an express service
(C) Postpone her trip
(D) Search for information online

35. Who most likely is the man?

(A) A technician
(B) A security guard
(C) A salesperson
(D) A new client

36. What problem does the woman mention?

(A) A door is locked shut.
(B) A business has closed.
(C) An area is off limits.
(D) An employee is absent.

37. What does the man ask about?

(A) Where to submit an invoice
(B) When some equipment will arrive
(C) Where to park his truck
(D) When the work will be completed

38. What is the conversation mainly about?

(A) A real estate contract
(B) An apartment renovation
(C) A government regulation
(D) A moving service

39. What does the woman suggest doing?

(A) Taking a citywide tour
(B) Booking a weekday appointment
(C) Reading a company brochure
(D) Making a payment in advance

40. What will the man most likely do next?

(A) Confirm a deposit
(B) Make another phone call
(C) Give the woman his address
(D) E-mail his landlord

41. What happened this morning?

(A) A new branch was opened.
(B) A report was released.
(C) A delivery was made.
(D) A meeting was held.

42. What is the man concerned about?

(A) Losing a document
(B) Damaging some equipment
(C) Upsetting senior employees
(D) Exceeding a budget

43. What will the man receive from one of the women?

(A) Some discount coupons
(B) An updated contract
(C) Some contact details
(D) An overtime payment

GO ON TO THE NEXT PAGE

Test 10

44. What does the man ask the woman to do?

(A) Pick up an important client
(B) Reserve a meeting space
(C) Give him driving directions
(D) Book some train tickets

45. What does the woman recommend doing?

(A) Postponing an activity
(B) Borrowing a company car
(C) Checking a report online
(D) Using public transportation

46. What does the woman offer to do?

(A) Answer the man's phone
(B) Send a reminder
(C) Copy some documents
(D) Accompany the man

47. What most likely is the man's occupation?

(A) Real estate agent
(B) Construction worker
(C) Bank teller
(D) Interior designer

48. What does the woman mean when she says, "that point is nonnegotiable"?

(A) She refuses to delete some contract terms.
(B) She will not agree to pay a higher price.
(C) She wants a certain number of rooms.
(D) She needs to live close to her office.

49. What does the man say he will do?

(A) Perform some research
(B) Refund a payment
(C) E-mail some information
(D) Visit the woman in person

50. What task have the speakers been assigned?

(A) Collecting some purchase orders
(B) Stocking the checkout aisle shelves
(C) Organizing a storage area
(D) Finding a new supplier

51. What does the man ask the woman to do?

(A) Get detailed instructions
(B) Print a contract
(C) Change the opening hours
(D) Prepare some labels

52. Where will the man go next?

(A) To the front entrance
(B) To the maintenance department
(C) To the break room
(D) To the IT department

53. What are the speakers planning?

(A) A musical performance
(B) A park tour
(C) A sports competition
(D) A volunteer recruitment drive

54. What problem does the woman mention?

(A) Prices have gone up sharply.
(B) Ticket sales have been slow.
(C) Bad weather is expected.
(D) A site has been double-booked.

55. What do the speakers decide to do?

(A) Schedule a newspaper interview
(B) Change an advertising method
(C) Ask for additional funding
(D) Postpone the event

56. What is the conversation mainly about?

(A) A company restructuring
(B) A neighborhood festival
(C) A new restaurant
(D) A cooking class

57. Where did the man get some information?

(A) From a magazine advertisement
(B) From an online review
(C) From a friend's recommendation
(D) From a promotional poster

58. Why is the woman unavailable tomorrow?

(A) She is attending an industry trade show.
(B) She needs to prepare for a presentation.
(C) She is holding a meeting with a client.
(D) She has plans to go out of town.

---

59. What is the purpose of the man's call?

(A) To set up an interview
(B) To make a medical appointment
(C) To promote a newspaper
(D) To respond to a request

60. According to the woman, what will happen next month?

(A) Workers will start a building expansion.
(B) The ownership of a hospital will change.
(C) An advertising campaign will begin.
(D) The hospital will raise money for a project.

61. Why does the woman say, "How about now"?

(A) To get the man's opinion about a change
(B) To suggest completing a task by phone
(C) To find out if an improvement was made
(D) To check that the phone volume is loud enough

Product Type: Curtains Brand: Callaghan / Width: 52 inches	
Length	Price (includes 2 panels)
54 inches	$79.99
63 inches	$84.99
72 inches	$109.99
84 inches	$129.99

62. What does the man mention about the Callaghan brand of curtains?

(A) They are good at blocking light.
(B) They are available in a variety of fabrics.
(C) They come with a money-back guarantee.
(D) They have been manufactured domestically.

63. Look at the graphic. How much will the woman pay for her purchase?

(A) $79.99
(B) $84.99
(C) $109.99
(D) $129.99

64. What does the man encourage the woman to do?

(A) Take a survey
(B) Use a gift-wrap service
(C) Copy the receipt
(D) Pick up a catalog

GO ON TO THE NEXT PAGE

```
┌─────────────────────────────────┐
│  ┌───────────────────────────┐  │
│  │   Holburn Hall            │  │
│  │   presents                │  │
│  │                      ONE  │  │
│  │  George Russell           │  │
│  │                      ADMIT│  │
│  │  Friday, November 8, 6:30 P.M. │
│  └───────────────────────────┘  │
└─────────────────────────────────┘
```

Holburn Hall
presents

George Russell

Friday, November 8, 6:30 P.M. | ONE ADMIT

Holbrook Theater Schedule
Week of September 5

Sept. 5 [Sun]	Belgium Dance Troupe
Sept. 9 [Thurs]	Comedy Showcase
Sept. 10 [Fri]	The McKenzie Brothers
Sept. 11 [Sat]	Jazz Extravaganza

65. What is the conversation mainly about?

   (A) An art exhibition
   (B) An academic lecture
   (C) A rock concert
   (D) A comedy show

66. Look at the graphic. When does the man plan to arrive at the venue?

   (A) At 5:30 P.M.
   (B) At 6:00 P.M.
   (C) At 7:00 P.M.
   (D) At 7:30 P.M.

67. What does the man offer to do for the woman?

   (A) Save her a seat
   (B) Purchase a ticket
   (C) Bring her a document
   (D) Record an event

68. Look at the graphic. Which show is affected by the cancellation?

   (A) Belgium Dance Troupe
   (B) Comedy Showcase
   (C) The McKenzie Brothers
   (D) Jazz Extravaganza

69. Why will a show be canceled?

   (A) A performer had a medical emergency.
   (B) Not enough tickets have been sold.
   (C) The venue was double-booked for that date.
   (D) Some essential equipment is malfunctioning.

70. What does the woman ask for?

   (A) Some entertainers' names
   (B) A Web site address
   (C) Some login information
   (D) An area code

PART 4

Directions: You will hear some talks given by a single speaker. You will be asked to answer three questions about what the speaker says in each talk. Select the best response to each question and mark the letter (A), (B), (C), or (D) on your answer sheet. The talks will not be printed in your test book and will be spoken only one time.

71. According to the speaker, what will happen at the business next month?

    (A) The hours of operation will change.
    (B) A customer survey will be conducted.
    (C) The employees will start wearing uniforms.
    (D) A new manager will be hired for the store.

72. Why should the listeners talk to Mr. Burke?

    (A) To express a preference
    (B) To request a work shift
    (C) To volunteer for a task
    (D) To get their questions answered

73. What does the speaker invite the listeners to do?

    (A) Take a group photo
    (B) Stop by her office
    (C) Make some suggestions
    (D) Look at some pictures

74. What is scheduled to happen on Saturday?

    (A) A music contest
    (B) A community parade
    (C) A food festival
    (D) A fireworks show

75. According to the speaker, how is this year's event different from last year's?

    (A) It will last for a longer period of time.
    (B) It will take place earlier in the day.
    (C) It will be held at a different location.
    (D) It will charge a higher admission fee.

76. What does the speaker recommend doing?

    (A) Using a public parking lot
    (B) Arriving at a site early
    (C) Consulting a map online
    (D) Purchasing group tickets

77. What is the speaker calling about?

    (A) An address change
    (B) A promotional offer
    (C) A loss of service
    (D) A billing error

78. What is the listener asked to do?

    (A) Return a software package
    (B) Send a new document
    (C) Contact the listener's manager
    (D) E-mail an updated contract

79. Why is the speaker unavailable this afternoon?

    (A) He will attend a training session.
    (B) He will take a trip out of town.
    (C) He will visit an important client.
    (D) He will shop for some merchandise.

80. What is the speaker mainly discussing?

    (A) A business relocation
    (B) Some property damage
    (C) A legal fee
    (D) Some regulation changes

81. What problem is mentioned?

    (A) A new employee is not qualified.
    (B) A computer system is not working.
    (C) A service is no longer available.
    (D) A contract's terms were rejected.

82. What does the speaker suggest doing?

    (A) Holding another meeting
    (B) Voting on an issue
    (C) Hiring a professional consultant
    (D) Announcing a decision

GO ON TO THE NEXT PAGE

Test 10

83. Who most likely are the listeners?

(A) Restaurant workers
(B) Delivery personnel
(C) Construction workers
(D) Appliance salespeople

84. What does the speaker suggest when he says, "it only happened once"?

(A) A class will take one day.
(B) A course will not be repeated.
(C) A problem has been resolved.
(D) A test will be easy to pass.

85. What will the speaker do in fifteen minutes?

(A) Check attendance
(B) Show a video
(C) Answer some questions
(D) Distribute a handout

86. What topic will Dr. Clark discuss with the speaker?

(A) Technological advancements
(B) Sleeping habits
(C) New medicines
(D) Learning languages

87. What has Dr. Clark recently done?

(A) Opened an institute
(B) Published his first book
(C) Received an award
(D) Returned from a trip abroad

88. According to the speaker, what can listeners do on the Web site?

(A) Sign up for an upcoming research study
(B) Submit questions for the guest
(C) Browse the findings of a study
(D) Download an interview schedule

89. What is the purpose of the event?

(A) To observe a national holiday
(B) To celebrate an anniversary
(C) To welcome some visitors
(D) To present some awards

90. What does the speaker suggest when she says, "It's not the first time you've heard it"?

(A) Some well-known songs will be played for the listeners.
(B) The listeners are familiar with the company's history.
(C) Some items were accidentally repeated in the program.
(D) The speaker thinks a discussion topic should not be covered again.

91. What does the speaker say she appreciates about the listeners?

(A) Their prompt response
(B) Their creative ideas
(C) Their hard work
(D) Their teamwork skills

92. What kind of event is the listener planning?

(A) A career fair
(B) A training session
(C) A product launch
(D) A retirement party

93. What does the speaker suggest when he says, "we'll have at least eighty people"?

(A) He is not accepting more volunteers.
(B) More food will be needed.
(C) He is pleased with the turnout.
(D) A larger room should be reserved.

94. What problem does the speaker mention?

(A) A deadline has already passed.
(B) An unexpected charge was imposed.
(C) A business is closing soon.
(D) A guest is missing an invitation.

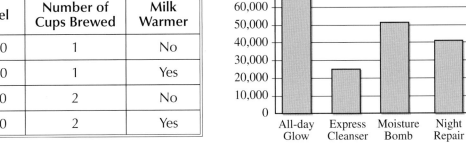

Home Styles Coffee Maker		
Model	Number of Cups Brewed	Milk Warmer
B-300	1	No
B-450	1	Yes
L-600	2	No
L-780	2	Yes

Monthly Sales

95. What is the purpose of the talk?

(A) To show how to operate a device
(B) To demonstrate a sales technique
(C) To explain a store's discount prices
(D) To gather feedback about a product

96. Look at the graphic. Which model is the speaker talking about?

(A) B-300
(B) B-450
(C) L-600
(D) L-780

97. What will some of the listeners most likely do next?

(A) Watch a video
(B) Sit down
(C) Read a handout
(D) Ask questions

98. What is the purpose of the meeting?

(A) To introduce a new employee
(B) To assign some projects
(C) To explain a company policy
(D) To adjust a product line

99. Look at the graphic. Which item will be available in two sizes?

(A) All-Day Glow
(B) Express Cleanser
(C) Moisture Bomb
(D) Night Repair

100. What most likely is Ms. Fitzgerald's occupation?

(A) Researcher
(B) Market analyst
(C) Actress
(D) Photographer

This is the end of the Listening test.

ANSWER SHEET

YBM 실전토익 LC 1000 (2)

수험번호

응시일자 : 20   년   월   일

성명
한글	
한자	
영자	

Test 01 (Part 1~4)

1–20	21–40	41–60	61–80	81–100
1	21	41	61	81
2	22	42	62	82
3	23	43	63	83
4	24	44	64	84
5	25	45	65	85
6	26	46	66	86
7	27	47	67	87
8	28	48	68	88
9	29	49	69	89
10	30	50	70	90
11	31	51	71	91
12	32	52	72	92
13	33	53	73	93
14	34	54	74	94
15	35	55	75	95
16	36	56	76	96
17	37	57	77	97
18	38	58	78	98
19	39	59	79	99
20	40	60	80	100

Test 02 (Part 1~4)

1–20	21–40	41–60	61–80	81–100
1	21	41	61	81
2	22	42	62	82
3	23	43	63	83
4	24	44	64	84
5	25	45	65	85
6	26	46	66	86
7	27	47	67	87
8	28	48	68	88
9	29	49	69	89
10	30	50	70	90
11	31	51	71	91
12	32	52	72	92
13	33	53	73	93
14	34	54	74	94
15	35	55	75	95
16	36	56	76	96
17	37	57	77	97
18	38	58	78	98
19	39	59	79	99
20	40	60	80	100

ANSWER SHEET

YBM 실전토익 LC 1000 (2)

수험번호

응시일자 : 20   년   월   일

성명	한글
	한자
편명	영자

Test 03 (Part 1~4)

Test 04 (Part 1~4)

ANSWER SHEET

YBM 실전토익 LC 1000 (2)

수험번호

응시일자 : 20   년   월   일

성명 한글 / 한자 / 영자

Test 05 (Part 1~4)

Test 06 (Part 1~4)

ANSWER SHEET

YBM 실전토익 LC 1000 (2)

수험번호

응시일자 : 20   년   월   일

성명
한글
한자
영자

Test 07 (Part 1~4)

Test 08 (Part 1~4)

ANSWER SHEET

YBM 실전토익 LC 1000 (2)

수험번호

응시일자 : 20   년   월   일

성명 | 한글 | 한자 | 영자

Test 09 (Part 1~4)

Test 10 (Part 1~4)

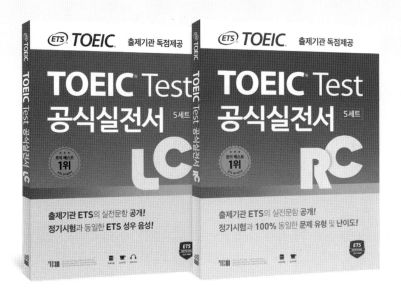

YBM
실전토익
LC 1000
2

YBM

1 (B)	2 (D)	3 (B)	4 (C)	5 (A)
6 (A)	7 (A)	8 (C)	9 (B)	10 (A)
11 (C)	12 (A)	13 (B)	14 (B)	15 (C)
16 (C)	17 (B)	18 (C)	19 (A)	20 (B)
21 (C)	22 (B)	23 (C)	24 (C)	25 (B)
26 (B)	27 (A)	28 (A)	29 (C)	30 (A)
31 (A)	32 (D)	33 (A)	34 (D)	35 (B)
36 (A)	37 (D)	38 (A)	39 (B)	40 (B)
41 (C)	42 (B)	43 (D)	44 (C)	45 (B)
46 (B)	47 (D)	48 (D)	49 (C)	50 (D)
51 (C)	52 (D)	53 (A)	54 (D)	55 (D)
56 (B)	57 (D)	58 (A)	59 (D)	60 (C)
61 (C)	62 (D)	63 (B)	64 (C)	65 (B)
66 (D)	67 (A)	68 (A)	69 (C)	70 (B)
71 (A)	72 (B)	73 (D)	74 (C)	75 (D)
76 (D)	77 (B)	78 (C)	79 (A)	80 (A)
81 (A)	82 (C)	83 (C)	84 (C)	85 (A)
86 (B)	87 (B)	88 (B)	89 (C)	90 (B)
91 (D)	92 (D)	93 (C)	94 (C)	95 (A)
96 (C)	97 (C)	98 (A)	99 (A)	100 (C)

PART 1

1 M-Au

(A) He's looking for a writing utensil.
(B) He's taking notes on a clipboard.
(C) He's repairing some equipment.
(D) He's adjusting a machine's dial.

(A) 남자가 필기도구를 찾고 있다.
(B) 남자가 클립보드에 메모를 하고 있다.
(C) 남자가 장비를 수리하고 있다.
(D) 남자가 기계의 눈금판을 조절하고 있다.

어휘 look for ~을 찾다 writing utensil 필기도구 take notes 메모하다 clipboard 클립보드 repair 수리하다 equipment 장비 adjust 조절하다 machine 기계 dial 눈금판, 다이얼

해설 1인 등장 사진 – 사람의 상태 묘사

(A) 동사 오답. 사진에 필기도구가 보이지만 남자가 필기도구를 찾는(is looking for a writing utensil) 모습은 아니므로 오답.
(B) 정답. 남자가 클립보드에 메모하고 있는(is taking notes on a clipboard) 모습이므로 정답.
(C) 동사 오답. 사진에 장비가 있지만 남자가 장비를 수리하는(is repairing some equipment) 모습이 아니므로 오답.
(D) 동사 오답. 사진에 눈금판이 보이지만 남자가 기계의 눈금판을 조절하는(is adjusting a machine's dial) 모습이 아니므로 오답.

2 W-Am

(A) Both of the men are leaving the construction site.
(B) One of the men is rolling up a document.
(C) Both of the men are putting on hard hats.
(D) One of the men is reaching out his arm.

(A) 두 남자가 건설 현장을 떠나고 있다.
(B) 남자들 중 한 명이 서류를 말고 있다.
(C) 두 남자가 안전모를 착용하는 중이다.
(D) 남자들 중 한 명이 팔을 뻗고 있다.

어휘 both 둘 다 leave 떠나다 construction site 건설 현장 roll up (둥글게) 말다 document 서류 put on ~을 입다[착용하다] hard hat 안전모 reach out ~을 뻗다 arm 팔

해설 2인 이상 등장 사진 – 사람의 동작 묘사

(A) 동사 오답. 두 남자가 건설 현장에 있지 건설 현장을 떠나는(are leaving the construction site) 모습이 아니므로 오답.
(B) 동사 오답. 사진에 서류가 보이지만 남자들 중 한 명이 서류를 말고 있는(is rolling up a document) 동작을 하고 있지 않으므로 오답.
(C) 동사 오답. 사진에 안전모가 보이지만 두 남자가 안전모를 착용하는(are putting on hard hats) 동작을 하고 있지 않으므로 오답.
(D) 정답. 남자들 중 한 명이 팔을 뻗고 있는(is reaching out his arm) 모습이므로 정답.

3 M-Cn

(A) One of the women is passing out papers.
(B) The people are gathered around a computer.
(C) One of the men is purchasing a laptop.
(D) The people are setting up a meeting room.

(A) 여자들 중 한 명이 종이를 나누어 주고 있다.
(B) 사람들이 컴퓨터 주위에 모여 있다.
(C) 남자들 중 한 명이 노트북 컴퓨터를 구입하고 있다.
(D) 사람들이 회의실을 준비하고 있다.

어휘 pass out ~을 나누어 주다 gather 모으다 purchase 구입하다 laptop 노트북 컴퓨터 set up 준비하다 meeting room 회의실

해설 2인 이상 등장 사진 – 사람의 동작 묘사

(A) 동사 오답. 사진에 종이가 있지만 여자들 중 한 명이 종이를 나누어 주는(is passing out papers) 동작을 하고 있지 않으므로 오답.
(B) 정답. 사람들이 컴퓨터 주위에 모여 있는(are gathered around a computer) 모습이므로 정답.
(C) 동사 오답. 사진에 노트북 컴퓨터가 보이지만 남자들 중 한 명이 노트북 컴퓨터를 구입하는(is purchasing a laptop) 모습이 아니므로 오답.

(D) 동사 오답. 사람들이 회의실 안에 있는 상태이지 회의실을 준비하는(are setting up a meeting room) 모습이 아니므로 오답.

4 W-Br

(A) Some vegetables are being harvested.
(B) A woman is adding food to a bag.
(C) Some produce is sorted by type.
(D) A shopper is returning some items.

(A) 채소가 수확되고 있다.
(B) 여자가 음식을 가방에 넣고 있다.
(C) 농산물이 종류별로 분류되어 있다.
(D) 쇼핑객이 상품 몇 개를 반품하고 있다.

어휘 vegetable 채소 harvest 수확하다 add 더하다, 첨가하다
produce 농산물 sort 분류하다 shopper 쇼핑객 return
반품하다, 돌려주다 item 품목, 상품

해설 1인 등장 사진 – 사람 또는 사물 중심 묘사
(A) 동사 오답. 사진에 채소가 있지만 채소가 수확되고 있는(are being harvested) 모습은 아니므로 오답.
(B) 동사 오답. 여자가 음식을 가방에 넣고 있지(is adding food to a bag) 않으므로 오답.
(C) 정답. 농산물이 종류별로 분류되어 있는(is sorted by type) 상태이므로 정답.
(D) 동사 오답. 쇼핑객이 상품 몇 개를 반품하는(is returning some items) 모습이 아니므로 오답.

5 W-Am

(A) The women are shaking hands.
(B) The men are greeting each other.
(C) The women are seated at the table.
(D) The men are opening some windows.

(A) 여자들이 악수하고 있다.
(B) 남자들이 서로 인사하고 있다.
(C) 여자들이 탁자에 앉아 있다.
(D) 남자들이 창문을 열고 있다.

어휘 shake hands 악수하다 greet 인사하다 each other 서로
seat 앉히다

해설 2인 이상 등장 사진 – 사람의 동작 묘사
(A) 정답. 여자들이 악수하고 있는(are shaking hands) 모습이므로 정답.

(B) 동사 오답. 남자들이 여자들을 쳐다보는 모습이지 서로 인사하는(are greeting each other) 모습이 아니므로 오답.
(C) 동사 오답. 여자들이 서 있는 상태이지 탁자에 앉아 있는(are seated at the table) 모습이 아니므로 오답.
(D) 동사 오답. 사진에 창문이 보이지만 남자들이 창문을 여는(are opening some windows) 동작을 하고 있지 않으므로 오답.

6 M-Au

(A) A sofa has been placed against the wall.
(B) A rug has been spread in the corner.
(C) Some cushions are scattered on the floor.
(D) Some curtains have been pulled closed.

(A) 소파가 벽을 등지고 배치되어 있다.
(B) 양탄자가 모퉁이에 펼쳐져 있다.
(C) 쿠션 몇 개가 바닥에 흩어져 있다.
(D) 커튼이 쳐져 있다.

어휘 place 배치하다 against the wall 벽을 등지고, 벽에 기대어 rug
깔개, 양탄자 spread 펼치다 corner 모퉁이 scatter 흩뿌리다
pull closed (잡아당겨) 닫다

해설 사물/배경 사진 – 사물의 위치 묘사
(A) 정답. 소파가 벽을 등지고 배치되어 있는(has been placed against the wall) 모습이므로 정답.
(B) 전치사구 오답. 양탄자가 중앙에 펼쳐져 있는 상태이지 모퉁이에 펼쳐져 있는(has been spread in the corner) 상태가 아니므로 오답.
(C) 동사 오답. 사진에 쿠션이 있지만 쿠션 몇 개가 바닥에 흩어져 있는(are scattered on the floor) 모습이 아니므로 오답.
(D) 동사 오답. 커튼이 열려 있는 상태이지 커튼이 쳐져 있는(have been pulled closed) 상태가 아니므로 오답.

PART 2

7

W-Br When will the contest winners be announced?
M-Cn (A) Probably sometime after January twelfth.
(B) Congratulations—you deserved it!
(C) The contract was announced yesterday.

대회 우승자는 언제 발표되나요?
(A) 아마 1월 12일 이후가 될 것 같아요.
(B) 축하해요. 당신은 그럴 자격이 있어요.
(C) 계약은 어제 발표되었어요.

어휘 contest 대회 winner 우승자 announce 발표하다
congratulations 축하해(요) deserve ~할 자격이 있다
contract 계약

해설 발표 시점을 묻는 When 의문문

(A) 정답. 대회 우승자 발표 시점을 묻는 질문에 1월 12일 이후가 될 거라는 구체적인 시점으로 응답하고 있으므로 정답.

(B) 연상 단어 오답. 질문의 contest winners에서 연상 가능한 Congratulations를 이용한 오답.

(C) 유사 발음 오답. 질문의 contest와 발음이 유사한 contract를 이용한 오답.

8

W-Am How far is it to the regional airport?

M-Au (A) At seven o'clock this evening.
　　　(B) A non-stop flight to Dallas.
　　　(C) Approximately five miles.

지역 공항까지 거리가 얼마나 되나요?
(A) 오늘 저녁 7시요.
(B) 댈러스행 직항기요.
(C) 약 5마일이요.

어휘 regional 지역의 non-stop flight 직항기 approximately 거의

해설 거리를 묻는 How far 의문문

(A) 질문과 상관없는 오답. 시간을 묻는 When 의문문에 적절한 응답이므로 오답.

(B) 연상 단어 오답. 질문의 airport에서 연상 가능한 non-stop flight를 이용한 오답.

(C) 정답. 공항까지 거리를 묻는 질문에 five miles이라는 구체적인 단위를 언급하고 있으므로 정답.

9

M-Cn Which meeting space should I use for the interview?

M-Au (A) For the manager position.
　　　(B) Whichever one is free.
　　　(C) I think it went better than expected.

면접을 위해 어떤 회의실을 사용해야 하나요?
(A) 관리자 직책이요.
(B) 어느 회의실이든 비어 있어요.
(C) 예상보다 잘 진행된 것 같아요.

어휘 meeting space 회의실 manager position 관리자 직책 whichever 어느 쪽의 ~이든 free (장소 등이) 비어 있는, 사용 중이 아닌 go (일이) 진행되다 better than expected 예상보다 더 잘 expect 예상하다

해설 사용 가능 회의실을 묻는 Which 의문문

(A) 연상 단어 오답. 질문의 interview에서 연상 가능한 manager position을 이용한 오답.

(B) 정답. 사용 가능 회의실을 묻는 질문에 어느 회의실이든 비어 있다고 응답하고 있으므로 정답.

(C) 연상 단어 오답. 질문의 interview를 듣고 면접 결과를 묻는 질문으로 잘못 이해했을 때 연상 가능한 답변이므로 오답.

10

M-Au Can I renew my license over the phone, or do I have to come in?

W-Am (A) It can only be done in person.
　　　(B) Yes, it's a new company policy.
　　　(C) What's your home phone number?

전화상으로 면허증을 갱신할 수 있나요, 아니면 직접 가야 하나요?
(A) 직접 오셔서 하는 것만 가능해요.
(B) 네, 새로운 회사 방침이에요.
(C) 집 전화번호가 어떻게 되나요?

어휘 renew 갱신하다 license 면허증, 자격증 over the phone 전화상으로 come in (상대방에게로) 가다 in person 직접 policy 정책

해설 문장을 연결한 선택의문문

(A) 정답. 전화상으로 면허증을 갱신하는 것과 직접 가는 것 중 어느 쪽이 가능한지 묻는 질문에 직접 오는 것만 가능하다고 응답하고 있으므로 정답.

(B) 질문과 상관없는 오답. 전화상으로 가능한지 또는 방문하는 것만 가능한지를 묻는 선택의문문에 맥락과 상관없는 회사 방침이라는 응답을 했으므로 오답.

(C) 단어 반복 오답. 질문에 나온 phone을 반복한 오답.

11

M-Cn Who labeled the folders in the file cabinet?

W-Br (A) I think it's still locked.
　　　(B) Patients' confidential medical records.
　　　(C) One of the part-time interns.

서류 캐비닛의 폴더에 누가 라벨을 붙였나요?
(A) 아직 잠겨 있는 거 같아요.
(B) 환자의 기밀 의료 기록이요.
(C) 파트타임 인턴 중 한 명이요.

어휘 label 라벨을 붙이다, (라벨을 붙여) 분류하다 folder 서류철, 폴더 file cabinet 문서 보관함, 서류 캐비닛 lock 자물쇠를 잠그다 patient 환자 confidential 기밀의 medical record 의료 기록 part-time 파트타임인, 시간제의 intern 인턴

해설 문서를 분류한 직원을 묻는 Who 의문문

(A) 질문과 상관없는 오답. 서류 캐비닛의 폴더에 누가 라벨을 붙였는지를 묻는 질문에 아직 잠겨 있다는 답변은 질문의 맥락에서 벗어난 것이므로 오답.

(B) 연상 단어 오답. 질문의 folders와 file cabinet에서 연상 가능한 medical records를 이용한 오답.

(C) 정답. 누가 라벨을 붙였는지를 묻는 질문에 파트타임 인턴 중 하나라고 구체적인 인물을 언급하고 있으므로 정답.

12

W-Am Where will I have a layover during my trip?

M-Cn (A) Somewhere on the West Coast, I think.
　　　(B) About an hour and a half.
　　　(C) A ticket in the first-class section.

여행 중 경유지는 어디인가요?

(A) 서해안 어디쯤 일 거예요.
(B) 약 1시간 30분이요.
(C) 1등석 티켓이요.

어휘 layover 경유, 도중하차 first-class section 1등석

해설 경유지를 묻는 Where 의문문
(A) 정답. 여행 중 경유지를 묻는 질문에 서해안이라는 구체적인 장소를 언급하고 있으므로 정답.
(B) 질문과 상관없는 오답. 경유 시간을 묻는 How long 의문문에 적절한 응답이므로 오답.
(C) 연상 단어 오답. 질문의 layover에 대해 경유 비행기 좌석 측면에서 연상 가능한 first-class를 이용한 오답.

13

M-Au How about purchasing another sofa for the employee lounge?

W-Am (A) Taking short breaks every hour.
(B) Sure, the staff would appreciate that.
(C) At the furniture store across the street.

직원 휴게실에 놓을 소파를 하나 더 구입하는 것은 어떨까요?
(A) 매 시간 짧은 휴식을 갖는 거요.
(B) 물론이죠, 직원들이 고마워할 거예요.
(C) 길 건너 가구점이요.

어휘 purchase 구입하다 employee lounge 직원 휴게실, 직원 라운지 take a break 잠시 휴식을 취하다 appreciate 고맙게 생각하다 furniture store 가구점

해설 제안/권유의 의문문
(A) 연상 단어 오답. 질문의 lounge에서 연상 가능한 short breaks를 이용한 오답.
(B) 정답. 직원 휴게실에 놓을 소파를 구입하자는 제안에 Sure로 긍정적 응답을 한 후, 직원들이 고마워할 거라고 부연 설명을 하고 있으므로 정답.
(C) 연상 단어 오답. 질문의 sofa에서 연상 가능한 furniture store를 이용한 오답.

14

W-Br Why was Ms. Dennison's application rejected?

W-Am (A) A computer technician job.
(B) She wasn't qualified enough.
(C) OK, I'll let her know.

데니슨 씨의 원서는 왜 탈락한 건가요?
(A) 컴퓨터 기사 업무요.
(B) 자격이 충분하지 못했어요.
(C) 네, 제가 그녀에게 알려줄게요.

어휘 application 지원(서) reject 불합격시키다 technician 기사 qualify 자격을 갖추다

해설 불합격 이유를 묻는 Why 의문문
(A) 연상 단어 오답. 질문의 application에 대해 지원 업무 측면에서 연상 가능한 computer technician job을 이용한 오답.
(B) 정답. 데니슨 씨의 원서가 불합격한 이유를 묻는 질문에 자격이 충분하지 못했다고 구체적인 이유를 언급하고 있으므로 정답.

(C) Yes/No 불가 오답. Why 의문문에는 Yes를 의미하는 OK 응답은 불가능하므로 오답.

15

M-Cn Which charity will the company donate to this year?

W-Am (A) No, it's every six months.
(B) Your donation is tax deductible.
(C) The local food bank.

회사는 올해 어떤 자선 단체에 기부할 건가요?
(A) 아니요, 6개월마다요.
(B) 기부금은 세금 공제가 돼요.
(C) 지역 푸드뱅크요.

어휘 charity 자선 단체 donate to ~에 기부하다 donation 기부, 기부금 tax deductible 세금 공제가 되는 local 지역의 food bank 푸드뱅크(식품을 기탁 받아 복지 시설 등에 제공하는 단체)

해설 기부할 자선 단체를 묻는 Which 의문문
(A) Yes/No 불가 오답. Which 의문문에는 Yes/No 응답이 불가능하므로 오답.
(B) 파생어 오답. 질문의 donate와 파생어 관계인 donation을 이용한 오답.
(C) 정답. 회사가 기부금을 낼 자선 단체를 묻는 질문에 지역 푸드뱅크라는 구체적인 복지 관련 단체를 언급하고 있으므로 정답.

16

M-Au This Web site takes a long time to load.

W-Br (A) The loan was finally approved.
(B) It's a new e-mail address.
(C) There must be a problem.

이 웹사이트는 로딩되는 데 시간이 오래 걸려요.
(A) 대출이 마침내 승인되었어요.
(B) 그건 새 이메일 주소예요.
(C) 문제가 있는 게 틀림없어요.

어휘 load (데이터나 프로그램을) 로딩하다[되다] loan 대출 approve 승인하다 must ~임에 틀림없다

해설 사실/정보 전달의 평서문
(A) 유사 발음 오답. 질문의 load와 부분적으로 발음이 유사한 loan을 이용한 오답.
(B) 연상 단어 오답. 질문의 Web site에서 연상 가능한 e-mail을 이용한 오답.
(C) 정답. 웹사이트가 로딩되는 데 시간이 오래 걸린다는 말에 문제가 있는 게 틀림없다고 응답하고 있으므로 정답.

17

W-Br Have you hiked both trails at Crystal Lake?

M-Cn (A) I hike on the weekends.
(B) Actually, there are three.
(C) Swimming and fishing.

크리스털 레이크에 있는 두 산책로에서 하이킹을 해 봤나요?

(A) 저는 주말에 하이킹을 해요.
(B) 사실은, 세 개가 있어요.
(C) 수영과 낚시요.

어휘 hike 하이킹(도보 여행)을 하다 trail 산길, 산책로 actually 사실은

해설 하이킹 경험을 묻는 조동사(Have) 의문문

(A) 단어 반복 오답. 질문의 hike를 반복한 오답.
(B) 정답. 특정 장소에 있는 두 산책로에서 하이킹을 해 보았는지 묻는 질문에 세 개가 있다며 새로운 정보를 제공하고 있으므로 정답.
(C) 연상 단어 오답. 질문의 lake에서 연상 가능한 swimming, fishing을 이용한 오답

18

M-Au Could you pick something up at the pharmacy for me?

W-Am (A) No, it's not that far to go.
(B) We picked the best option.
(C) Yes, but not until this afternoon.

저 대신 약국에서 뭔가 좀 받아 올 수 있나요?
(A) 아니오, 그렇게 멀지 않아요.
(B) 우리는 최선의 선택을 했어요.
(C) 네, 하지만 오늘 오후는 되어야 해요.

어휘 pharmacy 약국 option 선택(지)

해설 부탁/요청의 의문문

(A) 질문과 상관없는 오답. 약국에서 뭔가를 받아 올 수 있는지 묻는 질문에 안 된다(No)고 한 후 그렇게 멀지 않다고 답변한 것은 질문의 맥락에서 벗어난 것이므로 오답.
(B) 단어 반복 오답. 질문의 pick를 picked(과거형)로 반복한 오답.
(C) 정답. 약국에서 뭔가를 받아 올 수 있는지 묻는 질문에 Yes로 긍정적인 응답을 한 후, 오늘 오후는 되어야 한다는 부연 설명을 하고 있으므로 정답.

19

W-Am Isn't the recruitment drive still going on?

M-Cn (A) We filled the necessary positions.
(B) No, he doesn't have a driver's license.
(C) A professional recruitment agency.

모집 활동이 아직 진행되고 있는 것 아닌가요?
(A) 필요한 자리는 다 채웠어요.
(B) 아니오, 그는 운전면허증이 없어요.
(C) 취업 전문 알선업체요.

어휘 recruitment 모집, 채용 drive (조직적인) 운동, 활동 go on 계속되다 fill 채우다 necessary 필요한 position 직위, (일자리) driver's license 운전면허증 professional 전문적인 recruitment agency 취업 알선업체

해설 모집 진행 여부에 대한 부정의문문

(A) 정답. 모집이 진행 중인 것 아니냐는 질문에 필요한 자리는 다 채웠다고 응답한 것은 모집이 끝났다는 의미를 우회적으로 전달하는 것이므로 정답.
(B) 파생어 오답. 질문의 drive가 '운전하다'라는 의미일 경우 파생어 관계인 driver를 이용한 오답.

(C) 단어 반복 오답. 질문에 나온 recruitment를 반복한 오답.

20

M-Au You don't need any more office supplies, do you?

W-Br (A) It was a surprise for everyone.
(B) I have more than enough.
(C) My office is on the second floor.

사무용품이 더 필요하지 않죠, 그렇죠?
(A) 모두를 놀라게 했어요.
(B) 충분하고도 남아요.
(C) 내 사무실은 2층에 있어요.

어휘 office supplies 사무용품 surprise 놀라움, 뜻밖의 일

해설 사무용품 필요 여부를 확인하는 부가의문문

(A) 유사 발음 오답. 질문의 supplies와 발음이 유사한 surprise를 이용한 오답.
(B) 정답. 사무용품이 더 필요한지를 묻는 질문에 충분하고도 남는다고 응답하고 있으므로 정답.
(C) 단어 반복 오답. 질문에 나온 office를 반복한 오답.

21

M-Cn Does the furniture come assembled, or do we need to put it together?

W-Br (A) I'm not sure what color it is.
(B) Chairs in the lobby will be gathered.
(C) It'll be ready for use immediately.

가구가 조립되어 오나요, 아니면 우리가 조립해야 하나요?
(A) 그것이 어떤 색깔인지 모르겠어요.
(B) 로비에 있는 의자를 모아 놓을 거예요.
(C) 즉시 쓸 수 있도록 준비될 거예요.

어휘 assembled 조립된 put together 조립하다 gather 모으다 be ready for ~을 위한 준비가 되다 immediately 즉시

해설 문장을 연결한 선택의문문

(A) 질문과 상관없는 오답. 색상을 묻는 What color 의문문에 어울리는 응답이므로 오답.
(B) 연상 단어 오답. 질문의 furniture에서 연상 가능한 chairs를 이용한 오답.
(C) 정답. 가구가 조립되어 오는 것과 구매자가 조립해야 하는 것 중 어느 쪽인지 묻는 질문에 즉시 쓸 수 있도록 준비될 것이라고 응답한 것은 가구가 조립되어 온다는 것을 우회적으로 선택한 것이므로 정답.

22

W-Am I haven't been reimbursed for my business expenses.

W-Br (A) No, I wasn't able to afford it.
(B) Should I call accounting?
(C) A round-trip ticket to Tokyo.

업무 경비를 아직 상환받지 못했어요.
(A) 아니오, 여유가 되지 않았어요.
(B) 회계부서에 전화해야 하나요?
(C) 도쿄행 왕복 티켓이요.

어휘 reimburse 배상[상환]하다 business expense 업무 경비
afford ~할 여유가 되다 accounting 회계 round-trip 왕복의

해설 사실/정보 전달의 평서문

(A) 연상 단어 오답. 질문의 expenses에서 연상 가능한 afford를 이용한 오답.

(B) 정답. 업무 경비를 상환받지 못했다는 말에 회계부서에 (확인) 전화를 해야 하는지를 묻는 응답이므로 정답.

(C) 질문과 상관없는 오답. 업무 경비를 상환받지 못했다는 말에 도쿄행 왕복 티켓이라는 답변은 질문의 맥락에서 벗어난 것이므로 오답.

23

M-Au When will the receptionist's replacement start?

W-Am (A) Probably at the corporate headquarters.
(B) That's the perfect place for it.
(C) She's already begun training.

접수계원 후임자는 언제 일을 시작하나요?
(A) 아마도 회사 본사에서요.
(B) 그것을 위한 완벽한 장소예요.
(C) 그녀는 이미 교육을 받기 시작했어요.

어휘 receptionist 접수계원 replacement 후임자 corporate
headquarters 회사 본사 training 교육

해설 근무 시점을 묻는 When 의문문

(A) 질문과 상관없는 오답. 장소를 묻는 Where 의문문에 적절한 응답이므로 오답.

(B) 유사 발음 오답. 질문의 replacement와 부분적으로 발음이 유사한 place를 이용한 오답.

(C) 정답. 접수계원 후임자의 근무 시작 시점을 묻는 질문에 이미 교육을 받기 시작했다고 응답하고 있으므로 정답.

24

W-Br I'd like a deadline extension for the newsletter article.

M-Cn (A) The business expanded operations.
(B) It's sent to clients every month.
(C) How far behind are you at the moment?

소식지 기사 마감일을 연장해 주셨으면 해요.
(A) 회사는 사업체를 확장했어요.
(B) 매달 고객에게 보내요.
(C) 지금 얼마나 늦어지고 있나요?

어휘 deadline 기한, 마감 시간 extension 확장, 연장 newsletter
소식지 article 기사 expand 확장하다 operation 사업체
client 고객 behind 뒤떨어져[늦어] at the moment 바로 지금

해설 부탁/요청의 평서문

(A) 유사 발음 오답. 질문의 extension과 부분적으로 발음이 같은 expanded를 이용한 오답.

(B) 질문과 상관없는 오답. 빈도를 묻는 How often 의문문에 적절한 응답이므로 오답.

(C) 정답. 기사 마감일 연장을 원한다고 이야기하자 얼마나 늦어지고 있는지 되묻고 있으므로 정답.

25

M-Au Would you mind turning up the heat in the building?

W-Am (A) I'll send a copy to the building owner.
(B) The temperature is already at the maximum.
(C) Take a right at this intersection.

건물의 난방 온도를 좀 올려 주시겠어요?
(A) 건물주에게 사본을 보낼게요.
(B) 이미 최대 온도예요.
(C) 이 교차로에서 우회전하세요.

어휘 Would you mind -ing? ~해 주시겠어요? turn up the heat
난방 온도를 높이다 building owner 건물주 temperature 온도
maximum 최대 take a right 우회전하다 intersection 교차로

해설 부탁/요청의 평서문

(A) 단어 반복 오답. 질문에 나온 building을 반복한 오답.

(B) 정답. 난방 온도를 올려달라고 하자 이미 최대 온도라고 답하며 더 이상 올릴 수 없다는 점을 우회적으로 표현하고 있으므로 정답.

(C) 질문과 상관없는 오답. 난방 온도를 올려달라는 요청에 교차로에서 우회전하라는 답변은 질문의 맥락에서 벗어난 것이므로 오답.

26

W-Br Didn't Mr. Jacobs review the statistics in the report?

M-Au (A) How many figures do you need?
(B) Did you find an error?
(C) That's an interesting viewpoint.

제이콥 씨가 보고서의 통계 수치를 검토하지 않았나요?
(A) 수치가 얼마나 필요한가요?
(B) 오류를 발견했나요?
(C) 흥미로운 견해군요.

어휘 review 검토하다 statistics 통계 figure 수치, 숫자 error 오류,
실수 viewpoint 견해

해설 통계 수치 검토 여부를 묻는 부정의문문

(A) 연상 단어 오답. 질문의 statistics에 대해 수치 측면에서 연상 가능한 figures를 이용한 오답.

(B) 정답. 보고서의 통계 수치를 검토하지 않았냐는 질문에 오류를 발견했는지 되묻고 있으므로 정답.

(C) 유사 발음 오답. 질문의 review와 부분적으로 발음이 비슷한 viewpoint를 이용한 오답.

27

W-Am Are all of these light fixtures on sale?

M-Cn (A) Only a few brands in particular.
(B) To brighten up the room.
(C) The branches that you visited.

이 조명 기구 모두 할인되나요?
(A) 특정 상표 몇 개만요.
(B) 방을 환하게 하려고요.
(C) 방문하셨던 지점들이요.

어휘 light fixture 조명 기구 on sale 할인 중인 brand 상표 in particular 특히, 특정한 brighten up ~을 밝히다 branch 지사, 지점

해설 할인 여부를 묻는 Be동사 의문문
(A) 정답. 조명 기구 모두가 할인되는지 묻는 질문에 특정 상표 몇 개만 할인 중이라고 응답하고 있으므로 정답.
(B) 연상 단어 오답. 질문의 light fixtures에서 연상 가능한 brighten을 이용한 오답.
(C) 질문과 상관없는 오답. 조명 기구 모두가 할인되는지를 묻는 질문에 방문했던 지점들이라는 응답은 질문의 맥락에서 벗어난 것이므로 오답.

28
M-Cn Why was the itinerary changed at the last minute?
M-Au (A) A flight was canceled unexpectedly.
(B) He was able to assist you last month.
(C) Is the trip for business or pleasure?

여행 일정이 왜 막판에 변경되었나요?
(A) 비행편이 예상치 않게 취소되었어요.
(B) 그는 지난달에 당신을 도울 수 있었어요.
(C) 여행은 출장인가요, 아니면 관광인가요?

어휘 itinerary 여행 일정 at the last minute 막판에, 마지막 순간에 flight 비행기[편] cancel 취소하다 unexpectedly 예상치 않게 assist 돕다, 보조하다 trip for business 출장 pleasure 즐거움

해설 일정 변경 이유를 묻는 Why 의문문
(A) 정답. 여행 일정이 마지막 순간에 변경된 이유를 묻는 질문에 비행기가 예상치 않게 취소되었다고 구체적인 이유를 언급하고 있으므로 정답.
(B) 단어 반복 오답. 질문의 last를 반복한 오답.
(C) 연상 단어 오답. 질문의 itinerary에서 연상 가능한 trip을 이용한 오답.

29
W-Br Who has time to update the employee handbook?
M-Cn (A) Today at 4 P.M. at the latest.
(B) There are some changes to the dress code.
(C) Rachel doesn't have any urgent projects.

누가 직원 안내서를 개정할 시간이 있나요?
(A) 늦어도 오늘 오후 4시요.
(B) 복장 규정에 변경 사항이 좀 있어요.
(C) 레이첼이 급한 프로젝트가 없어요.

어휘 update 개정하다, 갱신하다 employee handbook 직원 안내서 at the latest 늦어도 dress code 복장 규정 urgent 긴급한

해설 개정할 직원을 묻는 Who 의문문
(A) 연상 단어 오답. 질문의 time에서 연상 가능한 4 P.M.을 이용한 오답.
(B) 연상 단어 오답. 질문의 employee handbook에서 연상 가능한 dress code를 이용한 오답.

(C) 정답. 직원 안내서를 개정할 시간이 있는 직원을 묻는 질문에 레이첼이 급한 프로젝트가 없다고 응답한 것은 시간이 있다는 말을 우회적으로 표현한 것이므로 정답.

30
M-Au Can I purchase souvenirs from the concert during intermission?
W-Br (A) Yes, and also following the show.
(B) A T-shirt and a poster for them.
(C) This is a ticket for February.

콘서트 중간 휴식 시간에 기념품을 구입할 수 있나요?
(A) 네, 콘서트 끝나고도 가능해요.
(B) 그들을 위한 티셔츠와 포스터요.
(C) 이건 2월달 표예요.

어휘 purchase 구입하다 souvenir 기념품 intermission 중간 휴식 시간 following ~ 후에

해설 기념품 구입 가능 여부를 묻는 조동사(Can) 의문문
(A) 정답. 콘서트 중간 휴식 시간 중 기념품 구입이 가능한지 묻는 질문에 Yes로 긍정적 응답을 한 후, 콘서트 끝나고도 가능하다는 추가 정보를 주고 있으므로 정답.
(B) 연상 단어 오답. 질문의 souvenirs에 대해 기념품 종류 측면에서 연상 가능한 T-shirt와 poster를 이용한 오답.
(C) 질문과 상관없는 오답. 콘서트 중간 휴식 시간 중에 기념품 구입이 가능한지를 묻는 질문에 2월달 표라는 응답은 맥락에 맞지 않으므로 오답.

31
W-Am Interpreters will be available at the conference, right?
M-Au (A) For the most common languages only.
(B) Chinese food, I think.
(C) They've selected a venue.

회의에서 통역사들을 쓸 수 있겠죠, 그렇죠?
(A) 가장 흔하게 사용되는 언어만요.
(B) 제 생각엔 중국 요리요.
(C) 그들이 장소를 선택했어요.

어휘 interpreter 통역사 available 이용 가능한 conference 회의 common 흔한 language 언어 fluent in ~에 유창한 select 선택하다 venue 개최 장소

해설 회의에서 통역 서비스가 가능한지를 확인하는 부가의문문
(A) 정답. 회의에서 통역사를 쓸 수 있는지 묻는 질문에 가장 흔하게 사용되는 언어만 가능하다고 긍정적인 응답을 하고 있으므로 정답.
(B) 연상 단어 오답. 질문의 interpreter에 대해 통역 언어 종류 측면에서 연상 가능한 Chinese를 이용한 오답.
(C) 연상 단어 오답. 질문의 conference에 대해 회의 개최 장소 측면에서 연상 가능한 venue를 이용한 오답.

PART 3

32-34

M-Au   Hi, my name is Peter Miller. ³²**I arrived from Boston this morning, but my bag was lost in transit. I'm calling to find out if you've found it yet.**

W-Br   Let's see … Yes, Mr. Miller. Fortunately, we have tracked it down, and it'll arrive sometime this afternoon. ³³**We can just deliver it to your hotel. Which one did you check into?**

M-Au   I'm at the Dovetail Inn.

W-Br   OK. The courier will be there around 3 P.M. ³⁴**Don't forget to have your passport ready to prove your identity when you sign for it.** And we're very sorry for the inconvenience.

남: 안녕하세요, 제 이름은 피터 밀러입니다. **오늘 아침 보스턴에서 도착했는데, 제 가방이 운송 중에 분실되었어요. 제 가방을 찾았는지 알아보려고 전화했어요.**

여: 한번 살펴볼게요… 네, 밀러 씨. 다행히 추적해서 찾았어요. 오늘 오후쯤 도착할 거예요. **저희가 호텔로 배달해 드릴게요. 어느 호텔에 투숙하셨나요?**

남: 도브테일 호텔에 있어요.

여: 좋아요. 배달원이 오후 3시쯤 도착할 거예요. **수령 시 본인 확인을 위한 여권 준비를 잊지 마세요.** 불편을 끼쳐 드려서 정말 죄송합니다.

어휘   lost 분실된 in transit 수송 중에, 운송 도중 fortunately 다행히도 track down ~을 찾아내다 deliver 배달하다 check into 투숙하다 inn (작은) 호텔, 여관 courier 배달원 passport 여권 prove 증명하다 identity 신원 inconvenience 불편함

32

What is the purpose of the man's call?

(A) To inquire about a transportation service
(B) To change a flight from Boston
(C) To complain about a damaged bag
(D) To follow up on a missing item

남자가 전화한 목적은 무엇인가?
(A) 운송 서비스에 대해 문의하려고
(B) 보스턴발 항공편을 변경하려고
(C) 파손된 가방에 대해 불만을 제기하려고
(D) 분실된 물건에 대해 알아보려고

어휘   purpose 목적 inquire about ~에 관해 문의하다 transportation service 운송 서비스 flight from Boston 보스턴발 항공편 complain about ~에 대해 불평하다 damaged 파손된 follow up on ~에 대해 후속 조치[사후 관리]를 하다 missing item 분실된 물건

해설   전체 내용 관련 - 전화의 목적

남자는 첫 번째 대사에서 보스턴에서 오는 중에 분실한 가방을 찾았는지 알아보려 전화한다(I arrived from Boston this morning, but my bag was lost in transit. I'm calling to find out if you've found it yet)고 했다. 이를 통해 남자가 분실된 물건에 대해 알아볼 목적으로 전화를 한 것임을 알 수 있으므로 정답은 (D)이다.

▸▸ Paraphrasing   대화의 find out → 정답의 follow up on

33

What does the woman ask about?

(A) Where the man is staying
(B) When the man will arrive
(C) What form the man completed
(D) Who originally helped the man

여자는 무엇에 대해 물어보는가?
(A) 남자가 머물고 있는 곳
(B) 남자가 도착할 시기
(C) 남자가 작성한 양식
(D) 처음 남자를 도와준 사람

어휘   complete a form 양식을 다 작성하다 originally 원래

해설   세부 사항 관련 - 여자가 물어보는 사항

여자의 첫 번째 대사에서 가방을 호텔로 보내주겠다며 어떤 호텔에 투숙했는지(We can just deliver it to your hotel. Which one did you check into) 물었으므로 정답은 (A)이다.

34

What does the woman remind the man to do?

(A) Read a sign carefully
(B) Provide a tracking number
(C) Call the woman this afternoon
(D) Prepare a form of identification

여자는 남자에게 무엇을 하라고 상기시키는가?
(A) 표지판 주의 깊게 읽기
(B) 추적 번호 제공하기
(C) 오늘 오후 여자에게 전화하기
(D) 신분증 준비하기

어휘   remind 상기시키다 provide 제공하다 tracking number 추적 번호 prepare 준비하다 a form of identification 신분증

해설   세부 사항 관련 - 여자가 상기시키는 사항

대화 마지막에서 여자가 수령 시 본인 확인을 위한 여권 준비를 잊지 말라(Don't forget to have your passport ready to prove your identity when you sign for it)고 했으므로 정답은 (D)이다.

▸▸ Paraphrasing   대화의 have your passport ready → 정답의 Prepare a form of identification

35-37

W-Am Hello. This is Yolanda Mendez calling from Room 506. ³⁵**I wanted to do some sightseeing today, so I'm wondering how to get to the Modern Art Museum on foot.**

M-Cn Well, the museum is fairly close to our hotel, about half an hour's walk. You just follow Eden Street north. ³⁶**However, it's really cold and windy outside, so I don't recommend walking.**

W-Am Oh, I see. Is there a bus or subway that goes there?

M-Cn ³⁷**Because it's such a short trip, you should just call a cab to take you.** The fare will be less than five dollars.

여: 안녕하세요. 506호의 올란다 멘데즈입니다. **오늘은 관광을 좀 하고 싶어 그러는데, 걸어서 현대미술관에 가는 방법을 알고 싶어요.**

남: 글쎄요, 박물관은 우리 호텔과 꽤 가까워서 걸어서 30분 정도 거리예요. 북쪽으로 에덴 스트리트를 따라가시면 돼요. **그런데 지금 몹시 춥고 바람이 심하니 걷는 것을 추천하지 않아요.**

여: 오, 그렇군요. 거기까지 가는 버스나 지하철이 있나요?

남: **아주 짧은 거리니 택시를 타고 가세요.** 요금도 5달러 미만일 거예요.

어휘 sightseeing 관광 on foot 걸어서, 도보로 fairly 꽤 walk 보행 거리 recommend 추천하다 cab 택시 trip 이동 fare 요금

35

What is the purpose of the woman's call?

(A) To make a complaint
(B) To get some directions
(C) To inquire about a bill
(D) To book a hotel room

여자가 전화한 목적은 무엇인가?

(A) 불만을 제기하려고
(B) 길 안내를 받으려고
(C) 청구서에 대해 문의하려고
(D) 호텔 객실을 예약하려고

어휘 make a complaint 불만을 제기하다 directions 길 안내 bill 청구서 book 예약하다

해설 전체 내용 관련 – 전화의 목적

여자의 첫 번째 대사에서 관광을 위해 걸어서 현대미술관에 가는 방법을 알고 싶다(I wanted to do some sightseeing today, so I'm wondering how to get to the Modern Art Museum on foot)고 했다. 이를 통해 여자가 길 안내를 받을 목적으로 전화한 것을 알 수 있으므로 정답은 (B)이다.

36

What does the man tell the woman about?

(A) Inclement weather conditions
(B) An entrance fee
(C) A closing time
(D) New company policies

남자는 여자에게 무엇에 관해 말하는가?

(A) 궂은 날씨 상태
(B) 입장료
(C) 폐점 시간
(D) 새로운 회사 방침

어휘 inclement 좋지 못한, 궂은 entrance fee 입장료 closing time 폐점 시간 policy 정책, 방침

해설 세부 사항 관련 – 남자가 여자에게 하는 말

남자의 첫 번째 대사에서 날씨가 춥고 바람이 부니 걷는 것을 추천하지 않는다(However, it's really cold and windy outside, so I don't recommend walking)고 했으므로 정답은 (A)이다.

> ▸▸ **Paraphrasing** 대화의 **cold and windy**
> → 정답의 **Inclement weather conditions**

37

What does the man suggest doing?

(A) Walking to a site
(B) Taking the subway
(C) Riding a bus
(D) Using a taxi

남자는 무엇을 하라고 제안하는가?

(A) 현장으로 걸어가기
(B) 지하철 타기
(C) 버스 타기
(D) 택시 이용하기

어휘 suggest 제안하다 site 현장, 사이트

해설 세부 사항 관련 – 남자가 제안하는 일

대화 마지막에서 남자가 짧은 거리니 택시를 타라(Because it's such a short trip, you should just call a cab to take you)고 했으므로 정답은 (D)이다.

> ▸▸ **Paraphrasing** 대화의 **cab** → 정답의 **taxi**

38-40

W-Br Hi, this is Mindy Ross. ³⁸**I'm supposed to get my hair cut at two, but I have a last-minute meeting with a client. Could I move it to later this week?**

M-Cn Let's see ... Sandra is full for the rest of the week. ³⁹**But Thomas can do it on Thursday at three o'clock.**

W-Br ³⁹**Sorry, but I'd really like Sandra to do it.** I'm flying to Hong Kong on Saturday. Couldn't she fit me in?

M-Cn Hmm... ⁴⁰**I'll ask her to add one more appointment after her shift ends on Friday.** She might be willing to do that.

W-Br Oh, I'd really appreciate that.

여:	안녕하세요, 민디 로스예요. 2시에 머리를 자르기로 예약했는데, 갑작스레 고객과 미팅이 잡혔어요. 예약을 이번 주 후반으로 옮길 수 있을까요?
남:	한번 볼게요 … 산드라는 오늘 이후로 주중 예약이 다 찼어요. **하지만 토마스는 목요일 3시에 가능해요.**
여:	미안하지만, 산드라가 꼭 해 주었으면 해요. 토요일에 홍콩에 가거든요. 산드라가 시간을 좀 낼 수 없을까요?
남:	음 … 산드라가 금요일 교대를 끝낸 후 예약 하나를 더 추가할 수 있는지 요청해 볼게요. 그럴 의향이 있을지도 몰라요.
여:	오, 그렇게 해 주면 정말 고맙겠어요.

어휘	be supposed to ~하기로 되어 있다 last-minute 갑작스러운 client 고객 move 옮기다, 바꾸다 fit in 시간을 내어 ~을 하다 add 더하다 appointment 약속 shift 교대 근무 be willing to 기꺼이 ~하다 appreciate 고마워하다

38

What is the purpose of the woman's call?

(A) To change an appointment
(B) To apply for a job opening
(C) To inquire about business hours
(D) To request a complimentary service

여자가 전화한 목적은 무엇인가?
(A) 예약을 변경하려고
(B) 일자리에 지원하려고
(C) 영업시간을 문의하려고
(D) 무료 서비스를 요청하려고

어휘   appointment 약속, 예약   apply for ~에 지원하다   job opening 일자리   business hours 영업시간   request 요청하다   complimentary 무료의

해설   전체 내용 관련 – 전화의 목적

여자가 첫 번째 대사에서 갑자기 고객과 미팅이 생겨서 예약을 2시에서 이번 주 후반으로 옮길 수 있는지(I'm supposed to get my hair cut at two, but I have a last-minute meeting with a client. Could I move it to later this week) 물어보았다. 따라서 여자가 예약 변경을 목적으로 전화한 것임을 알 수 있으므로 정답은 (A)이다.

▶ Paraphrasing   대화의 **move it to later this week**
→ 정답의 **change an appointment**

39

Why does the woman say she does not want to come on Thursday?

(A) She has to attend a business meeting.
(B) She prefers a haircut from a certain employee.
(C) She plans to take a flight that day.
(D) She lives too far from the business.

여자가 목요일에 오는 것을 원하지 않는 이유는?
(A) 업무 회의에 참석해야 한다.
(B) 특정 직원이 머리를 깎아 주길 선호한다.
(C) 그날 비행기를 탈 계획이다.
(D) 영업장에서 너무 먼 곳에 산다.

어휘   attend 참석하다   prefer 선호하다   certain 특정한   employee 직원   plan to ~할 계획이다   take a flight 비행기를 타다

해설   세부 사항 관련 – 여자가 목요일을 원하지 않는 이유

남자의 첫 번째 대사에서 토마스는 목요일에 할 수 있다(But Thomas can do it on Thursday at three o'clock)고 했다. 이에 대해 여자가 산드라가 해 주길 원한다(Sorry, but I'd really like Sandra to do it)고 응답했다. 여자가 특정 직원이 해 주길 선호한다는 것을 알 수 있으므로 정답은 (B)이다.

40

What does the man offer to do?

(A) Call the woman if a customer cancels
(B) Ask a coworker to work overtime
(C) Print a copy of a document
(D) Give directions to another branch

남자는 무엇을 해 주겠다고 하는가?
(A) 고객이 취소하면 여자에게 전화하기
(B) 동료에게 초과 근무 요청하기
(C) 문서 인쇄하기
(D) 다른 지점으로 가는 길 안내하기

어휘   customer 고객   cancel 취소하다   coworker 직장동료   work overtime 초과 근무하다   directions 길 안내   branch 지점, 지사

해설   세부 사항 관련 – 남자가 제안하는 일

남자의 마지막 대사에서 산드라가 금요일 교대를 끝낸 후 예약 하나를 추가해 달라고 요청하겠다(I'll ask her to add one more appointment after her shift ends on Friday)고 했으므로 정답은 (B)이다.

41-43

W-Am	Excuse me. **⁴¹This is my first time working out here, and I noticed that some of the treadmills and stationary bikes have red stickers on them.** Is that something I need to pay attention to?
M-Au	Yes. **⁴²That's our system for reserving equipment in advance.** Members can call to book a machine during a certain time.
W-Am	Oh, I see. That's a good idea for people who don't have time to wait around.
M-Au	Exactly. **⁴³A lot of our members asked for that feature when they filled out the questionnaire we gave them last month.** We hope the change will make things more convenient for everyone.

여:	실례합니다. 여기서 처음 운동하는데요. 러닝 머신과 고정 자전거 몇 대에 빨간 스티커가 붙어 있는 걸 봤어요 주의해야 할 점이 있는 건가요?
남:	네. 그것은 사전에 장비를 예약하는 저희 시스템입니다. 회원들이 전화로 특정 시간 동안 장비를 예약할 수 있어요.
여:	오, 그렇군요. 기다릴 시간이 없는 사람들에게는 좋겠네요.
남:	바로 그거죠. 지난달 설문지를 작성할 때 많은 회원이 그 기능을 요청했어요. 이 변화로 모든 사람이 더 편해졌으면 해요.

41

Where is the conversation most likely taking place?

(A) At a sporting goods store
(B) At an office
(C) At a fitness facility
(D) At a factory

대화는 어디에서 일어나겠는가?

(A) 스포츠 용품점
(B) 사무실
(C) **헬스클럽**
(D) 공장

어휘　take place 일어나다　sporting goods 스포츠 용품　fitness facility 헬스클럽　factory 공장

해설　전체 내용 관련 – 대화 장소
대화 첫 부분에서 여자가 처음 운동하는데 러닝 머신과 고정 자전거 몇 대에서 빨간 스티커를 보았다(This is my first time working out here, and I noticed that some of the treadmills and stationary bikes have red stickers on them)고 했다. 이로써 대화가 헬스클럽에서 이루어지고 있음을 알 수 있으므로 정답은 (C)이다.

42

According to the man, what does a red sticker on an item mean?

(A) It is currently on sale.
(B) It has been booked.
(C) It is not working.
(D) It is for advanced users.

남자에 따르면, 장비에 있는 빨간 스티커는 무엇을 의미하는가?

(A) 현재 할인 중이다.
(B) **예약되었다.**
(C) 작동하지 않는다.
(D) 상급자를 위한 것이다.

어휘　currently 현재　on sale 할인 중인　book 예약하다　work 작동하다　advanced 상급의, 고급의　user 사용자

해설　세부 사항 관련 – 빨간 스티커가 의미하는 것
남자가 첫 번째 대사에서 그것은 사전에 장비를 예약하는 시스템(That's our system for reserving equipment in advance)이라고 했으므로 정답은 (B)이다.

▸▸ Paraphrasing　대화의 **reserving** → 정답의 **booked**

43

What did the business do last month?

(A) Received an award
(B) Hired more workers
(C) Moved to a better location
(D) Conducted a survey

헬스클럽은 지난달에 무엇을 했는가?

(A) 상을 받았다
(B) 직원을 더 채용했다
(C) 위치가 더 좋은 곳으로 이사했다
(D) **설문 조사를 실시했다**

어휘　receive 받다　award 상　hire 고용하다　location 위치, 장소　conduct 실시하다　survey 설문 조사

해설　세부 사항 관련 – 지난달 헬스클럽이 한 일
대화 마지막에 남자가 지난달 설문지에서 많은 회원들이 그 기능을 요청했다(A lot of our members asked for that feature when they filled out the questionnaire we gave them last month)고 했으므로 정답은 (D)이다.

▸▸ Paraphrasing　대화의 **questionnaire** → 정답의 **survey**

44-46 3인 대화

W-Br	**44Our head chef's last day will be on June sixth, and his replacement, Guido Mazzi, will officially start on June seventh, though he's already completed the new menu.**
W-Am	All right. We're holding a special event on his first day to publicize the change so people can try the new dishes.
M-Cn	We've run into some trouble. **45We were supposed to have some fresh Atlantic salmon delivered yesterday, but it's still not here.**
W-Br	Really? I guess Chef Mazzi will have to come up with something else for the debut event we advertised.
M-Cn	**46In that case, how about I call the printer and ask them to halt our menu project until we're sure?**

여1:	우리 주방장님의 마지막 날은 6월 6일이고 후임자인 규도 마지 주방장님은 새 메뉴는 벌써 완성했지만, 공식적으로는 6월 7일에 업무를 시작해요.
여2:	좋아요. 첫날에 특별 행사로 주방장 교체를 알려서 손님들이 새 요리를 맛볼 수 있도록 할 거예요.
남:	문제가 좀 생겼어요. **대서양 생물 연어가 어제 배달되었어야 했는데, 아직 안 왔어요.**
여1:	정말요? 그럼 우리가 광고했던 데뷔 행사를 위해 마지 주방장님이 뭔가 다른 걸 내놓아야 할 것 같아요.
남:	그렇다면 제가 인쇄소로 연락해서 확정될 때까지 메뉴 인쇄를 중단하도록 요청하는 게 어떨까요?

어휘 head chef 주방장 replacement 후임자 officially 공식적으로 complete 완성하다 hold ~을 개최하다 event 행사 publicize 알리다, 홍보하다 dish 음식, 요리 run into ~에 부딪히다[마주치다] fresh 신선한, (냉동이 아닌) 생물의 salmon 연어 deliver 배달하다 come up with ~을 내놓다[떠올리다] debut 데뷔, 첫 출연 advertise 광고하다 printer 인쇄기, 인쇄소 halt 중지하다

44

What are the speakers discussing?

(A) A customer complaint
(B) A grand opening
(C) A staff change
(D) A restaurant inspection

화자들은 무엇을 논의하고 있는가?
(A) 고객 불만 사항
(B) 개장
(C) **직원 교체**
(D) 식당 검사

어휘 customer 고객 complaint 불평, 불만 inspection 검사, 점검

해설 전체 내용 관련 – 대화 주제
첫 번째 여자의 첫 대사에서 주방장의 마지막 근무 날짜가 6월 6일이고 후임자는 새 메뉴를 완성했지만 공식 업무 시작 날짜는 6월 7일(Our head chef's last day will be on June sixth, and his replacement, Guido Mazzi, will officially start on June seventh, though he's already completed the new menu)이라고 말했다. 이로써 화자들이 직원 교체를 논의하고 있다는 것을 알 수 있으므로 정답은 (C)이다.

45

What problem does the man mention?

(A) A dish is not selling well.
(B) A shipment has not arrived.
(C) An employee is inexperienced.
(D) An advertisement contained an error.

남자는 어떤 문제를 언급하는가?
(A) 요리가 잘 팔리지 않는다.
(B) **배달 물품이 아직 도착하지 않았다.**
(C) 직원이 미숙하다.
(D) 광고에 오류가 있다.

어휘 shipment 수송품, 배달 물품 employee 직원 inexperienced 경험이 부족한 advertisement 광고 contain 포함하다

해설 세부 사항 관련 – 남자가 언급하는 문제
남자의 첫 번째 대사에서 대서양 생물 연어가 어제 배달되었어야 했는데 아직 안 왔다(We were supposed to have some fresh Atlantic salmon delivered yesterday, but it's still not here)고 했다. 이로써 배달 물품이 아직 도착하지 않았다는 것을 알 수 있으므로 정답은 (B)이다.

46

What does the man offer to do?

(A) Proofread a menu
(B) Contact a print shop
(C) Call Chef Mazzi
(D) Create a new design

남자는 무엇을 해 주겠다고 하는가?
(A) 메뉴 교정하기
(B) **인쇄소에 연락하기**
(C) 마지 주방장에게 전화하기
(D) 새롭게 디자인하기

어휘 proofread 교정하다 contact 연락하다 print shop 인쇄소 create 창조하다, 만들다

해설 세부 사항 관련 – 남자가 제안하는 일
대화 마지막에 남자가 인쇄소에 연락해 확정될 때까지 메뉴 인쇄를 중단하도록 요청하겠다(In that case, how about I call the printer and ask them to halt our menu project until we're sure)고 했으므로 정답은 (B)이다.

▶▶ **Paraphrasing** 대화의 **call the printer**
→ 정답의 **Contact a print shop**

47-49

W-Am Thanks for letting me stop by, Mr. Friedman. [47]**I'm Chandra Badal, your real estate agent.**

M-Au It's nice to meet you. [47]**This is the first time I've sold a house, so I'm not very familiar with the process.**

W-Am That's why I'm here to walk you through every step of the way. Now, before we put the property on the market, you should invest in some cosmetic changes like painting to give the place a fresh look. [48]**This will help to maximize the return on your investment.**

M-Au I've set aside three thousand dollars for those kinds of improvements. [49]**I'm worried about going over that amount, though, because I don't want to empty my savings.**

여: 잠깐 들를 수 있게 해 주셔서 감사해요, 프리드먼 씨. 찬드라 바달입니다. 담당 부동산 중개인이에요.
남: 만나서 반가워요. 처음으로 집을 파는 거라서 절차에 익숙하지 않아요.
여: 그래서 단계별 절차를 차근차근 알려드리려고 온 겁니다. 이제 집을 시장에 내놓기 전에, 좀 더 산뜻한 모습을 위해 페인트칠 같은 외관 변화에 투자해야 해요. 그렇게 하면 투자 수익을 최대로 끌어올리는 데 도움이 될 거예요.
남: 그런 개선에 대비해 3천 달러를 따로 준비해 두었어요. 그래도 그 금액을 초과할까 봐 걱정되네요. 저축한 돈을 다 쓰고 싶지 않거든요.

어휘	stop by 잠깐 들르다 real estate agent 부동산 중개인 be familiar with ~에 익숙하다 process 절차, 과정 walk ~ through ... (어떤 것을 배우거나 익힐 수 있도록 단계별로 차례차례) ~에게 …을 보여주다 property 부동산 on the market 시장[시중]에 내놓은 invest in ~에 투자하다 cosmetic 표면적인, 장식적인 fresh look 산뜻한 모습 maximize 극대화하다 return on investment 투자 수익[이익]률 set aside 따로 떼어 놓다 improvement 개량, 개선 go over 초과하다 amount 총액, 금액 empty 비우다 savings 저축한 돈

47

Who most likely is the man?

(A) A construction worker
(B) A real estate agent
(C) An interior designer
(D) A homeowner

남자는 누구이겠는가?

(A) 건설 노동자
(B) 부동산 중개인
(C) 인테리어 디자이너
(D) 집주인

어휘 construction worker 건설 노동자 homeowner 집주인

해설 전체 내용 관련 – 남자의 직업

대화 첫 부분에서 여자가 본인이 담당 부동산 중개인이다(I'm Chandra Badal, your real estate agent)라고 했다. 이어서 남자가 처음으로 집을 팔기 때문에 절차에 익숙하지 않다(This is the first time I've sold a house, so I'm not very familiar with the process)라고 응답했다. 이로써 남자가 집주인이라는 것을 알 수 있으므로 정답은 (D)이다.

48

Why does the woman want to make some changes?

(A) To retain employees
(B) To follow a regulation
(C) To save time
(D) To increase profits

여자가 변화를 원하는 이유는 무엇인가?

(A) 직원을 붙잡아 두기 위해
(B) 규정을 준수하기 위해
(C) 시간을 절약하기 위해
(D) 수익을 높이기 위해

어휘 make changes 변화시키다 retain 유지하다 follow 따르다, 준수하다 regulation 규정 increase 증가시키다 profit 이익, 이윤

해설 세부 사항 관련 – 여자가 변화를 원하는 이유

여자의 두 번째 대사에서 그 변화가 프리드먼 씨의 투자 수익을 최대로 끌어올릴 것이다(This will help to maximize the return on your investment)라고 했으므로 정답은 (D)이다.

▸▸ Paraphrasing 대화의 **maximize the return on your investment** → 정답의 **increase profits**

49

What is the man concerned about?

(A) Opening an account
(B) Upsetting a customer
(C) Exceeding a budget
(D) Missing a deadline

남자는 무엇을 걱정하는가?

(A) 계좌를 개설하는 것
(B) 고객의 기분을 상하게 하는 것
(C) 예산을 초과하는 것
(D) 마감을 지키지 못하는 것

어휘 be concerned about ~을 걱정하다 open 개설하다 account 계좌 upset 속상하게 만들다 exceed 초과하다 budget 예산 miss 놓치다 deadline 마감 기한

해설 세부 사항 관련 – 남자가 걱정하는 것

대화 마지막에 남자가 금액을 초과할까 봐 걱정된다며 저축한 돈을 다 쓰고 싶지 않다(I'm worried about going over that amount, though, because I don't want to empty my savings)고 했으므로 정답은 (C)이다.

▸▸ Paraphrasing 대화의 **going over that amount** → 정답의 **Exceeding a budget**

50-52

M-Cn	**50Thanks again, Elizabeth, for helping me with the planning for the upcoming Technology Career Expo.**
W-Am	I'm happy to help, and we've made a lot of progress. I've already paid the rental fee at the Oakdale Center. **51The building has several entrances, so I've asked their staff to post signs to direct people to our event.**
M-Cn	Perfect. And I've ordered the refreshments from the caterer. We'll have coffee and cookies for about two thousand people.
W-Am	That should be enough. **52Since we'll be setting up the refreshments in the hall, I'd better call to find out how big the tables are so we know how many we need.** I can take care of that now.

남: 곧 다가올 테크놀로지 커리어 엑스포 기획을 도와줘서 다시 한 번 감사드려요, 엘리자베스.

여: 도울 수 있어서 기뻐요. 많이 진척되었어요. 오크데일 센터 임대료는 벌써 지불했어요. 그 건물에는 입구가 여러 개 있어서 우리 행사를 안내하는 표지판을 게시하도록 그쪽 직원에게 요청했어요.

남: 완벽해요. 그리고 출장 뷔페 업체에 다과를 주문했어요. 약 2천 명 분의 커피와 쿠키가 준비될 거예요.

여: 그 정도면 충분할 거예요. 다과를 복도에 놓을 거니까 전화로 테이블 크기를 물어봐서 필요한 테이블 개수를 알아봐야겠어요. 지금 처리할게요.

어휘 upcoming 다가올 career expo 취업 박람회(= job fair) make progress 진전을 보이다 rental 대여, 임대 fee 요금 several 몇몇의 entrance 입구 post 게시하다 sign 표지판 direct to ~로 가는 길을 가르쳐 주다 refreshments 다과 caterer 출장 뷔페 업체 set up 세우다, 놓다 take care of ~을 처리하다

50

What kind of event are the speakers planning?

(A) An academic lecture
(B) A technology course
(C) A product launch
(D) A job fair

화자들은 어떤 행사를 계획하는가?

(A) 학술 강연
(B) 기술 강좌
(C) 제품 출시
(D) 취업 박람회

어휘 academic 학문의 lecture 강연, 강의 technology 기술 course 강의, 강좌 product 제품 launch 출시, 개시 job fair 취업 박람회

해설 전체 내용 관련 – 화자들이 계획하는 행사

남자가 첫 번째 대사에서 여자에게 테크놀로지 커리어 엑스포 기획을 도와주어 고맙다(Thanks again, Elizabeth, for helping me with the planning for the upcoming Technology Career Expo)고 했다. 행사 이름이 Career Expo이므로 화자들이 취업 박람회 행사를 계획한다는 것을 알 수 있으므로 정답은 (D)이다.

51

What have Oakdale Center employees been asked to do?

(A) Confirm a booking date
(B) Decorate a venue
(C) Put up some signs
(D) Keep one entrance locked

오크데일 센터 직원은 무엇을 하라고 요청받았나?

(A) 예약 날짜 확인하기
(B) 개최지 장식하기
(C) 표지판 게시하기
(D) 입구 한 곳 잠그기

어휘 confirm 확인하다 decorate 장식하다 venue 개최지 put up 게시하다 lock 잠그다

해설 세부 사항 관련 – 센터 직원이 요청 받은 일

여자의 첫 번째 대사에서 건물에 입구가 여러 개 있어서 행사 안내 표지판을 게시하도록 직원에게 요청했다(The building has several entrances, so I've asked their staff to post signs to direct people to our event)고 했으므로 정답은 (C)이다.

▸▸ Paraphrasing 대화의 post signs
→ 정답의 put up some signs

52

What does the woman say she will check?

(A) The expected number of attendees
(B) The ingredients in some refreshments
(C) The cost of renting a facility
(D) The size of some tables

여자는 무엇을 확인하겠다고 말하는가?

(A) 예상 참석자 수
(B) 다과의 성분
(C) 시설 임대 비용
(D) 테이블의 크기

어휘 expected 예상되는 attendee 참석자 ingredient 재료, 성분 rent 임대하다 facility 시설

해설 세부 사항 관련 – 여자가 확인할 사항

대화 마지막에 여자가 다과를 복도에 둘 예정이니 전화로 테이블 크기를 물어봐서 테이블이 몇 개 필요한지 정하겠다(Since we'll be setting up the refreshments in the hall, I'd better call to find out how big the tables are so we know how many we need)고 했으므로 정답은 (D)이다.

▸▸ Paraphrasing 대화의 how big the tables are
→ 정답의 The size of some tables

53-55

M-Cn Excuse me. **53I need to buy a new router for my Wi-Fi connection in my studio apartment. I see you have a large selection here, but to me,** they all look the same.

W-Br I understand. The choices can seem overwhelming. **54How many devices would be using the router at a time?**

M-Cn Usually just two—my laptop and my smartphone.

W-Br Then since you don't need it to cover a large area, I'd recommend the Conway-HX. It is just a basic model, but it will do what you need it to do. **55It's our store's best-seller.**

M-Cn OK, I'll give that one a try. Thanks!

남: 실례합니다. 제 원룸 아파트의 와이파이 연결을 위해서 공유기를 구입해야 해요. 여기에 공유기 종류가 많네요. 하지만 저한테는 다 똑같이 보여요.

여: 이해해요. 종류가 많아서 좀 당황스러우실 거예요. 한 번에 몇 대의 장치가 공유기를 사용하나요?

남: 보통 2개뿐이에요— 노트북과 스마트폰이요.

여: 넓은 영역을 지원할 필요가 없으니 콘웨이-HX를 추천합니다. 그냥 기본 모델이지만 손님께 필요한 건 다 될 거예요. 이게 우리 가게에서 제일 잘 나가는 상품이에요.

남: 좋아요, 그걸로 한번 써 봐야겠어요. 감사합니다!

어휘 router 라우터[공유기] connection 연결 studio apartment 원룸 아파트 selection 선택의 대상이 되는 물품, 정선품 choice 선택된 것, 특선품, 정선물 overwhelming 압도적인, 당황하게 만드는 device 장비, 장치 at a time 한 번에 laptop 노트북 컴퓨터 cover 포함시키다, 사징 거리 안에 두다 basic 기본적인 best-seller 베스트셀러, 잘 나가는 상품 give ~ a try ~를 한번 해 보자

53

What does the man mean when he says, "they all look the same"?

(A) He needs help making a decision.
(B) He is disappointed with the store's options.
(C) He wants his devices to be the same color.
(D) He thinks the brand does not matter.

남자가 "다 똑같아 보인다"라고 말한 의도는 무엇인가?

(A) 결정을 내리는 데 도움이 필요하다.
(B) 가게가 보유하고 있는 상품이 실망스럽다.
(C) 그의 장치와 같은 색상이기를 바란다.
(D) 상표는 중요하지 않다고 생각한다.

어휘 make a decision 결정을 내리다 be disappointed with ~에 실망하다 option 선택지 brand 상표 matter 중요하다

해설 화자의 의도 파악 - 다 똑같아 보인다는 말의 의도

인용문에서 they는 앞 문장의 a large selection을 가리킨다. 즉 공유기의 종류는 많은데 다 똑같아 보이기 때문에 어떤 공유기를 구입할지 결정하는 데 도움이 필요하다는 의미가 내포되어 있으므로 정답은 (A)이다.

54

What does the woman ask the man about?

(A) The budget he has prepared for a purchase
(B) The brands of his laptop and smartphone
(C) The size of the area he wants to cover
(D) The number of machines that will be used

여자는 남자에게 무엇에 대해 물어보는가?

(A) 구입을 위해 준비한 예산
(B) 노트북과 스마트폰의 상표
(C) 지원하길 원하는 곳의 면적
(D) 사용될 기기의 수

어휘 budget 예산 prepare for ~를 준비하다 purchase 구입하다 the number of ~의 수 machine 기계, 기기

해설 세부 사항 관련 - 여자가 물어보는 것

여자가 남자에게 한 번에 몇 대의 장치가 공유기를 사용하는지(How many devices would be using the router at a time) 물어보았으므로 정답은 (D)이다.

▸▸ Paraphrasing 대화의 devices → 정답의 machines

55

What does the woman suggest about the Conway-HX?

(A) It is not enough for the man's needs.
(B) It is larger than the other models.
(C) It is currently offered at a discount.
(D) It is the most popular item.

여자가 콘웨이-HX에 대해 암시하는 것은 무엇인가?

(A) 남자의 요구에 비해 충분하지 않다.
(B) 다른 모델보다 더 크다.
(C) 현재 할인된 가격으로 제공된다.
(D) 가장 인기 있는 상품이다.

어휘 needs 요구 currently 현재 at a discount 할인하여 item 상품

해설 세부 사항 관련 - 여자가 콘웨이-HX에 대해 암시하는 것

여자의 두 번째 대사에서 그것이 가게에서 제일 잘 나가는 상품(It's our store's best-seller)이라고 했으므로 정답은 (D)이다.

▸▸ Paraphrasing 대화의 best-seller
→ 정답의 the most popular item

56-58

M-Au Welcome back, Christina. **56We missed you last week. I hope you've fully recovered from that case of the flu you had.**

W-Br Thanks. I'm feeling much better now. A few days of rest was just what I needed.

M-Au I'm glad to hear that. Now, while you were gone, Ms. Milton assigned groups for the presentations at Kenner International.

W-Br Oh, no! That's this Friday, isn't it? **57I'm going to be so far behind. I haven't even started any of the preparations.**

M-Au **57You don't have to do the work alone.** Arthur Hammond is on your team.

W-Br That's a relief. **58He's been working here the longest, so he'll know what to do.**

남: 돌아온 걸 환영해요. 크리스티나. 지난주에 모두 크리스티나를 보고 싶어 했어요. 독감에서 완전히 회복되었기를 바라요.

여: 고마워요. 이제 몸이 한결 나아졌어요. 나한테 필요했던 건 그저 며칠 동안의 휴식이었어요.

남: 반가운 소리네요. 크리스티나가 없는 사이에 밀턴 씨가 케너 인터내셔널에서 할 발표를 위해 조를 배정했어요.

여: 오, 이런! 발표가 이번 금요일이죠, 그렇죠? 너무 뒤처지겠는데요. 준비를 시작도 못했어요.

남: 크리스티나 혼자서 하지 않아도 돼요. 아서 하몬드가 같은 팀이에요.

여: 그럼 안심이네요. 하몬드는 여기서 가장 오래 근무했으니 어떻게 해야 하는지 알 거에요.

<table>
<tr><td>어휘</td><td>miss 그리워하다 fully 완전히 recover from ~에서
회복하다 case (질병·부상) 사례[환자] flu 독감 rest 휴식
be gone 부재 중이다 assign 배정하다 presentation
발표 be behind 뒤처지다 preparation 준비 relief 안도,
안심</td></tr>
</table>

56

Why was the woman absent last week?

(A) She visited another branch.
(B) She had an illness.
(C) She went on a business trip.
(D) She was taking a vacation.

여자가 지난주에 결근한 이유는 무엇인가?
(A) 다른 지점을 방문했다.
(B) 아팠다.
(C) 출장을 갔다.
(D) 휴가를 갔다.

어휘 absent 결석한, 결근한 branch 지점 go on a business trip
출장을 가다 take a vacation 휴가를 얻다

해설 세부 사항 관련 – 여자가 결근한 이유
대화 첫 부분에서 남자가 지난주 모두 여자를 보고 싶어 했다며 독감에서 회
복되었기를 바란다(We missed you last week. I hope you've fully
recovered from that case of the flu you had)고 했다. 이를 통해 여자가
지난주에 아파서 결근했음을 알 수 있으므로 정답은 (B)이다.

▸▸ **Paraphrasing** 대화의 flu → 정답의 illness

57

Why does the man say, "Arthur Hammond is on your
team"?

(A) To thank the woman for training a coworker
(B) To correct an error in a document sent to the woman
(C) To explain that he cannot answer the woman's
questions
(D) To reassure the woman about an assignment

남자가 "아서 하몬드가 같은 팀이에요"라고 말한 이유는 무엇인가?
(A) 동료를 교육시킨 것에 감사하려고
(B) 여자에게 보낸 문서에 있는 오류를 바로잡으려고
(C) 여자의 질문에 답할 수 없다는 것을 설명하려고
(D) 할당 업무에 대해 여자를 안심시키려고

어휘 coworker 직장동료 correct 바로잡다 error 실수, 오류
explain 설명하다 reassure 안심시키다 assignment 과제, 임무

해설 화자의 의도 파악 – 아서 하몬드가 같은 팀이라고 말한 이유
대화 중반부에서 여자는 너무 뒤처지겠다며 준비를 시작도 못했다(I'm going
to be so far behind. I haven't even started any of the preparations)
고 했다. 이어서 남자가 혼자서 하지 않아도 된다(You don't have to do the
work alone)며 아서 하몬드가 같은 팀이라고 했다. 따라서 발표를 걱정하는
여자를 안심시키기 위해 아서 하몬드가 같은 팀이라고 말했다는 것을 알 수 있
으므로 정답은 (D)이다.

58

What does the woman suggest about Mr. Hammond?

(A) He has a lot of experience.
(B) He used to work at Kenner International.
(C) He is behind schedule.
(D) He prefers to work alone.

여자가 하몬드에 대해 암시하는 것은 무엇인가?
(A) 경험이 많다.
(B) 케너 인터내셔널에서 일했다.
(C) 일정보다 늦어지고 있다.
(D) 혼자 일하기를 좋아한다.

어휘 experience 경험, 경력 used to (과거에) ~했다 behind
schedule 예정보다 늦게 prefer 선호하다, 좋아하다

해설 세부 사항 관련 – 여자가 하몬드에 대해 말하는 것
대화 마지막에서 여자가 하몬드는 회사에서 가장 오래 근무했기 때문에 무엇을
해야 하는지 안다(He's been working here the longest, so he'll know
what to do)고 했다. 이로써 하몬드가 경험이 많다는 것을 알 수 있으므로 정
답은 (A)이다.

▸▸ **Paraphrasing** 대화의 working here the longest
→ 정답의 has a lot of experience

59-61 3인 대화

<table>
<tr><td>M-Au</td><td>⁵⁹**When I was unloading the ingredients
shipment, I noticed that the walk-in
refrigerator is not as cold as it should
be.** We can't store food in there if it keeps
rising above forty degrees.</td></tr>
<tr><td>M-Cn</td><td>Is it having problems again? We were
penalized on our health inspection
because of that. Right, Stephanie?</td></tr>
<tr><td>W-Am</td><td>Yes. ⁶⁰**And we don't have enough
money to replace it, so we'd better
get a technician to look at it.** I can call
someone.</td></tr>
<tr><td>M-Cn</td><td>I know a maintenance company that has
reasonable rates. ⁶¹**Stephanie, I'll forward
you their phone number and e-mail
address.**</td></tr>
<tr><td>M-Au</td><td>Thanks to you two, I think we can get this
resolved before it causes a problem.</td></tr>
</table>

남1: 배달된 음식 재료를 내릴 때 대형 냉장실의 온도가 기준만큼 낮지
않다는 것을 알아챘어요. 냉장실 온도가 계속해서 (화씨) 40도 이상
올라가면 더 이상 음식을 보관할 수 없어요.
남2: 또 말썽인가요? 그것 때문에 지난번 위생 점검에서 제재를 받았죠.
그렇죠, 스테파니?
여: 네. 그리고 지금 냉장실을 교체할 돈이 없으니 기술자를 불러 살펴보게
하는 게 좋겠어요. 제가 전화 볼게요.
남2: 가격이 저렴한 정비 업체를 알고 있어요. 스테파니, 전화번호와 이메일
주소를 전달해 줄게요.
남1: 두 분 다 고마워요. 문제가 생기기 전에 해결할 수 있을 거예요.

어휘	unload (짐을) 내리다 ingredient 재료 shipment 배달품, 선적품 notice 알아채다 walk-in refrigerator 대형 냉장실 store 보관하다 keep -ing 계속해서 ~하다 rise 올라가다 penalize 처벌하다, 제재를 가하다 health inspection 위생 점검 replace 교체하다 technician 기술자 look at ~를 살펴보다 maintenance 유지 (관리), 정비 reasonable 합리적인, 저렴한 rate 가격 forward 보내다, 전달하다 resolve 해결하다 cause 유발하다

59

What problem are the speakers discussing?

(A) The restaurant lacks storage space.
(B) A delivery contained the wrong items.
(C) Some lighting in the kitchen is not working.
(D) The temperature of an area is too high.

화자들은 무슨 문제를 논의하고 있는가?
(A) 식당에 저장 공간이 부족하다.
(B) 배달된 물품에 엉뚱한 물건이 있다.
(C) 부엌의 일부 전등이 고장이다.
(D) 한 장소의 온도가 너무 높다.

어휘 lack 부족하다 storage space 저장 공간 delivery 배달 contain 포함하다 lighting 조명, 전등 work 작동하다 temperature 온도

해설 전체 내용 관련 - 논의하고 있는 문제
첫 번째 남자의 대사에서 배달된 음식 재료를 내릴 때 대형 냉장실의 온도가 낮지 않다는 것을 알아챘다(When I was unloading the ingredients shipment, I noticed that the walk-in refrigerator is not as cold as it should be)고 했다. 이를 통해 한 장소의 온도가 너무 높다는 것을 알 수 있으므로 정답은 (D)이다.

▶▶ Paraphrasing 대화의 not as cold as it should be → 정답의 too high

60

What does the woman think the business should do?

(A) Take out a small loan
(B) Purchase some new equipment
(C) Hire a repairperson
(D) Undergo another inspection

여자는 회사가 무엇을 해야 한다고 생각하는가?
(A) 소액 대출 받기
(B) 새 장비 구입하기
(C) 수리공 부르기
(D) 다른 점검 받기

어휘 take out (공식적인 서비스를) 받다 loan 대출 equipment 장비 hire (단기간 동안 사람을) 쓰다, 고용하다 repairperson 수리공 undergo 겪다, 받다 inspection 점검

해설 세부 사항 관련 - 회사가 해야 하는 일
여자는 냉장실을 교체할 돈이 없으니 기술자를 불러 살펴보게 하자(And we don't have enough money to replace it, so we'd better get a technician to look at it)고 했으므로 정답은 (C)이다.

▶▶ Paraphrasing 대화의 get a technician → 정답의 Hire a repairperson

61

What will be sent to the woman?

(A) A shipping address
(B) A pricing estimate
(C) Some contact details
(D) An application form

여자는 무엇을 받을 것인가?
(A) 배송 주소
(B) 가격 견적서
(C) 자세한 연락처
(D) 신청서

어휘 shipping 운송, 배송 pricing 가격 책정 estimate 견적서 contact 연락 (상대) application form 신청서

해설 세부 사항 관련 - 여자가 받을 것
두 번째 남자의 두 번째 대사에서 전화번호와 이메일 주소를 전달하겠다(Stephanie, I'll forward you their phone number and e-mail address)고 했으므로 정답은 (C)이다.

▶▶ Paraphrasing 대화의 phone number and e-mail address → 정답의 Some contact details

62-64 대화 + 통로 표시

M-Au Good news, Sally. We'll finally be getting some self-checkout machines—you know, the ones that let customers scan and check out their own groceries. 62**They'll be installed next week.**

W-Br Great. 63**I'll post an update on our Web page about that if you'd like.**

M-Au Sure. And speaking of that—there's some more news. 64**One of the popular snack products we carry is going to be discontinued soon—the Healthy Plus mixed nuts. You know, the one packaged in the convenient can.**

W-Br Oh, no. Really?

M-Au 64**Yes, I'll head over to the aisle they're in now, and then move them to the special "Buy Now Before It's Gone" display in the front of the store.**

남: 좋은 소식이 있어요, 샐리. 드디어 셀프 계산대 기계를 몇 대 놓을 거예요. 고객이 직접 식료품을 스캔하고 계산할 수 있는 기계 말이에요. 기계들이 다음 주에 설치될 거예요.
여: 잘됐네요. 원하시면 우리 웹사이트에 그 소식을 올릴게요.
남: 물론이죠. 그리고 말 나온 김에, 뉴스가 더 있어요. 인기 스낵 제품 하나가 단종될 예정이에요. 헬스 플러스 혼합 견과요. 간편 캔에 포장되어 있는 거예요.

18

여: 오, 안 돼요. 정말인가요?

남: 네, 현재 제품이 진열된 통로로 가서 가게 정면에 특별히 마련한 "판매 중지 전에 지금 구입하세요" 진열대로 그 제품들을 옮길 거예요.

어휘 finally 마침내 self-checkout 셀프 계산대 machine 기계 customer 고객 scan 스캔하다 check out (비용을 지불하고) 나가다 groceries 식료품 install 설치하다 post 게시하다 speaking of ~에 관해서 말한다면 product 제품 carry (물품을) 보유하고[팔고] 있다 discontinue 중단하다 package 포장하다 convenient 편리한 can 캔, 깡통 head over to ~를 향해 가다 aisle 통로 move 옮기다 gone 다 쓴[떨어진] display 진열

Aisle 1	Cleaning Supplies
Aisle 2	Meats and Fish
64Aisle 3	Packaged Snacks
Aisle 4	Teas and Coffees

통로 1	청소 용품
통로 2	육류 및 생선
통로 3	**포장 스낵**
통로 4	차 및 커피

어휘 supplies 물품 meat 고기, 육류

62

According to the man, what will happen at the store next week?

(A) A clearance sale will take place.
(B) An orientation session will be given.
(C) Some new equipment will be installed.
(D) Some safety inspectors will visit.

남자에 의하면, 다음 주 가게에서 무슨 일이 일어나는가?
(A) 재고 정리 할인 판매가 있다.
(B) 오리엔테이션이 있다.
(C) 새 장비가 설치된다.
(D) 안전 감독관이 방문한다.

어휘 clearance sale 재고 정리 판매, 염가 처분 판매 take place 일어나다 orientation session 오리엔테이션 equipment 장비 safety inspector 안전 감독관

해설 세부 사항 관련 – 다음 주에 있을 일
남자의 첫 번째 대사에서 기계들이 다음 주에 설치된다(They'll be installed next week)고 했으므로 정답은 (C)이다.

63

What does the woman offer to do?

(A) Create a large sign
(B) Update a Web site
(C) Work an additional shift
(D) Check on inventory levels

여자는 무엇을 해 주겠다고 제안하는가?
(A) 큰 간판 만들기
(B) 웹사이트 업데이트하기
(C) 추가 근무하기
(D) 재고 수준 점검하기

어휘 sign 간판 update 최신 정보를 알려주다 additional 추가적인 shift 교대 근무 check on (이상이 없는지) ~을 확인하다 inventory 재고

해설 세부 사항 관련 – 여자의 제안 사항
여자의 첫 번째 대사에서 웹사이트에 그 소식을 올리겠다(I'll post an update on our Web page about that if you'd like)고 했으므로 정답은 (B)이다.

64

Look at the graphic. Which aisle will the man most likely go to?

(A) Aisle 1
(B) Aisle 2
(C) Aisle 3
(D) Aisle 4

시각 정보에 의하면, 남자는 어떤 통로로 가겠는가?
(A) 통로 1
(B) 통로 2
(C) 통로 3
(D) 통로 4

해설 시각 정보 연계 – 통로
남자는 인기 스낵 제품인 간편 캔에 들어 있는 혼합 견과의 판매가 중단된다(One of the popular snack products we carry is going to be discontinued soon — the Healthy Plus mixed nuts. You know, the one packaged in the convenient can)고 했다. 대화 마지막에서는 제품이 있는 통로로 가서 그 제품들을 가게 정면에 있는 특별 진열대로 옮기겠다(I'll head over to the aisle they're in now, and then move them to the special "Buy Now Before It's Gone" display in the front of the store)고 했다. 표를 보면 포장 스낵이 있는 곳은 통로 3이므로 정답은 (C)이다.

65-67 대화 + 지도

M-Cn Good afternoon. My friend and I just opened a bakery. **65When I found out about your food festival in an Internet search, I knew it would be good exposure for us.** I'd like to reserve a spot.

W-Br Wonderful! If you want to be the first thing people see when they enter the festival, you should reserve one of our Premium spots.

M-Cn **66Well ... to keep costs down, I think we'd rather be by the soccer field.**

W-Br All right. **67And you should know that trucks are not allowed to drive here, so you'll have to park near the main entrance and take your goods to your spot in a cart.**

남: 안녕하세요. 제 친구와 저는 막 제과점을 열었어요. **인터넷 검색으로 음식 축제에 대해 보고 제과점을 알릴 좋은 기회라고 확신했어요.** 자리를 하나 예약하고 싶어요.

여: 좋습니다! 사람들이 축제에 와서 제일 먼저 보게 되는 자리를 원하시면 고급형 자리를 예약하세요.

남: 글쎄요 … 비용 절감을 위해 축구장 옆자리가 낫겠어요.

여: 알겠습니다. 그리고 트럭 운행이 허용되지 않으니 정문 근처에 주차하시고 상품은 카트에 넣어서 지정 자리까지 운반하셔야 합니다.

어휘 bakery 제과점 search 검색 exposure 알려짐, 노출
reserve 예약하다 premium 고급의 keep ~ down
~를 억제하다[낮추다] would rather (~보다는 차라리)
~하겠다[낫다] spot 자리 soccer field 축구장 allow
허용하다 park 주차하다 main entrance 정문 goods
상품

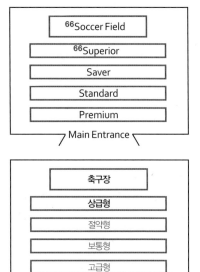

Main Entrance

```
┌─────────────────────────┐
│         축구장           │
├─────────────────────────┤
│         상급형           │
├─────────────────────────┤
│         절약형           │
├─────────────────────────┤
│         보통형           │
├─────────────────────────┤
│         고급형           │
└─────────────────────────┘
           정문
```

어휘 superior 상급의 standard 보통의 saver 절약되는 것

65

How did the man find out about the event?

(A) By seeing a poster
(B) By searching online
(C) By reading a newspaper
(D) By talking to a friend

남자는 행사에 대해 어떻게 알게 되었나?
(A) 포스터를 보고
(B) 온라인으로 검색해서
(C) 신문을 읽고
(D) 친구와 얘기해서

해설 세부 사항 관련 – 남자가 행사를 알게 된 경로
남자의 첫 번째 대사에서 인터넷 검색으로 음식 축제를 보고 제과점을 알릴 좋은 기회라고 확신했다(When I found out about your food festival in an Internet search, I knew it would be good exposure for us)고 했으므로 정답은 (B)이다.

▶▶ Paraphrasing 대화의 **Internet** → 정답의 **online**

66

Look at the graphic. In which section does the man want to reserve a space?

(A) Premium
(B) Standard
(C) Saver
(D) Superior

시각 정보에 의하면, 남자는 어떤 구역의 자리를 예약하길 원하는가?
(A) 고급형
(B) 보통형
(C) 절약형
(D) 상급형

해설 시각 정보 연계 – 예약할 자리
남자의 두 번째 대사에서 비용 절감을 위해 축구장 옆자리가 좋다(Well … to keep costs down, I think we'd rather be by the soccer field)고 했다. 표를 보면 축구장 옆이 상급이므로 정답은 (D)이다.

67

What does the woman tell the man about?

(A) A restriction on vehicles
(B) A parking fee
(C) A registration process
(D) A food regulation

여자는 남자에게 무엇에 대해 말하는가?
(A) 차량 제한
(B) 주차료
(C) 등록 절차
(D) 식품 규제

어휘 restriction 제한 vehicle 차량 parking fee 주차료
registration 등록 regulation 규제

해설 세부 사항 관련 – 여자가 말하는 사항
여자의 마지막 대사에서 트럭 운행이 허용되지 않으니 정문 근처에 주차하여 상품을 카트로 운반하라(And you should know that trucks are not allowed to drive here, so you'll have to park near the main entrance and take your goods to your spot in a cart)고 했으므로 정답은 (A)이다.

68-70 대화 + 주문서

M-Au Hi, Ms. Kimball. I'm calling from Rainbow Printing. **68I just noticed we've made a mistake with your order. I'm very sorry about that.**

W-Am We need those materials as soon as possible. Will there be a delay?

M-Au Only for one item. **69We only printed fifty calendars because someone misread the form.** We'll send everything that's finished today.

W-Am We were planning to give those out as gifts to our clients. How long will it take to get the rest of them?

M-Au We'll start working on them today so we can send them to you by Thursday morning. **⁷⁰And because of this problem, I'll include a voucher for twenty-five percent off with your package.**

남: 안녕하세요, 킴볼 씨. 레인보우 프린팅입니다. 귀사의 주문에 오류가 있다는 걸 방금 알게 됐습니다. 정말 죄송합니다.

여: 가능한 한 빨리 그 자료가 필요해요. 지연되나요?

남: 품목 한 개요. 저희 직원이 양식을 잘못 읽어서 달력을 50개만 인쇄했습니다. 오늘 완성되는 것은 모두 보낼게요.

여: 우리 고객들에게 선물로 줄 계획이었어요. 나머지는 언제 받을 수 있나요?

남: 오늘 작업을 시작해서 목요일 아침까지는 보내도록 하겠습니다. 이런 문제가 생겼으니 물품과 함께 25퍼센트 할인권을 같이 보내겠습니다.

어휘 notice 알아채다 make a mistake 실수하다 material 재료, 자료 delay 지연 print 인쇄하다 misread 잘못 읽다 client 고객 give out ~을 나눠 주다 rest 나머지 work on ~에 착수하다 include 포함하다 voucher 상품권, 할인권 off 할인되어 package 소포, 물품

Rainbow Printing

Customer: Marion Kimball

Item	Quantity
Banner (4'X8')	15
Business card 100-count pack	25
⁶⁹Photo calendar	150
Trifold brochure	350

레인보우 프린팅

고객: 마리온 킴볼

품목	수량
배너 (4'×8')	15
명함 100개짜리 한 묶음	25
사진 달력	150
3단 접이 소책자	350

68

What is the purpose of the man's call?

(A) To apologize for an error
(B) To request a payment
(C) To confirm a mailing address
(D) To promote a service

남자가 전화한 목적은 무엇인가?

(A) 오류에 대해 사과하려고
(B) 대금 지불을 요청하려고
(C) 우편 주소를 확인하려고
(D) 서비스를 홍보하려고

어휘 apologize 사과하다 request 요청하다 payment 지불 confirm 확인하다 promote 홍보하다

해설 전체 내용 관련 – 전화 통화의 목적

남자의 첫 번째 대사에서 남자가 주문에 오류가 있음을 방금 알게 되어 사과한다(I just noticed we've made a mistake with your order. I'm very sorry about that)고 했다. 이를 통해 남자가 오류에 대해 사과할 목적으로 전화를 한 것임을 알 수 있으므로 정답은 (A)이다.

▸▸ Paraphrasing 대화의 **a mistake** → 정답의 **an error**
대화의 **I'm very sorry** → 정답의 **apologize**

69

Look at the graphic. Which quantity is now incorrect?

(A) 15
(B) 25
(C) 150
(D) 350

시각 정보에 의하면, 무엇의 수량이 부정확한가?

(A) 15
(B) 25
(C) 150
(D) 350

해설 시각 정보 연계 – 부정확한 수량

남자의 두 번째 대사에서 직원이 양식을 잘못 읽어서 달력을 50개만 인쇄했다(We only printed fifty calendars because someone misread the form)고 했다. 표를 보면 달력의 수량은 150이므로 정답은 (C)이다.

70

What does the man say he will do?

(A) Give the woman store credit
(B) Send a discount coupon
(C) Report a problem to his manager
(D) Waive a delivery fee

남자는 무엇을 할 것이라고 말하는가?

(A) 여자에게 매장 포인트 주기
(B) 할인 쿠폰 보내기
(C) 매니저에게 문제 알리기
(D) 배송료 면제해 주기

어휘 store credit 매장에서 현금처럼 쓸 수 있는 포인트 waive 면제하다 delivery fee 배송료

해설 세부 사항 관련 – 남자가 할 일

남자의 마지막 대사에서 이런 문제가 생겼으니 물품과 함께 25% 할인권을 보내겠다(And because of this problem, I'll include a voucher for twenty-five percent off with your package)고 했으므로 정답은 (B)이다.

▸▸ Paraphrasing 대화의 **a voucher for twenty-five percent off** → 정답의 **a discount coupon**

PART 4

71-73 회의 발췌

> **W-Am** Good morning. **[71]I've gathered the sales team together for an important announcement about our line of solar panels. [72]I'm thrilled to announce that we have surpassed our goal of selling one thousand units.** Great job, everyone! The company would like to give each of you a special gift. You can choose between a luggage set and a watch. **[73]Please e-mail me by Friday to let me know which one you want.** Thank you for your hard work. Keep it up!

> 안녕하세요. 자사 태양 전지판에 관한 중대 발표를 위해 영업팀을 모이게 했습니다. 1천 개 판매라는 우리의 목표를 뛰어넘었다는 사실을 발표하게 되어 정말 기쁩니다. 훌륭해요, 모두들! 회사에서 여러분 모두에게 특별한 선물을 주고자 합니다. 여행용 가방 세트와 시계 중 하나를 선택할 수 있습니다. 금요일까지 저에게 이메일을 보내서 원하는 것을 알려 주세요. 여러분의 노고에 감사합니다. 계속 수고해 주세요!

> 어휘 gather 모으다 sales team 영업팀 announcement 발표 solar panel 태양 전지판 be thrilled to ~해서 신이 나다 surpass 넘어서다 goal 목표 unit 구성 단위, 한 개 choose 선택하다 luggage 가방, 수하물 keep up (동일한 정도로) ~을 계속하다

71

Who most likely are the listeners?

(A) Sales team members
(B) Product developers
(C) Company stockholders
(D) Solar panel technicians

청자들은 누구이겠는가?

(A) 영업팀 팀원
(B) 제품 개발자
(C) 회사 주주
(D) 태양 전지판 기술자

어휘 product 제품 developer 개발자 stockholder 주주 technician 기술자

해설 전체 내용 관련 – 청자들의 신분
지문 초반부에 화자가 태양 전지판에 관한 중대 발표를 위해 영업팀을 모이게 했다(I've gathered the sales team together for an important announcement about our line of solar panels)고 했으므로 정답은 (A)이다.

72

What is the speaker pleased about?

(A) A contract was approved.
(B) A goal was exceeded.
(C) A product won an award.
(D) A deadline was met.

화자는 무엇에 대해 기뻐하는가?

(A) 계약이 승인되었다.
(B) 목표를 초과했다.
(C) 제품이 상을 받았다.
(D) 마감 기한을 지켰다.

어휘 contract 계약 approve 승인하다 exceed 초과하다 award 상 deadline 마감 기한 meet 만족시키다, (기한 등을) 지키다

해설 세부 사항 관련 – 화자가 기뻐하는 이유
지문 초반부에 화자가 1천 개 판매라는 목표를 넘어서 기쁘다(I'm thrilled to announce that we have surpassed our goal of selling one thousand units)고 했으므로 정답은 (B)이다.

▸▸ **Paraphrasing** 지문의 **surpassed** → 정답의 **exceeded**

73

Why should the listeners e-mail the speaker?

(A) To confirm some figures
(B) To schedule a business trip
(C) To sign up for a group
(D) To express a preference

청자들은 왜 화자에게 이메일을 보내야 하는가?

(A) 일부 수치를 확인하기 위해
(B) 출장 일정을 잡기 위해
(C) 단체에 가입하기 위해
(D) 선호하는 것을 알리기 위해

어휘 confirm 확인하다 figure 수치 business trip 출장 sign up for ~을 신청하다 express 알리다, 표현하다 preference 선호도

해설 세부 사항 관련 – 이메일을 보내는 이유
지문 후반부에 화자가 금요일까지 이메일을 보내서 원하는 것을 알려 달라(Please e-mail me by Friday to let me know which one you want)고 했다. 즉 청자들이 선호하는 것을 알기 위해 이메일을 보내라고 한 것이므로 정답은 (D)이다.

▸▸ **Paraphrasing** 지문의 **let me know which one you want** → 정답의 **express a preference**

74-76 광고

> **M-Cn** **[74]Valley Solutions has the experienced landscapers you need to keep your yard looking its best.** We're more than just a maintenance service. We can totally transform your property with the strategic planting of flowers, bushes, and trees. **[75]Our designs have been featured in *Outdoors Magazine* as well as the hit TV show *Home with Us*, presented by Spencer Shaw.** Call us at 555-0141 to book a free consultation to get you started. **[76]And don't forget to visit our Web site, www.valleysolutions.com, to look through our gallery of photos posted by satisfied customers.**

밸리 솔루션에는 여러분의 정원을 최상의 상태로 유지하는 데 필요한 숙련된 조경사가 있습니다. 우리는 단순한 유지 관리 서비스 그 이상을 제공합니다. 꽃, 수풀 및 나무를 전략적으로 심어 여러분의 정원을 완전히 탈바꿈시킬 수 있습니다. 우리 디자인은 인기 TV 프로그램인 〈홈 위드 어스〉에서 스펜서 쇼가 소개했을 뿐 아니라 〈아웃도어 매거진〉에도 실렸습니다. 555-0141로 전화해 무료 상담 예약부터 시작하십시오. 웹사이트 www.valleysolutions.com을 방문해 만족한 고객들이 올린 사진을 살펴보는 것도 잊지 마십시오.

어휘 experienced 숙련된, 경험이 많은 landscaper 조경사 yard 마당, 정원 look one's best 가장 아름답게 보이다, 제일 돋보이다 be more than just ~ 이상이다, ~에 그치지 않다 maintenance 유지 (관리) transform 변형하다 totally 완전히 property 재산, 건물 strategic 전략적인 feature 싣다, (특집으로) 다루다 as well as ~뿐만 아니라 present 진행하다, 방송하다 book 예약하다 consultation 상담 get ~ started ~에게 시작하게 하다 look through ~을 살펴보다 post 게시하다 satisfied 만족한 customer 고객

74

What is being advertised?

(A) An interior design studio
(B) A landscaping business
(C) A transportation company
(D) A flower shop

무엇이 광고되고 있는가?
(A) 인테리어 디자인 스튜디오
(B) 조경 업체
(C) 운송 회사
(D) 꽃 가게

어휘 landscaping 조경 transportation 수송, 운송

해설 세부 사항 관련 – 광고 대상
지문 초반부에 화자가 밸리 솔루션에는 정원을 최고로 유지하는 데 필요한 숙련된 조경사가 있다(Valley Solutions has the experienced landscapers you need to keep your yard looking its best)고 했다. 조경 업체가 광고되고 있다는 것을 알 수 있으므로 정답은 (B)이다.

75

Who most likely is Spencer Shaw?

(A) An interior designer
(B) A maintenance worker
(C) A magazine journalist
(D) A television host

스펜서 쇼는 누구이겠는가?
(A) 인테리어 디자이너
(B) 유지 관리 작업자
(C) 잡지 기자
(D) TV 프로그램 진행자

어휘 journalist 기자 host (TV, 라디오 프로의) 진행자

해설 세부 사항 관련 – 스펜서 쇼의 직업
지문 중반부에 화자가 우리 디자인은 인기 TV 프로그램인 〈홈 위드 어스〉에서 스펜서 쇼가 소개했을 뿐 아니라 〈아웃도어 매거진〉에도 실렸다(Our designs

have been featured in *Outdoors Magazine* as well as the hit TV show *Home with Us*, presented by Spencer Shaw)고 했다. 스펜서 쇼가 TV 프로그램 진행자라는 것을 알 수 있으므로 정답은 (D)이다.

76

According to the speaker, what can listeners do on the Web site?

(A) View an updated price list
(B) Read customer comments
(C) Register for a free consultation
(D) Browse pictures of past projects

화자에 따르면, 청자들은 웹사이트에서 무엇을 할 수 있는가?
(A) 업데이트된 가격표 보기
(B) 고객 의견 읽기
(C) 무료 상담 등록하기
(D) 과거 프로젝트 사진 열람하기

어휘 view 보다 updated 업데이트된, 갱신된 comment 의견 register for ~에 등록하다 browse 열람[검색]하다

해설 세부 사항 관련 – 웹사이트에서 할 수 있는 일
지문 후반부에 화자가 웹사이트 www.valleysolutions.com을 방문해 만족한 고객들이 올린 사진을 살펴보라(And don't forget to visit our Web site, www.valleysolutions.com, to look through our gallery of photos posted by satisfied customers)고 했다. 따라서 고객이 찍은 조경 프로젝트 결과물을 볼 수 있을 것이므로 정답은 (D)이다.

▸▸ **Paraphrasing** 지문의 **photos** → 정답의 **pictures**

77-79 회의 발췌

W-Br Next, I'd like to update you on our library's annual Used Book Sale. **⁷⁷Normally we hold this sale in August, but we've decided to move it to June this year because a lot of people read books over the summer break.** We will have one library employee present during each shift of the five-day sale, and the rest of the workers will be volunteers. **⁷⁸We still need a few more volunteers, so please ask your friends and family if they would like to help out.** As donated books come in, they'll be stored in my office temporarily. **⁷⁹As you know, the Willow Room has flood damage that needs to be fixed.** Any questions?

다음으로, 우리 도서관의 연례 중고서적 판매에 대한 최신 정보입니다. 일반적으로 이 판매 행사는 8월에 개최되지만, 많은 사람들이 여름방학 때 책을 읽기 때문에 올해는 6월로 옮기기로 결정했습니다. 5일간의 판매에서 교대 근무마다 한 명의 도서관 직원을 두고 나머지 일손은 자원봉사자로 채울 겁니다. 자원봉사자 몇 명이 더 필요하니 친구나 가족에게 도와줄 수 있는지 문의해 주십시오. 기증 도서가 도착하면 제 사무실에 임시로 보관할 겁니다. 아시다시피, 윌로우 룸이 침수 피해로 보수가 필요합니다. 질문 있나요?

77

According to the speaker, what is different about the sale this year?

(A) It will be advertised in the newspaper.
(B) It will include donations from the public.
(C) It will last for more days than before.
(D) It will be held earlier in the year.

화자에 의하면, 올해 판매의 다른 점은 무엇인가?
(A) 신문에 광고된다.
(B) 일반인의 기부금이 포함된다.
(C) 이전보다 며칠 더 진행한다.
(D) 연초에 개최된다.

어휘   advertise 광고하다   include 포함한다   donations 기부금
      public 일반 대중   last 지속되다   be held 개최되다   earlier in
      the year 연초에

해설   세부 사항 관련 – 올해 판매의 다른 점
지문 초반부에서 보통 판매는 8월에 개최되지만 사람들이 여름방학 동안 책을
읽기 때문에 올해는 6월로 옮겼다(Normally we hold this sale in August,
but we've decided to move it to June this year because a lot of
people read books over the summer break)고 했으므로 정답은 (D)이다.

78

What are the listeners asked to do?

(A) Help set up an area
(B) Sign up for a shift
(C) Recruit some volunteers
(D) Make a financial donation

청자들은 무엇을 하라고 요청받는가?
(A) 장소 마련 돕기
(B) 교대 근무 신청하기
(C) 자원봉사자 모집하기
(D) 기부금 내기

어휘   set up ~을 마련하다   sign up for ~에 등록하다   shift 교대 근무
      recruit 모집하다   financial 재정적   make a donation 기부하다

해설   세부 사항 관련 – 청자들이 요청 받은 사항
지문 중반부에서 화자가 자원봉사자 몇 명이 더 필요하니 친구나 가족에게 도
와줄 수 있는지 문의해 달라(We still need a few more volunteers, so
please ask your friends and family if they would like to help out)고
했으므로 정답은 (C)이다.

79

What does the speaker mention about the Willow Room?

(A) It is in need of some repairs.
(B) It will be used to store extra books.
(C) It is the largest room in the library.
(D) It will be the site of the next meeting.

화자는 윌로우 룸에 대해 무엇을 언급하는가?
(A) 보수가 필요하다.
(B) 여러분의 책을 보관하는 데 사용될 것이다.
(C) 도서관에서 가장 큰 방이다.
(D) 다음 회의 장소이다.

어휘   repair 수리, 보수   store 보관하다   extra 여분의   site 장소

해설   세부 사항 관련 – 윌로우 룸에 대해 언급된 사항
후반부에서 화자가 윌로우 룸이 침수 피해로 보수가 필요하다(As you know,
the Willow Room has flood damage that needs to be fixed)고 했으므
로 정답은 (A)이다.

> ▸▸ **Paraphrasing**   지문의 **needs to be fixed**
> → 정답의 **in need of some repairs**

80-82 전화 메시지

M-Au Hi, Ms. Hong. This is Jack from Pyramid.
I'm calling to follow up on your accounting firm's
company retreat at the Rhoden Luxury Resort.
**⁸⁰You've hired us to transport your employees
between your office and the resort on April fifth
and seventh.** You said you'll have ninety-four
people total, so that's two buses. But... um... **⁸¹I
still need to know when you want to leave your
office.** I'll be gone this afternoon, but I'd still like
to hear from you today. **⁸²You can call and talk
to my assistant, James. He'll take a message
and pass it on to me.** Thanks!

안녕하세요, 홍 씨. 피라미드의 잭입니다. 로든 럭셔리 리조트에서 있을 귀하의
회계 법인 단합대회에 대한 추가 진행 사항 때문에 전화했습니다. 4월 5일과 7
일에 사무실에서 휴양지까지 귀하의 직원들을 이동시키기는 일을 의뢰하셨습니
다. 총 94명이고 버스 2대라고 했습니다. 그런데… 음… 사무실에서 언제 출발
하는지 알아야 합니다. 제가 오늘 오후에는 자리에 없지만 오늘까지 알려 주셨으
면 합니다. 전화해서 제 조수인 제임스에게 알려 주십시오. 제임스가 메시지를 받
아 저에게 내용을 전달할 겁니다. 감사합니다!

어휘   follow up on ~에 대해 후속 조치[사후 관리]를 하다
accounting firm 회계 법인[사무소]   retreat 휴양, 단합대회
resort 휴양지, 리조트   hire 고용하다   transport 운반하다   be
gone 부재 중이다   hear from ~에게서 소식을 듣다[연락을 받다]
assistant 조수   take a message 메시지를 받다   pass on to
~에게 전달하다

80

What kind of business is Pyramid?

(A) A transportation company
(B) A vacation resort
(C) An accounting firm
(D) A catering service

피라미드는 어떤 사업체인가?

(A) 운송 회사
(B) 휴양지
(C) 회계 법인
(D) 출장 뷔페 업체

어휘 transportation 운송, 운반 catering 음식 공급

해설 세부 사항 관련 – 피라미드의 업종

초반부에서 화자는 청자가 4월 5일과 7일에 사무실에서 휴양지까지 청자의 직원들을 이동시키는 일을 의뢰했다(You've hired us to transport your employees between your office and the resort on April fifth and seventh)고 했다. 이로써 화자가 일하는 피라미드는 운송 회사라는 것을 알 수 있으므로 정답은 (A)이다.

81

What information does the speaker ask for?

(A) The departure time
(B) The billing address
(C) The number of people
(D) The event date

화자는 어떤 정보를 요청하는가?

(A) 출발 시간
(B) 대금 청구 주소
(C) 인원 수
(D) 행사 날짜

어휘 departure 출발 billing 대금 청구, 청구서 발부

해설 세부 사항 관련 – 화자가 요청하는 정보

지문 중반부에서 화자가 사무실에서 언제 출발하는지 알아야 한다(I still need to know when you want to leave your office)고 했으므로 정답은 (A)이다.

▸▸ Paraphrasing 지문의 when you want to leave → 정답의 The departure time

82

What does the speaker want the listener to do?

(A) Provide some feedback about a service
(B) Send some information by e-mail
(C) Call him at his office tomorrow
(D) Leave a message with his coworker

화자는 청자가 무엇을 했으면 하는가?

(A) 서비스에 대한 의견 제공하기
(B) 이메일로 정보 보내기
(C) 그의 사무실로 내일 전화하기
(D) 동료에게 메시지 남기기

어휘 provide 제공하다 feedback 피드백, 의견 leave a message 메시지를 남기다 coworker 직장동료

해설 세부 사항 관련 – 화자가 청자에게 요청한 일

후반부에서 화자는 청자가 전화해서 조수인 제임스에게 메시지를 남기면 제임스가 화자에게 내용을 전달해 줄 것(You can call and talk to my assistant, James. He'll take a message and pass it on to me)이라고 했으므로 정답은 (D)이다.

▸▸ Paraphrasing 지문의 assistant → 정답의 coworker

83-85 견학 정보

W-Br Welcome to today's tour of the Purnex Ltd. manufacturing complex, which includes our production, testing, and distribution facilities. **83The highlight of our tour will be a visit to our state-of-the-art factory, where you'll see actual workers baking the delicious cakes and pies we're famous for.** Today's tour will last a full three hours. We'll see every part of the complex, and... the buildings are spread over a large area. **84There are places to sit along the way if anyone gets tired.** Now, to accommodate a slight change in our manufacturing schedule, we've adjusted our tour route. **85We'll begin our tour where we usually end it—at the gift shop.** Please follow me.

생산, 테스트 및 유통 시설을 포함하고 있는 퍼넥스 제조 단지 견학을 환영합니다. 오늘 견학의 하이라이트는 최첨단 공장을 방문하는 것으로, 그곳에서 여러분은 자사를 널리 알린 맛있는 케이크와 파이를 실제로 굽고 있는 작업자들을 볼 수 있습니다. 오늘의 견학은 3시간 동안 꼬박 지속됩니다. 단지의 구석구석을 보실 겁니다. 그리고 … 건물은 넓은 지역에 퍼져 있습니다. 피곤하시면 곳곳에 앉을 자리가 있습니다. 자, 제조 일정상 약간의 변경이 있어 그에 맞추어 견학 경로를 조정했습니다. 보통 견학을 마무리하는 장소인 선물 가게에서 오늘의 일정을 시작하겠습니다. 저를 따라오십시오.

어휘 manufacturing complex 제조 단지 include 포함하다 production 생산 distribution 분배, 유통 facility 시설 highlight 하이라이트, 가장 좋은 부분 tour 견학, 투어 state-of-the-art 최첨단의 factory 공장 actual 실제의 bake 굽다 be famous for ~로 유명하다 last 지속되다 full 완전한, 모든 spread over 퍼지다 along the way 그 과정에서 accommodate 맞추다, 부응하다 slight 사소한, 작은 adjust 조정하다 route 경로

83

What kind of products does Purnex Ltd. make?

(A) Beauty products
(B) Art supplies
(C) Baked goods
(D) Work uniforms

퍼넥스가 만드는 제품은 무엇인가?
(A) 미용 제품
(B) 미술 용품
(C) **제과제빵류**
(D) 작업복

어휘 beauty product 미용 제품 art supplies 미술 용품 baked goods 제과제빵류 uniform 제복, 군복, 유니폼

해설 전체 내용 관련 – 퍼넥스가 만드는 제품
지문 초반부에서 화자가 오늘 투어의 하이라이트는 최첨단 공장을 방문하는 것이며, 그곳에서 자사를 널리 알린 맛있는 케이크와 파이를 굽고 있는 작업자들을 볼 수 있다(The highlight of our tour will be a visit to our state-of-the-art factory, where you'll see actual workers baking the delicious cakes and pies we're famous for)고 했다. 따라서 화자의 회사인 퍼넥스는 제과제빵류 생산 업체임을 알 수 있으므로 정답은 (C)이다.

▸▸ Paraphrasing 지문의 **cakes and pies**
→ 정답의 **Baked goods**

84

Why most likely does the speaker say, "the buildings are spread over a large area"?
(A) To highlight a company's business expansion
(B) To warn that a tour has a lot of walking
(C) To give a reason for starting a tour late
(D) To apologize for the large size of a tour group

화자가 "건물은 넓은 지역에 퍼져 있습니다"라고 말한 이유는 무엇이겠는가?
(A) 회사의 사업 확장을 강조하기 위해
(B) **견학 중 많이 걷는다는 것을 경고하기 위해**
(C) 견학을 늦게 시작하는 이유를 밝히기 위해
(D) 견학에 인원이 많은 것을 사과하기 위해

어휘 highlight 강조하다 business expansion 사업 확장 warn 경고하다, 주의를 주다 give a reason 이유를 밝히다 apologize for ~에 대해 사과하다

해설 화자의 의도 파악 – 건물이 넓은 지역에 퍼져 있다고 말한 이유
인용문 바로 뒤 문장에서 피곤하면 곳곳에 앉을 자리가 있다(There are places to sit along the way if anyone gets tired)고 했다. 즉 견학 중 많이 걸어야 한다는 점을 경고하기 위한 것이므로 정답은 (B)이다.

85

What will the listeners most likely see next?
(A) A gift shop
(B) A production area
(C) A museum exhibit
(D) A research laboratory

청자들은 다음으로 무엇을 보겠는가?
(A) **선물 가게**
(B) 생산 구역
(C) 박물관 전시
(D) 연구 실험실

어휘 exhibit 전시 research 연구 laboratory 실험실

해설 세부 사항 관련 – 청자들이 다음으로 볼 것
지문 후반부에서 화자가 보통 견학을 마무리하는 장소인 선물 가게에서 오늘의 일정을 시작하겠다(We'll begin our tour where we usually end it—at the gift shop)고 했으므로 정답은 (A)이다.

86-88 방송

> M-Cn We're back on *Science Seekers* with our guest, Dr. Sanjay Batta of Toronto University. **86Dr. Batta has just finished creating an allergy medication that does not produce side effects in users.** An article about his work was published last month in the *National Medical Journal*. **87In June, Dr. Batta will travel to Rio de Janeiro to accept the prestigious Cardoso Prize at an event there.** **88If you would like to ask Dr. Batta a question about his work, call us on our hotline.** Our contact numbers are listed on our home page.

토론토대학의 산제이 바타 박사님과 함께 〈사이언스 시커스〉를 이어서 진행하겠습니다. 바타 박사님은 사용자에게 부작용을 일으키지 않는 알레르기 약 개발을 최근 완료했습니다. 박사님의 연구에 관한 기사가 지난달 〈내셔널 메디컬 저널〉에 실렸습니다. 6월에 바타 박사님은 리오데자네이루를 방문해 한 행사에서 권위 있는 카르도소상을 수상합니다. 바타 박사님의 연구에 대해 질문이 있으시면 직통 전화로 전화 주세요. 저희 연락처는 홈페이지에 있습니다.

어휘 allergy 알레르기 medication 약 produce 낳다, 초래하다 side effect 부작용 user 사용자 article 기사 publish 발행하다 accept 받다 prestigious 권위 있는, 명망 있는 hotline 직통 전화, 핫라인 contact number 연락처 list 목록에 싣다

86

What has Sanjay Batta recently done?
(A) Founded a university
(B) Developed a medicine
(C) Moved to another city
(D) Published a book

산제이 바타가 최근에 한 일은 무엇인가?
(A) 대학을 설립했다
(B) **의약품을 개발했다**
(C) 다른 도시로 이사했다
(D) 책을 출판했다

어휘 found 설립하다 develop 개발하다 medicine 의약품

해설 세부 사항 관련 – 산제이 바타가 한 일
지문 초반부에서 바타 박사가 사용자에게 부작용을 일으키지 않는 알레르기 약을 최근 개발했다(Dr. Batta has just finished creating an allergy medication that does not produce side effects in users)고 했으므로 정답은 (B)이다.

▸▸ Paraphrasing 지문의 **finished creating an allergy medication**
→ 정답의 **Developed a medicine**

87

According to the speaker, what will happen in Rio de Janeiro in June?

(A) An academic lecture will be given.
(B) A medical clinic will be opened.
(C) An award will be presented.
(D) A fundraiser will be hosted.

화자에 따르면, 6월 리오데자네이루에서 무슨 일이 있는가?
(A) 학술 강연이 있다.
(B) 병원을 개업한다.
(C) **상이 수여된다.**
(D) 기금 모금 행사가 열린다.

어휘   academic 학문적인   lecture 강연, 강의   medical clinic 병원
award 상   present 수여하다   fundraiser 기금 모금 행사   host
개최하다

해설   세부 사항 관련 – 리오데자네이루에서 있을 일
지문 중반부에서 6월에 바타 박사는 리오데자네이루를 방문해 한 행사에서 권위 있는 카르도소 상을 수상한다(In June, Dr. Batta will travel to Rio de Janeiro to accept the prestigious Cardoso Prize at an event there)고 했으므로 정답은 (C)이다.

▸▸ Paraphrasing   지문의 **the prestigious Cardoso Prize**
→ 정답의 **an award**

88

What are listeners encouraged to do?

(A) Enter a prize drawing
(B) Call the radio station
(C) E-mail their questions
(D) Attend an event

청자들은 무엇을 하도록 권유받는가?
(A) 경품 추첨에 참가하기
(B) **라디오 방송국에 전화하기**
(C) 질문을 이메일로 보내기
(D) 행사에 참석하기

어휘   encourage 권유하다   enter 참가하다   prize drawing 경품 추첨
radio station 라디오 방송국   attend 참석하다

해설   세부 사항 관련 – 청자들에게 권유되는 일
지문 후반부에서 바타 박사의 연구에 대해 질문이 있으면 직통 전화로 전화하라(If you would like to ask Dr. Batta a question about his work, call us on our hotline)고 했으므로 정답은 (B)이다.

89-91 회의 발췌

W-Am   **⁸⁹Next up, I'd like to inform you all that our elevators will undergo a safety inspection later today.** This will be performed by city employees, and it is part of the regulations for buildings of our size. Unfortunately, you'll have to use the stairs during the inspection, which is likely to happen while everyone is coming and going at lunchtime. **⁹⁰We were hoping it would be later, but** we don't set the schedule. **⁹¹We'll post signs explaining the procedure near the elevators and stairways in case you want to know more.** Thank you for your cooperation in this matter.

다음으로, 오늘 엘리베이터 안전 점검이 있다는 것을 여러분 모두에게 알려드립니다. 시 공무원들이 점검을 시행하며 이는 우리 건물 규모의 건물에 대한 규정의 일환입니다. 안타깝게도 점검이 진행되는 동안에는 계단을 이용해야 하며 모두가 오르내리는 점심 시간에 점검이 있을 것 같습니다. 점심 시간 이후에 점검하기를 바랐습니다만 우리가 일정을 정하는 것은 아닙니다. 자세한 사항을 알고 싶으시다면, 절차가 설명된 표지판을 엘리베이터와 계단 근처에 게시해 두겠습니다. 이 문제에 대해 협조해 주셔서 감사합니다.

어휘   inform 알리다   undergo 겪다, 받다   safety inspection
안전 점검   perform 실시하다, 수행하다   city employee 시
공무원   regulation 규정   stairs 계단   be likely to ~할 것
같다   set 정하다   post 게시하다   sign 표지판   explain 설명하다
procedure 절차, 과정   stairways 계단, 층계   in case ~할 경우에
대비해서   cooperation 협조   matter 문제

89

What does the speaker tell listeners about?

(A) A training workshop
(B) An equipment installation
(C) A safety check
(D) A health examination

화자는 청자들에게 무엇에 대해 말하는가?
(A) 교육 워크숍
(B) 장비 설치
(C) **안전 점검**
(D) 건강 검진

어휘   training 교육   workshop 워크숍, 연수회   equipment 장비
installation 설치   check 점검   health examination 건강 검진

해설   전체 내용 관련 – 안내문의 내용
지문 초반부에서 화자는 오늘 엘리베이터 안전 점검이 있다는 것을 여러분 모두에게 알린다(Next up, I'd like to inform you all that our elevators will undergo a safety inspection later today)고 했으므로 정답은 (C)이다.

▸▸ Paraphrasing   지문의 **safety inspection**
→ 정답의 **safety check**

90

What does the speaker suggest when she says, "we don't set the schedule"?

(A) Employees can take some time off.
(B) She thinks a plan is inconvenient.
(C) Employees can work anytime.
(D) She does not mind changing a deadline.

화자가 "우리가 일정을 정하는 것은 아닙니다"라고 말한 의도는 무엇인가?

(A) 직원들은 휴가를 낼 수 있다.
(B) **일정이 폐기 된다고 생각한다.**
(C) 직원들은 언제든지 일할 수 있다.
(D) 마감일 변경을 꺼리지 않는다.

어휘 take time off 휴가를 내다 inconvenient 불편한, 폐기 되는 mind -ing ~하는 것을 꺼리다[싫어하다] deadline 마감일, 기한

해설 화자의 의도 파악 – 우리가 일정을 정하는 것이 아니라는 말의 의도

인용문 바로 앞 문장에서 화자는 점심시간 지나서 점검하기를 바란다(We were hoping it would be later, but)고 했다. 즉 '우리가 일정을 정하는 것이 아닙니다'라는 인용문은 화자가 일정의 불편함을 드러낸 것이므로 정답은 (B)이다.

91

According to the speaker, how can listeners get more information?

(A) By calling the speaker
(B) By visiting a Web site
(C) By attending another meeting
(D) By reading some signs

화자에 따르면, 청자들은 어떻게 더 많은 정보를 얻을 수 있는가?

(A) 화자에게 전화해서
(B) 웹사이트를 방문해서
(C) 다른 회의에 참석해서
(D) **표지판을 읽어서**

어휘 attend 참석하다

해설 세부 사항 관련 – 청자들이 정보를 얻는 방법

후반부에서 화자가 자세한 사항에 대해서는 절차가 설명된 표지판을 엘리베이터와 계단 근처에 게시하겠다(We'll post signs explaining the procedure near the elevators and stairways in case you want to know more)고 했으므로 정답은 (D)이다.

92-94 공지

> M-Cn **92It's time once again for us to take inventory of the merchandise in our store. Next week, we'll have a team of people working on this after the store closes. 93We usually budget five days for this, but last year everyone cooperated well. It took three days. 93I hope we can have a similar result again.** Those who help with the inventory work will receive one-and-a-half times their usual hourly wage. **94If you'd like to add your name to the sign-up list, come to my office anytime today or tomorrow.** Thanks.

> 우리 가게의 상품 재고를 조사할 시기가 또 왔습니다. 다음 주에는 매장 영업 완료 후 이 업무를 맡아서 할 팀을 구성할 겁니다. 이 업무에 보통 5일을 할당하는데, 작년에는 모두가 잘 협력해 주었습니다. 업무가 3일 걸렸거든요. 비슷한 결과가 또 있기를 바랍니다. 재고 조사 업무를 도와주는 직원은 평소 시급의 1.5배를

받을 겁니다. 업무 지원자 목록에 이름을 추가하고 싶으면, 오늘이나 내일 중으로 언제든 내 사무실로 오십시오. 감사합니다.

> **어휘** take inventory 재고 조사를 하다 merchandise 상품 work on ~에 착수하다 budget 배분하다, 할당하다 cooperate 협력하다 result 결과 receive 받다 times (…) 배 usual 보통의, 평소의 hourly wage 시급, 시간당 임금 add to ~에 추가하다 sign-up list 등록[지원] 명부

92

What will some listeners do next week?

(A) Learn how to close the store
(B) Unpack some new merchandise
(C) Give demonstrations to customers
(D) Make a list of the store's goods

일부 청자들은 다음 주에 무엇을 할 것인가?

(A) 매장 문 닫는 방법 배우기
(B) 일부 신상품 포장 풀기
(C) 고객에게 시연하기
(D) **매장 제품 목록 만들기**

어휘 unpack 풀다 give a demonstration 시연하다 make a list 명단을 작성하다 goods 물건, 제품

해설 세부 사항 관련 – 다음 주에 일부 청자들이 할 일

초반부에서 화자는 가게의 상품 재고를 관리할 때라며 다음 주에는 매장 영업 완료 후 재고 조사 업무를 맡아서 할 팀을 구성할 예정(It's time once again for us to take inventory of the merchandise in our store. Next week, we'll have a team of people working on this after the store closes)이라고 했다. 일부 청자들이 매장 제품 목록을 다음 주에 만든다는 것을 알 수 있으므로 정답은 (D)이다.

> ▶ **Paraphrasing** 지문의 **take inventory of the merchandise in our store**
> → 정답의 **make a list of the store's goods**

93

What does the speaker imply when he says, "It took three days"?

(A) He was disappointed with a delayed shipment.
(B) He thinks a deadline for an assignment should be extended.
(C) He was impressed with how quickly a project was done.
(D) He wants to schedule another meeting later.

화자가 "업무가 3일 걸렸거든요"라고 말한 의도는 무엇인가?

(A) 선적 지연으로 실망했다.
(B) 과제 마감일이 연장되어야 한다고 생각한다.
(C) **프로젝트가 빨리 완료되어 인상 깊었다.**
(D) 나중에 다른 회의 일정을 잡고 싶다.

어휘 be disappointed with ~에 실망하다 delayed 지연된 shipment 선적 deadline 마감일 assignment 과제, 업무 extend 연장하다 be impressed with ~에 깊은 인상을 받다 schedule 일정을 잡다

해설 화자 의도 파악 – 업무가 3일 걸렸다는 말의 의도

인용문 바로 앞 문장에서 이 업무에 보통 5일을 할당하는데 작년에는 모두
가 잘 협력해 줬다(We usually budget five days for this, but last year
everyone cooperated well)고 했다. 이어서 인용문 바로 뒤 문장에서 비슷
한 결과가 또 있기를 바란다(I hope we can have a similar result again)
고 했다. 따라서 인용문은 프로젝트가 빨리 완료된 것이 인상 깊었다는 의미이
므로 정답은 (C)이다.

94

Why should listeners visit the speaker's office?

(A) To report missing items
(B) To make a suggestion
(C) To sign up for a task
(D) To check their hourly wage

청자들이 화자의 사무실에 방문해야 하는 이유는?

(A) 분실된 물품 보고를 위해
(B) 제안을 하기 위해
(C) 업무에 지원하기 위해
(D) 시급을 확인하기 위해

어휘 missing 분실된 item 물품 make a suggestion 제안하다
task 업무, 임무

해설 세부 사항 관련 – 사무실 방문 이유

후반부에서 화자가 업무 지원자 목록에 이름을 추가하고 싶으면 언제든 화자
의 사무실로 오라(If you'd like to add your name to the sign-up list,
come to my office anytime today or tomorrow)고 했으므로 정답은 (C)
이다.

▸▸ Paraphrasing 지문의 add your name to the sign-up list
→ 정답의 sign up for a task

95-97 담화 + 목록

W-Br Good morning, and welcome to the factory
tour here at Seneca Manufacturing. **95Today
you'll have the opportunity to see how we
make our wooden cabinets, tables, dressers,
and more.** We'll start out with a brief safety
review before you tour the production floor.
**96That will be followed by a live demonstration,
the longest part of the tour.** Then we'll wrap
things up by answering your questions. **97This is
a large facility, and we don't want anyone to get
lost, so remember to remain with the group at
all times.** If everyone is ready, let's get started.

안녕하세요. 세네카 매뉴펙처링 공장 견학을 환영합니다. 오늘 여러분은 목재 캐
비닛, 탁자, 옷장 등의 제조 방식을 직접 볼 기회를 갖게 됩니다. 생산 현장을 둘
러보기 전에 간단한 안전 점검부터 시작하겠습니다. 그런 다음 견학에서 가장 긴
시간을 차지하는 실황 시연입니다. 그리고 여러분의 질문에 답하는 것으로
마무리하겠습니다. 이곳은 대형 시설로, 길을 잃는 사람이 있으면 안 되므로 무리
에서 이탈하지 않도록 하십시오. 모두 준비되셨다면 시작하겠습니다.

어휘 manufacturing 제조(업) opportunity 기회 wooden
목재로 된 dresser 옷장 start out with ~부터 시작하다 brief
간단한 safety review 안전 점검 production floor 생산 현장
be followed by 이어서 ~이 계속되다 live demonstration 실황
시연 wrap up 마치다 facility 시설 get lost 길을 잃다 remain
남아 있다 at all times 항상 get started 시작하다

Group Activities	
Safety review	Takeshi
Production floor tour	Gloria
96Live demonstration	Ji-Hee
Question-and-answer session	William

단체 활동	
안전 점검	타케시
생산 현장 견학	글로리아
실황 시연	**지희**
질의응답	윌리엄

95

What kind of goods does the speaker's company
produce?

(A) Furniture
(B) Clothing
(C) Electronics
(D) Food

화자의 회사가 생산하는 제품을 무엇인가?

(A) 가구
(B) 의류
(C) 전자제품
(D) 식품

어휘 electronics 전자제품

해설 전체 내용 관련 – 화자의 회사가 생산하는 제품

초반부에서 화자가 오늘 여러분은 목재 캐비닛, 탁자, 옷장 등의 제조 방법을 직
접 볼 기회를 갖는다(Today you'll have the opportunity to see how we
make our wooden cabinets, tables, dressers, and more)고 했으므로
정답은 (A)이다.

▸▸ Paraphrasing 지문의 cabinets, tables, dressers, and
more → 정답의 furniture

96

Look at the graphic. Whose activity will be longer than all
the other parts?

(A) Takeshi's
(B) Gloria's
(C) Ji-Hee's
(D) William's

시각 정보에 의하면, 누구의 활동이 가장 오래 걸리는가?
(A) 타케시의 활동
(B) 글로리아의 활동
(C) 지희의 활동
(D) 윌리엄의 활동

해설 시각 정보 연계 – 가장 긴 활동

지문 중반부에서 화자가 안전 점검 다음에 견학에서 가장 긴 시간을 차지하는 실황 시연이 있다(That will be followed by a live demonstration, the longest part of the tour)고 했다. 표를 보면 실황 시연은 지희의 활동이므로 정답은 (C)이다.

97

What does the speaker remind listeners to do?

(A) Select a group
(B) Avoid taking photos
(C) Stay together
(D) Carry an ID card

화자는 청자들에게 무엇을 하라고 상기시키는가?
(A) 조 선택하기
(B) 사진 찍지 않기
(C) 함께 있기
(D) 신분증 소지하기

어휘 remind 상기시키다 avoid 피하다 carry 휴대하다, 가지고 다니다 ID card 신분증

해설 세부 사항 관련 – 화자가 상기시키는 내용

지문 후반부에서 화자가 이곳은 대형 시설로, 길을 잃으면 안 되므로 무리에서 이탈하지 않도록 하라(This is a large facility, and we don't want anyone to get lost, so remember to remain with the group at all times)고 했다. 화자가 청자들에게 함께 있으라고 주의를 주는 것이므로 정답은 (C)이다.

▶▶ Paraphrasing 지문의 **remain with the group**
→ 정답의 **Stay together**

98-100 담화 + 표

M-Au On behalf of the Redfield Gallery, I'd like to thank you all for attending this fundraising event. **⁹⁸Our goal is to continue making our extensive art collection available to the public, and your generosity helps us do that. ⁹⁹Tonight, we raised just enough to make the necessary upgrades to our Web site.** We'll start that project in January, and we hope it will attract more visitors. To wrap up this evening's proceedings, you'll hear a speech from one of our artists, Randy Edelman. **¹⁰⁰But first, I'd like to introduce him and give you some background information.**

레드필드 갤러리를 대표해서 기금 마련 행사에 참석해 주신 모든 분들께 감사드립니다. 우리의 목표는 폭넓은 미술 소장품을 계속 대중이 즐길 수 있도록 하는 것으로, 여러분의 아낌없는 마음이 도움이 되고 있습니다. 오늘밤 우리는 웹사이트 필수 업그레이드에 충분할 만큼 기금을 조성했습니다. 업그레이드 프로젝트는 1월에 시작하며 이것으로 웹사이트 방문자 수가 더 많아지길 희망합니다. 오늘 저녁 행사의 마무리로, 우리 갤러리의 작가인 랜디 에델만 씨가 연설을 하겠습니다. 먼저 에델만 씨를 소개하고 약력을 알려드리겠습니다.

어휘 on behalf of ~을 대표해서 attend 참석하다 fundraising event 기금 마련 행사 continue 계속하다 extensive 광범위한 art collection 미술 소장품 available to ~가 이용 가능한 public 대중 generosity 관대함, 인심 raise 조성하다 just enough 충족될 만큼 necessary 필요한 make upgrades 업그레이드[개선]하다 attract 유치하다 wrap up 마무리하다 proceeding 행사 background (개인의) 배경

Proposed Project	Projected Cost
⁹⁹Web site upgrades	$15,000
Landscaping changes	$25,000
Visitor center renovation	$30,000
Security upgrades	$60,000

예정된 프로젝트	예상 비용
웹사이트 업그레이드	1만 5천 달러
조경 변경	2만 5천 달러
방문자 센터 개조	3만 달러
보안 업그레이드	6만 달러

어휘 proposed 예정된 projected 예상된 landscaping 조경 renovation 수리, 개조 security 보안, 안전

98

Where most likely does the speaker work?

(A) At a museum
(B) At a music venue
(C) At a hospital
(D) At a government office

화자는 어디에서 일하겠는가?
(A) 미술관
(B) 음악공연장
(C) 병원
(D) 관공서

어휘 museum 미술관, 박물관 venue 장소 government office
관공서

해설 전체 내용 관련 – 화자의 근무지
지문 초반부에서 목표는 폭넓은 미술 소장품을 계속 대중이 즐길 수 있도록 하
는 것으로, 여러분의 아낌없는 마음이 도움이 된다(Our goal is to continue
making our extensive art collection available to the public, and
your generosity helps us do that)고 했다. 화자가 미술관에서 일하고 있음
을 알 수 있으므로 정답은 (A)이다.

99
Look at the graphic. About how much money was
collected during the fundraiser?
(A) $15,000
(B) $25,000
(C) $30,000
(D) $60,000

시각 정보에 의하면, 기금 마련 행사 동안 조성된 금액은 얼마인가?
(A) 1만 5천 달러
(B) 2만 5천 달러
(C) 3만 달러
(D) 6만 달러

해설 시각 정보 연계 – 조성된 금액
중반부에서 화자가 오늘밤 우리는 웹사이트 필수 업그레이드에 충분할 만큼 기
금을 조성했다(Tonight, we raised just enough to make the necessary
upgrades to our Web site)고 했다. 표를 보면 웹사이트 업그레이드의 예상
비용은 $15,000이므로 정답은 (A)이다.

100
What will the listeners do next?
(A) Watch a performance
(B) View some images
(C) Hear an introduction
(D) Review a document

청자들은 다음으로 무엇을 할 것인가?
(A) 공연 보기
(B) 이미지 보기
(C) 소개 듣기
(D) 문서 검토하기

어휘 performance 공연 view 보다 introduction 소개 review
검토하다

해설 세부 사항 관련 – 청자들이 다음으로 할 일
지문 후반부에서 화자가 에델만 씨를 소개하고 그 분의 약력을 알려주겠다
(But first, I'd like to introduce him and give you some background
information)고 했으므로 정답은 (C)이다.

TEST 2

1 (D)	**2** (A)	**3** (B)	**4** (B)	**5** (B)
6 (C)	**7** (B)	**8** (A)	**9** (B)	**10** (B)
11 (B)	**12** (A)	**13** (B)	**14** (B)	**15** (A)
16 (A)	**17** (A)	**18** (A)	**19** (A)	**20** (B)
21 (C)	**22** (A)	**23** (B)	**24** (A)	**25** (B)
26 (A)	**27** (B)	**28** (C)	**29** (C)	**30** (B)
31 (C)	**32** (D)	**33** (D)	**34** (B)	**35** (C)
36 (C)	**37** (A)	**38** (C)	**39** (D)	**40** (B)
41 (A)	**42** (C)	**43** (B)	**44** (C)	**45** (A)
46 (C)	**47** (B)	**48** (A)	**49** (D)	**50** (B)
51 (A)	**52** (D)	**53** (B)	**54** (C)	**55** (D)
56 (C)	**57** (A)	**58** (D)	**59** (A)	**60** (C)
61 (A)	**62** (B)	**63** (A)	**64** (B)	**65** (D)
66 (B)	**67** (C)	**68** (C)	**69** (D)	**70** (A)
71 (A)	**72** (B)	**73** (C)	**74** (A)	**75** (D)
76 (B)	**77** (C)	**78** (A)	**79** (D)	**80** (C)
81 (B)	**82** (A)	**83** (A)	**84** (B)	**85** (C)
86 (A)	**87** (C)	**88** (A)	**89** (D)	**90** (A)
91 (C)	**92** (A)	**93** (C)	**94** (B)	**95** (D)
96 (C)	**97** (B)	**98** (D)	**99** (B)	**100** (B)

PART 1

1 W-Am

(A) He's putting leaves into a waste bin.
(B) He's adjusting his glasses.
(C) He's trimming some trees.
(D) He's holding a box of fruit.

(A) 남자가 나뭇잎들을 쓰레기통에 넣고 있다.
(B) 남자가 안경을 고쳐 쓰고 있다.
(C) 남자가 나뭇가지를 다듬고 있다.
(D) **남자가 과일 한 상자를 들고 있다.**

어휘 put 넣다 waste bin 쓰레기통 adjust 조정하다, 바로잡다 trim 다듬다, 손질하다

해설 1인 등장 사진 – 사람의 상태 묘사
(A) 동사 오답. 남자가 나뭇잎을 만지고 있는 중이지 나뭇잎들을 쓰레기통에 넣고 있는(is putting leaves into a waste bin) 동작을 하고 있지 않으므로 오답.
(B) 동사 오답. 남자가 안경을 쓰고 있는 상태이지 고쳐 쓰고 있는(is adjusting his glasses) 동작을 하고 있지 않으므로 오답.
(C) 동사 오답. 남자가 나뭇가지를 다듬고 있는(is trimming some trees) 모습이 아니므로 오답.
(D) 정답. 남자가 과일 상자를 들고 있는(is holding a box of fruit) 상태이므로 정답.

2 M-Au

(A) One of the men is leaning on a table.
(B) One of the men is putting a cover over a laptop.
(C) They're arranging folders on a table.
(D) They're sitting in a circle.

(A) **남자들 중 한 명이 탁자에 기대어 있다.**
(B) 남자들 중 한 명이 노트북 위에 덮개를 씌우고 있다.
(C) 그들은 탁자 위에 있는 폴더를 정리하고 있다.
(D) 그들은 동그랗게 둘러 앉아 있다.

어휘 lean 기대다 put a cover 덮개를 씌우다 laptop 노트북 컴퓨터 arrange 정리하다 folder 서류철, 폴더 in a circle 원형으로

해설 2인 이상 등장 사진 – 사람의 상태 묘사
(A) 정답. 남자들 중 한 명(one of the men)이 탁자에 기대어 있는(is leaning on a table) 모습이므로 정답.
(B) 동사 오답. 남자들 중 한 명(one of the men)이 노트북 위에 덮개를 씌우고 있는(is putting a cover over a laptop) 모습이 아니므로 오답.
(C) 동사 오답. 사람들이 탁자 위에 있는 폴더를 정리하고 있는(are arranging folders on a table) 모습이 아니므로 오답.
(D) 동사 오답. 사람들이 동그랗게 둘러 앉아 있는(are sitting in a circle) 모습이 아니므로 오답.

3 W-Br

(A) A man is pulling a cart.
(B) A man is washing a vehicle.
(C) Some tires are stacked in rows.
(D) Some hoses are stretched across a garden.

(A) 남자가 카트를 당기고 있다.
(B) **남자가 세차를 하고 있다.**
(C) 타이어들이 줄지어 쌓여 있다.
(D) 호스들이 정원을 가로질러 뻗어 있다.

어휘 cart 손수레, 카트 wash a vehicle 세차하다 stack 쌓다 in rows 줄지어 stretch 뻗다 across 가로질러

해설 1인 등장 사진 – 사람의 동작 묘사
(A) 동사 오답. 남자가 카트를 당기고 있는(is pulling a cart) 모습이 아니므로 오답.
(B) 정답. 남자가 세차를 하고 있는(is washing a vehicle) 모습이므로 정답.
(C) 동사 오답. 사진에 타이어가 보이지만 줄지어 쌓여 있는(are stacked in rows) 모습이 아니므로 오답.

(D) 동사 오답. 사진에 호스가 보이지만 정원을 가로질러 뻗어 있는(are stretched across a garden) 모습이 아니므로 오답.

4 M-Au

(A) A woman's holding a door open.
(B) A woman's wearing a pair of safety goggles.
(C) A woman's clearing food from a table.
(D) A woman's mounting shelves on a wall.

(A) 여자가 문을 연 채 잡아 주고 있다.
(B) 여자가 보안경을 착용하고 있다.
(C) 여자가 식탁에서 음식을 치우고 있다.
(D) 여자가 벽에 선반을 설치하고 있다.

어휘 safety goggles 보안경 clear from ~에서 치우다 mount
설치하다 shelves 선반들

해설 1인 등장 사진 – 사람의 상태 묘사
(A) 명사 오답. 여자가 문을 연 채 잡아 주고 있는(is holding a door open) 모습이 아니므로 오답.
(B) 정답. 여자가 보안경을 착용하고 있는(is wearing a pair of safety goggles) 모습이므로 정답.
(C) 동사 오답. 여자가 식탁에서 음식을 치우는(is clearing food from a table) 모습이 아니므로 오답.
(D) 동사 오답. 여자가 벽에 선반을 설치하고 있는(is mounting shelves on a wall) 모습이 아니므로 오답.

5 W-Am

(A) A tree is being trimmed by a work crew.
(B) Pedestrians are walking in a plaza.
(C) People are boarding a shuttle bus.
(D) A pavement is being washed with a hose.

(A) 나무가 인부에 의해 다듬어지고 있다.
(B) 보행자들이 광장을 걷고 있다.
(C) 사람들이 셔틀버스에 탑승하고 있다.
(D) 보도가 호스 물로 씻겨지고 있다.

어휘 trim 다듬다, 손질하다 work crew 인부 pedestrian 보행자
plaza 광장 board 탑승하다 shuttle bus 셔틀버스 pavement
보도 wash with ~으로 씻다

해설 2인 이상 등장 사진 – 사람 또는 사물 중심 묘사
(A) 동사 오답. 나무가 인부에 의해 다듬어지고 있는(is being trimmed by a work crew) 모습이 아니므로 오답.
(B) 정답. 보행자들(pedestrians)이 광장을 걷고 있는(are walking in a plaza) 모습이므로 정답.
(C) 동사 오답. 사람들이 셔틀버스에 탑승하고 있는(are boarding a shuttle bus) 모습이 아니므로 오답.
(D) 동사 오답. 사진에 보도(pavement)가 보이지만 호스 물로 씻겨지고 있는(is being washed with a hose) 상황이 아니므로 오답.

6 M-Cn

(A) Some railings are being painted.
(B) Rope is being wrapped around a pipe.
(C) Some chairs are facing a round table.
(D) People are seated on a viewing platform.

(A) 철책 일부가 페인트칠 되고 있다.
(B) 밧줄이 파이프에 감겨지고 있다.
(C) 의자 몇 개가 둥근 탁자를 마주보고 있다.
(D) 사람들이 전망대에 앉아 있다.

어휘 railing 철책, 난간 rope 밧줄 wrap around 싸다, 감다 face
마주보다 seat 앉히다 viewing platform 전망대

해설 사물/배경 사진 – 사람 또는 사물 중심 묘사
(A) 동사 오답. 사진에 철책(railing)이 보이지만 현재 페인트칠 되고 있는(are being painted) 상황이 아니므로 오답.
(B) 동사 오답. 사진에 밧줄이 보이지만 파이프에 감겨지고 있는(is being wrapped around a pipe) 상황이 아니므로 오답.
(C) 정답. 의자 몇 개가 둥근 탁자를 마주보고 있는(are facing a round table) 모습이므로 정답.
(D) 사진에 없는 명사를 이용한 오답. 사진에 사람들(people)이 보이지 않으므로 오답.

PART 2

7

M-Cn Where are the organic fruit juices?
W-Am (A) Each bottle is five hundred milliliters.
        (B) In the aisle to your left.
        (C) No, several different uses.

유기농 과일 주스는 어디에 있나요?
(A) 각 병은 500밀리리터입니다.
(B) 왼쪽 통로예요.
(C) 아니요, 여러 가지 용도로요.

어휘 organic 유기농의 bottle 병 aisle 통로 several 몇몇의 use
용도

해설 유기농 주스 위치를 묻는 Where 의문문

(A) 질문과 상관없는 오답. 용량을 묻는 How much 의문문에 적절한 응답이
므로 오답.

(B) 정답. 유기농 주스의 위치를 묻는 질문에 왼쪽 통로라는 구체적인 장소를
언급하고 있으므로 정답.

(C) Yes/No 불가 오답. Where 의문문에는 Yes/No 응답이 불가능하므로 오답.

8

W-Br Why did the projector stop working?

M-Au (A) Because of a connection failure.

(B) She already finished that work.

(C) During the presentation.

프로젝터가 왜 작동이 안 되나요?
(A) 접속 장애 때문에요.
(B) 그녀는 이미 그 일을 마쳤어요.
(C) 발표 동안에요.

어휘 projector 프로젝터 work 작동하다 connection 연결, 접속
failure 정지, 고장 presentation 발표

해설 프로젝터 정지 이유를 묻는 Why 의문문

(A) 정답. 프로젝터가 안 되는 이유를 묻는 질문에 접속 장애라는 구체적인 이
유를 언급하고 있으므로 정답.

(B) 파생어 오답. 질문의 working과 파생어 관계인 work를 이용한 오답.

(C) 연상 단어 오답. 질문의 projector에서 연상 가능한 presentation을 이용
한 오답.

9

M-Au Who got transferred to our marketing division?

W-Am (A) I got it at a farmers' market.

(B) Wasn't it Sally Park?

(C) Transfer at Central Station.

누가 마케팅 부서로 왔나요?
(A) 농산물 직판장에서 샀어요.
(B) 샐리 박 아닌가요?
(C) 센트럴 역에서 환승하세요.

어휘 transfer 옮기다, 전근 가다 marketing department 마케팅 부서
farmers' market 농산물 직판장

해설 전근자를 묻는 Who의문문

(A) 유사 발음 오답. 질문의 marketing과 부분적으로 발음이 같은 market를
이용한 오답.

(B) 정답. 마케팅 부서로 옮긴 직원을 묻는 질문에 Sally Park이라는 특정 인
물을 언급하면서 되묻고 있으므로 정답.

(C) 단어 반복 오답. 질문의 transferred와 다른 의미로 쓰인 transfer를 반
복한 오답.

10

W-Br Would you prefer tea or coffee?

M-Cn (A) Two or three copies.

(B) Just water is fine, thanks.

(C) Five cups a day.

차를 드릴까요, 커피를 드릴까요?
(A) 두 장이나 석 장이요.
(B) 그냥 물이면 돼요, 고마워요.
(C) 하루에 다섯 잔이요.

어휘 prefer 선호하다 copy 사본

해설 단어를 연결한 선택의문문

(A) 유사 발음 오답. 질문의 coffee와 부분적으로 발음이 같은 copies를 이용
한 오답.

(B) 정답. 질문에서 선택 사항으로 언급된 차나 커피 대신 물이라는 제3의 선택
사항을 제시한 것이므로 정답.

(C) 연상 단어 오답. 질문의 tea, coffee에서 연상 가능한 cups를 이용한 오답.

11

M-Au Didn't you get this memo about the laboratory
remodeling?

W-Br (A) To the contractor.

(B) Oh, let me take a look at it.

(C) I have one of the older models.

실험실 리모델링에 관한 이 메모를 받지 못했나요?
(A) 계약자한테요.
(B) 아, 그거 좀 보여 주세요.
(C) 구형 모델 하나를 가지고 있어요.

어휘 laboratory 실험실 remodeling 리모델링, 개조 contractor
계약자 take a look at ~을 (한번) 보다

해설 메모 수령 여부를 묻는 부정의문문

(A) 연상 단어 오답. 질문의 remodeling에서 연상 가능한 contractor를 이용
한 오답.

(B) 정답. 실험실 리모델링에 관한 메모 수령 여부를 묻자 보여 달라고 요청하
고 있으므로 정답.

(C) 유사 발음 오답. 질문의 remodeling과 부분적으로 발음이 같은 models
를 이용한 오답.

12

M-Cn What restaurant did she pick for the department
lunch?

W-Am (A) She's about to look over the options.

(B) I ordered the tomato pasta.

(C) Ann is selling her apartment.

그녀는 부서 점심 회식 장소로 어떤 식당을 골랐나요?
(A) 그녀가 지금 갈 만한 데를 살펴보려는 참이에요.
(B) 저는 토마토 파스타를 주문했어요.
(C) 앤은 자신의 아파트를 팔 거예요.

어휘 pick 고르다, 선택하다 department 부서 be about to 막
~하려는 참이다 look over 살펴보다 option 선택지 order
주문하다

해설 어떤 식당을 선택했는지 묻는 What 의문문

(A) 정답. 부서 점심 회식 장소로 선택한 식당을 묻는 질문에 갈 만한 데를 살펴
볼 참이라며 아직 선택하지 못했다는 의미를 우회적으로 표현하고 있으므
로 정답.

(B) 연상 단어 오답. 질문의 restaurant, lunch에서 연상 가능한 tomato
pasta를 이용한 오답.

(C) 유사 발음 오답. 질문의 department와 부분적으로 발음이 같은
apartment를 이용한 오답.

13

W-Br Why are you taking that company laptop home
with you?

M-Au (A) An extended warranty period.

(B) My report is due tomorrow.

(C) Oh, did he do that?

회사 노트북 컴퓨터는 왜 집에 가지고 가나요?
(A) 연장된 보증 기간이요.
(B) 보고서 제출 기한이 내일이라서요.
(C) 오, 그가 그랬나요?

어휘 laptop 노트북 컴퓨터 extended 연장된 warranty period 보증
기간 due ~하기로 되어 있는, 예정인

해설 노트북을 집으로 가져가는 이유를 묻는 Why 의문문

(A) 연상 단어 오답. 질문의 laptop에 대해 보증 기간 측면에서 연상 가능한
extended warranty를 이용한 오답.

(B) 정답. 회사 노트북 컴퓨터를 집으로 가져가는 이유를 묻는 질문에 보고서
제출 기한이 내일이라는 구체적인 이유를 제시하고 있으므로 정답.

(C) 질문과 상관없는 오답. he가 가리키는 대상이 질문에 없으므로 오답.

14

W-Am How was the new accounting clerk trained?

M-Cn (A) They're being counted now.

(B) He already knew our system.

(C) The train is running late.

신입 경리 직원은 어떤 교육을 받았나요?
(A) 지금 세고 있는 중이에요.
(B) 그는 이미 우리 시스템을 알고 있더라고요.
(C) 열차가 예정보다 늦어지고 있어요.

어휘 accounting clerk 경리직원 train 교육하다 count 세다, 계산하다
run late 예정보다 늦다

해설 직원 교육 방법을 묻는 How 의문문

(A) 유사 발음 오답. 질문의 accounting과 부분적으로 발음이 같은 counted
를 이용한 오답.

(B) 정답. 신입 경리 직원의 교육 방법을 묻는 질문에 그가 이미 시스템을 알고
있다는 응답으로 교육이 필요 없었다는 것을 우회적으로 표현하고 있으므로
정답.

(C) 파생어 오답. 질문의 trained와 파생어 관계인 train을 이용한 오답.

15

M-Au Could you get me a computer headset?

W-Br (A) Do you need one with a microphone?

(B) The head of a technology firm.

(C) My commute is fairly short.

컴퓨터 헤드폰 좀 갖다 줄래요?
(A) 마이크가 달린 것이 필요한가요?
(B) 기술 회사의 책임자요.
(C) 통근 거리가 꽤 짧아요.

어휘 headset 헤드폰 microphone 마이크 head 책임자
technology 기술 firm 회사 commute 통근 (거리) fairly
상당히, 꽤

해설 부탁/요청의 의문문

(A) 정답. 헤드폰을 갖다 달라는 요청에 마이크가 달린 것이 필요하냐고 되묻고
있으므로 정답.

(B) 연상 단어 오답. 질문의 computer에서 연상 가능한 technology를 이용
한 오답.

(C) 유사 발음 오답. 질문의 computer와 부분적으로 발음이 같은 commute
를 이용한 오답.

16

M-Cn They seemed really satisfied with Mr. Jensen's
interview performance.

W-Am (A) He certainly is a great candidate.

(B) You can write a product review.

(C) The band will perform next week.

그들은 젠슨 씨의 면접 성적에 매우 만족했어요.
(A) 그는 정말 우수한 지원자예요.
(B) 제품평을 작성하셔도 돼요.
(C) 그 밴드는 다음 주에 연주할 거예요.

어휘 be satisfied with ~에 만족하다 interview 면접, 인터뷰
performance 성적, 성과 candidate 후보자 product review
제품평 band 밴드, 악단 perform 공연하다

해설 의견 제시의 평서문

(A) 정답. 젠슨 씨의 면접 성적에 만족한다는 말에 그가 우수한 지원자라는 말
로 우회적으로 공감을 표시하고 있으므로 정답.

(B) 유사 발음 오답. 질문의 interview와 부분적으로 발음이 같은 review를
이용한 오답.

(C) 파생어 오답. 질문의 performance와 파생어 관계인 perform을 이용한
오답.

17

M-Cn When will the next issue of the quarterly newsletter come out?

M-Au (A) On the twentieth of November.
(B) The article was quite useful.
(C) More than seven pages long.

계간 소식지 다음 호는 언제 나오나요?
(A) 11월 20일이에요.
(B) 그 기사는 꽤 유용했어요.
(C) 7페이지 이상이에요.

어휘 issue 호, 발행물 quarterly 분기별의 newsletter 소식지, 회보 come out 출간되다 article 기사 useful 유용한

해설 사보 발행 시점을 묻는 When 의문문
(A) 정답. 계간 소식지의 다음 호가 나오는 시점을 묻는 질문에 11월 20일이라는 구체적인 날짜로 응답하고 있으므로 정답.
(B) 연상 단어 오답. 질문의 newsletter에서 연상 가능한 article을 이용한 오답.
(C) 질문과 상관없는 오답. 페이지 수를 묻는 How many 의문문에 적절한 응답이므로 오답.

18

M-Cn Isn't the doctor supposed to arrive at the clinic by nine?

W-Br (A) That's right—he's setting up now.
(B) This is flu medicine.
(C) Almost a dozen appointments.

의사는 9시까지 병원에 도착해야 되지 않나요?
(A) 맞아요. 그는 지금 준비하는 중이에요.
(B) 이것은 감기약이에요.
(C) 진료 예약이 거의 12건 정도예요.

어휘 be supposed to ~하기로 되어 있다 set up 준비하다 clinic 진료소, 병원 flu 독감 medicine 약 dozen 12개의 appointment (진료 등의) 예약

해설 병원 도착 여부를 묻는 부정의문문
(A) 정답. 의사의 병원 도착 여부에 대해 긍정적 응답을 한 후, 지금 준비하고 있다는 부연 설명을 하고 있으므로 정답.
(B) 연상 단어 오답. 질문의 doctor와 clinic에서 연상 가능한 flu medicine을 이용한 오답.
(C) 연상 단어 오답. 질문의 doctor와 clinic에서 연상 가능한 appointments를 이용한 오답.

19

W-Am Will you need this rack installed or just delivered to your home?

M-Au (A) Actually, I'll pick it up myself.
(B) Right there is fine.
(C) For my kitchen towels.

이 선반을 설치해 드려야 하나요, 아니면 배달만 해드리면 되나요?
(A) 사실, 제가 직접 찾으러 갈 거예요.
(B) 바로 거기가 좋아요.
(C) 키친타월용이에요.

어휘 rack 선반, 걸이 install 설치하다 deliver 배달하다 actually 사실은 pick up ~을 찾다[찾아오다]

해설 구를 연결한 선택의문문
(A) 정답. 질문에서 선택 사항으로 언급된 설치나 단순 배달 대신 직접 찾으러 갈 것이라고 제3의 선택 사항을 제시한 것이므로 정답.
(B) 질문과 상관없는 오답. 배달품을 놓을 장소를 묻는 Where 의문문에 적절한 응답이므로 오답.
(C) 연상 단어 오답. 질문의 rack에서 연상 가능한 kitchen towels를 이용한 오답.

20

M-Au The air conditioner is really loud these days, isn't it?

W-Br (A) No, it's in the instructions.
(B) I haven't noticed.
(C) A thicker jacket, maybe.

요즘 에어컨이 정말 시끄러워요, 그렇죠?
(A) 아니요, 설명서에 있어요.
(B) 나는 눈치채지 못했어요.
(C) 아마도 더 두꺼운 재킷이요.

어휘 air conditioner 에어컨 loud 시끄러운 instructions 설명서 notice 알아채다 thick 두꺼운

해설 에어컨의 소음 여부를 확인하는 부가의문문
(A) 연상 단어 오답. 질문의 air conditioner에 대해 작동 방법 측면에서 연상 가능한 instructions를 이용한 오답.
(B) 정답. 에어컨 소음 여부에 대해 눈치채지 못했다는 말로 부정적 응답을 하고 있으므로 정답.
(C) 질문과 상관없는 오답. 에어컨 소음 여부를 묻는 질문에 아마도 더 두꺼운 재킷이라고 응답하는 것은 질문의 맥락에서 벗어난 것이므로 오답.

21

M-Cn Do we need a passcode to access the warehouse?

M-Au (A) I brought some extra boxes.
(B) A change of address form.
(C) Someone there can let you in.

창고에 들어가려면 비밀번호가 필요한가요?
(A) 제가 추가로 상자를 가져왔어요.
(B) 주소 양식 변경이요.
(C) 거기에 있는 사람이 당신을 들여보내 줄 거예요.

어휘 passcode 비밀번호, 암호 access 접근하다, 들어가다 warehouse 창고 extra 추가의 form 양식 let in ~을 들어오게 하다

해설 비밀번호가 필요한지 여부를 묻는 조동사(do) 의문문

(A) 연상 단어 오답. 질문의 warehouse에서 연상 가능한 box를 이용한 오답.

(B) 질문과 상관없는 오답. 창고에 들어가는 데 비밀번호가 필요한지 묻는 질문에 주소 양식 변경이라고 응답하는 것은 질문의 맥락에서 벗어난 것이므로 오답.

(C) 정답. 창고에 들어가는 비밀번호가 필요한지 묻는 질문에 거기에 있는 사람이 들여보내 줄 것이라고 우회적으로 답하고 있으므로 정답.

22

W-Am Who's going to pick up the clients from the hotel?

M-Cn (A) Mary booked a taxi for them.

(B) Room service, please.

(C) Is that so?

누가 호텔에서 고객들을 데려오나요?
(A) 메리가 그들을 위해 택시를 예약했어요.
(B) 룸서비스 부탁합니다.
(C) 그래요?

어휘 pick up 자동차로 마중 나가다, 태워 오다 client 고객 book 예약하다

해설 고객들을 차로 데려올 사람을 묻는 Who 의문문

(A) 정답. 공항에서 고객들을 차로 데려올 사람을 묻는 질문에 메리가 그들을 위해 택시를 예약했다고 우회적으로 응답하고 있으므로 정답.

(B) 연상 단어 오답. 질문의 hotel에서 연상 가능한 room service를 이용한 오답.

(C) 질문과 상관없는 오답. 공항에서 고객들을 데려올 사람을 묻는 Who 의문문에 그렇냐고 상대방의 말을 재확인하는 응답은 맥락에서 벗어난 것이므로 오답.

23

W-Br We're taking a photo for the Web site tomorrow, aren't we?

M-Au (A) The photographer's phone number.

(B) Nobody's mentioned it to me.

(C) A scheduled site inspection.

내일 웹사이트 사진을 찍을 예정이지요, 그렇죠?
(A) 사진가 전화번호요.
(B) 아무도 그런 말을 한 적이 없는데요.
(C) 정기 현장 점검이요.

어휘 scheduled 예정된 site 현장 inspection 점검

해설 정보 확인을 위한 부가의문문

(A) 유사 발음 오답. 질문의 photo와 부분적으로 발음이 비슷한 photographer를 이용한 오답.

(B) 정답. 내일 웹사이트 사진을 찍는지 확인하는 말에 대해 아무도 그런 말을 한 적이 없다고 불확실성 표현으로 응답하고 있으므로 정답.

(C) 단어 반복 오답. 질문에 나온 site를 반복한 오답.

24

M-Cn What day does the free shoe-polishing service end?

W-Am (A) I've never heard of that.

(B) By getting a gift certificate.

(C) On the way to the shoe store.

무료 구두닦이 서비스는 며칠에 끝나나요?
(A) 그런 말은 들은 적이 없는데요.
(B) 상품권을 얻어서요.
(C) 신발 가게로 가는 길이에요.

어휘 shoe-polishing service 구두닦이 서비스 gift certificate 상품권 on the way to ~로 가는 도중에

해설 서비스 마감 날짜를 묻는 What day 의문문

(A) 정답. 서비스 마감 날짜에 대해 들은 적이 없다고 불확실성 표현으로 응답하고 있으므로 정답.

(B) 질문과 상관없는 오답. 서비스 이용 방법을 묻는 질문에 어울리는 응답이므로 오답.

(C) 연상 단어 오답. 질문의 shoe-polishing에서 연상 가능한 shoe store를 이용한 오답.

25

W-Br How about hiring more temporary workers during the busy season?

M-Au (A) I did walk there quite often.

(B) Why didn't I think of that before?

(C) They should be hung higher up.

성수기 때 임시직을 더 고용하는 게 어때요?
(A) 나는 꽤 자주 거기까지 걸어 다녔죠.
(B) 왜 그 생각을 못한 걸까요?
(C) 그것들은 더 높이 걸어야 해요.

어휘 hire 고용하다 temporary worker 임시 직원 busy season 성수기 quite 꽤 hang 걸다

해설 제안의 의문문

(A) 유사 발음 오답. 질문의 workers와 부분적으로 발음이 같은 walk를 이용한 오답.

(B) 정답. 성수기 때 임시직을 고용하는 게 어떠냐는 말에 왜 그런 생각을 못했을까라는 말로 우회적으로 좋은 생각이라는 것을 표현하고 있으므로 정답.

(C) 동일 발음 오답. 질문의 hire와 발음이 같은 higher를 이용한 오답.

26

M-Cn What types of insurance are available?

W-Am (A) I'll send you the full list later.

(B) It's going to ensure our success.

(C) That's not my company's policy.

어떤 종류의 보험에 가입할 수 있나요?
(A) 제가 나중에 전체 목록을 보내드릴게요.
(B) 우리의 성공을 보장할 거예요.
(C) 그건 우리 회사 정책이 아니에요.

어휘 insurance 보험 available 이용할 수 있는 full 전부 갖추어진 list 목록 ensure 보장하다 policy 정책, 보험증권(증서)

해설 보험 종류를 묻는 What 의문문
(A) 정답. 가입 가능한 보험 종류를 묻는 질문에 나중에 전체 (보험) 목록을 보내주겠다고 우회적으로 답변하고 있으므로 정답.
(B) 유사 발음 오답. 질문의 insurance와 부분적으로 발음이 같은 ensure를 이용한 오답.
(C) 연상 단어 오답. 질문의 insurance에 대해 보험 약관 측면에서 연상 가능한 policy를 이용한 오답.

27

M-Au Has Jeremy completed the market research?
W-Br (A) From Mexican consumers.
(B) He's been busy with the interns.
(C) They're respected scientists.

제레미가 시장조사를 마쳤나요?
(A) 멕시코 소비자들로부터요.
(B) 그는 인턴들 때문에 바빴어요.
(C) 그들은 존경받는 과학자예요.

어휘 complete 끝내다 market research 시장조사 consumer 소비자 be busy with ~으로 바쁜 respected 존경받는

해설 시장조사 완료 여부를 묻는 현재완료 의문문
(A) 연상 단어 오답. 질문의 market research에서 연상 가능한 consumers를 이용한 오답.
(B) 정답. 제레미의 시장조사 완료 여부에 대해 그가 인턴들 때문에 바쁘다는 우회적인 표현으로 불확실성을 나타내고 있으므로 정답.
(C) 연상 단어 오답. 질문의 research에서 연상 가능한 scientists를 이용한 오답.

28

W-Br How many items are in the shop's inventory?
W-Am (A) From tomorrow's stock.
(B) He didn't invent it.
(C) Six or so.

매장에 재고품이 얼마나 있나요?
(A) 내일 재고에서요.
(B) 그가 발명하지 않았어요.
(C) 여섯 개 정도요.

어휘 inventory 재고 stock 재고품, 주식 invent 발명하다 or so ~쯤[정도]

해설 재고 개수를 묻는 How many 의문문
(A) 연상 단어 오답. 질문의 inventory에 대해 재고 측면에서 연상 가능한 stock을 이용한 오답.
(B) 유사 발음 오답. 질문의 inventory와 부분적으로 발음이 같은 invent를 이용한 오답.
(C) 정답. 재고 개수를 묻는 질문에 여섯 개 정도라는 구체적인 숫자를 언급하고 있으므로 정답.

29

W-Am This video game has the best graphics I've ever seen.
M-Au (A) Seven different characters to choose from.
(B) I'm done with the first level.
(C) I guess you haven't played *Sprag Quest*.

이 비디오게임의 그래픽은 지금까지 본 것 중 최고예요.
(A) 선택할 수 있는 캐릭터가 7개예요.
(B) 첫 단계는 끝냈어요.
(C) 〈스프래그 퀘스트〉는 아직 안 해 봤군요.

어휘 graphics 그래픽스, 삽화 character 캐릭터, 등장인물 choose from ~에서 선택하다 be done with ~을 다 처리하다[마치다]

해설 사실/정보 전달의 평서문
(A) 연상 단어 오답. 질문의 video game에 대해 등장인물 측면에서 연상 가능한 characters를 이용한 오답.
(B) 연상 단어 오답. 질문의 video game에 대해 게임 단계 측면에서 연상 가능한 first level을 이용한 오답.
(C) 정답. 이 비디오게임의 그래픽이 최고라는 말에 〈스프래그 퀘스트〉는 아직 안 해 본 것 같다는 말로 이 비디오게임의 그래픽이 최고가 아니라는 의미를 우회적으로 표현한 것이므로 정답.

30

M-Cn Where will the hands-on training sessions be held?
W-Br (A) About three or four hours.
(B) In the large meeting room.
(C) A group e-mail sent last week.

실무 교육은 어디에서 열리나요?
(A) 약 3~4 시간이요.
(B) 대회의실에서요.
(C) 지난주에 보낸 단체 이메일이요.

어휘 hands-on 직접 해보는, 실제의 training session 교육 hold 열다, 개최하다 meeting room 회의실

해설 실무 교육 개최 장소를 묻는 Where 의문문
(A) 질문과 상관없는 오답. 소요 시간을 묻는 How long 의문문에 대한 응답이므로 오답.
(B) 정답. 실무 교육을 할 수 있는 장소를 묻는 질문에 대회의실이라는 구체적인 장소로 응답하고 있으므로 정답.
(C) 질문과 상관없는 오답. 어디에서 열리냐는 질문에 지난주에 보낸 이메일이라고 응답하는 것은 맥락에서 벗어나는 것이므로 오답.

31

W-Am Is the downtown office space as expensive as they say?
M-Au (A) I'll let you know where he is.
(B) They said all office staff are invited.
(C) It's comparable to nearby properties.

도심에 위치한 그 사무실은 사람들 말처럼 비싼가요?
(A) 그가 어디에 있는지 알려 줄게요.
(B) 그들은 사무실 직원 모두 초대받았다고 말했어요.
(C) 인근 건물들과 비슷해요.

어휘 downtown 도심 office space 사무실 (공간) staff 직원 comparable 비슷한, 비교할 만한 nearby 근처 property 건물, 대지

해설 사무실이 비싼지 묻는 Be동사 의문문
(A) 질문과 상관없는 오답. he가 가리키는 대상이 질문에 없으므로 오답.
(B) 유사 발음 오답. 질문의 office space와 발음이 부분적으로 비슷한 office staff을 이용한 오답.
(C) 정답. 도심에 위치한 사무실이 비싼지 묻는 질문에 인근 건물들과 비슷하다고 응답하고 있으므로 정답.

Part 3

32-34

M-Cn Maria, can I make a suggestion? ³²I'm looking at our Web site, and... to enhance our position as the region's largest retailer of cooking equipment, I think we should add some features to the online product listings.

W-Am Yes, I agree. ³³The person who originally designed the site for us, Sarah Yoon, still works in that field as a freelancer. I'm sure she could upgrade the site for us. I'll call her today.

M-Cn Excellent. Uh, one thing I'd like to include is a product search by brand. ³⁴So first... this afternoon, I'll put together a list of all the brands we sell.

남: 마리아, 제가 제안 하나 할까요? 지금 우리 웹사이트를 보고 있어요, 우리가 지역 최대의 조리 장비 소매업체로서 입지를 강화하려면, 제 생각엔 온라인 제품 목록에 몇 가지 기능을 추가해야 할 것 같아요.

여: 네, 동의해요. 처음에 우리 웹사이트를 디자인해 준 사라 윤씨가 아직 동종업계에서 프리랜서로 일하고 있어요. 그분이 우리 웹사이트를 업그레이드해 줄 거예요. 오늘 제가 그분에게 전화할게요.

남: 좋아요. 음, 추가했으면 하는 게 한 가지 있는데 브랜드별 제품 검색 기능이에요. 그러면 일단 제가 오늘 오후에 우리 회사가 판매하는 모든 브랜드를 취합해 목록을 만들게요.

어휘 make a suggestion 제안하다 enhance 높이다[향상시키다] position 위상, 위치 region 지역 retailer 소매업체, 소매상 cooking equipment 조리 장비 add to ~에 추가하다 feature 특색, 특징, 기능 product 제품 listing 목록 originally 원래, 애초에 field 분야, 현장 freelancer 프리랜서 upgrade 개선하다 include 포함하다 search 검색 put together 한데 모으다

32

Where do the speakers work?

(A) At an event planning agency
(B) At a marketing firm
(C) At a magazine publisher
(D) At a cooking equipment store

화자들은 어디에서 일하는가?
(A) 행사 기획 대행사에서
(B) 마케팅 업체에서
(C) 잡지 출판사에서
(D) 조리 장비 매장에서

어휘 agency 대행사 firm 회사 publisher 출판사

해설 전체 내용 관련 – 화자들의 근무 장소
남자의 첫 번째 대사에서 지역 최대의 조리 장비 소매업체로서 우리의 입지를 강화하기 위해서(to enhance our position as the region's largest retailer of cooking equipment)라고 했으므로 화자들은 조리 장비 판매와 관련된 일을 하고 있음을 알 수 있다. 따라서 정답은 (D)이다.

▸▸ Paraphrasing 대화의 the region's largest retailer of cooking equipment
→ 정답의 a cooking equipment store

33

Who most likely is Ms. Yoon?

(A) A potential supplier
(B) A real estate agent
(C) A celebrity chef
(D) A Web site designer

윤 씨는 누구이겠는가?
(A) 잠재적 공급업체
(B) 부동산 중개업자
(C) 유명 요리사
(D) 웹사이트 디자이너

어휘 potential 잠재적인 supplier 공급업체 real estate 부동산 (중개업) agent 대리인, 중개인 celebrity 유명인사

해설 세부 사항 관련 – 대화 속 등장인물의 직업
여자의 첫 번째 대사에서 사라 윤이 회사의 웹사이트를 처음에 디자인해 준 사람(the person who originally designed the site for us, Sarah Yoon)이라고 했으므로 정답은 (D)이다.

▸▸ Paraphrasing 대화의 the person who originally designed the site for us
→ 정답의 a Web site designer

34

What does the man say he will do in the afternoon?

(A) Edit a digital video
(B) Assemble a list
(C) Install a computer
(D) Lead a facility tour

남자는 오후에 무엇을 할 거라고 말하는가?
(A) 디지털 비디오 편집하기
(B) 목록 정리하기
(C) 컴퓨터 설치하기
(D) 시설 견학 안내하기

어휘 edit 편집하다 assemble 취합하다 install 설치하다 facility 시설 tour 견학

남자의 두 번째 대사에서 남자가 오늘 오후에 회사가 판매하는 모든 브랜드를 취합해 목록을 만들 것(this afternoon, I'll put together a list of all the brands we sell)이라고 했으므로 정답은 (B)이다.

▸▸ Paraphrasing   대화의 put together → 정답의 assemble

35-37

M-Cn	Customer service. How may I help you?
W-Br	Hi, my name is Lisa Denby. **35I applied for a Kohlberg Store credit card online last week, and was approved, but I haven't yet received my card in the mail.** Can you find out what happened to it?
M-Cn	Sure, I'd be happy to do that. **36Could you spell your last name for me?**
W-Br	D-E-N-B-Y.
M-Cn	Got it. Let's figure out what went wrong here... Ah, it appears that you checked the box marked "In-Store Pickup", **37so we shipped your card to the Safton Heights branch. You'll have to go there to get it.**

남:	고객 서비스입니다. 무엇을 도와드릴까요?
여:	안녕하세요, 제 이름은 리사 덴비인데요. 제가 지난주에 인터넷에서 콜버그 매장 신용카드를 신청해서 승인을 받았는데요. 그런데 아직 카드를 우편으로 받지 못했어요. 어떻게 된 건지 알아봐 주시겠어요?
남:	물론이죠. 기꺼이 알아봐 드리죠. 성의 철자를 말씀해 주시겠어요?
여:	D-E-N-B-Y.
남:	알겠습니다. 뭐가 잘못됐는지 볼게요… "매장에서 수령"란에 체크하신 것 같아요. 그래서 우리가 카드를 사프톤 하이츠 지점으로 보냈어요. 그곳에 가서 카드를 수령하셔야 해요.

어휘	customer service 고객서비스 (부서) apply for ~에 지원하다, ~을 신청하다 credit card 신용카드 approve 승인하다 find out 알아보다 spell 철자하다; 철자 last name 성 figure out 이해하다 go wrong 잘못되다 pickup 수거

35

What does the woman hope to do?

(A) Modify an online order
(B) Return a defective product
(C) Obtain a store credit card
(D) Cancel a loyalty club membership

여자는 무엇을 하고 싶어 하는가?
(A) 온라인 주문 변경하기
(B) 불량품 반품하기
(C) 매장 신용카드 수령하기
(D) 포인트 적립 멤버십 카드 취소하기

어휘	modify 수정하다, 변경하다 order 주문 defective 결함 있는 obtain 얻다 cancel 취소하다 loyalty 충성 club membership 회원권

해설 세부 사항 관련 – 여자가 하려는 일

여자의 첫 번째 대사에서 남자에게 인터넷에서 매장 신용카드를 신청해서 승인을 받았는데 우편으로 카드를 받지 못했다(I applied for a Kohlberg Store credit card online last week, and was approved, but I haven't yet received my card in the mail)고 했으므로 정답은 (C)이다.

36

What information does the man ask for?

(A) An address
(B) An error code
(C) The spelling of a name
(D) The date of a transaction

남자는 무슨 정보를 요청하는가?
(A) 주소
(B) 오류 코드
(C) 이름의 철자
(D) 거래 날짜

어휘	error 오류 spelling 철자 transaction 거래, 매매

해설 세부 사항 관련 – 남자가 요청하는 정보

남자의 두 번째 대사에서 성의 철자를 말해 달라(Could you spell your last name for me)고 했으므로 정답은 (C)이다.

▸▸ Paraphrasing   대화의 spell your last name
→ 정답의 The spelling of a name

37

What does the man say the woman must do?

(A) Visit a store branch
(B) Pack an item for shipping
(C) Open a Web page
(D) Keep an invoice

남자는 여자에게 무엇을 해야 한다고 말하는가?
(A) 매장 지점 방문하기
(B) 배송용 물건 포장하기
(C) 웹페이지 개설하기
(D) 송장 보관하기

해설 세부 사항 관련 – 남자가 여자에게 요청하는 것

남자의 세 번째 대사에서 남자가 여자에게 카드를 사프톤 하이츠 지점으로 보냈으니 거기에 가서 카드를 찾으라(we shipped your card to the Safton Heights branch. You'll have to go there to get it)고 했으므로 정답은 (A)이다.

▸▸ Paraphrasing   대화의 go there to get it
→ 정답의 Visit a store branch

38-40

M-Au: Vicky, you've heard how I sometimes teach at the local community college, right? **38Well, I'd like our product development division to help the students understand the work we do.** So I was thinking of bringing the class here next week. Would that be all right with you?

W-Am: Sure. **39The golf simulator product we're developing is undergoing hands-on testing now, so we can have our quality assurance team walk them through that whole process.**

M-Au: That would be great. **40Could you talk to Donny, the quality assurance manager, and make sure he updates that project's progress report?** I'd like to show that to the students too.

남: 비키, 제가 이 지역 전문대에서 가끔 가르친다는 얘기 들었죠? 우리 제품개발부에서 학생들이 우리가 하는 일을 이해하도록 도와줬으면 해요. 그래서 다음 주 학생들을 이곳에 데려오려고 하는데요. 그래도 괜찮겠어요?

여: 물론이죠. 우리가 개발하고 있는 스크린골프 제품이 현재 실무 테스트 중이니 우리 품질보증팀이 그들에게 모든 테스트 과정을 하나 하나 보여줄 수 있어요.

남: 그거 좋겠군요. 품질보증팀장인 도니에게 말해서 해당 프로젝트의 경과 보고서를 꼭 업데이트하라고 얘기해 줄래요? 그 보고서를 학생들에게도 보여 주고 싶어요.

어휘 local 지역의 community college 지역 전문대학 product development 제품 개발 division 부문, 부 simulator 시뮬레이터, 모의 훈련 장치 undergo 겪다, 받다 hands-on 직접 해보는, 실제의 quality assurance team 품질보증팀 walk ~ through ~에게 …를 (단계별로) 보여주다 whole 전체의 process 과정, 절차 progress report 경과 보고(서) make sure 반드시 (꼭) ~하게 하다

38

Why does the man talk to the woman?

(A) To offer help with a development process
(B) To inform her of a financial difficulty
(C) To arrange an educational opportunity
(D) To remind her about an upcoming merger

남자는 왜 여자에게 말하는가?

(A) 개발 과정을 도와주기 위해
(B) 여자에게 자금난을 알리기 위해서
(C) **교육 기회를 마련하기 위해서**
(D) 다가오는 합병에 대해 상기시키기 위해서

어휘 financial 재정[금전]상의 difficulty 어려움 upcoming 다가오는 merger 합병

해설 세부 사항 관련 – 남자가 말하는 이유

남자의 첫 번째 대사에서 제품개발부에서 학생들이 우리가 하는 일을 이해하도록 도와줬으면 한다(I'd like our product development division to help the students understand the work we do)고 했으므로 정답은 (C)이다.

> ▸ Paraphrasing 대화의 **help the students understand the work we do** → 정답의 **arrange an educational opportunity**

39

What does the woman recommend doing?

(A) Hiring additional part-time staff
(B) Raising some quality standards
(C) Signing up for evening classes
(D) Showing product-testing methods

여자는 무엇을 하라고 권하는가?

(A) 시간제 직원을 추가로 고용하기
(B) 품질 기준 높이기
(C) 야간 수업 신청하기
(D) **제품 검사법 보여주기**

어휘 hire 고용하다 additional 추가적인 part-time staff 시간제 직원 raise 높이다 quality standard 품질 기준 sign up for ~을 신청하다 method 방법

해설 세부 사항 관련 – 여자가 권하고 있는 행동

여자의 첫 번째 대사에서 개발하고 있는 스크린골프 제품이 현재 실무 테스트 중이므로 품질보증팀이 그들에게 모든 테스트 과정을 하나 하나 보여줄 수 있다(The golf simulator product we're developing is undergoing hands-on testing now, so we can have our quality assurance team walk them through that whole process)고 했으므로 정답은 (D)이다.

> ▸ Paraphrasing 대화의 **have our quality assurance team walk them through that whole process** → 정답의 **Showing product-testing methods**

40

What does the man ask the woman to do?

(A) Clean a work area
(B) Speak with a team manager
(C) Update a software program
(D) Photocopy a report

남자는 여자에게 무엇을 하라고 요청하는가?

(A) 작업장 청소하기
(B) **팀 관리자와 대화하기**
(C) 소프트웨어 프로그램 업데이트하기
(D) 보고서 복사하기

어휘 photocopy 복사하다

해설 세부 사항 관련 – 남자가 여자에게 요청하는 것

남자의 두 번째 대사에서 품질보증팀장인 도니에게 말해서 해당 프로젝트의 경과 보고서를 꼭 업데이트하라고 얘기해 달라(Could you talk to Donny, the quality assurance manager, and make sure he updates that project's progress report)고 했으므로 정답은 (B)이다.

> ▸ Paraphrasing 대화의 **talk to Donny, the quality assurance manager** → 정답의 **speak with a team manager**

41-43

M-Au **⁴¹Hi, I came to find out about your vehicle painting service...** I'm interested in getting my company's logo, plus some graphics, painted onto the side and windows of this delivery van.

W-Br Sure. Do you have a design idea in mind?

M-Au **⁴²Well, I run a garment cleaning service**, and I just added a delivery option—I bring the clean laundry to customers' homes. So, a design that emphasizes speed and convenience...

W-Br OK. **⁴³We have many samples of graphic designs for your type of business here in our database. Take a look at them.** I'm sure we have something that'll work for your van.

남: 안녕하세요, 여기서 제공하는 차량 도색 서비스에 대해 알아보려고 왔는데요. 저희 회사 로고와 몇 가지 그림을 배달 차량 옆면과 창에 새기려고 합니다.

여: 네, 생각하고 계신 디자인이 있으신가요?

남: 제가 의류세탁업을 하고 있는데 최근에 배달 서비스를 추가했거든요. 세탁물들을 고객들의 집에 가져다 드리는 거죠. 그래서 빠른 배달과 편리함을 강조하는 디자인이었으면…

여: 알겠습니다. 저희 데이터베이스에 고객님 사업체 같은 업체용으로 나온 그래픽 디자인 샘플이 많이 있습니다. 한번 살펴보세요. 고객님 차량에 맞는 것이 있을 겁니다.

어휘 vehicle 차량 painting service 도색 서비스 logo 로고, 상징 graphic 그래픽(그림이나 사진) delivery van 배달용 차량 have ~ in mind ~를 염두에 두다 run 운영하다 garment 의류 cleaning service 세탁 서비스 add 추가하다 option 선택지 emphasize 강조하다 convenience 편의 database 데이터베이스 take a look at ~을 (한번) 보다 work 효과가 있다

41

What does the man want to have painted?

(A) A delivery vehicle
(B) Some store windows
(C) A warehouse floor
(D) Some furniture

남자가 도색하고 싶어 하는 것은 무엇인가?

(A) 배달용 차량
(B) 매장 창문
(C) 창고 바닥
(D) 가구

어휘 warehouse 창고

해설 세부 사항 관련 – 남자가 도색하기 원하는 것

남자의 첫 번째 대사에서 여기서 제공하는 차량 도색 서비스에 대해 알아보려고 왔다(I came to find out about your vehicle painting service)고 했으므로 정답은 (A)이다.

42

What kind of company does the man operate?

(A) A clothing shop
(B) A catering service
(C) A laundry-cleaning business
(D) A plumbing company

남자는 어떤 종류의 회사를 운영하는가?

(A) 의류 매장
(B) 출장 요리 서비스
(C) 세탁업체
(D) 배관업체

어휘 catering service 출장 요리 업체 plumbing 배관 공사[설비]

해설 세부 사항 관련 – 남자가 운영하는 회사의 종류

남자의 두 번째 대사에서 남자가 의류세탁업을 하고 있다(I run a garment cleaning service)고 했으므로 정답은 (C)이다.

> ▸▸ Paraphrasing 대화의 a garment cleaning service
> → 정답의 A laundry-cleaning business

43

What does the woman suggest the man do?

(A) Delay a promotional sale
(B) View some sample designs
(C) Load some packages into a van
(D) Choose a type of paint

여자는 남자에게 무엇을 하라고 제안하는가?

(A) 판촉 할인 미루기
(B) 몇 개의 샘플 디자인 보기
(C) 소포를 차량에 싣기
(D) 페인트 종류 고르기

어휘 delay 연기하다 promotional sale 판촉 할인 view 보다 load into ~에 싣다 package 소포 choose 고르다

해설 세부 사항 관련 – 여자가 남자에게 제안하는 것

여자의 두 번째 대사에서 데이터베이스에 세탁업체용으로 나온 그래픽디자인 샘플이 많이 있으니 한번 보라(We have many samples of graphic designs for your type of business here in our database. Take a look at them)고 했으므로 정답은 (B)이다.

44-46 3인 대화

W-Am Mr. Hilling, so nice to see you again. **⁴⁴How are the flowers you bought from us?** Do you need some more soil for them?

M-Cn No, they're doing just fine. **⁴⁵I'm actually here to buy a potted rosebush. I'm going to give it to a new neighbor tomorrow.**

W-Am Oh, in that case, you should talk to Jodie. She's our expert on roses. Jodie? Mr. Hilling is looking to buy some roses.

W-Br I'd be happy to help you with that. Hmm, since you are an experienced grower, how about this variety? It's very beautiful.

M-Cn **⁴⁶Well, it's not for me, so I think I'd better get something that doesn't require too much care.**

W-Br In that case, I recommend these.

여1: 다시 만나서 반갑습니다, 힐링 씨. **저희한테서 구입하신 화초는 어떤가요?** 흙이 더 필요하신가요?

남: 아뇨, 화초는 잘 자라고 있어요. 실은 장미 화분을 사려고 왔어요. 내일 새로 온 이웃에게 주려고요.

여1: 아, 그러면 조디와 이야기해 보세요. 장미 전문가예요. 조디, 힐링 씨가 장미를 사려고 하신대요.

여2: 기꺼이 도와 드리겠습니다. 음, 재배 경험이 있으시니까 이 품종은 어때세요? 정말 예쁘죠.

남: 음, 그건 제가 쓰려는 게 아니라서요, 신경을 많이 안 써도 되는 것으로 사는 게 좋을 것 같네요.

여2: 그러면 이것들을 추천해 드릴게요.

어휘 flower 화초 soil 흙, 토양 potted 화분에 심은 rosebush 장미나무, 장미덤불 neighbor 이웃 (사람) in that case 그런 경우라면 expert 전문가 look to ~하려고 하다 be happy to 기꺼이 ~하다 experienced 경험[경력]이 있는, 능숙한 variety (식물 등의) 품종 require 요구하다, 필요로 하다 care 돌봄, 보살핌

44

Where does the conversation most likely take place?

(A) At a nature park
(B) At an art gallery
(C) At a plant nursery
(D) At a toy store

대화는 어디에서 이루어지겠는가?

(A) 자연공원에서
(B) 미술관에서
(C) 화훼 판매장에서
(D) 장난감 매장에서

어휘 plant 화훼, 식물 nursery 묘목장

해설 전체 내용 관련 – 대화가 이루어지는 장소

첫 번째 여자의 첫 대사에서 남자에게 이곳에서 구입한 화초가 어떤지(How are the flowers you bought from us)를 묻고 있으므로 대화는 화초, 묘목 등을 판매하는 곳에서 이루어지고 있음을 알 수 있다. 따라서 정답은 (C)이다.

45

What does the man say he will do tomorrow?

(A) Give a gift
(B) Decorate an office
(C) Move to a new house
(D) Go on a picnic

남자는 내일 무엇을 할 거라고 말하는가?

(A) 선물 주기
(B) 사무실 장식하기
(C) 새집으로 이사하기
(D) 소풍 가기

해설 세부 사항 관련 – 남자가 내일 할 일

남자의 첫 번째 대사에서 장미 화분을 사러 왔다면서 그것을 내일 새로 온 이웃에게 주려고 한다(I'm actually here to buy a potted rosebush. I'm going to give it to a new neighbor tomorrow)고 했으므로 이웃에게 선물로 화분을 주려 한다는 것을 알 수 있다. 따라서 정답은 (A)이다.

> ▸▸ Paraphrasing 대화의 **give it to a new neighbor**
> → 정답의 **present a gift**

46

According to the man, what is most important about a product?

(A) How beautiful it is
(B) How inexpensive it is
(C) How easy it will be to maintain
(D) How soon it will be available

남자에 따르면 제품에 대해 가장 중요한 것은 무엇인가?

(A) 얼마나 아름다운가
(B) 얼마나 저렴한가
(C) 관리가 얼마나 쉬운가
(D) 얼마나 빨리 구입할 수 있는가

어휘 inexpensive 저렴한 maintain 유지[간수]하다 available 구입 가능한

해설 세부 사항 관련 – 제품에 대해 가장 중요한 것

남자의 두 번째 대사에서 화분은 자신이 쓸 것이 아니라고 말하면서 많이 신경을 쓰지 않아도 되는 것을 사는 게 좋겠다(it's not for me, so I think I'd better get something that doesn't require too much care)고 말하고 있으므로 정답은 (C)이다.

47-49

M-Au **⁴⁷Hi, I'm with Latrobe Courier Service. I have an envelope with paperwork for Mr. Max Beckley.**

W-Am Oh, you can leave it with me here at the reception desk and I'll make sure he gets it.

M-Au Thank you. **⁴⁸Also, I'm sorry to bother you, but I was looking for another business just now and it wasn't where my mobile app said it would be. Sometimes this technology is really frustrating. ⁴⁹Do you happen to know where Yelnick Associates is located?**

W-Am **⁴⁹Sure, their office is in the alley a little up the street. Once you turn left at the Garden Lights Café,** it's really noticeable.

M-Au Ah, OK. Thanks.

남:	안녕하세요, 저는 라트로브 택배 서비스 직원인데요. 맥스 베클리 씨 앞으로 서류가 담긴 봉투가 하나 있어서요.
여:	아, 여기 안내데스크에 두시면 베클리 씨 가져가시라고 하겠습니다.
남:	감사합니다. 그리고, 귀찮게 해드려 죄송합니다만 방금 전에 다른 업체를 찾는 중이었는데 제 핸드폰 앱이 알려 준 곳에 가 보니 없네요. 이 위치 찾기 기술이 가끔은 답답할 때가 있죠. 혹시 옐니크 어소시에이츠가 어디 있는지 아세요?
여:	그럼요. 이 길을 따라 조금만 올라가면 골목길에 있어요. 가든 라이츠 카페에서 왼쪽으로 가면 바로 보여요.
남:	아, 알겠습니다. 감사합니다.

어휘	courier 택배업체 envelope 봉투 paperwork 서류 (작업) bother 귀찮게 하다, 신경 쓰이게 하다 look for ~을 찾다 just now 방금 전에 app 애플리케이션(프로그램) frustrating 답답하게 하는 happen to 우연히[마침] ~하다 located ~에 위치한 noticeable 뚜렷한, 잘 보이는

47

What is the purpose of the man's visit?

(A) To meet a client for lunch
(B) To deliver some documents
(C) To conduct a site inspection
(D) To install some equipment

남자의 방문 목적은 무엇인가?
(A) 고객을 만나 점심을 먹으려고
(B) 문서를 배달하려고
(C) 현장 점검을 하려고
(D) 장비를 설치하려고

어휘 client 고객 deliver 배달하다 document 서류 conduct 시행하다 site 현장, 장소 inspection 검사, 점검 install 설치하다 equipment 장비

해설 세부 사항 관련 – 남자의 방문 목적
남자의 첫 번째 대사에서 라트로브 택배 서비스 직원인데 맥스 베클리 씨 앞으로 서류가 담긴 봉투가 하나 있다(I'm with Latrobe Courier Service. I have an envelope with paperwork for Mr. Max Beckley)고 말하고 있는 것으로 보아 택배회사의 직원임을 알 수 있다. 따라서 정답은 (B)이다.

▸▸ **Paraphrasing** 대화의 paperwork → 정답의 documents

48

What does the man express frustration with?

(A) A mobile app
(B) A carrying case
(C) A machine part
(D) A supervisor's instructions

남자는 무엇을 답답해 하는가?
(A) 핸드폰 앱
(B) 운반용 케이스
(C) 기계 부품
(D) 상사의 지시

어휘 carrying 운송, 적재 part 부품 supervisor 상사, 관리자 instruction 지시, 명령

해설 세부 사항 관련 – 남자가 답답해 하는 대상
남자의 두 번째 대사에서 귀찮게 해서 죄송하지만 방금 전에 다른 업체를 찾는 중이었는데 핸드폰 앱이 알려준 곳에 가 보니 없다(I'm sorry to bother you, but I was looking for another business just now and it wasn't where my mobile app said it would be)고 하면서 가끔 이 위치 찾기 기술이 답답할 때가 있다(Sometimes this technology is really frustrating)고 했으므로 정답은 (A)이다.

49

What does the woman imply when she says, "it's really noticeable"?

(A) She is proud of a project's results.
(B) The man cannot leave an item in the lobby.
(C) A problem must be addressed quickly.
(D) A location is not difficult to find.

여자가 "바로 보여요"라고 말한 의미는 무엇인가?
(A) 여자는 프로젝트의 결과가 자랑스럽다.
(B) 남자는 물건을 로비에 두고 갈 수 없다.
(C) 문제가 빨리 해결되어야 한다.
(D) 위치를 찾기가 어렵지 않다.

어휘 address (문제 등을) 해결[처리]하다 location 위치, 장소

해설 화자의 의도 파악 – 바로 보인다는 말의 의미
남자의 두 번째 대사에서 옐니크 어소시에이츠가 어디 있는지(Do you happen to know where Yelnick Associates is located) 묻자 여자가 길을 따라 조금만 올라가면 골목길에 있다면서 가든 라이츠 카페에서 왼쪽으로 가라(their office is in the alley a little up the street. Once you turn left at the Garden Lights Café)고 했으므로 길을 찾기 쉽다는 의미임을 알 수 있다. 따라서 정답은 (D)이다.

50-52

M-Cn	I just finished looking over the data from our study on green technology, and the results are very surprising. **⁵⁰We should run the experiment again to make sure that they're correct.**
W-Br	I agree. **⁵¹But if we're going to present the findings at the Riggins conference like we had hoped, we'll need to speed up the process.** That's the only way we'll be able to complete our analysis in time.
M-Cn	That's a good point. **⁵²I'll ask the team to gather this afternoon to talk over the experiment process.** They may have some ideas on how to shorten it without sacrificing accurate results.

남:	방금 우리 친환경 기술 연구 데이터 검토를 끝냈는데 결과가 정말 놀랍네요. 연구 결과가 정확한지 확인하려면 재실험을 실시해야 할 것 같아요.
여:	맞아요. 하지만 우리가 바란 대로 리긴스 회의에서 연구 결과를 발표하려면 절차를 서둘러야 할 거예요. 우리가 분석을 제시간에 마무리하려면 그게 유일한 방법이에요.

남: 좋은 지적이에요. 제가 연구팀에게 오늘 오후에 모여서 실험 과정에 대해 논의하자고 요청할게요. 정확한 연구 결과를 포기하지 않으면서도 과정을 단축할 아이디어가 있을지도 모르니까요.

50

What is the conversation mainly about?

(A) Improving laboratory conditions
(B) Repeating an experiment
(C) Selecting student interns
(D) Publishing a scientific paper

대화는 주로 무엇에 관한 것인가?

(A) 실험실 여건 개선하기
(B) 재실험 하기
(C) 학생 인턴 선정하기
(D) 과학 논문 출판하기

어휘   improve 개선하다   laboratory 실험실   condition (작업) 환경   repeat 반복하다   select 선정하다   publish 출간하다   scientific paper 과학논문

해설   전체 내용 관련 – 대화의 주제

남자의 첫 번째 대사에서 연구 결과가 정확한지 확인하려면 재실험을 실시해야 한다(We should run the experiment again to make sure that they're correct)고 말하고 있으므로 대화의 주제는 (B)이다.

▶ Paraphrasing   대화의 **run the experiment again** → 정답의 **repeating an experiment**

51

What does the woman want to change?

(A) A time frame
(B) The focus of a text
(C) A method of analysis
(D) The size of a budget

여자는 무엇을 변경하고 싶어 하는가?

(A) 소요 기간
(B) 글의 초점
(C) 분석 방법
(D) 예산의 규모

어휘   time frame 소요 시간[기간]   focus 초점   text 본문, 글   method 방법   analysis 분석   budget 예산

해설   세부 사항 관련 – 여자가 변경하고자 하는 것

여자의 첫 번째 대사에서 리긴스 회의에서 연구 결과를 발표하려면 절차를 서둘러야 한다(if we're going to present the findings at the Riggins conference like we had hoped, we'll need to speed up the process)고 말하고 있는 것으로 보아 실험의 일정을 앞당기려 한다는 것을 알 수 있다. 따라서 정답은 (A)이다.

52

What does the man say he will do?

(A) Buy a measuring device
(B) Register for a conference
(C) Edit some passages
(D) Schedule a meeting

남자는 무엇을 할 거라고 말하는가?

(A) 측정 장치 구매하기
(B) 회의에 등록하기
(C) 글 편집하기
(D) 회의 일정 잡기

어휘   measuring device 측정 장치   register for ~에 등록하다   edit 편집하다   passage 글   schedule 일정을 잡다

해설   전체 내용 관련 – 대화의 주제

남자의 두 번째 대사에서 연구팀에게 실험 과정을 논의하기 위해 오늘 오후에 모이라고 요청할 것(I'll ask the team to gather this afternoon to talk over the experiment process)이라고 말하고 있으므로 회의를 요청할 것임을 알 수 있다. 따라서 정답은 (D)이다.

▶ Paraphrasing   대화의 **ask the team to gather this afternoon** → 정답의 **schedule a meeting**

53-55 3인 대화

M-Au   Quentin, Serena, I have some news. **[53]Starting in early June, our staff parking area will be closed so that crews can upgrade its landscaping and lighting systems.**

M-Cn   That's a big project. That area might be off-limits for weeks.

M-Au   Right. So I was wondering if you two have ideas for easing the burden on staff.

W-Br   **[54]Hmm... at the Lake Avenue train station, there's a free shuttle bus connection that stops one block from this office.** The service just started up last week.

M-Cn   Most employees can access that station, so that would work.

M-Au   Sounds good. Serena, could you tell everyone else about the shuttle?

W-Br   **[55]Sure, I'll post the details on our staff Web site now.**

남 1:	퀜튼, 세레나, 소식이 있어요. **6월 초부터 조경 및 조명 설비 개선 작업을 위해 직원 주차 구역이 폐쇄될 예정입니다.**
남2:	대형 프로젝트네요. 몇 주 동안 출입 금지 구역이 될 수도 있겠어요.
남1:	맞아요. 그래서 직원들 부담을 덜어 줄 만한 아이디어가 있는지 궁금해서요.
여:	흠… 우리 사무실에서 한 블록 떨어진 곳에 정차하는 무료 셔틀버스가 레이크가 기차역에 운행되고 있어요. 셔틀버스 서비스는 지난주에 시작되었고요.
남2:	직원들 대부분이 그 역에 갈 수 있으니, 도움이 될 것 같아요.
남1:	좋네요. 세레나, 다른 사람들에게도 셔틀버스에 대해 알려 주실래요?
여:	**물론이죠, 제가 지금 바로 직원 웹사이트에 세부 사항을 게시할게요.**

어휘   starting ~부터 staff 직원 parking area 주차 구역
crew (함께 일하는) 팀, 반, 조 landscaping 조경, 경관 꾸미기
lighting 조명 (시설) off-limits 출입 금지의 ease 덜어
주다 burden 부담 shuttle bus 셔틀버스 connection
운행 수단, 운행편 start up 시작되다, 개시되다 access ~에
접근하다 work 효과가 있다 post 게시하다 details 세부
사항, 세목

53

What will happen in June?

(A) A recycling program will be introduced.
(B) A parking area will be upgraded.
(C) A job recruitment campaign will begin.
(D) A series of staff workshops will be held.

6월에 무슨 일이 있는가?
(A) 재활용 프로그램이 도입될 것이다.
(B) 주차 구역이 개선될 것이다.
(C) 채용 캠페인이 시작될 것이다.
(D) 일련의 직원 워크숍이 열릴 것이다.

어휘   recycling 재활용 introduce 도입하다 job recruitment 채용
campaign 캠페인, 활동 a series of 일련의 hold 개최하다

해설   세부 사항 관련 – 6월에 있을 일

남자의 첫 번째 대사에서 6월부터 조경 및 조명 작업을 위해 회사 주차 구역
이 폐쇄될 것(Starting in early June, our staff parking area will be
closed so that crews can upgrade its landscaping and lighting
systems)이라고 했으므로 정답은 (B)이다.

54

What does the woman suggest doing?

(A) Spending more money on office electronics
(B) Providing staff discounts on goods
(C) Using a new transportation link
(D) Allowing staff to work from home

여자는 무엇을 할 것을 제안하는가?
(A) 사무실 전자 제품 구입 비용 늘리기
(B) 제품에 직원 할인가 적용하기
(C) 새로운 연결교통편을 이용하기
(D) 직원 재택 근무 허용하기

어휘   electronics 전자 기기 staff discount 직원할인 goods 상품
transportation 교통 수단 link (교통) 연결 수단 allow 허가하다
work from home 재택 근무하다

해설   세부 사항 관련 – 여자가 제안하는 것

여자의 첫 번째 대사에서 레이크 가 기차역에 사무실에서 한 블록 떨어진 곳
에 정차하는 무료셔틀이 운행되고 있다(at the Lake Avenue train station,
there's a free shuttle bus connection that stops one block from
this office)고 했으므로 셔틀버스를 통한 새로운 교통편을 이용하는 것을 제안
하고 있다. 따라서 정답은 (C)이다.

▶▶ Paraphrasing   대화의 **a free shuttle bus connection**
→ 정답의 **a new transportation link**

55

Where will the woman share some information with
others?

(A) On a bulletin board near a door
(B) At an all-staff meeting
(C) In a text message
(D) On a company Web site

여자는 다른 사람과 어디에서 정보를 공유할 것인가?
(A) 문 옆 게시판에
(B) 전 직원 회의에서
(C) 문자 메시지로
(D) 회사 웹사이트에

어휘   bulletin board 게시판 text message 문자 메시지

해설   세부 사항 관련 – 여자가 정보를 공유할 통로

여자의 두 번째 대사에서 지금 바로 직원 웹사이트에 세부 사항을 게시할 것(I'll
post the details on our staff Web site now)이라고 했으므로 정답은 (D)
이다.

▶▶ Paraphrasing   대화의 **our staff Web site**
→ 정답의 **a company Web site**

56-58

W-Am	Mr. York, this is Dr. Lloyd. You called the clinic earlier today?
M-Au	Yes, Doctor. **56I want to talk to you about the cream you prescribed for my skin condition. I'm applying it as directed, but my symptoms are getting worse.**
W-Am	Well, I warned you that this medication may do that at first.
M-Au	I know, but it wasn't supposed to last this long. **57I'm going to the beach for vacation next week**, and I'm afraid I'll have to cover up to keep my condition from appearing in any pictures.

W-Am **58In that case, you should lower the dosage amount by applying it just once a day, before bed.** But we should avoid stopping the treatment altogether.

여: 요크 씨, 로이드입니다. 오전에 병원에 전화하셨죠?

남: 네, 로이드 선생님. 선생님이 제 피부 상태 때문에 처방해 주신 크림에 대해 얘기 좀 하려고요. 처방된 대로 크림을 바르고 있는데 증세가 더 악화되고 있어요.

여: 음, 그 약이 처음에는 그런 증세를 보일 수 있다고 주의 드렸지요.

남: 알고 있지만, 증세가 이렇게 오래 지속될지는 몰랐죠. 제가 다음 주에 해변으로 휴가를 가는데 제 피부상태가 사진에 나오지 않게 옷을 껴입어야 할 것 같아요.

여: 그러면 크림 사용량을 줄여서 하루에 한 번 잠자기 전에만 바르도록 하세요. 그렇지만 치료를 완전히 중단하지는 말아야 합니다.

어휘 clinic 병원, 진료소 prescribe 처방하다 condition 상태 apply (크림 등을) 바르다 as directed 지시받은 대로, 처방대로 symptom 증상 get worse 더 안 좋아지다, 악화되다 worn 주의를 주다 medication 약, 약물 at first 처음에는 be supposed to ~할 예정이다, ~하게 되어 있다 last 지속되다, 계속되다 cover up 옷을 더 껴입다 keep ~ from ~가 …하지 못하게 하다 appear 나타나다 in that case 그런 경우에는 lower 낮추다, 내리다 dosage amount (약의) 복용[투여]량 avoid 피하다 treatment 치료 altogether 완전히, 전적으로

56

Why does the man want to speak to the woman?

(A) To order a refill of a medication
(B) To reschedule an appointment
(C) To complain about a treatment
(D) To find out the results of a test

남자는 왜 여자와 이야기하고 싶어하는가?

(A) 약의 재조제를 주문하려고
(B) 진료일을 다시 잡으려고
(C) 치료에 대해 불만을 제기하려고
(D) 시험 결과를 알아보려고

어휘 order 주문하다 refill (약의) 재조제 reschedule 일정을 다시 잡다 appointment 진료 약속 complain about ~에 대해 불만을 제기하다

해설 세부 사항 관련 – 남자가 여자와 통화하고 싶어 하는 이유
남자의 첫 번째 대사에서 처방받은 크림에 대해 얘기하고 싶다 말하면서 처방대로 약을 발랐지만 증세가 악화되고 있다(I want to talk to you about the cream you prescribed for my skin condition. I'm applying it as directed, but my symptoms are getting worse)고 말하고 있는 것으로 보아 남자는 치료에 대해 불만족스럽게 생각하고 있다는 것을 알 수 있다. 따라서 정답은 (C)이다.

57

What will the man do next week?

(A) Take a vacation
(B) Appear in a performance
(C) Increase his insurance coverage
(D) Undergo a surgical procedure

남자는 다음 주에 무엇을 할 것인가?

(A) 휴가 가기
(B) 공연에 출연하기
(C) 보험 보장 금액 올리기
(D) 시술 받기

어휘 appear 출연하다 performance 공연 increase 증가시키다 insurance 보험 coverage 보장 범위, 담보 금액 undergo 겪다, 받다 surgical 수술의 procedure 수술, 처치

해설 세부 사항 관련 – 남자가 할일
남자의 두 번째 대사에서 다음 주에 해변으로 휴가를 간다(I'm going to the beach for vacation next week)고 했으므로 정답은 (A)이다.

▸▸ Paraphrasing 대화의 **going to the beach for vacation** → 정답의 **take a vacation**

58

What does the woman recommend?

(A) Going to sleep earlier
(B) Avoiding excessive sunlight
(C) Seeing another doctor
(D) Reducing the amount of medication used

여자는 무엇을 권하는가?

(A) 일찍 잠자리에 들기
(B) 과도한 햇빛 피하기
(C) 다른 병원에 가기
(D) 사용중인 약 투여량 줄이기

어휘 excessive 과도한 sunlight 햇빛 qualified 자격을 갖춘 reduce 줄이다

해설 세부 사항 관련 – 여자가 권하는 것
여자의 세 번째 대사에서 남자에게 바르는 양을 취침 전 한번으로 줄이라(you should lower the dosage amount by applying it just once a day, before bed)고 했으므로 정답은 (D)이다.

▸▸ Paraphrasing 대화의 **lower the dosage amount** → 정답의 **reducing the amount of medication used**

59-61

W-Br Mr. Norris, did you know there's an empty storefront in downtown Rissville? **59How about buying it and opening a second branch of Norris Stationery?**

M-Cn ⁶⁰Hmm, I don't think so. I've heard from other small business owners that that kind of thing is always more difficult than it seems.

W-Br **You may be right. It's just that business has been really good recently.**

M-Cn I suppose...

W-Br Why don't I put together a formal proposal for you? ⁶¹I'll spend some time in Rissville looking into its current market conditions.

M-Cn All right. But make sure you also think about how a location there might affect this branch.

여: 노리스 씨, 리스빌 시내에 대로변 건물 하나가 비어 있는 거 아셨어요? 그걸 구매해서 노리스 스테이셔너리의 두 번째 지점을 여는 게 어떨까요?

남: 음. 제 생각은 다른데요. 다른 소규모 자영업자들에게 들었는데 그런 일은 항상 보기보다 훨씬 어렵다더군요.

여: 그럴지도 몰라요. 최근에 사업이 정말 잘되고 있어서 그런 거예요.

남: 그렇긴 하죠…

여: 제가 정식으로 제안서를 작성해 보면 어떨까요? 리스빌을 둘러보면서 현재 시장 상황을 살펴볼게요.

남: 좋아요. 하지만 그곳에 지점을 두는 게 이 지점에 영향을 주지는 않을지도 반드시 생각해 봐야 해요.

어휘 empty 비어 있는 storefront 거리에 면한 점포[건물] downtown 번화가[도심 / 상업 지구]의[에 있는] branch 지사, 분점 business owner 사업주, 자영업자 It's just that 단지 ~한 것뿐이다 recently 최근에, 얼마 전에 suppose 생각하다, 추측하다 put together 준비하다 formal 정식의 proposal 제안(서), 제의 look into ~을 조사하다[알아보다] current 현재의 market condition 시장 상황, 시장 여건 location 장소, 위치 affect 영향을 미치다

59

What possibility is being discussed?

(A) The expansion of a company
(B) The renovation of a store
(C) The creation of an association
(D) The purchase of an appliance

어떤 가능성이 논의되고 있는가?

(A) 회사 확장
(B) 매장 보수
(C) 협회 창설
(D) 기기 구매

어휘 expansion 확장, 확대 renovation 개조, 보수 creation 창설 association 협회 purchase 구매 appliance 가전 제품

해설 전체 내용 관련 – 화자들이 논의하는 것
여자의 첫 번째 대사에서 남자에게 비어 있는 시내 점포를 구입해 노리스 스테이셔너리의 두 번째 지점을 여는 것이 어떠냐(How about buying it and opening a second branch of Norris Stationery)고 묻고 있으므로 화자들은 회사의 확장에 관해 이야기하고 있음을 알 수 있다. 따라서 정답은 (A)이다.

▶▶ Paraphrasing 대화의 opening a second branch → 정답의 expansion of a company

60

What does the woman imply when she says, "It's just that business has been really good recently"?

(A) She needs help with some work.
(B) She is surprised by a criticism.
(C) She is dissatisfied with a decision.
(D) She thinks a change is unnecessary.

여자가 "최근에 사업이 정말 잘되고 있어서 그런 거예요"라고 말하는 의도는 무엇인가?

(A) 업무에 도움이 필요하다.
(B) 비판에 놀랐다.
(C) 판단에 아쉬워하고 있다.
(D) 변화가 불필요하다고 생각한다.

어휘 criticism 비판 be dissatisfied with ~에 아쉬워하다[불만스럽다] unnecessary 불필요한

해설 화자의 의도 파악 – 사업이 잘돼서 하는 말이라고 한 의도
남자의 첫 번째 대사에서 여자에게 새 지점을 여는 일이 보기보다 훨씬 어렵다고 다른 소규모 자영업자들에게서 들었다(I've heard from other small business owners that that kind of thing is always more difficult than it seems)고 하자 여자가 남자에게 동의하면서 최근에 사업이 잘돼서 얘기해 본 것뿐(You may be right. It's just that business has been really good recently)이라고 말하는 것으로 보아 여자가 남자의 판단에 아쉬워하고 있음을 알 수 있다. 따라서 정답은 (C)이다.

61

Why will the woman go to Rissville?

(A) To conduct market research
(B) To look into an application process
(C) To talk to a construction contractor
(D) To hand out promotional flyers

여자는 왜 리스빌로 갈 것인가?

(A) 시장조사를 하기 위해
(B) 지원 절차를 살펴보기 위해
(C) 공사 계약자와 이야기를 나누기 위해
(D) 판촉용 전단지를 나눠 주기 위해

어휘 conduct market research 시장조사를 하다 look into ~을 조사하다 application 지원 process 절차[과정] construction 건설 contractor 계약자 hand out 나눠 주다 promotional 판촉용의 flyer 전단(지)

해설 세부 사항 관련 – 여자가 리스빌로 가는 이유
여자의 마지막 대사에서 리스빌을 둘러보면서 현재 시장 상황을 살펴보겠다(I'll spend some time in Rissville looking into its current market conditions)고 했으므로 정답은 (A)이다.

▶▶ Paraphrasing 대화의 **looking into its current market conditions** → 정답의 **conduct market research**

W-Am	Excuse me. Do you sell glass beads?
M-Au	Yes, they're over here. We're actually having a sale on Reilly beads right now, so I recommend those.
W-Am	**62Hmm, they are very pretty.** Do the discounts apply to all the different sizes of beads available?
M-Au	Yes, they do—here's a coupon. But if you're looking for variety, these boxes of assorted beads are a good choice.
W-Am	Oh, I see. **63Yes, I think just one assorted box would do.**
M-Au	Sure—the counter is this way. So, you make jewelry?
W-Am	Well, not usually. **64But I'm going to make a bracelet to give my friend for her birthday this year.**
M-Au	Oh, that's nice.

여:	실례합니다. 유리구슬 판매하나요?
남:	네, 여기 있습니다. 지금 할인 중인 레일리 구슬을 추천해 드려요.
여:	**음. 정말 예쁘네요.** 구매 가능한 다른 크기의 구슬에도 모두 할인이 적용되나요?
남:	네, 그렇습니다. 여기 쿠폰을 드릴게요. 다양한 구슬을 찾으신다면 이 모듬 구슬 세트를 사시는 게 좋고요.
여:	아, 그렇군요. **그럼 이 모듬 구슬 세트 하나면 될 것 같아요.**
남:	그러세요. 계산대는 이쪽입니다. 장신구를 만드시나요?
여:	응, 직업은 아니에요. **하지만 올해 친구 생일에 줄 팔찌를 만들 생각이에요.**
남:	오, 멋지네요.

어휘 glass bead 유리구슬 have a sale 세일하다, 할인 판매하다 discount 할인 apply to ~에 적용되다(해당되다) variety 여러 가지, 다양성 assorted 여러 가지의, 갖은 choice 선택 do 적절하다, 충분하다 jewelry 보석류, 장신구 bracelet 팔찌

Sale on Reilly-brand beads!

Amount	Savings
631 box	5%
2 boxes	10%
3 boxes	15%
4 boxes	20%

레일리 브랜드 구슬 할인

수량	할인율
1상자	5퍼센트
2상자	10퍼센트
3상자	15퍼센트
4상자	20퍼센트

62

What does the woman say about Reilly beads?

(A) They are durable.
(B) They are attractive.
(C) They are cheap.
(D) They are small.

여자는 레일리 구슬에 대해 뭐라고 말하는가?

(A) 튼튼하다.
(B) 매력적이다.
(C) 저렴하다.
(D) 작다.

어휘 durable 내구성 있는 attractive 매력적인

해설 세부 사항 관련 – 여자가 구슬에 대해 말하는 것

여자의 두 번째 대사에서 구슬이 정말 예쁘다(they are very pretty)고 말하고 있으므로 정답은 (B)이다.

▸▸ **Paraphrasing** 대화의 **pretty** → 정답의 **attractive**

63

Look at the graphic. Which discount does the woman qualify for?

(A) 5%
(B) 10%
(C) 15%
(D) 20%

시각 정보에 의하면, 여자는 얼마나 할인을 받을 수 있는가?

(A) 5퍼센트
(B) 10퍼센트
(C) 15퍼센트
(D) 20퍼센트

해설 시각 정보 연계 – 적용 할인율

여자의 세 번째 대사에서 모듬 구슬 세트 하나면 충분할 것 같다(I think just one assorted box would do)고 말하고 있으므로 하나만 구입할 것임을 알 수 있다. 시각 정보에 따르면 한 상자의 할인율이 5퍼센트이므로 정답은 (A)이다.

64

What does the woman plan to do?

(A) Take a crafting class
(B) Make a birthday present
(C) Compete in a costume contest
(D) Sell handmade jewelry

여자는 무엇을 할 계획이라고 말하는가?

(A) 공예 수업 듣기
(B) 생일 선물 만들기
(C) 코스프레 대회 참가하기
(D) 수공예 보석 판매하기

어휘 take a class 수업을 듣다 craft 공예품을 만들다 compete in ~에 참가하다 costume 복장 handmade 수제의

해설 세부 사항 관련 – 여자가 계획하는 것

여자의 마지막 대사에서 올해 친구 생일에 줄 팔찌를 만들려고 한다(But I'm going to make a bracelet to give my friend for her birthday this year)고 말하고 있으므로 정답은 (B)이다.

▸ Paraphrasing 대화의 **make a bracelet to give my friend for her birthday**
→ 정답의 **Make a birthday present**

65-67 대화 + 전화번호부

W-Am	Raynor University campus helpline.
M-Cn	**65Hi, my name is Neal Powell, and I'm an undergraduate majoring in chemistry here.**
W-Am	Hello, Neal. What can I do for you today?
M-Cn	Well, my parents are coming to visit me this semester, and they need a place to stay. I live on campus, so I don't know the city very well. I was hoping you could recommend some inexpensive hotels.
W-Am	**66Hmm, you should talk to the housing department.** I'll transfer you. **67The staff there has been specially trained to handle these sorts of inquiries, so they can offer you some good ideas.** Please stay on the line while I look up the number.

여:	레이너 대학 캠퍼스 전화 상담 서비스입니다.
남:	안녕하세요, 제 이름은 닐 파월이라고 하는데요, 이곳에서 화학을 전공하고 있는 학부생입니다.
여:	안녕하세요, 닐. 오늘 무엇을 도와드릴까요?
남:	부모님이 이번 학기에 방문하실 예정인데요, 계실 곳이 필요한 상황입니다. 저는 기숙사에 있어서 도심은 잘 모르거든요. 저렴한 호텔을 몇 군데만 추천해 주셨으면 해서요.
여:	음, 그러면 주거 담당 부서에 연락해 보셔야 할 것 같습니다. 제가 연결해 드리도록 하겠습니다. 그 부서 직원들은 해당 문의 사항을 처리해 드리는 전문 교육을 받은 분들이라 적합한 곳을 알려드릴 수 있을 겁니다. 번호를 찾아보는 동안 잠시 대기해 주시기 바랍니다.

어휘 helpline 전화 상담 서비스 undergraduate 학부생, 대학생 major in ~을 전공하다 chemistry 화학 semester 학기 live on campus 기숙사에 살다 housing department 주거 담당 부서 transfer (전화를) 연결하다 train 교육하다 handle 다루다[처리하다] sort 종류 inquiry 질문, 문의 stay on the line (전화를) 끊지 않고 기다리다, 대기하다 look up ~을 찾아보다

Department	Extension #
Admissions	101
66Housing	102
Purchasing	103
Security	104

부서	내선 번호
입학	101
주거	**102**
구매	103
보안	104

65

Who most likely is the man?

(A) A government researcher
(B) A science professor
(C) An educational administrator
(D) A university student

남자는 누구이겠는가?

(A) 정부 기관 연구원
(B) 이공계 교수
(C) 교육행정가
(D) 대학생

어휘 government 정부 researcher 연구자 educational administrator 교육행정가

해설 전체 내용 관련 – 남자의 직업

남자의 첫 번째 대사에서 이 대학교에서 화학을 전공하는 학부생(I'm an undergraduate majoring in chemistry here at the university)이라고 말하고 있으므로 남자의 직업은 대학생임을 알 수 있다. 따라서 정답은 (D)이다.

▸ Paraphrasing 대화의 **undergraduate**
→ 정답의 **a university student**

66

Look at the graphic. Which number will the woman dial?

(A) 101
(B) 102
(C) 103
(D) 104

시각 정보에 의하면, 여자는 몇 번으로 전화를 걸 것인가?

(A) 101번
(B) 102번
(C) 103번
(D) 104번

해설 세부 사항 관련 – 여자가 걸 전화번호

여자의 마지막 대사에서 남자에게 주거 담당 부서에 전화를 걸어야 한다고 말하고, 해당 번호로 연결해 주겠다(you should talk to the housing department. I'll transfer you)고 했다. 시각 정보에 따르면 주거 담당 부서의 내선 번호는 102번이므로 정답은 (B)이다.

67

According to the woman, what makes some staff able to help?

(A) Their artistic skills
(B) Their convenient schedule
(C) Their relevant training
(D) Their access to an online database

50

여자에 따르면 일부 직원들이 도와줄 수 있는 이유는 무엇인가?
(A) 예술적 역량을 갖추고 있기 때문에
(B) 편한 일정 때문에
(C) **관련 교육을 받았기 때문에**
(D) 온라인 데이터베이스에 접근할 수 있기 때문에

어휘 artistic 예술적인 skill 기술, 역량 convenient 편리한 relevant 관련 있는 access to ~에의 접근[출입]

해설 세부 사항 관련 – 특정 직원들이 도움을 줄 거라고 말하는 이유

여자의 마지막 대사에서 주거 담당 부서 직원들이 이러한 문의를 처리하도록 전문적으로 교육을 받았기 때문에 적절한 제안을 해 줄 수 있다(The staff there has been specially trained to handle these sorts of inquiries, so they can offer you some good ideas)고 말하고 있으므로 주거 담당 부서 직원들은 관련 교육을 받았음을 알 수 있다. 따라서 정답은 (C)이다.

68-70 대화 + 가격표

M-Au	Hi, I'm interested in getting satellite television service for my home, and heard your company has packages with lots of sports channels. **68I especially like classic football matches.**
W-Br	Yes, our standard package has more than twenty sports channels, and some of them show that kind of content. This brochure has the current list.
M-Au	Wow, these channels are awesome! How much does this package cost?
W-Br	It varies by the length of your contract. Here's a price chart.
M-Au	Hmm... **69I guess I'd better go with a two-year contract.**
W-Br	Great choice. Just a second. **70I'll check our calendar to see when we could send a technician out to your home.**

남:	안녕하세요, 집에 위성 TV를 설치할까 하던 차에 귀사에 스포츠 채널이 다양한 패키지 상품이 있다고 들었어요. **저는 특히 유명 축구 경기를 좋아합니다.**
여:	네, 일반 패키지에는 20개 이상의 스포츠 채널이 있고 일부 채널에서 말씀하신 경기 방송을 보여줍니다. 이 안내 책자에 현재 방송되는 목록이 있습니다.
남:	와, 괜찮은 채널들이네요! 이 패키지는 얼마인가요?
여:	계약 기간에 따라 달라집니다. 여기 가격표가 있어요.
남:	흠… **2년 약정이 좋겠어요.**
여:	훌륭한 선택입니다. 잠시만요. **댁으로 기사를 언제 보낼 수 있는지 일정을 확인해 볼게요.**

어휘 be interested in ~에 관심 있다 satellite television 위성 TV package 세트 판매 상품 classic (시합이) 유명한 match 경기 standard 일반적인 content 콘텐츠 brochure 소책자 current 현재의 list 목록 awesome 굉장한 cost (비용이) 들다 vary 각기 다르다 length (시간 등의) 길이 contract 계약(서) go with (제안 등을) 받아들이다 technician 기술자, 기사

Duration of contract	Price per month
1 month	$60
6 months	$45
1 year	$40
69 2 years	$35

약정 기간	월정액
1개월	60달러
6개월	45달러
1년	40달러
2년	35달러

68

What most likely does the man like to watch?
(A) Music programs
(B) Travel documentaries
(C) Sports games
(D) Classic films

남자가 시청하고 싶은 것은 무엇이겠는가?
(A) 음악 프로그램
(B) 여행 다큐멘터리
(C) **스포츠 경기**
(D) 명화

해설 세부 사항 관련 – 남자가 시청하고 싶은 것

남자의 첫 번째 대사에서 특히 유명한 축구 경기를 좋아한다(I especially like classic football matches)고 했으므로 정답은 (C)이다.

▸▸ **Paraphrasing** 대화의 football matches → 정답의 Sports games

69

Look at the graphic. How much will the man most likely pay per month?
(A) $60
(B) $45
(C) $40
(D) $35

시각 정보에 의하면, 남자는 매달 얼마를 지불하겠는가?
(A) 60달러
(B) 45달러
(C) 40달러
(D) **35달러**

해설 시각 정보 연계 – 남자가 지불할 요금

남자의 마지막 대사에서 2년 약정이 좋겠다(I guess I'd better go with a two-year contract)고 했다. 시각 정보에 따르면 2년 약정은 35달러이므로 정답은 (D)이다.

70

What will the woman do next?

(A) Look at a calendar
(B) Call a technician
(C) Provide a paper contract
(D) Turn on a model television

여자는 다음으로 무엇을 할 것인가?

(A) 일정 살펴보기
(B) 기술자에게 전화하기
(C) 약정서 제공하기
(D) 모델 TV 켜기

어휘 turn on (전원을) 켜다

해설 세부 사항 관련 – 여자가 다음으로 할 일
여자의 마지막 대사에서 댁에 기술자를 언제 보낼 수 있는지 일정을 확인하겠다(I'll check our calendar to see when we could send a technician out to your home)고 했으므로 정답은 (A)이다.

> ▸▸ Paraphrasing 대화의 **check our calendar**
> → 정답의 **Look at a calendar**

Part 4

71-73 공지

W-Br **71I gathered you all here today to announce that a film crew will be visiting us here at the factory over the next few days.** They're going to film some of you at work in order to create a video about how washing machines are made, from raw materials to shipping preparation. It's going to be posted on the Web site for the Organization of Appliance Manufacturers. **72This is a chance to impress distributors and consumers with our skill and high standards. 73I've posted a memo with more information on the break room board, and I need everyone to look it over before leaving today.** If you have any questions, you can ask your managers. Thank you.

앞으로 며칠간 영상촬영팀이 이 공장을 방문한다는 것을 알리기 위해 여러분을 소집했습니다. 영상촬영팀은 원자재부터 운송 준비에 이르는 세탁기 제조 과정에 대한 동영상 제작을 위해 근무 중인 여러분 몇몇을 촬영할 것입니다. 해당 동영상은 가전 제품 제조사 협회 웹사이트에 게시될 예정입니다. 이는 유통업체 및 소비자들에게 우리의 기술과 높은 수준으로 깊은 인상을 남길 수 있는 기회입니다. 휴게실 게시판에 더 자세한 정보가 담긴 메모를 게시하였으니 오늘 퇴근 전에 모두 검토해 주시길 바랍니다. 질문이 있으면 관리자에게 문의하십시오. 감사합니다.

어휘 gather 모으다 announce 발표하다, 알리다 film 영상, 영화; 촬영하다 crew (함께 일하는) 조, 반, 팀 factory 공장 at work 근무 중인, 작업 중인 in order to ~하기 위해 create 제작하다 washing machine 세탁기 raw material 원자재 shipping 운송 preparation 준비 post 게시하다 organization 조직, 단체 appliance 가전 제품 manufacturer 제조사 impress with ~로 강한 인상을 남기다 distributor 유통업체 consumer 소비자 skill 기술 standard 수준, 기준 break room 휴게실 board 게시판 look over ~을 살펴보다

71

Where does the speaker work?

(A) At a manufacturing plant
(B) At an appliance store
(C) At a shipping center
(D) At an industry association

화자는 어디에서 근무하는가?

(A) 제조 공장
(B) 가전 제품 대리점
(C) 물류 센터
(D) 산업 협회

어휘 manufacturing plant 제조 공장 industry 산업, 업계 association 협회

해설 전체 내용 관련 – 화자의 근무지
지문 초반부에서 화자가 영상촬영팀이 공장을 방문한다는 것을 알리기 위해 소집했다(I gathered you all here today to announce that a film crew will be visiting us here at the factory over the next few days)라고 했으므로 정답은 (A)이다.

> ▸▸ Paraphrasing 담화의 **factory** → 정답의 **manufacturing plant**

72

What does the company plan to use the video for?

(A) Organizing a celebration
(B) Publicizing its strengths
(C) Educating its employees
(D) Discovering potential problems

회사는 동영상을 어디에 쓸 계획인가?

(A) 축하 행사 기획하기
(B) 회사의 장점 홍보하기
(C) 직원 교육하기
(D) 잠재적 문제들 발견하기

어휘 organize 조직하다, 준비하다 celebration 축하 행사 publicize 홍보하다 strength 장점, 강점 educate 교육하다 employee 직원 discover 발견하다 potential 잠재적인

해설 세부 사항 관련 – 동영상 활용 계획
지문 중반부에서 화자가 유통업체 및 소비자들에게 우리의 기술과 높은 수준으로 깊은 인상을 남길 수 있는 기회(This is a chance to impress distributors and consumers with our skill and high standards)라고 했으므로 정답은 (B)이다.

▸▸ Paraphrasing 담화의 impress distributors and consumers with our skill and high standards
→ 정답의 Publicizing its strengths

73

What does the speaker instruct listeners to do?

(A) Write down any questions
(B) Leave at a certain time
(C) Read a notice
(D) Tidy up a space

화자는 청자들에게 무엇을 하라고 지시하는가?

(A) 질문 적기
(B) 특정 시간에 퇴근하기
(C) 공고 읽기
(D) 공간 정리하기

어휘 write down 적다, 쓰다 notice 공고문 tidy up 깔끔하게 정리하다 space 공간

해설 세부 사항 관련 – 청자에게 지시하는 것

지문 후반부에서 화자가 청자들에게 휴게실 게시판에 자세한 정보가 담긴 메모를 게시하였으니 퇴근 전에 모두 검토해 주길 바란다(I've posted a memo with more information on the break room board, and I need everyone to look it over before leaving today)라고 했으므로 정답은 (C)이다.

▸▸ Paraphrasing 담화의 memo → 정답의 notice

74-76 회의 발췌

W-Am Let's get started. 74I called today's staff meeting to discuss some complaints we've received from our patients. 75The negative feedback has all been related to the advertisements promoting our cosmetic dentistry services. It seems the problem is with the design—patients say the print explaining the restrictions on the promotion is too small. So there are misunderstandings about the costs of the services, and what's included. We've canceled these ads, but I'm worried about the people affected already. 76We're going to decide on a way to make it up to these customers by the end of the day. If you have any ideas, please let me know.

시작합시다. 환자들로부터 접수한 불만 사항을 논의하기 위해 오늘 직원회의를 소집했습니다. 부정적 의견은 모두 우리 미용치과 서비스를 홍보하는 광고와 관련되어 있습니다. 문제는 디자인에 있는 듯 합니다. 환자들은 그 광고에 제한 사항을 설명하는 글자가 너무 작다고 합니다. 그래서 서비스 비용 및 서비스 내용에

대해 오해가 있습니다. 해당 광고를 취소했지만 이미 그렇게 서비스를 적용받은 분들이 있어서 우려됩니다. 해당 고객들에게 보상할 방안을 오늘 퇴근 전까지 결정할 것입니다. 좋은 방안이 있으면 알려주십시오.

어휘 get started 시작하다 call 소집하다 staff meeting 직원 회의 discuss 논의하다 complaint 불만 사항 receive 받다, 접수하다 patient 환자 negative 부정적인 feedback 피드백, 의견 be related to ~와 관련 있다 advertisement 광고 promote 홍보하다 cosmetic dentistry services 미용치과 서비스 seem ~처럼 보이다 print 인쇄된 활자 explain 설명하다 restriction on ~에 대한 제약[제한] promotion 홍보[판촉] 활동 misunderstanding 오해, 착오 cost 비용 include 포함하다 cancel 취소하다 ads 광고 be worried about ~에 대해 걱정하다[우려하다] affect 영향을 주다, (불리하게) 작용하다 decide on ~에 대해 결정하다 way 방법 make it up to ~에게 보상하다 customer 고객

74

Who most likely are the listeners?

(A) Dental clinic workers
(B) Tax accountants
(C) Hair salon staff
(D) Travel agents

청자들은 누구이겠는가?

(A) 치과 직원
(B) 세무사
(C) 미용실 직원
(D) 여행사 직원

어휘 dental clinic 치과 tax 세금 accountant 회계사 hair salon 미용실 agent 대리인, 중개인

해설 전체 내용 관련 – 청자의 신분

지문 초반부에서 화자가 환자들로부터 접수한 불만 사항을 논의하기 위해 직원회의를 소집했다(I called today's staff meeting to discuss some complaints we've received from our patients)고 했으므로 정답은 (A)이다.

▸▸ Paraphrasing 담화의 dentistry services
→ 정답의 dental clinic

75

What problem is the speaker discussing?

(A) Mislabeled computer files
(B) Undersized equipment
(C) Unsatisfactory customer service
(D) Misleading advertisements

화자가 논의하는 문제는 무엇인가?

(A) 제목이 틀린 컴퓨터 파일
(B) 소형 장비
(C) 만족스럽지 못한 고객 서비스
(D) 오해의 소지가 있는 광고

어휘 mislabel 라벨을 잘못 붙이다 undersized 소형의 equipment 장비 unsatisfactory 만족스럽지 못한 misleading 오도하는, 오해의 소지가 있는

지문 중반부에서 화자가 부정적 의견은 모두 미용치과 서비스를 홍보하는 광고와 관련 있다(The negative feedback has all been related to the advertisements promoting our cosmetic dentistry services)고 하면서 문제는 디자인인데 그 광고에 제한 사항을 설명하는 글자가 너무 작아 서비스 비용 및 서비스 내용에 대해 오해가 있었다(It seems the problem is with the design ~ So there are misunderstandings about the costs of the services, and what's included)고 했다. 따라서 정답은 (D)이다.

>> Paraphrasing 담화의 misunderstandings
→ 정답의 misleading

76

What will happen by the end of the day?

(A) A workshop will be announced.
(B) A form of compensation will be determined.
(C) Part of the workplace will be cleared out.
(D) Some coupons will be distributed.

오늘 퇴근 전에 무슨 일이 있을 것인가?

(A) 워크숍 공지가 있을 것이다.
(B) 보상 방식이 결정될 것이다.
(C) 작업장 일부가 정리될 것이다.
(D) 쿠폰이 배부될 것이다.

어휘 announce 공지하다 form 형태, 방식 compensation 보상 determine 결정하다 workplace 직장, 업무 현장 clear out 청소하다, 정리하다 distribute 나누어 주다, 배부하다

해설 세부 사항 관련 – 퇴근 전에 있을 일

지문 후반부에서 화자가 해당 고객들에게 보상할 방안을 퇴근 전까지 결정할 것이다(We're going to decide on a way to make it up to these customers by the end of the day)라고 했으므로 정답은 (B)이다.

>> Paraphrasing 담화의 are going to decide on a way to make it up → 정답의 compensation will be determined

77-79 전화 메시지

M-Cn Hi, this is Bill Johnson with Standec Real Estate. **77I'm glad I could show you around the new Courtway apartment building last Thursday.** I just want to confirm that you're still interested in renting the one-bedroom unit— its rental price is, of course, quite affordable. Now... you'd be among the first residents to move in. **78Uh, you may need a little patience as crews finish up painting and electrical work.** Still, I think it's a great option for you. **79I'm going to e-mail you the rental contract right now, so take a look at it when you get a chance.** Then, I'll call you later this week to discuss it.

안녕하세요, 스탠덱 부동산의 빌 존슨입니다. **지난 목요일에 신축 코트웨이 아파트 건물을 보여드릴 수 있어서 기뻤습니다.** 여전히 침실 한 개짜리 아파트 임차에 관심 있으신지 확인하려고 하는데요. 물론 임대료는 매우 저렴합니다. 그리고 **… 귀하는 첫 입주자들 중 한 분이 될 겁니다.** 음, 직원들이 페인트 작업과 전기 작업을 마무리해야 하니 조금 기다리셔야 할 수도 있습니다. 그래도 귀하께 훌륭한 선택이라고 생각합니다. **지금 바로 임대 계약서를 이메일로 보내겠습니다. 시간 날 때 계약서를 봐주시기 바랍니다.** 주말께 전화해서 계약서에 관해 논의하도록 하지요.

어휘 real estate 부동산 (중개) show around 구경시켜 주다 confirm 확인하다 be interested in ~에 관심이 있다 rent 임차하다, 임대하다 unit (공동 주택 내의) 한 가구 rental price 임대료 affordable 저렴한 resident 거주자, 주민 move in 이사 오다 patience 인내심 crew (함께 일하는) 조, 반, 팀 finish up ~을 끝내다, 마무리 짓다 electrical work 전기 작업 option 선택지 contract 계약 chance 기회 discuss 논의하다

77

What most likely did the speaker do last Thursday?

(A) He attended a seminar.
(B) He trained a sales associate.
(C) He gave a building tour.
(D) He helped renovate an office.

화자는 지난 목요일에 무엇을 했겠는가?

(A) 세미나에 참석했다.
(B) 판매 사원을 교육했다.
(C) 건물 견학을 안내했다.
(D) 사무실 개조를 도왔다.

어휘 attend 참석하다 train 교육하다 sales 판매[영업]의 associate (사업·직장) 동료 renovate 개조하다, 보수하다

해설 세부 사항 관련 – 화자가 지난 목요일에 한 일

지문 초반부에서 화자가 지난 목요일에 신축 코트웨이 아파트 건물을 보여줄 수 있어서 기뻤다(I'm glad I could show you around the new Courtway apartment building last Thursday)고 했으므로 정답은 (C)이다.

>> Paraphrasing 담화의 **show you around the new Courtway apartment building** → 정답의 **gave a building tour**

78

Why does the speaker say, "you'd be among the first residents to move in"?

(A) To highlight possible inconveniences
(B) To express frustration with a timeline
(C) To emphasize that an area is quiet
(D) To recommend seizing an opportunity

화자가 "귀하는 첫 입주자들 중 한 분이 될 겁니다"라고 말한 이유는 무엇인가?

(A) 발생 가능한 불편함을 강조하기 위해
(B) 시간표에 불만을 나타내기 위해
(C) 어떤 지역이 조용하다는 것을 강조하기 위해
(D) 기회를 잡으라고 권하기 위해

어휘 highlight 강조하다 possible 가능한 inconvenience 불편 express 표현하다 frustration 좌절, 불만 timeline 시간표 emphasize 강조하다 seize 잡다 opportunity 기회

해설 화자의 의도 파악 – 첫 입주자들 중 한 사람이 될 거라는 말한 이유

인용문 뒤에 직원들이 페인트 작업과 전기 작업을 마무리해야 하므로 조금 기다려야 할 수도 있다(you may need a little patience as crews finish up painting and electrical work)고 했다. 따라서 문맥상 첫 입주자들 중 한 사람이 될 거라는 말은 추후 발생할 수 있는 불편 사항을 강조하기 위한 것임을 알 수 있으므로 정답은 (A)이다.

79

What is the listener asked to do?

(A) Fill out a form
(B) Return a phone call
(C) Look for a contact list
(D) Check an e-mail

청자는 무엇을 하라는 요청을 받는가?

(A) 양식 작성하기
(B) 회신 전화하기
(C) 연락처 목록 찾기
(D) 이메일 확인하기

어휘 fill out 작성하다 return 회답하다 contact 연락(처)

해설 세부 사항 관련 – 청자가 요청받은 일

지문 후반부에서 화자가 지금 바로 임대 계약서를 이메일로 보낼 테니 시간 날 때 계약서를 보라(I'm going to e-mail you the rental contract right now, so take a look at it when you get a chance)고 했으므로 정답은 (D)이다.

▸▸ Paraphrasing 담화의 take a look at it
→ 정답의 Check an e-mail

80-82 담화

W-Br 80All right, it's almost time to begin auditions for the Kench City Orchestra's new violinist, so let me explain our process to you. Each of you will be asked to take the stage individually and play the musical pieces that were listed in the online job posting. To determine the order, please take a ticket from the box on this table. 81The person who draws the ticket numbered "one" will go first, "two" will go second, and so on. 82Shortly after you've all finished, our judges will choose three candidates to move on to the second and final stage, which will take place later this week. Good luck, everyone.

자, 켄츠 시티 오케스트라의 신입 바이올리니스트 오디션을 시작할 시간이 다 됐군요. 제가 절차를 설명해 드리겠습니다. 각자 단독으로 무대에 올라 온라인 구인 광고에 제시된 음악 작품을 연주하라는 요청을 받을 것입니다. 순서를 정하기 위해서, 탁자 위에 있는 상자에서 표를 꺼내주십시오. "1"번 표를 뽑으신 분이 첫 번째, "2"번이 두 번째 등으로 이어집니다. 모두 마치는 대로 심사위원들이 이번 주말로 예정된 두 번째이자 최종 무대에 설 세 명의 후보자들을 선정할 것입니다. 모두 행운을 빕니다.

어휘 all right (상대방의 관심을 끌 때) 자, 저 almost 거의 begin 시작하다 audition 오디션 explain 설명하다 process 절차, 진행 each 각각 take the stage 무대에 오르다 individually 개별적으로 musical piece 음악 작품 be listed 열거되다 job posting 구인 광고 determine 결정하다 order 순서 ticket 표 draw 뽑다 and so on 기타 등등 shortly after ~직후에 judge 심사위원 choose 선택하다, 선정하다 candidate 후보자 move on to ~로 옮기다[이동하다] take place 개최되다, 일어나다 good luck 행운을 빕니다

80

What is the speaker preparing to do?

(A) Rehearse a performance
(B) Photograph a concert hall
(C) Hold auditions for a position
(D) Make supplies for a play

화자는 무엇을 하려고 준비하는가?

(A) 공연 리허설
(B) 콘서트홀 사진 촬영
(C) 일자리를 위한 오디션 개최
(D) 연극을 위한 소품 만들기

어휘 rehearse 리허설을 하다, 예행연습을 하다 performance 공연 hold 열다 position 일자리 supplies 물품, 비품 play 연극

해설 세부 사항 관련 – 화자가 준비하는 일

지문 초반부에서 화자가 켄츠 시티 오케스트라의 신입 바이올리니스트 오디션을 시작할 시간이 다 됐다(it's almost time to begin auditions for the Kench City Orchestra's new violinist)고 했으므로 정답은 (C)이다.

▸▸ Paraphrasing 담화의 begin auditions for the Kench City Orchestra's new violinist
→ 정답의 hold auditions for a position

81

What are the listeners asked to take from a box?

(A) A piece of sheet music
(B) A numbered ticket
(C) A cleaning tool
(D) A pencil sketch

청자들은 상자에서 무엇을 꺼내라고 요청받는가?

(A) 악보 한 장
(B) 번호가 매겨진 티켓
(C) 청소 도구
(D) 연필 스케치

어휘 sheet music 악보 numbered 번호가 매겨진 tool 도구

해설 세부 사항 관련 – 청자들이 상자에서 꺼내야 하는 것
지문 중반부에서 화자가 "1"번 티켓을 뽑으면 첫 번째, "2"번이 두 번째 등으로 이어진다(The person who draws the ticket numbered "one" will go first, "two" will go second, and so on)고 했으므로 정답은 (B)이다.

82

What will happen after the session?

(A) Finalists will be chosen.
(B) Permits will be issued.
(C) A song will be recorded.
(D) A stage will be redecorated.

이 시간 이후에는 무슨 일이 있는가?

(A) 결선 진출자가 선정될 것이다.
(B) 허가증이 발급될 것이다.
(C) 노래가 녹음될 것이다.
(D) 무대가 새롭게 단장될 것이다.

어휘 finalist 결승전 출전자 permit 허가증 issue 발급하다 record 녹음하다, 녹화하다 stage 무대 redecorate 개조하다, 다시 꾸미다

해설 세부 사항 관련 – 오디션 이후에 일어날 일
지문 후반부에서 화자가 모두 마치는 대로 심사위원들이 이번 주말로 예정된 두 번째이자 최종 무대에 설 세 명의 후보자들을 선정할 것(Shortly after you've all finished, our judges will choose three candidates to move on to the second and final stage, which will take place later this week)이라고 했으므로 정답은 (A)이다.

▸▸ Paraphrasing 담화의 candidates to move on to the second and final stage → 정답의 finalists

83-85 방송

M-Au This is Terry Ruiz with a local news update. **83The City of Lamott has announced that the new cycling trail at Lamott City Park will open this Friday.** The trail development project began a year ago thanks to the persistence of the Lamott Association, a citizens' group. **84Its members repeatedly asked the city council to set aside government funds for a new trail.** Once the council finally approved the idea in March, construction proceeded quickly. **85Everyone in the community is encouraged to come out and ride the trail on opening day, and the park district will provide visitors with free lemonade and juice drinks all day long.**

지역 뉴스를 전해 드리는 테리 루이즈입니다. 라모트 시는 새로운 자전거 전용 도로가 오는 금요일에 개통된다고 발표했습니다. 이 전용 도로 개발 사업은 시민 단체인 라모트 어소시에이션의 끈기 덕에 일년 전에 시작되었습니다. 단체 회원

들은 새로운 전용 도로를 위한 정부 지원금을 확보해 달라고 시의회에 여러 차례 요구했습니다. 3월에 의회가 마침내 이 안을 승인하자마자 공사는 신속하게 진행되었습니다. 지역 주민 모두 개통일에 참석하셔서 전용 도로를 이용해 주시기 바라며, 공원 지구에서는 방문객들에게 하루 종일 무료 레모네이드 및 주스를 제공할 예정입니다.

어휘 local 지역의 update 최신 소식 announce 발표하다 cycling trail 자전거 전용 도로 open 개통하다 development project 개발 사업 thanks to ~ 덕분에 persistence 고집, 끈기 citizen 시민 repeatedly 여러 차례 city council 시의회 set aside (특정 목적을 위해 돈 등을) 따로 떼어 두다 fund 자금 once ~하자마자 approve 승인하다 construction 공사 proceed 진행되다 community 지역사회 be encouraged to ~하라고 장려되다 opening day 개장일 district 지역, 지구 provide with ~을 제공하다 visitor 방문객 free 무료의 all day long 하루 종일

83

What does the speaker say is opening this week?

(A) A bicycle trail
(B) A concert venue
(C) A roller coaster
(D) A water fountain

화자는 이번 주에 무엇이 개통된다고 말하는가?

(A) 자전거 도로
(B) 콘서트 장소
(C) 롤러코스터
(D) 분수

어휘 venue 장소, 개최지 fountain 분수

해설 세부 사항 관련 – 이번 주에 개통되는 것
지문 초반부에서 화자가 라모트 시는 새로운 자전거 전용 도로가 오는 금요일에 개통된다고 발표했다(The City of Lamott has announced that the new cycling trail at Lamott City Park will open this Friday)고 했으므로 정답은 (A)이다.

▸▸ Paraphrasing 담화의 cycling trail → 정답의 bicycle trail

84

What did a citizens' group do to support the project?

(A) Removed trash from the park
(B) Spoke to government officials
(C) Donated necessary funds
(D) Assisted with construction

프로젝트를 지원하기 위해 시민 단체가 한 일은 무엇인가?

(A) 공원에서 쓰레기를 치웠다
(B) 공무원들에게 이야기했다
(C) 필요한 자금을 기부했다
(D) 공사를 도왔다

어휘 remove 제거하다 trash 쓰레기 government official 관리, 국가 공무원 donate 기부하다 necessary 필요한 assist with ~를 돕다

해설 세부 사항 관련 – 사업 지연의 원인

지문 중반부에서 단체 회원들은 새로운 전용 도로를 위한 정부 지원금을 확보해 달라고 시의회에 여러 차례 요구했다(Its members repeatedly asked the city council to set aside government funds for a new trail)고 했으므로 정답은 (B)이다.

▸▸ Paraphrasing 담화의 **the city council**
→ 정답의 **government officials**

85

What will park visitors get for free on Friday?

(A) Parking
(B) Fitness instruction
(C) Beverages
(D) T-shirts

공원 방문객들은 금요일에 어떤 무료 혜택을 받을 것인가?
(A) 주차
(B) 체력 단련 지도
(C) 음료
(D) 티셔츠

어휘 parking 주차 fitness 신체 단련 instruction 가르침, 지도
beverage 음료

해설 세부 사항 관련 – 방문객들에게 무료로 제공되는 것

지문 후반부에서 개통일에 지역 주민 모두 개통일에 참석해 전용 도로를 이용해 주길 바라며, 공원 지구에서는 방문객들에게 하루 종일 무료 레모네이드 및 주스를 제공할 예정이다(Everyone in the community is encouraged to come out and ride the trail on opening day, and the park district will provide visitors with free lemonade and juice drinks all day long)라고 했으므로 정답은 (C)이다.

▸▸ Paraphrasing 담화의 **lemonade and juice drinks**
→ 정답의 **beverages**

86-88 전화 메시지

M-Cn Hi, Griffin. It's Yasser from work. 86I wanted to let you know my thoughts on the paper you wrote summarizing your suggestion for how to spend the team's budget surplus. Sorry to bother you on the weekend, but I couldn't catch you before you left yesterday. 87Now, I know you mostly do technical tasks, but if you're interested, I'd like to assign you more writing work in the future. 88There's a shortage of specialists, and reading the paper, I was struck by how you explained a complicated idea in such clear, persuasive language. Not everyone can do that. I believe you have a promising future in our company. Please give my offer some thought.

안녕하세요, 그리핀 씨. 야세르입니다. 팀의 흑자 예산을 어떻게 쓸지를 요약한 귀하의 제안서에 대해 제 의견을 말씀드리고 싶습니다. 주말에 방해해서 죄송합니다만, 어제 퇴근 전에 뵙지를 못해서요. 저, 대체로 기술적인 업무를 맡고 계시다는 건 알지만 관심이 있다면 앞으로는 문서 작성 업무를 더 맡기고 싶습니다. 전문가가 부족한 상황인데 문서를 읽어 보니 복잡한 생각을 그렇게 명료하고 설득력 있는 언어로 설명하셔서 놀랐습니다. 아무나 할 수 있는 일은 아니죠. 전도 유망한 직원이라는 생각이 드네요. 한번 생각해 보세요.

어휘 thoughts 의견, 견해 summarize 요약하다 suggestion 제안 spend 지출하다, 소비하다 budget surplus 흑자 예산 bother 방해하다, 귀찮게 하다 weekend 주말 catch 만나다, 보다 mostly 대체로 technical 기술적인 task 임무, 업무 assign 할당하다 shortage 부족 specialist 전문가 be struck by ~에 감명받다 complicated 복잡한 clear 분명한, 명료한 persuasive 설득력 있는 promising 유망한 give a thought 고려하다

86

What is the telephone message mainly about?

(A) A written proposal
(B) A team's decision
(C) A colleague's retirement
(D) A malfunctioning machine

전화 내용은 주로 무엇에 관한 것인가?
(A) 서면 제안서
(B) 팀의 결정
(C) 동료의 은퇴
(D) 오작동하는 기계

어휘 written 서면으로 된 proposal 제안 decision 결정 colleague 동료 retirement 은퇴 malfunction 오작동하다

해설 전체 내용 관련 – 전화의 내용

지문 초반부에서 화자가 팀의 흑자 예산 지출 방법을 요약한 제안서에 대한 의견을 이야기하고 싶다(I wanted to let you know my thoughts on the paper you wrote summarizing your suggestion for how to spend the team's budget surplus)고 했으므로 정답은 (A)이다.

▸▸ Paraphrasing 담화의 **the paper you wrote summarizing your suggestion**
→ 정답의 **written proposal**

87

What does the speaker offer to do?

(A) Circulate a technical memo
(B) Revise a detail of a financial plan
(C) Assign a certain type of task to the listener
(D) Obtain an outside specialist's input on an idea

화자는 무엇을 해 주겠다고 하는가?
(A) 업무 회람 배포하기
(B) 재무 계획의 세부 사항 수정하기
(C) 청자에게 특정 업무 할당하기
(D) 아이디어에 대해 외부 전문가로부터 조언 구하기

circulate 배포하다 technical 전문적인 memo 회람 revise 변경하다, 수정하다 detail 세부 사항 financial 재정의, 금융의 obtain 얻다, 획득하다 specialist 전문가 input 조언

해설 세부 사항 관련 – 화자의 제안 사항

지문 중반부에서 화자가 대체로 기술적인 업무를 맡고 있다는 건 알지만 관심이 있다면 앞으로는 문서 작성 업무를 더 맡기고 싶다(I know you mostly do technical tasks, but if you're interested, I'd like to assign you more writing work in the future)고 했으므로 정답은 (C)이다.

> ▸▸ Paraphrasing 담화의 **assign you more writing work in the future**
> → 정답의 **Assign a certain type of task**

88

Why does the speaker say, "Not everyone can do that"?

(A) To give a compliment
(B) To oppose a recommendation
(C) To clarify his job duties
(D) To offer an apology

화자가 "아무나 할 수 있는 일은 아니죠."라고 말한 이유는 무엇인가?

(A) 칭찬하기 위해
(B) 추천을 반대하기 위해
(C) 업무를 명확하게 하기 위해
(D) 사과를 하기 위해

어휘 compliment 칭찬 oppose 반대하다 duties 직무, 직책 clarify 명확하게 하다 offer an apology 사과하다

해설 화자의 의도 파악 – 아무나 할 수 있는 일이 아니라고 말하는 이유

인용문 바로 앞 문장에서 화자가 문서를 읽어 보니 복잡한 생각을 명료하고 설득력 있는 언어로 설명해서 놀랐다(reading the paper, I was struck by how you explained a complicated idea in such clear, persuasive language)고 말한 후 아무나 할 수 있는 일이 아니라고 했다. 따라서 문맥상 청자가 한 일을 칭찬하기 위한 것임을 알 수 있으므로 정답은 (A)이다.

89-91 담화

W-Br All right. **89I'd like to briefly go over our company's procedures for reimbursing expenses that are incurred while on business trips.** All staff must submit paper receipts to the finance department for expenses to be repaid, and all travel must be authorized. **90I'm raising this subject now because our recent good fortune in convincing Jackson Welter Holdings to bring their business to us will mean an increased number of business trips.** Management wants to make sure that this change doesn't cause unnecessary problems. **91For easy reference, all our corporate expense policies are covered in this paper guidebook. I'll hand one out to each of you now.**

자, 출장 중 발생한 경비 환급과 관련한 회사 절차를 간략히 살펴보겠습니다. 모든 직원은 비용을 환급받으려면 반드시 서면 영수증을 재무부에 제출해야 하며 모든 출장은 반드시 허가를 받아야 한다는 점을 알려드립니다. 이 의제를 제기하는 이유는 최근에 다행히 잭슨 웰터 홀딩스를 설득해 거래를 확보함에 따라 출장이 늘어날 예정이기 때문입니다. 경영진은 이러한 변화로 쓸데없는 문제가 발생하지 않도록 분명히 하고자 합니다. 쉽게 참고하실 수 있도록 회사 경비 정책이 모두 나와 있는 편람을 준비했습니다. 지금 한 부씩 나누어 드리겠습니다.

어휘 briefly 간단히 go over ~을 검토하다 procedure 절차 reimburse 배상하다, 환급하다 expenses (업무상의) 경비 incur 발생시키다 on business trips 출장 중인 submit 제출하다 receipt 영수증 finance department 재무부 repay 상환하다 authorize 인가하다 raise 제기하다 recent 최근의 good fortune 행운 convince 설득하다 increased 증가한 management 경영진 cause 유발하다 unnecessary 불필요한, 쓸데없는 reference 참고 corporate 기업의, 회사의, 법인의 policy 정책, 방침 cover 다루다, 포함시키다 guidebook 편람 hand out to ~에게 나누어 주다

89

What is the speaker mainly discussing?

(A) Product demonstration procedures
(B) Strategies for negotiating contracts
(C) Nominations for staff awards
(D) Travel reimbursement policies

화자는 주로 무엇에 대해 논의하고 있는가?

(A) 제품 시연 절차
(B) 계약 협상 전략
(C) 사원상 후보 지명
(D) 출장 경비 환급 정책

어휘 product 제품 demonstration 시연 strategy 전략 negotiate 협상하다, 교섭하다 contract 계약 nomination 지명, 추천, 임명 award 상 reimbursement 상환, 환급

해설 전체 내용 관련 – 화자의 논의 사항

지문 초반부에서 화자가 출장 중 발생한 경비 환급과 관련한 회사의 절차를 간략히 살펴보겠다(I'd like to briefly go over our company's procedures for reimbursing expenses that are incurred while on business trips)고 했으므로 정답은 (D)이다.

> ▸▸ Paraphrasing 담화의 **procedures for reimbursing expenses that are incurred while on business trips**
> → 정답의 **travel reimbursement policies**

90

What recently happened at the speaker's company?

(A) A new client was acquired.
(B) An executive was transferred.
(C) Some departments were restructured.
(D) Some rules were changed.

화자의 회사에 최근 무슨 일이 있었는가?

(A) 새로운 고객을 확보했다.
(B) 임원 한 사람이 전근을 갔다.
(C) 일부 부서들이 구조조정되었다.
(D) 일부 규칙들이 변경되었다.

어휘 client 고객 acquire 얻다 executive 임원, 간부 transfer 옮기다, 전근 보내다 department 부서 restructure 구조조정하다 rule 규칙

해설 세부 사항 관련 – 최근 회사에 일어난 일

지문 중반부에서 화자가 이 의제를 제기하는 이유는 최근에 다행히 잭슨 웰터 홀딩스를 설득해 거래를 확보함에 따라 출장이 늘어날 것(I'm raising this subject now because our recent good fortune in convincing Jackson Welter Holdings to bring their business to us will mean an increased number of business trips)이라고 했으므로 잭슨 웰터 홀딩스라는 새로운 고객을 확보했음을 알 수 있다. 따라서 정답은 (A)이다.

▶▶ Paraphrasing 담화의 convincing Jackson Welter Holdings to bring their business to us → 정답의 A new client was acquired.

91

What will the speaker give to the listeners?

(A) Corporate credit cards
(B) Hotel vouchers
(C) Reference guides
(D) Photo ID badges

화자는 청자들에게 무엇을 줄 것인가?

(A) 법인 신용카드
(B) 호텔 쿠폰
(C) 참고용 안내서
(D) 사진 부착 신분증 배지

어휘 voucher 상품권, 할인권, 쿠폰 reference 참고, 참조 guide 안내서

해설 세부 사항 관련 – 화자가 청자들에게 나누어 줄 것

지문 후반부에서 화자가 쉽게 참고할 수 있도록 회사 경비 정책이 모두 나와 있는 편람을 준비했다(For easy reference, all our corporate expense policies are covered in this paper guidebook)고 하면서 지금 한 부씩 나누어 주겠다(I'll hand one out to each of you now)고 했으므로 정답은 (C)이다.

▶▶ Paraphrasing 담화의 guidebook → 정답의 guides

92-94 회의 발췌

M-Au Now, I'd like to finish this meeting with an update on our budget. As you know, we've set aside unusually high levels of funding for developing our Amidar-3 software package. It now looks like we'll have to make up for this by reducing some of our other expenses. **⁹²To start with, we should find less expensive vendors to**

---

provide us with office supplies. **⁹³Let's research some options online this morning, and then I'll contact you through the company messenger service this afternoon to compare results.** Probably around three P.M. **⁹⁴Uh, this isn't an urgent matter, though, so those of you with a lot of other work to do**—use your best judgment. All right, that'll be all for today.

자, 예산에 관한 소식을 끝으로 본 회의를 마치고자 합니다. 여러분도 아시다시피, 우리는 에이미더-3 소프트웨어 패키지 개발에 전례 없는 매우 높은 금액의 자금을 배정했습니다. 다른 비용을 절감해서 이를 메워야 할 것 같습니다. 우선 좀 더 저렴한 사무용품 납품업체를 찾아야 합니다. 오전에 온라인으로 몇 가지 옵션을 찾아봅시다. 그런 다음 오후에 회사 메신저 서비스로 연락해 결과를 비교하겠습니다. 오후 3시쯤이 되겠네요. 음, 하지만 긴급한 사안은 아니니 해야 할 업무가 많은 분들은 적절히 판단하시기 바랍니다. 좋습니다. 오늘은 여기까지입니다.

어휘 update on ~에 대한 최신 정보 budget 예산 set aside 챙겨두다, 확보하다 unusually 평소와 달리 level 수준, 규모 funding 자금, 재정 지원 develop 개발하다 make up for ~을 벌충하다[메우다] reduce 줄이다 expenses (업무상의) 경비 to start with 우선 vendor 판매[공급]업체 provide 제공하다 office supplies 사무용품 research 조사하다 option 선택지 contact 연락[접촉]하다 compare 비교하다 urgent 긴급한 matter 사안 judgement 판단

92

What does the speaker suggest doing?

(A) Finding cheaper sources of office supplies
(B) Rehearsing for future sales presentations
(C) Updating a company's customer list
(D) Moving up a production deadline

화자는 무엇을 하라고 제안하는가?

(A) 더 저렴한 사무용품 공급처 찾기
(B) 향후 제품 소개를 위한 예행연습하기
(C) 회사의 고객 목록 갱신하기
(D) 생산 마감일 앞당기기

어휘 source 공급자 sales presentation 제품 소개 rehearse 리허설을 하다, 예행연습을 하다 update 갱신하다 customer 고객 move up 앞당기다 production 생산 deadline 마감일

해설 세부 사항 관련 – 화자의 제안 사항

지문 중반부에서 화자가 우선 좀 더 저렴한 사무용품 납품업체를 찾아야 한다(To start with, we should find less expensive vendors to provide us with office supplies)고 했으므로 정답은 (A)이다.

▶▶ Paraphrasing 담화의 less expensive vendors to provide us with office supplies → 정답의 cheaper sources of office supplies

93

What does the speaker say he will do in the afternoon?

(A) Drive to a research center
(B) Schedule client visits
(C) Use a messaging service
(D) Design a consumer survey

화자는 오후에 무엇을 할 것이라고 말하는가?

(A) 차를 몰고 연구소로 가기
(B) 고객 방문 일정 잡기
(C) **메시지 서비스 이용하기**
(D) 소비자 설문조사 기획하기

어휘 research 연구 schedule 일정을 잡다 client 고객 design 기획하다 survey 설문 조사

해설 세부 사항 관련 – 화자가 오후에 할 일

지문 후반부에서 화자가 오전에 온라인으로 몇 가지 옵션을 찾아본 다음 오후에 회사 메신저 서비스를 통해 연락해 결과를 비교하겠다(Let's research some options online this morning, and then I'll contact you through the company messenger service this afternoon to compare results)고 했으므로 정답은 (C)이다.

▸▸ Paraphrasing   담화의 **the company messenger service** → 정답의 **a messaging service**

94

What does the speaker mean when he says, "use your best judgment"?

(A) There is no fixed dress code for an event.
(B) Listeners may prioritize other assignments.
(C) Listeners can decide when to go home.
(D) He will not be available all day today.

화자가 "적절히 판단하시기 바랍니다"라고 말하는 의미는 무엇인가?

(A) 행사에 정해진 복장 규정이 없다.
(B) **청자들은 다른 임무를 우선시할 수도 있다.**
(C) 청자들은 언제 집에 갈지 결정할 수 있다.
(D) 화자는 하루 종일 시간이 안 날 것이다.

어휘 fixed 고정된, 정해진 dress code 복장 규정 prioritize 우선시하다 assignment 임무, 과제 available 시간[여유]이 있는

해설 화자의 의도 파악 – 적절히 판단하라고 말한 의도

인용문 바로 앞 문장에서 화자가 하지만 긴급한 사안은 아니라고 말하면서 해야 할 업무가 많은 사람들(this isn't an urgent matter, though, so those of you with a lot of other work to do)을 지칭하고 있으므로, 긴급하지 않으니 다른 일이 많은 사람들은 잘 생각해서 업무의 우선순위를 따지라는 의미이다. 따라서 정답은 (B)이다.

95-97 전화 메시지 + 일정

W-Am Arturo, I just got a call from *Keller's Monthly* about doing a photo shoot featuring our botanical gardens. **96The photographers want to come for an entire day to capture the** plants in different lighting conditions. It's a great opportunity, but... **95I'm worried that the magazine staff will get in the way of our paying visitors. 96I'll post a notice near the entrance that explains the situation to visitors.** That way, it won't be a surprise for them. **97Uh, as for the date, I'd like to suggest the day before the Homenway picnic so that we have time to prepare after the weekly lecture.** How does that sound?

아르투로 씨. 우리 식물원 사진 촬영과 관련해 〈월간 켈러스〉로부터 방금 전화를 받았습니다. 사진가들이 다양한 채광 조건에서 식물들을 촬영하기 위해 종일 식물원에 있고 싶다고 합니다. 굉장한 기회지만… 잡지사 직원들이 유료 관람 방문객들에게 방해가 되지 않을지 걱정입니다. 방문객들에게 상황을 설명하는 공지문을 입구 근처에 게시할게요. 그렇게 하면 방문객들이 당황하지 않겠죠. 음, 주간 강연 이후에 준비할 시간을 확보할 수 있도록 날짜는 홈앤웨이 야유회 전날로 잡고 싶습니다. 어때요?

어휘 get a call from ~로부터 전화를 받다 photo shoot 사진 촬영 feature 특집으로 다루다 botanical garden 식물원 entire 전체의 capture 포착하다 plant 화초, 식물 lighting 조명 condition 조건 opportunity 기회 get in the way of ~를 방해하다 paying visitor 유료 방문객 post 게시하다 notice 공지 entrance 입구 explain 설명하다 situation 상황 as for ~에 대해서 말하자면 suggest 제안하다 picnic 야유회 so that ~하도록 prepare 준비하다 lecture 강연

Mon.	Tues.	Wed.	97Thurs.	Fri.	Sat.
12 Weekly Lecture	13	14	**15** Homenway Company Picnic	16	**17** Mendoza Wedding

월요일	화요일	수요일	목요일	금요일	토요일
12 주간 강연	13	14	15 홈앤웨이 야유회	16	17 멘도자 결혼식

95

What is the speaker concerned about?

(A) Inaccurate reporting
(B) Damage to plants
(C) Bad weather conditions
(D) Inconvenience to visitors

화자는 무엇을 걱정하는가?

(A) 부정확한 보고
(B) 식물에 대한 피해
(C) 악천후
(D) **방문객에게 초래되는 불편**

어휘 inaccurate 부정확한 damage to ~에 대한 피해 bad weather 악천후 condition 상태, 상황, 날씨 inconvenience 불편

지문 전반부에서 화자가 잡지사 직원들이 유료 관람 방문객들에게 방해가 되지 않을지 걱정(I'm worried that the magazine staff will get in the way of our paying visitors)이라고 했으므로 정답은 (D)이다.

▸▸ **Paraphrasing** 담화의 **get in the way of our paying visitors** → 정답의 **inconvenience to visitors**

96

What will the speaker post a notice about?

(A) The opening hours of a business
(B) The requirements for obtaining a refund
(C) The presence of photographers on site
(D) The remodeling of an indoor space

화자는 무엇에 대한 공지 사항을 게시할 것인가?
(A) 업체의 영업시간
(B) 환불 요건
(C) 현장에 자리 잡은 사진 작가
(D) 실내 공간 보수

어휘 opening hours 영업시간 requirement 요건 obtain 얻다, 획득하다 refund 환불(금) presence 존재 on site 현장에 있는 remodel 개조하다 indoor 실내의

해설 전체 내용 관련 - 공지 사항의 내용

지문 전반부에서 화자가 사진가들이 다양한 채광 조건에서 식물들을 촬영하기 위해 종일 식물원에 있고 싶어 한다(The photographers want to come for an entire day to capture the plants in different lighting conditions)고 말한 후 지문 중반부에서 방문객들에게 상황을 설명하는 공지문을 입구 근처에 게시하겠다(I'll post a notice near the entrance that explains the situation to visitors)고 했으므로 정답은 (C)이다.

▸▸ **Paraphrasing** 담화의 **The photographers want to come for an entire day** → 정답의 **The presence of photographers on site**

97

Look at the graphic. Which day does the speaker suggest scheduling the photo shoot for?

(A) Tuesday
(B) Wednesday
(C) Thursday
(D) Friday

시각 정보에 의하면, 화자는 무슨 요일에 사진 촬영 일정을 잡자고 제안하는가?
(A) 화요일
(B) 수요일
(C) 목요일
(D) 금요일

해설 시각 정보 연계 - 사진 촬영 희망일

지문 후반부에서 화자가 주간 강연 이후에 준비할 시간을 확보할 수 있도록 날짜는 홈앤웨이 야유회 전날로 잡고 싶다(as for the date, I'd like to suggest the day before the Homenway picnic so that we have time to prepare after the weekly lecture)고 했다. 시각 정보에 따르면 홈앤웨이 야유회는 목요일이므로 정답은 (B)이다.

98-100 공지 + 흐름도

M-Cn OK, quick announcement about hiring. **98Human Resources has responded to our department's concerns and agreed to let us test out a new hiring stage in the search for our newest Information Technology Specialist.** I'll just put the hiring process flow chart up on the screen... **99All right, there's the new step, after the document screening.** I really think this move is going to be beneficial. **100And we'll find out soon, because we've received dozens of applications for the specialist position just in the short time since the opening was posted.** Now, before I let you all go, I want to thank Yumiko again for proposing this idea. Excellent work.

자, 채용에 대한 간단한 안내 말씀 드립니다. 인사부에서 우리 부서의 염려를 감안해 신입 IT 전문가 모집시 새로운 채용 단계를 시험하는 데 동의했습니다. 화면에 채용 절차 순서도를 띄울게요… 됐네요. 저기 서류 심사 후에 새로운 단계가 있어요. 이 조치가 정말 유익하리라 생각합니다. 곧 알게 되겠죠. 일자리 공고 후 단시간에 수십 명이 전문가 직책에 지원했으니까요. 자, 자리를 마무리하기 전에 이 아이디어를 제안해 준 유미코 씨에게 다시 한 번 감사 드려요. 아주 훌륭해요.

어휘 quick 신속한, 빠른 announcement 안내, 발표 hiring 채용 respond to ~에 응답하다 department 부서 concern 걱정, 우려 agree to ~하기로 동의하다 test out ~을 시험해 보다 stage 단계 search 수색, 물색 Information Technology 정보통신기술(IT) specialist 전문가 process 절차 put up 게시하다 flow chart 흐름도 step 단계 document screening 서류 심사 move 조치 beneficial 이로운, 유익한 receive 받다 dozens of 수십의 application 지원(서) position (일)자리 opening 공석, 일자리 post 게시하다 let go 보내다 propose 제안하다

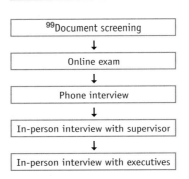

```
        99Document screening
               ↓
          Online exam
               ↓
        Phone interview
               ↓
  In-person interview with supervisor
               ↓
  In-person interview with executives
```

Test 2

서류 심사
↓
온라인 시험
↓
전화 면접
↓
관리자 대면 면접
↓
임원진 대면 면접

98

What department does the speaker most likely work for?

(A) Customer Service
(B) Public Relations
(C) Human Resources
(D) Information Technology

화자는 어느 부서에서 일하겠는가?

(A) 고객서비스부
(B) 홍보부
(C) 인사부
(D) IT부

어휘 public relations 홍보 human resources 인사부, 인적 자원

해설 전체 내용 관련 – 화자가 일하는 부서

지문 초반부에서 인사부에서 우리 부서의 염려를 감안해 신입 IT 전문가 모집 시 새로운 채용 단계를 시험하는 데 동의했다(Human Resources has responded to our department's concerns and agreed to let us test out a new hiring stage in the search for our newest Information Technology Specialist)고 했으므로 화자는 IT부에 근무한다는 것을 알 수 있다. 따라서 정답은 (D)이다.

99

Look at the graphic. Which step does the speaker say was added recently?

(A) Document screening
(B) Online exam
(C) Phone interview
(D) In-person interview with executives

시각 정보에 의하면, 화자는 최근에 무슨 단계가 추가되었다고 말하는가?

(A) 서류 심사
(B) 온라인 시험
(C) 전화 면접
(D) 임원진 대면 면접

어휘 interview 면접 in-person 대면의 executive 임원

해설 시각 정보 연계 – 최근 추가된 단계

지문 중반부에서 화자가 서류 심사 후에 새로운 단계가 있다(there's the new step, after the document screening)고 했고 시각 정보에 따르면 서류 심사 뒤에는 온라인 시험(Online exam)이 있으므로 정답은 (B)이다.

100

What does the speaker say about the position?

(A) It comes with excellent benefits.
(B) It is attracting many applicants.
(C) It is currently held by Yumiko.
(D) It will be temporary.

화자는 그 직위에 대해 뭐라고 하는가?

(A) 복지 혜택이 훌륭하다.
(B) 지원자가 많이 몰리고 있다.
(C) 현재 유미코 씨가 맡고 있다.
(D) 임시직이다.

어휘 come with ~이 딸려 있다 benefits (수당 등의) 복지 혜택 attract 끌어들이다 applicant 지원자 currently 현재 hold (직위를) 차지하다 temporary 일시적인, 임시적인

해설 세부 사항 관련 – 직위에 관한 화자의 언급

지문 후반부에서 화자가 일자리가 공지된 뒤로 단시간에 전문가 직책에 수십 명이 지원했다(because we've received dozens of applications for the specialist position just in the short time since the opening was posted)고 했으므로 정답은 (B)이다.

> ▸▸ Paraphrasing 담화의 **dozens of applications**
> → 정답의 **many applicants**

TEST 3

1 (B)	**2** (C)	**3** (D)	**4** (D)	**5** (A)
6 (C)	**7** (B)	**8** (C)	**9** (B)	**10** (A)
11 (A)	**12** (C)	**13** (C)	**14** (C)	**15** (A)
16 (A)	**17** (C)	**18** (B)	**19** (C)	**20** (C)
21 (B)	**22** (C)	**23** (A)	**24** (B)	**25** (C)
26 (A)	**27** (C)	**28** (B)	**29** (A)	**30** (C)
31 (B)	**32** (B)	**33** (C)	**34** (A)	**35** (D)
36 (A)	**37** (C)	**38** (A)	**39** (D)	**40** (A)
41 (A)	**42** (B)	**43** (B)	**44** (C)	**45** (B)
46 (B)	**47** (D)	**48** (A)	**49** (B)	**50** (D)
51 (A)	**52** (B)	**53** (D)	**54** (C)	**55** (A)
56 (D)	**57** (D)	**58** (C)	**59** (C)	**60** (C)
61 (A)	**62** (C)	**63** (B)	**64** (D)	**65** (C)
66 (C)	**67** (B)	**68** (D)	**69** (B)	**70** (A)
71 (C)	**72** (C)	**73** (B)	**74** (C)	**75** (B)
76 (A)	**77** (B)	**78** (D)	**79** (B)	**80** (C)
81 (D)	**82** (D)	**83** (A)	**84** (B)	**85** (C)
86 (D)	**87** (D)	**88** (C)	**89** (D)	**90** (B)
91 (C)	**92** (A)	**93** (A)	**94** (C)	**95** (A)
96 (B)	**97** (A)	**98** (D)	**99** (A)	**100** (B)

PART 1

1 W-Br

(A) A patient is leaving a doctor's office.
(B) A doctor is examining a patient.
(C) A woman is lifting up her arm.
(D) A physician is looking for medical equipment.

(A) 환자가 진료실을 떠나고 있다.
(B) 의사가 환자를 진찰하고 있다.
(C) 여자가 팔을 들어 올리고 있다.
(D) 의사가 진료 기구를 찾고 있다.

어휘 patient 환자 leave 떠나다 doctor's office 병원, 진료실
examine 진료하다 lift up 들어 올리다 physician 내과의사
look for ~을 찾다 medical equipment 의료 기구, 진료 기구

해설 2인 이상 등장 사진 – 사람의 동작 묘사
(A) 동사 오답. 환자가 진료를 받고 있는 상태이지 진료실을 나가는(is leaving a doctor's office) 모습이 아니므로 오답.
(B) 정답. 의사가 환자를 진찰하는(is examining a patient) 모습이므로 정답.
(C) 동사 오답. 여자가 팔을 내려 놓고 있는 상태이지 팔을 들어 올리고 있는(is lifting up her arm) 모습이 아니므로 오답.
(D) 명사 오답. 사진에 진료 기구가 보이지만 의사가 진료 기구를 찾는(is looking for medical equipment) 모습이 아니므로 오답.

2 W-Am

(A) She is plugging in a vacuum.
(B) She is making a bed.
(C) She is cleaning a carpet.
(D) She is putting on a uniform.

(A) 여자가 진공 청소기의 전원을 연결하고 있다.
(B) 여자가 침대를 정돈하고 있다.
(C) 여자가 카펫 청소하고 있다.
(D) 여자가 유니폼을 입고 있는 중이다.

어휘 plug in ~의 전원을 연결하다 vacuum 진공 청소기 make a bed
침대를 정돈하다 carpet 카펫, 양탄자 put on ~을 입다 uniform
유니폼, 제복

해설 1인 등장 사진 – 사람의 동작 묘사
(A) 명사 오답. 사진에 진공 청소기가 있지만 여자가 진공 청소기의 전원을 연결하는(is plugging in a vacuum) 모습은 아니므로 오답.
(B) 동사 오답. 여자가 침대를 정돈하는(is making a bed) 모습이 아니므로 오답.
(C) 정답. 여자가 카펫을 청소하고 있는(is cleaning a carpet) 모습이므로 정답.
(D) 동사 오답. 여자가 유니폼을 입은 상태이지 유니폼을 입는(is putting on a uniform) 동작을 하고 있지 않으므로 오답.

3 M-Cn

(A) The man is attaching some tiles to a wall.
(B) The man is cutting some electrical wires.
(C) The man is picking up a screwdriver.
(D) The man is leaning on a counter.

(A) 남자가 타일을 벽에 붙이고 있다.
(B) 남자가 전선을 자르고 있다.
(C) 남자가 드라이버를 집어 들고 있다.
(D) 남자가 카운터에 기대어 있다.

어휘 attach to ~에 부착하다 electrical wire 전선 pick up
집다, 들어 올리다 screwdriver 드라이버 lean on ~에 기대다
counter 카운터(길고 좁은 테이블)

해설 1인 등장 사진 – 사람의 상태 묘사
(A) 명사 오답. 사진에 타일이 보이지만 남자가 타일을 벽에 붙이는(is attaching some tiles to a wall) 모습은 아니므로 오답.
(B) 동사 오답. 남자가 전선을 자르는(is cutting some electrical wires) 모습이 아니므로 오답.
(C) 명사 오답. 사진에 드라이버가 있지만 남자가 드라이버를 집어 드는(is picking up a screwdriver) 모습이 아니므로 오답.

(D) 정답. 남자가 카운터에 기대어 있는(is leaning on a counter) 상태이므로 정답.

4 M-Au

(A) All of the people are seated in a circle.
(B) One of the people is exiting the room.
(C) Two of the people are touching a keyboard.
(D) One of the people is standing up.

(A) 사람들이 모두 둘러앉아 있다.
(B) 사람들 중 한 명이 방을 나가고 있다.
(C) 사람들 중 두 명이 키보드를 만지고 있다.
(D) 사람들 중 한 명이 일어서 있다.

어휘 seat 앉히다 in a circle 둥그렇게 exit 나가다 keyboard 키보드
stand up 일어서다

해설 2인 이상 등장 사진 – 사람의 동작 묘사
(A) 전치사구 오답. 두 사람이 나란히 앉아 있는 모습이지 사람들이 모두 둘러
앉아 있는(are seated in a circle) 상태가 아니므로 오답.
(B) 동사 오답. 사람들 중 한 명이 방을 나가는(is exiting the room) 모습이
아니므로 오답.
(C) 명사 오답. 사람들 중 한 명이 키보드를 만지는 모습이지 사람들 중 두 명
(Two of the people)이 키보드를 만지는 모습이 아니므로 오답.
(D) 정답. 사람들 중 한 명이 일어서 있는(is standing up) 모습이므로 정답.

5 M-Cn

(A) Some lights are suspended from a ceiling.
(B) Some stools are arranged in a circle.
(C) Some flowers have been placed by a sofa.
(D) Some windows are covered with a curtain.

(A) 전등들이 천장에 매달려 있다.
(B) 의자들이 둥그렇게 놓여 있다.
(C) 꽃이 소파 옆에 놓여 있다.
(D) 창문이 커튼에 가려져 있다.

어휘 light 전등 suspend from ~에 매달다 ceiling 천장 stool
(등받이가 없는) 의자 arrange 배열하다 place 놓다 be covered
with ~로 덮여 있다

해설 사물/배경 사진 – 사물의 위치 묘사
(A) 정답. 전등들이 천장에 매달려 있는(are suspended from a ceiling) 상
태이므로 정답.
(B) 전치사구 오답. 의자들이 일렬로 놓여 있는 상태이지 의자들이 둥그렇게 놓
여 있는(are arranged in a circle) 상태가 아니므로 오답.
(C) 전치사구 오답. 꽃이 카운터 위에 놓여 있는 상태이지 꽃이 소파 옆에 놓여
있는(have been placed by a sofa) 상태가 아니므로 오답.
(D) 사진에 없는 명사를 이용한 오답. 사진에 커튼(curtain)이 보이지 않으므로
오답.

6 W-Br

(A) A stripe is being painted on an aircraft.
(B) Some passengers are boarding an airplane.
(C) Parcels have been loaded onto some carts.
(D) A plane is taking off from an airport.

(A) 줄무늬가 항공기에 그려지는 중이다.
(B) 승객 몇 명이 비행기에 오르고 있다.
(C) 화물이 카트 몇 대에 실려 있다.
(D) 비행기가 공항에서 이륙하고 있다.

어휘 stripe 줄무늬 aircraft 항공기 passenger 승객 board 타다
parcel 소포, 화물 꾸러미 load onto ~에 (짐을) 싣다 cart 손수레,
카트 take off 이륙하다

해설 사물/배경 사진 – 사람 또는 사물 중심 묘사
(A) 동사 오답. 줄무늬가 항공기에 이미 그려져 있는 상태이지 줄무늬가 항공기에
그려지고 있는(is being painted on an aircraft) 상황이 아니므로 오답.
(B) 사진에 없는 명사를 이용한 오답. 사진에 승객들(passengers)이 보이지
않으므로 오답.
(C) 정답. 화물이 카트 몇 대에 실려 있는(have been loaded onto some
carts) 상태이므로 정답.
(D) 동사 오답. 비행기가 공항에 착륙해 있는 모습이지 공항에서 이륙하는(is
taking off from an airport) 모습이 아니므로 오답.

PART 2

7

W-Am Where should the file cabinets be delivered?
M-Au (A) Early in the morning.
(B) To the second-floor offices.
(C) Three drawers each, I think.

서류 캐비닛은 어디로 배달해야 하나요?
(A) 아침 일찍이요.
(B) 2층 사무실로요.
(C) 각각 서랍이 세 개인 것 같아요.

어휘 file 서류철 cabinet 캐비닛 deliver 배달하다 second floor 2층 drawer 서랍

해설 배달 장소를 묻는 Where 의문문

(A) 질문과 상관없는 오답. 시간을 묻는 When 의문문에 적절한 응답이므로 오답.

(B) 정답. 서류 캐비닛 배달 장소를 묻는 질문에 2층 사무실이라는 구체적인 장소를 언급하고 있으므로 정답.

(C) 연상 단어 오답. 질문의 cabinets에서 연상 가능한 drawers를 이용한 오답.

8

W-Br Why is this leather jacket's price marked down so much?

M-Cn (A) I'll count them all again for you.

(B) Only if you have a valid coupon.

(C) There's a noticeable scratch on the sleeve.

이 가죽 재킷은 왜 이렇게 할인을 많이 하나요?
(A) 당신 대신 다시 수를 세어 놓을게요.
(B) 유효한 쿠폰이 있어야만요.
(C) 소매에 눈에 띄게 긁힌 자국이 있어요.

어휘 leather jacket 가죽 재킷 mark down 가격을 인하하다 count 세다 valid 유효한 noticeable 눈에 띄는 scratch 긁힌 자국 sleeve 소매

해설 할인이 많이 되는 이유를 묻는 Why 의문문

(A) 질문과 상관없는 오답. 가죽 재킷이 왜 할인을 많이 하는지를 묻는 질문에 다시 수를 세겠다는 응답은 맥락에 맞지 않으므로 오답.

(B) 연상 단어 오답. 질문의 price 및 marked down에서 연상 가능한 coupon을 이용한 오답.

(C) 정답. 가죽 재킷이 왜 할인이 많이 되는지를 묻는 질문에 소매에 눈에 띄게 긁힌 자국이 있다는 구체적인 이유를 제시하고 있으므로 정답.

9

M-Au Did you call the cable company about the reception problem yet?

W-Am (A) He's fully capable of completing it.

(B) No, I've been busy all day.

(C) My cell phone number would be best.

수신 문제에 대해 케이블 회사에 전화해 봤어요?
(A) 그는 그것을 완수할 능력이 충분해요.
(B) 아니오, 하루 종일 바빴어요.
(C) 내 휴대전화 번호가 최고일 거예요.

어휘 reception problem 수신 문제 yet 이미, 이제 be capable of ~할 능력이 있다 fully 충분히 complete 완료하다 cell phone 휴대전화

해설 전화 통화 여부를 묻는 조동사(did) Yes/No 의문문

(A) 유사 발음 오답. 질문의 cable과 부분적으로 발음이 동일한 capable을 이용한 오답.

(B) 정답. 케이블 회사에 전화를 했는지 묻는 질문에 No로 부정적 응답을 한 후, 하루 종일 바빴다는 부연 설명을 하고 있으므로 정답.

(C) 연상 단어 오답. 질문의 reception problem에서 연상 가능한 cell phone을 이용한 오답.

10

M-Cn Has Ms. Lang had a chance to check out the new logo yet?

W-Am (A) Yes, and she simply adored it.

(B) It's a great opportunity for you.

(C) A professional graphic designer.

랭 씨가 새로운 로고를 확인할 기회가 있었대요?
(A) 네, 그리고 아주 마음에 들어 했어요.
(B) 그건 당신에게 아주 좋은 기회예요.
(C) 전문 그래픽 디자이너요.

어휘 chance 기회 check out 확인하다 logo 로고 adore 아주 좋아하다 simply 정말로, 아주 opportunity 기회 professional 전문적인

해설 로고 확인 여부를 묻는 조동사(has) 의문문

(A) 정답. 랭 씨가 새로운 로고를 확인했는지 묻는 질문에 Yes로 긍정적 응답을 한 후, 아주 마음에 들어 했다는 부연 설명을 하고 있으므로 정답.

(B) 연상 단어 오답. 질문의 chance에서 연상 가능한 opportunity를 이용한 오답.

(C) 연상 단어 오답. 질문의 logo에서 연상 가능한 graphic designer를 이용한 오답.

11

W-Br How many floral centerpieces do we need for the banquet?

M-Cn (A) One for each table of guests.

(B) For the twenty-fifth anniversary party.

(C) I like the pink and white roses.

연회를 위한 꽃 장식은 몇 개가 필요한가요?
(A) 손님 테이블당 한 개씩이요.
(B) 25주년 기념 파티를 위해서요.
(C) 분홍색 장미와 흰색 장미를 좋아해요.

어휘 floral 꽃으로 장식된 centerpiece 중앙부 장식 banquet 연회 guest 손님 anniversary 기념일

해설 필요한 꽃 장식 개수를 묻는 How many 의문문

(A) 정답. 연회에 몇 개의 꽃 장식이 필요한지 묻는 질문에 손님 테이블당 한 개씩이라는 구체적인 개수를 제시하고 있으므로 정답.

(B) 연상 단어 오답. 질문의 banquet에서 연상 가능한 anniversary party를 이용한 오답.

(C) 연상 단어 오답. 질문의 floral centerpieces에서 연상 가능한 roses를 이용한 오답.

12

M-Au Which room needs to have its carpets steam-cleaned?

W-Am (A) I prefer wooden floors.

(B) The third building on the right.

(C) All of them, if we can afford it.

카펫 증기 청소가 필요한 방은 어디인가요?
(A) 저는 나무 바닥이 좋아요.
(B) 오른쪽 세 번째 건물이요.
(C) 여유가 된다면 모두 다요.

어휘 steam-clean 증기 청소를 하다 prefer 선호하다 wooden floor 나무 바닥 afford ~할 여유가 있다

해설 카펫 증기 청소가 필요한 방을 묻는 Which 의문문
(A) 연상 단어 오답. 질문의 Which room을 듣고 선호하는 방의 종류를 묻는 질문으로 잘못 이해했을 때 연상 가능한 답변이므로 오답.
(B) 질문과 상관없는 오답. 어떤 방이 청소가 필요한지 묻는 질문에 세 번째 건물이라고 응답했으므로 오답.
(C) 정답. 카펫 증기 청소가 필요한 방이 어디인지 묻는 질문에 여유가 된다면 모두 해 달라고 답하고 있으므로 정답.

13

M-Cn The museum's fundraiser had record attendance.
M-Au (A) My phone can record audio and video.
(B) To renovate the building's lobby.
(C) That's fantastic news!

박물관의 기금 모금 행사가 기록적인 참석률을 보였어요.
(A) 내 휴대전화는 녹화와 녹음이 가능해요.
(B) 건물 로비를 보수하기 위해서요.
(C) 정말 대단한 소식이군요!

어휘 fundraiser 기금 모금 행사 record 기록적인 attendance 참석 renovate 개조[보수]하다 fantastic 환상적인, 대단한

해설 사실/정보 전달의 평서문
(A) 단어 반복 오답. 질문에 나온 record를 반복한 오답.
(B) 평서문과 상관없는 오답. 이유를 묻는 Why 의문문에 적절한 응답이므로 오답.
(C) 정답. 박물관의 기금 모금 행사가 기록적인 참석률을 보였다는 말에 정말 대단한 소식이라고 기쁨을 표현하고 있으므로 정답.

14

M-Au What time does the bank usually close on Fridays?
W-Br (A) To exchange some foreign currency.
(B) It's fairly close to my office.
(C) You'll have to look that up online.

그 은행은 금요일에 보통 언제 문을 닫나요?
(A) 외화 환전을 위해서요.
(B) 내 사무실과 꽤 가까워요.
(C) 인터넷으로 알아보셔야 해요.

어휘 exchange 환전하다 foreign currency 외화 fairly 꽤 look up (정보를) 찾아보다 online 온라인으로, 인터넷으로

해설 은행 마감 시간을 묻는 What time 의문문
(A) 연상 단어 오답. 질문의 bank에서 연상 가능한 exchange와 foreign currency를 이용한 오답.
(B) 단어 반복 오답. 질문에 나온 close를 반복한 오답.
(C) 정답. 은행 마감 시점을 묻는 질문에 인터넷으로 알아봐야 한다는 불확실한 표현으로 응답하고 있으므로 정답.

15

W-Br Should I make the necessary revisions on this paper copy?
M-Cn (A) No, on the original document, please.
(B) To update the figures for accuracy.
(C) Yes, my vision has improved greatly.

이 서류 사본에 필요한 수정을 할까요?
(A) 아니요, 원본에 해 주세요.
(B) 수치를 정확하게 고치기 위해서요.
(C) 네, 시력이 많이 향상되었어요.

어휘 make revisions 수정하다 necessary 필요한 paper copy 서류 사본 original 원본의, 최초의 document 문서 update 갱신하다 figure 수치 accuracy 정확성 vision 시력 improve 향상되다

해설 수정 여부를 묻는 조동사(should) Yes/No 의문문
(A) 정답. 서류 사본을 수정해야 하는지 묻는 질문에 No로 부정적 응답을 한 후, 원본에 해 달라고 요청하고 있으므로 정답.
(B) 질문과 상관없는 오답. 이유를 묻는 Why 의문문에 적절한 응답이므로 오답.
(C) 유사 발음 오답. 질문의 revisions와 부분적으로 발음이 동일한 vision을 이용한 오답.

16

W-Br The CEO isn't taking any calls now, is he?
M-Au (A) He doesn't want to be interrupted.
(B) You can call me after lunch.
(C) Feel free to take it in to him.

최고경영자가 지금 어떤 전화도 받지 않는 거죠, 그렇죠?
(A) 그는 방해받기 싫어해요.
(B) 점심 식사 후에 전화하면 돼요.
(C) 그에게 언제든지 갖다 주세요.

어휘 CEO 최고경영자 interrupt 방해하다 feel free to 마음대로 ~하다

해설 전화 수신 여부를 확인하는 부가의문문
(A) 정답. 최고경영자가 어떤 전화도 받지 않는지 확인하는 질문에 방해받기 싫어한다는 표현으로 부정의 대답을 대신하고 있으므로 정답.
(B) 단어 반복 오답. 질문의 calls를 동사형 형태인 call로 반복한 오답.
(C) 파생어 오답. 질문의 taking과 파생어 관계인 take를 이용한 오답.

17

M-Cn How much milk would you like in your coffee?
W-Am (A) A few days is enough for me.
(B) In a to-go container, please.
(C) Actually, I take it black.

커피에 우유는 얼마나 넣을까요?
(A) 며칠이면 충분해요.
(B) 테이크아웃 용기에 주세요.
(C) 사실 저는 블랙으로 마셔요.

어휘 to-go (음식을 식당에서 먹지 않고) 가지고 갈 container 용기 actually 사실은

해설 커피에 넣을 우유 양을 물어보는 How much 의문문
(A) 질문과 상관없는 오답. 커피에 우유를 얼마나 넣을지 묻는 질문에 며칠이면 충분하다는 답변은 질문의 맥락에서 벗어난 것이므로 오답.
(B) 연상 단어 오답. 질문의 coffee에 대해 커피를 담는 컵 측면에서 연상 가능한 to-go container를 이용한 오답.
(C) 정답. 커피에 우유를 얼마나 넣을지 묻는 질문에 블랙으로 마신다(우유를 넣지 않는다)고 밝히고 있으므로 정답.

18

W-Br Will you have time to compile the statistics from our study tomorrow?
W-Am (A) We studied for most of the night.
(B) Sure, I'm available after lunch.
(C) In three piles, please.

내일 우리 연구 자료에서 통계를 집계할 시간이 있나요?
(A) 우리는 저녁 시간 대부분을 공부하며 보내요.
(B) 물론이죠, 점심 식사 후에 시간이 돼요.
(C) 세 겹으로요.

어휘 compile 수집하다, 집계하다 statistics 통계 available 시간이 되는 pile 포개 놓은 것, 무더기

해설 부탁/요청의 의문문
(A) 단어 반복 오답. 질문의 study를 과거 동사 형태인 studied로 반복한 오답.
(B) 정답. 연구 자료에서 통계를 집계할 시간이 있느냐는 요청에 Sure로 긍정적 응답을 한 후, 점심 식사 후에 시간이 된다는 부연 설명을 하고 있으므로 정답.
(C) 유사 발음 오답. 질문의 compile과 부분적으로 발음이 동일한 piles를 이용한 오답.

19

W-Br Isn't the shipping service included in the listed price?
M-Cn (A) It's shipped overnight by courier.
(B) To 744 Conifer Avenue.
(C) I don't think so.

운송비가 표시 가격에 포함되어 있지 않나요?
(A) 그건 속달로 보내드렸습니다.
(B) 코니퍼 애비뉴 744번지로요.
(C) 아닐걸요.

어휘 shipping service 운송 서비스, 운송비 listed price 표시 가격 include 포함하다 ship 운송하다 overnight 익일 배달의 courier 급송 택배

해설 운송비 포함 여부에 대한 부정의문문
(A) 파생어 오답. 질문의 shipping과 파생어 관계인 shipped를 이용한 오답.
(B) 질문과 상관없는 오답. 장소를 묻는 Where 의문문에 적절한 응답이므로 오답.
(C) 정답. 운송비가 표시 가격에 포함되지 않느냐는 질문에 아니라고 부정으로 답하고 있으므로 정답.

20

M-Au Where do you think I should stay while visiting Barcelona?
M-Cn (A) I recommend three or four nights.
(B) We had a wonderful time there.
(C) How much is your budget?

바르셀로나를 방문하는 동안 어디에 머무르는 게 좋을까요?
(A) 사나흘 밤을 추천해요.
(B) 우리는 그곳에서 정말 즐거운 시간을 보냈어요.
(C) 예산이 얼마나 되나요?

어휘 recommend 추천하다 budget 예산

해설 바르셀로나에서 머물 장소를 물어보는 Where 의문문
(A) 질문과 상관없는 오답. 기간을 묻는 How long 의문문에 적절한 응답이므로 오답.
(B) 연상 단어 오답. 질문의 visiting Barcelona에서 연상 가능한 wonderful time을 이용한 오답.
(C) 정답. 바르셀로나에서 머물 장소를 묻는 질문에 숙박비 측면에서 예산이 얼마나 되는지 되묻고 있으므로 정답.

21

W-Am I can use this coupon at your store, right?
M-Au (A) For our rewards club members.
(B) Unfortunately, it's already expired.
(C) We used to be located at the mall.

당신 가게에서 이 쿠폰을 사용할 수 있죠, 맞죠?
(A) 멤버십 고객을 위해서요.
(B) 안타깝게도 유효 기간이 이미 만료되었어요.
(C) 우리 가게는 쇼핑몰에 있었어요.

어휘 rewards club 멤버십 고객(특별 혜택 등이 제공되는 회원) unfortunately 안타깝게도, 불행하게도 expire (기간이) 만료되다 used to ~하곤 했다 be located ~에 있다[위치하다] mall 쇼핑몰

해설 쿠폰 사용 여부를 확인하는 부가의문문
(A) 질문과 상관없는 오답. 가게에서 쿠폰을 사용할 수 있는지 묻는 질문에 멤버십 고객을 위해서라는 답변은 질문의 맥락에서 벗어난 것이므로 오답.
(B) 정답. 가게에서 쿠폰을 사용할 수 있는지 묻는 질문에 유효 기간이 끝났다는 말로 부정적 응답을 하고 있으므로 정답.
(C) 단어 반복 오답. 질문의 use를 used의 형태로 반복한 오답.

22

M-Cn Who do you think has the most creative costume?
W-Br (A) Yes, for most of the participants.
(B) He needs to go through customs.
(C) I like them all equally.

누가 가장 창의적인 의상을 보유하고 있다고 생각하나요?
(A) 네, 대부분의 참가자를 위해서요.
(B) 그는 세관을 통과해야 해요.
(C) 모두 똑같이 마음에 들어요.

어휘 creative 창의적인 costume 의상 participant 참가자 go through ~을 통과하다 customs 세관 equally 동등하게

해설 가장 창의적인 의상 소유자를 묻는 Who 의문문

(A) Yes/No 불가 오답. Who 의문문에 Yes/No 응답은 불가능하므로 오답.

(B) 유사 발음 오답. 질문의 costume과 발음이 유사한 customs를 이용한 오답.

(C) 정답. 누구의 의상이 가장 창의적인지 묻는 질문에 모두 다 똑같이 마음에 든다고 답하고 있으므로 정답.

23

M-Au This prescription for pain medication can be renewed, right?

W-Am (A) Yes, up to two more times.

(B) It's a highly effective product.

(C) The description is very detailed.

이 진통제 처방전은 다시 사용할 수 있죠, 맞죠?

(A) 네, 최대 두 번 더요.
(B) 아주 효과적인 제품이에요.
(C) 설명이 아주 자세하네요.

어휘 prescription 처방전 pain medication 진통제 renew 갱신하다 up to ~까지 highly 매우 effective 효과적인 product 제품 description 서술, 설명 detailed 상세한

해설 처방전 재사용 여부를 확인하는 부가의문문

(A) 정답. 진통제 처방전을 다시 사용할 수 있는지 묻는 질문에 Yes로 긍정적 응답을 한 후, 최대 두 번 더라는 부연 설명을 하고 있으므로 정답.

(B) 연상 단어 오답. 질문의 medication에서 연상 가능한 effective를 이용한 오답.

(C) 유사 발음 오답. 질문의 prescription과 부분적으로 발음이 동일한 description을 이용한 오답.

24

M-Cn Wasn't this film nominated for several prestigious awards?

W-Br (A) I saw it at the theater.

(B) That's what I heard.

(C) You can get a rewards card.

이 영화는 몇몇 권위 있는 상의 후보로 지명되지 않았나요?

(A) 극장에서 봤어요.
(B) 그렇다고 들었어요.
(C) 적립 카드를 받으실 수 있어요.

어휘 film 영화 nominate 지명하다 several 몇몇의 prestigious 권위 있는 award 상 theater 극장 rewards card (포인트) 적립 카드

해설 후보 지명 여부에 대한 부정의문문

(A) 연상 단어 오답. 질문의 film에서 연상 가능한 theater를 이용한 오답.

(B) 정답. 영화가 권위 있는 상의 후보로 지명되었는지 묻는 질문에 그렇다고 들었다는 말로 긍정적 응답을 하고 있으므로 정답.

(C) 유사 발음 오답. 질문의 awards과 발음이 유사한 rewards를 이용한 오답.

25

W-Am Would you like to drive to Manchester or take the train?

W-Br (A) For a business strategy meeting.

(B) About three hours from here.

(C) Isn't there a direct flight?

맨체스터까지 운전해서 가시겠어요, 기차를 타시겠어요?

(A) 사업 전략 회의를 위해서요.
(B) 여기에서 약 3시간 정도요.
(C) 직항편은 없나요?

어휘 strategy 전략 direct flight 직항 비행기[편]

해설 구를 연결한 선택의문문

(A) 질문과 상관없는 오답. 이유를 묻는 Why 의문문에 적절한 응답이므로 오답.

(B) 질문과 상관없는 오답. 시간을 묻는 How long 의문문에 적절한 응답이므로 오답.

(C) 정답. 질문에서 선택 사항으로 언급된 차와 기차 대신 맨체스터까지 직항 비행기는 없는지를 되물어 제3의 선택 사항을 제시한 것이므로 정답.

26

W-Br Is Gourmet Grub catering the welcome reception next month?

M-Cn (A) Only if we can agree on a reasonable price.

(B) An event to welcome the new employees.

(C) It'll probably be on June twenty-fifth.

고멧 그럽이 다음 달 환영회에서 음식을 공급할 건가요?

(A) 합리적인 가격에 합의할 경우에 한해서요.
(B) 신입 사원을 환영하기 위한 행사예요.
(C) 아마 6월 25일일 거예요.

어휘 cater (행사에) 음식을 공급하다 reception 리셉션, 환영 연회 only if ~할 경우에 한해 agree on ~에 합의하다, 동의하다 reasonable 합리적인, (가격이) 비싸지 않은

해설 환영회 음식 공급 여부를 묻는 Be동사 Yes/No 의문문

(A) 정답. 고멧 그럽이 환영회에 음식을 공급하는지를 묻는 질문에 합리적인 가격에 합의할 경우에 한해서라는 조건을 제시하고 있으므로 정답.

(B) 단어 반복 오답. 질문에 나온 welcome을 반복한 오답.

(C) 질문과 상관없는 오답. 시점을 묻는 When 의문문에 적절한 응답이므로 오답.

27

W-Br This rug is too wide to be used in the entryway.

M-Au (A) What kind of textile do you need?

(B) The checkered pattern.

(C) I must have measured it wrong.

이 깔개는 입구에 쓰기에는 너무 넓어요.

(A) 어떤 종류의 직물이 필요한가요?
(B) 체크 무늬요.
(C) 제가 치수를 잘못 잰 게 틀림없어요.

어휘 rug 깔개 too ~ to … 너무 ~해서 …할 수 없는 entryway 입구
textile 직물, 섬유 checkered pattern 체크 무늬 must ~임에
틀림없다 measure (치수 등을) 측정하다

해설 사실/정보 전달의 평서문
(A) 연상 단어 오답. 질문의 rug에 대해 깔개의 재질 측면에서 연상 가능한
textile을 이용한 오답.
(B) 연상 단어 오답. 질문의 rug에 대해 깔개의 무늬 측면에서 연상 가능한
checkered pattern을 이용한 오답.
(C) 정답. 입구에 사용하기에는 깔개가 너무 넓다는 말에 치수를 잘못 잰 게 틀
림없다고 응답하고 있으므로 정답.

28
W-Am Did you do a lot of sightseeing while you were
traveling overseas?
M-Au (A) Yes, I can see the tour bus from here.
(B) There wasn't much spare time, I'm afraid.
(C) To learn a foreign language.

해외 여행하는 동안 관광을 많이 했나요?
(A) 네, 여기서 관광 버스가 보이네요.
(B) 아쉽게도 자유 시간이 많지 않았어요.
(C) 외국어를 배우기 위해서요.

어휘 sightseeing 관광 overseas 해외로 spare time 여가[여유]
시간 I'm afraid (유감이지만) ~이다 foreign language 외국어

해설 관광 여부를 묻는 조동사(did) Yes/No 의문문
(A) 연상 단어 오답. 질문의 sightseeing에서 연상 가능한 tour bus를 이용한
오답.
(B) 정답. 해외 여행 중에 관광을 많이 했는지를 묻는 질문에 아쉽게도 자유 시
간이 많지 않았다는 말로 부정적 응답을 하고 있으므로 정답.
(C) 연상 단어 오답. 질문의 overseas에서 연상 가능한 foreign language를
이용한 오답.

29
W-Br The spokesperson for Moonlight Cosmetics made
a lot of good points.
M-Cn (A) He certainly convinced me.
(B) I'll point it out to you if necessary.
(C) A daily moisturizing cream.

문라이트 코스메틱스의 대변인은 좋은 지적을 많이 했어요.
(A) 그는 정말 설득력이 있었어요.
(B) 필요하면 제가 알려드리죠.
(C) 매일 쓰는 보습 크림이요.

어휘 spokesperson 대변인 make a point (주장이 옳음을) 역설하다
certainly 확실히 convince 설득하다 point ~ out to … …에게
~를 가리켜 보이다[알려주다] if necessary 필요하면 daily 매일
일어나는, 나날의 moisturizing cream 보습 크림

해설 의견 제시의 평서문
(A) 정답. 대변인이 좋은 지적을 많이 했다는 의견에 그의 말이 설득력이 있었
다는 응답으로 의견에 대한 동의를 나타냈으므로 정답.
(B) 단어 반복 오답. 질문의 points를 동사원형인 point로 반복한 오답.
(C) 연상 단어 오답. 질문의 Cosmetics에서 연상 가능한 moisturizing
cream을 이용한 오답.

30
W-Am How can I have the chance to be selected as a
conference leader?
M-Au (A) Everyone enjoyed the sessions at the event.
(B) She was elected by a wide margin last month.
(C) You have to fill out a form and submit it.

어떻게 하면 학회 대표자로 선출될 기회를 얻을 수 있나요?
(A) 모두가 행사에서 그 시간을 즐겼어요.
(B) 그녀는 지난달에 큰 표 차이로 선출되었어요.
(C) 양식을 작성해서 제출해야 해요.

어휘 select 선택하다 conference 회의, 학회 leader 리더, 대표
session (특정 활동을 위한) 시간, 기간 elect 선출하다 by a wide
margin 큰 차이로 fill out a form 양식을 작성하다 submit
제출하다

해설 선출 기회 획득 방법을 묻는 How 의문문
(A) 질문과 상관없는 오답. 학회 대표자 선출 기회 획득 방법을 묻는 질문에 모
두가 행사에서 그 시간을 즐겼다는 답변은 질문의 맥락에서 벗어난 것이므
로 오답.
(B) 질문과 상관없는 오답. She가 가리키는 대상이 질문에 없으므로 오답.
(C) 정답. 학회 대표자 선출 기회 획득 방법을 묻는 질문에 양식을 작성해서 제
출해야 한다는 구체적인 방법을 제시하고 있으므로 정답.

31
M-Cn I don't think that environmental legislation will be
passed.
W-Am (A) I try to help the environment too.
(B) But a lot of voters support it.
(C) You don't need an entrance pass.

환경 법안이 통과될 것 같지 않아요.
(A) 나도 환경에 도움이 되려고 노력해요.
(B) 하지만 많은 유권자들이 그것을 지지해요.
(C) 입장권은 필요 없어요.

어휘 environmental 환경의 legislation 법규, 법안 pass 통과하다
voter 유권자 support 지지하다 entrance pass 입장권

해설 의견 제시의 평서문
(A) 파생어 오답. 질문의 environmental과 파생어 관계인 environment를
이용한 오답.
(B) 정답. 환경 법안이 통과되지 않을 것이라는 의견에 많은 유권자들이 지지한
다는 응답으로 간접적으로 동의하지 않음을 나타낸 것이므로 정답.
(C) 파생어 오답. 질문의 passed와 파생어 관계인 pass를 이용한 오답.

Part 3

32-34

M-Au Excuse me. **³²I own a small housekeeping business, and I'm wondering what kind of cleanser you recommend for cleaning kitchen surfaces.**

W-Br V-Max is popular for residential use. But if you're dealing with major stains, Sparkwell is much more effective. It's nearly twice the price, though. **³³About how much are you planning to spend?**

M-Au The final result is much more important than the cost.

W-Br You'll really want to consider this one then. **³⁴I'd be happy to show you how it works.** I'm sure you'll be impressed.

남: 실례합니다. 전 작은 가사 대행업체를 소유하고 있는데 주방 싱크대 청소에 좋은 세제를 좀 추천해 주세요.

여: V-맥스가 가정용으로 인기가 좋아요. 하지만 심한 얼룩 처리에는 스파크웰이 훨씬 더 효과적이죠. 가격은 거의 두 배지만요. **대략 얼마를 쓰실 계획이세요?**

남: 최종 결과가 비용보다 훨씬 더 중요해요.

여: 그러면 이 제품을 고려해 보세요. **이 제품이 얼마나 효과적인지 기꺼이 보여드리죠.** 분명 깊은 인상을 받으실 거예요.

어휘 own 소유하다 housekeeping 살림, 집안 돌보는 일 wonder 궁금하다 cleanser 세제 surface 작업대(의 표면) residential 주거의 deal with ~다루다 major 심각한 stain 얼룩 effective 효과적인 nearly 거의 consider 고려하다 work 작동되다, 작용을 하다 impress 깊은 인상을 주다

32

What kind of item is the man shopping for?

(A) A piece of furniture
(B) A cleaning product
(C) A kitchen appliance
(D) A laundry detergent

남자가 구매하려는 물건은 무엇인가?

(A) 가구
(B) 청소용품
(C) 주방용품
(D) 세탁세제

어휘 cleaning product 세정제, 청소용품 appliance (가정용) 기기 laundry detergent 세탁세제

해설 세부 사항 관련 – 남자가 구매하려는 물건

남자의 첫 번째 대사에서 남자가 작은 가사 대행업체를 소유하고 있고 주방 싱크대 청소에 좋은 세제를 추천해 달라(I own a small housekeeping business, and I'm wondering what kind of cleanser you recommend for cleaning kitchen surfaces)고 했으므로 정답은 (B)이다.

▸▸ Paraphrasing 대화의 cleanser
→ 정답의 A cleaning product

33

What does the woman ask the man about?

(A) His schedule
(B) His business model
(C) His budget
(D) His mailing address

여자는 남자에게 무엇에 관해 물어보는가?

(A) 일정
(B) 사업 모델
(C) 예산
(D) 메일 주소

어휘 budget 예산 mailing address 메일 주소

해설 세부 사항 관련 – 여자가 물어보는 것

여자의 첫 번째 대사에서 지출하려는 금액은 얼마인지(About how much are you planning to spend) 물어보았으므로 정답은 (C)이다.

▸▸ Paraphrasing 대화의 planning to spend → 정답의 budget

34

What does the woman offer to do?

(A) Give a demonstration
(B) Check another store
(C) Provide a guarantee
(D) Reduce a price

여자는 무엇을 해 주겠다고 하는가?

(A) 시연하기
(B) 다른 매장 확인하기
(C) 품질보증서 제공하기
(D) 가격 할인해 주기

어휘 demonstration (작동 과정이나 사용법에 대한) 시범, 시연 provide 제공하다 guarantee 품질보증서 reduce (가격 등을) 낮추다, 할인하다

해설 세부 사항 관련 – 여자의 제안 사항

여자의 마지막 대사에서 이 제품이 얼마나 효과적인지 보여주겠다(I'd be happy to show you how it works)고 했다. 여자가 시연을 제안하고 있음을 알 수 있으므로 정답은 (A)이다.

▸▸ Paraphrasing 대화의 show you how it works
→ 정답의 Give a demonstration

35-37

W-Am Oh, I'm glad you're here, Brett. I'm catching up on a project, so I came to do some work on the weekend. **³⁵But I forgot to bring my keycard for the laboratory, so I can't get in.**

M-Cn I wish I could help you, but my keycard only works for my office and the third-floor lab. **³⁶You should talk to Kevin Lee. He's working security today.**

W-Am	Thanks, but I already tried stopping by his office. No one was there.
M-Cn	[37]**I've got a business card with his cell phone number on it. You're welcome to have it so you can get in touch with him.**

여	오, 브렛, 여기 와줘서 기뻐요. 전 밀린 프로젝트 일을 하려고 주말인데도 출근했어요. 그런데 실험실 키카드를 안 가지고 와서 들어갈 수가 없어요.
남	도와주고 싶지만 제 키카드는 제 사무실과 3층 실험실에만 사용할 수 있어요. 케빈 리에게 얘기해 보세요. 오늘 당직 경비원이에요.
여	고마워요. 그런데 경비실에 들렀는데, 아무도 없었어요.
남	케빈의 휴대전화 번호가 적힌 명함이 저한테 있어요. 이걸 줄 테니 케빈에게 연락해 보세요.

어휘	catch up on (뒤처진 일을) 만회하다 keycard 키카드(문을 열기 위한 출입 카드) laboratory 실험실(= lab) security 보안 stop by 들르다 business card 명함 welcome to 자유로이 ~하다 get in touch with ~와 연락하다

35

What is the woman's problem?

(A) Her laboratory project was canceled.
(B) She lost a parking pass.
(C) Her computer password is not working.
(D) She cannot access a room.

여자의 문제는 무엇인가?
(A) 실험 프로젝트가 취소되었다.
(B) 주차권을 잃어버렸다.
(C) 컴퓨터 비밀번호가 틀리다.
(D) 방에 들어갈 수가 없다.

어휘	parking pass 주차권 password 비밀번호 access 접근하다

해설 전체 내용 관련 – 여자의 문제점

여자의 첫 번째 대사에서 실험실 카드를 안 가지고 와서 들어갈 수가 없다(But I forgot to bring my keycard for the laboratory, so I can't get in)고 했다. 방에 들어갈 수 없다는 것이 여자의 문제라는 것을 알 수 있으므로 정답은 (D)이다.

▸▸ Paraphrasing 대화의 **get in** → 정답의 **access**

36

Who does the man suggest speaking with?

(A) A security guard
(B) A department manager
(C) A building owner
(D) A software technician

남자는 누구와 이야기하라고 제안하는가?
(A) 경비원
(B) 부서장
(C) 건물주
(D) 소프트웨어 기술자

어휘	security guard 경비원 department manager 부서장 owner 소유자 technician 기술자

해설 세부 사항 관련 – 남자가 이야기하라고 제안하는 사람

남자의 첫 번째 대사에서 오늘 당직 경비원인 케빈 리에게 얘기하라(You should talk to Kevin Lee. He's working security today)고 했으므로 정답은 (A)이다.

37

What does the man offer to do?

(A) Let the woman borrow his cell phone
(B) Take a message for a coworker
(C) Give the woman a business card
(D) Accompany the woman to the third floor

남자는 무엇을 해 주겠다고 제안하는가?
(A) 여자에게 휴대전화를 빌려 주기
(B) 동료를 위해 메시지를 받아 놓기
(C) 여자에게 명함 주기
(D) 3층까지 여자와 동행하기

어휘	take a message 메시지를 받다 coworker 직장 동료 accompany to ~까지 동행하다

해설 세부 사항 관련 – 남자의 제안 사항

남자의 마지막 대사에서 케빈의 휴대전화 번호가 적힌 명함이 있는데 그 명함을 줄 테니 케빈에게 연락해 보라(I've got a business card with his cell phone number on it. You're welcome to have it so you can get in touch with him)고 했으므로 정답은 (C)이다.

38-40

W-Br	Good afternoon, Pinewood Furnishings. What can I help you with today?
M-Cn	Hello. [38]**I ordered a crystal light fixture a few days ago. Your Web site said it would be delivered between January seventh and tenth. I'd like to know if you have the exact date.** The order number is 4221.
W-Br	Let's see … It looks like you can expect it on January tenth.
M-Cn	Oh, I'm going to be out of town then. Can I change the delivery date?
W-Br	[39]**Yes, but there's an extra charge of twenty dollars.**
M-Cn	Hmm… [40]**in that case, I'll ask my neighbor to sign for it instead.** Her apartment is right next door.
W-Br	OK, I'll make a note in our system.

여	안녕하세요. 파인우드 퍼니싱즈입니다. 오늘은 무엇을 도와드릴까요?
남	안녕하세요. 며칠 전에 크리스털 전등을 주문했어요. 웹사이트에는 1월 7일에서 10일 사이에 배송된다고 했는데, 정확한 날짜를 알고 싶어요. 주문번호는 4221이에요.
여	한번 볼게요. 1월 10일에 배송될 것 같네요.
남	오, 제가 그때 타지에 있을 거예요. 배송 날짜를 바꿀 수 있을까요?
여	네, 대신 20달러의 추가 요금이 있어요.

Test 3

남: 음… 그렇다면, 이웃에게 대신 받아달라고 부탁해야겠어요. 아파트가 바로 옆집이에요.

여: 좋아요, 전산에 그렇게 입력해 놓을게요.

<table>
<tr><td>어휘</td><td>light fixture 전등 deliver 배달하다 exact 정확한
expect 기대하다, 예상하다 out of town 도시를 떠나서
delivery 배송 extra charge 추가 요금 in that case
그렇다면 neighbor 이웃 주민 sign for (~을 수령했다고)
서명하다 instead 대신 make a note 써 놓다</td></tr>
</table>

38

Why is the man calling?

(A) To follow up on an order
(B) To report being overcharged
(C) To complain about a shipping delay
(D) To inquire about installation

남자가 전화한 이유는?

(A) 주문에 대해 더 알아보려고
(B) 과다 청구를 알리려고
(C) 운송 지연을 항의하려고
(D) 설치에 대해 문의하려고

어휘 follow up on ~에 대해 후속 조치[사후 관리]를 하다 overcharge
과다 청구하다 complain about ~에 대해 불평하다[항의하다]
shipping delay 운송 지연 inquire 문의하다 installation 설치

해설 전체 내용 관련 – 남자가 전화한 이유
남자의 첫 번째 대사에서 크리스털 전등을 주문했다며 웹사이트에는 1월 7일에서 10일 사이에 배송된다고 하는데 정확한 날짜가 궁금하다(I ordered a crystal light fixture a few days ago. Your Web site said it would be delivered between January seventh and tenth. I'd like to know if you have the exact date)고 했다. 주문에 대해 더 알아보기 위해 전화했다는 것을 알 수 있으므로 정답은 (A)이다.

39

What does the woman tell the man about?

(A) A promotional sale
(B) A return policy
(C) A delivery route
(D) An additional fee

여자는 남자에게 무엇에 관해 말하는가?

(A) 판촉 할인
(B) 반품 정책
(C) 배송 경로
(D) 추가 요금

어휘 promotional 판촉의 return 반품 policy 정책, 규정 route
경로 additional 추가적인 fee 수수료, 요금

해설 세부 사항 관련 – 여자가 남자에게 하는 말
여자의 세 번째 대사에서 대신 20달러의 추가 요금이 있다(Yes, but there's an extra charge of twenty dollars)고 했으므로 정답은 (D)이다.

> ▸▸ Paraphrasing 대화의 an extra charge
> → 정답의 An additional fee

40

What does the man plan to do?

(A) Get help from a neighbor
(B) Cancel an out-of-town trip
(C) Sign a new contract
(D) Change a delivery date

남자는 무엇을 할 계획인가?

(A) 이웃에게 도움 받기
(B) 타지 여행 취소하기
(C) 새 계약 체결하기
(D) 배송 날짜 바꾸기

어휘 out-of-town trip 타지 여행 sign a contract 계약을 체결하다

해설 세부 사항 관련 – 남자의 계획
남자의 세 번째 대사에서 이웃에게 대신 받아달라고 부탁해야겠다(in that case, I'll ask my neighbor to sign for it instead)고 했다. 남자가 이웃에게 도움을 받을 계획이라는 것을 알 수 있으므로 정답은 (A)이다.

> ▸▸ Paraphrasing 대화의 ask my neighbor to sign for it
> → 정답의 Get help from a neighbor

41-43

<table>
<tr><td>M-Cn</td><td>Good morning. 41I'd like to book a cab from the Kirkland Hotel to Sea-Tac Airport for this Friday, March twentieth. 42I have a lot of luggage and boxes, so I was concerned that I couldn't manage the express train on my own.</td></tr>
<tr><td>W-Am</td><td>All right, sir. Please give me your name and the exact pick-up time you need.</td></tr>
<tr><td>M-Cn</td><td>My name is Arnold Fujimoto, and I'd like to be picked up at eight A.M.</td></tr>
<tr><td>W-Am</td><td>OK. A car has been reserved for you, Mr. Fujimoto. 43You'll receive an automated text from us on March nineteenth reminding you about the pick-up time.</td></tr>
</table>

남: 안녕하세요. 3월 20일, 이번 금요일에 커크랜드 호텔에서 씨-택 공항까지 택시를 예약하고 싶어요. 짐과 박스가 많아 급행열차를 혼자서 못 탈까 걱정돼서요.

여: 네, 손님. 성함과 정확한 승차 시간을 알려주세요.

남: 제 이름은 아놀드 후지모토이고 아침 8시에 차가 왔으면 해요.

여: 알겠습니다. 예약되었습니다, 후지모토 씨. 저희가 3월 19일에 차 도착 시간을 알려드리는 자동 문자를 보내겠습니다.

<table>
<tr><td>어휘</td><td>book 예약하다 cab 택시 luggage 짐, 수화물 manage
해내다 express 급행의 on my own 혼자서 exact
정확한 pick-up 픽업, (사람을) 태우러 감 reserve 예약하다
automated 자동화된 text 문자 remind 상기시키다,
알려주다</td></tr>
</table>

41

What kind of business is the man calling?

(A) A taxi service
(B) An airline
(C) A train operator
(D) A hotel

남자는 어떤 업체에 전화하는가?

(A) 택시 회사
(B) 항공사
(C) 철도 공사
(D) 호텔

어휘 airline 항공사 train operator 철도 공사

해설 전체 내용 관련 – 남자가 전화한 업체

남자의 첫 번째 대사에서 3월 20일 금요일에 커크랜드 호텔에서 씨-택 공항까지 택시를 예약하고 싶다(I'd like to book a cab from the Kirkland Hotel to Sea-Tac Airport for this Friday, March twentieth)고 했으므로 정답은 (A)이다.

42

What was the man concerned about?

(A) Overspending on transportation
(B) Carrying a lot of items
(C) Arriving at a site late
(D) Getting lost during a journey

남자가 걱정하는 것은 무엇인가?

(A) 교통에 과다 지출하는 것
(B) 많은 물건을 운반하는 것
(C) 장소에 늦게 도착하는 것
(D) 여행 중 길을 잃는 것

어휘 overspend 과다 지출하다 transportation 교통 carry 옮기다 site 장소 get lost 길을 잃다 journey 여행

해설 세부 사항 관련 – 남자가 걱정하는 사항

남자의 첫 번째 대화 마지막 부분에서 짐과 박스가 많아 급행열차를 혼자서 못 탈까 봐 걱정된다(I have a lot of luggage and boxes, so I was concerned that I couldn't manage the express train on my own)고 했다. 짐 운반을 걱정한다는 것을 알 수 있으므로 정답은 (B)이다.

▸▸ Paraphrasing 대화의 **luggage and boxes** → 정답의 **items**

43

What does the woman say the business will do?

(A) Call the man again
(B) Send a reminder
(C) Charge a credit card
(D) E-mail a receipt

여자는 업체에서 무엇을 할 것이라고 말하는가?

(A) 남자에게 다시 전화하기
(B) 알림 문자 보내기
(C) 신용카드로 청구하기
(D) 이메일로 영수증 보내기

어휘 reminder (메모·문자 등) 알리는 것 charge 청구하다 receipt 영수증

해설 세부 사항 관련 – 회사가 할 일

여자의 마지막 대사에서 업체에서 3월 19일에 차 도착 시간을 알리는 자동 문자를 보낼 것이다(You'll receive an automated text from us on March nineteenth reminding you about the pick-up time)라고 했다. 업체가 알림 문자를 보낸다는 것을 알 수 있으므로 정답은 (B)이다.

44-46

M-Au	Hi, Rita. It's Oliver. **⁴⁴You mentioned that you're going to the food festival at Wilson Park this weekend. I plan on driving there, so I was wondering if you wanted a ride.**
W-Br	Thanks, but you're not taking the bus? **⁴⁵I was worried about taking my own car because there's hardly any parking in that neighborhood.**
M-Au	Don't worry. **⁴⁶I contacted the park's visitor center, and they mailed me a pass for that day, so I'll have a guaranteed spot.**
W-Br	That's great! In that case, I'd love to join you. Thank you!

남	안녕하세요, 리타. 올리버예요. 이번 주말에 윌슨 파크에서 열리는 음식 축제에 갈 거라고 했죠. 제가 그곳에 차로 갈 계획인데 같이 타고 가면 어떨까 해서요.
여	고마워요. 그런데 버스를 안 타시려고요? 저도 차를 가져가려 했는데 그 근처에 주차 공간이 거의 없어서 걱정하고 있었어요.
남	걱정 마세요. 제가 공원 관광안내소에 연락했더니 그날 주차권을 우편으로 보내 줘서 주차 공간을 확보했어요.
여	아주 좋아요! 그렇다면 저야 같이 가면 좋죠. 고마워요!

어휘	mention 언급하다 plan on -ing ~할 예정이다 ride 차를 얻어 타는 것 hardly 거의 없는 neighborhood 인근, 동네 contact 연락하다 visitor center 관광안내소 pass 통행증, 출입증 guaranteed 보장된 spot 곳, 장소

44

Why is the man calling?

(A) To cancel some weekend plans
(B) To inquire about festival tickets
(C) To offer a ride to an event
(D) To change a meeting place

남자가 전화한 이유는 무엇인가?

(A) 주말 계획을 취소하려고
(B) 축제 티켓에 대해 문의하려고
(C) 행사장까지 차를 태워 주려고
(D) 만나는 장소를 변경하려고

어휘 cancel 취소하다 inquire 문의하다

해설 전체 내용 관련 – 남자가 전화한 이유

남자의 첫 번째 대사에서 주말에 윌슨 파크에서 열리는 음식 축제에 갈 거라고 하지 않았냐(You mentioned that you're going to the food festival at Wilson Park this weekend)며 그곳에 차로 갈 계획인데 같이 타고 가고 싶은지(I plan on driving there, so I was wondering if you wanted a ride) 물어보고 있다. 남자가 행사장까지 차를 태워 주려고 전화했다는 것을 알 수 있으므로 정답은 (C)이다.

45

What is the woman concerned about?

(A) A car malfunction
(B) A lack of parking
(C) A crowded bus
(D) A high admission fee

여자가 걱정하는 것은 무엇인가?
(A) 자동차 고장
(B) 주차 공간 부족
(C) 만원 버스
(D) 비싼 입장료

어휘 malfunction 오작동, 고장 lack 부족, 결핍 crowded 혼잡한 admission fee 입장료

해설 세부 사항 관련 – 여자가 걱정하는 사항

여자의 첫 번째 대사에서 차를 가져가려 했는데 주차 공간이 없어서 걱정했다(I was worried about taking my own car because there's hardly any parking in that neighborhood)고 했으므로 정답은 (B)이다.

▶▶ Paraphrasing 대화의 there's hardly any parking
→ 정답의 A lack of parking

46

What does the man say he has done?

(A) Checked a neighborhood map
(B) Received a pass in advance
(C) Confirmed a booking online
(D) Requested a group discount

남자는 무엇을 했다고 말하는가?
(A) 동네 지도를 확인했다
(B) 주차권을 미리 받았다
(C) 온라인으로 예약을 확인했다
(D) 단체 할인을 요구했다

어휘 receive 받다 in advance 미리 confirm 확인하다 booking 예약 request 요청하다 discount 할인

해설 세부 사항 관련 – 남자가 한 일

남자의 마지막 대사에서 공원 관광안내소에 연락해 주차권을 우편으로 받아서 주차 공간을 확보했다(I contacted the park's visitor center, and they mailed me a pass for that day, so I'll have a guaranteed spot)고 했으므로 정답은 (B)이다.

47-49

M-Au **47Ellen, I'm glad we'll be working together on inputting the dental patient files into the new database.**

W-Am Yeah. It'll go much faster with two people.

M-Au **48I know Dr. Perkins spent a lot of time deciding whether it was worth the cost, but in the end, I think she made the right move.**

W-Am I agree. Once all the files are available digitally, it'll be easier to search for information.

M-Au Now... um... **49we're supposed to get started on the work in the file room tomorrow, but that room is really small.**

W-Am **49Maybe we could use one of the empty exam rooms so we could have more space.**

M-Au I'll ask Dr. Perkins.

남: 엘렌, 우리가 치과 환자 파일을 새 데이터베이스에 입력하는 일을 같이 하게 되어 기뻐요.

여: 네, 둘이 같이 하면 훨씬 빨리 진행될 거예요.

남: 퍼킨스 박사님이 비용이 그만한 값어치를 하는지 판단하느라 오래 걸렸다고 하던데, 결국에는 박사님이 옳은 조치를 취했다고 생각해요.

여: 맞아요. 일단 모든 파일을 디지털로 이용할 수 있게 되면 정보 검색이 수월해질 거예요.

남: 이제… 음… 내일 서류 보관실에서 작업을 시작하기로 되어 있는데 그 방은 정말 작아요.

여: 아마 비어 있는 검사실 중 하나를 쓸 수 있으면 좀 더 넓은 공간에서 작업할 수 있을 거예요.

남: 퍼킨스 박사님에게 물어볼게요.

어휘 input into ~에 입력하다 dental 치과의 patient 환자 database 데이터베이스 spend time -ing ~하는 데 시간을 보내다 worth 가치 있는 in the end 마침내 make a move 행동에 들어가다, 조치를 취하다 available 이용 가능한 digitally 디지털 방식으로 search for ~를 찾아보다 be supposed to ~하기로 되어 있다 get started 시작하다 empty 텅 빈 exam room 검사실 space 공간

47

What task have the speakers been assigned?

(A) Installing a computer system
(B) Reviewing files for errors
(C) Recruiting new dental patients
(D) Adding information to a database

화자들에게 배정된 업무는 무엇인가?
(A) 컴퓨터 시스템 설치하기
(B) 파일에 오류가 있는지 검토하기
(C) 신규 치과 환자 유치하기
(D) 데이터베이스에 정보 추가하기

어휘 assign 맡기다, 배정하다 task 일, 과제 install 설치하다 review 검토하다 recruit 모집하다 add to ~에 추가하다

해설 전체 내용 관련 – 화자들의 업무
남자의 첫 번째 대사에서 치과 환자 파일의 데이터베이스 입력 업무를 같이 하게 되어 기쁘다(Ellen, I'm glad we'll be working together on inputting the dental patient files into the new database)라고 했으므로 정답은 (D)이다.

> ▸▸ Paraphrasing 대화의 inputting the dental patient files into the new database
> → 정답의 Adding information to a database

48

What does the man mention about Dr. Perkins?

(A) Her decision was a good one.
(B) She has no time to assist the speakers.
(C) Her business is growing steadily.
(D) She thinks the project should start today.

남자가 퍼킨스 박사에 대해 언급한 것은 무엇인가?
(A) 옳은 결정을 내렸다.
(B) 화자들을 도와줄 시간이 없다.
(C) 사업이 꾸준히 성장하고 있다.
(D) 프로젝트를 오늘 시작해야 한다고 생각한다.

어휘 decision 결정 assist 보조하다, 도와주다 grow 성장하다 steadily 꾸준히

해설 세부 사항 관련 – 퍼킨스 박사에 대해 언급된 사항
남자의 두 번째 대사에서 퍼킨스 박사가 비용이 그만한 값어치를 하는지 판단하느라 오래 걸렸다고 하던데, 결국에는 옳은 조치를 취했다고 생각한다(I know Dr. Perkins spent a lot of time deciding whether it was worth the cost, but in the end, I think she made the right move)고 했으므로 정답은 (A)이다.

> ▸▸ Paraphrasing 대화의 made the right move
> → 정답의 decision was a good one

49

What do the speakers want to do?

(A) Work in the evening
(B) Get a larger workspace
(C) Collect files from coworkers
(D) Perform an online search

화자들이 하고 싶어 하는 일은 무엇인가?
(A) 저녁에 작업하기
(B) 더 넓은 작업 공간 확보하기
(C) 동료로부터 파일 수집하기
(D) 온라인 검색하기

어휘 workspace 작업 공간 collect from ~에서[로부터] 수집하다 coworker 동료 perform 수행하다

해설 세부 사항 관련 – 화자가 원하는 것
남자의 세 번째 대사에서 서류 보관실에서 작업을 시작하는데 그 방은 정말 작다(we're supposed to get started on the work in the file room tomorrow, but that room is really small)고 했다. 이어서 여자가 비어

있는 검사실 중 하나를 쓰면 좀 더 넓은 공간에서 작업할 수 있다(Maybe we could use one of the empty exam rooms so we could have more space)고 했다. 화자들이 더 넓은 공간에서 작업하고 싶어 한다는 것을 알 수 있으므로 정답은 (B)이다.

> ▸▸ Paraphrasing 대화의 have more space
> → 정답의 Get a larger workspace

50-52 3인 대화

M-Cn	Ablex Property Development, how may I help you?
W-Am	I'm trying to reach Mr. David Kim. **50He's the person in charge of the Denbold Heights construction project, isn't he?**
M-Cn	Yes, he is. Let me put you through.
M-Au	David Kim speaking.
W-Am	Hello. It's Judy Marston with Sellway Building Supply. **51I just want to let you know that, because of an issue with our distributor, the exterior doors you ordered will be delivered tomorrow morning rather than this afternoon.** Uh…
M-Au	Oh, that's no problem. Our crews are actually working in a different area today. **52And I'll probably call you back later to order more railings once we've taken measurements.**
W-Am	All right. I'll talk to you later then.

남1: 애블렉스 프로퍼티 디벨롭먼트입니다. 어떻게 도와드릴까요?
여: 데이비드 김 씨와 통화하려 하는데요. 김 씨가 덴볼드 하이츠 건설 프로젝트 담당자죠, 아닌가요?
남1: 네, 맞아요. 연결해 드릴게요.
남2: 데이비드 김입니다.
여: 안녕하세요. 셀웨이 빌딩 서플라이의 주디 마스턴입니다. 우리 납품업체에 문제가 생겨서, 주문하신 현관문이 오늘 오후가 아니라 내일 아침에 배송될 예정이라고 알려드리려 전화했어요. 어…
남2: 오, 문제 없어요. 사실 오늘은 우리 팀원들이 다른 지역에서 작업하고 있어요. 그리고 측정을 다 마치면 나중에 다시 전화해서 철책을 추가로 주문할 수도 있어요.
여: 알겠어요. 그럼 나중에 연락드리겠습니다.

어휘 reach (전화로) 연락하다 in charge of ~을 담당하는 construction 건설 put through (전화를) 연결해 주다 issue 문제 distributor 납품업체 exterior door 현관문 deliver 배달하다 crew 팀, 조 actually 사실은 railing 철책(울타리) take measurements 측정하다

50

Who most likely is Mr. Kim?

(A) A building supply company owner
(B) An apartment rental agent
(C) A delivery driver
(D) A project manager

김 씨는 누구이겠는가?

(A) 건축 자재 회사 소유자
(B) 아파트 임대 중개사
(C) 배송 트럭 기사
(D) 프로젝트 매니저

어휘 building supply 건축 자재 owner 소유자 rental agent 임대 중개사

해설 전체 내용 관련 – 김 씨의 직업
여자의 첫 번째 대사에서 김 씨가 덴볼드 하이츠 건설 프로젝트 담당자가 맞는 지(He's the person in charge of the Denbold Heights construction project, isn't he) 확인했다. 김 씨가 프로젝트 매니저라는 것을 알 수 있으므로 정답은 (D)이다.

> ▸▸ Paraphrasing 대화의 **the person in charge of the Denbold Heights construction project** → 정답의 **A project manager**

51

What problem does the woman mention?

(A) A shipment will be delayed.
(B) A document is missing.
(C) A measurement is incorrect.
(D) A forecast calls for bad weather.

여자가 언급하는 문제는 무엇인가?

(A) 배송이 지연될 것이다.
(B) 문서가 분실되었다.
(C) 측정이 잘못되었다.
(D) 일기 예보에서 날씨가 나쁘다고 한다.

어휘 shipment 배송 delay 지연시키다 missing 없어진, 분실된 measurement 치수, 측정 incorrect 부정확한 forecast (날씨) 예보 call for (특정 날씨를) 예보하다

해설 세부 사항 관련 – 여자가 언급하는 문제
여자의 두 번째 대사에서 유통업체에 문제가 생겨 현관문이 오늘 오후가 아니라 내일 아침에 배송된다(I just want to let you know that, because of an issue with our distributor, the exterior doors you ordered will be delivered tomorrow morning rather this afternoon)고 했으므로 정답은 (A)이다.

52

What does Mr. Kim say he will most likely do later?

(A) Train some crew members
(B) Place an additional order
(C) Pay an overdue bill
(D) Approve a project

김 씨는 나중에 무엇을 하겠다고 말하는가?

(A) 일부 팀원 교육시키기
(B) 추가 주문하기
(C) 연체료 지불하기
(D) 프로젝트 승인하기

어휘 place an order 주문하다 overdue bill 연체료 approve 승인하다

해설 세부 사항 관련 – 남자가 할 일
두 번째 남자의 두 번째 대사에서 측정을 마치면 다시 전화해서 철책을 추가로 주문할 수도 있다(And I'll probably call you back later to order more railings once we've taken measurements)고 했으므로 정답은 (B)이다.

> ▸▸ Paraphrasing 대화의 **order more railings** → 정답의 **Place an additional order**

53-55 3인 대화

W-Br **53Jae-Young, I heard you were selected to present a talk at the National Energy Summit this fall.** Congratulations!

M-Cn Thank you. **53I'm excited about the opportunity, but I have no idea what I'll talk about.** It has to be about sustainable energy.

M-Au I've been researching how residential solar power is becoming more common. How about that?

M-Cn It's a great idea, Gregory, but it won't work. **54The keynote speech by award-winning scientist Rania Shenoy will be closely related to that.**

W-Br I've got a monthly subscription to *Green Future magazine*. **55I'm sure you could find some ideas in the old editions. You're more than welcome to borrow them.**

여: 재영 씨, 올 가을 국가에너지 정상회의에서 발표자로 뽑혔다고 들었어요. 축하해요!
남1: 고마워요. 이런 기회를 갖게 되어 설레지만, 무엇에 대해 발표해야 할지 모르겠어요. 지속 가능 에너지에 관한 것이어야 할 텐데요.
남2: 제가 주거용 태양열 발전이 더 보편화되는 양상을 연구하고 있는데, 이 주제는 어때요?
남1: 아주 좋은 생각이지만 안 될 것 같아요, 그레고리. 수상 경력이 있는 과학자인 래니아 쉐노이의 기조연설이 그 주제와 밀접하게 관련이 있어요.
여: 전 〈녹색 미래〉 잡지를 매달 구독하고 있어요. 지난 호에서 아이디어를 얻을 수 있을 거예요. 기꺼이 빌려줄게요.

어휘 select 선발하다 summit 정상회담 present a talk 발표하다, 연설하다 opportunity 기회 sustainable 지속 가능한 research 연구하다 residential 주거의 solar power 태양열 발전 common 보편적인, 흔한 keynote speech 기조연설 award-winning 상을 받은 closely 밀접하게 related to ~와 연관성이 있는[관련 있는] subscription to ~의 구독 edition 판, 호 You're more than welcome to 얼마든지 ~해도 된다 borrow 빌리다

53

What is the conversation mainly about?

(A) Articles for a magazine
(B) Venues for a conference
(C) Nominees for an award
(D) Topics for a presentation

대화의 주요 내용은 무엇인가?
(A) 잡지 기사
(B) 회의 장소
(C) 수상 후보자
(D) 발표 주제

어휘 article 기사　venue 개최지　conference 회의　nominee 후보자

해설 전체 내용 관련 – 대화의 주제
여자의 첫 번째 대사에서 첫 번째 남자가 국가에너지 정상회의에서 연설자로 뽑혔다(Jae-Young, I heard you were selected to present a talk at the National Energy Summit this fall)고 했다. 이어서 첫 번째 남자가 그런 기회를 가져 설레지만 무엇에 대해 말해야 할지 모르겠다(I'm excited about the opportunity, but I have no idea what I'll talk about)고 했다. 대화의 주요 내용이 발표 주제라는 것을 알 수 있으므로 정답은 (D)이다.

54

Why is Gregory's suggestion rejected?

(A) It will be too complex for the audience.
(B) It is not supported by evidence.
(C) It is too similar to another talk.
(D) It will take a long time to research.

그레고리의 제안이 거절된 이유는 무엇인가?
(A) 청중이 이해하기에 너무 복잡하다.
(B) 뒷받침할 증거가 없다.
(C) 다른 연설과 너무 비슷하다.
(D) 조사하는 데 시간이 오래 걸린다.

어휘 suggestion 제안　reject 거절하다　complex 복잡한 audience 청중, 관객　support 지지하다, 뒷받침하다　evidence 증거　too ~ to ... 너무 ~해서 …하지 못하는　take a long time 시간이 오래 걸리다

해설 세부 사항 관련 – 제안이 거절된 이유
첫 번째 남자의 두 번째 대사에서 수상 경력이 있는 과학자인 래니아 쉐노이의 기조연설이 그 주제와 밀접하게 관련이 있다(The keynote speech by award-winning scientist Rania Shenoy will be closely related to that)고 했다. 제안이 거절된 이유가 다른 연설과 너무 비슷해서라는 것을 알 수 있으므로 정답은 (C)이다.

▸▸ **Paraphrasing**　대화의 **closely related** → 정답의 **too similar**

55

What does the woman offer to do?

(A) Lend some publications to Jae-Young
(B) Contact an event coordinator
(C) Check Jae-Young's speech for errors
(D) Renew a magazine subscription

여자는 무엇을 해 주겠다고 하는가?
(A) 출판물을 재영에게 빌려 주기
(B) 행사 진행자에게 연락하기
(C) 재영의 연설문에서 오류 찾기
(D) 잡지 구독 갱신하기

어휘 lend to ~에게 빌려주다　publication 출판물　contact 연락하다 coordinator 코디네이터, 진행자　speech 연설　renew 갱신하다

해설 세부 사항 관련 – 여자의 제안 사항
대화 마지막에 여자가 지난 호에서 몇 가지 아이디어를 찾을 수 있을 거라며 기꺼이 빌려주겠다(I'm sure you could find some ideas in the old editions. You're more than welcome to borrow them)고 했으므로 정답은 (A)이다.

▸▸ **Paraphrasing**　대화의 **old editions** → 정답의 **some publications**

56-58

W-Br	Good evening. **⁵⁶While I was driving home from work, I noticed your banner saying that your restaurant was having a grand opening.** I love to give new restaurants a try. **⁵⁷Do you accept takeout orders?**
M-Au	Of course. We can box up anything in an insulated container for you. Here's a copy of our menu.
W-Br	Hmm… **⁵⁸I'm trying to cut down on junk food and eat things with more nutritional value.**
M-Au	The fish special comes with a side of vegetables. **⁵⁸Of all the things on the menu, I'd say that's the lightest option.**
W-Br	OK, thanks. I'll have that and a bottle of water, please.

여:	안녕하세요. **차를 몰고 퇴근하는 길에 이 식당의 개장 현수막을 봤어요.** 새로운 식당의 음식을 먹어 보는 것을 아주 좋아해요. **포장도 되나요?**
남:	물론이죠. 코팅 처리된 용기에 모든 메뉴가 포장됩니다. 여기 메뉴판이 있어요.
여:	흠 … **정크푸드를 줄이고 영양가 높은 음식을 먹으려고 하고 있어요.**
남:	생선 특선 요리에 채소가 같이 나와요. **전체 메뉴 중 가장 기름지지 않은 음식이죠.**
여:	알겠어요, 감사해요. 그럼 그것과 생수 한 병 주세요.

어휘 banner 플래카드, 현수막　grand opening 개장, 개업　give ~ a try ~를 한번 해 보다　accept 받아들이다　takeout 테이크아웃 음식　box up 상자에 담다　insulate 절연 처리를 하다　special 특별 메뉴　cut down on ~을 줄이다　junk food 정크푸드(건강에 안 좋은 인스턴트 음식)　nutritional 영양이 있는　value 가치　come with ~이 딸려 있다　side 곁들여 나오는 요리　vegetable 채소　light (음식이) 기름지지 않은[담백한]

56

What did the woman find out about the restaurant through?

(A) A flyer in the mail
(B) A friend's recommendation
(C) An online advertisement
(D) A sign near a roadway

여자는 무엇을 통해 식당에 대해 알게 되었나?

(A) 우편물 속 전단지
(B) 친구의 추천
(C) 온라인 광고
(D) 도로 위 안내판

어휘 flyer (광고·안내용) 전단 recommendation 추천
advertisement 광고 roadway 도로

해설 세부 사항 관련 – 여자가 식당을 알게 된 경로
여자의 첫 번째 대화에서 차를 몰고 퇴근하는 길에 식당의 개장 현수막을 보았다(While I was driving home from work, I noticed your banner saying that your restaurant was having a grand opening)고 했으므로 정답은 (D)이다.

> ▸▸ **Paraphrasing** 대화의 banner → 정답의 sign

57

What does the woman ask about?

(A) Which entrées are the most popular
(B) When the restaurant first opened
(C) How much a meal will cost
(D) Whether food can be packed to go

여자는 무엇에 대해 물어보는가?
(A) 가장 인기 있는 주요리
(B) 식당이 개점한 시기
(C) 음식 가격
(D) 음식 포장 여부

어휘 entrée (스테이크를 제외한) 주요 요리 meal 음식 pack 포장하다

해설 세부 사항 관련 – 여자가 물어보는 사항
여자의 첫 번째 대사에서 포장도 되는지(Do you accept takeout orders) 물었으므로 정답은 (D)이다.

> ▸▸ **Paraphrasing** 대화의 takeout → 정답의 be packed to go

58

Why does the man say, "The fish special comes with a side of vegetables"?

(A) To describe a change in the menu
(B) To suggest that an order is large enough
(C) To recommend a healthy dish
(D) To estimate a cooking time

남자가 "생선 특선 요리에 채소가 같이 나와요"라고 말한 이유는 무엇인가?
(A) 메뉴의 변경 사항을 설명하려고
(B) 주문 요리 하나가 충분히 많다는 것을 암시하려고
(C) 건강에 좋은 음식을 추천하려고
(D) 조리 시간을 예측하려고

어휘 describe 설명하다 enough ~할 만큼 충분히 healthy 건강에 좋은 estimate 예측하다 cooking time 조리 시간

해설 화자의 의도 파악 – 생선 특선 요리에 채소가 같이 나온다고 말한 의도
인용문 바로 앞 문장에서 여자가 정크푸드를 줄이고 영양가 높은 음식을 먹으려고 한다(I'm trying to cut down on junk food and eat things with more nutritional value)고 했다. 인용문 바로 뒤 문장에서 남자가 전체 메뉴

중 가장 기름지지 않다(Of all the things on the menu, I'd say that's the lightest option)고 했다. 따라서 건강에 좋은 음식을 추천하려고 한 말임을 알 수 있으므로 정답은 (C)이다.

59-61

M-Cn Hello, Ms. Bailey? This is Min-jae Moon from Otis Electronics. **59We were impressed with your résumé, and we'd like you to come to our headquarters for an interview for the field sales position. Are you free next Tuesday at four?**

W-Am Thank you for the opportunity. I usually work until five, but my manager knows I am looking for a new job. **60If it's all right with you, I'll talk to her to get approval to leave early, and then I'll call you back.**

M-Cn That's fine. My number is 555-0172. **61And you don't have to worry about speaking to a room full of HR employees. There are only three.** We think that's enough to provide an accurate assessment.

남: 안녕하세요, 베일리 씨? 오티스 일렉트로닉스의 문민재입니다. 베일리 씨의 이력서에 깊은 인상을 받았고, 현장 영업직 면접을 위해 본사로 방문해 주셨으면 합니다. 다음 주 화요일 4시가 괜찮을까요?

여: 기회를 주셔서 감사해요. 보통 5시까지 일하지만, 매니저가 제가 새 직장을 찾고 있다는 것을 알고 있어요. 괜찮다면 일찍 퇴근할 수 있는지 매니저와 얘기하고 다시 전화하겠습니다.

남: 좋아요. 제 번호는 555-0172입니다. 인사부 직원이 가득한 곳에서 면접을 보게 될까 봐 걱정하지 않아도 돼요. 3명뿐이니까요. 정확한 평가를 하는 데는 그 정도로 충분하다고 생각합니다.

어휘 impress 깊은 인상을 주다 résumé 이력서 headquarters 본사 field sale 현장 영업 opportunity 기회 look for ~을 찾다 approval 승인 full of ~로 가득 찬 HR 인사부(= human resources) employee 직원 provide 제공하다, 공급하다 accurate 정확한 assessment 평가

59

Why is the man calling the woman?

(A) To request a résumé
(B) To explain a job's duties
(C) To schedule an interview
(D) To make a job offer

남자가 여자에게 전화한 이유는 무엇인가?
(A) 이력서를 요청하기 위해
(B) 직무를 설명하기 위해
(C) 면접 일정을 잡기 위해
(D) 일자리를 제안하기 위해

어휘 request 요청하다 résumé 이력서 explain 설명하다 duties 직무, 업무

해설 전체 내용 관련 – 남자가 전화한 이유

남자의 첫 번째 대사에서 여자의 이력서에 깊은 인상을 받았고(We were impressed with your résumé) 현장 영업직 면접을 위해 본사로 방문해 달라며(we'd like you to come to our headquarters for an interview for the field sales position) 다음 주 화요일 4시가 괜찮은지(Are you free next Tuesday at four) 묻고 있다. 남자가 면접 일정을 잡기 위해 전화했다는 것을 알 수 있으므로 정답은 (C)이다.

60

What does the woman say she will do?

(A) Provide proof of purchase
(B) E-mail the man later
(C) Speak to a supervisor
(D) Arrive at the headquarters early

여자는 무엇을 할 것이라고 말하는가?

(A) 구매 증명 제공하기
(B) 나중에 남자에게 이메일 보내기
(C) 상사에게 이야기하기
(D) 본사에 일찍 도착하기

어휘 proof 증명 purchase 구매 supervisor 관리자, 직장 상사

해설 세부 사항 관련 – 여자가 할 일

여자의 대사에서 일찍 퇴근할 수 있는지 매니저와 이야기하고 다시 전화하겠다(If it's all right with you, I'll talk to her to get approval to leave early, and then I'll call you back)고 했으므로 정답은 (C)이다.

▸▸ Paraphrasing 대화의 talk to → 정답의 Speak to

61

What does the man mean when he says, "There are only three"?

(A) A group size will be small.
(B) Some time slots are filling up quickly.
(C) A task will not take very long.
(D) Some documents are still missing.

남자가 "3명뿐이니까요"라고 말한 의도는 무엇인가?

(A) 그룹 인원이 적을 것이다.
(B) 일부 시간대가 빨리 채워지고 있다.
(C) 업무는 그리 오래 걸리지 않을 것이다.
(D) 일부 문서가 여전히 누락되었다.

어휘 slot 자리, 틈, 시간 task 과제, 업무 missing 누락된

해설 화자의 의도 파악 – 3명뿐이라는 말의 의미

인용문 바로 앞 문장에서 남자가 인사부 직원이 가득한 곳에서 면접 보는 것에 대해서는 걱정하지 말라(And you don't have to worry about speaking to a room full of HR employees)고 했다. 즉 3명뿐(There are only three)이라는 말은 면접관이 적을 것이라는 의미가 내포되어 있으므로 정답은 (A)이다.

62-64 대화 + 쿠폰

W-Br Excuse me. Is this all the Marcos brand furniture you have? 62**I like the dark brown color of this sofa, but it's too wide.** I'm wondering if you have one that seats just two people.

M-Cn Usually, yes, but we're out of stock at the moment. 63**But we're getting another shipment next week.** Would you like me to give you a call when it comes in?

W-Br Thanks, but that won't be necessary. 64**I'll just get this lamp for now, and I'll come by again next week.** This coupon is still valid, isn't it?

M-Cn Yes. It expires today, so you are using it just in time.

여: 실례합니다. 이게 이 가게에 있는 마르코스 가구 전부인가요? 이 진한 갈색 소파가 마음에 드는데, 너무 넓어요. 2인용 소파가 있는지 궁금하네요.

남: 보통은 그렇습니다만, 현재 재고가 없어요. 하지만 다음 주에 배송품이 들어올 거예요. 배송품이 들어오면 전화를 드릴까요?

여: 감사하지만, 그럴 필요 없어요. 지금은 이 램프를 사고 다음 주에 다시 들를게요. 이 쿠폰 아직 사용할 수 있죠, 그렇죠?

남: 네, 오늘 만료되니까 제때 쓰시는 거예요.

어휘 out of stock 재고가 없는 shipment 배송품, 배달품 necessary 필요한 come by 들르다 valid 유효한 expire 만기가 되다 just in time 마침, 시간에 맞춰

Traverse Furniture
Discount Coupon

Sofas	$50 off
Chairs	$25 off
Bookcases	$15 off
64Lamps	$10 off

Valid until June 30

트레버스 퍼니처
할인 쿠폰

소파	50달러 할인
의자	25달러 할인
책장	15달러 할인
램프	**10달러 할인**

6월 30까지 유효

62

What does the woman dislike about the Marcos product?

(A) Its color
(B) Its price
(C) Its size
(D) Its warranty

여자는 마르코스 제품의 어떤 점이 마음에 들지 않는가?

(A) 색상
(B) 가격
(C) 크기
(D) 품질보증서

어휘 warranty 품질보증서

해설 세부 사항 관련 – 여자가 제품에서 마음에 들지 않는 것

여자의 첫 번째 대사에서 진한 갈색 소파가 마음에 드는데 너무 넓다(I like the dark brown color of this sofa, but it's too wide)고 했으므로 정답은 (C)이다.

63

According to the man, what will happen next week?

(A) A new branch location will open.
(B) Some merchandise will arrive.
(C) A store's promotional sale will end.
(D) Some products will be discontinued.

남자에 따르면, 다음 주에 무슨 일이 있는가?

(A) 새 지점이 개장한다.
(B) 일부 상품이 도착한다.
(C) 상점의 판촉 할인이 끝난다.
(D) 일부 제품이 단종된다.

어휘 branch 지점 merchandise 상품, 제품 promotional 홍보의, 판촉의 discontinue 중단하다

해설 세부 사항 관련 – 다음 주에 있을 일

남자의 첫 번째 대사에서 다음 주에 배송품이 들어온다(But we're getting another shipment next week)고 했으므로 정답은 (B)이다.

▸▸ Paraphrasing 대화의 we're getting another shipment
→ 정답의 Some merchandise will arrive.

64

Look at the graphic. How much will the woman save on her purchase?

(A) $50
(B) $25
(C) $15
(D) $10

시각 정보에 의하면, 여자는 구입 시 얼마를 절약할 것인가?

(A) 50달러
(B) 25달러
(C) 15달러
(D) 10달러

해설 시각 정보 연계 – 절약되는 금액

여자의 두 번째 대사에서 지금은 이 램프를 사고 다음 주에 다시 들르겠다(I'll just get this lamp for now, and I'll come by again next week)고 했다. 표를 보면 램프는 10달러 할인이므로 정답은 (D)이다.

65-67 대화 + 정보

M-Cn **65Jillian, you've just come off your lunch break, right?** I need your help right away.

W-Am OK, I was assigned to handle incoming luggage at the Bag Drop area. Do you need me to do something else?

M-Cn Yes. The computers at the Economy Class counter are down, so the lines are getting out of control. **66We're processing economy passengers at the Group Check-in area, so I need you to go there instead.**

W-Am All right. I'm on my way. **67I don't want any travelers to get angry about the long wait.**

남 질리언, 점심 휴식시간이 끝났죠? 당장 당신 도움이 필요해요.

여 알겠어요. 수하물 접수 구역에서 들어오는 수하물을 처리해야 하는데, 그 외에 다른 할 일이 있는 건가요?

남 네. 이코노미석 창구의 컴퓨터가 고장 나서 대기줄이 너무 길어졌네요. 이코노미석 승객들을 단체 탑승 수속 창구에서 처리해야 하니, 대신 그곳으로 가주세요.

여 알았어요. 지금 갈게요. 오래 기다리느라 화내는 여행객들이 있으면 안 돼죠.

어휘 come off (~에서) 떨어지다 lunch break 점심 시간 assign 배정하다 handle 처리하다 incoming 들어오는, 도착하는 luggage 수화물 bag drop 수화물 접수 counter 창구 down 고장 난 get out of control 제어할 수 없게 되다 process 처리하다 check-in 탑승 수속(대) instead 대신 on one's way 가는 중인

Sheenan Airlines Check-In

First/Business Class: Counter A
Economy Class: Counter B
66Group Check-in: Counter C
Bag Drop: Counter D

쉬난 항공 탑승 수속

1등석/비즈니스석: A 창구
이코노미석: B 창구
단체 탑승 수속: C창구
수화물 접수: D 창구

65

What has the woman just finished doing?

(A) Sorting luggage
(B) Fixing a computer
(C) Taking a break
(D) Ordering dinner

여자가 방금 끝낸 일은 무엇인가?

(A) 수화물 분류
(B) 컴퓨터 수리
(C) 휴식하기
(D) 저녁 식사 주문

어휘 sort 분류하다 fix 고치다

해설 세부 사항 관련 – 여자가 방금 끝낸 일
남자의 첫 번째 대사에서 여자에게 점심 휴식 시간이 끝났는지(Jillian, you've just come off your lunch break, right) 확인하고 있으므로 정답은 (C)이다.

66

Look at the graphic. Where will the woman most likely go next?

(A) Counter A
(B) Counter B
(C) Counter C
(D) Counter D

시각 정보에 의하면, 여자는 다음으로 어디에 가겠는가?

(A) A 창구
(B) B 창구
(C) C 창구
(D) D 창구

해설 시각 정보 연계 – 여자가 갈 곳
남자의 두 번째 대사에서 이코노미석 승객들을 단체 탑승 수속 창구에서 처리해야 하니 그곳으로 가달라(We're processing economy passengers at the Group Check-in area, so I need you to go there instead)라고 했다. 표를 보면 단체 탑승 수속은 C창구이므로 정답은 (C)이다.

67

What is the woman concerned about?

(A) Missing a flight
(B) Making passengers upset
(C) Losing some luggage
(D) Using a new system

여자가 걱정하는 것은 무엇인가?

(A) 비행기를 놓치는 것
(B) 승객을 화나게 하는 것
(C) 수화물을 분실하는 것
(D) 새 시스템을 사용하는 것

어휘 miss 놓치다 upset 화난

해설 세부 사항 관련 – 여자가 걱정하는 사항
여자의 마지막 대사에서 오래 기다리느라 화내는 여행객들이 있으면 안 된다 (I don't want any travelers to get angry about the long wait)고 했으므로 정답은 (B)이다.

▸▸ **Paraphrasing** 대화의 **angry** → 정답의 **upset**

68-70 대화 + 보고서

Test 3

W-Br Michael, we've had more complaints than usual lately. **68It seems a lot of customers are dissatisfied with the electrical work our company provides.**

M-Au Oh, really? I thought both of our teams were doing well.

W-Br Some of the problems are out of our control. **69For example, I just got off the phone with someone who was charged too much.** But take a look at the rest of the complaints.

M-Au I see what you mean. There is definitely room for improvement.

W-Br Right. Maybe some of the junior staff members are not being professional.

M-Au **70In that case, how about I conduct a workshop on basic etiquette and dealing with customers?** I think that will help.

여: 마이클, 최근에 평소보다 불만 제기가 늘었어요. 우리 회사가 제공하는 전기 작업에 불만을 가진 고객이 많은 것 같아요.

남: 오, 그래요? 우리 두 팀 모두 잘하고 있다고 생각했는데요.

여: 일부 문제는 우리가 수습할 수 없는 거예요. 가령 요금이 너무 많이 부과됐다고 방금 통화한 고객과 방금 통화한 것처럼. 그래도 나머지 불만 사항을 좀 봐 주세요.

남: 무슨 말인지 알겠어요. 개선의 여지가 있는 부분이 확실히 있네요.

여: 그렇죠. 일부 신입 직원들이 좀 미숙한 것 같아요.

남: 그런 경우라면, 기본 에티켓과 고객을 대하는 태도를 주제로 제가 워크숍을 진행해 보면 어떨까요? 그러면 도움이 될 것 같은데요.

어휘 complaint 불만사항 dissatisfied with ~에 불만인 out of control 통제할 수 없는 get off the phone with ~와 방금 통화를 끝내다 charge 요금을 부과하다 definitely 절대적으로 room 여지 improvement 향상, 개선 junior staff 하급 사원, 신입 직원 professional 능숙한, 전문가의 솜씨를 가진 conduct 실시하다 etiquette 에티켓, 예의 deal with ~을 다루다

Customer	Reported Issue
Victoria Castro	Late arrival
Motokazu Sai	Mess left behind
69Chun Deng	Overcharged on bill
Rohan Baria	Unfriendly staff

고객	보고된 문제
빅토리아 캐스트로	도착 지체
모토카즈 사이	깔끔하지 못한 마무리
천 뎅	**과다 청구된 요금**
로한 바리아	불친절한 직원

68

Who most likely are the speakers?

(A) Gardeners
(B) Taxi drivers
(C) Housekeepers
(D) Electricians

화자들은 누구이겠는가?

(A) 조경사
(B) 택시 기사
(C) 가사 도우미
(D) 전기 기사

어휘 gardener 조경사 housekeeper 가사 도우미 electrician 전기
기사

해설 전체 내용 관련 – 화자들의 직업

여자의 첫 번째 대사에서 회사에서 제공하는 전기 작업에 불만을 가진 고객이
많다(It seems a lot of customers are dissatisfied with the electrical
work our company provides)고 했다. 화자들이 전기 기사라는 것을 알 수
있으므로 정답은 (D)이다.

69

Look at the graphic. Whom did the woman speak to
earlier today?

(A) Victoria Castro
(B) Motokazu Sai
(C) Chun Deng
(D) Rohan Baria

시각 정보에 의하면, 여자가 오늘 통화한 사람은 누구인가?

(A) 빅토리아 캐스트로
(B) 모토카즈 사이
(C) 천 뎅
(D) 로한 바리아

해설 시각 정보 연계 – 여자가 통화한 사람

여자의 두 번째 대사에서 요금이 너무 많이 부과됐다는 고객과 방금 통화했
다(For example, I just got off the phone with someone who was
charged too much)고 했다. 표를 보면 과다 청구된 요금을 보고한 사람은
Chun Deng이므로 정답은 (C)이다.

▸▸ Paraphrasing 대화의 **charged too much**
→ 시각 정보의 **Overcharged**

70

What does the man offer to do?

(A) Lead a training session
(B) Visit a customer
(C) Work on the weekend
(D) Hire more junior employees

남자는 무엇을 해 주겠다고 하는가?

(A) 교육 진행하기
(B) 고객 방문하기
(C) 주말에 근무하기
(D) 신입 직원 고용하기

어휘 lead 지휘하다, 이끌다 training session 교육 (과정) customer
고객 hire 고용하다 junior employee 신입 직원

해설 세부 사항 관련 – 남자의 제안 사항

남자의 마지막 대사에서 그런 경우라면 기본 에티켓과 고객을 대하는 태
도를 주제로 내가 워크숍을 진행해 보면 어떻겠냐(In that case, how
about I conduct a workshop on basic etiquette and dealing with
customers)고 제안하고 있다. 따라서 남자가 교육을 진행할 것을 제안하고 있
으므로 정답은 (A)이다.

▸▸ Paraphrasing 대화의 **conduct a workshop**
→ 정답의 **Lead a training session**

PART 4

71-73 전화 메시지

M-Au Hello, Mr. Osmond. This is Leo from the
company headquarters. **71We received your
paperwork asking to move to the Salem branch.**
I'm pleased to say there is an opening there,
so we can approve your request. Your first day
will be Monday, October eighth. **72The company
will reimburse you for a portion of your moving
expenses, so don't forget to hang onto your
receipts. 73Your office hasn't been assigned yet,
but I'll e-mail the directions to you as soon as
they're ready.** I'll be in touch later this week.

안녕하십니까, 오스몬드 씨. 본사의 레오입니다. 살렘 지점으로 전근을 요청하는
문서를 받았습니다. 그 지점에 자리가 나서 오스몬드 씨의 요청을 승인할 수 있
음을 알리게 되어 기쁩니다. 근무일은 10월 8일 월요일부터입니다. 회사에서 이
사 비용 일부를 상환해 주니 잊지 말고 영수증을 보관하세요. 오스몬드 씨의 사무
실이 아직 배정되지 않아서 준비되는 대로 약도를 이메일로 보내겠습니다. 이번
주 후반에 연락하겠습니다.

어휘 headquarters 본사 paperwork 서류, 문서 branch
지점, 지사 opening 공석 approve 승인하다 request 요청
reimburse 상환하다 a portion of 일부, 약간의 expense
경비 hang onto ~을 보관하다 receipt 영수증 assign 할당하다,
배정하다 directions 약도, 길 안내 as soon as ~하자마자 be in
touch 연락하고 지내다

71

What has the listener recently done?

(A) Received a job promotion
(B) Purchased a home in Salem
(C) Requested a branch transfer
(D) Found some missing paperwork

청자가 최근에 한 일은 무엇인가?

(A) 승진했다
(B) 살렘에 주택을 구입했다
(C) 지점 전근을 요청했다
(D) 일부 누락 문서를 찾았다

어휘 job promotion 승진 purchase 구입하다 transfer 전근 가다
request 요청하다 missing 분실된

해설 전체 내용 관련 – 청자가 최근에 한 일
지문 초반부에 화자가 살렘 지점으로 전근을 요청하는 문서를 받았다(We received your paperwork asking to move to the Salem branch)고 했으므로 정답은 (C)이다.

> ▸▸ Paraphrasing 지문의 asking to move to the Salem branch
> → 정답의 Requested a branch transfer

72

What does the speaker remind the listener to do?
(A) Read some training materials
(B) Stay within a budget
(C) Keep some receipts
(D) E-mail him an update

화자는 청자에게 무엇을 하라고 상기시키는가?
(A) 교육 자료 읽기
(B) 예산을 초과하지 않기
(C) 일부 영수증 보관하기
(D) 이메일로 최신 정보 알리기

어휘 remind 상기시키다, 알리다 material 자료 stay within ~에서 벗어나지 않다 budget 예산 update 최신 정보

해설 세부 사항 관련 – 화자가 상기시키는 내용
지문 중반부에서 화자가 회사에서 이사 비용 일부를 상환해 주니 잊지 말고 영수증을 보관하라(The company will reimburse you for a portion of your moving expenses, so don't forget to hang onto your receipts)고 했으므로 정답은 (C)이다.

> ▸▸ Paraphrasing 지문의 hang onto → 정답의 keep

73

What information does the speaker plan to send?
(A) A colleague's number
(B) An office location
(C) A list of responsibilities
(D) An updated schedule

화자가 보내려고 계획하는 정보는 무엇인가?
(A) 동료의 전화번호
(B) 사무실 위치
(C) 직무 목록
(D) 업데이트된 일정

어휘 colleague 동료 responsibility 책임, 책무

해설 세부 사항 관련 – 화자가 보내려는 정보
지문 후반부에 청자의 사무실이 아직 배정되지 않아서 준비되는 대로 약도를 이메일로 보내겠다(Your office hasn't been assigned yet, but I'll e-mail the directions to you as soon as they're ready)고 했으므로 정답은 (B)이다.

74-76 공지

W-Am Good evening, ladies and gentlemen. **74It's wonderful to see so many people here tonight to watch our two main mayoral candidates—business owner Diego Silva and current mayor Jesse Sundburg—debate the important issues.** As you came in, you were handed a small white card. **75If you have any questions you want to ask the candidates, please write them on the card and pass it to an usher.** We'll try to get to as many as possible. **76Moderating this event will be Lily Nolan, a top-class reporter from the _Clemensville Times_**, and we'll begin shortly.

안녕하십니까, 신사 숙녀 여러분. 우리의 주요 시장 후보 두 명인 기업가 디에고 실바 씨와 제시 선드버그 현 시장님이 펼칠 주요 현안 토론회에 이렇게 많은 분들이 오신 것을 보니 정말 놀랍습니다. 여러분께서는 들어오실 때, 작은 흰색 카드를 받으셨습니다. 후보자에게 질문이 있으면 그 카드에 적어서 안내원에게 전달해 주십시오. 최대한 많은 질문을 다루도록 노력하겠습니다. 〈클레멘스빌 타임즈〉의 최고 기자인 릴리 놀란이 사회를 보겠습니다. 곧 시작하겠습니다.

어휘 mayoral 시장의 candidate 후보자 business owner 경영주, 기업주 current 현재의 mayor 시장 debate 토론하다 issue 문제, 쟁점 hand 건네다 pass to ~에게 넘기다 usher 안내원 get to ~에 착수하다 moderate (공정한 토론이 진행되도록) 사회를 보다 top-class 최고의 reporter 기자 shortly 곧

74

Where is the announcement taking place?
(A) At an annual election
(B) At a community fundraiser
(C) At a political debate
(D) At a publication launch

공지는 어디에서 이루어지고 있는가?
(A) 연례 선거
(B) 지역사회 기금 모금 행사
(C) 정치 토론회
(D) 출판물 발행 행사

어휘 annual 연례의 election 선거 community 지역사회 fundraiser 기금 모금 행사 political 정치적인 debate 토론 publication 출판 launch 출시(하는 행사)

해설 전체 내용 관련 – 발표 장소
지문 초반부에 화자가 주요 시장 후보인 기업가 디에고 실바 씨와 제시 선드버그 현 시장이 펼칠 주요 현안 토론회에 많은 사람들이 온 것을 보니 놀랍다(It's wonderful to see so many people here tonight to watch our two main mayoral candidates—business owner Diego Silva and current mayor Jesse Sundburg—debate the important issues)고 했다. 따라서 정치 토론회에서 안내하는 내용임을 알 수 있으므로 정답은 (C)이다.

75

How can the listeners use the card they were given?

(A) To register for a service
(B) To share an inquiry
(C) To cast a vote
(D) To make a donation

청자들이 받은 카드의 사용처는 무엇인가?

(A) 서비스에 등록하기 위해
(B) 질문을 공유하기 위해
(C) 투표를 하기 위해
(D) 기부를 하기 위해

어휘   register for ~에 등록하다   inquiry 질문, 문의   cast 던지다   vote
표   make a donation 기부하다

해설   세부 사항 관련 – 청자들이 받은 카드의 사용처

지문 중반부에서 후보자에게 질문이 있으면 카드에 적어서 안내원에게 전달하
라(If you have any questions you want to ask the candidates, please
write them on the card and pass it to an usher)고 했다. 따라서 청자들
은 질문 공유를 위해 카드를 사용한다는 것을 알 수 있으므로 정답은 (B)이다.

>> **Paraphrasing**   지문의 **questions** → 정답의 **inquiry**

76

Who most likely is Lily Nolan?

(A) A journalist
(B) A city official
(C) A business owner
(D) An actress

릴리 놀란은 누구이겠는가?

(A) 기자
(B) 시 공무원
(C) 기업가
(D) 여배우

어휘   journalist 기자, 언론인   city official 시 공무원   actress 여배우

해설   세부 사항 관련 – 릴리 놀란의 직업

지문 마지막에서 화자가 〈클레멘스빌 타임즈〉의 최고 기자인 릴리 놀란이 사
회를 보겠다(Moderating this event will be Lily Nolan, a top-class
reporter from the *Clemensville Times*)고 했으므로 정답은 (A)이다.

>> **Paraphrasing**   지문의 **a top-class reporter**
→ 정답의 **A journalist**

77-79 전화 메시지

M-Cn   Hello, Ms. Fleming? My name's Ted, and
I'm calling from Lawson Incorporated. **77We're
supposed to visit your property tomorrow to
trim some bushes and remove a dead tree. 78I
have your address, but I'm wondering whether
or not we'll be able to park on your street. Will
there be any open spots?** Our truck might be too
big for your driveway, so I wanted to check in
advance. Please call me back at 555-0133. **79Our
office is open until six P.M., but I'm leaving an
hour before that. So, please try to call while I'm
still here, if possible.** Thanks a lot!

안녕하세요, 플레밍 씨? 저는 로슨 인코퍼레이티드의 테드입니다. 내일 플레밍
씨 댁을 방문해서 일부 덤불을 손질하고 죽은 나무를 제거하기로 되어 있습니다.
귀하의 주소는 있는데, 거리에 주차 공간이 있는지 알고 싶습니다. 개방된 장소가
있나요? 우리 트럭이 귀하의 진입로로 너무 클지 몰라서 미리 확인하고 싶습니
다. 555-0133으로 전화 주십시오. 우리 사무실은 오후 6시까지 열지만 저는 1
시간 일찍 퇴근할 겁니다. 그러니 가능하면 제가 사무실에 있는 동안 전화해 주세
요. 대단히 감사합니다!

어휘   be supposed to ~하기로 되어 있다   property 건물, 부동산
trim 다듬다   bush 덤불   remove 제거하다   park 주차하다   open
개방된   spot 장소   driveway 진입로   in advance 미리

77

What kind of business most likely is Lawson
Incorporated?

(A) A construction firm
(B) A landscaping company
(C) A catering service
(D) A transportation firm

로슨 인코퍼레이티드는 어떤 사업체이겠는가?

(A) 건설 회사
(B) 조경 회사
(C) 음식 공급 업체
(D) 운송 회사

어휘   construction 건축, 건설   landscaping 조경   catering 음식
공급, 출장 뷔페   transportation 운송

해설   전체 내용 관련 – 로슨 인코퍼레이티드의 사업 분야

지문 초반부에서 내일 청자의 집을 방문해서 일부 덤불을 손질하고 죽은 나무
를 제거하기로 했다(We're supposed to visit your property tomorrow
to trim some bushes and remove a dead tree)고 했으므로 정답은 (B)
이다.

78

What does the speaker ask the listener about?

(A) The billing method
(B) The address for a service
(C) The arrival time
(D) The parking availability

화자가 청자에게 물어보는 것은 무엇인가?

(A) 청구 방법
(B) 서비스를 위한 주소
(C) 도착 시간
(D) 주차 가능성

어휘   billing 청구   method 방법   arrival 도착   parking 주차
availability 가능성

해설 세부 사항 관련 - 화자가 물어보는 사항

지문 중반부에서 주소는 있는데 주차가 가능한 공간이 있는지 알고 싶다며 개방된 장소가 있는지(I have your address, but I'm wondering whether or not we'll be able to park on your street. Will there be any open spots) 물어보았다. 따라서 화자는 주차가 가능한지를 묻고 있으므로 정답은 (D)이다.

▸▸ Paraphrasing 지문의 **whether or not we'll be able to park** → 정답의 **parking availability**

79

When should the listener call the speaker?

(A) By three o'clock
(B) By five o'clock
(C) By six o'clock
(D) By eight o'clock

청자는 화자에게 언제 전화해야 하는가?
(A) 3시까지
(B) 5시까지
(C) 6시까지
(D) 8시까지

해설 세부 사항 관련 - 청자가 전화해야 하는 시간

지문 후반부에서 사무실은 오후 6시까지 열지만 1시간 일찍 퇴근하니 사무실에 있는 동안 전화하라(Our office is open until six P.M., but I'm leaving an hour before that. So, please try to call while I'm still here, if possible)고 했다. 청자가 화자에게 5시까지 전화해야 함을 알 수 있으므로 정답은 (B)이다.

80-82 공지

> W-Br ⁸⁰**I have some great news regarding our new line of athletic shoes.** ⁸¹**I'm thrilled to say that I've just received word that professional basketball player Kevin Murphy has agreed to endorse the line.** We'll hold a product launch event where he'll be signing autographs. There will also be a drawing for one of his jerseys, part of the official uniform he wore in a championship game. ⁸²**Having a big star like this on board is going to be great for our profits.** We can expect major growth. I'll keep you posted on the rest of the details of Mr. Murphy's involvement as they unfold.

자사 운동화 신제품에 관한 좋은 소식이 있습니다. 프로 농구 선수 케빈 머피가 신제품을 홍보하기로 했다는 것을 알리게 되어 아주 기쁩니다. 머피가 사인회를 하는 곳에서 제품 출시 행사를 개최할 예정입니다. 챔피언십 경기에서 그가 입은 공식 유니폼을 경품으로 내건 추첨 행사도 있을 겁니다. 이처럼 대스타가 합류한 것은 자사 수익에 좋은 영향을 미칠 것입니다. 큰 성장을 기대할 수 있습니다. 머피 씨의 합류에 대한 나머지 자세한 소식이 들어오는 대로 계속 알려드리겠습니다.

어휘 regarding ~에 대한 athletic shoes 운동화 thrilled 아주 신이 난 endorse (유명인이 광고에 나와서 특정 상품을) 보증[홍보]하다 launch 출시하다 autograph (유명인의) 사인 drawing 제비뽑기, 추첨 jersey 운동복 on board 합류한 profit 수익 keep posted (최신 정보를) 계속 알려 주다 involvement 개입, 관여 unfold 전개되다, 펼치다

80

What does the speaker's company sell?

(A) Camping gear
(B) Uniforms
(C) Footwear
(D) Jewelry

화자의 회사가 판매하는 것은 무엇인가?
(A) 캠핑 장비
(B) 유니폼
(C) 신발류
(D) 보석

어휘 gear 장비 footwear 신발(류) jewelry 보석

해설 전체 내용 관련 - 회사 판매품

지문 초반부에 화자가 자사 운동화 신제품에 관한 좋은 소식이 있다(I have some great news regarding our new line of athletic shoes)고 했으므로 정답은 (C)이다.

▸▸ Paraphrasing 지문의 **athletic shoes** → 정답의 **Footwear**

81

What is the speaker pleased about?

(A) A product launch had high attendance.
(B) A new product experienced record sales.
(C) A professional consultant approved a plan.
(D) A celebrity will provide an endorsement.

화자는 무엇에 대해 기뻐하는가?
(A) 제품 출시 행사에 사람들이 많이 왔다.
(B) 신제품이 기록적인 판매고를 올렸다.
(C) 전문 컨설턴트가 계획을 승인했다.
(D) 유명 인사가 제품을 홍보할 것이다.

어휘 launch 출시 (행사) attendance 출석(률), 참석(률) experience 경험하다 record sales 기록적인 판매 consultant 상담가, 컨설턴트 approve 승인하다 celebrity 유명 인사 provide 제공하다 endorsement 홍보, 보증

해설 세부 사항 관련 - 화자가 기뻐하는 일

지문 초반부에 프로 농구 선수 케빈 머피가 신제품을 홍보하기로 했다는 것을 알리게 되어 아주 기쁘다(I'm thrilled to say that I've just received word that professional basketball player Kevin Murphy has agreed to endorse the line)라고 했으므로 정답은 (D)이다.

▸▸ Paraphrasing 지문의 **endorse** → 정답의 **provide an endorsement**

82

What does the speaker most likely mean when she says, "We can expect major growth"?

(A) Some competitors have left the market.
(B) Another branch will be opened.
(C) Many more employees will be hired.
(D) The company's revenue will increase.

여자가 "큰 성장을 기대할 수 있습니다"라고 말한 의도는 무엇인가?

(A) 일부 경쟁사들이 시장을 떠났다.
(B) 다른 지점이 개장할 것이다.
(C) 더 많은 직원이 고용될 것이다.
(D) 회사 수익이 증가할 것이다.

어휘 competitor 경쟁자, 경쟁사 branch 지사 employee 직원
hire 고용하다 revenue 수익, 수입 increase 증가하다

해설 화자 의도 파악 – 큰 성장을 기대한다는 말의 의도
인용문 바로 앞 문장에서 이처럼 대스타가 합류한 것은 수익에 좋은 영향을 미칠 것(Having a big star like this on board is going to be great for our profits)이라고 했다. 따라서 큰 성장은 문맥상 수익 증대를 의미하므로 정답은 (D)이다.

83-85 회의 발췌

W-Am Good morning, everyone. **83I've called this meeting to let you know about a loan type that we'll be adding to our bank's borrowing options.** This product is called the Flex Loan, and its funds can be spent on a variety of uses such as renovations, vehicle purchases, and even vacations. **84I'm passing out the details about the terms of the loan. Please commit them to memory so you don't have to refer to the sheet when speaking to customers.** **85Vigil Bank and Rochester Bank have offered something similar for a long time, so it's a good thing we're finally doing this ourselves.**

여러분, 안녕하세요. 우리 은행의 대출 상품에 추가되는 대출 유형에 대해 알려드리려고 회의를 소집했습니다. 이 상품은 플렉스론으로 수리, 차량 구매 및 심지어 휴가와 같은 다양한 용도로 자금을 사용할 수 있습니다. 대출 조건에 대한 세부 사항을 나누어 주겠습니다. 고객과 상담할 때 인쇄물을 참조할 필요가 없도록 세부 사항을 외워두십시오. 비질 뱅크와 로체스터 뱅크는 벌써 오래전부터 비슷한 대출을 제공하고 있는데, 마침내 우리도 이런 대출을 제공하게 되니 잘된 일입니다.

어휘 call a meeting 회의를 소집하다 loan 대출 borrowing
option 대출 상품 product 상품 a variety of 다양한 fund 자금
renovation 수리 vehicle 차량 purchase 구입 pass out
~을 나누어 주다 details 세부 사항 term 조건 commit ~ to
memory ~를 기억하다, 암기하다 refer to ~을 참조하다 sheet
종이, 인쇄물 offer 제공하다 similar 비슷한

83

According to the speaker, what is the purpose of the meeting?

(A) To introduce a loan type
(B) To announce a change in leadership
(C) To explain a hiring process
(D) To remind listeners about a policy

화자에 따르면, 회의의 주제는 무엇인가?

(A) 대출 유형 소개
(B) 임원진 교체 발표
(C) 채용 절차 설명
(D) 청자들에게 정책 알리기

어휘 introduce 소개하다 announce 발표하다 leadership
지도부 explain 설명하다 hiring process 채용 절차 remind
상기시키다, 알리다 policy 정책

해설 전체 내용 관련 – 회의 주제
지문 초반부에 화자가 은행의 대출 상품에 추가할 대출 유형에 대해 알리려고 회의를 소집했다(I've called this meeting to let you know about a loan type that we'll be adding to our bank's borrowing options)고 했다. 따라서 회의의 주제가 대출 상품 소개라는 것을 알 수 있으므로 정답은 (A)이다.

84

What are the listeners asked to do?

(A) Report their vacation time
(B) Memorize some information
(C) Be more friendly to customers
(D) Fill out a consent form

청자들은 무엇을 하라는 요청을 받았는가?

(A) 휴가 시점 보고하기
(B) 몇 가지 정보 외우기
(C) 고객을 더 친절하게 대하기
(D) 동의서 작성하기

어휘 report 보고하다 memorize 암기하다 friendly 친절한
customer 고객 fill out a form 양식을 작성하다 consent 동의

해설 세부 사항 관련 – 청자들이 요청 받은 사항
지문 중반부에서 대출 조건에 대한 세부 사항을 나누어 줄 테니 고객과 상담할 때 인쇄물을 참조할 필요가 없도록 외워 두라(I'm passing out the details about the terms of the loan. Please commit them to memory so you don't have to refer to the sheet when speaking to customers)고 했으므로 정답은 (B)이다.

▸▸ Paraphrasing 지문의 **commit them to memory**
→ 정답의 **memorize some information**

85

What benefit does the speaker mention?

(A) Catching up with competitors
(B) Keeping fees low
(C) Improving employee motivation
(D) Boosting productivity

화자가 언급하는 이점은 무엇인가?

(A) 경쟁사들 따라잡기
(B) 수수료 저렴하게 유지하기
(C) 직원 의욕 고취하기
(D) 생산성 증진하기

어휘 benefit 혜택, 이점 catch up with 따라잡다 competitor 경쟁사 fee 수수료 motivation 적극성, 의욕 boost 증진하다, 북돋우다 productivity 생산성

해설 세부 사항 관련 - 화자가 언급하는 혜택

지문 마지막에 화자가 비질 뱅크와 로체스터 뱅크는 벌써 오래 전부터 비슷한 대출을 제공하고 있는데, 마침내 우리도 이런 대출을 제공하게 되니 잘된 일 (Vigil Bank and Rochester Bank have offered something similar for a long time, so it's a good thing we're finally doing this ourselves) 이라고 했다. 경쟁사들을 따라잡는 것이 화자가 언급하는 이점임을 알 수 있으므로 정답은 (A)이다.

86-88 광고

M-Au Work your way to a healthier you at Daily Fit Gym, located at 701 18th Street. We're the area's largest fitness facility, with modern workout equipment and challenging group classes that will get you in shape. [86]**We're now open later than usual, until 11 P.M., to better fit our members' busy schedules.** [87]**We also offer additional services such as food consultations with nutritionist Chris Abner and massages from our on-site therapist, Min-Ji Williams.** Not sure Daily Fit Gym is right for you? [88]**Visit us at no cost for the entire first week of April.** We're sure you'll want to make Daily Fit Gym your new workout home.

18번가 701번지에 위치한 데일리 핏 짐에서 열심히 운동해 더욱 건강한 사람이 되십시오. 저희는 이 지역 최대 규모의 피트니스 시설로서, 현대식 운동 장비와 도전 의식을 북돋는 단체 수업을 통해 여러분의 건강을 지켜 줍니다. **이제 회원들의 바쁜 일정에 맞추어 평소보다 늦은 밤 11시까지 문을 엽니다. 크리스 에브너 영양사의 식단 상담, 민지 윌리엄스 상주 치료사의 마사지 등과 같은 추가 서비스도 제공합니다.** 데일리 핏 짐이 여러분에게 딱 맞는지 확신할 수 없다면요? **4월 첫 주 내내 무료로 방문해 보십시오.** 데일리 핏 짐을 여러분의 새로운 운동 시설로 원하시리라 확신합니다.

어휘 work one's way to (노력하여) ~에 도달하다 healthier 더 건강한 fitness facility 피트니스 시설, 운동 시설 equipment 장비 challenging 도전적인, 어려운 get in shape 좋은 몸 상태[몸매]를 유지하다 fit 맞추다 additional 추가의 consultation 상담 nutritionist 영양사 on-site 현장의, 상주하는 therapist 치료사 at no cost 무료로 entire 전체의 workout 운동

86

What has Daily Fit Gym recently done?

(A) Expanded its building
(B) Added new exercise classes
(C) Purchased more equipment
(D) Extended its business hours

데일리 핏 짐이 최근에 한 것은 무엇인가?

(A) 건물을 확장했다
(B) 신규 운동 강좌를 추가했다
(C) 추가 장비를 구입했다
(D) 영업시간을 연장했다

어휘 expand 확장하다 add 추가하다 purchase 구입하다 extend 연장하다 business hours 영업시간

해설 세부 사항 관련 - 데일리 핏 짐이 최근에 한 일

지문 중반부에 화자가 회원들의 바쁜 스케줄에 맞추어 평소보다 늦은 밤 11시까지 문을 연다(We're now open later than usual, until 11 P.M., to better fit our members' busy schedules)고 했다. 데일리 핏 짐이 최근에 영업시간을 연장했다는 것을 알 수 있으므로 정답은 (D)이다.

▶▶ Paraphrasing 지문의 open later than usual
→ 정답의 Extended its business hours

87

Who most likely is Mr. Abner?

(A) The Daily Fit Gym owner
(B) A fitness instructor
(C) A massage therapist
(D) A diet consultant

애브너 씨는 누구이겠는가?

(A) 데일리 핏 짐 주인
(B) 피트니스 강사
(C) 마사지 치료사
(D) 식단 상담가

어휘 owner 소유주 instructor 강사 diet 식단, 다이어트 consultant 상담사, 컨설턴트

해설 세부 사항 관련 - 애브너 씨의 신분

지문 중반부에서 크리스 에브너 영양사의 식단 상담, 민지 윌리엄스 상주 치료사의 마사지 등과 같은 추가 서비스도 제공한다(We also offer additional services such as food consultations with nutritionist Chris Abner and massages from our on-site therapist, Min-Ji Williams)고 했다. 애브너 씨가 영양사라고 언급했으므로 정답은 (D)이다.

▶▶ Paraphrasing 지문의 food consultations
→ 정답의 diet consultant

88

According to the advertisement, what can listeners do in the first week of April?

(A) Attend a welcome reception
(B) Enroll in some group classes
(C) Use the facility for free
(D) Sign up for a building tour

TEST 3   **87**

광고에 따르면, 청자들이 4월 첫 주에 할 수 있는 일은 무엇인가?

(A) 환영회 참석하기
(B) 일부 단체 수업에 등록하기
(C) **무료로 시설 이용하기**
(D) 건물 견학 신청하기

어휘 attend 참석하다 welcome reception 환영회 enroll in ~에 등록하다 for free 무료로 sign up for ~을 신청하다 building tour 건물 견학

해설 세부 사항 관련 – 4월 첫 주에 할 수 있는 일

지문 후반부에서 4월 첫 주 내내 무료로 방문하라(Visit us at no cost for the entire first week of April)고 했다. 4월 첫 주에 무료로 시설을 이용할 수 있음을 알 수 있으므로 정답은 (C)이다.

▶▶ Paraphrasing 지문의 **visit us at no cost**
→ 정답의 **use the facility for free**

89-91 전화 메시지

W-Br Hi, Samantha. I just wanted to thank you again for giving me a private tour of your hair salon. **89I hope you have a lot of customers when you open next week.** I loved the way you've decorated the waiting area. I especially liked the brightly colored chairs. Were they from a local store? **90They would look great in my living room.** Anyway, I'm sure your hard work will pay off. **91I'll encourage all of my friends to go to your salon.** If there's anything else I can do, just let me know.

안녕하세요, 사만다. 미용실을 개인적으로 구경시켜 준 것에 다시 한 번 감사해요. 다음 주 개점 때 손님이 많이 오길 바라요. 대기실 장식이 아주 마음에 들었어요. 특히 밝은색 의자가 좋았어요. 이 지역에 있는 가게 물건인가요? 우리 집 거실에도 잘 어울릴 것 같아요. 어쨌든 사만다가 열심히 한 결실이 있을 거예요. 내 친구 모두에게 사만다의 미용실을 권할게요. 뭐든 내가 도울 일이 있으면 알려 주세요.

어휘 give a tour of ~에 대해 안내하다 private 개인적인, 비밀의 customer 고객 decorate 장식하다 waiting area 대기 장소 especially 특히 brightly 밝게 local 지역의, 지방의 pay off 성과를 올리다, 결실을 맺다 encourage 권장하다

89

What is the listener preparing to do?

(A) Apply for a job
(B) Move to a new city
(C) Purchase a home
(D) Open a business

청자가 준비하는 것은 무엇인가?

(A) 일자리 지원하기
(B) 다른 도시로 이사하기
(C) 집 구입하기
(D) **사업 개시하기**

어휘 apply for ~에 지원하다 move to ~로 옮기다

해설 전체 내용 관련 – 청자가 준비하는 것

지문 초반부에 화자가 다음 주 개점 때 손님이 많이 오길 바란다(I hope you have a lot of customers when you open next week)고 했으므로 정답은 (D)이다.

90

What does the speaker suggest when she says, "Were they from a local store"?

(A) She is trying to reduce the shipping time on some items.
(B) She wants to buy some furniture for herself.
(C) She thinks the listener should support the local economy.
(D) She hopes returning the furniture will be easy.

화자가 "이 지역에 있는 가게 물건인가요?"라고 말한 의도는 무엇인가?

(A) 일부 품목의 운송 시간을 줄이려 한다.
(B) **자신을 위해 가구를 몇 점 사고 싶다.**
(C) 청자가 지역 경제를 뒷받침해야 한다고 생각한다.
(D) 가구 반납이 쉽기를 바란다.

어휘 reduce 줄이다 shipping time 운송 시간 furniture 가구 support 지원하다 local 지역의 economy 경제 return 돌려주다

해설 화자 의도 파악 – 이 지역 가게 제품인지 묻는 말의 의도

이 지역 가게 물건인지(Were they from a local store)를 물은 후 화자의 집 거실에도 잘 어울릴 것 같다(They would look great in my living room)고 했다. 따라서 인용문은 화자가 자기 집에도 둘 수 있게 그 가구를 사고 싶다는 의미이므로 정답은 (B)이다.

91

What does the speaker say she will do?

(A) Visit a site again
(B) Provide her friends' numbers
(C) Recommend a business
(D) Call the listener later

화자는 무엇을 해 주겠다고 말하는가?

(A) 사이트 다시 방문하기
(B) 친구들의 전화번호 제공하기
(C) **가게 추천하기**
(D) 나중에 청자에게 전화하기

어휘 provide 제공하다 recommend 추천하다

해설 세부 사항 관련 – 화자의 제안 사항

지문 후반부에서 화자의 친구 모두에게 청자의 미용실을 권하겠다(I'll encourage all of my friends to go to your salon)고 했으므로 정답은 (C)이다.

▶▶ Paraphrasing 지문의 **encourage** → 정답의 **recommend**

M-Cn   This is Matt Hershell for WTTR Radio reporting live from the newly opened Fincham Stadium. **92I'm here for the National Soccer Tournament's championship game between the Everton Eagles and the Webster Tigers.** **93The game will begin in about ten minutes, and I'm surrounded by the crowd's cheers. It's unlike anything I've experienced before. I can hardly hear myself.** **94Up next, I'll be talking with former Webster coach Ron Frazier to get his thoughts on what we can expect this evening, so stay tuned because you won't want to miss that.**

새로 문을 연 핀챔 스타디움에서 생방송으로 소식을 전하고 있는 WTTR 라디오의 매트 허쉘입니다. 지금 저는 에버튼 이글스와 웹스터 타이거즈의 전국 축구 선수권대회 결승전 현장에 나와 있습니다. 경기는 약 10분 후에 시작되고 저는 군중의 환호에 둘러싸여 있습니다. 이런 경험은 처음입니다. 제 목소리가 거의 들리지 않을 정도입니다. 곧이어 론 프레이저 전 웹스터 코치와 이야기를 나누며 오늘 저녁 예상되는 경기에 대한 의견을 들어보겠습니다. 놓치고 싶지 않다면 주파수를 고정하십시오.

어휘 report 보고하다, 보도하다 live 생방송으로 newly 새롭게 championship 선수권 대회, 챔피언전 surround 둘러싸다 crowd 군중 cheer 환호 unlike ~과 다르게 hardly 거의 ~않다 up next 다음 순서로는 former 이전의 thought 생각 expect 기대하다 stay tuned 채널을 고정하다 miss 놓치다

92

What is the report mainly about?

(A) A sports competition
(B) An awards ceremony
(C) A music festival
(D) A construction project

보도의 주제는 무엇인가?
(A) 스포츠 대회
(B) 시상식
(C) 음악 축제
(D) 건설 프로젝트

어휘 competition 경쟁, 대회 awards ceremony 시상식 construction 건설

해설 전체 내용 관련 – 보도의 주제
지문 초반부에서 화자가 지금 에버튼 이글스와 웹스터 타이거즈의 전국 축구 선수권대회 결승전 현장에 나와 있다(I'm here for the National Soccer Tournament's championship game between the Everton Eagles and the Webster Tigers)고 했다. 따라서 보도의 주제가 스포츠 대회라는 것을 알 수 있으므로 정답은 (A)이다.

▶▶ Paraphrasing   지문의 National Soccer Tournament's championship game → 정답의 sports competition

93

What does the speaker most likely mean when he says, "I can hardly hear myself"?

(A) The attendees are excited.
(B) Some equipment is not working.
(C) The report is getting interrupted.
(D) An area is too small.

화자가 "제 목소리가 거의 들리지 않을 정도입니다"라고 말한 의도는 무엇인가?
(A) 관중이 흥분해 있다.
(B) 일부 장비가 작동하지 않는다.
(C) 보도가 중단되고 있다.
(D) 장소가 너무 좁다.

어휘 attendee 참석자 equipment 장비 interrupt 방해하다

해설 화자 의도 파악 – 목소리를 들을 수 없다는 말의 의도
인용문 바로 앞 문장에서 경기는 10분 후에 시작되고 화자는 군중의 환호에 둘러싸여 있으며 이런 경험은 처음이다(The game will begin in about ten minutes, and I'm surrounded by the crowd's cheers. It's unlike anything I've experienced before)라고 했다. 그런 다음 화자의 목소리가 들리지 않는다(I can hardly hear myself)는 말을 한 것은 관중의 함성이 크다는 의미이므로 정답은 (A)이다.

94

What will the listeners hear next?

(A) Some music
(B) A commercial
(C) An interview
(D) A weather update

청자들이 다음으로 듣게 되는 것은 무엇인가?
(A) 음악
(B) 광고
(C) 인터뷰
(D) 날씨 정보

어휘 commercial 광고 update 최신 정보

해설 세부 사항 관련 – 청자들이 듣게 될 것
지문 마지막에서 다음으로 론 프레이저 전 웹스터 코치와 이야기를 나누며 오늘 저녁 예상되는 경기에 대한 의견을 들어보겠다(Up next, I'll be talking with former Webster coach Ron Frazier to get his thoughts on what we can expect this evening)며 놓치고 싶지 않다면 주파수를 고정하라(so stay tuned because you won't want to miss that)고 했으므로 정답은 (C)이다.

▶▶ Paraphrasing   지문의 talking with → 정답의 interview

95-97 공지 + 지도

M-Au   Attention, customers. Dewdrop Fashions is offering an amazing seventy-five percent off certain brands of coats. **95We accidentally ordered too many Albers Incorporated and**

Berea coats, so we need to get rid of them fast. ⁹⁶You can find the sale items at the back section of the store on the left. ⁹⁷This offer is valid for today only, so don't miss your chance to pick up fashionable and durable coats at a fraction of the usual price. And don't forget, next week we're opening our second store in Ramosville. With two stores, it's twice the fun at Dewdrop Fashions!

고객님, 주목해 주십시오. 듀드롭 패션즈는 특정 브랜드 코트를 75퍼센트 할인하여 놀라운 가격에 제공하고 있습니다. 뜻하지 않게 앨버스 인코퍼레이티드와 베리아 코트를 너무 많이 주문하는 바람에 빨리 처분해야 합니다. 할인 품목은 상점 뒤편 구역 왼쪽에 있습니다. 이번 할인은 오직 오늘만 유효하니 세련되고 튼튼한 코트를 정상가보다 훨씬 저렴하게 구입할 수 있는 기회를 절대 놓치지 마십시오. 그리고 다음 주 래모스빌에 2호점을 개점한다는 것도 잊지 마십시오. 2개의 매장으로 듀드롭 패션즈에서는 쇼핑이 두 배 더 재미있습니다.

어휘 attention 알립니다, 주목하세요 customer 고객 off 할인되어 certain 특정한 brand 상표 accidentally 뜻하지 않게 get rid of ~을 처리하다[없애다] section 부분, 구역 valid 유효한 fraction 극히 일부 durable 내구성 있는, 튼튼한 usual price 정상가

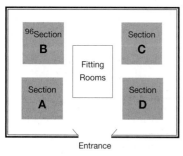

Entrance

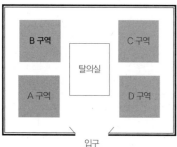

입구

95

Why is the store having a sale?

(A) To correct an ordering error
(B) To celebrate an anniversary
(C) To promote a grand opening
(D) To introduce a new brand

상점이 할인을 하는 이유는?

(A) 주문 실수를 바로잡으려고
(B) 기념일을 축하하려고
(C) 개장을 홍보하려고
(D) 새 상표를 소개하려고

어휘 correct 바로잡다, 정정하다 celebrate 축하하다 anniversary 기념일 promote 홍보하다 grand opening 개장 introduce 소개하다 brand 상표

해설 세부 사항 관련 – 상점이 할인하는 이유

지문 초반부에서 화자는 실수로 앨버스 인코퍼레이티드와 베리아 코트를 너무 많이 주문하는 바람에 빨리 처분해야 한다(We accidentally ordered too many Albers Incorporated and Berea coats, so we need to get rid of them fast)고 했다. 상점이 할인하는 이유는 주문 실수를 바로잡기 위한 것이므로 정답은 (A)이다.

96

Look at the graphic. Where can listeners find discounted items?

(A) In Section A
(B) In Section B
(C) In Section C
(D) In Section D

시각 정보에 의하면, 청자들이 할인 품목을 찾을 수 있는 곳은 어디인가?

(A) A 구역
(B) B 구역
(C) C 구역
(D) D 구역

해설 시각 정보 연계 – 할인 품목을 찾을 수 있는 곳

지문 중반부에 화자가 할인 품목은 상점 뒤편 왼쪽에 있다(You can find the sale items at the back section of the store on the left)고 했다. 표를 보면 상점 뒤편 왼쪽은 B 구역이므로 정답은 (B)이다.

97

When will the sale end?

(A) At the end of the day
(B) Tomorrow evening
(C) At the end of the week
(D) Next week

할인은 언제 끝나는가?

(A) 그날 폐점 때
(B) 내일 저녁
(C) 주가 끝날 때
(D) 다음 주

해설 세부 사항 관련 – 할인이 끝나는 시기

지문 중반부에서 세일은 오직 오늘만 유효하니 세련되고 튼튼한 코트를 정상가보다 훨씬 저렴하게 구입할 수 있는 기회를 놓치지 말라(This offer is valid for today only, so don't miss your chance to pick up fashionable and durable coats at a fraction of the usual price)고 했으므로 정답은 (A)이다.

98-100 전화 메시지 + 양식

W-Am Hi, Mr. Barkley. This is Konomi Okano from the PR department, um... department code 423. **⁹⁸I was sorting and arranging the items in our supply closet this morning, and I noticed that we had some leftover supplies from last month.** I don't want to purchase items we don't need. **⁹⁹So, I'd like only four binders instead of the number I ordered. ¹⁰⁰I won't be here on Friday when the shipment comes in, so please just drop off the supplies with Regina Marino, who also works in my department.** Thank you.

안녕하세요, 바클리 씨. 홍보실의 코노미 오카노입니다, 음… 부서 코드는 423이고요. 오늘 아침 비품 창고에서 물품을 분류하고 정리했는데 지난달에 쓰고 남은 물품을 좀 발견했어요. 필요하지 않은 물품은 구입하고 싶지 않아요. 그래서 주문한 개수 대신 바인더는 4개만 있으면 좋겠어요. 배송품이 들어오는 금요일에는 제가 여기 없을 거예요. 그러니 같은 부서에 근무하는 레지나 마리노에게 물품을 건네주시면 됩니다. 감사합니다.

어휘 PR 홍보(= public relations) department 부서 sort 분류하다 arrange 정리하다 supply closet 비품 창고 notice 알아채다 leftover supply 남은 물품 purchase 구입하다 binder 바인더 instead of ~ 대신에 shipment 배송품 drop off 갖다 놓다

Monthly Supply Request
Department Code: 423

Description	Quantity
⁹⁹Three-ring binder	12
Box of printing paper	7
Ink cartridge	4
Pack of address labels	3

월간 비품 요청
부서 코드: 423

세부 사항	수량
3공 링바인더	12
인쇄 용지 1박스	7
잉크 카트리지	4
주소 라벨 1팩	3

98

What did the speaker do in the morning?

(A) Received the wrong supplies
(B) Changed a department code
(C) Completed a PR campaign
(D) Organized a storage area

화자가 아침에 한 일은 무엇인가?

(A) 엉뚱한 물품을 받았다
(B) 부서 코드를 변경했다
(C) 홍보 캠페인을 완료했다
(D) 보관 구역을 정리했다

어휘 receive 받다 supply 물품 complete 완료하다 organize 정리하다 storage 보관

해설 세부 사항 관련 – 화자가 아침에 한 일
지문 초반부에서 오늘 아침 비품 창고에서 물품을 분류하고 정리했는데 지난달에 사용하고 남은 물품을 발견했다(I was sorting and arranging the items in our supply closet this morning, and I noticed that we had some leftover supplies from last month)고 했으므로 정답은 (D)이다.

▸▸ Paraphrasing 지문의 was sorting and arranging the items in our supply closet
→ 정답의 organized a storage area

99

Look at the graphic. Which item's quantity is now incorrect?

(A) 12
(B) 7
(C) 4
(D) 3

시각 정보에 의하면, 어느 물품의 수량이 잘못되었는가?

(A) 12
(B) 7
(C) 4
(D) 3

해설 시각 정보 연계 – 수량이 잘못된 물품
지문 중반부에 화자가 주문한 개수 대신 바인더는 4개만 있으면 된다(I'd like only four binders instead of the number I ordered)고 했다. 표를 보면 3공 링바인더의 주문 수량은 12개이므로 정답은 (A)이다.

100

What does the speaker ask the listener to do?

(A) Provide a catalog of supplies
(B) Give the items to a coworker
(C) Confirm that a change has been made
(D) Drop off another order form

화자가 청자에게 해 달라고 요청하는 것은 무엇인가?

(A) 물품 카탈로그 제공하기
(B) 물품을 동료에게 주기
(C) 변경되었는지 확인하기
(D) 다른 주문 양식 가져다 주기

어휘 provide 제공하다 coworker 동료 confirm 확인하다 order form 주문 양식

해설 세부 사항 관련 – 화자가 요청하는 일
지문 후반부에서 배송품이 들어오는 금요일에는 화자가 없으니 같은 부서에 근무하는 레지나 마리노에게 물품을 건네주라(I won't be here on Friday when the shipment comes in, so please just drop off the supplies with Regina Marino, who also works in my department)고 했으므로 정답은 (B)이다.

TEST 4

1 (B)	**2** (C)	**3** (B)	**4** (A)	**5** (D)
6 (B)	**7** (C)	**8** (C)	**9** (C)	**10** (A)
11 (B)	**12** (B)	**13** (A)	**14** (A)	**15** (B)
16 (C)	**17** (B)	**18** (B)	**19** (B)	**20** (C)
21 (B)	**22** (B)	**23** (A)	**24** (B)	**25** (C)
26 (A)	**27** (C)	**28** (B)	**29** (B)	**30** (A)
31 (B)	**32** (A)	**33** (C)	**34** (A)	**35** (B)
36 (A)	**37** (C)	**38** (A)	**39** (D)	**40** (C)
41 (C)	**42** (D)	**43** (D)	**44** (C)	**45** (C)
46 (A)	**47** (B)	**48** (A)	**49** (D)	**50** (B)
51 (A)	**52** (C)	**53** (A)	**54** (B)	**55** (B)
56 (C)	**57** (D)	**58** (C)	**59** (D)	**60** (C)
61 (A)	**62** (B)	**63** (D)	**64** (B)	**65** (D)
66 (B)	**67** (A)	**68** (A)	**69** (B)	**70** (C)
71 (D)	**72** (B)	**73** (A)	**74** (C)	**75** (D)
76 (B)	**77** (A)	**78** (A)	**79** (B)	**80** (A)
81 (D)	**82** (A)	**83** (B)	**84** (D)	**85** (C)
86 (B)	**87** (D)	**88** (C)	**89** (D)	**90** (B)
91 (A)	**92** (C)	**93** (B)	**94** (D)	**95** (C)
96 (A)	**97** (B)	**98** (B)	**99** (C)	**100** (B)

PART 1

01 W-Br

(A) She's pushing a shopping cart.
(B) She's reaching for a product.
(C) She's wiping off a counter.
(D) She's piling up serving trays.

(A) 여자가 쇼핑 카트를 밀고 있다.
(B) 여자가 제품을 향해 손을 뻗고 있다.
(C) 여자가 카운터를 닦아 내고 있다.
(D) 여자가 서빙 쟁반을 쌓고 있다.

어휘 push 밀다 reaching for ~을 향해 (손을) 뻗다 product 제품 wipe off 닦아 내다 counter 판매대, 카운터 pile up 쌓다 serving tray 서빙 쟁반

해설 1인 등장 사진 – 사람의 동작 묘사
(A) 동사 오답. 사진에 쇼핑 카트가 보이지만 여자가 쇼핑 카트를 밀고 있는(is pushing a shopping cart) 모습이 아니므로 오답.
(B) 정답. 여자가 제품을 향해 손을 뻗고 있는(is reaching for a product) 모습이므로 정답.
(C) 동사 오답. 사진에 판매대가 보이지만 여자가 판매대를 닦아 내고 있는(is wiping off a counter) 모습이 아니므로 오답.
(D) 사진에 없는 명사를 이용한 오답. 사진에 서빙 쟁반(serving tray)이 보이지 않으므로 오답.

02 M-Au

(A) Some people are climbing up a staircase.
(B) A wheelbarrow is being loaded with plants.
(C) Some people are working near an open flame.
(D) A cable is hanging from a ceiling.

(A) 몇 사람이 계단을 올라가고 있다.
(B) 손수레에 화분들을 싣고 있다.
(C) 몇 사람이 화염 근처에서 일하고 있다.
(D) 전선이 천정에 매달려 있다.

어휘 climb up 오르다 staircase 계단 wheelbarrow 손수레 load with ~을 싣다 plant 화초, 식물 open flame 화염 cable 케이블, 전선 hang from ~에 매달리다 ceiling 천정

해설 2인 이상 등장 사진 – 사람 또는 사물 중심 묘사
(A) 사진에 없는 명사를 이용한 오답. 사진에 계단(staircase)이 보이지 않으므로 오답.
(B) 사진에 없는 명사를 이용한 오답. 사진에 수레(wheelbarrow)나 화분들(plants)이 보이지 않으므로 오답.
(C) 정답. 몇 사람이 화염 근처에서 일하고 있는(are working near an open flame) 모습이므로 정답.
(D) 동사 오답. 사진에 전선이 보이지만 천정에 매달려 있는(is hanging from a ceiling) 모습이 아니므로 오답.

03 W-Am

(A) A man is placing soil into a pot.
(B) A man is working with a rake.
(C) A man is holding a tree branch.
(D) A man is putting on a hat.

(A) 남자가 항아리에 흙을 넣고 있다.
(B) 남자가 갈퀴로 작업하고 있다.
(C) 남자가 나뭇가지에 손을 뻗치고 있다.
(D) 남자가 모자를 쓰고 있는 중이다.

어휘 place 놓다, 두다 soil 흙 pot 냄비, 항아리 rake 갈퀴 hold 들고 있다 branch 나뭇가지 put on 입다, 쓰다

해설 1인 등장 사진 – 사람의 동작 묘사
(A) 동사 오답. 남자가 항아리에 흙을 넣는(is placing soil into a pot) 모습이 아니므로 오답.
(B) 정답. 남자가 갈퀴로 작업하는(is working with a rake) 모습이므로 정답.

(C) 동사 오답. 남자가 나뭇가지를 들고 있는(is holding a tree branch) 모습이 아니므로 오답.

(D) 동사 오답. 남자가 모자를 쓰고 있는 상태이지 쓰고 있는(is putting on a hat) 동작을 하고 있지 않으므로 오답.

04 M-Cn

(A) They are examining a file.
(B) They are moving a table.
(C) The man is closing a notebook computer.
(D) The woman is pouring coffee into a cup.

(A) 그들은 서류를 검토하고 있다.
(B) 그들은 탁자를 옮기고 있다.
(C) 남자가 노트북 컴퓨터를 닫고 있다.
(D) 여자가 컵에 커피를 따르고 있다.

어휘 examine 검토하다 file 파일, 서류(철), 자료 move 옮기다 pour 붓다, 따르다

해설 2인 이상 등장 사진 – 사람의 동작 묘사
(A) 정답. 두 사람이 서류를 검토하고 있는(are examining a file) 모습이므로 정답.
(B) 동사 오답. 사진에 탁자가 보이지만 두 사람이 탁자를 옮기고 있는(are moving a table) 모습은 아니므로 오답.
(C) 동사 오답. 사진에 노트북 컴퓨터가 보이지만 남자가 노트북 컴퓨터를 닫고 있는(is closing a notebook computer) 모습은 아니므로 오답.
(D) 동사 오답. 사진에 컵이 보이지만 여자가 컵에 커피를 따르고 있는(is pouring coffee into a cup) 모습이 아니므로 오답.

05 W-Br

(A) Some people are folding napkins.
(B) Bottles are being arranged on a shelf.
(C) Glasses have been placed in a dishwasher.
(D) Some people are gathered at a table.

(A) 몇 사람이 냅킨을 접고 있다.
(B) 병이 선반 위에 놓여지고 있다.
(C) 유리컵이 식기세척기 안에 있다.
(D) 몇 사람이 식탁에 모여 있다.

어휘 fold 접다 arrange 배열하다, 정리하다 shelf 선반 place 놓다, 두다 dishwasher 식기세척기 gather 모이다

해설 2인 이상 등장 사진 – 사람 또는 사물 중심 묘사
(A) 동사 오답. 사진에 냅킨이 보이지만 사람들이 냅킨을 접고 있는(are folding napkins) 모습이 아니므로 오답.

(B) 동사 오답. 사진에 병이 보이지만 병이 선반 위에 놓여지고 있는(are being arranged on a shelf) 모습이 아니므로 오답.
(C) 사진에 없는 명사를 이용한 오답. 사진에 식기세척기(dishwasher)가 보이지 않으므로 오답.
(D) 정답. 몇 사람이 식탁에 모여 있는(are gathered at a table) 모습이므로 정답.

06 M-Cn

(A) Plants are lined up along a ramp.
(B) Some chairs are unoccupied.
(C) A table is being removed from a room.
(D) A painting is propped against a chair.

(A) 화분이 경사로를 따라 줄지어 있다.
(B) 몇몇 의자가 비어 있다.
(C) 식탁이 방에서 치워지고 있다.
(D) 그림이 의자에 기대어져 있다.

어휘 line up 줄을 서다 ramp 경사로, 램프 unoccupied 비어 있는 remove 제거하다, 치우다 painting 그림 prop (받침대 등으로) 받치다

해설 사물/배경 사진 – 사물의 상태 묘사
(A) 동사 오답. 사진에 화분이 보이지만 경사로를 따라 줄지어 있는(are lined up along a ramp) 모습이 아니므로 오답.
(B) 정답. 몇몇 의자들이 비어 있는(are unoccupied) 모습이므로 정답.
(C) 동사 오답. 사진에 식탁이 있지만 방에서 치워지고 있는(is being removed from a room) 모습이 아니므로 오답.
(D) 동사 오답. 사진에 그림이 보이지만 의자에 기대어져 있는(is propped against a chair) 모습이 아니므로 오답.

Part 2

07

M-Au How long will the meeting take?
W-Am (A) I prefer the bus.
　　　(B) A couple of feet.
　　　(C) Most of the afternoon.

회의가 얼마나 걸릴까요?
(A) 전 버스가 좋아요.
(B) 2피트요.
(C) 오후 내내요.

어휘 take (시간이) 걸리다 a couple of 둘의

해설 회의 소요 시간을 묻는 How long 의문문
(A) 질문과 상관없는 오답. 회의 소요 시간을 묻는 How long 의문문에 버스가 더 좋다는 답변은 질문의 맥락에서 벗어난 것이므로 오답.

(B) 연상 단어 오답. How long을 듣고 길이에 대한 질문으로 잘못 이해했을 때 연상 가능한 a couple of feet를 이용한 오답.

(C) 정답. 회의 소요 시간을 묻는 질문에 오후 내내라는 구체적인 시간을 언급하고 있으므로 정답.

08

W-Br The sign is smaller than I anticipated.

M-Cn (A) Sorry, I can't do that.
(B) In a wide range.
(C) Yes, it's hard to read.

표지판이 예상했던 것보다 작네요.
(A) 죄송해요, 저는 그렇게 할 수 없어요.
(B) 넓은 범위로요.
(C) 맞아요. 읽기가 어려워요.

어휘 sign 간판, 표지판 anticipate 예상, 기대하다 range 범위

해설 사실/정보 전달의 평서문
(A) 질문과 상관없는 오답. that이 가리키는 대상이 평서문에 없으므로 오답.
(B) 연상 단어 오답. 질문의 smaller에 대해 크기 측면에서 연상되는 단어인 wide를 이용한 오답.
(C) 정답. 표지판이 예상보다 작다는 말에 긍정으로 응답한 후 읽기가 어렵다는 부연 설명을 하고 있으므로 정답.

09

M-Cn When is Janice supposed to be away at the conference?

M-Au (A) That's the shortest route possible.
(B) No, she's giving a presentation.
(C) Late August, I believe.

재니스 씨가 언제 회의 때문에 자리를 비울 건가요?
(A) 그게 가능한 최단 경로예요.
(B) 아뇨, 그녀는 발표를 할 예정이에요.
(C) 8월 말일 거예요.

어휘 be supposed to ~하기로 되어 있다 be away 부재 중이다 conference 회의 route 경로 give a presentation 발표하다

해설 자리를 비우는 시점을 묻는 When 의문문
(A) 질문과 상관없는 오답. 재니스 씨가 언제 회의 때문에 자리를 비울지 묻는 질문에 그게 가능한 최단 경로라는 답변은 질문의 맥락에서 벗어난 것이므로 오답.
(B) Yes/No 불가 오답. When 의문문에 Yes/No 응답은 불가능하므로 오답.
(C) 정답. 재니스 씨가 언제 회의 때문에 자리를 비울지 묻는 질문에 8월 말이라는 구체적인 시점을 제시하고 있으므로 정답.

10

M-Au Does he want any more help carrying those pots next door?

W-Br (A) It looks like he can manage it.
(B) Packing services are free.
(C) Some carrying cases.

그가 화분들을 옆집으로 옮기는 데 도움이 더 필요할까요?
(A) 그가 어떻게든 할 수 있을 것 같아요.
(B) 포장 서비스는 무료예요.
(C) 휴대용 케이스 몇 개요.

어휘 carry 나르다 pot 화분 next door 옆방[집]에 manage (어떻게든) 해내다 packing service 포장 서비스 carrying case 휴대용 케이스

해설 도움 필요 여부를 묻는 조동사(does) Yes/No 의문문
(A) 정답. 화분을 옆집으로 옮기는 데 도움이 필요한지 여부에 대해 그가 혼자 할 수 있다고 응답한 것은 도움이 필요하지 않다는 의미를 우회적으로 표현하는 것이므로 정답.
(B) 연상 단어 오답. 질문의 box에 대하여 포장 측면에서 연상 가능한 packing services를 이용한 오답.
(C) 단어 반복 오답. 질문의 carrying을 반복한 오답.

11

M-Cn Would you mind hanging these paintings on the wall?

W-Br (A) In the wooden frames.
(B) Sure, show me where you want them.
(C) They're landscape painters.

이 그림들을 벽에 걸어 주시겠어요?
(A) 목재 틀 안에요.
(B) 그러죠, 어디에 걸면 되는지 알려 주세요.
(C) 그들은 풍경 화가예요.

어휘 hang 걸다 wooden 목재의 frame 틀 landscape 풍경 painter 화가

해설 부탁/요청의 의문문
(A) 연상 단어 오답. 질문의 paintings에 대해 그림 액자의 틀 측면에서 연상 가능한 wooden frames를 이용한 오답.
(B) 정답. 그림을 벽에 걸어 달라고 하자 흔쾌히 승낙하면서(Sure) 그림을 어디에 걸면 되는지 알려 달라고 응답했으므로 정답.
(C) 파생어 오답. 질문의 paintings와 파생어 관계인 painters를 이용한 오답.

12

M-Cn Who is going to supervise our new night shift?

W-Am (A) By adding part-time staff.
(B) Mr. Jung, most likely.
(C) From four to midnight.

누가 우리의 새 야간 교대 근무를 감독할 예정인가요?
(A) 시간제 직원을 투입해서요.
(B) 아마도 정 씨일 거예요.
(C) 4시부터 자정까지요.

어휘 supervise 감독하다 shift 교대 근무 add 추가하다 part-time 시간제의 staff 직원 most likely 아마, 필시 midnight 자정

해설 교대 근무 감독자를 묻는 Who 의문문
(A) 연상 단어 오답. 질문의 night shift에 대해 야간 교대 근무 충원 측면에서 연상 가능한 part-time staff를 이용한 오답.

(B) 정답. 새 야간 교대 근무 감독자를 묻는 질문에 Mr. Jung이라는 특정 인물을 언급하고 있으므로 정답.

(C) 파생어 오답. 질문의 night와 파생어 관계인 midnight를 이용한 오답.

13

W-Br No tickets are left for tonight's performance.

W-Am (A) Have the ushers put up a notice.

(B) Two seats near the front.

(C) My friend really liked it.

오늘 밤 공연 표가 한 장도 안 남았어요.

(A) 안내원에게 공지를 올리라고 하세요.

(B) 앞쪽 근처에 두 자리 주세요.

(C) 친구가 정말 좋아했어요.

어휘 performance 공연 usher 좌석 안내원 put up 게시하다 notice 공지 front 앞쪽

해설 사실/정보 전달의 평서문

(A) 정답. 오늘 밤 공연표가 하나도 남지 않았다는 말에 안내원이 공지를 올리게 하라는 응답으로 대처 방안을 제시하고 있으므로 정답.

(B) 연상 단어 오답. 질문의 tickets에서 연상 가능한 seats를 이용한 오답.

(C) 질문과 상관없는 오답. 오늘 밤 공연표가 없다는 말에 친구가 좋아했다는 대답은 맥락에 어긋난 응답이므로 오답.

14

W-Am What does Table Five want for dessert?

M-Cn (A) They're about to order now.

(B) No, thank you — I'm full.

(C) Another set of spoons.

5번 테이블은 디저트로 무엇을 원하나요?

(A) 지금 주문하려는 차예요.

(B) 고맙지만 괜찮아요. 배가 부르네요.

(C) 숟가락 한 벌 더 주세요.

어휘 be about to 막 ~하려 하다 order 주문하다 vegetarian 채식주의자 special 특별 요리[메뉴], 정식 a set of 한 벌[세트]의

해설 디저트 메뉴를 묻는 What 의문문

(A) 정답. 5번 테이블 손님이 디저트로 무엇을 원하는지를 묻는 질문에 지금 주문하려고 한다고 답하고 있으므로 정답.

(B) 질문과 상관없는 오답. 5번 테이블 손님이 디저트로 무엇을 원하는지 묻는 질문에 괜찮다, 배부르다는 응답은 맥락에 어긋나므로 오답.

(C) 연상 단어 오답. 질문의 dessert에 대해 식기 측면에서 연상 가능한 set of spoons를 이용한 오답.

15

M-Cn Did you return those poetry books?

W-Br (A) Traditional pottery.

(B) Yes, I dropped them off earlier.

(C) An informational booklet.

그 시집들을 반납했나요?

(A) 전통 도자기요.

(B) 네, 일찌감치 갖다 줬어요.

(C) 정보 책자요.

어휘 return 돌려주다, 반납하다 poetry 시 traditional 전통적인 pottery 도자기 drop off (가는 도중에) 내려[갖다] 주다 booklet 소책자

해설 시집 반납 여부를 묻는 조동사(did) Yes/No 의문문

(A) 유사 발음 오답. 질문의 poetry와 부분적으로 발음이 유사한 pottery를 이용한 오답.

(B) 정답. 시집들을 반납했냐는 질문에 Yes로 긍정적 응답을 한 후 일찌감치 갖다 줬다는 부연 설명을 하고 있으므로 정답.

(C) 파생어 오답. 질문의 books와 파생어 관계인 booklet을 이용한 오답.

16

M-Au Last year's team-building event was wonderful, wasn't it?

W-Am (A) It's at the convention center.

(B) Our whole company.

(C) I wasn't working here then.

작년 단합대회는 정말 좋았어요, 그렇죠?

(A) 컨벤션 센터에 있어요.

(B) 회사 전체요.

(C) 그때 전 여기서 근무하지 않았어요.

어휘 team-building 팀의 결속력을 다져 주는, 팀워크의 convention center 컨벤션 센터, 대회장 whole 전체의

해설 의견에 대한 동의를 구하는 부가의문문

(A) 연상 단어 오답. 질문의 team-building event에 대해 행사 장소 측면에서 연상 가능한 convention center를 이용한 오답.

(B) 연상 단어 오답. 질문의 team-building event에 대해 행사 참가자 측면에서 연상 가능한 whole company를 이용한 오답.

(C) 정답. 작년 단합대회는 좋지 않았냐는 질문에 당시에는 여기서 근무하지 않았다는 응답으로 우회적으로 표현하고 있으므로 정답.

17

W-Br Where can I find the women's clothing section?

M-Cn (A) Some formal suits.

(B) It's on the second floor.

(C) I'll look in the fitting rooms.

여성복 코너는 어디에 있나요?

(A) 정장 몇 벌이요.

(B) 2층에 있어요.

(C) 탈의실에서 볼게요.

어휘 clothing 의복, 의류 section 부분, 구획 formal 격식을 갖춘, 정중한 suit 정장 fitting room 탈의실

해설 여성복 코너 위치를 묻는 Where 의문문

(A) 연상 단어 오답. 질문의 clothing에서 연상 가능한 suits를 이용한 오답.

(B) 정답. 여성복 코너 위치를 묻는 질문에 2층이라는 구체적인 장소를 언급하고 있으므로 정답.

(C) 연상 단어 오답. 질문의 clothing에서 연상 가능한 fitting rooms를 이용한 오답.

18

W-Am Why did we purchase all these new pieces of equipment?

M-Au (A) Try plugging it in.
(B) They were on sale.
(C) By next week, at the latest.

이 새 장비들은 왜 구입한 건가요?
(A) 전원을 연결해 보세요.
(B) 할인 중이었어요.
(C) 늦어도 다음 주까지요.

어휘 purchase 구입하다 equipment 장비 plug in 플러그를 꽂다, 전원을 연결하다 on sale 세일(할인) 중인 at the latest 늦어도

해설 새 장비를 구입한 이유를 묻는 Why 의문문
(A) 연상 단어 오답. 질문의 equipment에서 연상 가능한 plug in을 이용한 오답.
(B) 정답. 새 장비를 구입한 이유를 묻는 질문에 할인 중이었다고 응답하고 있으므로 정답.
(C) 연상 단어 오답. 질문의 purchase와 new pieces of equipment에 대하여 배달 측면에서 연상 가능한 by next week를 이용한 오답.

19

M-Cn Are you interested in an individual tour or a customized group tour?

W-Br (A) The display seems quite visible.
(B) It depends on what the costs are.
(C) Yes, it was an interesting trip.

개별 관광과 맞춤형 단체 관광 중 어느 것에 관심이 있나요?
(A) 화면이 꽤 또렷하게 보이네요.
(B) 비용에 따라 달라요.
(C) 네, 흥미로운 여행이었어요.

어휘 be interested in ~에 관심이 있다 individual 개별의, 개인의 tour 관광 customized 개개인의 요구에 맞춘 display 화면 표시 장치 quite 꽤 visible 가시적인, 뚜렷한 depend on ~에 달려 있다 cost 비용

해설 구를 연결한 선택의문문
(A) 유사 발음 오답. 질문의 individual과 부분적으로 발음이 유사한 visible을 이용한 오답.
(B) 정답. 개별 관광과 맞춤형 단체 관광 중 어느 것에 관심 있는지에 대해 비용에 달려 있다고 답한 것은 비용을 듣고 선택하겠다는 의미를 우회적으로 표현한 것이므로 정답.
(C) 파생어 오답. 질문의 interested와 파생어 관계인 interesting을 이용한 오답.

20

W-Am Won't the company banquet be held at Acorn Steakhouse?

M-Au (A) It's an investment bank.
(B) I put both of the calls on hold.
(C) Nothing has been announced yet.

회사 연회가 에이콘 스테이크하우스에서 열리지 않을까요?
(A) 투자 은행이에요.
(B) 두 전화 모두 대기 상태예요.
(C) 아직 아무런 공지도 없었어요.

어휘 banquet 연회 be held 열리다 investment 투자 put on hold ~을 보류[연기]하다

해설 연회 장소를 묻는 부정의문문
(A) 유사 발음 오답. 질문의 banquet과 부분적으로 발음이 유사한 bank를 이용한 오답.
(B) 파생어 오답. 질문의 held와 파생어 관계인 hold를 이용한 오답.
(C) 정답. 회사 연회가 에이콘 스테이크하우스에서 열리지 않겠느냐는 질문에 아직 아무런 공지도 없었다는 답변으로 불확실성을 나타내고 있으므로 정답.

21

W-Br When did Zack make plans to replace the office's light fixtures?

M-Au (A) From the hardware store.
(B) As soon as our energy bills rose.
(C) The one in my office is bright enough.

잭은 언제 사무실 전등을 교체하기로 계획한 건가요?
(A) 철물점에서요.
(B) 전기 요금이 많이 나오자마자요.
(C) 제 사무실 전구는 충분히 밝아요.

어휘 make plans 계획을 세우다 replace 교체하다 light fixture 조명 기구, 전등 hardware store 철물점 as soon as ~하자마자 energy bills 전기세 고지서 rise 증가하다

해설 결정 시기를 물어보는 When 의문문
(A) 연상 단어 오답. 질문의 replace와 light fixtures에 대해 전등 교체 측면에서 연상 가능한 hardware store를 이용한 오답.
(B) 정답. 잭이 사무실 전등을 교체하기로 계획한 시점을 묻는 질문에 전기 요금이 많이 나오자마자라고 구체적인 시점으로 응답하고 있으므로 정답.
(C) Yes/No 불가 오답. When 의문문에 Yes/No 응답은 불가능하므로 오답.

22

M-Au How often does this shop refresh its inventory?

M-Cn (A) Mine seemed rather old.
(B) About every two months.
(C) By pressing the "screen" key.

이 상점은 물건이 얼마마다 재입고되나요?
(A) 제 건 다소 오래돼 보였어요.
(B) 두 달에 한 번 정도요.
(C) "화면"키를 눌러서요.

어휘 refresh 다시 채우다 inventory 재고 rather 다소 every ~마다
press 누르다

해설 재입고 빈도를 물어보는 How often 의문문

(A) 질문과 상관없는 오답. 재입고 빈도를 물어보는 질문에 내 것은 다소 오래
되어 보였다는 답변은 질문의 맥락에서 벗어난 것이므로 오답.

(B) 정답. 재입고 빈도를 물어보는 질문에 두 달에 한 번 정도라는 구체적인 횟
수로 응답하고 있으므로 정답.

(C) 연상 단어 오답. 질문의 refresh에 대해 컴퓨터에서 최신 정보로 재생하는
측면에서 연상 가능한 "screen" key를 이용한 오답.

23

W-Am Diego hasn't repaired the printer yet, has he?

W-Br (A) I believe he has.

(B) The print edition.

(C) Oh, we only need two?

디에고가 아직 프린터를 수리하지 않았죠, 그렇죠?

(A) 수리한 것 같아요.

(B) 인쇄판이요.

(C) 오, 두 개만 있으면 되나요?

어휘 repair 수리하다 edition 판(版)

해설 프린터 수리 여부를 확인하는 부가의문문

(A) 정답. 디에고가 프린터를 수리했는지를 묻는 질문에 그런 것 같다고 긍정적
인 응답을 하고 있으므로 정답.

(B) 파생어 오답. 질문의 printer와 파생어 관계인 print를 이용한 오답.

(C) 질문과 상관없는 오답. 필요한 양을 묻는 질문에 어울리는 응답이므로 오답.

24

W-Br Who's the new sales team leader?

M-Au (A) About four promising candidates.

(B) A former consultant, I heard.

(C) In the building's East Wing.

새 영업팀장은 누구인가요?

(A) 약 4명의 유망한 후보자요.

(B) 전직 컨설턴트라고 들었어요.

(C) 건물의 동쪽에 있는 부속 건물이요.

어휘 sales team leader 영업팀장 promising 유망한 candidate
후보자 former 이전의 wing 동, 부속 건물

해설 새 영업팀장을 묻는 Who 의문문

(A) 연상 단어 오답. 질문의 new sales team leader에 대해 후보자 측면에
서 연상 가능한 promising applicants를 이용한 오답.

(B) 정답. 새 영업팀장을 묻는 질문에 전직 컨설턴트라는 특정 인물을 언급하고
있으므로 정답.

(C) 질문과 상관없는 오답. 장소를 묻는 Where 의문문에 적절한 응답이므로
오답.

25

M-Cn Where will the staff seminars be held?

W-Am (A) In less than two hours.

(B) By a local entrepreneur.

(C) We didn't know you were interested.

직원 세미나는 어디에서 열리나요?

(A) 2시간 이내예요.

(B) 지역 사업가에 의해서요.

(C) 우린 당신이 관심 있는지 몰랐어요.

어휘 staff 직원 seminar 세미나 be held 열리다, 개최되다 local
지역의 entrepreneur 사업가 interested 관심 있어 하는

해설 세미나 개최지를 묻는 Where 의문문

(A) 질문과 상관없는 오답. 시점을 묻는 When 의문문에 적절한 응답이므로
오답.

(B) 연상 단어 오답. 질문의 staff seminars에 대해 주최자나 연설자 측면에
서 연상 가능한 entrepreneur를 이용한 오답.

(C) 정답. 직원 세미나 개최지를 묻는 질문에 관심 있는지 몰랐다면서 놀라움을
나타내고 있으므로 정답.

26

W-Br Can I assist you in finding anything today?

M-Au (A) I'm just looking around.

(B) It was a small fine.

(C) Sorry, we don't have any.

찾으시는 데 도움이 필요하신가요?

(A) 그냥 둘러보는 중이에요.

(B) 적은 액수의 벌금이었어요.

(C) 죄송해요, 없어요.

어휘 assist in ~을 돕다 look around 둘러보다 fine 벌금

해설 제안/권유의 의문문

(A) 정답. 찾는 것을 도와주겠다는 제안에 그냥 둘러보는 중이라는 말로 간접적
으로 부정적인 응답을 하고 있으므로 정답.

(B) 유사 발음 오답. 질문의 finding과 부분적으로 발음이 유사한 fine을 이용
한 오답.

(C) 질문과 상관없는 오답. 찾는 것을 도와주겠다는 제안에 미안하지만 없다는
답변은 질문의 맥락에서 벗어난 것이므로 오답.

27

M-Cn Didn't you already book a seat at this conference?

W-Am (A) A brand new phonebook.

(B) Metal folding chairs.

(C) That was for Ms. Fuller.

이 회의의 좌석은 이미 예약하지 않았나요?

(A) 새 전화번호부예요.

(B) 금속 접이자요.

(C) 그건 풀러 씨를 위한 거였어요.

Test 4

어휘　book 예약하다　conference 회의　brand new 완전 새 것인
phonebook 전화번호부　metal 금속의　folding 접을 수 있는

해설　좌석 예약 여부를 묻는 부정의문문

(A) 파생어 오답. 질문의 book과 파생어 관계인 phonebook을 이용한 오답.

(B) 연상 단어 오답. 질문의 seat에서 연상 가능한 chairs를 이용한 오답.

(C) 정답. 좌석 예약 여부를 묻는 질문에 그 좌석 예약 건은 풀러 씨를 위한 거였다는 답변은 예약을 한 건 사실이지만 다른 사람을 위한 일이었음을 밝히고 있으므로 정답.

28

M-Au　Why are these books in the conference room?

W-Br　(A) Thanks, I appreciate that.

(B) Harold was working on some research.

(C) At a stationery store down the street.

왜 이 책들이 회의실에 있나요?

(A) 고마워요, 그래 주시면 감사하죠.

(B) **해럴드가 조사를 좀 하고 있었어요.**

(C) 길 아래에 있는 문구점에서요.

어휘　conference room 회의실　work on ~에 착수하다, ~에 공을 들이다　research 연구, 조사　stationery store 문구점　down the street 길 아래편에

해설　책들이 회의실에 있는 이유를 묻는 Why 의문문

(A) 질문과 상관없는 오답. 이유를 묻는 질문에 고맙다고 감사를 표하는 것은 질문의 맥락에서 벗어난 것이므로 오답.

(B) 정답. 책들이 회의실에 있는 이유를 묻는 질문에 해럴드가 조사를 하고 있었다며 구체적인 이유로 응답하고 있으므로 정답.

(C) 연상 단어 오답. 질문의 books, conference에서 연상 가능한 stationery를 이용한 오답.

29

M-Au　Do you want to lead the facility tour, or should I?

W-Am　(A) Yes, I led him there.

(B) I'll start things off.

(C) That sounds good to me.

시설 견학을 맡으시겠어요, 아니면 제가 할까요?

(A) 네, 제가 그를 그곳으로 안내했어요.

(B) **제가 맡아서 할게요.**

(C) 저는 괜찮은 것 같아요.

어휘　lead 안내하다　facility 시설　start off 시작하다

해설　문장을 연결한 선택의문문

(A) 파생어 오답. 질문의 lead와 파생어 관계인 led를 이용한 오답.

(B) 정답. 상대방에게 시설 견학을 맡고 싶은지 아니면 본인이 해야 하는지를 묻는 질문에 상대방이 하겠다는 간접적인 대답으로 선택을 제시한 것이므로 정답.

(C) 질문과 상관없는 오답. 시설 견학을 누가 해야 할지를 묻는 질문에 괜찮은 것 같다는 답변은 질문의 맥락에서 벗어난 것이므로 오답.

30

W-Br　Have you made a decision about the job transfer offer?

M-Cn　(A) I'd like to think about it some more.

(B) From the branch manager.

(C) Click here to send it.

부서 이동 제안에 대해 결정을 내렸나요?

(A) **좀 더 생각해 보고 싶어요.**

(B) 지점장한테서요.

(C) 보내려면 여기를 클릭하세요.

어휘　make a decision 결정하다　job transfer 부서[직무] 이동　offer 제안　branch manager 지점장

해설　결정 여부를 묻는 조동사(Have) 의문문

(A) 정답. 부서 이동 제안에 대한 결정 여부를 묻는 질문에 좀 더 생각해 보고 싶다는 불확실성 표현으로 응답하고 있으므로 정답.

(B) 연상 단어 오답. 질문의 job에 대해 직책 측면에서 연상 가능한 branch manager를 이용한 오답.

(C) 질문과 상관없는 오답. 부서 이동 제안에 대한 결정 여부를 묻는 질문에 보내려면 여기를 클릭하라는 답변은 질문의 맥락에서 벗어난 것이므로 오답.

31

W-Am　When do staff take their summer vacation?

M-Cn　(A) Among the Human Resources staff.

(B) Anytime, but they have to ask in advance.

(C) How long is the summary you saw?

직원들은 여름 휴가를 언제 가나요?

(A) 인사부 직원 중에서요.

(B) **언제든지요. 하지만 미리 요청해야 해요.**

(C) 당신이 본 요약문은 얼마나 긴가요?

어휘　staff 직원　take a vacation 휴가를 가다　Human Resources 인사부　anytime 언제든지　in advance 미리, 사전에　summary 요약

해설　여름 휴가 시점을 묻는 When 의문문

(A) 단어 반복 오답. 질문에 나온 staff를 반복한 오답.

(B) 정답. 직원이 여름 휴가를 언제 가는지 묻는 질문에 언제든지 가도 된다고 시점을 말한 후에 미리 요청해야 한다고 부연 설명을 하고 있으므로 정답.

(C) 유사 발음 오답. 질문의 summer와 부분적으로 발음이 유사한 summary를 이용한 오답.

Part 3

32-34

W-Br: Hi, this is Dana from Orwig Printing. **³²I was told that you called about a company name being left off of some T-shirts we printed for your upcoming fundraiser.** I'm terribly sorry about that. How can we make it up to you?

M-Cn: **³³Well, that company is one of the major sponsors of our fundraiser, and I'm concerned that this mistake could damage our good relationship with them.** Could you print up new shirts without the defect?

W-Br: **³⁴Yes, we'd be happy to provide a replacement batch for free.** We'll begin right away so that you can pick it up by Friday.

여: 안녕하세요, 오르윅 프린팅의 다나입니다. 다가오는 모금 행사용으로 저희 회사에서 제작해 드린 티셔츠 일부에서 회사명이 누락된 건으로 전화하셨다고 들었습니다. 정말 죄송합니다. 어떻게 보상해 드리면 될까요?

남: 음, 그 회사는 우리 모금 행사의 주요 후원 업체 중 하나예요. 그래서 이 실수로 해당 업체와의 우호 관계가 훼손될까 걱정입니다. 불량 없는 새 셔츠를 제작해 줄 수 있나요?

여: 네, 교체품을 기꺼이 무료로 제공해 드리겠습니다. 지금 당장 착수해서 금요일까지는 찾으실 수 있도록 하겠습니다.

어휘: leave off ~을 빼다 print (up) 무늬를 찍다, 날염하다 upcoming 다가오는 fundraiser 모금 행사 make it up to ~에게 (손해를) 보상하다 major 주요[중대]한 sponsor 후원 업체 damage 훼손하다 relationship 관계 defect 결함 replacement 교체, 대체 batch 1회분(한 번에 만들어 내는 양) for free 공짜로, 무료로 so that ~하도록 pick up ~을 찾아오다

32

What is the problem?

(A) A missing name
(B) An outdated logo
(C) A blurred image
(D) A dull color

무엇이 문제인가?

(A) 누락된 이름
(B) 구식 로고
(C) 흐린 이미지
(D) 칙칙한 색상

어휘: missing 빠진 outdated 구식인 logo 로고 blurred 흐릿한 dull 칙칙한

해설: 전체 내용 관련 – 언급된 문제

여자의 첫 번째 대사에서 제작해 준 티셔츠 일부에서 회사명이 누락된 건에 대해 남자가 전화했다고 들었다(I was told that you called about a company name being left off of some T-shirts we printed for your upcoming fundraiser)고 했다. 따라서 누락된 회사명이 문제라는 것을 알 수 있으므로 정답은 (A)이다.

▸▸ **Paraphrasing** 대화의 a company name being left off → 정답의 a missing name

33

Why is the man concerned?

(A) An event may be postponed.
(B) A type of shirt may not sell well.
(C) A sponsor may be displeased.
(D) An event budget may be exceeded.

남자가 걱정하는 이유는 무엇인가?

(A) 행사가 연기될 수 있다.
(B) 셔츠가 잘 안 팔릴 수 있다.
(C) 후원 업체가 불쾌할 수 있다.
(D) 행사 예산이 초과될 수 있다.

어휘: postpone 연기하다 displeased 불쾌한, 마음에 들지 않는 budget 예산 exceed 초과하다

해설: 세부 사항 관련 – 남자가 걱정하는 것

남자의 두 번째 대사에서 그 회사는 우리 모금 행사의 주요 후원 업체 중 하나인데 이 실수로 해당 업체와의 우호 관계가 훼손될까 걱정(that company is one of the major sponsors of our fundraiser, and I'm concerned that this mistake could damage our good relationship with them)이라고 했다. 따라서 후원 업체의 심기를 불편하게 할까 봐 걱정한다는 것을 알 수 있으므로 정답은 (C)이다.

34

What does the woman offer to do?

(A) Waive a production charge
(B) Dispose of some items
(C) Expedite a delivery
(D) Conceal some defects

여자는 무엇을 해 주겠다고 하는가?

(A) 생산 비용 면제하기
(B) 일부 제품 폐기하기
(C) 신속 배송하기
(D) 일부 결함 은폐하기

어휘: waive 포기하다 production 생산 charge 요금 dispose of ~을 없애다 expedite 더 신속히 처리하다 delivery 배달 conceal 감추다

해설: 세부 사항 관련 – 여자의 제안 사항

여자의 마지막 대사에서 교체품을 기꺼이 무료로 제공하겠다(we'd be happy to provide a replacement batch for free)고 했으므로 정답은 (A)이다.

▸▸ **Paraphrasing** 대화의 provide a replacement batch for free → 정답의 waive a production charge

W-Am **35Hi, I heard your store started a used-item exchange deal for all the electronic items you sell here.** Could you tell me how that works?

M-Cn Sure. You simply bring in your older device in good condition, and we'll give you a gift card to use toward purchasing a newer device.

W-Am Oh. How much could I get for this DX7 mobile phone?

M-Cn **36The DX7's current value is listed on our Web site. But, uh, the site is down for maintenance at the moment. 37So... let me find Jeff, our floor manager, to help you.**

W-Am I'd appreciate that.

여: 안녕하세요. 귀사에서 판매하는 전자 제품 일체에 대해 중고품 교환 거래를 시작했다고 들었어요. 그 거래가 어떻게 진행되는지 알려 주시겠어요?

남: 물론이죠. 소유하고 계신 전자 제품 중 상태가 양호한 제품을 그냥 가져오시면 돼요. 그러면 새 제품을 구입할 수 있는 상품권을 드립니다.

여: 오. 이 DX7 휴대 전화는 얼마나 받을 수 있을까요?

남: DX7의 시가가 저희 웹사이트에 나와 있어요. 그런데 지금 사이트가 보수 중이라 사용하실 수 없어요. 그럼… 손님을 도와드릴 매장 관리자인 제프를 찾아볼게요.

여: 감사합니다.

어휘 used-item 중고품 exchange 교환 deal 거래 electronic 전자의 work 작동되다, 기능하다 simply 그냥, 그저 bring 가져오다 device 장치, 기구 good condition 양호한 상태 gift card 상품권 toward ~를 얻기 위하여 purchase 구입하다 current value 시가(時價) list 리스트[목록 / 명단]에 포함시키다 down 작동이 안 되는, 다운된 maintenance 유지 (관리) at the moment 바로 지금 floor manager 매장[상점] 관리자 appreciate 고마워하다

35

Where most likely are the speakers?

(A) In a job placement agency
(B) In an electronics store
(C) In a bank
(D) In a dental clinic

화자들은 어디에 있겠는가?

(A) 취업 알선 기관
(B) 전자 제품 매장
(C) 은행
(D) 치과 진료소

어휘 job placement agency 취업 알선 기관 electronics 전자 장치 dental clinic 치과 진료소

해설 전체 내용 관련 – 화자들이 있는 장소

여자의 첫 번째 대사에서 남자의 가게에서 판매하는 전자 제품 일체에 대해 중고품 교환 거래를 시작했다고 들었다(I heard your store started a used-item exchange deal for all the electronic items you sell here)고 했다. 따라서 화자들이 전자 제품 매장에 있다는 것을 알 수 있으므로 정답은 (B)이다.

36

According to the man, what is a problem?

(A) A Web site is not operating.
(B) A promotional offer has ended.
(C) A mobile phone has no power.
(D) A meeting room is unavailable.

남자에 따르면, 무엇이 문제인가?

(A) 웹사이트가 작동하지 않는다.
(B) 판촉용 할인이 끝났다.
(C) 휴대전화에 전력이 없다.
(D) 회의실을 이용할 수 없다.

어휘 operate 운용하다, 작동하다 promotional 판촉용의 offer (일정 기간의) 할인 power (공급) 전기 unavailable 이용할 수 없는

해설 세부 사항 관련 – 남자가 언급하는 문제점

남자의 두 번째 대사에서 DX7 시가가 나와 있는 웹사이트가 보수 중이라 사용할 수 없다(The DX7's current value is listed on our Web site. But, uh, the site is down for maintenance at the moment)고 했으므로 정답은 (A)이다.

▶▶ Paraphrasing 대화의 **the site is down**
→ 정답의 **a Web site is not operating**

37

What does the man say he will do?

(A) Lower a price
(B) Supply an additional form
(C) Find a manager
(D) Reschedule an appointment

남자는 무엇을 하겠다고 말하는가?

(A) 가격 인하하기
(B) 추가 양식 제공하기
(C) 관리자 찾기
(D) 약속 일정 변경하기

어휘 lower 낮추다 supply 제공하다 additional 추가의 form 양식 reschedule 일정을 변경하다 appointment 약속

해설 세부 사항 관련 – 남자의 제안 사항

남자의 두 번째 대사에서 도움을 줄 매장 관리자를 찾아보겠다(let me find Jeff, our floor manager, to help you)고 했으므로 정답은 (C)이다.

▶▶ Paraphrasing 대화의 **our floor manager**
→ 정답의 **a manager**

38-40

W-Am	Thank you for coming in. **38As I mentioned on the phone, our insurance company is looking for software that will allow employees to work from home.**
M-Au	OK. So, your employees will need to open and edit company files remotely, right? Are there any other features you need?
W-Am	Not really. But since some of the files will contain sensitive information, the software should be extremely secure.
M-Au	Let me see... **39BaxterShare fully protects data from unauthorized access.** It's probably your best choice.
W-Am	OK. Tell me more.
M-Au	**40Well, if you'd like, I could show you how it works, using the copy on my notebook.**
W-Am	**40That would be great.**

여	방문해 주셔서 감사해요. 전화로 언급했듯이, 우리 보험회사는 직원들이 재택근무를 할 수 있도록 해 주는 소프트웨어를 찾고 있어요.
남	알겠습니다. 그럼 직원들이 원격으로 컴퓨터 파일을 열고 편집해야 한다는 거죠? 그 밖에 필요한 기능은 없으신가요?
여	없어요. 하지만 일부 파일에는 민감한 정보가 있기 때문에 소프트웨어는 매우 안전해야 합니다.
남	어디 보자… 백스터쉐어는 허용되지 않은 접근으로부터 데이터를 완벽히 보호해 줍니다. 이게 최선의 선택일 겁니다.
여	그렇군요. 자세히 얘기해 주세요.
남	괜찮으시면 제 노트북 컴퓨터 복사본을 이용해서 어떻게 작동하는지 보여드릴 수 있어요.
여	좋아요.

어휘 mention 언급하다 insurance 보험 allow to ~하도록 허용하다 work from home 재택근무 하다 edit 편집하다 remotely 원격으로 feature 기능, 특징 contain 포함하다 sensitive 민감한 extremely 극도로 secure 안전한, 보안의 fully 완전히 protect 보호하다 unauthorized 허가 받지 않은 access 접근 choice 선택 work 작동되다 copy 복사본

38

Where most likely does the woman work?

(A) At an insurance provider
(B) At a marketing company
(C) At a paper manufacturer
(D) At a customer service call center

여자는 어디에서 일하겠는가?

(A) 보험회사
(B) 마케팅 회사
(C) 제지 업체
(D) 고객서비스 콜센터

어휘 provider 제공자, 제공 업체 manufacturer 제조 업체

해설 전체 내용 관련 - 여자가 일하는 회사

여자의 첫 번째 대사에서 보험회사는 직원들이 재택근무를 할 수 있도록 해 주는 소프트웨어를 찾고 있다(our insurance company is looking for software that will allow employees to work from home)고 했다. 따라서 보험회사에서 일하고 있음을 알 수 있으므로 정답은 (A)이다.

> **Paraphrasing** 대화의 insurance company
> → 정답의 insurance provider

39

What does the man say about BaxterShare?

(A) It is difficult to use.
(B) It has limited features.
(C) It is available in a trial version.
(D) It offers strong security.

남자는 백스터쉐어에 대해 뭐라고 하는가?

(A) 사용하기 어렵다.
(B) 기능이 제한되어 있다.
(C) 시험 버전에서 사용 가능하다.
(D) 강력한 보안을 제공한다.

어휘 limited 제한된 available 가능한 trial version 시험 버전 offer 제공하다 security 보안

해설 세부 사항 관련 - 백스터쉐어에 관한 남자의 말

남자의 두 번째 대사에서 백스터쉐어가 허용되지 않은 접근으로부터 데이터를 완벽히 보호한다(BaxterShare fully protects data from unauthorized access)고 했으므로 정답은 (D)이다.

> **Paraphrasing** 대화의 fully protects data from unauthorized access → 정답의 offers strong security

40

What does the woman agree to do?

(A) Copy some important files
(B) Download some software
(C) View a demonstration
(D) Buy a notebook computer

여자는 무엇을 하는 데 동의하는가?

(A) 중요한 파일 복사하기
(B) 소프트웨어 다운로드하기
(C) 시연 보기
(D) 노트북 컴퓨터 구입하기

어휘 copy 복사하다 download (데이터를) 내려받다 view 보다 demonstration 시연

해설 세부 사항 관련 - 남자의 권유 사항

남자의 마지막 대사에서 노트북 컴퓨터 복사본을 이용해서 어떻게 작동하는지 보여주겠다(I could show you how it works, using the copy on my notebook)고 했고 여자가 마지막 대사에서 좋다(That would be great)고 했다. 따라서 소프트웨어 시연에 동의했으므로 정답은 (C)이다.

> **Paraphrasing** 대화의 show you how it works
> → 정답의 view a demonstration

41-43

W-Br   ⁴¹**Well, Andy, it's hard to believe, but… our coffee shop's second store is set to open in mid-July. That's only one month away.**

M-Au   Yes, it's quite soon. But I think our preparations are going well, don't you?

W-Br   Actually, I think we could be doing more to promote the opening.

M-Au   Hmm… ⁴²**If you'd like, I could head out to Third Street and take some pictures of the storefront.** Then we can post them on social media to build excitement in the community.

W-Br   Good idea. ⁴³**Oh, and I'll visit some Web sites that target specialty coffee enthusiasts to find out how much it would cost to run text advertisements on them.** We may have enough of a budget to do that.

여: 음, 앤디, 믿기 힘들겠지만… 우리 커피숍의 두 번째 매장이 7월 중순에 개장할 예정이에요. 이제 한 달밖에 안 남았어요.

남: 네, 꽤 빠르네요. 하지만 준비는 잘 되어 가고 있겠죠, 그렇죠?

여: 사실, 개점을 홍보하기 위해 할 수 있는 일이 더 있는 것 같아요.

남: 음, 괜찮으시면 3번가로 가서 가게 정면 사진을 찍을게요. 그런 다음 사진을 소셜 미디어에 올리면 이 지역 사람들의 관심을 끌 수 있을 거예요.

여: 좋은 생각이에요. 오, 난 프리미엄 커피 애호가를 대상으로 하는 웹사이트를 몇 군데 방문해서 사이트에서 문자 광고를 하려면 비용이 얼마나 드는지 알아볼게요. 이런 광고를 할 만한 예산이 충분할 수도 있어요.

어휘   be set to ~할 예정이다 mid-July 7월 중순 preparation 준비 promote 홍보하다 head out to ~으로 향하다 storefront 가게 정면 post 게시하다 social media 소셜 미디어 excitement 흥분 community 지역사회 target 목표로 삼다 specialty coffee (엄선된 생두를 로스팅해 신선하게 추출한) 프리미엄 커피 enthusiast 열렬한 지지자 run 운영[제공]하다 text 문자 advertisement 광고 budget 예산

41

What does the woman say will happen next month?

(A) Special shipments will arrive.
(B) A city festival will take place.
(C) A new location will open.
(D) Temporary employees will be hired.

여자는 다음 달에 무슨 일이 있다고 말하는가?
(A) 특별 배송품이 도착한다.
(B) 시 축제가 열린다.
(C) 새 지점이 개장된다.
(D) 임시 직원이 채용된다.

어휘   shipment 배송(품) location 위치, 장소 temporary 임시의, 일시의

해설   세부 사항 관련 – 다음 달에 있을 일

여자의 첫 번째 대사에서 두 번째 커피숍 매장이 7월 중순에 개장할 예정이고 이제 한 달밖에 안 남았다(our coffee shop's second store is set to open in mid-July. That's only one month away)고 했으므로 정답은 (C)이다.

▸▸ Paraphrasing   대화의 our coffee shop's second store is set to open → 정답의 a new location will open

42

What does the man offer to do?

(A) Clean a sidewalk area
(B) Print some flyers
(C) Move a display case
(D) Take some photographs

남자는 무엇을 해 주겠다고 하는가?
(A) 보도 구역 청소하기
(B) 전단지 인쇄하기
(C) 진열대 옮기기
(D) 사진 찍기

어휘   sidewalk 보도 flyer 전단지 display case 진열 상자, 진열 선반

해설   세부 사항 관련 – 남자의 제안 사항

남자의 두 번째 대사에서 3번가로 가서 가게 정면 사진을 찍겠다(If you'd like, I could head out to Third Street and take some pictures of the storefront)고 했으므로 정답은 (D)이다.

▸▸ Paraphrasing   대화의 take some pictures → 정답의 take photographs

43

What does the woman say she will research?

(A) The layout of a store showroom
(B) The best place to buy some kitchen equipment
(C) The wholesale price of a coffee drink
(D) The costs for some online advertisements

여자는 무엇에 대해 알아보겠다고 말하는가?
(A) 매장 전시실의 배치
(B) 부엌 용품을 살 최적의 장소
(C) 커피의 도매가
(D) 일부 온라인 광고 비용

어휘   layout 배치, 설계 showroom 전시실 equipment 장비, 용품 wholesale 도매의 advertisement 광고

해설   세부 사항 관련 – 여자가 알아볼 것

여자의 마지막 대사에서 프리미엄 커피 애호가를 대상으로 하는 웹사이트를 몇 군데 방문해서 사이트에서 문자 광고를 하려면 비용이 얼마나 드는지 알아보겠다(I'll visit some Web sites that target specialty coffee enthusiasts to find out how much it would cost to run text advertisements on them)고 했으므로 정답은 (D)이다.

▸▸ Paraphrasing   대화의 cost to run text advertisements on them → 정답의 The costs for some online advertisements

44-46

W-Am Thank you for visiting the information desk here at Patton Train Station. How can I help you?

M-Cn **⁴⁴Well, a client of mine is coming in on the train, and I'm supposed to pick him up.** He'll be here any minute. **⁴⁵But I can't find the place we're supposed to meet.**

W-Am **⁴⁵OK. Just tell me the name of the place, and I'll direct you there.**

M-Cn Thanks. It's the Jorgens store. I was told it would be hard to miss, but I don't see it.

W-Am Oh, that store closed down last month. **⁴⁶I'm afraid you'll have to choose a different place to meet.** The West Exit has a nice waiting area.

여: 패튼 기차역 안내 데스크를 방문해 주셔서 감사합니다. 무엇을 도와 드릴까요?

남: 저, 제 고객이 기차를 타고 오고 있는데, 제가 그분을 마중하기로 되어 있거든요. 곧 오실 거예요. 근데 만나기로 한 장소를 찾을 수가 없네요.

여: 그렇군요. 장소 이름만 말씀해 주세요. 제가 그리로 안내할게요.

남: 감사합니다. 조르겐스 가게예요. 찾기 쉽다고 들었는데 안 보이네요.

여: 아, 그 가게는 지난 달에 문을 닫았어요. **다른 곳에서 만나셔야 할 것 같네요.** 서쪽 출구에 좋은 대합실이 있습니다.

어휘 information desk 안내 데스크 client 고객 be supposed to ~하기로 되어 있다, ~할 의무가 있다 pick ~ up ~를 (차에) 태우러 가다 direct 길을 가르쳐 주다, 안내하다 miss 놓치다 close down 닫다, 폐쇄하다 choose 고르다 waiting area 대합실, 대기실

44

Why has the man come to the train station?

(A) To reserve a ticket
(B) To work in a shop
(C) To pick up a client
(D) To leave on a train

남자가 기차역에 온 이유는 무엇인가?
(A) 표를 예매하기 위해
(B) 매장에서 일하기 위해
(C) 고객을 마중하기 위해
(D) 기차를 타기 위해

어휘 reserve 예약하다

해설 전체 내용 관련 – 남자가 기차역에 온 이유

남자의 첫 번째 대사에게 고객이 기차를 타고 오고 있는데, 내가 마중하기로 되어 있다(a client of mine is coming in on the train, and I'm supposed to pick him up)고 했으므로 정답은 (C)이다.

45

What does the woman offer to help the man do?

(A) Carry some luggage
(B) Understand a wall display
(C) Locate a meeting site
(D) Obtain an access card

여자는 어떤 일로 남자를 돕겠다고 제안하는가?
(A) 수하물 옮기기
(B) 벽면 전시 이해하기
(C) 약속 장소 찾기
(D) 출입 카드 얻기

어휘 luggage 수하물 display 전시 locate 정확한 위치를 찾아내다 obtain 얻다, 획득하다

해설 세부 사항 관련 – 여자가 도울 일

남자의 첫 번째 대사에서 만나기로 한 장소를 찾을 수가 없다(I can't find the place we're supposed to meet)고 하자 여자가 장소 이름만 말하면 그리로 안내하겠다(Just tell me the name of the place, and I'll direct you there)고 했다. 따라서 남자가 장소 찾는 일을 돕는다는 것을 알 수 있으므로 정답은 (C)이다.

46

What is the man told to do?

(A) Make a change to a plan
(B) Wait for an attendant
(C) Save some printed receipts
(D) Double-check some instructions

남자는 무엇을 하라는 말을 듣는가?
(A) 계획 변경하기
(B) 안내원 기다리기
(C) 인쇄된 영수증 챙기기
(D) 몇 가지 지침 재확인하기

어휘 attendant 안내원 save 챙기다, 확보하다 printed 인쇄된 double-check 재확인하다 instructions 지침, 설명

해설 세부 사항 관련 – 남자가 해야 할 일

대화 마지막에 여자가 남자에게 다른 곳에서 만나야 할 것 같다(I'm afraid you'll have to choose a different place to meet)고 했다. 따라서 당초 약속 장소를 변경하라는 의미이므로 정답은 (A)이다.

▸▸ Paraphrasing 대화의 choose a different place to meet → 정답의 make a change to a plan

47-49

M-Au OK, that's it. **⁴⁷I hope this orientation session has taught you everything you'll need to know about being a sewing machine operator in this factory.**

W-Br Yes, it was very helpful. Uh, but you mentioned that I'll be expected to perform minor repairs on the machine myself. **⁴⁸Do I need to bring in my own tools for that?**

M-Au It's not a bad idea. We have all of the required items, but sometimes other operators may be using them.

W-Br I see. ⁴⁹**Let me write that down, so that tonight I'll remember to collect everything I might want.**

남: 좋아요, 끝입니다. 이번 오리엔테이션 시간으로 이 공장에서 재봉사로서 알아야 할 모든 것을 배웠기를 바라요.

여: 네, 아주 유익했어요. 어, 그런데 사소한 수리는 제가 직접 해야 한다고 하셨는데요. **수리를 위해 제 도구를 가져와야 하나요?**

남: 그것도 좋은 생각이에요. 필요한 도구는 다 있지만 때로는 다른 재봉사들이 사용하고 있을 수도 있어요.

여: 알겠어요. **오늘밤에 필요한 것을 모두 잊지 않고 챙겨 놓도록 적을게요.**

어휘 orientation 오리엔테이션 session 시간, 기간 sewing machine 재봉틀 operator 조작자, 운영자 factory 공장 mention 언급하다 be expected to ~하도록 기대되다 perform 수행하다 minor 사소한 repair 수리 tool 도구 required 필수의 collect 모으다

47

Who most likely is the woman?

(A) A safety inspector
(B) A new employee
(C) A board member
(D) A potential vendor

여자는 누구이겠는가?
(A) 안전 감독관
(B) 신입 사원
(C) 중역
(D) 잠재적 판매상

어휘 safety inspector 안전 감독관 board member (이사회에 참석하는) 중역 potential 잠재적인 vendor 판매상, 판매업체

해설 전체 내용 관련 – 여자의 직업
남자의 첫 번째 대사에서 남자가 이번 오리엔테이션 시간으로 이 공장에서 재봉사로서 알아야 할 모든 것을 배웠기를 바란다(I hope this orientation session has taught you everything you'll need to know about being a sewing machine operator in this factory)고 했다. 이를 통해 여성이 직무 관련 오리엔테이션을 받는 신입 사원임을 알 수 있으므로 정답은 (B)이다.

48

What does the woman ask about?

(A) The need for some repair instruments
(B) The speed of some machines
(C) The placement of a workstation
(D) The difficulty of hiring technicians

여자는 무엇에 대하여 묻는가?
(A) 수리 도구의 필요성
(B) 일부 기계의 속도
(C) 작업 장소의 배치
(D) 기술자 채용 과정

어휘 instrument 기구 placement 배치 workstation 작업 장소 hire 고용하다 technician 기술자

해설 세부 사항 관련 – 여자의 질문 사항
여자의 첫 번째 대사에서 수리를 위해 자신의 도구를 직접 가져와야 하는지(Do I need to bring in my own tools for that)를 묻고 있으므로 정답은 (A)이다.

▶▶ Paraphrasing 대화의 **need to bring in my own tools** → 정답의 **the need for some repair instruments**

49

What will the woman most likely do next?

(A) Put on a uniform
(B) Monitor some procedures
(C) Gather some supervisors
(D) Make a reminder note

여자는 다음으로 무엇을 하겠는가?
(A) 유니폼 입기
(B) 일부 절차 관찰하기
(C) 몇몇 감독관 소집
(D) 알림 메모 만들기

어휘 monitor 관찰하다 procedure 절차 gather 모으다 supervisor 감독관 reminder 상기시키는 것

해설 세부 사항 관련 – 여자가 할 일
여자의 마지막 대사에서 오늘밤에 필요한 것을 모두 잊지 않고 챙겨 놓도록 적어 두겠다(Let me write that down, so that tonight I'll remember to collect everything I might want)고 했으므로 정답은 (D)이다.

▶▶ Paraphrasing 대화의 **write that down** → 정답의 **make a reminder note**

50-52

W-Am Carl, it's good to see you again. Have you been enjoying the conference?

M-Cn Hi, Mi-Jung. ⁵⁰**Yes, I've picked up some good tips on how to make science enjoyable for my students.**

W-Am Me too. ⁵⁰**And I just attended a great workshop on getting funding for classroom projects.**

M-Cn Oh, I wanted to go to that workshop, but I registered too late.

W-Am ⁵¹**Yeah, every available seat was taken.** I can understand why—the speaker was excellent.

M-Cn I'd heard that. ⁵²**I'd love to meet him.**

W-Am ⁵²**Well, here's your chance—that's him next to the banquet table. Do you see him?** He's wearing a green shirt.

M-Cn Ah, OK. Thanks!

50

Who most likely are the speakers?

(A) Financial consultants
(B) School teachers
(C) Travel photographers
(D) Research scientists

화자들은 누구이겠는가?
(A) 재무 컨설턴트
(B) 교사
(C) 여행 사진가
(D) 연구원

어휘 financial 재정의, 금융의 consultant 자문 위원, 상담가
research 연구

해설 전체 내용 관련 – 화자들의 직업
남자의 첫 번째 대사에서 학생들이 과학을 즐길 수 있는 방법에 관한 좋은 정보를 얻었다(I've picked up some good tips on how to make science enjoyable for my students)고 했고 여자의 두 번째 대사에서 방금 교실 프로젝트 자금 조달에 관한 유익한 워크숍에 참석했다(I just attended a great workshop on getting funding for classroom projects)고 했다. 따라서 화자들은 교사임을 알 수 있으므로 정답은 (B)이다.

51

What does the woman say about a workshop?

(A) It was full.
(B) It began late.
(C) It was recorded.
(D) It involved role-playing.

여자는 워크숍에 대해 무엇이라고 말하는가?
(A) 만석이었다.
(B) 늦게 시작했다.
(C) 녹화되었다.
(D) 역할 연기가 포함되었다.

어휘 record 녹화[녹음]하다 role-playing 역할 연기

해설 세부 사항 관련 – 여자가 한 말
여자의 세 번째 대사에서 이용 가능한 자리가 모두 찼다(every available seat was taken)고 했으므로 정답은 (A)이다.

▸▸ Paraphrasing 대화의 **every available seat was taken**
→ 정답의 **full**

52

Why does the woman say, "He's wearing a green shirt"?

(A) To complain about a person's appearance
(B) To clarify why some lighting is unsuitable
(C) To help the man identify a person
(D) To indicate what the man should wear

여자가 "그는 초록색 셔츠를 입고 있어요"라고 말하는 이유는 무엇인가?
(A) 어떤 사람의 겉모습에 대해 불평하려고
(B) 일부 조명이 적절치 않은 이유를 설명하려고
(C) 남자가 사람을 식별하는 것을 도우려고
(D) 남자가 입어야 할 옷을 알려주려고

어휘 appearance 외관 clarify 명확히 설명하다 unsuitable 부적절한, 어울리지 않는 identify 식별하다 indicate 나타내다, 알리다

해설 화자의 의도 파악 – 초록색 셔츠를 입고 있다는 말의 의도
남자의 세 번째 대사에서 그 사람 만나 보고 싶다(I'd love to meet him)고 하자 인용문 앞 여자의 마지막 대사에서 지금 기회가 왔다며 연회 테이블 옆에 있는 사람(Well, here's your chance—that's him next to the banquet table)이라면서 보이는지(Do you see him) 물었다. 따라서 남자가 누구인지 알아보도록 한 말이므로 정답은 (C)이다.

53-55

53

What does the woman want to do?

(A) Attend an upcoming event
(B) Apply for a position
(C) Place a special order
(D) Promote her work

여자는 무엇을 하고 싶어 하는가?
(A) 다가오는 행사 참석하기
(B) 일자리에 지원하기
(C) 특별 주문하기
(D) 자신의 작품 홍보하기

어휘 apply for ~에 지원하다 place an order 주문하다 promote 홍보하다, 장려하다

해설 세부 사항 관련 – 여자가 하려는 일

여자의 첫 번째 대사에서 가게 유리창에 붙은 표지판을 보니 현지 저자들의 낭독회가 있다고 하던데(I saw the sign on your bookstore's window, about book readings by local authors) 거기 가고 싶다(I'd like to go to one)고 했다. 따라서 여자는 저자의 행사에 가고 싶다는 것을 알 수 있으므로 정답은 (A)이다.

▸▸ Paraphrasing   대화의 book readings by local authors → 정답의 an upcoming event

54

What does the man warn the woman about?

(A) An extra fee
(B) A new restriction
(C) A possible delay
(D) A dissatisfied customer

남자는 여자에게 무엇에 관해 주의를 주는가?
(A) 추가 요금
(B) 새로운 규제
(C) 지연 가능성
(D) 불만을 제기한 고객

어휘 extra 추가의 fee 요금 restriction 제한, 규제 delay 지연, 연기 dissatisfied 불만 있는, 불만족한

해설 세부 사항 관련 – 남자가 주의를 주는 것

남자의 첫 번째 대사에서 전단지에 안 나와 있지만 가게에서는 더 이상 고객의 간식 반입을 허용하지 않는다(Just one thing that's not on the flyer—we no longer allow customers to bring in any snacks)고 했다. 따라서 새로 생긴 규제에 관해 주의를 주고 있으므로 정답은 (B)이다.

55

What does the man encourage the woman to do?

(A) Enter a writing contest
(B) Register for an e-mail update program
(C) Participate in a local trade show
(D) Visit another store location

남자는 여자에게 무엇을 하라고 권하는가?
(A) 작문 경연 대회 참가하기
(B) 이메일 업데이트 프로그램 등록하기
(C) 지역 무역 박람회 참가하기
(D) 다른 상점 방문하기

어휘 enter 참가 신청을 하다 register for ~에 등록하다 participate in ~에 참가하다 trade show 무역 박람회 location 장소, 위치

해설 세부 사항 관련 – 남자의 권유 사항

남자의 마지막 대사에서 웹사이트의 이메일 소식지 프로그램에 가입하여 할인 및 행사에 대한 업데이트를 받아보길 권한다(I'd encourage you to visit our Web site to sign up for our e-mail newsletter program—for updates on sales and other events)고 했으므로 정답은 (B)이다.

▸▸ Paraphrasing   대화의 sign up for our e-mail newsletter program—for updates on sales and other events → 정답의 register for an e-mail update program

56-58

W-Br	56Mike, I need to edit some figures with the new database software. But I still don't know how to use the "data merge" feature. Could you give me a tutorial on that before I start?
M-Cn	I wanted to talk to you about that program. It's been running slowly, and it's making calculation errors. 57I looked through all the troubleshooting tips in the user's manual yesterday—nothing helped.
W-Br	Oh, I see. 58Well, I guess we'll have to call technical support. Could you do it, since you know the program best?
M-Cn	Well, I was on my way to a meeting...
W-Br	OK. You can just try to get it worked out by the end of the day.

여: 마이크, 제가 새로운 데이터베이스 소프트웨어로 일부 수치를 수정해야 해요. 하지만 아직 "데이터 병합" 기능 사용법을 모르겠어요. 시작 하기 전에 사용 지침을 좀 알려 주시겠어요?
남: 그 프로그램에 대해 말하려고 했어요. 프로그램이 느리게 실행되고, 계산 오류가 발생하고 있어요. 어제 사용 설명서의 문제 해결 팁을 다 살펴보았지만 아무런 도움이 되지 않았네요.
여: 아, 알겠어요. 그러면 기술 지원을 요청해야 할 것 같아요. 당신이 프로그램을 제일 잘 아니까 요청하시겠어요?
남: 음, 지금 회의하러 가던 참이어서…
여: 좋아요. 오늘 퇴근 전까지 한번 고쳐보세요.

56

What does the woman ask the man to do?

(A) Start preparing a presentation
(B) Proofread a section of an article
(C) Explain a feature of a software program
(D) Purchase some office supplies online

여자는 남자에게 무엇을 하라고 요청하는가?
(A) 발표 준비 시작하기
(B) 기사의 한 부분 교정 보기
(C) **소프트웨어 프로그램의 특징 설명**
(D) 온라인으로 사무용품 구매하기

어휘 proofread (원고의) 교정을 보다 article 기사 purchase 구매하다 office supplies 사무용품

해설 세부 사항 관련 – 여자의 요청 사항

여자의 첫 번째 대사에서 남자에게 새로운 데이터베이스 소프트웨어로 일부 수치를 수정해야 하는데(I need to edit some figures with the new databases software) 아직 '데이터 병합' 기능 사용법을 모르겠다(But I still don't know how to use the "data merge" feature)며 사용 지침을 알려 달라(Could you give me a tutorial on that before I start)고 했다. 따라서 소프트웨어 프로그램의 특징을 설명해 달라는 의미임을 알 수 있으므로 정답은 (C)이다.

57

What did the man do yesterday?

(A) Paid a utility bill
(B) Toured a warehouse
(C) Met a technician
(D) Reviewed a manual

남자는 어제 무엇을 했다고 말하는가?
(A) 공공요금을 납부했다
(B) 창고를 돌아보았다
(C) 기술자를 만났다
(D) **설명서를 검토했다**

어휘 pay 지불하다, 납부하다 utility bill (전기·수도 요금 등) 공공요금 warehouse 창고 technician 기술자, 기사

해설 세부 사항 관련 – 남자가 어제 한 일

남자의 첫 번째 대사에서 어제 사용 설명서의 문제 해결 팁을 다 살펴보았지만 아무런 도움이 되지 않았다(I looked through all the troubleshooting tips in the user's manual yesterday—nothing helped)고 했으므로 정답은 (D)이다.

▶ Paraphrasing 대화의 looked through all the troubleshooting tips in the user's manual → 정답의 reviewed a manual

58

What does the man mean when he says "I was on my way to a meeting"?

(A) He traveled to a site separately from others.
(B) He was not in the area when a problem occurred.
(C) He will not be able to make a phone call immediately.
(D) He can make an announcement to a group of staff.

남자가 "지금 회의하러 가던 참이어서"라고 말한 의도는 무엇인가?
(A) 다른 사람들과 떨어져 따로 현장으로 이동했다.
(B) 문제가 발생했을 때 그곳에 없었다.
(C) **전화를 바로 할 수 없을 것이다.**
(D) 한 무리의 직원 앞에서 발표를 할 수 있다.

어휘 travel 이동하다 site 위치, 현장 separately 따로 occur 일어나다, 발생하다 make a phone call 전화하다 immediately 당장 make an announcement 발표하다

해설 화자의 의도 파악 – 회의하러 가던 참이라는 말의 의미

인용문의 바로 앞 문장에서 여자는 기술 지원을 요청해야 할 것 같은데(I guess we'll have to call technical support) 당신이 프로그램을 제일 잘 아니까 요청하겠느냐(Could you do it, since you know the program best) 물었다. 따라서 회의 때문에 기술 지원 요청을 당장 할 수 없다는 의미를 나타낸 것이므로 정답은 (C)이다.

59-61 3인 대화

W-Am	Hi, Itaru. It's Nicole in the accounting department. We're having an issue with one of our wall fans. **59Every time it rotates, there's a loud clicking sound.** It's really annoying.
M-Cn	**60I'd like to help you, but I need to deal with a serious plumbing problem now.** Let me put you on with Adam. He's new here at the maintenance department, but he's very skilled.
W-Am	OK. Thank you.
M-Au	Hi, this is Adam. I can take a look at your fan right now. **61But I'm sorry, I don't know my way around yet—what floor is the accounting department?**
W-Am	It's the sixth. Once you're up here, please wait for me at the elevators.

여1: 안녕, 이타루. 경리부 니콜이에요. 우리 벽걸이 선풍기 중 하나가 말썽이에요. **돌아갈 때마다 덜커덕 소리가 나요.** 너무 거슬려요.
남1: **도와드리고 싶은데 지금 심각한 배관 문제를 해결해야 해서요.** 아담을 바꿔줄게요. 관리부 신입이지만 아주 솜씨가 좋아요.
여1: 좋아요. 고마워요.
남2: 안녕하세요, 이담입니다. 지금 당장 선풍기를 봐 드릴 수 있어요. **그런데 죄송하지만 길을 아직 잘 몰라서요. 경리부는 몇 층인가요?**
여1: 6층이에요. 6층에 올라오시면 엘리베이터 앞에서 기다리세요.

59

According to the woman, what is the problem with the fan?

(A) It cannot be turned on.
(B) It has stopped rotating.
(C) It may fall off of the wall.
(D) It is making loud noises.

여자에 따르면 선풍기에는 어떤 문제가 있는가?
(A) 전원이 켜지지 않는다.
(B) 회전을 멈추었다.
(C) 벽에서 떨어졌다.
(D) 시끄러운 소음이 난다.

어휘 turn on 전원을 켜다 fall off 떨어지다 noise 소음

해설 세부 사항 관련 – 선풍기의 문제
여자의 첫 번째 대사에서 돌아갈 때마다 덜커덕 소리가 난다(Every time it rotates, there's a loud clicking sound)고 했으므로 정답은 (D)이다.

▸▸ Paraphrasing 대화의 a loud clicking sound
→ 정답의 loud noises

60

Why is Itaru unable to assist the woman?

(A) His work space is being used by a colleague.
(B) He does not have the necessary skills.
(C) He has to handle another task.
(D) His job description does not allow it.

이타루가 여자를 도울 수 없었던 이유는 무엇인가?
(A) 그의 작업 공간을 동료가 사용하고 있다.
(B) 필요한 기술이 없다.
(C) 다른 업무를 해야 한다.
(D) 그의 직무기술서상 해당 업무는 포함되지 않는다.

어휘 colleague 동료 necessary 필요한 task 과업, 과제 job
description 직무기술서 allow 고려하다, 감안하다

해설 세부 사항 관련 – 이타루 씨가 여자를 도울 수 없는 이유
남자의 첫 번째 대사에서 도와주고 싶지만 지금 심각한 배관 문제를 해결해야 한다(I'd like to help you, but I need to deal with a serious plumbing problem now)고 했다. 따라서 남자는 다른 일이 있다는 것을 알 수 있으므로 정답은 (C)이다.

▸▸ Paraphrasing 대화의 need to deal with a serious
plumbing problem
→ 정답의 has to handle another task

61

What does Adam ask about?

(A) A building floor
(B) A contact method
(C) A department name
(D) A vacation period

아담은 무엇에 관해 묻는가?
(A) 건물의 층
(B) 연락 방법
(C) 부서 이름
(D) 휴가 기간

어휘 contact 연락 method 방법 department 부서

해설 세부 사항 관련 – 아담이 묻는 것
대화 후반부 아담의 대사에서 미안하지만 길을 아직 모른다(I'm sorry, I don't know my way around yet)고 하면서 경리부는 몇 층인지(what floor is the accounting department) 물었으므로 정답은 (A)이다.

62-64 대화 + 이메일 받은 편지함

M-Au Good morning, Lynette. **62Wow, there are a lot of dishes in the sink.**

W-Br Good morning, Barry. Yes, it's a bit messy in here. Oh, I just remembered something. I know you're in here to relax, but could I talk to you about a problem I've been having?

M-Au Sure.

W-Br **63Well, it's taking me a long time to complete the action plan—you know, an outline of our sales strategies and targets.** Finding information about our competitors has been hard.

M-Au **64Oh—actually, there was a team e-mail just now about a change to our project timetable.** It said that the deadline will be pushed back a little. You should be fine.

남: 안녕, 리네트. 와, 싱크대에 접시가 아주 많네요.
여: 안녕, 베리. 맞아요, 여기 좀 지저분해요. 아, 방금 생각났어요. 여기 쉬러 온 건 알지만 제 고민을 얘기해도 될까요?
남: 그럼요.
여: 음, 시행 계획을 완성하는 데 시간이 오래 걸리네요. 그게, 영업 전략과 목표에 대한 개요죠. 경쟁사들에 관한 정보를 찾는 게 어렵네요.
남: 아, 실은 프로젝트 일정 변경에 관한 팀 이메일이 방금 왔어요. 마감일이 약간 미뤄질 거라고 하네요. 괜찮을 거예요.

Inbox - Unread Messages

From	Subject
Mariana Sanchez	Estimate of expenses
[64]Georgina Lewis	Revision to timeline
Wyatt Rayburn	Copy machine tips
Suraj Sidhu	Team outing

받은 편지함 - 읽지 않은 메시지

발신인	제목
마리아나 산체스	비용 견적
조지나 루이스	**일정 변경**
와이어트 레이번	복사기 사용 팁
수라 시듀	팀 야유회

어휘 estimate 추정, 견적 expense 비용 revision 수정, 변경
timeline 시각표, 일정 copy machine 복사기 outing 야유회

62

Where is the conversation most likely taking place?

(A) In a copy room
(B) In a break area
(C) In a reception area
(D) In a conference room

대화는 어디에서 이루어지고 있겠는가?
(A) 복사실
(B) 휴게실
(C) 안내실
(D) 회의실

어휘 break area 휴식 공간, 휴게실 reception area 안내실, 로비 제품
conference room 회의실

해설 전체 내용 관련 – 대화가 이루어지는 장소
남자의 첫 번째 대화에서 싱크대에 접시가 아주 많다(there are a lot of dishes in the sink)고 했으므로 음식을 먹을 수 있는 공간임을 알 수 있다. 따라서 정답은 (B)이다.

63

What is the woman having trouble with?

(A) Designing new merchandise
(B) Completing a training course
(C) Using a filing system
(D) Developing a sales plan

여자는 어떤 문제를 겪고 있는가?
(A) 새로운 상품 디자인하기
(B) 교육 강좌 수료하기
(C) 파일 분류 시스템 사용하기
(D) 영업 계획 짜기

어휘 merchandise 상품 filing 서류 철하기 develop 개발하다

해설 세부 사항 관련 – 남자의 제안 사항
여자의 두 번째 대사에서 시행 계획을 완성하는 데 시간이 오래 걸린다(it's taking me a long time to complete the action plan)고 하면서 영업 전략과 목표에 대한 개요(an outline of our sales strategies and targets)라고 부연 설명했으므로 정답은 (D)이다.

▸▸ Paraphrasing 대화의 complete the action plan
→ 정답의 Developing a sales plan

64

Look at the graphic. Who sent the e-mail that the man mentions?

(A) Mariana Sanchez
(B) Georgina Lewis
(C) Wyatt Rayburn
(D) Suraj Sidhu

시각 정보에 의하면, 남자가 언급한 이메일은 누가 보냈는가?
(A) 마리아나 산체스
(B) 조지나 루이스
(C) 와이어트 레이번
(D) 수라 시듀

해설 시각 정보 연계 – 이메일의 발신인
남자의 마지막 대사에서 실은 프로젝트 일정 변경에 관한 팀 이메일이 방금 왔다(there was a team e-mail just now about a change to our project timetable)고 했다. 시각 정보에 따르면 '일정 변경'이란 제목의 이메일의 발신인이 조지나 루이스이므로 정답은 (B)이다.

65-67 대화 + 청구서

M-Au	OK, Ms. Brody, thank you for holding. I'm looking at the invoice for your evening visit now. What was the problem?
W-Am	[65]My coupon for five percent off the entire bill wasn't applied.
M-Au	Oh, I apologize. I remember seeing that coupon. I'll send you out a new invoice with a total that reflects the discount.
W-Am	Great. [66]Uh, and I'd also like to ask a question for a friend of mine who needs her carpets cleaned.
M-Au	Go ahead.
W-Am	Well, she doesn't want all the services included in your basic package. [67]So I was wondering what kind of customized cleaning services you offer.
M-Au	Sure, I'd be happy to go over those with you.

남: 좋아요, 브로디 씨. 기다려 주셔서 감사해요. 야간 방문 청구서를 보고 있어요. 무슨 문제였나요?
여: 전체 청구서에 대한 5퍼센트 할인 쿠폰이 적용되지 않았어요.
남: 오, 죄송합니다. 그 쿠폰을 본 기억이 나요. 할인을 반영한 총계로 새 청구서를 보내 드리겠습니다.

여: 좋아요. 어, 카펫 청소가 필요한 제 친구를 대신해서 문의도 하고 싶어요.

남: 말씀하세요.

여: 친구는 기본 패키지에 포함된 서비스를 전부 원하지는 않아요. 그래서 어떤 맞춤 청소 서비스를 제공하는지 궁금했어요.

남: 좋아요. 그럼 같이 살펴보시죠.

어휘 invoice 송장 entire 전체의 apply 적용하다 apologize 사과하다 reflect 반영하다 customized 맞춤의 go over 검토하다, 살펴보다

Basic package	$110.00
Evening visit surcharge	$35.00
Local taxes	$8.00
65Total	**$153.00**

기본 패키지	110달러
야간 방문 할증료	35달러
지방세	8달러
합계	153달러

65

Look at the graphic. What amount from the invoice will be modified?

(A) $110.00
(B) $35.00
(C) $8.00
(D) $153.00

시각 정보에 의하면, 청구서에서 어떤 금액이 수정될 것인가?

(A) 110달러
(B) 35달러
(C) 8달러
(D) 153달러

해설 시각 정보 연계 – 청구서에서 수정될 금액

여자의 첫 번째 대사에서 전체 청구서에 대한 5퍼센트 할인 쿠폰이 적용되지 않았다(My coupon for five percent off the entire bill wasn't applied)고 했다. 시각 정보에 따르면, 합계 금액은 153달러이므로 정답은 (D)이다.

66

What service does the man's company most likely provide?

(A) Commercial moving
(B) Carpet cleaning
(C) Garden care
(D) Grocery delivery

남자의 업체는 어떤 서비스를 제공하겠는가?

(A) 업체 이사
(B) 카펫 세탁
(C) 정원 관리
(D) 식료품 배달

어휘 commercial 상업적인 moving 이사 care 관리 grocery 식료품 delivery 배달

해설 전체 내용 관련 – 남자가 제공하는 서비스

여자의 두 번째 대사에서 카펫 청소가 필요한 친구를 대신해 문의를 하고 싶다(I'd also like to ask a question for a friend of mine who needs her carpets cleaned)고 했다. 따라서 남자가 카펫 청소 업계에 종사하고 있음을 알 수 있으므로 정답은 (B)이다.

67

What does the woman want to know about?

(A) Customized services
(B) Rewards for client referrals
(C) Appointment cancellation policies
(D) Employment opportunities

여자는 무엇에 대해 알고 싶어 하는가?

(A) 맞춤 서비스
(B) 고객 추천에 대한 보상
(C) 예약 취소 규정
(D) 취업 기회

어휘 reward 보상, 대가 referral 추천 cancellation 취소 policy 정책 employment 고용, 취업 opportunity 기회

해설 세부 사항 관련 – 여자가 알고자 하는 것

여자의 마지막 대화에서 어떤 종류의 맞춤 청소 서비스를 제공하는지 궁금했다(So I was wondering what kind of customized cleaning services you offer)고 했으므로 정답은 (A)이다.

68-70 대화 + 요금표

M-Cn Welcome to the Sharula Hotel. Do you have a reservation?

W-Am No, I don't. This was a sudden decision. **68A friend of mine had an urgent problem at her job, so she gave me her ticket for a concert in this area.**

M-Cn Oh, I see. Well, we do have several rooms available. **69Would you like a view of the sea?**

W-Am **69That won't be necessary. But I'd like to have breakfast here before going home tomorrow morning.**

M-Cn All right. Uh, is the concert at Ladden Center, by chance?

W-Am Yes, it is.

M-Cn **70In that case, you should use our downtown shuttle bus.** Its second stop is right in front of there.

남: 샤룰라 호텔에 오신 것을 환영합니다. 예약하셨나요?

여: 아니요, 갑자기 결정해서요. 제 친구가 직장에서 급한 문제가 생겨서 이 지역에서 열리는 공연표를 제게 줬거든요.

남: 그렇군요. 음, 빈 객실이 몇 개 있어요. 바다 전망을 원하시나요?

여: 아뇨. 하지만 내일 아침 집으로 떠나기 전에 여기서 아침을 먹고 싶어요.

남: 좋습니다. 어, 혹시 래든 센터에서 열리는 공연인가요?

여: 맞아요.

남: **그렇다면 시내 셔틀버스를 이용하세요.** 두 번째 정거장이 바로 거기 앞이에요.

어휘	reservation 예약 sudden 갑작스러운 decision 결정, 결심 urgent 긴급한 several 몇몇의 available 이용 가능한 view 전망, 시야 necessary 필요한 by chance 우연히, 혹시 in that case 그렇다면 in front of ~ 앞에

Sharula Hotel Pricing

	Sea view	No sea view
With breakfast	£130	69£100
Without breakfast	£115	£85

샤룰라 호텔 가격

	바다 전망	바다 안 보임
조식 포함	130파운드	100파운드
조식 미포함	115파운드	85파운드

68

Why is the woman in the area?

(A) To see a performance

(B) To interview for a job

(C) To speak at a conference

(D) To spend time with a friend

여자가 그 지역에 있는 이유는 무엇인가?

(A) 공연을 보기 위해

(B) 취업 면접을 위해

(C) 회의에서 강연하기 위해

(D) 친구와 시간을 보내기 위해

어휘 performance 공연 interview 면접을 보다 spend time 시간을 보내다

해설 세부 사항 관련 – 여자가 이 지역에 온 이유

여자의 첫 번째 대사에서 친구가 직장에서 급한 문제가 생겨서 이 지역에서 열리는 공연표를 줬다(A friend of mine had an urgent problem at her job, so she gave me her ticket for a concert in this area)고 했으므로 여자는 공연을 보러 왔음을 알 수 있다. 따라서 정답은 (A)이다.

▸▸ Paraphrasing   대화의 a concert → 정답의 a performance

69

Look at the graphic. How much will the woman most likely pay?

(A) £130

(B) £100

(C) £115

(D) £85

시각 정보에 의하면, 여자는 얼마를 지불하겠는가?

(A) 130파운드

(B) **100파운드**

(C) 115파운드

(D) 85파운드

해설 시각 정보 연계 – 여자가 지불할 금액

남자의 두 번째 대사에서 바다 전망을 원하는지(Would you like a view of the sea) 물었고 여자는 바다 전망은 필요 없지만(That won't be necessary) 집으로 가기 전 아침은 먹고 싶다(I'd like to have breakfast here before going home tomorrow morning)고 했다. 시각 정보에 따르면 조식이 포함된 바다 전망 없는 객실은 100파운드이므로 정답은 (B)이다.

70

What does the man recommend doing?

(A) Arriving early for a meal

(B) Parking in front of a hotel

(C) Taking a shuttle bus downtown

(D) Getting a second room key

남자는 무엇을 하라고 권하는가?

(A) 식사를 위해 일찍 도착하기

(B) 호텔 앞에 주차하기

(C) **시내 셔틀버스 타기**

(D) 추가 객실 열쇠 받기

어휘 park 주차하다

해설 세부 사항 관련 – 남자가 권하는 것

남자의 마지막 대사에서 그렇다면 시내 셔틀버스를 이용하라(In that case, you should use our downtown shuttle bus)고 했으므로 정답은 (C)이다.

Part 4

71-73 공지

W-Br ⁷¹**Is your boat not running as smoothly as it used to?** Make an appointment to bring it down to Grizzard's Marine today. Our experienced mechanics will find out the problem and fix it quickly—and for a reasonable price. No problem is too big or too small. ⁷²**There's a reason why people like renowned water-skier Trisha Harliss entrust their boats only to Grizzard's.** Our excellent service is just a short drive away. ⁷³**And during your service appointment, tell us you heard this ad to get a free fishing hat branded with the Grizzard's logo.**

보트가 전처럼 원활하게 작동되지 않습니까? 오늘 예약하셔서 그리자즈 마린으로 가져오세요. 숙련된 기술자가 문제를 찾아 신속하게 합리적인 가격으로 해결해 드립니다. 사소한 문제도, 심각한 문제도 모두 해결해 드립니다. 유명한 수상 스키 선수인 트리샤 할리스 같은 분이 보트를 그리자즈에만 맡기는 데에는 그만한 이유가 있습니다. 차로 조금만 오시면 탁월한 서비스를 받으실 수 있습니다. 서비스 예약 시, 이 광고를 들었다고 언급하시고 그리자즈 로고가 새겨진 낚시 모자를 무료로 받으세요.

어휘 run 작동하다, 운행하다 smoothly 부드럽게, 순조롭게, 원활하게 make an appointment 약속하다, 예약하다 bring 가져오다 experienced 숙련된 mechanic 정비사, 기술자 find out 알아내다, 찾다 fix 고치다 reasonable 합리적인 renowned 유명한, 명성 있는 water-skier 수상스키 선수 entrust (일을) 맡기다 away (시간적·공간적으로) 떨어져 ad 광고 fishing 낚시 hat 모자 branded with ~ 상표가 붙어 있는, ~ 브랜드의

71

What kind of business is being advertised?

(A) An ocean cruise provider
(B) A sportswear store
(C) A seaside café
(D) A boat repair shop

어떤 사업체가 광고되고 있는가?
(A) 유람선 공급업체
(B) 운동복 매장
(C) 바닷가 카페
(D) 보트 수리점

어휘 cruise 유람선, 크루즈 sportswear 운동복 seaside 해변(의) repair 수리, 수선

해설 전체 내용 관련 – 광고되는 사업체
지문 초반부에서 보트가 전처럼 원활하게 작동되지 않는다면 예약을 해서 그리자즈 마린으로 가져오라(Is your boat not running as smoothly as it used to? Make an appointment to bring it down to Grizzard's Marine today)고 말하며 숙련된 기술자가 문제를 찾아 신속하게 합리적인 가격으로 해결해 준다(Our experienced mechanics will find out the problem and fix it quickly—and for a reasonable price)고 했으므로 정답은 (D)이다.

72

What does the speaker emphasize about the business?

(A) Its numerous branches
(B) Its famous customers
(C) Its advanced technology
(D) Its relaxed atmosphere

업체에 관해 화자가 강조하는 점은 무엇인가?
(A) 수많은 지점
(B) 유명한 고객들
(C) 앞선 기술
(D) 편안한 분위기

어휘 numerous 많은 branch 지사, 분점, 지점 advanced 앞선, 진보된 relaxed 편안한 atmosphere 분위기

해설 세부 사항 관련 – 그리자즈의 특별한 점
지문 중반부에서 유명한 수상스키 선수인 트리샤 할리스와 같은 사람들이 보트를 그리자즈에만 맡기는 데에는 그만한 이유가 있다(There's a reason why people like renowned water-skier Trisha Harliss entrust their boats only to Grizzard's)라고 했으므로 정답은 (B)이다.

▶ **Paraphrasing** 지문의 **people like renowned water-skier Trisha Harliss** → 정답의 **famous customers**

73

How can listeners get a free gift?

(A) By mentioning an advertisement
(B) By signing up for a loyalty card
(C) By visiting on a certain day
(D) By referring a friend

청자들은 어떻게 무료 선물을 받을 수 있는가?
(A) 광고를 언급해서
(B) 고객 카드를 신청해서
(C) 특정 날짜에 방문해서
(D) 친구에게 추천해서

어휘 mention 언급하다 sign up for ~을 신청하다 certain 특정한 refer 추천하다

해설 세부 사항 관련 – 광고 언급 시 받는 것
지문 후반부에서 서비스 예약 시, 광고를 언급하고 그리자즈 로고가 새겨진 낚시 모자를 무료로 받으라(during your service appointment, tell us you heard this ad to get a free fishing hat branded with the Grizzard logo)고 했으므로 정답은 (A)이다.

▶ **Paraphrasing** 지문의 **tell us you heard this ad** → 정답의 **mentioning an advertisement**

74-76 공지

W-Am **74You're listening to *Mofford Money*, the only radio show that provides financial advice to Mofford-area residents.** Before we finish today, I'd like to promote an exciting upcoming event. **75Curtis Jensen will give a talk on personal money management at the Botkins Center on October sixteenth.** I have often recommended his work to those who are looking for useful tips, so I urge you to take advantage of this rare opportunity. **76Attendees will even be able to speak with Mr. Jensen personally at a reception afterwards.** Visit the Botkins Center Web site for details. All right, that's it for this week on *Mofford Money*.

여러분은 모포드 지역 주민들에게 재정 조언을 제공하는 유일한 라디오 프로그램인 〈모포드 머니〉를 듣고 계십니다. 오늘 마치기 전에, 다가오는 흥미로운 행사를 홍보하고 싶습니다. 커티스 젠슨 씨가 10월 16일 보트킨스 센터에서 개인 금융 관리에 관해 강연할 예정입니다. 유용한 조언을 구하는 분들에게 그의 책을 추천해 드린 적이 많기에 여러분께도 이 드문 기회를 활용하실 것을 권합니다. 참가자들은 강연 이후에 연회에서 개인적으로 젠슨 씨와 이야기를 나누실 수 있습니다. 자세한 내용은 보트킨스 센터 웹사이트를 방문하십시오. 자, 이번 주 〈모포드 머니〉 마치겠습니다.

어휘 provide 제공하다, 공급하다 financial 재정의, 금융의 resident 거주자, 주민 promote 홍보하다 upcoming 다가오는, 곧 있을 give a talk 강연을 하다 management 관리, 운용 personal 개인의 recommend 추천하다, 권고하다 work 작품, 저작물, 책 tip 조언, 정보 urge 권고하다, 촉구하다 take advantage of ~을 이용하다, ~을 기회로 활용하다 rare 드문, 희귀한 opportunity 기회 attendee 참석자 be able to ~을 할 수 있다 personally 개인적으로 reception 리셉션, 환영 연회 afterwards 나중에, 그 뒤에 detail 세부 사항

74
Who most likely is making the announcement?
(A) A public official
(B) An event coordinator
(C) A bank manager
(D) A radio program host

공지하는 사람은 누구이겠는가?
(A) 공무원
(B) 이벤트 진행자
(C) 은행 지점장
(D) 라디오 프로그램 진행자

어휘 public official 공무원 coordinator 진행자, 책임자 host (프로그램) 진행자

해설 전체 내용 관련 – 화자의 신분
지문 초반부에서 청취자들은 모포드 지역 주민들에게 재정 조언을 제공하는 유일한 라디오 프로그램인 〈모포드 머니〉를 듣고 있다(You're listening to *Mofford Money*, the only radio show that provides financial advice to Mofford-area residents)고 했다. 따라서 말하는 사람은 프로그램 진행자라는 것을 알 수 있으므로 정답은 (D)이다.

75
What will Mr. Jensen speak about at the event?
(A) A regional economy
(B) A negotiation method
(C) Business management
(D) Personal finance

젠슨 씨는 행사에 관해 무엇에 대해 강연할 것인가?
(A) 지역 경제
(B) 협상 방법
(C) 사업 운영
(D) 개인 금융

어휘 regional 지역의 economy 경제 negotiation 협상 method 방법 personal 개인의 finance 금융

해설 세부 사항 관련 – 젠슨 씨의 전문 분야
지문 중반부에서 청자들에게 커티스 젠슨 씨가 10월 16일 보트킨스 센터에서 개인 금융 관리에 관해 강연할 예정(Curtis Jensen will give a talk on personal money management at the Botkins Center on October sixteenth)이라고 했으므로 정답은 (D)이다.

▸▸ Paraphrasing 지문의 money → 정답의 finance

76
What is mentioned about the event?
(A) Its attendees will be given handouts.
(B) It will be followed by a reception.
(C) Its date has been moved.
(D) It is predicted to sell out.

행사에 대해 언급된 것은 무엇인가?
(A) 참가자들에게 유인물이 제공될 것이다.
(B) 행사 후 연회가 있을 예정이다.
(C) 날짜가 변경되었다.
(D) 매진되리라 예상된다.

어휘 attendee 참석자 handout 유인물, 인쇄물 follow 뒤따르다 predict 예측하다 sell out 매진되다

해설 세부 사항 관련 – 행사에 대해 언급된 내용
지문 후반부에서 참가자들은 강연 이후에 연회에서 개인적으로 젠슨 씨와 이야기를 나눌 수 있다(Attendees will even be able to speak with Mr. Jensen personally at a reception afterwards)고 했다. 따라서 행사 후 연회가 있을 예정이라는 것을 알 수 있으므로 정답은 (B)이다.

77-79 전화 메시지

M-Cn Hi, Ms. Lundquist. **77It's Ted calling from Artisan's Central Furniture Shop about the small bookshelf you were supposed to pick up from us tomorrow. 78Unfortunately, it still hasn't been delivered to our store.** We've contacted our wholesale supplier and are waiting to hear back from them. But uh... don't get your hopes up. Anyway, we should talk before tomorrow. **79I'll be leaving for the day shortly, but please call the store and speak to Lisa, the assistant manager, and she'll help you.** Thanks.

안녕하세요, 룬트퀴스트 씨. 아티잔스 센트럴 퍼니처 숍의 테드인데요. 내일 가지러 오실 예정이었던 작은 책꽂이 관련해 전화드렸어요. 아쉽게도 아직 저희 매장에 배송이 되지 않았네요. 도매 업체에 연락했고 답변을 기다리고 있습니다. 하지만 어... 큰 기대는 하지 마십시오. 어쨌든 오늘 중으로 말씀드릴게요. 저는 곧 퇴근합니다만, 다시 매장에 전화해서 부매니저 리사와 이야기하세요. 그녀가 도와드릴 겁니다. 감사합니다.

77

What is the speaker calling about?

(A) A furniture order
(B) A broken appliance
(C) A rental contract
(D) A delivery van

화자는 무엇에 관해 전화하고 있는가?
(A) 가구 주문
(B) 고장 난 가전 제품
(C) 임대 계약
(D) 배송 트럭

어휘 broken 고장 난, 망가진 appliance 가전 제품 rental 임대의,
대여의 contract 계약

해설 전체 내용 관련 – 화자의 전화 목적

지문 초반부에서 아티잔스 센트럴 퍼니처 숍의 테드라고 자기소개를 한 후 내
일 가지러 올 예정이었던 작은 책꽂이 관련해 전화했다(It's Ted calling from
Artisan's Central Furniture Shop about the small bookshelf you
were supposed to pick up from us tomorrow)고 했다. 따라서 남자가
주문한 가구에 관해 전화하고 있음을 알 수 있으므로 정답은 (A)이다.

78

What does the speaker imply when he says, "don't get
your hopes up"?

(A) An item may not arrive on time.
(B) A phone number may not be correct.
(C) A space may be too small for a vehicle.
(D) An item may be damaged in transit.

화자가 "큰 기대는 하지 마십시오"라고 말한 의도는 무엇인가?
(A) 물품이 제시간에 도착하지 않을 수도 있다.
(B) 전화번호가 정확하지 않을 수도 있다.
(C) 장소가 자동차가 들어가기에는 너무 좁을 수도 있다.
(D) 물품이 운송 중에 손상될 수도 있다.

어휘 on time 제시간에 correct 정확한 vehicle 차량 damage
훼손하다 in transit 수송 중에

해설 화자의 의도 파악 – 큰 기대는 하지 말라는 말의 의미

인용문 앞 부분에서 화자가 청자에게 아쉽게도 아직 매장에 배송이 되지 않았
다(Unfortunately, it still hasn't been delivered to our store)고 했다.
즉 배송이 지연될 수 있다는 의미이므로 정답은 (A)이다.

79

What does the speaker request that the listener do?

(A) Leave a message on a door
(B) Speak to his coworker
(C) Look for some records
(D) Take some measurements

화자는 청자에게 무엇을 하라고 요청하는가?
(A) 문에 메시지 남기기
(B) 동료와 이야기하기
(C) 일부 기록 찾기
(D) 측정하기

어휘 coworker 동료 measurement 측정

해설 세부 사항 관련 – 화자의 요청 사항

지문 후반부에서 자신은 곧 퇴근하지만 다시 매장에 전화해서 부매니저 리사와
이야기하면 도와줄 것이다(I'll be leaving for the day shortly, but please
call the store and speak to Lisa, the assistant manager, and she'll
help you)라고 했으므로 정답은 (B)이다.

▸▸ Paraphrasing   지문의 the assistant manager
→ 정답의 his coworker

80-82 담화

M-Au My colleague and I really appreciate this
chance to tell you all about the great products we
offer at Dodmac Company. **80By the time we're
finished, I'm sure you'll agree that they would
be the perfect addition to your store's inventory.
81Now, as you know, we specialize in making
durable and attractive journals, notebooks,
and notepads.** Our unique designs and high-
quality materials have proved appealing to
customers throughout the region. And our
popularity is rising. **82As you can see from the
chart I'm putting up on the screen, our sales
have increased steadily since our founding five
years ago.** Considering that we only partner with
boutique stores, I think you'll agree that these
numbers are remarkable.

제 동료와 저는 저희 도드맥 컴퍼니에서 제공하는 훌륭한 제품에 관해 여러분께
말씀드릴 수 있는 이번 기회에 정말 감사드립니다. 끝날 때쯤이면 여러분 매장
의 물품 목록에 추가할 완벽한 제품이라는 사실에 동의하시리라 확신합니다. 아
시다시피 저희는 튼튼하고 멋진 일기장, 공책, 메모장을 전문으로 합니다. 저희의
독특한 디자인과 고품질 자재는 이 지역에서 두루 고객들의 관심을 받고 있다는
것이 입증되었습니다. 게다가 인기도 많아지고 있습니다. 화면에 나오는 차트에
서도 볼 수 있듯 5년 전에 창립한 이후 매출이 꾸준히 상승하고 있습니다. 고급
매장만 상대로 거래한다는 것을 고려하면 이 수치들이 대단하다는 것에 동의하
실 겁니다.

80

What is the purpose of the talk?

(A) To persuade the listeners to purchase some items
(B) To educate listeners about a manufacturing process
(C) To report on the progress of a design project
(D) To introduce the new head of a department

담화의 목적은 무엇인가?

(A) 청자들을 설득해 물품을 구매하게 만들기
(B) 제조 과정에 대해 청자들을 교육시키기
(C) 디자인 프로젝트 진행에 대해 보고하기
(D) 신임 부서장 소개하기

어휘 persuade 설득하다 educate 교육시키다 manufacturing process 제조 과정 progress 진행, 진척 상황 head 장(長), 우두머리

해설 전체 내용 관련 – 담화의 목적

지문 초반부에서 끝날 때쯤이면 여러분 매장의 물품 목록에 추가할 완벽한 제품이라는 사실에 동의하리라 확신한다(By the time we're finished, I'm sure you'll agree that they would be the perfect addition to your store's inventory)고 했다. 따라서 제품을 판매하려는 것임을 알 수 있으므로 정답은 (A)이다.

81

What does the speaker's company make?

(A) Portable electronic devices
(B) Skin care goods
(C) Food packaging
(D) Stationery products

화자의 회사는 무엇을 만드는가?

(A) 휴대용 전자 기기
(B) 피부 관리 제품
(C) 음식 포장 용기
(D) 문구 제품

어휘 portable 휴대 가능한 electronic device 전자 기기 skin care 피부 관리 goods 제품 packaging 포장 용기 stationery 문구

해설 세부 사항 관련 – 화자의 회사가 생산하는 제품

지문 중반부에서 튼튼하고 멋진 일기장, 공책, 메모장을 전문으로 한다(we specialize in making durable and attractive journals, notebooks, and notepads)고 했으므로 정답은 (D)이다.

▸▸ Paraphrasing 지문의 attractive journals, notebooks, and notepads → 정답의 Stationery products

82

What does the speaker show on a screen?

(A) A sales chart
(B) A regional map
(C) Pictures of an event
(D) Results from a survey

화자는 화면으로 무엇을 보여 주는가?

(A) 매출 차트
(B) 지역 지도
(C) 행사 사진
(D) 설문 조사 결과

어휘 sales 매출(액), 판매 regional 지역의 survey 설문 조사

해설 세부 사항 관련 – 화면에 보여 주는 것

지문 후반부에서 화면에 띄운 차트에서도 볼 수 있듯 5년 전에 창립한 이후 매출이 꾸준히 상승하고 있다(As you can see from the chart I'm putting up on the screen, our sales have increased steadily since our founding five years ago)고 했으므로 정답은 (A)이다.

83-85 회의 발췌

W-Am Now, I've saved the best part of today's meeting for last. **83As you know, our new line of greeting cards will appear in stores nationwide at the end of the year, just in time to benefit from the winter holidays.** Well, upper management is so thankful for the hard work that made this possible that they want to give you a recognition reward—something like bonus pay or some time off. **84You'll get an e-mail later today outlining the options, so please vote for the one you like best.** Isn't that exciting? **85You certainly earned it with the great job you all did producing that creative content so quickly. That was really something.** All right, that's all.

자, 마지막으로 오늘 직원 회의에서 가장 중요한 부분이 남았군요. **아시다시피 우리의 새 연하장이 겨울 연휴 대목을 맞아 전국 매장에 나올 예정입니다.** 회사 경영진은 이런 성과를 낸 분들의 노고를 치하하고자 보너스나 휴가와 같은 포상을 해 드리고자 합니다. **오늘 선택 사항을 요약한 이메일을 보내드릴 테니 가장 마음에 드는 것에 투표해 주세요.** 신나지 않나요? **창의적인 콘텐츠를 그토록 신속하게 훌륭히 만들어 낸 덕분에 얻은 것입니다. 정말 대단해요.** 좋아요, 이것으로 마칩니다.

어휘 greeting card 인사장, 연하장 appear 나타나다, 나오다 nationwide 전국적으로 in time 제시간에 benefit from ~에서 혜택을 보다 upper 위쪽의, 상부의 management 경영진, 관리진 recognition 인정, 인식 reward 보상 bonus 보너스, 상여금 time off 휴가 outline 요약하다 option 선택지 vote 투표(하다) earn 노력해서) 얻다 produce 생산하다 creative 창의적인 content 내용 something 대단한(중요한) 일

83

What will take place at the end of the year?

(A) The launch of a product line
(B) A retirement ceremony
(C) The renovation of a store
(D) A holiday banquet

연말에 무슨 일이 있을 것인가?

(A) 제품군 출시
(B) 은퇴식
(C) 매장 개조
(D) 휴일 연회

어휘 launch 출시 retirement 은퇴 ceremony 의식 renovation 개조 banquet 연회

해설 세부 사항 관련 – 연말에 일어날 일

지문 초반부에서 새 연하장이 겨울 연휴 대목을 맞아 전국 매장에 나올 예정 (our new line of greeting cards will appear in stores nationwide at the end of the year, just in time to benefit from the winter holidays)이라고 했다. 따라서 연말에 신제품을 출시할 것이라는 의미이므로 정답은 (A)이다.

> ▸▸ Paraphrasing 지문의 **new line of greeting cards will appear**
> → 정답의 **The launch of a product line**

84

What are the listeners asked to do?

(A) Forward an e-mail to some contacts
(B) Stay later than usual today
(C) Outline some goals
(D) Participate in a vote

청자들은 무엇을 하라는 요청을 받는가?

(A) 일부 연락처로 이메일 전달하기
(B) 오늘 평소보다 늦게까지 일하기
(C) 몇 가지 목표 요약
(D) 투표 참가

어휘 forward 전달하다 than usual 평소보다 participate in ~에 참여하다

해설 세부 사항 관련 – 청자의 요청 사항

지문 마지막에서 선택 사항을 요약한 이메일을 보내겠으니 가장 마음에 드는 것에 투표하라(You'll get an e-mail later today outlining the options, so please vote for the one you like best)고 했으므로 정답은 (D)이다.

> ▸▸ Paraphrasing 지문의 **please vote**
> → 정답의 **Participate in a vote**

85

What does the speaker imply when she says, "That was really something"?

(A) She hopes to avoid repeating a mistake.
(B) Customers appreciated a special service.
(C) An achievement was impressive.
(D) A proposal was too impractical.

화자가 "정말 대단해요"라고 말한 의도는 무엇인가?

(A) 실수를 되풀이하지 않기를 바란다.
(B) 고객들이 특별 서비스에 감사해했다.
(C) 업적이 인상적이었다.
(D) 제안이 너무 비현실적이었다.

어휘 avoid 피하다 repeat 반복하다 appreciate 고마워하다 achievement 업적 impressive 인상적인 proposal 제안 impractical 터무니없는, 비현실적인

해설 화자의 의도 파악 – 대단하다는 말의 의미

인용문 바로 앞 문장에서 창의적인 콘텐츠를 그토록 신속하게 훌륭히 만들어 낸 덕분에 얻은 것이다(You certainly earned it with the great job you all did producing that creative content so quickly)라고 했다. 따라서 업적을 칭찬하는 의미로 한 말이므로 정답은 (C)이다.

86-88 방송

M-Cn Hello, and welcome to *Nightly Entertainment*. **86On tonight's show, we're going to talk about** ***Trandell City*, currently the most popular drama on TV.** Its second season has just finished, with a thrilling episode that left its main character, politician Devin Grant, in a difficult position. In contrast, John Tarver, the actor that plays him, is enjoying a career high point. And we're lucky enough to have him here today. **87I'm going to speak with Mr. Tarver about** ***Trandell City*, his costars, and his experiences traveling to exotic locations in Mexico, where one memorable episode was filmed last year.** We'll also show exclusive behind-the-scenes footage from this season. **88But first, let me start by summarizing the last episode for viewers who may not have seen it.**

안녕하세요, 〈나이틀리 엔터테인먼트〉입니다. 오늘 밤 쇼에서는 현재 가장 인기 있는 TV 드라마 〈트랜델 시티〉에 관해 이야기하겠습니다. 주인공인 정치인 데번 그랜트가 곤경에 빠지는 긴장감 넘치는 에피소드와 함께 두 번째 시즌이 막 끝 났죠. 반면 주인공 배역을 맡은 존 타버 씨는 연기자로서 전성기를 누리고 있죠. 오늘 저희는 운 좋게도 타버 씨를 여기 모시게 되었습니다. 타버 씨와 함께 〈트 랜델 시티〉, 조연 배우들, 그리고 지난 해 인상적인 에피소드를 찍었던 멕시코의 이국적인 촬영지를 여행한 경험에 대해 이야기 나누겠습니다. 또한 이번 시즌 촬 영 현장 뒷이야기도 단독 공개하겠습니다. 그 전에 방송을 놓친 시청자들을 위해 마지막 에피소드를 요약해 드리겠습니다.

어휘 entertainment 연예, 오락 currently 현재 thrilling 긴장감 넘치는, 짜릿한 character 등장인물 main character 주인공 politician 정치인 in a difficult position 곤경에 처한 in contrast 반면, 반대로 play 배역을 맡다 career 경력 high point 전성기 costar 조연 배우 exotic 이국적인, 진귀한 location 장소, 야외 촬영지 memorable 인상적인 film 촬영하다 exclusive 독점적인, 유일한 behind-the-scenes 은밀한, 무대 뒤의 footage 장면 summarize 요약하다 viewer 시청자

86

What is the main topic of the broadcast?

(A) A video game
(B) A television series
(C) A classic novel
(D) A recent film

방송의 주제는 무엇인가?

(A) 비디오 게임
(B) TV 연속극
(C) 고전 소설
(D) 최근 영화

어휘 series 연재물 classic 고전의

해설 전체 내용 관련 – 방송의 주제
지문 초반부에서 화자가 오늘 밤 쇼에서는 현재 가장 인기 있는 TV 드라마 〈트랜델 시티〉에 관해 이야기하겠다(On tonight's show, we're going to talk about *Trandell City*, currently the most popular drama on TV)고 했으므로 정답은 (B)이다.

▶▶ Paraphrasing   지문의 **drama on TV**
→ 정답의 **A television series**

87

According to the speaker, what did Mr. Tarver do last year?

(A) He starred in a commercial.
(B) He met a politician.
(C) He wrote a play.
(D) He traveled abroad.

화자에 따르면, 타버 씨는 지난해에 무엇을 했는가?

(A) 광고에 출연했다.
(B) 정치인을 만났다.
(C) 희곡을 썼다.
(D) 해외로 여행했다.

어휘 star 주연을 맡다 commercial 광고 play 희곡

해설 세부 사항 관련 – 타버 씨가 지난해에 한 일
지문 중반부에서 타버 씨와 함께 〈트랜델 시티〉, 조연 배우들, 그리고 지난해 인상적인 에피소드를 찍었던 멕시코의 이국적인 촬영지를 여행한 경험에 대해 이야기를 나누겠다(I'm going to speak with Mr. Tarver about *Trandell City*, his costars, and his experiences traveling to exotic locations in Mexico, where one memorable episode was filmed last year)고 했으므로 타버 씨는 지난해에 해외로 나갔음을 알 수 있다. 따라서 정답은 (D)이다.

▶▶ Paraphrasing   지문의 **his experiences traveling to exotic locations** → 정답의 **He traveled abroad.**

88

What will the speaker do next?

(A) Bring out a guest
(B) Give a Web site address
(C) Describe a story's contents
(D) Read letters from viewers

화자는 다음으로 무엇을 할 것인가?

(A) 초대 손님 소개하기
(B) 웹사이트 주소 주기
(C) 줄거리 내용 설명하기
(D) 시청자 편지 읽기

어휘 bring out 소개하다 describe 묘사하다, 설명하다 content 내용

해설 세부 사항 관련 – 화자가 다음에 할 일
지문 후반부에서 방송을 놓친 시청자들을 위해 마지막 에피소드를 요약하겠다(But first, let me start by summarizing the last episode for viewers who may not have seen it)고 했으므로 정답은 (C)이다.

▶▶ Paraphrasing   지문의 **summarizing the last episode**
→ 정답의 **Describe a story's contents.**

89-91 공지

M-Au   Thank you for using the District Transit Authority's commuter railway system. **[89]This is a special express train offering direct service to the downtown Central Square railway station. We will not be stopping at other stations in the city. [90]It looks like we'll arrive at our destination at one-twenty P.M., which is actually five minutes ahead of schedule.** To connect to city bus and subway services, please refer to the boarding information on the large electronic signs throughout the station. **[91]Also, on behalf of the transit authority, I'd like to encourage all passengers to spend some time exploring the new shops and boutiques at our recently-renovated Central Square station.**

지구 교통국의 통근 열차를 이용해 주셔서 감사합니다. 이 열차는 시내 센트럴 스퀘어 기차역까지 직행으로 운행되는 급행 열차입니다. 시내 다른 역에서는 정차하지 않습니다. 오후 1시 20분에 목적지에 도착할 예정이며 이는 일정보다 5분 앞선 시간입니다. 시내 버스 및 지하철로 환승하시려면 역 곳곳에 있는 대형 전자 표지판의 탑승 정보를 참고하십시오. 또한 교통국을 대신하여 최근 새롭게 단장한 센트럴 스퀘어 역의 새 상점 및 부티크를 둘러봐 주시길 권하는 바입니다.

어휘 district 지구, 지역 transit authority 교통 당국 commuter 통근자 express 급행의 direct 직접적인, 직통의 destination 목적지, 도착지 actually 사실은 ahead of schedule 예정보다 빨리 connect 연결하다 refer to ~를 참고하다 boarding information 탑승 정보 electronic 전자의 sign 표지판, 간판 throughout 도처에 on behalf of ~을 대신하여, 대표하여 encourage 권장하다, 장려하다 explore 답사하다, 둘러보다 boutique 부티크, 고급 매장 recently 최근에 renovate 개조하다, 보수하다

89

What is mentioned about the train?

(A) It does not go above ground.
(B) It offers wireless Internet service.
(C) It crosses a national border.
(D) It does not stop at all stations.

열차에 관해 언급된 것은 무엇인가?
(A) 지상으로는 운행하지 않는다.
(B) 무선 인터넷 서비스를 제공한다.
(C) 국경을 건넌다.
(D) 모든 역에서 정차하지는 않는다.

어휘 ground 지상 wireless 무선의 cross 건너다 national border 국경선

해설 세부 사항 관련 – 열차에 관해 언급된 것

지문 초반부에서 이 열차는 시내 센트럴 스퀘어 기차역까지 직행으로 운행되는 급행 열차이며(This is a special express train offering direct service to the downtown Central Square railway station) 시내 다른 역에서는 정차하지 않는다(We will not be stopping at other stations in the city)고 했다. 따라서 열차가 정차하지 않는 역이 있음을 알 수 있으므로 정답은 (D)이다.

> ▸▸ **Paraphrasing** 지문의 **will not be stopping at other stations in the city**
> → 정답의 **does not stop at all stations**

90

What information does the speaker announce?

(A) The number of passengers on board
(B) The time of an arrival
(C) The location of a dining car
(D) The charge for transferring to a bus

화자는 어떤 정보를 공지하는가?
(A) 탑승한 승객 수
(B) 도착 시간
(C) 식당칸의 위치
(D) 버스 환승 요금

어휘 on board 탑승한 location 위치 charge 요금 transfer 환승하다

해설 세부 사항 관련 – 공지하는 정보

지문 중반부에서 열차는 오후 1시 20분 목적지에 도착하는데 이는 일정보다 5분 앞선 시간(It looks like we'll arrive at our destination at one-twenty P.M., which is actually five minutes ahead of schedule)이라고 했으므로 정답은 (B)이다.

91

What does the speaker encourage listeners to do?

(A) Browse around some stores
(B) Buy special transport passes
(C) Use a short-term storage facility
(D) Install a new mobile app

화자는 청자들에게 무엇을 하라고 권하는가?
(A) 일부 상점 둘러보기
(B) 특별 교통 카드 구매하기
(C) 단기 화물 보관소 이용하기
(D) 신규 휴대폰 앱 설치하기

어휘 browse 둘러보다 pass 탑승권 short-term 단기의 storage facility 저장[보관] 시설 install 설치하다

해설 세부 사항 관련 – 화자의 권고 사항

지문 마지막에서 최근 새롭게 단장한 센트럴 스퀘어 역의 새 상점과 부티크를 둘러보는 시간을 가지시길 권한다(I'd like to encourage all passengers to spend some time exploring the new shops and boutiques at our recently-renovated Central Square station)고 했으므로 정답은 (A)이다.

> ▸▸ **Paraphrasing** 지문의 **exploring the new shops and boutiques**
> → 정답의 **Browse around some stores**

92-94 회의 발췌

W-Am **92All right, those of you who've worked here for a while have probably noticed that businesses in our neighborhood have been struggling since the Market District across town was revitalized.** It appears that we'll need to work harder to ensure that our restaurant remains an attractive dining destination. **93I'm going to start by extending our hours of operation to eleven P.M. 94This is going to bring some changes to your working schedule that may require flexibility on your part. But with luck, it will be a temporary situation.** OK, any questions about this?

자, 여기에서 한동안 일한 직원이라면 누구라도 마을 건너편의 마켓 디스트릭트가 활성화된 이후 동네 가게들이 어려움을 겪고 있다는 사실을 잘 알고 있을 것입니다. 우리 식당이 명물 맛집으로 남아 있으려면 더 열심히 일해야 할 것 같습니다. 우선 영업시간을 오후 11시까지 연장하려고 합니다. 그렇게 되면 여러분의 작업 일정에 변동이 생겨 여러분 입장에서도 융통성을 발휘해야 할 수도 있습니다. 하지만 운이 좋으면 일시적인 상황이 될 것입니다. 자, 여기에 대해 질문 있으신가요?

어휘 for a while 얼마 동안, 한동안 notice (보거나 들어서) 알다 neighborhood 근처, 인근 struggle 분투하다, 고생하다 across 건너서, 가로질러서 revitalize 새로운 활력을 주다, 재활성화시키다 appear ~인 것 같다 ensure 반드시 ~하게 하다, 보장하다 remain 계속 ~이다 attractive 매력적인 dining 식사, 식당 destination 행선지 extend 연장하다 opening hours 영업시간 flexibility 융통성, 유연성 on one's part ~쪽으로서는 with luck 일이 잘 되면, 운이 좋으면 temporary 일시적인

118

92

What has caused a problem?

(A) Shortages of special ingredients
(B) New city regulations for restaurants
(C) Improvements to another neighborhood
(D) Negative customer reviews posted online

문제를 일으킨 원인은 무엇인가?
(A) 특정 재료의 부족
(B) 시에서 새로 마련한 식당 규정
(C) 다른 인근 지역의 발전
(D) 온라인에 게시된 부정적인 고객 평가

어휘 shortage 부족 ingredient 재료 regulation 규제
improvement 개선, 발전 negative 부정적인 customer
review 고객 평가 post 게시하다

해설 세부 사항 관련 – 문제의 원인
지문 초반부에서 여기에서 한동안 일한 직원이라면 누구라도 마을 건너편의
마켓 디스트릭트가 활성화된 이후 동네 가게들이 어려움을 겪고 있는 사실
을 알 것(those of you who've worked here for a while have probably
noticed that businesses in our neighborhood have been struggling
since the Market District across town was revitalized)이라고 했다. 건
너편 지구가 활성화된 이후 어려움을 겪고 있으므로 정답은 (C)이다.

▸▸ Paraphrasing 지문의 the Market District across town
was revitalized → 정답의 Improvements to
another neighborhood

93

What does the speaker intend to do?

(A) Build some parking garages
(B) Extend some opening hours
(C) Schedule a press conference
(D) Reconsider a hiring requirement

화자는 무엇을 하려고 하는가?
(A) 주차 전용 건물 건설하기
(B) 영업시간 연장하기
(C) 기자회견 일정 잡기
(D) 채용 요건 재고하기

어휘 parking garage 주차 전용 건물 press conference 기자 회견
reconsider 재고하다 hiring 고용 requirement 요건, 조건

해설 세부 사항 관련 – 화자가 하려는 일
지문 중반부에서 우선 영업시간을 오후 11시까지 연장하려고 한다(I'm going
to start by extending our hours of operation to eleven P.M.)고 했으므
로 정답은 (B)이다.

▸▸ Paraphrasing 지문의 extending our hours of operation
→ 정답의 Extend some opening hours

94

Why does the speaker say, "it will be a temporary situation"?

(A) To give a reason for a decision
(B) To express frustration with an agreement
(C) To suggest postponing an announcement
(D) To reassure the listeners about a change

화자가 "일시적인 상황이 될 것입니다"라고 말하는 이유는 무엇인가?
(A) 결정의 이유를 제시하기 위해
(B) 합의에 대한 실망을 나타내기 위해
(C) 발표 연기를 제안하기 위해
(D) 청자들에게 변동 사항에 대해 안심시키기 위해

어휘 decision 결정, 판단 frustration 낙심, 실망 agreement
합의 suggest 제안하다, 제시하다 postpone 연기하다
announcement 발표, 공지 reassure 안심시키다

해설 세부 사항 관련 – 화자가 일시적인 상황이라고 말하는 이유
지문 후반부에서 작업 일정에 변동이 생겨 청자 입장에서도 융통성을 발휘해
야 할 수도 있다(This is going to bring some changes to your working
schedule that may require flexibility on your part)고 우려되는 사항을
말한 뒤, 운이 좋으면(But with luck) 일시적인 상황이 될 수도 있다고 했다.
따라서 변경이 일시적일 수도 있다는 말로 청자들을 안심시키고 있음을 알 수
있으므로 정답은 (D)이다.

95-97 회의 발췌 + 지출품의서

M-Au **95Now, if you'll turn to page three of the
expense report, we can talk about balancing
the library's magazine budget.** We're going to
have a slight deficit in this area next year, and I
was hoping to cancel one of our subscriptions.
**96So I read the latest edition of the most
expensive periodical—and I wasn't impressed.**
I'm not sure that it's a good fit for our facility.
But I think we may need it to keep drawing in
visitors, especially younger ones. What do you
all think? **97Should we subscribe to it again next
year? Let's talk it over.**

자, 지출품의서 3페이지를 보면서 도서관 잡지 예산 균형에 대해 이야기하겠습니
다. 내년에 이 분야에서 소액 적자가 예상돼서 구독 잡지 중 하나를 취소하고 싶
었습니다. 그래서 가장 비싼 정기 간행물의 최신 호를 읽어봤죠. 별로더군요. 우
리 시설에 잘 맞는지 모르겠어요. 하지만 이용객들 중에서도, 특히 젊은 이용자
들을 유치하려면 그 잡지가 필요할지도 모르겠어요. 다들 어떻게 생각하세요?
내년에도 구독해야 할까요? 논의해 봅시다.

어휘 expense report 지출품의서 balance the budget
예산 균형을 맞추다 slight 약간의 deficit 적자 cancel 취소하다,
해지하다 subscription 정기 구독 latest 최신의 edition 호,
판 periodical 정기 간행물 impressed 감동 받은 fit 적합성, 맞는
것 facility 시설 draw 끌다 visitor 방문객 especially 특히
subscribe to ~을 정기 구독하다 talk over 의논하다

Expense Report
Section: Magazines

Title	Cost per year
96Celebrity Gossip	£96
Wise Consumer	£55
Games for Children	£48
Earth in Photographs	£27

지출품의서
부문: 잡지

제목	연간 비용
유명인 뒷이야기	96파운드
현명한 소비자	55파운드
아동용 게임	48파운드
사진으로 보는 지구	27파운드

어휘 celebrity 유명 인사 gossip 소문, 험담 consumer 소비자
earth 지구

95

Who most likely are the listeners?

(A) Medical clinic staff
(B) Magazine designers
(C) Librarians
(D) Journalism students

청자들은 누구이겠는가?
(A) 병원 직원들
(B) 잡지 디자이너들
(C) 사서들
(D) 신문방송학과 학생들

어휘 medical clinic 병원 librarian (도서관) 사서 journalism
저널리즘, 신문방송학

해설 전체 내용 관련 – 청자의 신분
지문 초반부에서 화자가 지출품의서 3페이지를 보면서 도서관의 잡지 예산
균형에 대해 이야기하겠다(if you'll turn to page three of the expense
report, we can talk about balancing the library's magazine budget)
고 했다. 따라서 도서관 사서들의 회의임을 알 수 있으므로 정답은 (C)이다.

96

Look at the graphic. Which title did the speaker read recently?

(A) Celebrity Gossip
(B) Wise Consumer
(C) Games for Children
(D) Earth in Photographs

시각 정보에 의하면, 화자가 최근에 읽은 간행물의 제목은 무엇인가?

(A) 유명인 뒷이야기
(B) 현명한 소비자
(C) 아동용 게임
(D) 사진으로 보는 지구

해설 시각 정보 연계 – 화자가 최근에 읽은 간행물
지문 초반부에서 가장 비싼 정기 간행물의 최신 호를 읽어봤는데 별로였다
(I read the latest edition of the most expensive periodical—and I
wasn't impressed)고 했다. 시각 정보에 따르면, 가장 비싼 구독료의 잡지는
96파운드의 〈유명인 뒷이야기(Celebrity Gossip)〉이므로 정답은 (A)이다.

97

What will most likely be discussed next?

(A) Who will take on an assignment
(B) Whether to renew a subscription
(C) How to arrange a magazine rack
(D) Why some expenses have increased

다음으로 무엇이 논의되겠는가?
(A) 업무를 담당할 사람
(B) 구독 갱신 여부
(C) 잡지 서가 배열 방법
(D) 일부 경비가 늘어난 이유

어휘 assignment 과제, (할당된) 업무 renew 갱신하다 arrange
정리하다, 배열하다 increase 증가하다, 오르다

해설 세부 사항 관련 – 다음으로 논의할 사항
지문 후반부에서 내년에도 구독해야 할지(Should we subscribe to it again
next year) 논의해 보자(Let's talk it over)고 했으므로 정답은 (B)이다.

▶▶ Paraphrasing 지문의 subscribe to it again
→ 정답의 renew a subscription

98-100 전화 메시지 + 일기 예보

W-Br Hi, Norman. This is Jackie from SeaDeck Resort. **98I know that we were planning to meet this week so I could show you our outdoor terrace, but the weather forecast said it's supposed to rain that day.** You'll appreciate the terrace's pleasant atmosphere much more if you come on a sunnier day, so I'd like to reschedule. **99Please know that we're still very interested in being the site for the launch of your company's new line of tableware.** I'll call you again tomorrow, but in the meantime, you should stop by our Web site. **100We just uploaded a video tour of our facilities.** It'll give you a good sense of what we offer.

안녕하세요, 노먼 씨. 씨데크 리조트의 잭키입니다. **이번 주에 만나서 옥외 테라스를 보여드릴 계획이었지만 일기예보에 따르면 그날 비가 온다고 합니다.** 더 화창한 날에 오시면 테라스의 쾌적한 분위기를 좀 더 음미하실 수 있을 테니 일정을 다시 잡고 싶습니다. **귀사의 신제품 식기류 출시 행사 장소를 마련해 드리는 데 여전히 큰 관심을 두고 있다는 점을 알아 주시기 바랍니다.** 내일 다시 전화드리기 전에 저희 웹사이트에 한번 들러주십시오. **저희 시설을 둘러보실 수 있는 동영상을 막 올렸습니다.** 그 동영상이면 저희가 제공해 드리는 장소를 자세히 살펴보실 수 있을 겁니다.

어휘 outdoor 야외의 terrace 테라스 weather forecast 기상예보 be supposed to ~하기로 되어 있다 appreciate 감상하다, 음미하다 atmosphere 분위기 reschedule 일정을 다시 잡다, 일정을 조정하다 site 현장, 장소 launch 출시 line 상품군 tableware 식기류 in the meantime 그동안 stop by 들르다 upload 데이터를 전송하다 facility 시설

98

Look at the graphic. On what day was a meeting scheduled?

(A) Tuesday
(B) Wednesday
(C) Thursday
(D) Friday

시각 정보에 의하면, 회의는 어느 요일로 예정돼 있었는가?
(A) 화요일
(B) 수요일
(C) 목요일
(D) 금요일

해설 시각 정보 연계 – 회의 일정
지문 초반부에 화자가 이번 주에 만나서 옥외 테라스를 보여줄 계획이었지만 기상예보에 따르면 그날 비가 온다(I know that we were planning to meet this week so I could show you our outdoor terrace, but the weather forecast said it's supposed to rain that day) 고 했다. 시각 정보에 따르면, 수요일에는 비가 예상되므로 정답은 (B)이다.

99

What is the speaker offering to provide for an event?

(A) The transportation
(B) The refreshments
(C) The venue
(D) The decorations

화자는 행사를 위해 무엇을 제공하겠다고 제안하는가?
(A) 교통편
(B) 다과
(C) 장소
(D) 장식물

어휘 transportation 교통 수단 refreshment 다과 decoration 장식(물)

해설 세부 사항 관련 – 화자가 제공하는 것
지문 중반부에 화자가 여전히 귀사의 신제품 식기류 출시 장소를 제공하는 데 관심이 있다는 점을 알아 달라(Please know that we're still very interested in being the site for the launch of your company's new line of tableware)고 했으므로 정답은 (C)이다.

▸▸ Paraphrasing 지문의 **the site** → 정답의 **The venue**

100

Why should the listener visit a Web site?

(A) To obtain a coupon
(B) To watch a video
(C) To join a mailing list
(D) To make a tour reservation

청자가 웹사이트를 방문해야 하는 이유는 무엇인가?
(A) 쿠폰을 얻기 위해
(B) 동영상을 보기 위해
(C) 메일링 리스트에 가입하기 위해
(D) 견학 예약을 하기 위해

어휘 obtain 얻다, 획득하다 join 합류하다, 들어가다 mailing list 우편물 수신자 명단, 메일링 리스트(수신자 이메일 주소록) make a reservation 예약하다

해설 세부 사항 관련 – 청자가 웹사이트를 방문해야 하는 이유
지문 후반부에 화자가 시설을 둘러볼 수 있는 동영상을 막 올렸다(We just uploaded a video tour of our facilities)고 했으므로 정답은 (B)이다.

TEST 5

1 (D)	**2** (C)	**3** (A)	**4** (D)	**5** (C)
6 (C)	**7** (A)	**8** (B)	**9** (B)	**10** (C)
11 (A)	**12** (B)	**13** (C)	**14** (B)	**15** (A)
16 (A)	**17** (C)	**18** (B)	**19** (A)	**20** (C)
21 (B)	**22** (C)	**23** (B)	**24** (B)	**25** (C)
26 (B)	**27** (A)	**28** (A)	**29** (C)	**30** (A)
31 (C)	**32** (B)	**33** (B)	**34** (A)	**35** (B)
36 (D)	**37** (A)	**38** (C)	**39** (D)	**40** (C)
41 (A)	**42** (D)	**43** (B)	**44** (C)	**45** (D)
46 (B)	**47** (A)	**48** (D)	**49** (C)	**50** (A)
51 (C)	**52** (B)	**53** (C)	**54** (C)	**55** (D)
56 (C)	**57** (D)	**58** (B)	**59** (C)	**60** (D)
61 (C)	**62** (B)	**63** (C)	**64** (C)	**65** (B)
66 (A)	**67** (D)	**68** (B)	**69** (A)	**70** (C)
71 (D)	**72** (B)	**73** (A)	**74** (C)	**75** (B)
76 (D)	**77** (C)	**78** (C)	**79** (D)	**80** (C)
81 (D)	**82** (C)	**83** (D)	**84** (B)	**85** (B)
86 (B)	**87** (A)	**88** (C)	**89** (D)	**90** (B)
91 (C)	**92** (A)	**93** (D)	**94** (B)	**95** (C)
96 (A)	**97** (D)	**98** (A)	**99** (C)	**100** (D)

PART 1

1 W-Am

(A) He's hanging art on a wall.
(B) He's carrying a bucket.
(C) He's rinsing a paintbrush.
(D) He's using a tool.

(A) 남자가 벽에 미술품을 걸고 있다.
(B) 남자가 양동이를 나르고 있다.
(C) 남자가 그림 붓을 헹구고 있다.
(D) 남자가 연장을 사용하고 있다.

어휘 hang 걸다, 매달다 carry 나르다 bucket 양동이 rinse 헹구다
paintbrush 그림 붓 tool 연장

해설 1인 등장 사진 – 사람의 동작 묘사

(A) 사진에 없는 명사를 이용한 오답. 사진에 미술품(art)이 보이지 않으므로 오답.
(B) 동사 오답. 사진에 양동이가 보이지만 남자가 양동이를 나르는(is carrying a bucket) 모습이 아니므로 오답.
(C) 동사 오답. 사진에 그림 붓이 있지만 남자가 그림 붓을 헹구는(is rinsing a paintbrush) 모습이 아니므로 오답.
(D) 정답. 남자가 도구를 사용하는(is using a tool) 모습이므로 정답.

2 M-Au

(A) Both of the men are operating equipment.
(B) One of the men is holding a pen.
(C) Both of the men are wearing hard hats.
(D) One of the men is pointing at a document.

(A) 남자 두 명 모두 장비를 작동시키고 있다.
(B) 남자들 중 한 명이 펜을 들고 있다.
(C) 남자 두 명 모두 안전모를 쓰고 있다.
(D) 남자들 중 한 명이 서류를 가리키고 있다.

어휘 operate 가동[조작]하다 equipment 장비 hard hat 안전모
point at ~를 가리키다

해설 2인 이상 등장 사진 – 사람의 동작 묘사

(A) 사진에 없는 명사를 이용한 오답. 사진에 장비(equipment)가 보이지 않으므로 오답.
(B) 동사 오답. 남자 중 한 명이 펜을 들고 있는(is holding a pen) 모습이 아니므로 오답.
(C) 정답. 두 남자가 모두 안전모를 쓴(are wearing hard hats) 상태이므로 정답.
(D) 명사 오답. 사진에 서류가 보이지만 남자 중 한 명이 서류를 가리키는(is pointing at a document) 모습이 아니므로 오답.

3 W-Br

(A) A handbag hangs on the woman's arm.
(B) The woman is trying on a shoe.
(C) Some merchandise is being arranged.
(D) A shopper is exchanging an item.

(A) 여자의 팔에 손가방이 매달려 있다.
(B) 여자는 신발을 신어 보고 있다.
(C) 몇몇 상품이 진열되고 있다.
(D) 쇼핑객이 상품을 교환하고 있다.

어휘 hang on ~에 매달다[걸다] try on ~을 입어 보다, 신어 보다
merchandise 상품 arrange 정리하다, 배열하다 exchange 교환하다

해설 1인 등장 사진 – 사람 또는 사물 중심 묘사

(A) 정답. 여자의 팔에 손가방이 매달려 있는(hangs on the woman's arm) 상태이므로 정답.
(B) 동사 오답. 사진에 신발이 있지만 여자가 신발을 신어 보고 있는(is trying on a shoe) 모습이 아니므로 오답.
(C) 동사 오답. 상품이 진열된 상태이지 진열하는(is being arranged) 모습이 아니므로 오답.

(D) 동사 오답. 쇼핑객이 상품을 들고 있지 상품을 교환하는(is exchanging an item) 모습이 아니므로 오답.

4 W-Am

(A) One of the men is writing on a board.
(B) Some of the men are shaking hands.
(C) Some paperwork is being distributed.
(D) Meeting attendees are seated at a table.

(A) 남자 중 한 명이 칠판에 쓰고 있다.
(B) 남자 중 몇 명이 악수를 하고 있다.
(C) 서류가 배포되고 있다.
(D) **회의 참석자들이 탁자에 앉아 있다.**

어휘 shake hands 악수를 하다 paperwork 서류 distribute 나누어 주다, 분배하다 attendee 참석자

해설 2인 이상 등장 사진 – 사람 또는 사물 중심 묘사
(A) 동사 오답. 남자 중 한 명이 칠판에 적고 있는(is writing on a board) 모습이 아니므로 오답.
(B) 동사 오답. 남자 중 몇 명이 악수를 하는(are shaking hands) 모습이 아니므로 오답.
(C) 동사 오답. 사진에 서류가 보이지만 배포하는(is being distributed) 모습이 아니므로 오답.
(D) 정답. 회의 참석자들이 탁자에 앉아 있는(are seated at a table) 모습이므로 정답.

5 M-Cn

(A) The people are assisting a hospital patient.
(B) The woman is wearing a lab coat and stethoscope.
(C) The people are looking at the same item.
(D) One of the men is standing with his arms crossed.

(A) 사람들이 병원 환자를 돕고 있다.
(B) 여자가 실험실 가운을 입고 청진기를 걸치고 있다.
(C) **사람들이 같은 물건을 바라보고 있다.**
(D) 남자들 중 한 명이 팔짱을 끼고 서 있다.

어휘 assist 돕다 patient 환자 lab coat 실험실 가운 stethoscope 청진기 with one's arms crossed 팔짱을 낀 채

해설 2인 이상 등장 사진 – 사람의 동작 묘사
(A) 사진에 없는 명사를 이용한 오답. 사진에 환자(hospital patient)가 보이지 않으므로 오답.
(B) 동사 오답. 사진에 실험실 가운과 청진기가 보이지만 여자가 실험실 가운을 입고 청진기를 걸치고 있는(is wearing a lab coat and stethoscope) 모습이 아니므로 오답.

(C) 정답. 사람들이 같은 물건을 보고 있는(are looking at the same item) 모습이므로 정답.
(D) 명사 오답. 여자가 팔짱을 끼고 서 있는 모습이지 남자들 중 한 명이(One of the men) 팔짱을 끼고 서 있는 모습이 아니므로 오답.

6 M-Au

(A) A wooden shelf has been left empty.
(B) Some books have been stacked in a box.
(C) A broom is leaning against a bookcase.
(D) Some dishes are placed inside a basket.

(A) 나무 선반이 텅 비었다.
(B) 책들이 상자에 쌓여 있다.
(C) **빗자루가 책장에 기대어져 있다.**
(D) 접시들이 바구니 안에 놓여 있다.

어휘 wooden 나무로 된 shelf 선반 empty 비어 있는 stack 쌓다, 포개다 broom 빗자루 lean against ~에 기대다 place 놓다

해설 사물/배경 사진 – 사물의 위치 묘사
(A) 명사 오답. 사진에 나무 선반이 있지만 나무 선반이 텅 비어 있는(has been left empty) 상태는 아니므로 오답.
(B) 전치사구 오답. 책들이 책장에 쌓여 있는 상태이지 상자에 쌓여 있는(in a box) 상태가 아니므로 오답.
(C) 정답. 빗자루가 책장에 기대어 있는(is leaning against a bookcase) 상태이므로 정답.
(D) 전치사구 오답. 접시들이 책 위에 놓여 있는 상태이지 바구니 안에 놓여 있는(inside a basket) 상태가 아니므로 오답.

PART 2

7
W-Br You are a homeowner, aren't you?
M-Au (A) No, I can't afford it.
　　　 (B) I'll be there later.
　　　 (C) He works from home.

집주인이시군요, 그렇죠?
(A) **아닙니다. 그럴 형편이 안 돼요.**
(B) 나중에 거기로 가겠습니다.
(C) 그는 재택근무를 합니다.

어휘 afford 여유가 있다, 형편이 되다 work from home 재택근무를 하다

해설 집주인인지를 확인하는 부가의문문
(A) 정답. 집주인(homeowner)인지에 대한 질문에 먼저 No라는 부정적인 응답을 한 후, 그럴 만한 형편이 안 된다(I can't afford it)고 부연 설명을 하고 있으므로 정답.
(B) 질문과 상관없는 오답. 집주인인지를 묻는 질문에 나중에 거기로 가겠다(I'll be there later)는 답변은 질문의 맥락에서 벗어난 것이므로 오답.

(C) 유사 발음 오답. 질문의 homeowner와 부분적으로 발음이 동일한 home을 이용한 오답.

8

M-Cn Where should I send Mr. Basak's invitation?

W-Am (A) By Thursday afternoon.

(B) To his residence.

(C) For a retirement party.

바자크 씨의 초대장을 어디로 보내야 합니까?
(A) 목요일 오후까지요.
(B) 그의 거주지로요.
(C) 은퇴 기념 파티를 위해서요.

어휘 invitation 초대(장) residence 거주지 retirement 은퇴

해설 초대장 발송지를 묻는 Where 의문문
(A) 질문과 상관없는 오답. 시기를 묻는 When 의문문에 적절한 응답이므로 오답.
(B) 정답. 초대장을 어디로 보내야 하는지 묻는 질문에 그의 거주지라는 구체적인 장소를 언급하고 있으므로 정답.
(C) 연상 단어 오답. 질문의 invitation에서 연상 가능한 party를 이용한 오답.

9

M-Au When will the negotiations be completed?

M-Cn (A) At the Giles Incorporated headquarters.

(B) By the end of the week.

(C) For the corporate merger agreement.

협상은 언제 완료되나요?
(A) 자일스 주식회사 본사에서요.
(B) 이번 주 말까지요.
(C) 회사 합병 계약을 위해서요.

어휘 negotiation 협상 complete 완료하다 incorporated 주식회사 headquarters 본사 corporate 회사의 merger 합병 agreement 협정, 계약

해설 협상 완료 시점을 묻는 When 의문문
(A) 질문과 상관없는 오답. 장소를 묻는 Where 의문문에 적절한 응답이므로 오답.
(B) 정답. 협상이 언제 완료될지를 묻는 질문에 이번 주 말이라는 구체적인 시점을 언급하고 있으므로 정답.
(C) 연상 단어 오답. 질문의 negotiations에서 연상 가능한 corporate merger agreement를 이용한 오답.

10

W-Br Does the performance have an intermission?

M-Cn (A) Our mission is to help the environment.

(B) It'll be performed live.

(C) Yes, after the second act.

공연에 중간 휴식 시간이 있나요?
(A) 저희 임무는 환경에 도움이 되는 것입니다.
(B) 라이브로 공연될 겁니다.
(C) 네, 2막 후예요.

어휘 performance 공연 intermission 중간 휴식 시간 mission 임무 perform live 라이브 공연을 하다 act (연극 등의) 막

해설 중간 휴식 시간 여부를 묻는 조동사(does) Yes/No 의문문
(A) 유사 발음 오답. 질문의 intermission과 부분적으로 발음이 동일한 mission을 이용한 오답.
(B) 파생어 오답. 질문의 performance와 파생어 관계인 performed를 이용한 오답.
(C) 정답. 중간 휴식 시간이 공연 중에 있는지에 대해 먼저 Yes라는 긍정적인 응답을 한 후, 2막 후에 있다고 부연 설명을 하고 있으므로 정답.

11

W-Am Which charts should I attach to the budget report?

M-Au (A) Hasn't it already been turned in?

(B) A minimum of five thousand dollars.

(C) Certainly, if you have enough time.

예산보고서에 어떤 도표를 첨부해야 하나요?
(A) 이미 제출되지 않았나요?
(B) 최소 5천 달러요.
(C) 그럼요. 시간이 충분하다면요.

어휘 attach to ~에 붙이다 budget report 예산보고서 turn in 제출하다 a minimum of 최소한의 ~ certainly 그럼요, 물론이지요

해설 첨부할 도표를 묻는 Which 의문문
(A) 정답. 예산보고서에 첨부해야 할 도표를 묻는 질문에 이미 제출되지 않았냐고 되묻고 있으므로 정답.
(B) 연상 단어 오답. 질문의 budget에 대해 예산 금액 측면에서 연상 가능한 five thousand dollars를 이용한 오답.
(C) Yes/No 불가 오답. Which 의문문에 Certainly와 같은 긍정적 응답은 불가능하므로 오답.

12

W-Am Am I allowed to bring my dog on the ferry?

W-Br (A) The boat will depart at 2 P.M. sharp.

(B) Yes, but it must be kept on a leash.

(C) I think cats are more practical pets.

개를 데리고 배를 타도 됩니까?
(A) 배는 오후 2시 정각에 출발할 겁니다.
(B) 네, 하지만 줄을 매어 두어야 합니다.
(C) 고양이가 더 실용적인 애완동물이라고 생각해요.

어휘 be allowed to ~하는 것이 허용되다 bring 데리고 가다 ferry 배, 연락선 depart 출발하다 sharp (특정 시간 뒤에 쓰여) 정각 keep ~ on a leash ~을 가죽끈으로 매어 두다 practical 현실적인, 실용적인

해설 배에 개의 동승 여부를 확인하는 Be동사 Yes/No 의문문
(A) 연상 단어 오답. 질문의 ferry에서 연상 가능한 boat를 이용한 오답.
(B) 정답. 개를 데리고 배를 타도 되는지를 묻는 질문에 먼저 Yes라는 긍정적인 응답을 한 후, 줄에 매어 두어야 한다는 조건을 제시하고 있으므로 정답.
(C) 연상 단어 오답. 질문의 dog에서 연상 가능한 cats와 pets를 이용한 오답.

13

M-Au Who can use the gym's swimming pool?

W-Am (A) We usually carpool together.

(B) Yes, to get in better shape.

(C) Anyone with a valid membership.

체육관의 수영장은 누가 사용할 수 있죠?
(A) 우리는 보통 승용차를 함께 타요.
(B) 네, 더 나은 체력을 위해서요.
(C) 유효한 회원권을 가진 누구나 가능해요.

어휘 carpool 카풀[합승]하다 get in shape 좋은 몸 상태[몸매]를 유지하다
valid 유효한

해설 수영장 사용이 가능한 사람을 묻는 Who 의문문
(A) 유사 발음 오답. 질문의 pool과 부분적으로 발음이 동일한 carpool을 이용한 오답.
(B) Yes/No 불가 오답. Who 의문문에 Yes/No 응답이 불가능하므로 오답.
(C) 정답. 체육관의 수영장 사용이 가능한 사람을 묻는 질문에 유효한 회원권을 가진 사람은 누구든지 가능하다고 언급했으므로 정답.

14

M-Au How much is the postage to send this package?

W-Br (A) It contains fragile items.

(B) Let's check its weight first.

(C) That was thoughtful of you.

이 소포를 보내는 데 드는 우편료는 얼마인가요?
(A) 깨지기 쉬운 물건이 들어 있습니다.
(B) 먼저 무게부터 확인해 봅시다.
(C) 사려 깊으시군요.

어휘 postage 우편 요금 package 소포 contain ~이 들어 있다
fragile 깨지기 쉬운 weight 무게 thoughtful 사려 깊은, 배려심
있는

해설 우편료를 묻는 How much 의문문
(A) 연상 단어 오답. 질문의 package에서 연상 가능한 fragile items를 이용한 오답.
(B) 정답. 소포 우편료를 묻는 질문에 먼저 무게를 확인하자고 답함으로써 무게에 따라 가격이 다르다는 것을 의미하고 있으므로 정답.
(C) 질문과 상관없는 오답. 소포 우편료를 묻는 질문에 사려 깊다는 대답은 맥락에 맞지 않으므로 오답.

15

W-Br Should we make a donation now or wait for the fundraiser?

W-Am (A) The sooner the better.

(B) Yes, to support adult literacy.

(C) I appreciate your generosity.

지금 기부를 해야 하나요, 아니면 모금행사를 기다려야 하나요?
(A) 빠를수록 좋아요.
(B) 네, 성인의 문맹률을 낮추기 위해서요.
(C) 너그러움에 감사드립니다.

어휘 make a donation 기부하다 fundraiser 모금 행사
the sooner the better 빠를수록 좋다 support 지지[지원]하다
literacy 읽고 쓸 줄 아는 능력 generosity 관대함, 너그러움

해설 구를 연결한 선택 의문문
(A) 정답. 지금 기부하는 것과 모금 행사를 기다리는 것 중 어느 쪽을 선택해야 하는지를 묻는 질문에 빠를수록 좋다는 답변으로 간접적으로 지금 기부하는 쪽을 선택한 것이므로 정답.
(B) Yes/No 불가 오답. 구를 연결한 선택의문문에 Yes/No 응답이 불가능하므로 오답.
(C) 연상 단어 오답. 질문의 donation과 fundraiser에서 연상 가능한 generosity를 이용한 오답.

16

W-Am Would you like to assist in developing our new prototype?

M-Au (A) Yes, that'd be a fascinating project.

(B) Ms. Klein will be in charge of it.

(C) Probably three or four months.

저희 새 시제품 개발을 도와주시겠어요?
(A) 네, 아주 흥미로운 프로젝트가 되겠군요.
(B) 클라인 씨가 맡을 거예요.
(C) 아마 서너 달일 거예요.

어휘 assist in ~을 돕다 prototype 원형, 시제품 fascinating
매력적인, 대단히 흥미로운 be in charge of ~를 맡다

해설 부탁/요청의 의문문
(A) 정답. 새 시제품 개발을 도와달라고 하자 Yes로 긍정적 응답을 한 후, 아주 흥미로운 프로젝트가 되겠다고 관심을 보이고 있으므로 정답.
(B) 질문과 상관없는 오답. 책임자를 묻는 Who 의문문에 적절한 응답이므로 오답.
(C) 질문과 상관없는 오답. 기간을 묻는 How long 의문문에 적절한 응답이므로 오답.

17

M-Cn Why did you move the site of the training session?

W-Br (A) Just a few hours ago.

(B) For all newly hired employees.

(C) Because the projector was broken.

교육 강좌 장소를 왜 옮긴 거죠?
(A) 불과 몇 시간 전이에요.
(B) 신입 직원 전부를 위해서요.
(C) 프로젝터가 고장 났거든요.

어휘 site 부지, 장소 training session 교육[연수] (과정) newly 새로
hired 채용된

해설 장소 변경 이유를 묻는 Why 의문문
(A) 질문과 상관없는 오답. 시기를 묻는 When 의문문에 적절한 응답이므로 오답.
(B) 연상 단어 오답. 질문의 training session에서 연상 가능한 newly hired employees를 이용한 오답.
(C) 정답. 교육 강좌 장소를 왜 옮겼는지 묻는 질문에 프로젝터가 고장 났다는 구체적인 이유를 말하고 있으므로 정답.

18

W-Am How can I make changes to my travel itinerary?

M-Cn (A) To stay a few additional days.

(B) The airline has a direct line.

(C) Within one week of the trip.

제 여행 일정표를 어떻게 변경할 수 있나요?

(A) 며칠 더 묵기 위해서요.

(B) 그 항공사는 직통 전화가 있어요.

(C) 여행 1주일 이내예요.

어휘 make a change 변경하다 itinerary 여행일정표 additional 추가의 direct line 직통 전화

해설 변경 방법을 묻는 How 의문문

(A) 질문과 상관없는 오답. 이유를 묻는 Why 의문문에 적절한 응답이므로 오답.

(B) 정답. 여행 일정표를 어떻게 변경할 수 있는지 묻는 질문에 그 항공사는 직통 전화가 있다고 답하며 항공사에 물어보라는 의미를 우회적으로 나타냈으므로 정답.

(C) 연상 단어 오답. 질문의 travel에서 연상 가능한 trip을 이용한 오답.

19

W-Br Who will perform the renovation work at the chapel?

M-Au (A) We still haven't decided yet.

(B) No, I lack the necessary time.

(C) OK, let's meet there tomorrow.

예배당 개조 작업은 누가 할 예정인가요?

(A) 아직 결정 못했어요.

(B) 아니오, 필요한 시간이 부족해요.

(C) 좋아요. 내일 거기서 만나요.

어휘 perform 수행하다 renovation 개조 chapel 예배당 lack 부족하다 necessary 필요한

해설 개조 작업자를 묻는 Who 의문문

(A) 정답. 예배당의 개조 작업을 누가할지 묻는 질문에 아직 결정 못했다고 응답하고 있으므로 정답.

(B) Yes/No 불가 오답. Who 의문문에 Yes/No 응답이 불가능하므로 오답.

(C) Yes/No 불가 오답. Who 의문문에 OK와 같은 긍정의 응답이 불가능하므로 오답.

20

W-Am Shall I pick up your medication for you?

M-Cn (A) That's the one I would pick.

(B) He works at a pharmacy nearby.

(C) The prescription isn't ready yet.

약을 찾아다 드릴까요?

(A) 저라면 그걸 고르겠어요.

(B) 그는 인근 약국에서 일해요.

(C) 처방전이 아직 나오지 않았어요.

어휘 pick up ~을 찾아오다 medication 약 pharmacy 약국 nearby 근처에 prescription 처방전

해설 제안/권유의 의문문

(A) 단어 반복 오답. 질문에 나온 pick을 반복 이용한 오답.

(B) 연상 단어 오답. 질문의 medication에서 연상 가능한 pharmacy를 이용한 오답.

(C) 정답. 약을 찾아다 주겠다는 제안에 처방전이 아직 나오지 않았다는 부정적 응답을 하고 있으므로 정답.

21

M-Au Is this sweater included in the half-off sale?

M-Cn (A) We sell styles for all tastes.

(B) No, just the items with red tags.

(C) I think it's very flattering.

이 스웨터는 반값 할인에 포함되나요?

(A) 저희는 모든 취향에 맞는 스타일을 판매합니다.

(B) 아니오, 빨간 꼬리표가 붙은 상품만요.

(C) 굉장히 돋보이게 하는 것 같아요.

어휘 half-off sale 반값 할인 taste 취향 tag 꼬리표 flattering (옷 등이 사람을) 돋보이게 하는

해설 할인 포함 여부를 묻는 Be동사 Yes/No 의문문

(A) 연상 단어 오답. 질문의 sale에서 연상 가능한 sell을 이용한 오답.

(B) 정답. 스웨터에 반값 할인이 적용되는지 묻는 질문에 No로 부정적 응답을 한 후, 빨간 꼬리표가 붙은 상품만이라고 할인의 조건을 제시하고 있으므로 정답.

(C) 연상 단어 오답. 질문의 sweater를 듣고 스웨터가 잘 어울리는지를 묻는 질문으로 잘못 이해했을 때 연상 가능한 답변이므로 오답.

22

M-Cn How do I get a permit to park in this neighborhood?

W-Br (A) One more ticket, please.

(B) No, but there are some benches over here.

(C) You have to be a resident.

이 근처에 주차하려면 허가를 어떻게 받나요?

(A) 표 한 장 더요.

(B) 아니요. 하지만 이쪽에 벤치가 있어요.

(C) 거주민이어야 합니다.

어휘 get a permit 허가를 받다 neighborhood 인근, 근처 resident 주민

해설 주차 허가 방법을 묻는 How 의문문

(A) 연상 단어 오답. 질문의 a permit to park에서 주차증과 관련해 연상 가능한 ticket을 이용한 오답.

(B) 연상 단어 오답. 질문의 park를 공원으로 이해했을 때 연상 가능한 benches를 이용한 오답.

(C) 정답. 주차 허가 방법을 묻는 질문에 거주민이어야 한다는 구체적인 조건을 알려주고 있으므로 정답.

23

M-Au Employees receive their paychecks on the fifteenth, right?

W-Am (A) She deserves the recognition.

(B) Yes, for the previous month's work.

(C) Wouldn't ten be sufficient?

직원들은 15일에 급여를 받죠, 그렇죠?

(A) 그녀는 인정을 받을 만해요.

(B) 네, 지난달 근무에 대해서요.

(C) 열 개면 충분하지 않을까요?

어휘 paycheck 급료 deserve ~을 받을 만하다 recognition (공로에 대한) 인정 previous 이전의 sufficient 충분한

해설 급여 지급 날짜를 확인하는 부가의문문

(A) 연상 단어 오답. 질문의 Employees receive에서 연상 가능한 deserves the recognition을 이용한 오답.

(B) 정답. 직원들이 15일에 급여를 받는지 묻는 질문에 먼저 Yes라는 긍정의 응답을 한 후, 지난달 근무에 대해서 그렇다는 부연 설명을 하고 있으므로 정답.

(C) 연상 단어 오답. 질문의 fifteenth에서 연상 가능한 ten을 이용한 오답.

24

M-Cn Didn't Marcia work for a nonprofit organization?

M-Au (A) I'm pleased about the boost in profits.

(B) It was a homeless shelter.

(C) A very organized person.

마르시아는 비영리단체에서 일하지 않았나요?

(A) 이윤이 증가해서 흐뭇합니다.

(B) 노숙자 쉼터였어요.

(C) 매우 체계적인 사람이에요.

어휘 nonprofit organization 비영리단체 boost in ~의 증가 profit 이윤 homeless 노숙자의 shelter 쉼터 organized 체계적인, 조직적인

해설 비영리단체에서 일했는지 묻는 부정의문문

(A) 유사 발음 오답. 질문의 nonprofit과 부분적으로 발음이 동일한 profits를 이용한 오답.

(B) 정답. 마르시아가 비영리단체에서 일하지 않았는지 묻는 질문에 노숙자 쉼터였다고 단체를 구체적으로 언급하고 있으므로 정답.

(C) 파생어 오답. 질문의 organization과 파생어 관계인 organized를 이용한 오답.

25

M-Au Where should I set up the workstation for our new intern?

W-Br (A) Tomorrow morning at nine.

(B) She lives near the subway station.

(C) See what Mr. Dong thinks.

새 인턴을 위한 업무 공간은 어디에 마련해야 하죠?

(A) 내일 아침 9시예요.

(B) 그녀는 지하철역 근처에 살아요.

(C) 동 씨가 어떻게 생각하는지 알아보세요.

어휘 set up 설치하다, 마련하다 workstation 작업 장소

해설 업무 장소를 묻는 Where 의문문

(A) 질문과 상관없는 오답. 시점을 묻는 When 의문문에 적절한 응답이므로 오답.

(B) 유사 발음 오답. 질문의 workstation과 부분적으로 발음이 같은 station을 이용한 오답.

(C) 정답. 인턴의 업무 공간을 어디에 마련할지 묻는 질문에 동 씨의 생각을 알아보라며 동 씨에게 물어볼 것을 우회적으로 표현하고 있으므로 정답.

26

W-Am Why don't we post a transcript of the interview on our Web site?

M-Cn (A) The interviewer might offer me the job.

(B) Unfortunately, we didn't prepare one.

(C) He transferred to another department.

웹사이트에 인터뷰 녹취록을 게시하면 어때요?

(A) 면접관은 저에게 일자리를 줄지도 몰라요.

(B) 안타깝게도 준비하지 못했어요.

(C) 그는 다른 부서로 옮겼어요.

어휘 post 게시하다 transcript 글로 옮긴 기록 prepare 준비하다 transfer to ~로 옮기다[전근하다] department 부서

해설 제안/권유의 의문문

(A) 파생어 오답. 질문의 interview와 파생어 관계인 interviewer를 이용한 오답.

(B) 정답. 웹사이트에 인터뷰 녹취록을 게시하자는 제안에 Unfortunately로 부정적 응답을 한 후, 준비하지 못했다고 부연 설명을 하고 있으므로 정답.

(C) 유사 발음 오답. 질문의 transcript와 부분적으로 발음이 유사한 transferred를 이용한 오답.

27

W-Br How about collaborating with the R&D team on this project?

M-Cn (A) Let's see if they're available.

(B) Thanks, it was a great accomplishment.

(C) By adjusting the schedule.

이 프로젝트는 R&D팀과 협업하는 건 어때요?

(A) 그들이 시간이 되는지 봅시다.

(B) 감사합니다. 대단한 성과였어요.

(C) 일정을 조정해서요.

어휘 collaborate with ~와 협력하다 available 시간이 있는 accomplishment 업적, 성과, 성취 adjust 조정하다

해설 제안/권유의 의문문

(A) 정답. R&D팀과 협력하자는 제안에 그들이 시간이 되는지 보자고 응답했으므로 정답.

(B) 연상 단어 오답. 질문의 project에 대해 결과 측면에서 연상 가능한 great accomplishment를 이용한 오답.

(C) 질문과 상관없는 오답. 그 프로젝트에 대해 R&D팀과 협력하자는 제안에 일정을 조정해서라는 답변은 질문의 맥락에서 벗어난 것이므로 오답.

28

W-Br These assembly instructions are in French.

W-Am (A) Could you search for the English version online?

(B) You don't need any tools to put it together.

(C) I apologize for the broken merchandise.

이 조립 설명서는 프랑스어로 되어 있어요.

(A) 온라인으로 영어 버전을 찾아주겠어요?
(B) 조립하는 데 연장이 필요하지 않아요.
(C) 고장 난 상품에 대해 사과드립니다.

어휘 assembly 조립 instructions 설명서 search for ~를 찾다 put together 조립하다 apologize for ~에 대해 사과하다 broken 고장 난 merchandise 상품

해설 사실/정보 전달의 평서문

(A) 정답. 조립 설명서가 프랑스어로 되어 있다는 말에 온라인으로 영어 버전을 찾을 수 있는지 묻는 응답이므로 정답.
(B) 연상 단어 오답. 질문의 assembly에서 연상 가능한 tools와 put it together를 이용한 오답.
(C) 평서문과 상관없는 오답. 조립 설명서가 프랑스어로 되어 있다는 말에 고장 난 상품에 대해 사과한다는 답변은 질문의 맥락에서 벗어난 것이므로 오답.

29

W-Br Who's succeeding the company president when he steps down?

M-Au (A) To spend more time with his family.

(B) Congratulations on your success.

(C) The board will appoint someone.

회사 회장이 물러나면 누가 후임이 되나요?

(A) 가족과 더 많은 시간을 보내기 위해서요.
(B) 성공을 축하합니다.
(C) 이사회가 누군가를 임명할 겁니다.

어휘 succeed 뒤를 잇다, 후임이 되다 step down 물러나다, 사임하다 congratulations on ~을 축하합니다 board 이사회 appoint 임명하다

해설 회장 후임자를 묻는 Who 의문문

(A) 질문과 상관없는 오답. 이유를 묻는 Why 의문문에 적절한 응답이므로 오답.
(B) 파생어 오답. 질문의 succeeding과 파생어 관계인 success를 이용한 오답.
(C) 정답. 회장 후임자를 묻는 질문에 이사회가 누군가를 임명할 것이라는 불확실성 표현으로 응답하고 있으므로 정답.

30

M-Cn How can I update my contact details in the electronic directory?

W-Am (A) Speak to someone in IT.

(B) It's sixty-three Landover Street.

(C) The electrician repaired it.

전자 전화번호부에서 제 연락처를 어떻게 업데이트합니까?

(A) IT 직원에게 말씀하세요.
(B) 랜드로버 가 63번지입니다.
(C) 전기 기사가 수리했어요.

어휘 update 최신 정보를 알려주다 contact details 연락처 electronic directory 전자 전화번호부 electrician 전기 기사

해설 업데이트 방법을 묻는 How 의문문

(A) 정답. 전자 전화번호부에 연락처 업데이트 방법을 묻는 질문에 (잘 모르니) IT 직원에게 말해 보라고 답변한 것이므로 정답.
(B) 질문과 상관없는 오답. 장소를 묻는 Where 의문문에 적절한 응답이므로 오답.
(C) 유사 발음 오답. 질문의 electronic과 발음이 유사한 electrician을 이용한 오답.

31

M-Au Has the rise in the exchange rate affected our profits?

W-Am (A) We're currently understaffed.

(B) My account is in euros.

(C) Not as much as we feared.

환율 상승이 우리 수익에 영향을 미쳤나요?

(A) 우리는 현재 인원이 부족합니다.
(B) 제 계좌는 유로화 계좌입니다.
(C) 우려했던 것만큼은 아닙니다.

어휘 rise in ~의 상승 exchange rate 환율 affect 영향을 미치다 profit 수익, 이익 currently 현재 understaffed 인원이 부족한 account 계좌

해설 환율 상승의 영향 여부를 묻는 조동사(have) Yes/No 의문문

(A) 질문과 상관없는 오답. 환율 상승이 수익에 영향을 주었는지 묻는 질문에 현재 인원이 부족하다는 응답은 맥락에 어울리지 않으므로 오답.
(B) 연상 단어 오답. 질문의 exchange rate에서 연상 가능한 euros를 이용한 오답.
(C) 정답. 환율 상승이 수익에 영향을 주었는지 묻는 질문에 우려했던 것만큼의 영향은 아니라고 답하고 있으므로 정답.

PART 3

32-34

W-Am Excuse me, sir. **32Are you interested in seeing the features of the recently released Rev-55 coffee maker? I'm giving a demonstration in just a few minutes.**

M-Cn I've heard great reviews about that device, and I'd love to see it in action, but I'm in a hurry this afternoon. **33I want to take bus 103 downtown, and it's departing soon.**

W-Am No problem. **³⁴How about I give you a brochure so you can read up on the Rev-55 in your spare time?**

M-Cn Sure.

여: 실례합니다. 최근 출시된 Rev-55 커피메이커의 기능들을 보는 데 관심 있으신가요? 몇 분 후 시연할 예정입니다.

남: 그 기기에 대해 좋은 평을 들었습니다. 작동하는 모습을 보고 싶지만 오늘 오후엔 바쁘군요. 시내로 가는 103번 버스를 타려고 하는데 곧 출발하거든요.

여: 괜찮습니다. 제가 안내 책자를 드릴 테니 시간 나실 때 Rev-55에 대해 읽어 보시면 어떨까요?

남: 좋습니다.

어휘 be interested in ~에 관심이 있다 feature 기능, 특징 recently released 최근 출시된 give a demonstration 시연하다 review 평가 in action 동작 중인 be in a hurry 서두르다 depart 출발하다 brochure 안내 책자 read up on ~에 대해 많이 읽다, 공부하다

32

What does the woman want the man to do?

(A) View an instructional video
(B) Watch a demonstration
(C) Try a sample of coffee
(D) Provide customer feedback

여자는 남자가 무엇을 하기를 바라는가?
(A) 설명용 영상 시청하기
(B) 시연 보기
(C) 커피 샘플 시음하기
(D) 고객 의견 제공하기

어휘 instructional 교육의 provide 제공하다 feedback 의견

해설 전체 내용 관련 – 여자가 바라는 일
대화 첫 부분에서 여자가 최근 출시된 Rev-55 커피메이커의 기능을 보고 싶은지 물어보며 몇 분 후 시연할 예정(Are you interested in seeing the features of the recently released Rev-55 coffee maker? I'm giving a demonstration in just a few minutes)이라고 했다. 따라서 여자는 남자가 제품 시연을 보길 바란다는 것을 알 수 있으므로 정답은 (B)이다.

33

Why does the man want to leave quickly?

(A) He will meet up with someone.
(B) He needs to catch a bus.
(C) He parked in a restricted area.
(D) He has to start a work shift.

남자는 왜 빨리 떠나야 하는가?
(A) 누군가를 만날 예정이다.
(B) 버스를 타야 한다.
(C) 금지 구역에 주차했다.
(D) 교대 근무를 시작해야 한다.

어휘 meet up with ~와 만나다 park 주차하다 restricted 제한된, (출입이) 제한된 work shift 근무 교대

해설 세부 사항 관련 – 남자가 떠나는 이유
남자의 첫 번째 대사에서 남자가 시내로 가는 103번 버스를 타야 하는데 버스가 곧 출발한다(I want to take bus 103 downtown, and it's departing soon)고 했으므로 정답은 (B)이다.

▸▸ **Paraphrasing** 대화의 take bus → 정답의 catch a bus

34

What does the woman offer to do?

(A) Give the man some product information
(B) Mail a brochure to the man's address
(C) Add the man to a waiting list
(D) Start an activity earlier than usual

여자는 무엇을 해 주겠다고 하는가?
(A) 남자에게 제품 정보 제공하기
(B) 우편으로 남자의 주소로 안내책자 보내기
(C) 남자를 대기 명단에 올리기
(D) 평소보다 일찍 활동 시작하기

어휘 mail to ~로 부치다 add to ~에 추가하다 waiting list 대기 명단 than usual 평소보다

해설 세부 사항 관련 – 여자의 제안 사항
대화 마지막에 여자가 안내 책자를 줄 테니 시간 날 때 Rev-55에 대해 읽어 보면 어떻겠냐(How about I give you a brochure so you can read up on the Rev-55 in your spare time)고 제안했다. 따라서 여자가 남자에게 제품 정보를 제공하려고 함을 알 수 있으므로 정답은 (A)이다.

▸▸ **Paraphrasing** 대화의 brochure 정답의 product information

35-37

M-Au Good afternoon. **³⁵I'd like to use one of the library's computers to do some research on Renaissance art.** Could you show me how to sign in?

W-Am **³⁶I'm sorry, but the computers are being used for a class at the moment, so they're not currently available to patrons.** That'll be finished shortly, though, um... in about fifteen minutes.

M-Au Oh, I see. Then should I stop by here again?

W-Am **³⁷To save time, you should just go straight to the lab upstairs and wait there.** Sign-in instructions are posted on the door.

남: 안녕하세요. 르네상스 미술에 대한 조사를 위해 도서관 컴퓨터 중 한 대를 사용하고 싶은데요. 로그인 방법을 알려 주시겠어요?

여: 죄송하지만 현재 컴퓨터를 수업에 쓰고 있어서 지금은 회원분들이 사용할 수 없습니다. 하지만 곧, 음… 15분쯤 후에 끝날 겁니다.

남: 아, 알겠습니다. 그럼 이곳에 다시 들려야 할까요?

여: 시간을 아끼시려면 바로 위층 컴퓨터실로 가셔서 거기서 기다리셔야 합니다. 로그인 방법 설명이 문에 게시되어 있습니다.

어휘 | research 조사, 연구 sign in 로그인하다 at the moment 지금, 당장 currently 현재 available to ~가 이용 가능한 patron 고객, 단골 손님 shortly 곧 stop by 들르다 lab 실험실, 실습실 post 게시하다

35

Where does the conversation take place?

(A) At an art museum
(B) At a library
(C) At an electronics store
(D) At a hotel

대화는 어디에서 이루어지는가?

(A) 미술관
(B) 도서관
(C) 전자제품 매장
(D) 호텔

어휘 art museum 미술관 electronics 전자 기기, 전자 제품

해설 전체 내용 관련 - 대화 장소

대화 초반부에서 남자가 르네상스 미술에 대한 조사를 위해 도서관 컴퓨터 중 한 대를 사용하고 싶다(I'd like to use one of the library's computers to do some research on Renaissance art)고 했다. 따라서 대화가 도서관에서 이루어지고 있다는 것을 알 수 있으므로 정답은 (B)이다.

36

Why is the woman unable to help the man?

(A) A service has been discontinued.
(B) The business closes in fifteen minutes.
(C) A system has not been upgraded.
(D) Some equipment is in use.

여자가 남자를 도울 수 없는 이유는 무엇인가?

(A) 서비스가 중단됐다.
(B) 업무가 15분 후 마감된다.
(C) 시스템이 업그레이드되지 않았다.
(D) 일부 기기가 사용 중이다.

어휘 discontinue 중단하다 upgrade 개선하다 equipment 장비, 기기 be in use 사용되고 있다

해설 세부 사항 관련 - 여자가 남자를 도울 수 없는 이유

여자의 첫 번째 대사에서 현재 컴퓨터를 수업에 쓰고 있어서 지금은 회원들이 사용할 수 없다(I'm sorry, but the computers are being used for a class at the moment, so they're not currently available to patrons)고 했다. 따라서 일부 기기가 사용 중이어서 여자가 남자를 도울 수 없다는 것을 알 수 있으므로 정답은 (D)이다.

> ▸▸ Paraphrasing 대화의 **computers are being used** → 정답의 **some equipment is in use**

37

What does the woman suggest doing?

(A) Waiting on another floor
(B) Coming back later
(C) Calling for an update
(D) Verifying a time online

여자는 무엇을 하라고 제안하는가?

(A) 다른 층에서 기다리기
(B) 나중에 다시 오기
(C) 업데이트 요청하기
(D) 온라인으로 시간 확인하기

어휘 call for ~을 요청하다 update 업데이트(기존 정보를 최신 정보로 바꿈) verify 확인하다, 증명하다

해설 세부 사항 관련 - 여자가 제안하는 일

대화 마지막에 여자가 시간을 아끼려면 위층 컴퓨터실로 가서 기다려야 한다(To save time, you should just go straight to the lab upstairs and wait there)고 했으므로 정답은 (A)이다.

> ▸▸ Paraphrasing 대화의 **upstairs** → 정답의 **another floor**

38-40

M-Au	Hello. ³⁸I saw your advertisement for the community marathon, and I'm wondering if I can sign up for it over the phone.
W-Br	Sorry, but that can only be done through our Web site, using the form posted on the homepage. ³⁹However, please be aware that registration closes at midnight tonight. It was supposed to be next week, but we can't handle more than five thousand athletes, so we had to adjust the enrollment period.
M-Au	Thanks for letting me know. ⁴⁰I'm flying out for a business trip tomorrow, so I'll make sure to take care of this tonight.
W-Br	That's the best way to guarantee that you don't miss out.

남:	안녕하세요. 지역 마라톤에 관해 광고하신 것을 보았는데요. 전화로 신청할 수 있는지 궁금합니다.
여:	죄송합니다만, 홈페이지에 게시된 양식을 이용해 웹사이트를 통해서만 가능합니다. 하지만 등록이 오늘 자정에 마감된다는 점을 유념하시기 바랍니다. 다음 주에 마감하려고 했는데 5천 명 이상의 선수들을 수용할 수 없어 등록 기간을 조정해야 했거든요.
남:	알려 주셔서 감사합니다. 내일 출장을 떠날 예정이니 오늘밤에 반드시 처리할 겁니다.
여:	놓치지 않으시려면 그게 최선의 방법입니다.

어휘 advertisement 광고 community 지역 사회 sign up for ~를 신청하다 post 게시하다 be aware 알다 registration 등록 be supposed to ~하기로 되어 있다

handle 다루다, 처리하다 athlete 경기자, 운동 선수
adjust 조정하다 enrollment 등록 fly out 비행기로
출발하다 business trip 출장 take care of ~를 처리하다
guarantee 보장하다

38

What is the man trying to do?

(A) Arrange some advertising
(B) Volunteer for a fundraiser
(C) Register for a race
(D) Sign up for a community picnic

남자는 무엇을 하려고 하는가?
(A) 광고 준비하기
(B) 모금 행사에 지원하기
(C) 달리기 시합에 등록하기
(D) 지역 야유회 신청하기

어휘 arrange 마련하다 volunteer for ~에 지원하다 fundraiser
모금 행사 register for ~에 등록하다

해설 전체 내용 관련 – 남자가 하려는 일

대화 초반부에서 남자가 지역 마라톤에 대한 광고를 보았다며 전화로 신청할 수 있는지 궁금하다(I saw your advertisement for the community marathon, and I'm wondering if I can sign up for it over the phone)고 했다. 남자가 달리기 시합에 등록하려 한다는 것을 알 수 있으므로 정답은 (C)이다.

▸▸ Paraphrasing 대화의 the community marathon
→ 정답의 a race

39

What does the woman tell the man about?

(A) A meeting place
(B) An enrollment fee
(C) A Web site upgrade
(D) A deadline change

여자는 남자에게 무엇에 대해 이야기하는가?
(A) 만남 장소
(B) 등록비
(C) 웹사이트 업그레이드
(D) 마감 기한 변경

어휘 enrollment 등록 fee 요금

해설 세부 사항 관련 – 여자가 남자에게 이야기하는 사항

여자의 첫 번째 대사에서 등록이 오늘 자정에 마감된다(please be aware that registration closes at midnight tonight)는 것을 유념하라고 한 후, 다음 주에 마감하려 했으나 5천 명 이상의 선수들을 수용할 수 없어 등록 기간을 조정했다(It was supposed to be next week, but we can't handle more than five thousand athletes, so we had to adjust the enrollment period)고 말했다. 따라서 여자는 남자에게 마감 기한 변경에 대해 이야기하고 있다는 것을 알 수 있으므로 정답은 (D)이다.

▸▸ Paraphrasing 대화의 adjust the enrollment period
→ 정답의 a deadline change

40

What does the man plan to do tomorrow?

(A) Submit a form
(B) Call the woman again
(C) Go out of town
(D) Send a payment

남자는 내일 무엇을 할 계획인가?
(A) 양식 제출하기
(B) 여자에게 다시 전화하기
(C) 타지에 가기
(D) 대금 보내기

어휘 submit 제출하다 go out of town (출장 등으로) 도시를 떠나다
payment 대금, 지불(금)

해설 세부 사항 관련 – 남자의 계획

남자의 두 번째 대사에서 내일 출장을 떠나니 오늘밤 반드시 처리하겠다(I'm flying out for a business trip tomorrow, so I'll make sure to take care of this tonight)고 했으므로 정답은 (C)이다.

▸▸ Paraphrasing 대화의 flying out for a business trip
→ 정답의 go out of town

41-43

W-Br	Mr. Rajan, did you receive the memo regarding the investors' meeting? **41We're going to meet in Willow Hall instead of Pine Hall, as the sound system in Pine Hall is malfunctioning.**
M-Cn	Are you sure that's wise? **42Willow Hall can only seat twenty-five people. I thought our guest list was closer to forty.**
W-Br	**43It is, but Mr. Padilla is going to take the table out and set up the chairs in rows, facing forward, so I don't anticipate any issues.**
M-Cn	OK. If he needs assistance, tell him I can lend him a hand.

여: 라잔 씨, 투자자 회의에 관한 메모 받으셨어요? **파인 홀의 음향 시스템이 제대로 작동하지 않아서 파인홀 대신 윌로우 홀에 모일 예정입니다.**

남: 그게 신중한 조치일까요? **윌로우 홀은 25석밖에 없는데요.** 방문객 명단은 40명에 가까웠던 것 같아요.

여: 그렇기는 하지만 파딜라 씨가 테이블을 밖으로 꺼내고 앞쪽을 향해 의자를 여러 줄로 놓을 거예요. 그래서 문제가 생기지 않을 것 같아요.

남: 알겠어요. 도움이 필요하면 제가 도울 수 있다고 파딜라 씨에게 얘기해 주세요.

어휘 regarding ~에 관해 investor 투자자 malfunction
제대로 작동하지 않다 wise 신중한 take out 제거하다, 빼다
set up 놓다 in rows 여러 줄로, 줄지어 face forward
앞쪽을 향하다 anticipate 예상하다, 기대하다 issue 문제
assistance 도움 lend a hand 도움을 주다

41

What has changed about the meeting?

(A) Its location
(B) Its start time
(C) Its duration
(D) Its guest list

회의에 대해 어떤 변경 사항이 생겼는가?

(A) 장소
(B) 시작 시간
(C) 기간
(D) 방문객 명단

어휘　location 장소　duration 기간　guest 손님　list 명단

해설　전체 내용 관련 – 회의에서의 변경 사항

여자의 첫 번째 대사에서 파인홀의 음향 시스템이 제대로 작동하지 않아서 파인홀 대신 윌로우 홀에 모일 예정(We're going to meet in Willow Hall instead of Pine Hall, as the sound system in Pine Hall is malfunctioning)이라고 했다. 회의 장소가 변경됐다는 것을 알 수 있으므로 정답은 (A)이다.

42

Why is the man concerned about the change?

(A) He believes people cannot be informed on short notice.
(B) He does not know how to use the sound system.
(C) He worries that it will cause confusion among guests.
(D) He thinks there will not be enough space.

남자가 변경 사항에 대해 우려하는 이유는 무엇인가?

(A) 촉박해서 사람들에게 알릴 수 없다고 생각한다.
(B) 음향 시스템 사용법을 모른다.
(C) 방문객들에게 혼란을 줄까 봐 염려한다.
(D) 공간이 충분치 않을 것이라고 생각한다.

어휘　be informed 통지를 받다　on short notice 촉박하게, 갑자기
　　cause 야기하다　confusion 혼란

해설　세부 사항 관련 – 남자가 우려하는 이유

남자의 첫 번째 대사에서 윌로우 홀은 25석밖에 없다며 방문객 명단은 40명에 가깝다(Willow Hall can only seat twenty-five people. I thought our guest list was closer to forty)고 했다. 따라서 남자가 공간이 충분치 않을까 봐 우려하고 있으므로 정답은 (D)이다.

43

According to the woman, what will Mr. Padilla do?

(A) Handle the first presentation to investors
(B) Remove a piece of furniture
(C) Set up some electrical equipment
(D) Call visitors to inform them

여자에 따르면, 파딜라 씨는 무엇을 할 것인가?

(A) 투자자들에게 첫 번째 발표하기
(B) 가구 치우기
(C) 전자 기기 설치하기
(D) 투자자들에게 통보 전화하기

어휘　remove 치우다, 제거하다　set up 설치하다　electrical 전기의
　　inform 알리다

해설　세부 사항 관련 – 파딜라 씨가 할 일

여자의 두 번째 대사에서 파딜라 씨가 테이블을 밖으로 꺼내고 앞쪽을 향해 의자를 여러 줄로 놓을 것이라서 문제가 안 된다(It is, but Mr. Padilla is going to take the table out and set up the chairs in rows, facing forward, so I don't anticipate any issues)라고 했으므로 정답은 (B)이다.

> ▶▶ Paraphrasing　대화의 take the table out
> 　　　　　　　　→ 정답의 Remove a piece of furniture

44-46

M-Cn	**44Teresa, I've just finished analyzing the responses to the customer survey you created.**
W-Am	Did you identify any trends that need our immediate attention?
M-Cn	**45We scored well on most categories, but there were numerous complaints about raising our prices last month.** We're charging nearly ten percent more than our competitors.
W-Am	There's not much we can do about that because of the supplier's charge for raw materials. **46However, I'll speak with the finance team to see if they have any ideas about where we could make other cuts.**

남:	테레사 씨, 작성하신 고객 설문조사 응답에 대한 분석을 막 끝마쳤어요.
여:	즉각적인 대처를 요하는 동향이 보이나요?
남:	대부분의 범주에서 점수가 좋았는데, 지난달 가격 인상에 대한 불만이 아주 많았어요. 경쟁업체보다 거의 10퍼센트 더 비싸니까요.
여:	공급업체 원자재 가격 때문에 저희가 할 수 있는 부분이 많지 않아요. 하지만 절감할 수 있는 부분으로 뭐가 있을지 재무팀과 이야기해 볼게요.

어휘　analyze 분석하다　response 응답　customer survey
　　고객 설문 조사　identify 파악하다　trend 동향, 추세
　　immediate 즉각적인　attention 주목　score 점수를 받다
　　category 범주　numerous 수많은　complaint 불만
　　raise 올리다　charge (요금을) 청구(하다)　competitor
　　경쟁사　supplier 공급업체　raw material 원자재, 원료
　　finance 재무, 재정　make a cut 삭감하다

44

What does the man say he has done?

(A) Created a customer questionnaire
(B) Analyzed some sales techniques
(C) Reviewed feedback from patrons
(D) Contacted some regular customers

남자는 무엇을 했다고 말하는가?

(A) 고객 설문지를 작성했다
(B) 영업 기법을 분석했다
(C) 고객 의견을 검토했다
(D) 단골 고객들에게 연락했다

어휘 questionnaire 설문서 sales 판매 업무, 영업 technique 기법 patron 고객 regular customer 단골 손님

해설 전체 내용 관련 – 남자가 한 일

남자의 첫 번째 대화에서 작성한 고객 설문조사 응답에 대한 분석을 끝마쳤다(Teresa, I've just finished analyzing the responses to the customer survey you created)고 했다. 따라서 남자가 고객 의견을 검토했다는 것을 알 수 있으므로 정답은 (C)이다.

> ▸▸ Paraphrasing 대화의 finished analyzing the responses to the customer survey
> → 정답의 Reviewed feedback from patrons

45

What did the speakers' company do last month?

(A) Discontinued unpopular items
(B) Changed to a new supplier
(C) Added a shipping fee
(D) Increased its product prices

화자들의 회사는 지난달에 무엇을 했는가?
(A) 비인기 품목을 단종했다
(B) 신규 공급업체로 변경했다
(C) 배송료를 추가했다
(D) 제품 가격을 인상했다

어휘 discontinue 중단하다 unpopular 인기 없는 shipping fee 배송료

해설 세부 사항 관련 – 회사가 지난달에 한 일

남자의 두 번째 대사에서 대부분의 범주에서 점수가 좋았으나 지난달 가격 인상에 대한 불만이 많았다(We scored well on most categories, but there were numerous complaints about raising our prices last month)고 했다. 따라서 회사가 지난달에 제품 가격을 인상했음을 알 수 있으므로 정답은 (D)이다.

> ▸▸ Paraphrasing 대화의 raising our prices
> → 정답의 Increased its product prices

46

What does the woman plan to do?

(A) Research information about new suppliers
(B) Have a discussion with some coworkers
(C) Prepare an application for financial assistance
(D) Publish some information about a trend

여자는 무엇을 할 계획인가?
(A) 신규 공급업체에 대한 정보 조사하기
(B) 동료들과 의논하기
(C) 재정 지원 신청 준비하기
(D) 동향 정보 발표하기

어휘 have a discussion 토론하다 coworker 동료 prepare for ~을 준비하다 application 지원(서) financial 재정의, 금융의 assistance 도움, 지원 publish (공식적으로) 발표하다

해설 세부 사항 관련 – 여자가 계획하는 일

여자의 마지막 대화에서 절감할 수 있는 부분으로 뭐가 있을지 재무팀과 이야

기해 보겠다(However, I'll speak with the finance team to see if they have any ideas about where we could make other cuts)고 했다. 따라서 여자가 동료들과 의논할 계획임을 알 수 있으므로 정답은 (B)이다.

> ▸▸ Paraphrasing 대화의 speak with the finance team
> → 정답의 Have a discussion with some coworkers

47-49

W-Br	Hello, Mr. Zellers. This is Caitlin calling from the Orchard Dental Clinic. **47You have an appointment for tomorrow at 9:30 A.M., but I noticed that no one has input the name of your insurance provider or policy number.**
M-Au	I don't currently have a provider, so I was planning to pay the entire fee on my own. I'm confident that I can personally cover any costs. **48You accept credit cards and cash, don't you?**
W-Br	Yes, we do. The initial checkup fee is eighty euros. **49Our Web site lists the prices for other services, such as teeth whitening. You might want to check those out before you come.**

여:	안녕하세요, 젤러스 씨. 오차드 치과의 케이틀린입니다. 내일 오전 9시 30분에 진료 예약이 되어 있습니다만, 보험사 이름이나 보험증권번호가 입력되지 않아서요.
남:	현재는 보험업체가 없습니다. 그래서 제가 전액을 다 내려고 하고 있었어요. 개인적으로 모든 비용을 부담할 수 있을 것이라고 확신하는데요. 신용카드와 현금을 받으시죠, 그렇죠?
여:	네, 그렇습니다. 초진료는 80유로입니다. 저희 웹사이트에 치아 미백과 같은 다른 서비스 요금도 나와 있습니다. 오시기 전에 확인하시면 됩니다.

어휘 dental 치아[치과]의 clinic 병원 appointment (병원 진료 등의) 예약 input 입력하다 insurance provider 보험회사 policy number 보험증권번호 currently 현재 entire 전체의 on one's own 혼자서 personally 직접, 개인적으로 cover 충당하다 accept 받아 주다 initial 처음의 checkup 검진 list (명부에) 오르다 teeth whitening 치아 미백

47

Why did the woman call the man?

(A) To request insurance information
(B) To introduce a new service
(C) To explain a clinic's policy
(D) To reschedule an appointment

여자가 남자에게 전화를 건 이유는 무엇인가?
(A) 보험 정보를 요청하려고
(B) 새로운 서비스를 소개하려고
(C) 병원의 정책을 설명하려고
(D) 예약 일정을 다시 잡으려고

어휘 policy 정책, 규정 explain 설명하다 reschedule 일정을 다시 잡다

해설 전체 내용 관련 – 전화 통화의 목적

여자의 첫 번째 대사에서 내일 오전 9시 30분에 진료 예약이 되어 있는데 보험사 이름이나 보험증권번호를 입력하지 않은 것을 알게 되었다(You have an appointment for tomorrow at 9:30 A.M., but I noticed that no one has input the name of your insurance provider or policy number)고 했다. 따라서 여자는 보험 정보 요청을 위해 남자에게 전화했음을 알 수 있으므로 정답은 (A)이다.

▸▸ Paraphrasing 대화의 name of your insurance provider or policy number
→ 정답의 insurance information

48

What does the man inquire about?

(A) The duration of some procedures
(B) The expertise of some employees
(C) Confidentiality rights
(D) Payment methods

남자는 무엇에 대해 문의하는가?
(A) 절차 소요 기간
(B) 직원의 전문성
(C) 기밀유지 권한
(D) 지불 방식

어휘 duration 기간 procedure 절차 expertise 전문성, 전문지식
confidentiality 기밀 right 권한, 권리 payment 지불
method 방식

해설 세부 사항 관련 – 남자가 문의하는 사항

남자는 여자에게 신용카드와 현금을 받는지(You accept credit cards and cash, don't you) 물었다. 따라서 지불 방식을 문의하고 있음을 알 수 있으므로 정답은 (D)이다.

49

What does the woman recommend doing?

(A) Arriving early to complete a form
(B) Checking a schedule online
(C) Reviewing some rates in advance
(D) Settling a service fee by mail

여자는 무엇을 하라고 권유하는가?
(A) 양식 작성을 위해 일찍 도착하기
(B) 일정을 온라인으로 확인하기
(C) 비용을 미리 확인하기
(D) 우편으로 서비스 비용 정산하기

어휘 complete a form 양식을 작성하다 rate 요금 in advance
사전에 settle 정산하다, 해결하다

해설 세부 사항 관련 – 여자가 권유하는 일

대화 마지막에 여자가 웹사이트에 치아 미백과 같은 다른 서비스 요금이 나와 있으니 오기 전에 확인하라(Our Web site lists the prices for other services, such as teeth whitening. You might want to check those out before you come)고 했으므로 정답은 (C)이다.

▸▸ Paraphrasing 대화의 check those out before you come
→ 정답의 Reviewing some rates in advance

50-52

M-Cn Hello. My name is Frank Charla. I reserved a taxi to pick me up tomorrow morning at 6:30 A.M. from 891 Blair Street and take me to Kenyon Airport. ⁵⁰I'm wondering if I can change to a van because there will be three additional people with me.

W-Am Unfortunately, Mr. Charla, all of our vans are booked at that time. But I can reserve two taxis for you instead.

M-Cn Is that the only way? ⁵¹It'll be much more expensive than I had planned.

W-Am I know what you mean. ⁵²The best I can do is give you twenty-five percent off the second taxi. That will help to keep your costs down.

남: 안녕하세요. 저는 프랭크 샤를라입니다. 내일 아침 6시 30분에 블레어가 891번지에서 케니언 공항으로 데려다 줄 택시를 예약했는데요. 저와 함께 가는 사람이 세 명 더 있을 예정이라 밴으로 바꿀 수 있는지 궁금합니다.

여: 샤를라 씨, 안타깝게도 그 시간에는 저희 밴이 모두 예약됐습니다. 하지만 대신 택시 두 대를 예약해 드릴 수 있습니다.

남: 그 방법밖에 없나요? 제가 계획한 것보다 훨씬 비쌀 텐데요.

여: 무슨 말씀이신지 압니다. 제가 해 드릴 수 있는 최선은 두 번째 택시를 25퍼센트 할인해 드리는 겁니다. 비용을 낮추시는 데 도움이 될 겁니다.

어휘 pick up (차에) 태우러 가다 reserve 예약하다 additional
추가의 unfortunately 아쉽게도, 안타깝게도 book 예약하다
instead 대신에 off 할인되어 keep ~ down 낮추다 cost
비용

50

What does the man want to change about his reservation?

(A) The type of vehicle
(B) The pick-up time
(C) The duration of a service
(D) The drop-off destination

남자가 예약에서 바꾸고 싶어 하는 것은 무엇인가?
(A) 차량 유형
(B) 픽업 시간
(C) 서비스 기간
(D) 내릴 목적지

어휘 vehicle 차량 pick-up 태우러 가는 drop-off 내리기, (렌터카 이용
후) 인계하는 destination 목적지

해설 전체 내용 관련 – 남자가 변경하려는 예약 사항

남자의 첫 번째 대사에서 함께 가는 사람이 세 명 더 있을 예정이라 밴으로 바꿀 수 있는지 궁금하다(I'm wondering if I can change to a van because there will be three additional people with me)고 말했다. 따라서 남자가 예약 사항에서 차량 유형을 바꾸고 싶어 한다는 것을 알 수 있으므로 정답은 (A)이다.

51

Why does the man say, "Is that the only way"?

(A) To suggest another driving route
(B) To accept a suggestion
(C) To express disappointment
(D) To point out an error

남자가 "그 방법밖에 없나요?"라고 말한 이유는 무엇인가?

(A) 다른 길을 제안하려고
(B) 제안을 수락하려고
(C) **실망감을 표현하려고**
(D) 실수를 지적하려고

어휘 route 경로, 길 accept 받아들이다 express 표현하다
disappointment 실망 point out 지적하다

해설 화자의 의도 파악 – 그 방법밖에 없는지 물어본 이유

인용문 바로 뒤 문장에서 계획보다 훨씬 비쌀 것(It'll be much more expensive than I had planned)이라고 했다. 즉 그 방법밖에 없는지 물어본 것은 비싼 가격에 대한 실망감을 표현하려는 것이므로 정답은 (C)이다.

52

What does the woman offer to do?

(A) Credit the man's account
(B) Reduce the price of a service
(C) Issue a partial refund
(D) Send a discount coupon

여자는 무엇을 해 주겠다고 하는가?

(A) 남자의 계좌에 입금하기
(B) **서비스 요금 낮추기**
(C) 일부 환불해 주기
(D) 할인 쿠폰 보내기

어휘 credit 입금하다 account 계좌 reduce 줄이다 issue 발행하다
partial 부분적인 refund 환불

해설 세부 사항 관련 – 여자가 제안하는 일

여자의 마지막 대사에서 해 줄 수 있는 최선은 두 번째 택시를 25퍼센트 할인해 주는 것(The best I can do is give you twenty-five percent off the second taxi)이라고 했으므로 정답은 (B)이다.

▸▸ **Paraphrasing** 대화의 **twenty-five percent off the second taxi** → 정답의 **Reduce the price of a service**

53-55 3인 대화

W-Am	Good luck tonight, you two. ⁵³**You've both been nominated in the Best New Employee category, right?**
W-Br	Yes, it's quite an honor.
M-Cn	Right. I'm pleased just to be recognized as a nominee.
W-Am	What would you do if you won? Have you prepared a speech to give on stage?
W-Br	I haven't. I didn't want to assume anything.

M-Cn	⁵⁴**I wrote down some notes, but that's only because I am terrified of public speaking, especially in such a formal setting.**
W-Am	Well, no matter what happens, I'm proud of you.
W-Br	Thanks. Oh, it looks like the company president is about to take the stage.
M-Cn	⁵⁵**We'd better get seated somewhere.**

여1:	두 분, 오늘밤 행운을 빕니다. **두 분 모두 최고의 신입사원 부문 후보로 지명되셨죠, 그렇죠?**
여2:	네, 무척 영광입니다.
남:	맞습니다. 후보로 거론된 것만 해도 기쁩니다.
여1:	수상하시면 뭘 하시겠어요? 무대 위에서 할 말을 준비하셨나요?
여2:	아뇨. 아무것도 지레짐작하고 싶지 않았어요.
남:	저는 특히 공식적인 자리에서 대중 앞에서 말하는 걸 겁나서 메모를 해 두긴 했어요.
여1:	어떻게 되든 자랑스럽습니다.
여2:	감사합니다. 아, 회장님께서 무대에 오르시려나 봅니다.
남:	**어디 좀 앉아야겠어요.**

어휘 nominate (후보자로) 지명하다 category 범주 honor 영광
recognize 인정[표창]하다 nominee 후보자 speech
연설 assume 짐작하다 write down 적다 be terrified
of ~을 두려워하다 public speaking 대중 연설 formal
공식적인 setting 환경 no matter what 비록 무엇이
~한다 해도 be about to 막 ~하려는 참이다 take the
stage 무대에 오르다 had better ~하는 편이 낫다

53

Where most likely are the speakers?

(A) At a fundraising dinner
(B) At a coworker's birthday party
(C) At an awards banquet
(D) At a new staff orientation

화자들은 어디에 있겠는가?

(A) 기금 모금 만찬
(B) 동료 생일 파티
(C) **시상식 연회**
(D) 신입 사원 오리엔테이션

어휘 fundraising 모금 banquet 연회 staff 직원

해설 전체 내용 관련 – 대화 장소

첫 번째 여자의 첫 번째 대사에서 두 명 모두 최고의 신입사원 부문 후보로 지명되었는지(You've both been nominated in the Best New Employee category, right?) 물어보았다. 따라서 화자들이 시상식 연회에 있음을 짐작할 수 있으므로 정답은 (C)이다.

54

What does the man say he is nervous about?

(A) Sending a copy of some notes
(B) Meeting the company's president
(C) Speaking in front of others
(D) Making a formal complaint

남사는 무엇이 걱정된다고 말하는가?
(A) 메모 사본 보내기
(B) 회장과의 면담
(C) 사람들 앞에서 말하기
(D) 공식적으로 항의하기

어휘 in front of ~ 앞에서   make a complaint 불만을 제기하다

해설 세부 사항 관련 – 남자가 걱정하는 사항

남자의 두 번째 대사에서 특히 공식적인 자리에서는 대중 앞에서 말하는 게 겁나 메모를 해 두었다(I wrote down some notes, but that's only because I am terrified of public speaking, especially in such a formal setting)고 했으므로 정답은 (C)이다.

> **▸▸ Paraphrasing**   대화의 **public speaking**
> → 정답의 **Speaking in front of others**

55

What will the speakers most likely do next?

(A) Make a meal selection
(B) Put on some name tags
(C) Greet the company's president
(D) Find a place to sit

화자들은 다음으로 무엇을 할 것인가?
(A) 식사 선택하기
(B) 이름표 착용하기
(C) 회장 맞이하기
(D) 앉을 자리 찾기

어휘 meal 식사   make a selection 선택하다   put on 착용하다
name tag 명찰   greet 맞이하다

해설 세부 사항 관련 – 화자들이 다음에 할 일

남자의 마지막 대사에서 어디 좀 앉아야겠다(We'd better get seated somewhere)고 했으므로 정답은 (D)이다.

56-58

M-Au	Ms. Berhane, have you had any success in filling the job opening in the development office?
W-Br	Not yet. **56Plenty of candidates responded to our job posting, but none of them have the experience we need to manage the fundraising efforts of the university.**
M-Au	I know someone who would be perfect for the job. **57His name is Theo Gomez, and he lives in the apartment across the hall from mine.** He's been doing fundraising work for over five years now, and he's looking for a new job these days.
W-Br	I'd love to see his résumé. **58Would you give him my e-mail address so he can send it to me?**

남:	버헤인 씨, 개발실 공석을 메우는 데 성공했나요?
여:	아직이요. 많은 지원자들이 저희 구인 공고에 회신했는데 그중 우리에게 필요한 교내 모금 활동을 운영해 본 경험이 있는 사람은 아무도 없어요.
남:	그 일자리에 완벽히 들어맞는 사람을 알아요. 이름은 테오 고메즈이고, 제가 사는 아파트 복도 건너편에 삽니다. 5년 이상 모금 활동을 해 오고 있는데 요즘 새 일자리를 찾고 있어요.
여:	이력서를 보고 싶네요. 그 사람이 제게 이력서를 보내도록 제 이메일 주소를 주시겠어요?

어휘 success in ~에서의 성공   fill 메우다   job opening (직장 내의) 공석   plenty of 많은   candidate 후보자, 지원자   respond to ~에 응답하다   job posting 채용 공고   fundraising 모금   effort 노력, 공   look for ~을 찾다   résumé 이력서

56

What problem does the woman mention about the recruitment process?

(A) The number of responses to the posting was low.
(B) Many candidates do not want to commute to the university.
(C) The applicants lack the necessary qualifications.
(D) Some information on the job posting was incorrect.

여자는 채용 절차에 대해 어떤 문제를 언급하는가?
(A) 공고에 대한 회신 수가 적다.
(B) 많은 지원자가 대학교로 통근하기를 원치 않는다.
(C) 지원자들의 필수 자격 요건이 부족하다.
(D) 구인 공고의 정보 일부가 부정확하다.

어휘 posting 공고   commute to ~로 통근하다   applicant 지원자   lack 부족하다, 결핍되다   necessary 필요한   qualification 자격 요건   incorrect 부정확한

해설 세부 사항 관련 – 여자가 언급하는 채용 문제

여자의 첫 번째 대사에서 많은 지원자들이 구인 공고에 회신했는데 그중 회사에 필요한 교내 모금 활동 운영 경험이 있는 사람은 아무도 없다(Plenty of candidates responded to our job posting, but none of them have the experience we need to manage the fundraising efforts of the university)고 했다. 즉 여자가 언급하는 문제는 지원자들의 필수 자격 요건 부족임을 알 수 있으므로 정답은 (C)이다.

> **▸▸ Paraphrasing**   대화의 **the experience we need**
> → 정답의 **the necessary qualifications**

57

How does the man know Mr. Gomez?

(A) They met at a fundraising event.
(B) They are former coworkers.
(C) They had university classes together.
(D) They live in the same building.

남자는 고메즈 씨를 어떻게 아는가?
(A) 모금 행사에서 만났다.
(B) 예전 동료이다.
(C) 대학 수업을 함께 들었다.
(D) 같은 건물에 산다.

어휘 former 이전의 coworker 동료

해설 **세부 사항 관련 – 남자가 고메즈 씨를 알게 된 경위**
남자의 두 번째 대사에서 테오 고메즈는 남자가 사는 아파트 복도 건너편에 산다(His name is Theo Gomez, and he lives in the apartment across the hall from mine)고 했으므로 정답은 (D)이다.

58

What does the woman ask the man to do?

(A) E-mail Mr. Gomez a link to the job posting
(B) Give her e-mail address to Mr. Gomez
(C) Send a copy of Mr. Gomez's résumé
(D) Ask Mr. Gomez to call her office

여자는 남자에게 무엇을 하라고 요청하는가?
(A) 고메즈 씨에게 구인 공고 링크를 이메일로 보내기
(B) 여자의 이메일 주소를 고메즈 씨에게 주기
(C) 고메즈 씨의 이력서 사본 보내기
(D) 고메즈 씨에게 여자의 사무실로 전화하라고 요청하기

어휘 link (컴퓨터) 링크

해설 **세부 사항 관련 – 여자의 요청 사항**
여자의 두 번째 대사에서 그 사람이 이력서를 보내도록 자신의 이메일 주소를 줄 수 있는지(Would you give him my e-mail address so he can send it to me) 물었으므로 정답은 (B)이다.

59-61 3인 대화

> W-Am Greg, we're nearly set for our team's strategy meeting. But there's a problem with Room Two. **⁵⁹Its projector and screens have been removed.**
>
> M-Au Ah, we can use the client lounge. There's a projector in there. One thing, though— I'd like for Randy from the product development team to come to this meeting, if he can.
>
> M-Cn Hi, guys. Did I hear my name?
>
> M-Au **⁶⁰Yes, I'm wondering if you can attend our team's strategy meeting this afternoon…**
>
> M-Cn Oh! Well, actually… I just started a new project today.
>
> M-Au **⁶⁰I understand. No worries.**
>
> W-Am All right then. **⁶¹We may need more chairs in that lounge, so I'll move a few in there now.**

여: 그레그 씨, 팀 전략회의 준비가 거의 되었습니다. 하지만 2번 회의실에 문제가 있어요. **누군가 프로젝터와 스크린을 치워버렸어요.**
남1: 아, 고객 라운지를 쓰면 돼요. 거기 프로젝터가 있어요. 그런데 한 가지, 가능하다면 제품개발팀의 랜디 씨가 회의에 들어왔으면 합니다.
남2: 안녕하세요, 여러분. 제 이름이 들리는데요?
남1: 네, 오늘 오후 저희 팀 전략회의에 참석하실 수 있는지 궁금하군요…

남2: 아, 사실은… **오늘 새 프로젝트를 막 시작했거든요.**
남1: 알겠습니다. 괜찮습니다.
여: 그럼 됐어요. **라운지에 의자가 더 필요할지도 모르니 지금 몇 개 옮겨 놓을게요.**

어휘 set for ~할 준비를 갖춘 strategy 전략 remove 치우다 lounge 대합실 attend 참석하다 no worries 괜찮아요

59

According to the woman, what is a problem with a room?

(A) It is too large.
(B) It has been double-booked.
(C) It is missing some equipment.
(D) It is being cleaned.

여자에 따르면, 회의실에 어떤 문제가 있는가?
(A) 너무 크다.
(B) 이중으로 예약됐다.
(C) 일부 장비가 없다.
(D) 청소하는 중이다.

어휘 double-book 이중으로 예약을 받다 missing 없어진

해설 **세부 사항 관련 – 회의실의 문제점**
여자의 첫 번째 대사에서 누군가 프로젝터와 스크린을 치워버렸다(Its projector and screens have been removed)고 했다. 따라서 회의실에 일부 장비가 없다는 것이 문제임을 알 수 있으므로 정답은 (C)이다.

▸▸ Paraphrasing 대화의 **projector and screens** → 정답의 **some equipment**

60

Why most likely does Randy say, "I just started a new project today"?

(A) To explain a deadline
(B) To seek extra help
(C) To show excitement
(D) To decline an invitation

랜디가 "오늘 새 프로젝트를 막 시작했거든요"라고 말한 의도는 무엇인가?
(A) 마감 기한에 대해 해명하려고
(B) 추가로 도움을 구하려고
(C) 설렘을 나타내려고
(D) 초청을 거절하려고

어휘 explain 해명하다 deadline 마감일 seek 구하다 extra 추가의 decline 거절하다

해설 **화자의 의도 파악 – 새 프로젝트를 막 시작했다는 말의 의미**
인용문 앞 문장에서 첫 번째 남자가 두 번째 남자에게 오늘 오후 팀 전략회의에 참석할 수 있는지 궁금하다(Yes, I'm wondering if you can attend our team's strategy meeting this afternoon)고 했고, 두 번째 남자가 오늘 새 프로젝트를 막 시작했다(I just started a new project today)고 말했다. 이에 첫 번째 남자가 괜찮다(I understand. No worries)고 했다. 따라서 오늘 새 프로젝트를 막 시작했다는 말은 전략회의 초청을 거절하려는 의미이므로 정답은 (D)이다.

61

What will the woman probably do next?

(A) Update a Web site
(B) Edit an e-mail message
(C) Move some furniture
(D) Take a meal break

여자는 다음으로 무엇을 하겠는가?

(A) 웹사이트 업데이트하기
(B) 이메일 메시지 편집하기
(C) 가구 옮기기
(D) 식사 시간 갖기

어휘 update 최신 정보를 알려주다 edit 편집하다 meal break 식사 시간

해설 세부 사항 관련 – 여자가 다음에 할 일

여자의 마지막 대사에서 라운지에 의자가 더 필요할지도 모르니 지금 몇 개 옮겨 놓겠다(We may need more chairs in that lounge, so I'll move a few in there now)고 했으므로 정답은 (C)이다.

62-64 대화 + 정보

> W-Br **62Aren't you going out for lunch today, Kevin? I thought you usually eat with some of your team members on Wednesdays.**
>
> M-Cn Usually I do, but today I brought some soup so I could eat quickly and get back to work. **63It's called Swift-Cup, and I tried a sample of it when I was at Eagle Supermarket yesterday.**
>
> W-Br It looks like it's easy to prepare. You just heat it up in the microwave, right?
>
> M-Cn Yeah, the heating instructions are on the packaging here. **64Let's see... This microwave has a wattage of nine hundred, so my soup will be ready fairly shortly.**

여: 케빈 씨, 오늘은 점심 먹으러 안 가세요? 수요일마다 보통 팀원들과 함께 드신다고 생각했는데요.
남: 보통은 그렇지만 오늘은 수프를 가져왔어요. 빨리 먹고 다시 일하려고요. 스위프트컵이라는 건데 어제 이글 슈퍼마켓에 가서 음식 샘플을 시식해 봤어요.
여: 준비하기 쉬워 보이네요. 전자레인지에 데우기만 하면 되죠, 그렇죠?
남: 네, 가열 설명이 여기 포장에 적혀 있네요. 어디 봅시다. 이 전자레인지는 900와트니까 제 수프가 아주 금방 준비되겠군요.

어휘 go out for lunch 점심 먹으러 가다 get back to ~으로 돌아가다 heat up 데우다 instructions 설명 packaging 포장 wattage (와트로 표현되는) 전력량 fairly 꽤 shortly 곧

Heating Instructions

Microwave Wattage	Cooking Time
650	6 minutes
800	4 minutes
64900	3 minutes
1,000	2.5 minutes

가열 설명서

전자레인지 전력량	조리 시간
650	6분
800	4분
900	3분
1,000	2분 30초

62

Where is the conversation most likely taking place?

(A) In a food production facility
(B) In an office break room
(C) In a grocery store
(D) In an electronics store

대화는 어디에서 이루어지겠는가?

(A) 식품 생산시설
(B) 사무실의 휴게실
(C) 식료품점
(D) 전자제품 매장

어휘 production 생산 facility 시설 break 휴식 grocery 식료품

해설 전체 내용 관련 – 대화 장소

여자의 첫 번째 대사에서 남자에게 점심 먹으러 안 가는지 물어보며 수요일마다 팀원들과 함께 먹는다고 생각했다(Aren't you going out for lunch today, Kevin? I thought you usually eat with some of your team members on Wednesdays)고 했다. 대화가 사무실의 휴게실에서 이루어지고 있음을 알 수 있으므로 정답은 (B)이다.

63

What does the man indicate about Swift-Cup?

(A) It contains healthy ingredients.
(B) It does not need to be refrigerated.
(C) It was distributed as a free sample.
(D) It is available in different flavors.

남자가 스위프트 컵에 대해 명시한 것은 무엇인가?

(A) 건강에 좋은 성분이 들어 있다.
(B) 냉장 보관할 필요가 없다.
(C) 무료 음식 샘플로 나눠 줬다.
(D) 다양한 맛이 나와 있다.

어휘 contain 포함하다 healthy 건강에 좋은 ingredient 재료, 성분 refrigerate 냉장하다 distribute 배포하다, 나누어 주다 available 이용 가능한 flavor 맛

남자의 첫 번째 대사에서 스위프트컵이라는 제품으로 어제 이글 슈퍼마켓에 가서 음식 샘플을 시식해 보았다(It's called Swift-Cup, and I tried a sample of it when I was at Eagle Supermarket yesterday)고 했으므로 정답은 (C)이다.

64

Look at the graphic. For how long should the man run the microwave?

(A) 6 minutes
(B) 4 minutes
(C) 3 minutes
(D) 2.5 minutes

시각 정보에 의하면, 남자는 얼마 동안 전자레인지를 돌려야 하는가?

(A) 6분
(B) 4분
(C) 3분
(D) 2분 30초

해설 시각 정보 연계 – 전자레인지 작동 시간

남자의 마지막 대화에서 이 전자레인지는 900와트니까 수프가 아주 금방 준비되겠다(Let's see… This microwave has a wattage of nine hundred, so my soup will be ready fairly shortly)고 했다. 표를 보면 900와트는 3분이므로 정답은 (C)이다.

65-67 대화 + 쿠폰

M-Au	Good afternoon. ⁶⁷I'd like to purchase this Plymouth brand watch. ⁶⁵I love the sophisticated look of the leather strap and the sleek design.
W-Br	I'm glad you found something you like, sir. Your total comes to eighty-nine dollars and sixty cents. ⁶⁶Do you plan to give the watch as a gift?
M-Au	No, I'm just buying it for myself.
W-Br	All right. We just started offering a gift-wrapping service, but I guess you don't need that.
M-Au	Not this time, but I'll keep that in mind. And this coupon is valid until the end of the month, right?
W-Br	⁶⁷Yes, but you aren't eligible to use it for this purchase, so I'll let you hang onto that.

남: 안녕하세요. 이 플리머스 시계를 사고 싶은데요. 가죽끈의 세련된 모양과 매끈한 디자인이 마음에 들어요.
여: 마음에 드는 걸 발견하셔서 다행입니다. 총 89달러 60센트입니다. 시계를 선물할 계획이신가요?
남: 아니오, 제가 하려고 사는 겁니다.
여: 알겠습니다. 저희가 선물 포장 서비스를 막 시작했는데, 필요 없으실 것 같네요.

남: 이번엔 아니지만 기억해 두겠습니다. 이 쿠폰은 이번 달 말까지 유효하죠, 그렇죠?
여: 네, 하지만 이 구입품에는 사용하실 수 없으니 가지고 계셔야겠네요.

어휘 sophisticated 세련된, 정교한 look 모양새 strap 끈 sleek (모양이) 매끈한 total 총액 come to ~이 되다 gift-wrapping 선물 포장 keep ~ in mind ~를 명심하다 valid 유효한 be eligible to ~할 자격이 되다 purchase 구입품 hang onto ~를 유지하다

Val's Accessories
Discount Coupon

⁶⁷15% off

any Evans brand watch

Minimum purchase: $60
Expiration Date: July 31

밸즈 액세서리
할인 쿠폰

에반스 시계 전체 15% 할인

최소 구매 금액: 60달러
만료일자: 7월 31일

65

What does the man mention that he likes about the item?

(A) Its warranty
(B) Its appearance
(C) Its price
(D) Its technology

남자는 상품의 어떤 점이 마음에 든다고 언급하는가?

(A) 품질보증
(B) 외관
(C) 가격
(D) 기술

어휘 warranty 품질보증 appearance 외관, 겉모습

해설 세부 사항 관련 – 남자가 상품에 대해 마음에 드는 사항

남자의 첫 번째 대사에서 가죽끈의 세련된 모양과 매끈한 디자인이 마음에 든다(I love the sophisticated look of the leather strap and the sleek design)고 했으므로 정답은 (B)이다.

▸▸ Paraphrasing 대화의 look → 정답의 appearance

66

What does the woman ask the man about?

(A) What he intends to do with the item
(B) Which wrapping paper he prefers
(C) How he will pay for the merchandise
(D) Whether he is a rewards club member

Test 5

여사는 남자에게 무엇에 대해 질문하는가?

(A) 남자가 상품으로 무엇을 하려는지
(B) 남자가 어떤 포장지를 선호하는지
(C) 남자가 상품 가격을 어떻게 지불할지
(D) 남자가 멤버십 고객인지

어휘 intend to ~할 의향이 있다 wrapping paper 포장지
merchandise 상품 rewards club 멤버십 고객(특별 혜택 등이
제공되는 회원)

해설 세부 사항 관련 – 여자의 질문 사항
여자의 첫 번째 대사에서 시계를 선물할 계획인지(Do you plan to give the
watch as a gift) 물었으므로 정답은 (A)이다.

67

Look at the graphic. Why is the man most likely unable
to use the coupon?

(A) It cannot be used for a clearance item.
(B) It has passed its expiration date.
(C) His total purchase is not large enough.
(D) He is purchasing the wrong brand.

시각 정보에 의하면, 남자가 쿠폰을 사용할 수 없는 이유는 무엇이겠는가?
(A) 재고정리 품목에는 사용할 수 없다.
(B) 만료일자가 지났다.
(C) 총 구매 금액이 모자란다.
(D) 다른 상표를 구매했다.

어휘 clearance 재고정리 expiration date 만료일자

해설 시각 정보 연계 – 쿠폰을 사용할 수 없는 이유
남자의 첫 번째 대사에서 이 플리머스 시계를 사고 싶다(I'd like to purchase
this Plymouth brand watch)고 했다. 표를 보면 에반스 시계 전체 15퍼센
트 할인(15% off any Evans brand watch)이라고 나와 있으므로 남자가 쿠
폰을 사용할 수 없는 이유는 다른 상표를 구매했기 때문임을 알 수 있다. 따라서
정답은 (D)이다.

68-70 대화 + 지도

W-Am Preparations for Thursday's meeting
are underway. **68Once they see the
demonstration of our prototype, I'm sure
they'll be interested in investing in the
product.**

M-Cn I agree. You're holding the meeting in the
conference room on the third floor, right?

W-Am Yes. **69Since we've just completed the
renovation work for all of the offices and
meeting spaces on that floor, I think it'll
make a good impression.** I've drawn a
layout of how the room is to be set up.

M-Cn All right. That looks reasonable.
**70Remember that the representatives
from Tully Incorporated are arriving late,
so they should sit nearest to the exit.** And
the visitors from the Swanson Corporation
have requested to be up front.

여: 목요일 회의 준비는 진행 중입니다. 저희 시제품 시연을 보면 분명 제품
투자에 관심이 생길 겁니다.

남: 동의해요. 3층 회의실에서 회의하실 거죠, 그렇죠?

여: 네, 그 층에 있는 모든 사무실과 회의 공간 개조 작업이 막 완료됐기
때문에 좋은 인상을 줄 수 있을 것 같아요. 회의실을 어떻게 준비할지
배치도를 그렸습니다.

남: 좋습니다. 합리적인 듯하네요. 털리 주식회사 직원들이 늦게 도착하니
출구 가장 가까운 자리에 앉아야 한다는 점을 기억하세요. 스완슨
코퍼레이션에서 오시는 분들은 앞자리를 요청했어요.

어휘 preparation for ~에 대한 준비 be underway
진행 중이다 once 일단 ~하면 demonstration 시연
prototype 시제품, 원형 be interested in ~에 관심이
있다 invest in ~에 투자하다 hold 개최하다 conference
room 회의실 renovation 개조, 보수 make a good
impression 좋은 인상을 남기다 layout 배치도
set up 마련하다, 세우다[놓다] reasonable 합리적인
representative 직원 exit 출구 request 요청하다
up front 앞자리에

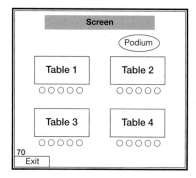

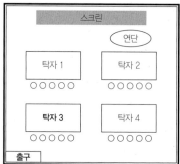

68

What is the purpose of Thursday's meeting?

(A) To demonstrate a service
(B) To secure funding
(C) To introduce new employees
(D) To develop a product

목요일 회의의 목적은 무엇인가?
(A) 서비스 시연하기
(B) 자금 확보하기
(C) 신입 사원 소개하기
(D) 제품 개발하기

어휘 demonstrate 시연하다, 보여주다 secure 확보하다 funding 자금 develop 개발하다

해설 전체 내용 관련 – 회의 목적

여자의 첫 번째 대사에서 시제품 시연을 보면 분명 제품 투자에 관심이 생길 것 (Once they see the demonstration of our prototype, I'm sure they'll be interested in investing in the product)이라고 했다. 따라서 목요일 회의의 목적이 자금 확보라는 것을 알 수 있으므로 정답은 (B)이다.

69

What has the speakers' company recently done?

(A) Renovated some rooms
(B) Merged with a competitor
(C) Moved to a new building
(D) Expanded a meeting space

화자의 회사가 최근에 한 일은 무엇인가?

(A) 일부 회의실을 개조했다
(B) 경쟁 업체와 합병했다
(C) 새 건물로 이사했다
(D) 회의 공간을 확장했다

어휘 renovate 개조하다 merge with ~와 합병하다 competitor 경쟁사 expand 확장하다

해설 세부 사항 관련 – 회사가 최근에 한 일

여자의 두 번째 대사에서 그 층에 있는 모든 사무실과 회의 공간 개조 작업이 막 완료됐기 때문에 좋은 인상을 줄 수 있다(Since we've just completed the renovation work for all of the offices and meeting spaces on that floor, I think it'll make a good impression)고 했으므로 정답은 (A)이다.

▸▸ Paraphrasing 대화의 completed the renovation work for all of the offices and meeting spaces → 정답의 Renovated some rooms

70

Look at the graphic. Where should the representatives from Tully Incorporated sit?

(A) Table 1
(B) Table 2
(C) Table 3
(D) Table 4

시각 정보에 의하면, 털리 주식회사 직원들은 어디에 앉아야 하는가?

(A) 탁자 1
(B) 탁자 2
(C) 탁자 3
(D) 탁자 4

해설 시각 정보 연계 – 털리 직원들이 앉을 자리

남자의 마지막 대사에서 털리 주식회사 직원들이 늦게 도착하니 출구 가장 가까운 자리에 앉아야 한다는 점을 기억하라(Remember that the representatives from Tully Incorporated are arriving late, so they should sit nearest to the exit)고 했다. 표를 보면 출구에서 가장 가까운 자리는 탁자 3이므로 정답은 (C)이다.

PART 4

71-73 광고

W-Br Do you love to travel abroad? [71]Make the most of your experience by learning to communicate with the locals in their native language. At the Coulter Institute, we'll help you to learn French, Chinese, Arabic, and more. [72]We guarantee that you will improve your skills and achieve your personal goals. If you don't pass the class you pay for, you can take it again for free. [73]Visit www.coulterinstitute.com to find out more. There you can also check your ability to see which level would be right for you with our free ten-minute online exam.

해외여행 좋아하세요? 지역 사람들의 모국어로 소통하는 법을 배워 해외 여행을 한껏 만끽하세요. 콜터 인스티튜트에서는 여러분이 프랑스어, 중국어, 아랍어 등을 배울 수 있도록 도와드립니다. 여러분이 실력을 향상시키고 개인 목표를 달성하게 될 것임을 보장합니다. 비용을 지불한 수업을 통과하지 못할 경우 무료로 재수강할 수 있습니다. 더 자세한 내용은 www.coulterinstitute.com에서 알아보세요. 10분짜리 무료 온라인 시험으로 실력을 확인해 어떤 레벨이 여러분에게 적당한지 확인하실 수도 있습니다.

어휘 make the most of ~를 최대한 활용하다 native language 모국어 institute 기관 guarantee 보장하다 achieve 달성하다 personal goal 개인의 목표 for free 무료로 ability 능력

71

What is being advertised?

(A) A volunteer program
(B) A travel agency
(C) A cooking institute
(D) A language school

무엇을 광고하는가?

(A) 자원봉사 프로그램
(B) 여행사
(C) 요리학원
(D) 어학원

해설 전체 내용 관련 – 광고되는 것

지문 초반부에서 지역 사람들의 모국어로 소통하는 법을 배워 해외 여행을 한껏 만끽하라(Make the most of your experience by learning to communicate with the locals in their native language)며 콜터 인스티튜트에서는 프랑스어, 중국어, 아랍어 등을 배울 수 있도록 도와준다(At the Coulter Institute, we'll help you to learn French, Chinese, Arabic, and more)고 했으므로 정답은 (D)이다.

72

What does the business offer to customers?

(A) A first-time discount
(B) Assurance of achievement
(C) A money-back guarantee
(D) A free trial period

업체는 고객에게 무엇을 제공하는가?

(A) 최초 할인
(B) 목표 달성 보장
(C) 환불 보장
(D) 무료 체험 기간

어휘 assurance 보장, 확신   achievement 성취, 업적   money-back
환불이 가능한   free trial 무료 체험

해설 세부 사항 관련 - 업체가 제공하는 것
지문 중반부에서 화자는 실력을 향상시키고 개인 목표를 달성하게 될 것임
을 보장한다(We guarantee that you will improve your skills and
achieve your personal goals)고 했으므로 정답은 (B)이다.

▶▶ Paraphrasing   지문의 achieve your personal goals
→ 정답의 Assurance of achievement

73

According to the speaker, what can listeners do online?

(A) Take a test
(B) View a schedule
(C) Request a brochure
(D) Check availability

화자에 따르면, 청자들은 온라인으로 무엇을 할 수 있는가?

(A) 시험 보기
(B) 일정 확인하기
(C) 안내 책자 요청하기
(D) 이용 가능 여부 확인하기

해설 세부 사항 관련 - 온라인으로 할 수 있는 것
지문 후반부에서 더 자세한 내용은 www.coulterinstitute.com에서 알아보
라(Visit www.coulterinstitute.com to find out more)며 10분짜리 무료
온라인 시험으로 실력을 확인해 어떤 레벨이 적당한지 확인할 수 있다(There
you can also check your ability to see which level would be right
for you with our free ten-minute online exam)고 했다. 레벨 진단을 위
한 시험을 볼 수 있다는 것을 알 수 있으므로 정답은 (A)이다.

▶▶ Paraphrasing   지문의 our free ten-minute online exam
→ 정답의 a test

74-76 담화

> M-Cn Good afternoon, everyone. **74We're
> pleased to have so many people here for the
> factory tour.** Today you'll discover how we
> produce our furniture, with every step from
> constructing the frame to adding the finishing
> touches. **75You'll be especially interested to see
> the Bolton-360, a cutting device whose unique
> design results in the lowest number of accidents
> and injuries compared to all other cutting
> equipment used in the industry.** **76Before we
> begin, I'd like to introduce you to Steven Spinelli,**

> **who founded this company seven years ago.**
> **He'll be happy to answer any questions you may
> have.**

> 여러분, 안녕하세요. **공장 견학에 이렇게 많은 분을 모시게 되어 기쁩니다.** 오늘
> 틀 제조부터 마무리 작업까지 저희 가구가 어떻게 생산되는지 알게 되실 겁니
> 다. 특히 독특한 디자인으로 업계에서 사용하는 여타 절단 장비에 비해 사고 및
> 부상률이 가장 낮은 절단 장치인 볼튼-360에 관심이 가실 텐데요. 시작하기 전
> 여러분께 스티븐 스피넬리 씨를 소개하고자 합니다. 7년 전 이 회사를 창립하신
> 분입니다. 어떤 질문이든 흔쾌히 대답해 주실 겁니다.

어휘 discover 발견하다   produce 생산하다   step 단계
construct 만들다, 건설하다   frame 틀   finishing touch 마무리
작업   cutting device 절단 장치   unique 독특한   result in
(결과로) ~을 낳다   low 낮은   injury 부상   compared to ~와
비교하여   industry 산업, 업계   found 설립하다

74

Where most likely are the listeners?

(A) At a construction site
(B) At a furniture store
(C) At a production facility
(D) At a textile warehouse

청자들이 있는 곳은 어디이겠는가?

(A) 공사 현장
(B) 가구점
(C) 생산 시설
(D) 직물 창고

어휘 site 현장, 장소   textile 직물   warehouse 창고

해설 전체 내용 관련 - 청자들이 있는 장소
지문 초반부에서 공장 견학에 많은 분을 모시게 되어 기쁘다(We're pleased
to have so many people here for the factory tour)고 했다. 청자들이 생
산 시설에 있다는 것을 알 수 있으므로 정답은 (C)이다.

▶▶ Paraphrasing   지문의 factory → 정답의 production facility

75

What does the speaker suggest about the Bolton-360?

(A) It was recently released on the market.
(B) It has an impressive safety record.
(C) It is the company's best-seller.
(D) It is made from recycled materials.

화자가 볼튼-360에 대해 암시하는 것은 무엇인가?

(A) 최근 시중에 출시됐다.
(B) 인상적인 안전 기록을 보유하고 있다.
(C) 업체에서 가장 잘 팔리는 제품이다.
(D) 재활용된 자재로 만들어졌다.

어휘 recently 최근에   release 출시하다   safety record
안전(성)[무사고] 기록   recycled 재활용된   material 재료, 자재

해설 세부 사항 관련 – 볼튼-360에 대해 암시된 것

지문 중반부에 화자가 특히 독특한 디자인으로 업계에서 사용하는 여타 절단 장비에 비해 사고 및 부상률이 가장 낮은 절단 장치 볼튼-360에 관심이 갈 것(You'll be especially interested to see the Bolton-360, a cutting device whose unique design results in the lowest number of accidents and injuries compared to all other cutting equipment used in the industry)이라고 했으므로 볼튼-360이 인상적인 안전 기록을 보유하고 있다는 것을 알 수 있다. 따라서 정답은 (B)이다.

▸▸ Paraphrasing 지문의 the lowest number of accidents and injuries
→ 정답의 an impressive safety record

76
Who most likely is Mr. Spinelli?

(A) A government inspector
(B) A tour guide
(C) A raw materials supplier
(D) A business's owner

스피넬리 씨는 누구이겠는가?
(A) 정부 조사관
(B) 여행가이드
(C) 원자재 공급자
(D) 업체 소유주

어휘 inspector 조사관 raw material 원자재 supplier 공급자, 공급 업체

해설 세부 사항 관련 – 스피넬리 씨의 신분

지문 후반부에서 화자가 견학 시작 전에 7년 전 회사를 창립한 스티븐 스피넬리 씨를 소개하겠다(Before we begin, I'd like to introduce you to Steven Spinelli, who founded this company seven years ago)고 했으므로 정답은 (D)이다.

▸▸ Paraphrasing 지문의 Steven Spinelli, who founded this company → 정답의 The business's owner

77-79 방송

W-Am You're listening to KVVL Radio. I'm Marissa Gilmore with the top-of-the-hour update. **77Roadways in the southern part of the city are looking clear, which is good news for commuters. However, if you're traveling on northbound Highway 106, expect delays because there has been a two-car accident. 78And this evening, avoid the downtown area if you can, as congestion is expected for the National Hockey Tournament. 79Don't forget that resurfacing work begins next week, so visit our Web site, www.kvvlradio.com to see a schedule of which roads will be closed so you can take an alternative route.**

여러분께서는 지금 KVVL 라디오를 듣고 계십니다. 저는 정시 교통 상황을 전해드리는 마리사 길모어입니다. 도시 남부 도로들은 원활한 상태입니다. 통근자들에게 좋은 소식이네요. 그러나 북쪽 방향 106번 고속도로를 이용하신다면 차량 두 대가 충돌하는 사고가 있으니 지체를 예상하시기 바랍니다. 그리고 오늘 저녁에는 전국 하키대회로 혼잡이 예상되니 가능하면 도심 지역을 피하십시오. 다음 주에 재포장 작업이 시작되니 저희 웹사이트 www.kvvlradio.com을 방문하셔서 어느 도로가 폐쇄되는지 일정을 확인하시어 다른 길을 택하도록 하십시오.

어휘 top-of-the-hour 정시 clear 트인 commuter 통근자 northbound 북쪽으로 향하는 delay 지체 avoid 피하다 congestion 혼잡 resurfacing 재포장 alternative 대안이 되는 route 길

77
What is the main purpose of the broadcast?

(A) To advertise a community event
(B) To provide a weather update
(C) To report on traffic conditions
(D) To explain a new city regulation

방송의 주요 목적은 무엇인가?
(A) 지역 행사를 광고하려고
(B) 날씨 정보를 전하려고
(C) 교통 상황을 알리려고
(D) 새로운 시 규정을 설명하려고

어휘 advertise 광고하다 community 지역사회 traffic 교통 condition 상태 regulation 규정, 정책

해설 전체 내용 관련 – 방송의 주요 목적

지문 초반부에서 도시 남부 도로들은 소통이 원활해 통근자들에게 좋은 소식이지만 북쪽 방향 106번 고속도로를 이용한다면 차량 두 대가 충돌한 사고가 있으니 지체를 예상하라(Roadways in the southern part of the city are looking clear, which is good news for commuters. However, if you're traveling on northbound Highway 106, expect delays because there has been a two-car accident)고 했다. 즉 교통 상황을 알려 주고 있으므로 정답은 (C)이다.

78
What is happening downtown this evening?

(A) A community parade
(B) A political debate
(C) A sporting event
(D) A theater show

오늘 저녁 도심에서 어떤 일이 있을 것인가?
(A) 마을 퍼레이드
(B) 정치 토론
(C) 스포츠 행사
(D) 연극 공연

어휘 political 정치의 debate 토론 sporting 스포츠의 theater 극장, 연극

해설 세부 사항 관련 – 도심에서 있을 일

지문 중반부에서 오늘 저녁에는 전국 하키대회로 혼잡이 예상되니 가능하면 도심 지역을 피하라(And this evening, avoid the downtown area if you can, as congestion is expected for the National Hockey Tournament)고 했으므로 정답은 (C)이다.

어휘 priced 값이 붙은 cost (비용이) ~이다 in excess of ~를 초과하여, ~ 이상의 rarely 좀처럼 ~ 않는 perform 공연하다 live 라이브로 critic 비평가 report 보도하다 truly 진정으로 once-in-a-lifetime 일생일대의 opportunity 기회 box office 매표소 regular business hours 평일 정규 영업시간

79

According to the speaker, why should listeners visit a Web site?

(A) To review the hours of operation
(B) To view a broadcasting schedule
(C) To send questions to the speaker
(D) To get road closure information

화자에 따르면, 청자들이 웹사이트를 방문해야 하는 이유는 무엇인가?
(A) 영업시간을 확인하기 위해
(B) 방송 일정을 보기 위해
(C) 화자에게 질문을 보내기 위해
(D) **도로 폐쇄 정보를 얻기 위해**

어휘 operation 운영, 영업 view 보다 broadcasting 방송 closure 폐쇄

해설 세부 사항 관련 – 웹사이트 방문 이유
지문 마지막에 다음 주에 재포장 작업이 시작되니 웹사이트 www.kvvlradio. com을 방문해서 어느 도로가 폐쇄되는지 일정을 확인해 다른 길을 택하라(Don't forget that resurfacing work begins next week, so visit our Web site, www.kvvlradio.com to see a schedule of which roads will be closed so you can take an alternative route)고 했으므로 정답은 (D)이다.

▶▶ **Paraphrasing** 지문의 **see a schedule of which roads will be closed**
→ 정답의 **get road closure information**

80-82 방송

> M-Au **80If you're looking for something to do this weekend, tickets are still available to see comedian Marcus Dorsett at Elmsford Hall on Saturday, April twenty-second.** The lowest-priced seats are seventy dollars each, with VIP seats costing in excess of two hundred dollars. **81That might seem like a lot for one event,** but Marcus Dorsett rarely performs live. Critics from newspapers all over the country are reporting that this is truly a once-in-a-lifetime opportunity that you won't forget. **82To find out more about the event, call Elmsford Hall's box office during regular business hours.**

> 이번 주말에 할 일을 찾으신다면, 4월 22일 토요일 엘름스포드 홀에서 코미디언 마커스 도셋을 볼 수 있는 입장권을 아직 구입하실 수 있습니다. 가장 저렴한 좌석은 70달러이며 VIP 좌석은 200달러가 넘습니다. 1회 공연치고 많은 금액처럼 보일 수 있습니다. 하지만 마커스 도셋의 라이브 공연은 흔치 않습니다. 전국 신문의 비평가들은 진정 일생일대의 잊지 못할 기회라고 보도하고 있습니다. 공연에 대한 더 자세한 내용을 알아보시려면 평일 정규 영업시간에 엘름스포드 매표소로 전화하시기 바랍니다.

80

What is the broadcast mainly about?

(A) A film
(B) A musical
(C) A comedy show
(D) A theater performance

방송의 주요 내용은 무엇인가?
(A) 영화
(B) 뮤지컬
(C) **코미디 쇼**
(D) 연극 공연

어휘 performance 공연

해설 전체 내용 관련 – 방송의 주요 내용
지문 초반부에 화자가 이번 주말에 할 일을 찾는다면, 4월 22일 토요일 엘름스포드 홀에서 코미디언 마커스 도셋을 볼 수 있는 입장권을 아직 구입할 수 있다(If you're looking for something to do this weekend, tickets are still available to see comedian Marcus Dorsett at Elmsford Hall on Saturday, April twenty-second)고 했으므로 정답은 (C)이다.

81

What does the speaker suggest when he says, "but Marcus Dorsett rarely performs live"?

(A) Mr. Dorsett is inexperienced.
(B) An event's tickets are sold out.
(C) Mr. Dorsett plans to retire soon.
(D) An experience is worth the cost.

남자가 "하지만 마커스 도셋의 라이브 공연은 흔치 않습니다"라고 말한 의도는 무엇인가?
(A) 도셋 씨는 경험이 부족하다.
(B) 공연 입장권은 매진됐다.
(C) 도셋 씨는 곧 은퇴할 계획이다.
(D) **비용을 내고 경험할 가치가 있다.**

어휘 inexperienced 미숙한, 경험이 없는 sold out 매진된 retire 은퇴하다 worth the cost 비용을 지불할 값어치가 있는

해설 화자의 의도 파악 – 마커스 도셋의 공연은 흔치 않다는 말의 의도
인용문 바로 앞 문장에서 화자는 1회 공연치고 많은 금액처럼 보일 수 있다 (That might seem like a lot for one event)고 말했고, 인용문 바로 뒤 문장에서는 전국 신문의 비평가들이 진정 일생일대의 잊지 못할 기회라고 보도하고 있다(Critics from newspapers all over the country are reporting that this is truly a once-in-a-lifetime opportunity that you won't forget)고 했다. 즉 마커스 도셋의 공연은 흔치 않다는 말은 비용을 내고 경험할 가치가 있다는 의미이므로 정답은 (D)이다.

82

According to the speaker, how can listeners get more information?

(A) By visiting a Web site
(B) By reading a review in a newspaper
(C) By contacting a venue directly
(D) By calling the radio station

화자에 따르면 청자들은 더 많은 정보를 어떻게 얻을 수 있는가?

(A) 웹사이트 방문하기
(B) 신문의 비평 읽어 보기
(C) **해당 장소로 직접 연락하기**
(D) 라디오 방송국에 전화하기

어휘 review 평가, 비평 contact 연락하다 venue (행사 등이 열리는) 장소 directly 직접, 바로 radio station 라디오 방송국

해설 세부 사항 관련 – 추가 정보 얻는 방법

지문 마지막에 화자가 공연에 대한 더 자세한 내용을 알아보려면 평일 정규 영업시간에 엘름스포드 매표소로 전화하라(To find out more about the event, call Elmsford Hall's box office during regular business hours)고 했으므로 정답은 (C)이다.

▸▸ **Paraphrasing** 지문의 **call Elmsford Hall's box office**
→ 정답의 **contacting a venue directly**

83-85 연설

M-Cn **83It is a pleasure to be here to celebrate the first day of construction for the Bernard Department Store project.** Once completed, this building will be the hub of the community. The process for selecting a location for our store was not easy, as we visited dozens of plots. **84But when we saw this spot, we knew our search was over.** It was the one. Surrounded by a thriving neighborhood of businesses and having easy access to public transportation, Bernard Department Store will be well-positioned to reach its revenue goals. **85I'd now like to introduce Oliver Estevez, who designed the building and has won several awards in his field.**

버나드 백화점 건설 공사 첫날을 기념하기 위해 이곳에 오게 되어 기쁩니다. 이 건물은 완공되면 지역사회의 중심지가 될 것입니다. 수십 곳의 부지를 돌아보는 등, 매장 위치를 선정하는 과정은 쉽지 않았습니다. 그러나 이 부지를 보았을 때 이제 부지 물색은 끝났음을 알 수 있었죠. 바로 그곳이었습니다. 업체로 번화한 인근 지역에 둘러싸여 있고 대중교통을 쉽게 이용할 수 있는 버나드 백화점은 수익 목표에 도달하기에 아주 유리한 조건입니다. 이제 올리버 에스테베즈 씨를 소개하려고 합니다. 이 건물을 디자인했고 건축 분야에서 여러 번 수상한 분입니다.

어휘 celebrate 경축하다, 기념하다 construction 건설 once 일단 ~하면 hub 중심지, 중추 process 절차, 과정 select 선택하다 location 위치 dozens of 수십 개의 plot 대지, 부지 spot 장소, 자리 search 물색 be over 끝나다 be surrounded by ~에 둘러싸인 thriving 번화한, 번영하는 neighborhood 인근, 근처 have easy access to ~에 손쉽게 접근하다 public transportation 대중교통 be well-positioned to ~하기에 유리한 조건이다 revenue 수익 goal 목표 award 상; 수여하다 field 분야

83

Where is the speech most likely taking place?

(A) At an employee orientation
(B) At an awards banquet
(C) At a store's grand opening
(D) At a groundbreaking ceremony

연설은 어디에서 이루어지겠는가?

(A) 직원 오리엔테이션
(B) 시상식 연회
(C) 매장 개업식
(D) **기공식**

어휘 banquet 연회 groundbreaking 착공 ceremony 의식

해설 전체 내용 관련 – 연설 장소

지문 초반부에서 버나드 백화점 건설 공사 첫날을 기념하기 위해 오게 되어 기쁘다 (It is a pleasure to be here to celebrate the first day of construction for the Bernard Department Store project)고 했으므로 정답은 (D)이다.

▸▸ **Paraphrasing** 지문의 **celebrate the first day of construction**
→ 정답의 **a groundbreaking ceremony**

84

What does the speaker imply when he says, "It was the one"?

(A) He was impressed with a product.
(B) He thought a site was perfect.
(C) He found the cause of an achievement.
(D) He was pleased to find a corporate partner.

화자가 "바로 그곳이었습니다"라고 말한 의도는 무엇인가?

(A) 제품에 감명받았다.
(B) **부지가 완벽하다고 생각했다.**
(C) 성취의 계기를 찾았다.
(D) 협력 업체를 찾아서 기뻤다.

어휘 cause 원인 achievement 성취, 업적 be pleased to ~하게 되어 기쁘다 corporate 회사의

해설 화자의 의도 파악 – 바로 그곳이었다는 말의 의도

인용문 바로 앞 문장에서 화자가 이 부지를 보았을 때 이제 부지 물색은 끝났음을 알 수 있었다(But when we saw this spot, we knew our search was over)고 했다. 따라서, 바로 그곳이었다는 말은 그만큼 부지가 완벽하다는 의미이므로 정답은 (B)이다.

85

Who will speak next?

(A) A graphic designer
(B) An architect
(C) A city official
(D) A store manager

다음으로 연설할 사람은 누구인가?

(A) 그래픽 디자이너
(B) 건축가
(C) 시 공무원
(D) 매장 관리자

어휘 architect 건축가 official 공무원, 관계자

해설 세부 사항 관련 – 다음 연설자

지문 마지막에 화자가 이 건물을 디자인했고 건축 분야에서 여러 번 수상한 올리버 에스테베즈 씨를 소개하겠다(I'd now like to introduce Oliver Estevez, who designed the building and has won several awards in his field)고 했으므로 정답은 (B)이다.

> **▸ Paraphrasing** 지문의 **Oliver Estevez, who designed the building** → 정답의 **An architect**

86-88 담화

W-Br Good morning, and thank you for volunteering to attend this workshop. **⁸⁶Today I'll be teaching you about the methods we have in place for safely getting everyone out of the building in case of a fire or other emergency.** **⁸⁷We have selected one employee from each floor so that someone knowledgeable will always be nearby.** **⁸⁸Now that you're in your small groups, I'd like to pass out a map of the offices and corridors.** You should note that elevators are not safe to use in times of emergency, and you must learn several routes in case one area is blocked.

안녕하세요. 이 워크숍에 자진해서 참석해 주셔서 감사합니다. **오늘 저는 여러분께 화재 또는 다른 비상사태 시 모두를 안전하게 건물 밖으로 대피시키는 데 적절한 방법을 가르쳐 드리겠습니다.** 각 층에서 한 명씩 직원을 뽑아서 (대피 요령을) 잘 아는 사람이 항상 근처에 있을 수 있도록 했습니다. 이제 여러분이 조별로 모였으니 사무실 및 통로 지도를 나눠드리고자 합니다. 비상시 엘리베이터는 사용하기에 안전치 않음을 명심하시고, 한 구역이 봉쇄될 경우에 대비해 여러 경로를 알아 두셔야 합니다.

어휘 volunteer to 자진해서 ~하다 attend 참석하다 in place 준비된, 제자리에 있는 safely 무사히 in case of ~의 경우에 emergency 비상(사태) knowledgeable 잘 아는, 해박한 now that ~이므로, ~이기 때문에 pass out ~을 나눠주다 corridor 복도, 통로 note ~에 주의하다 route 경로, 길 in case ~할 경우에 대비해서 block 막다

86

What will the listeners learn about?

(A) Fire prevention methods
(B) Evacuation procedures
(C) Customer service skills
(D) Volunteer opportunities

청자들은 무엇에 대해 배울 것인가?

(A) 화재 예방법
(B) 대피 절차
(C) 고객 서비스 기술
(D) 자원봉사 기회

어휘 prevention 예방 evacuation 대피 procedure 절차 skill 기술 volunteer 자원봉사 opportunity 기회

해설 전체 내용 관련 – 청자들이 배울 것

지문 초반부에서 화자가 오늘 화재 또는 다른 비상사태 시 모두를 안전하게 건물 밖으로 대피시키는 데 적절한 방법을 가르쳐 주겠다(Today I'll be teaching you about the methods we have in place for safely getting everyone out of the building in case of a fire or other emergency)고 했으므로 정답은 (B)이다.

> **▸ Paraphrasing** 지문의 **safely getting everyone out of the building** → 정답의 **Evacuation**

87

What is indicated about the listeners?

(A) They work on different floors of the building.
(B) They were recommended by their supervisors.
(C) They will be financially compensated for their time.
(D) They must pass a test at the end of the session.

청자들에 대해 명시된 것은 무엇인가?

(A) 각각 건물의 다른 층에서 일한다.
(B) 상관이 추천했다.
(C) 시간에 대해 금전적으로 보상받을 것이다.
(D) 강의 마지막에 시험을 통과해야 한다.

어휘 floor 층 recommend 추천하다 supervisor 상사, 관리자 financially 재정적으로, 금전적으로 compensate for ~에 대해 보상하다 pass 통과하다 session 수업 (시간), 강습회

해설 세부 사항 관련 – 청자들에 대해 명시된 것

지문 중반부에 화자가 각 층에서 한 명씩 직원을 뽑아서 (대피 요령을) 잘 아는 사람이 항상 근처에 있을 수 있도록 했다(We have selected one employee from each floor so that someone knowledgeable will always be nearby)고 했다. 청자들이 각각 다른 층에서 일한다는 것을 알 수 있으므로 정답은 (A)이다.

88

What will the speaker do next?

(A) Assign people to groups
(B) Respond to questions
(C) Distribute a map
(D) Examine the corridors

화자는 다음으로 무엇을 할 것인가?

(A) 사람들을 조에 배정하기
(B) 질문에 대답하기
(C) 지도 나눠 주기
(D) 복도 조사하기

어휘 assign to ~에 배정하다[할당하다] respond to ~에 대답하다[반응하다] distribute 배포하다, 나누어 주다

해설 세부 사항 관련 – 화자가 할 일

지문 후반부에 화자가 현재 청자들은 조에 속해 있으니 사무실 및 통로 지도를 나눠 주겠다(Now that you're in your small groups, I'd like to pass out a map of the offices and corridors)고 했으므로 정답은 (C)이다.

▸▸ **Paraphrasing** 지문의 **pass out** → 정답의 **Distribute**

89-91 전화 메시지

W-Am Hi, this message is for Mr. Wu Huh. This is Natalia from GBT. **89I'm calling about the vehicle you reserved to be picked up at Kearnes Airport on September fifteenth and dropped off at our location near Stewart Hotel on September twentieth.** You asked for a two-door compact car. **90I'm very sorry, but I just found the reservation form, and it was never entered into our system.** We're all out of that particular vehicle class, so we'd like to give you a four-door sedan instead. It has more space in the trunk and back seat and comes with the same features. **91Please call me back at 555-0168 to let me know that this is OK with you.** Thanks!

안녕하세요. 우 허 씨에게 남기는 메시지입니다. 저는 GBT의 나탈리아입니다. 9월 15일 컨즈 공항에서 픽업하여 9월 20일 스튜어트 호텔 근처 저희 회사로 가져다 놓도록 예약하신 차량에 관해 전화 드립니다. 2도어 소형 차량을 요청하셨는데요. 무척 죄송합니다만 예약서를 방금 발견했는데 저희 시스템에 미처 입력되지 않았습니다. 해당 차량 등급은 모두 예약 중이라 대신 4도어 세단 차량을 드리고자 합니다. 트렁크 공간과 뒷좌석이 더 넓고 기능은 같습니다. 괜찮으신지 555-0168로 연락해서 알려 주십시오. 감사합니다.

어휘 vehicle 차량 reserve 예약하다 pick up ~을 찾아오다 location 소재지, 위치 drop off 갖다 놓다 two-door 문이 두 개인 compact car 소형차 reservation form 예약서 enter into ~에 입력하다 be out of ~을 다 써서 없다 come with ~이 딸려 있다 feature 기능, 특징

89

Where does the speaker work?

(A) At a luxury hotel
(B) At a regional airport
(C) At an insurance company
(D) At a car rental firm

화자는 어디에서 일하는가?

(A) 고급 호텔
(B) 지역 공항
(C) 보험회사
(D) 차량 대여 업체

어휘 luxury 고급의 regional 지역의 insurance 보험 rental firm 대여 업체

해설 전체 내용 관련 – 화자의 근무지

지문 초반부에서 화자가 9월 15일 컨즈 공항에서 픽업하여 9월 20일 스튜어트 호텔 근처 회사로 가져다 놓도록 예약한 차량에 관해 전화한다(I'm calling about the vehicle you reserved to be picked up at Kearnes Airport on September fifteenth and dropped off at our location near Stewart Hotel on September twentieth)고 했다. 화자가 차량 대여업체에서 일하고 있음을 알 수 있으므로 정답은 (D)이다.

90

What problem does the speaker mention?

(A) A payment is still owed.
(B) A request was not processed.
(C) A price has recently increased.
(D) A service has been canceled.

화자는 어떤 문제를 언급하는가?

(A) 아직 지불이 이뤄지지 않았다.
(B) 요청이 처리되지 않았다.
(C) 최근에 가격이 인상됐다.
(D) 서비스가 취소됐다.

어휘 payment 지불 owe 빚지고 있다 request 요청 process 처리하다 recently 최근에 increase 오르다 cancel 취소하다

해설 세부 사항 관련 – 화자가 언급하는 문제

지문 중반부에 화자가 미안하지만 예약서를 방금 발견했는데 시스템에 미처 입력되지 않았다(I'm very sorry, but I just found the reservation form, and it was never entered into our system)고 했다. 요청이 처리되지 않은 것이 문제이므로 정답은 (B)이다.

▸▸ **Paraphrasing** 지문의 **it was never entered into our system**
→ 정답의 **A request was not processed.**

91

What is the listener asked to do?

(A) Provide a form of ID
(B) Pay a deposit
(C) Approve a change
(D) Sign a form

청자는 무엇을 해 달라는 요청을 받는가?

(A) 신분증 제공하기
(B) 보증금 지불하기
(C) 변경 사항 승인하기
(D) 서류에 서명하기

어휘 ID 신분증(= identification) deposit 보증금 approve 승인하다 sign 서명하다

해설 세부 사항 관련 - 청자가 요청받은 사항

지문 마지막에 화자가 괜찮은지 555-0168로 연락해서 알려 달라(Please call me back at 555-0168 to let me know that this is OK with you)고 했으므로 정답은 (C)이다.

92-94 공지

M-Au May I have your attention, please? I have a brief announcement for all staff members. **⁹²As you know, this Friday the office will be closed in honor of our country's Independence Day. ⁹³To celebrate, we're changing the dress code for Thursday. On that day, you are welcome to come to the office in casual clothing instead of your regular office attire. Of course, this is not mandatory.** It's up to you. **⁹³Some of you may prefer suits and blouses anyway. ⁹⁴Please let me know what you think of this idea.** We hope everyone enjoys experiencing a more relaxed atmosphere at work.

잠시 주목해 주십시오. 전 직원 여러분께 간단한 공지 사항이 있습니다. 아시다시피 이번 금요일에 독립기념일을 기념하여 사무실이 문을 닫을 예정입니다. 기념하기 위해 목요일 복장 규정을 변경합니다. 해당일에 사무실 근무 복장 대신 평상복을 입고 출근해도 좋습니다. 물론 의무 사항은 아닙니다. 알아서 하시면 됩니다. 일부는 정장과 블라우스를 더 선호할 수도 있으니까요. 이에 대한 의견을 알려 주십시오. 모두가 더 편안한 업무 환경을 경험했으면 합니다.

어휘 attention 주목 announcement 공지, 발표 staff 직원 in honor of ~를 기념하여 Independence Day 독립기념일 dress code 복장 규정 be welcome to ~을 자유로이 할 수 있다 casual clothing 평상복 attire 복장 mandatory 의무적인 be up to ~가 결정할 일이다 relaxed 편안한 atmosphere 분위기

92

According to the speaker, what is the purpose of the change?

(A) To recognize an upcoming holiday
(B) To make a good impression on clients
(C) To respond to customer requests
(D) To make employees easier to recognize

화자에 따르면, 변경의 목적은 무엇인가?

(A) 다가오는 국경일을 인식하기 위해
(B) 고객들에게 좋은 인상을 주기 위해
(C) 고객 요청에 부응하기 위해
(D) 직원들이 더 인식하기 쉽도록 하기 위해

어휘 recognize 인식하다, 인정하다 upcoming 다가오는 respond to ~에 대응하다

해설 전체 내용 관련 - 변경의 목적

지문 초반부에서 이번 금요일에 독립기념일을 기념하여 사무실이 문을 닫을 예정이고 이를 기념하기 위해 목요일 복장 규정을 변경한다(As you know, this Friday the office will be closed in honor of our country's

Independence Day. To celebrate, we're changing the dress code for Thursday)고 했으므로 정답은 (A)이다.

▸▸ Paraphrasing 지문의 in honor of our country's Independence Day
→ 정답의 recognize an upcoming holiday

93

What does the speaker mean when he says, "It's up to you"?

(A) The start date of the change could be postponed.
(B) Staff members should vote on their preferences.
(C) The listeners do not need attire approved in advance.
(D) Employees are not required to dress casually.

남자가 "알아서 하시면 됩니다"라고 말한 의도는 무엇인가?

(A) 변경 시작일이 연기될 수 있다.
(B) 직원들이 선호하는 바를 투표로 결정해야 한다.
(C) 청자들은 복장을 미리 승인받을 필요가 없다.
(D) 직원들은 반드시 평상복을 입을 필요는 없다.

어휘 postpone 연기하다 vote on 표결에 부치다 preference 선호 approve 승인하다 in advance 사전에 attire 복장 approve 승인하다 in advance 사전에 be required to ~하라는 요구를 받다 dress casually 평상복 차림을 하다

해설 화자의 의도 파악 - 알아서 하면 된다는 말의 의도

인용문 바로 앞 문장에서 기념하기 위해 목요일 복장 규정을 변경한다(To celebrate, we're changing the dress code for Thursday)며 해당일에 사무실 근무 복장 대신 평상복을 입고 출근해도 좋고 의무 사항은 아니(On that day, you are welcome to come to the office in casual clothing instead of your regular office attire. Of course, this is not mandatory)라고 했다. 인용문 바로 뒤 문장에서 화자는 일부는 정장과 블라우스를 더 선호할 수도 있다(Some of you may prefer suits and blouses anyway)고 했다. 즉 알아서 하면 된다는 말은 직원들이 평상복을 꼭 입을 필요가 없다는 것이므로 정답은 (D)이다.

94

What does the speaker ask the listeners to do?

(A) View some examples
(B) Share their opinions
(C) Attend a brief meeting
(D) Confirm their participation

화자는 청자들에게 무엇을 하라고 요청하는가?

(A) 견본 보기
(B) 의견 공유하기
(C) 짧은 회의 참석하기
(D) 참석 여부 확정하기

어휘 share 공유하다, 나누다 opinion 의견 brief 짧은, 간단한 confirm 확정하다 participation 참석

해설 세부 사항 관련 - 청자들이 요청받은 사항

지문 후반부에서 화자는 이에 대한 의견을 알려 달라(Please let me know what you think of this idea)고 했으므로 정답은 (B)이다.

▸▸ Paraphrasing 지문의 let me know what you think of this idea → 정답의 Share their opinions

W-Br **95As many of you know, I've been asked to organize the annual staff retreat, which will take place at the end of this month.** I distributed a survey to the entire staff to determine which venue people would prefer for the event, and you can see the results here on this chart. **96Unfortunately, I just found out yesterday that the most popular venue was already fully booked for the dates we need, so I'll call the one with the second-most votes today to make a reservation. 97Regarding the event itself, I need some ideas for icebreakers and team-building exercises, so I'd like you all to brainstorm with me now.**

많은 분들이 아시다시피, 저는 연례 직원 야유회를 기획해 달라는 요청을 받았는데요. 야유회는 이번 달 말에 개최될 예정입니다. 행사 장소로 선호하는 곳을 결정하기 위한 설문조사지를 전 직원께 나눠 드렸는데요. 이 도표에서 결과를 확인하실 수 있습니다. 안타깝게도 가장 인기 있는 장소는 우리가 원하는 날에 이미 예약이 다 찼다는 사실을 어제 알았습니다. 그래서 오늘 두 번째 인기 장소로 뽑힌 곳에 전화해 예약할 예정입니다. 행사 자체에 관해서는 분위기 조성 및 팀 단합 활동 등에 대한 아이디어가 필요합니다. 여러분 모두 지금 저와 함께 자유롭게 의견을 제시해 주셨으면 합니다.

어휘 organize 조직하다 annual 연례의 retreat 야유회 take place 일어나다, 개최되다 distribute 분배하다 entire 전체의 determine 결정하다 venue 장소 fully-booked 예약이 다 친 make a reservation 예약하다 regarding ~에 관해 icebreaker 어색한 분위기를 깨기 위한 말이나 행동 team-building 팀 단합 exercise 활동 brainstorm 어떤 주제에 대해 자유롭게 의견을 제시하다

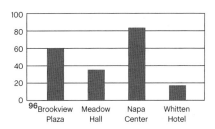

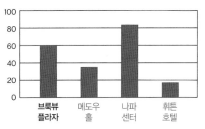

95

What is the speaker in charge of doing?

(A) Organizing a product launch
(B) Selecting a site for a new branch
(C) Planning an employee retreat
(D) Holding a recruitment event

화자는 어떤 일을 맡고 있는가?

(A) 제품 출시 준비
(B) 신규 지점 부지 선정
(C) 직원 야유회 기획
(D) 채용 행사 개최

어휘 be in charge of ~을 담당하다 launch 출시 select 고르다 site 장소, 부지 hold 개최하다 recruitment 채용, 모집

해설 전체 내용 관련 - 화자의 업무

지문 초반부에서 많은 사람들이 알 듯이 연례 직원 야유회를 기획해 달라는 요청을 받았고 이번 달 말에 개최될 예정(As many of you know, I've been asked to organize the annual staff retreat, which will take place at the end of this month)이라고 했으므로 정답은 (C)이다.

> **▸▸ Paraphrasing** 지문의 organize the annual staff retreat → 정답의 Planning an employee retreat

96

Look at the graphic. Which venue will the speaker contact today?

(A) Brookview Plaza
(B) Meadow Hall
(C) Napa Center
(D) Whitten Hotel

시각 정보에 의하면, 화자는 오늘 어떤 장소에 연락할 것인가?

(A) 브룩뷰 플라자　　(B) 메도우 홀
(C) 나파 센터　　(D) 휘튼 호텔

해설 시각 정보 연계 - 화자가 연락할 장소

지문 중반부에 화자가 가장 인기 있는 장소는 이미 예약이 다 찼다는 사실을 어제 알았다며 오늘 두 번째 인기 장소로 뽑힌 곳에 전화해 예약할 예정(Unfortunately, I just found out yesterday that the most popular venue was already fully booked for the dates we need, so I'll call the one with the second-most votes today to make a reservation)이라고 했다. 그래프를 보면 두 번째 인기 장소는 브룩뷰 플라자이므로 정답은 (A)이다.

97

What will the listeners most likely do next?

(A) Have a workout
(B) Sign up for an event
(C) Review a report
(D) Suggest some activities

청자들은 다음으로 무엇을 하겠는가?

(A) 운동하기　　(B) 행사 신청하기
(C) 보고서 검토하기　　**(D) 활동 제안하기**

해설 세부 사항 관련 - 청자들이 할 일

지문 후반부에서 행사 자체에 관해서는 분위기 조성 및 팀 단합 활동 등에 대한 아이디어가 필요하니 의견을 자유롭게 제시해 달라(Regarding the event itself, I need some ideas for icebreakers and team-building exercises, so I'd like you all to brainstorm with me now)고 했다. 청자들이 활동에 관한 의견을 제안할 것임을 알 수 있으므로 정답은 (D)이다.

▶ Paraphrasing　지문의 **icebreakers and team-building exercises** → 정답의 **some activities**

98-100 전화 메시지 + 목록

M-Cn　Hi, Marcy. It's Gerald. **98I wanted to let you know that I compiled the weekly inventory list today instead of tomorrow because I'll be spending most of tomorrow instructing the new housekeeping staff on how to clean guest rooms.** **99However, I just noticed that Victoria had two extra bottles of glass cleaner on her cart, which I didn't count.** **100There's no need to fix the error right away, as Ms. Edwards isn't placing the order until after the weekend**, but I just wanted to let you know in case you run out. Thanks!

안녕하세요, 마시 씨. 제럴드입니다. 제가 내일 대부분의 시간을 객실 관리 신입 직원들에게 객실 청소법을 가르치며 보낼 것 같아서, 대신 오늘 주간 재고 목록을 작성했음을 알려드리고자 합니다. 하지만 빅토리아 씨가 카트 안에 유리 세정제 두 병을 더 갖고 있었는데, 그건 세지 않았다는 것을 방금 알았습니다. 지금 당장 오류를 수정할 필요는 없습니다. 에드워즈 씨는 주말이 지나야 주문을 넣으니까요. 하지만 다 쓰실 경우를 대비해 알려드립니다. 감사합니다.

어휘　compile 엮다, 편집하다　inventory 재고　instruct 가르치다　housekeeping (호텔 등의) 객실 관리　notice 알아차리다　extra 추가의　count 세다　fix 바로잡다　right away 당장　place an order 주문하다　run out 다 써버리다

Inventory List

Product	Quantity
Carpet Cleaner	12 boxes
Deodorizing Spray	7 bottles
99Glass Cleaner	3 bottles
Bleach	9 bottles

재고 목록

제품	수량
카펫 세정제	12상자
탈취 스프레이	7병
유리 세정제	3병
표백제	9병

98

Why did the speaker do a task early?

(A) He needs to train some coworkers.
(B) His other project was canceled.
(C) He plans to go out of town.
(D) His manager requested it.

화자가 일을 빨리 한 이유는 무엇인가?

(A) 동료들을 교육해야 한다.
(B) 다른 프로젝트가 취소됐다.
(C) 출장을 떠날 예정이다.
(D) 그의 관리자가 요청했다.

해설 세부 사항 관련 - 일을 빨리 한 이유

지문 초반부에서 화자가 내일 대부분의 시간을 객실 관리 신입 직원들에게 객실 청소법을 가르치며 보낼 것 같아서 오늘 주간 재고 목록을 작성했다(I wanted to let you know that I compiled the weekly inventory list today instead of tomorrow because I'll be spending most of tomorrow instructing the new housekeeping staff on how to clean guest rooms)고 했으므로 정답은 (A)이다.

▶ Paraphrasing　지문의 **instructing the new housekeeping staff on how to clean guest rooms** → 정답의 **train some coworkers**

99

Look at the graphic. Which amount is incorrect?

(A) 12
(B) 7
(C) 3
(D) 9

시각 정보에 의하면, 어떤 수량이 잘못되었는가?

(A) 12　　　　　　　(B) 7
(C) 3　　　　　　　(D) 9

해설 시각 정보 연계 - 수량이 잘못된 것

지문 중반부에서 빅토리아 씨가 카트 안에 유리 세정제 두 병을 더 갖고 있었는데 세지 않았다는 것을 방금 알았다(However, I just noticed that Victoria had two extra bottles of glass cleaner on her cart, which I didn't count)고 했다. 표를 보면 유리 세정제는 3병이므로 정답은 (C)이다.

100

When will Ms. Edwards place the next order?

(A) Today
(B) Tomorrow
(C) On the weekend
(D) Next week

에드워즈 씨는 언제 다음 주문을 할 것인가?

(A) 오늘　　　　　　(B) 내일
(C) 주말　　　　　　(D) 다음 주

해설 세부 사항 관련 - 다음 주문 시점

지문 마지막에서 에드워즈 씨는 주말 이후에야 주문을 넣으므로 지금 당장 오류를 수정할 필요는 없다(There's no need to fix the error right away, as Ms. Edwards isn't placing the order until after the weekend)고 했으므로 정답은 (D)이다

TEST 6

1 (B)	**2** (C)	**3** (A)	**4** (D)	**5** (D)
6 (B)	**7** (B)	**8** (C)	**9** (C)	**10** (A)
11 (C)	**12** (B)	**13** (B)	**14** (C)	**15** (C)
16 (B)	**17** (B)	**18** (A)	**19** (C)	**20** (B)
21 (C)	**22** (A)	**23** (C)	**24** (A)	**25** (B)
26 (B)	**27** (B)	**28** (A)	**29** (C)	**30** (B)
31 (B)	**32** (B)	**33** (D)	**34** (D)	**35** (C)
36 (B)	**37** (A)	**38** (D)	**39** (A)	**40** (C)
41 (A)	**42** (C)	**43** (D)	**44** (B)	**45** (D)
46 (B)	**47** (D)	**48** (B)	**49** (A)	**50** (C)
51 (C)	**52** (A)	**53** (D)	**54** (C)	**55** (C)
56 (A)	**57** (D)	**58** (B)	**59** (D)	**60** (A)
61 (B)	**62** (C)	**63** (C)	**64** (D)	**65** (B)
66 (D)	**67** (A)	**68** (A)	**69** (B)	**70** (B)
71 (A)	**72** (A)	**73** (B)	**74** (D)	**75** (C)
76 (A)	**77** (C)	**78** (D)	**79** (C)	**80** (A)
81 (B)	**82** (B)	**83** (A)	**84** (D)	**85** (A)
86 (D)	**87** (B)	**88** (D)	**89** (C)	**90** (C)
91 (B)	**92** (B)	**93** (A)	**94** (B)	**95** (C)
96 (D)	**97** (D)	**98** (A)	**99** (C)	**100** (C)

PART 1

1　W-Am

(A) He's testing a water faucet.
(B) He's kneeling on the ground.
(C) He's painting a wall.
(D) He's rolling up his sleeves.

(A) 남자가 수도꼭지를 테스트하고 있다.
(B) 남자가 바닥에 무릎을 꿇고 있다.
(C) 남자가 벽에 페인트를 칠하고 있다.
(D) 남자가 소매를 걷어 올리고 있다.

어휘　faucet 수도꼭지　kneel on ~에 무릎을 꿇다　roll up one's
sleeves 소매를 걷어 올리다

해설　1인 등장 사진 – 사람의 상태 묘사
(A) 명사 오답. 남자가 테스트하고 있는 것은 수도꼭지(a water faucet)가 아
니므로 오답.
(B) 정답. 남자가 바닥에 무릎을 꿇고 있는(is kneeling on the ground) 모
습이므로 정답.
(C) 동사 오답. 남자가 벽에 페인트를 칠하고 있는(is painting a wall) 모습이
아니므로 오답.
(D) 동사 오답. 남자가 소매를 걷어 올린 상태이지 지금 걷어 올리고 있는(is
rolling up his sleeves) 동작을 하고 있지 않으므로 오답.

2　M-Au

(A) The man is handing papers to the woman.
(B) The man is stirring coffee with a spoon.
(C) The woman is writing on paper.
(D) The woman is tying a scarf.

(A) 남자가 여자에게 서류를 건네주고 있다.
(B) 남자가 숟가락으로 커피를 젓고 있다.
(C) 여자가 종이에 무언가를 쓰고 있다.
(D) 여자가 스카프를 매고 있다.

어휘　hand 건네주다　papers 서류　stir (휘)젓다, 뒤섞다　tie 묶다, 매다

해설　2인 등장 사진 – 사람의 동작 묘사
(A) 동사 오답. 사진에 서류가 보이지만 남자가 여자에게 서류를 건네주고 있는
(is handing papers to the woman) 모습은 아니므로 오답.
(B) 동사 오답. 사진에 커피와 숟가락이 보이지만 남자가 숟가락으로 커피를 젓
고 있는(is stirring coffee with a spoon) 모습이 아니므로 오답.
(C) 정답. 여자가 종이에 무언가를 쓰고 있는(is writing on paper) 모습이므
로 정답.
(D) 동사 오답. 여자가 스카프를 맨 상태이지 지금 스카프를 매고 있는(is tying
a scarf) 동작을 하고 있지 않으므로 오답.

3　W-Br

(A) Some sticky notes are attached to a monitor.
(B) A woman is looking at a television screen.
(C) An ink cartridge is being removed from a copier.
(D) A document tray is being assembled.

(A) 접착 메모지가 모니터에 붙어 있다.
(B) 여자가 TV 화면을 보고 있다.
(C) 복사기에서 잉크 카트리지를 빼고 있다.
(D) 서류 정리함을 조립하고 있다.

어휘　sticky note 접착 메모지, 포스트잇　attach to ~에 붙이다　ink
cartridge (복사기용) 잉크 카트리지　remove ~ from ~를
…에서 빼내다　copier 복사기　document tray 서류[문서] 정리함
assemble 조립하다

해설　1인 등장 사진 – 사람 또는 사물 중심 묘사
(A) 정답. 접착 메모지(Some sticky notes)가 모니터에 붙어 있는(are
attached to a monitor) 상태이므로 정답.
(B) 사진에 없는 명사를 이용한 오답. 사진에 텔레비전(television)이 보이지
않으므로 오답.

(C) 사진에 없는 명사를 이용한 오답. 사진에 잉크 카트리지(ink cartridge)가 보이지 않으므로 오답.

(D) 동사 오답. 사진에 서류 정리함이 보이지만, 여자가 서류 정리함(document tray)을 조립하고 있는(is being assembled) 모습은 아니므로 오답.

---

4 M-Cn

(A) A walking path is being resurfaced.
(B) A line of trees stands next to a parking area.
(C) There are some blankets spread on the grass.
(D) Some benches have been installed.

(A) 산책로를 재포장하고 있다.
(B) 주차장 옆에 나무들이 줄지어 서 있다.
(C) 잔디 위에 담요가 펼쳐져 있다.
(D) 벤치들이 설치되어 있다.

어휘 walking path 산책로 resurface (도로를) 새로 포장하다, 재포장하다 next to ~ 옆에 parking area 주차장 spread 펼쳐지다 install 설치하다

해설 사물/배경 사진 – 사물의 상태 묘사
(A) 동사 오답. 사진에 산책로는 보이지만 현재 재포장되고 있는(is being resurfaced) 상황이 아니므로 오답.
(B) 사진에 없는 명사를 이용한 오답. 사진에 주차장(parking area)은 보이지 않으므로 오답.
(C) 사진에 없는 명사를 이용한 오답. 사진에 잔디는 보이지만 담요(some blankets)는 보이지 않으므로 오답.
(D) 정답. 벤치들이 설치되어 있는(have been installed) 모습이므로 정답.

---

5 W-Am

(A) Safety helmets have been set on racks.
(B) Some construction workers are taking a break.
(C) Cars are entering an underground tunnel.
(D) A beam is being moved into place.

(A) 안전모들이 선반 위에 놓여 있다.
(B) 건설 노동자들이 휴식을 취하고 있다.
(C) 자동차들이 지하 터널로 들어가고 있다.
(D) 목재를 옮기고 있다.

어휘 safety helmet 안전모 set 놓다 rack 선반, 걸이 construction 건설, 공사 take a break 휴식을 취하다 underground 지하의 beam (용도에 따라 가공된) 목재, 철재 move into ~로 이동하다

해설 2인 이상 등장 사진 – 사람 또는 사물 중심 묘사
(A) 동사 오답. 사람들이 안전모를 착용한 상태이지 안전모가 선반 위에 놓여 있는 상태는 아니므로 오답.
(B) 동사 오답. 사진에 건설 노동자들이 보이지만 휴식을 취하고 있는(are taking a break) 모습이 아니므로 오답.
(C) 사진에 없는 명사를 이용한 오답. 사진에 자동차(cars)나 지하 터널(underground tunnel)은 보이지 않으므로 오답.
(D) 정답. 사람들이 목재를 옮기고 있는(is being moved into place) 모습이므로 정답.

---

6 M-Au

(A) A stream runs between rows of houses.
(B) Streetlights extend from buildings.
(C) Flowers have been planted in a garden.
(D) Some tables are being cleared.

(A) 늘어서 있는 주택들 사이로 시내가 흐르고 있다.
(B) 가로등이 건물에서 돌출되어 있다.
(C) 정원에 꽃들이 심어져 있다.
(D) 탁자를 치우고 있다.

어휘 stream 시내, 개울 run 흐르다 a row of 한 줄로 늘어서 있는 streetlight 가로등 extend from ~에서 돌출하다 plant 심다 clear 치우다

해설 사물/배경 사진 – 사물의 위치 묘사
(A) 사진에 없는 명사를 이용한 오답. 사진에 시내(stream)는 보이지 않으므로 오답.
(B) 정답. 가로등(streetlights)이 건물 외부에서 돌출되어(extend from buildings) 있으므로 정답.
(C) 사진에 없는 명사를 이용한 오답. 사진에 정원(garden)이 보이지 않으므로 오답.
(D) 동사 오답. 사진에 탁자가 보이지만 현재 치우고 있는(are being cleared) 상황이 아니므로 오답.

PART 2

07

W-Br Would you like our company's brochure?
M-Cn (A) Nobody will accompany them.
　　　(B) Yes, that would be helpful.
　　　(C) We can certainly meet the deadline.

우리 회사의 안내 책자를 보시겠어요?
(A) 아무도 그들과 동행하지 않을 거예요.
(B) 네, 그게 도움이 되겠네요.
(C) 우리는 확실히 마감일을 지킬 수 있을 거예요.

어휘 brochure 안내 책자 accompany 동행하다, 동반하다 certainly 분명히 meet the deadline 마감 시간에 맞추다

해설 제안/권유의 의문문

(A) 유사 발음 오답. 질문의 company와 부분적으로 발음이 유사한 accompany를 이용한 오답.

(B) 정답. 회사의 안내 책자를 보라는 제안에 책자가 도움이 될 거라는 긍정적인 응답을 하고 있으므로 정답.

(C) 질문과 상관없는 오답. 회사 안내 책자를 보라는 제안에 마감일을 지킬 수 있을 거라고 말하는 것은 질문의 맥락에서 벗어난 응답이므로 오답.

8

W-Am Where should I take the package?

M-Au (A) As soon as possible.
       (B) We used packing tape.
       (C) To the second floor.

소포를 어디로 가져다 드릴까요?
(A) 가능한 한 빨리요.
(B) 저희는 포장용 테이프를 사용했어요.
(C) 2층으로요.

어휘 package 소포 packing tape 포장(용) 테이프 floor 층, 바닥

해설 소포를 가져다 줄 위치를 묻는 Where 의문문

(A) 질문과 상관없는 오답. 시점을 묻는 When 의문문에 대한 응답이므로 오답.

(B) 연상 단어 오답. 질문의 package에서 연상 가능한 packing tape을 이용한 오답.

(C) 정답. 소포를 어디로 가져다 주어야 할지를 묻는 질문에 2층이라는 구체적인 장소로 응답하고 있으므로 정답.

9

M-Au Who's organizing the games for the company picnic?

W-Br (A) At the end of September.
       (B) No, the table was by the field.
       (C) Dylan Nam, I believe.

누가 회사 야유회 게임을 준비하고 있나요?
(A) 9월 말에요.
(B) 아뇨, 식탁은 들가에 있었어요.
(C) 아마 딜런 남이 준비할 거예요.

어휘 organize 계획하다, 준비하다 company picnic 회사 야유회

해설 야유회 게임 준비 담당자를 묻는 Who 의문문

(A) 질문과 상관없는 오답. 시점을 묻는 When 의문문에 대한 응답이므로 오답.

(B) Yes/No 불가 오답. 인물을 묻는 Who 의문문에 Yes/No 응답은 불가능하므로 오답.

(C) 정답. 누가 회사 야유회의 게임을 준비하는지를 묻는 질문에 딜런 남이라는 구체적인 인물로 응답하고 있으므로 정답.

10

W-Am Have we received the audit data yet?

M-Cn (A) No, it's not expected until Monday.
       (B) Sure, I'm free on that date.
       (C) Auditions for the next play.

우리가 회계 감사 자료를 받았나요?
(A) 아니오, 월요일이나 되어야 받을 거예요.
(B) 네, 그 날짜에는 시간이 돼요.
(C) 다음 연극을 위한 오디션이에요.

어휘 audit (회계) 감사 data 자료 expect 기대하다 conference 컨퍼런스, 회의 audition 오디션, 심사

해설 회계 감사 자료를 받았는지를 묻는 조동사(have) Yes/No 의문문

(A) 정답. 회계 감사 자료를 받았는지를 묻는 질문에 No라고 대답한 후, 월요일이나 되어야 받을 것이라고 부연 설명을 하고 있으므로 정답.

(B) 유사 발음 오답. 질문의 data와 부분적으로 발음이 유사한 date를 이용한 오답.

(C) 파생어 오답. 질문의 audit과 파생어 관계인 auditions를 이용한 오답.

11

M-Au You wanted some help connecting the printer, didn't you?

W-Br (A) Both winter and spring.
       (B) They're older sales projections.
       (C) I got it working now, thanks.

프린터를 연결하는 데 도움이 필요하다고 하셨죠, 그렇죠?
(A) 겨울과 봄 둘 다요.
(B) 이전 예상 매출액이에요.
(C) 이제 해결했어요, 고마워요.

어휘 connect 연결하다 sales projections 예상 매출(액), 판매 예상치 work 작동되다

해설 도움 필요 여부를 확인하는 부가의문문

(A) 유사 발음 오답. 질문의 printer와 부분적으로 발음이 유사한 winter를 이용한 오답.

(B) 질문과 상관없는 오답. 프린터를 연결하는 데 도움이 필요한지를 확인하는 질문에 예전 예상 매출액이라고 말하는 것은 질문의 맥락에서 벗어난 응답이므로 오답.

(C) 정답. 프린터를 연결하는 것에 대한 도움 필요 여부를 확인하는 질문에 이제 해결했다면서 고맙다고 응답하고 있으므로 정답.

12

W-Am When was that fountain installed in the park?

M-Cn (A) By planting new types of trees.
       (B) About three months ago.
       (C) To provide a rest area.

공원에 언제 저 분수가 설치되었나요?
(A) 새로운 종류의 나무를 심어서요.
(B) 석 달 전쯤에요.
(C) 휴식 공간을 제공하기 위해서요.

어휘 fountain 분수 install 설치하다 plant 심다 rest 휴식

해설 분수가 설치된 시점을 묻는 When 의문문
(A) 연상 단어 오답. 질문의 park에서 연상 가능한 trees를 이용한 오답.
(B) 정답. 공원에 분수가 설치된 시점을 묻는 질문에 석 달 전쯤이라는 구체적인 시점으로 응답하고 있으므로 정답.
(C) 연상 단어 오답. 질문의 park에서 연상 가능한 rest area를 이용한 오답.

13

M-Au How was the apartment you went to see yesterday?

W-Am (A) Beside the subway station.
　　　(B) I found it really appealing.
　　　(C) Through a real estate agency.

어제 보러 간 아파트는 어땠어요?
(A) 지하철역 옆에요.
(B) 정말 마음에 들었어요.
(C) 부동산 중개소를 통해서요.

어휘 appealing 매력적인, 흥미로운 real estate agency 부동산 중개소

해설 어제 본 아파트가 어땠는지 의견을 묻는 How 의문문
(A) 질문과 상관없는 오답. 위치를 묻는 Where 의문문에 어울리는 응답이므로 오답.
(B) 정답. 어제 보러 간 아파트가 어땠는지 묻는 질문에 정말 마음에 들었다고 자신의 의견을 밝히고 있으므로 정답.
(C) 연상 단어 오답. 질문의 apartment에서 연상 가능한 real estate agency를 이용한 오답.

14

W-Br Were your classes taught online or in person?

M-Cn (A) An additional teacher.
　　　(B) Yeah, I learned a lot.
　　　(C) They were online classes.

수업은 온라인으로 듣나요, 아니면 직접 참석하나요?
(A) 추가 교사요.
(B) 네, 많이 배웠어요.
(C) 온라인 강좌예요.

어휘 in person 직접, 몸소 additional 추가의

해설 구를 연결한 선택의문문
(A) 파생어 오답. 질문의 taught와 파생어 관계인 teacher를 이용한 오답.
(B) 연상 단어 오답. 질문의 classes에서 연상 가능한 learn을 이용한 오답.
(C) 정답. 온라인 수업인지 현장 수업인지를 묻는 질문에 온라인 수업이라고 응답하고 있으므로 정답.

15

W-Am Why has the office fridge been replaced?

W-Br (A) Well, there's traffic on the bridge.
　　　(B) Right next to the microwave.
　　　(C) Did you notice how often it broke down?

사무실 냉장고는 왜 교체했나요?
(A) 음, 대교에는 차가 다녀요.
(B) 전자레인지 바로 옆이요.
(C) 얼마나 자주 고장 나는지 보셨죠?

어휘 fridge 냉장고(= refrigerator) replace 교체하다, 대체하다 traffic 교통(량), 차량 next to ~ 옆에 microwave 전자레인지 notice 알아채다 break down 고장 나다

해설 사무실 냉장고를 교체한 이유를 묻는 Why 의문문
(A) 질문과 상관없는 오답. 냉장고 교체 이유를 묻는 질문에 그 대교에는 차가 다닌다고 응답하는 것은 질문의 맥락에서 벗어난 것이므로 오답.
(B) 연상 단어 오답. 질문의 fridge에서 연상 가능한 microwave를 이용한 오답.
(C) 정답. 사무실 냉장고를 교체한 이유를 묻는 질문에 얼마나 자주 고장이 나는지 봤냐고 되물음으로써 자주 고장이 났기 때문이라는 의미를 우회적으로 표현하고 있으므로 정답.

16

M-Cn Where can I find an extra stapler?

W-Am (A) While you were at the market.
　　　(B) In the storage room downstairs.
　　　(C) They're on a business trip.

여분의 스테이플러는 어디에 있나요?
(A) 당신이 시장에 있는 동안이요.
(B) 아래층 창고요.
(C) 그들은 지금 출장 중이에요.

어휘 extra 추가의, 여분의 stapler 스테이플러 market 시장 storage room 창고 downstairs 아래층 on a business trip 출장 중인

해설 스테이플러가 있는 장소를 묻는 Where 의문문
(A) 질문과 상관없는 오답. 시점을 묻는 When 의문문에 어울리는 응답이므로 오답.
(B) 정답. 여분의 스테이플러가 있는 장소를 묻는 질문에 아래층 창고에 있다는 말로 구체적인 장소를 언급하고 있으므로 정답.
(C) 질문과 상관없는 오답. 여분의 스테이플러가 있는 장소를 묻는 질문에 출장 중이라고 응답하는 것은 질문의 맥락에서 벗어난 것이므로 오답.

17

W-Br Let's talk about industry trends as well as sales results.

M-Au (A) Oh, those aren't on sale.
　　　(B) But we'll only have half an hour.
　　　(C) A regular companywide meeting.

매출 실적뿐 아니라 산업 동향에 대해서도 얘기해 봅시다.
(A) 오, 그건 할인되지 않아요.
(B) 하지만 30분밖에 없어요.
(C) 정기적으로 하는 전 직원 회의요.

어휘 industry trend 산업 동향 as well as ~뿐만 아니라 sales result 매출 실적, 판매 결과 on sale 할인 중인 regular 정기적인 companywide 회사 전반의

(A) 유사 발음 오답. 평서문의 sales와 부분적으로 발음이 동일한 sale을 이용한 오답

(B) 정답. 산업 동향에 관해 이야기하자는 제안에 대해 30분밖에 없다고 말하며 그럴 시간이 없다는 의미를 우회적으로 표현하고 있으므로 정답.

(C) 연상 단어 오답. 평서문의 talk about에서 연상 가능한 meeting을 이용한 오답.

18

M-Au **Don't you need an access badge to get into the mailroom?**

W-Am (A) Oh, I assumed you had one.

(B) There's room in that mailbox.

(C) No, he's never been a mail handler.

우편물실에 들어가려면 출입증이 필요하지 않나요?
(A) 아, 당신이 갖고 있는 줄 알았어요.
(B) 그 우편함에 공간이 있어요.
(C) 아니오, 그는 우편물을 처리해 본 적이 없어요.

어휘 access badge 출입증 mailroom 우편물실 assume 생각하다, 짐작하다 room 공간, 여유 mailbox 우편함, 우체통 handler 취급하는[다루는] 사람

해설 출입증 필요 여부에 대한 부정의문문

(A) 정답. 우편물실에 들어가려면 출입증이 필요하지 않냐는 질문에 당신이 출입증을 갖고 있는 줄 알았다고 우회적으로 응답하고 있으므로 정답.

(B) 유사 발음 오답. 질문의 mailroom과 부분적으로 발음이 동일한 room과 mailbox를 이용한 오답.

(C) 유사 발음 오답. 질문의 mailroom과 부분적으로 발음이 동일한 mail을 이용한 오답.

19

M-Cn **How long is the bus ride to the resort?**

W-Am (A) Our seats are near the back.

(B) Over a mountain road.

(C) You should ask the tour guide.

리조트까지 버스를 타고 가는 데 얼마나 걸리나요?
(A) 우리 좌석은 뒤쪽이에요.
(B) 산길을 넘어서요.
(C) 여행 가이드에게 물어보세요.

어휘 ride 타고 가기 resort 리조트, 유원지 seat 좌석, 자리

해설 소요 시간을 묻는 How long 의문문

(A) 연상 단어 오답. 질문의 bus에서 연상 가능한 seats를 이용한 오답.

(B) 연상 단어 오답. 질문의 resort에서 연상 가능한 mountain를 이용한 오답.

(C) 정답. 리조트까지 버스를 타고 가는 데 걸리는 시간을 묻는 질문에 여행 가이드에게 물어보라고 우회적으로 응답하고 있으므로 정답.

20

W-Br **Will the finance workshops still be held in Boston?**

M-Au (A) I'd prefer to register in advance.

(B) **No, the venue was changed to San Diego.**

(C) She's studying to become an accountant.

재무 워크숍은 변동 없이 보스턴에서 열릴 건가요?
(A) 미리 등록하는 게 좋겠어요.
(B) **아니오, 장소가 샌디에이고로 변경되었어요.**
(C) 그녀는 회계사가 되려고 공부하고 있어요.

어휘 finance 재정, 금융 workshop 워크숍, 연수, 교육 be held 열리다 register 등록하다 in advance 미리 venue 장소, 개최지 accountant 회계사

해설 워크숍 장소를 묻는 조동사(will) Yes/No 의문문

(A) 질문과 상관없는 오답. 재무 워크숍이 변동 없이 보스턴에서 열릴 것인지를 묻는 질문에 사전 등록을 선호한다고 응답하는 것은 질문의 맥락에서 벗어난 것이므로 오답.

(B) 정답. 재무 워크숍이 보스턴에서 변동 없이 열릴 것인지를 묻는 질문에 먼저 No라는 부정적인 응답을 한 후 장소가 샌디에이고로 변경되었다는 부연 설명을 하고 있으므로 정답.

(C) 연상 단어 오답. 질문의 finance에서 연상 가능한 accountant를 이용한 오답.

21

M-Cn **I'd like to try a sample of your new ice cream flavor.**

W-Br (A) Yes, it's a full-screen player.

(B) They're simple to follow.

(C) **The mint chocolate one?**

새로운 아이스크림 맛을 시식해 보고 싶어요.
(A) 네, 전체 화면 플레이어예요.
(B) 따라 하기가 쉬워요.
(C) **민트 초콜릿 맛이요?**

어휘 flavor 맛 full-screen 전체 화면의 player 재생 장치

해설 문의/요청의 평서문

(A) 유사 발음 오답. 평서문의 flavor와 부분적으로 발음이 유사한 player를 이용한 오답.

(B) 유사 발음 오답. 평서문의 sample과 부분적으로 발음이 유사한 simple을 이용한 오답.

(C) 정답. 새로운 아이스크림 맛을 시식해 보고 싶다는 요청에 대해 민트 초콜릿 맛을 가리키는 것인지를 되물으며 요청을 우회적으로 수락하고 있으므로 정답.

22

W-Am **You're on duty until check-in ends tonight, aren't you?**

M-Au (A) Yes, I traded shifts with Fiona.

(B) Sorry, we're fully booked for tonight.

(C) Those were checked for mistakes.

오늘 밤은 당신이 체크인 끝날 때까지 근무죠, 그렇죠?
(A) 네, 피오나와 근무 시간을 바꿨어요.
(B) 죄송해요. 오늘 밤은 예약이 꽉 찼어요.
(C) 그건 오류 검사를 한 거예요.

어휘 be on duty 근무 중이다 check-in 체크인, 탑승[숙박] 수속 trade 교환하다, 맞바꾸다 shift 근무 시간, 근무조 fully booked 예약이 꽉 찬 mistake 오류, 실수

해설 근무 여부를 확인하는 부가의문문
(A) 정답. 오늘 밤 체크인이 끝날 때까지 근무인지를 묻는 질문에 Yes라고 긍정적인 대답을 한 후 피오나와 근무 시간을 바꾸었다고 부연 설명을 하고 있으므로 정답.
(B) 연상 단어 오답. 질문의 check-in에서 연상 가능한 booked를 이용한 오답.
(C) 단어 반복 오답. 질문에 나온 check를 다른 의미의 check로 반복한 오답.

23

M-Cn When is our car insurance payment due?
W-Am (A) From the side entrance.
(B) They drive delivery trucks.
(C) I highlighted it on the bill.

우리 자동차 보험금 납입 기한이 언제죠?
(A) 옆문에서요.
(B) 그들은 배달 트럭을 운전해요.
(C) 청구서에 표시해 뒀어요.

어휘 car insurance 자동차 보험 payment 지불 (금액) due (지급·제출) 기일이 된 side entrance 옆문 delivery truck 배달 트럭 highlight 두드러지게 하다, 강조하다 bill 계산서, 청구서

해설 자동차 보험금 납입일을 묻는 When 의문문
(A) 유사 발음 오답. 질문의 insurance와 부분적으로 발음이 유사한 entrance를 이용한 오답.
(B) 연상 단어 오답. 질문의 car에서 연상 가능한 trucks를 이용한 오답.
(C) 정답. 자동차 보험금을 언제까지 내야 하는지를 묻는 질문에 구체적인 시점으로 응답하는 대신 청구서에 표시를 해 두었다고 우회적으로 응답하고 있으므로 정답.

24

M-Au Who's working at the security guard desk?
M-Cn (A) This morning it was Alex.
(B) That's a good idea.
(C) Another backup disk.

경비원 데스크에서는 누가 근무하고 있나요?
(A) 오늘 아침은 알렉스였어요.
(B) 좋은 생각이에요.
(C) 다른 백업 디스크요.

어휘 security guard 경비원

해설 경비원 데스크 근무 담당자를 묻는 Who 의문문
(A) 정답. 경비원 데스크 근무 담당자가 누구인지를 묻는 질문에 Alex라는 구체적인 인물로 응답하고 있으므로 정답.
(B) 질문과 상관없는 오답. 근무 담당자를 묻는 질문에 좋은 생각이라는 대답은 맥락에서 벗어난 응답이므로 오답.
(C) 유사 발음 오답. 질문의 desk와 부분적으로 발음이 유사한 disk를 이용한 오답.

25

W-Br Should we box up all of the paper files or just the older ones?
M-Cn (A) By tomorrow at the latest.
(B) We only rented one storage unit.
(C) The name of your client.

종이 파일을 모두 포장할까요, 아니면 예전 것만 포장할까요?
(A) 늦어도 내일까지요.
(B) 우리는 보관함을 하나만 빌렸어요.
(C) 고객의 이름이요.

어휘 box up 상자에 넣다, 포장하다 paper file 종이 파일, 서류꽂이 at the latest 늦어도 rent 빌리다 storage unit 보관함

해설 구를 연결한 선택의문문
(A) 질문과 상관없는 오답. 시기를 묻는 When 의문문에 적절한 응답이므로 오답.
(B) 정답. 종이 파일을 모두 포장할 것인지 아니면 예전 것만 포장할 것인지를 묻는 질문에 대해 보관함을 하나만 빌렸다고 말하는 것은 예전 것만 포장하라는 의미를 우회적으로 표현한 것이므로 정답.
(C) 질문과 상관없는 오답. 종이 파일을 모두 포장할 것인지 아니면 예전 것만 포장할 것인지를 묻는 질문에 고객의 이름이라고 대답한 것은 맥락에서 벗어난 응답이므로 오답.

26

M-Au Did you see the poster for that new action movie?
W-Br (A) A cinema in my neighborhood.
(B) Yes, and I'd like to get tickets.
(C) Elliot can send them for you.

새 액션 영화 포스터 봤어요?
(A) 우리 동네에 있는 극장이요.
(B) 네, 표를 사고 싶네요.
(C) 엘리어트가 당신 대신 보내 줄 수 있어요.

어휘 neighborhood 동네, 인근

해설 신작 영화 포스트를 봤는지 묻는 조동사(do) Yes/No 의문문
(A) 연상 단어 오답. 질문의 action movie에서 연상 가능한 cinema를 이용한 오답.
(B) 정답. 새 액션 영화 포스터를 봤는지 확인하는 질문에 Yes라고 대답한 후 표를 사고 싶다는 부연 설명을 하고 있으므로 정답.
(C) 질문과 상관없는 오답. 새 액션 영화 포스터를 봤느냐는 질문에 엘리어트가 대신 보낼 수 있다는 대답은 맥락에서 벗어난 응답이므로 오답.

27

W-Am Didn't Dorothy say there were more file folders in the supply closet?

M-Au (A) Jane will have the cabinet repaired.

(B) That was last week, though.

(C) Because they're on back order.

도로시가 비품 창고에 서류철이 더 있다고 말하지 않았어요?

(A) 제인이 캐비닛 수리를 맡길 거예요.

(B) 하지만 그건 지난주였어요.

(C) 이월 주문이기 때문이에요.

어휘 file folder 서류철, 파일 폴더　supply closet 비품 창고　repair 수리하다, 고치다　back order 이월 주문

해설 비품 창고에 서류철이 있는지를 확인하는 부정의문문

(A) 연상 단어 오답. 질문의 file folders나 supply closet에서 연상 가능한 cabinet을 이용한 오답.

(B) 정답. 비품 창고에 서류철이 더 있다고 말하지 않았느냐는 질문에 그건 지난주였다고 응답하며 지금은 없다는 것을 우회적으로 표현하고 있으므로 정답.

(C) 유사 발음 오답. 질문의 folders와 부분적으로 발음이 유사한 order를 이용한 오답.

28

M-Cn Can I have a few more napkins for our table?

W-Am (A) They're up at the buffet counter.

(B) He sat down with the rest of them.

(C) Do you have a reservation?

저희 테이블에 냅킨 좀 더 주시겠어요?

(A) 뷔페 진열대 위에 있어요.

(B) 그는 나머지 사람들과 동석했어요.

(C) 예약하셨나요?

어휘 counter 계산대, 진열대　rest 나머지　have a reservation 예약하다

해설 냅킨을 더 줄 수 있는지를 묻는 조동사(can) 제안/요청 의문문

(A) 정답. 냅킨을 더 줄 수 있는지를 묻는 질문에 대해, 뷔페 진열대 위에 있다고 말하며 직접 가져다 쓰라는 의미를 우회적으로 표현하고 있으므로 정답.

(B) 연상 단어 오답. 질문의 table에서 연상 가능한 sat down을 이용한 오답.

(C) 연상 단어 오답. 질문의 napkin에서 연상 가능한 reservation을 이용한 오답.

29

M-Au What floor is Nelson Dental Clinic located on?

W-Br (A) Just a regular check-up.

(B) The one on Main Street.

(C) It's posted on the directory.

넬슨 치과가 몇 층에 있나요?

(A) 그냥 정기 검진이에요.

(B) 메인 가에 있는 거요.

(C) 건물 안내판에 게시되어 있어요.

어휘 floor 층　dental clinic 치과 의원　be located ~에 위치하다　regular check-up 정기 검진　post 게시하다　directory (층수·호수가 표시된) 건물 안내판

해설 층수를 묻는 What 의문문

(A) 연상 단어 오답. 질문의 Dental Clinic에서 연상 가능한 check-up을 이용한 오답.

(B) 연상 단어 오답. 질문의 located에서 연상 가능한 Main Street를 이용한 오답.

(C) 정답. 넬슨 치과의 층수를 묻는 질문에 구체적인 층수로 응답하는 대신 안내판에 게시되어 있다고 우회적으로 표현한 것이므로 정답.

30

W-Am When do you think you'll get started on writing the market research report?

M-Au (A) The Internet search results.

(B) I'm working on the introduction now.

(C) They were very informative, I thought.

언제부터 시장조사 보고서를 작성할 건가요?

(A) 인터넷 검색 결과요.

(B) 지금 도입부를 작성하고 있어요.

(C) 제 생각에 그것들은 아주 유용했어요.

어휘 market research 시장조사　Internet search 인터넷 검색　work on ~에 착수하다　introduction 서론, 도입부　informative 유익한, 교육적인

해설 시장조사 보고서를 언제부터 작성할 것인지 묻는 간접의문문

(A) 유사 발음 오답. 질문의 research와 일부 발음이 유사한 search를 이용한 오답.

(B) 정답. 시장조사 보고서를 언제부터 작성할 것인지를 묻는 질문에 지금 도입부를 작성하고 있다고 응답하며 이미 시작했다는 의미를 우회적으로 표현하고 있으므로 정답.

(C) 질문과 상관없는 오답. they가 가리키는 대상이 질문에 없으며, 의견을 묻는 How 의문문에 어울리는 응답이므로 오답.

31

W-Br There must be a quicker route to get to the wholesale supplier.

M-Cn (A) There were very few bargains.

(B) You can check the map if you want.

(C) Well, cash is the best payment method.

분명 도매상으로 가는 더 빠른 길이 있을 거예요.

(A) 특가품이 별로 없어요.

(B) 원하시면 지도를 확인해 보세요.

(C) 음, 현금이 가장 좋은 결제 수단이에요.

어휘 route 길, 노선　get to ~에 도착하다　wholesale 도매의　supplier 납품업체, 공급업체　bargain (싸게) 산 물건, 특가품　map 지도　payment method 결제 수단

해설 의견 제시의 평서문

(A) 연상 단어 오답. 평서문의 wholesale에서 연상 가능한 bargains를 이용한 오답.

(B) 정답. 도매상으로 가는 더 빠른 길이 있을 것이라는 의견을 제시하는 말에 지도를 확인해 보라고 말하며 지도에는 빠른 길이 나와 있을 거라는 의미를 우회적으로 표현하고 있으므로 정답.

(C) 질문과 상관없는 오답. 도매상으로 가는 더 빠른 길이 있을 것이라는 의견을 제시하는 말에 현금이 가장 좋은 결제 수단이라는 대답은 맥락에서 벗어난 응답이므로 오답.

PART 3

32-34

M-Cn	Hi, this is Doug Silvers. Something has come up and I won't have time today to pick up the prescription I called in earlier. **³²What time are you open on Saturday?**
W-Am	Oh, Mr. Silvers, we were just about to call you. **³³I'm sorry, but we've just run out of that medication.**
M-Cn	Really? That's never happened before. Uh...
W-Am	We should get a new shipment by Wednesday. **³⁴In the meantime, the pharmacist said that you can take a similar medication instead. I'd recommend that.**

남	안녕하세요. 저는 더그 실버스입니다. 일이 생겨서 오늘은 앞서 요청했던 처방약을 찾을 시간이 없을 것 같습니다. **토요일에는 몇 시에 문을 엽니까?**
여	아, 실버스 씨. 막 전화하려던 참이었습니다. **죄송하지만 그 약이 떨어졌습니다.**
남	그래요? 전에는 그런 일이 없었는데요. 음…
여	수요일쯤에는 약이 새로 들어올 겁니다. **약사 말로는 당분간 비슷한 약을 대신 복용하실 수 있다고 합니다. 그렇게 하시기를 권합니다.**

어휘	come up 생기다, 발생하다 pick up 찾아오다 prescription 처방전, 처방된 약 be about to 막 ~하려던 참이다 run out of ~가 떨어지다 medication 약 shipment 선적물, 수송품 in the meantime 그동안, 당분간 pharmacist 약사

32

Why is the man calling?

(A) To confirm a treatment technique
(B) To find out some business hours
(C) To order some prescriptions
(D) To give an authorization

남자가 전화를 건 이유는 무엇인가?

(A) 치료법을 확인하려고
(B) 영업시간을 확인하려고
(C) 처방약을 주문하려고
(D) 허가를 내 주려고

어휘   confirm 확인하다   treatment 치료   technique 기법 business hours 영업시간   order 주문하다   authorization 허가

해설 전체 내용 관련 – 남자가 전화를 건 이유
남자의 첫 번째 대사에서 토요일에는 몇 시에 문을 여는지(What time are you open on Saturday) 질문했으므로 정답은 (B)이다.

> ▸▸ Paraphrasing   대화의 **What time are you open** → 정답의 **business hours**

33

What problem does the woman mention?

(A) A pharmacist has not yet arrived.
(B) A pharmacy is closed on weekends.
(C) A handwritten message is unclear.
(D) A product is not in stock.

여자는 어떤 문제를 언급하는가?

(A) 약사가 아직 도착하지 않았다.
(B) 약국이 주말에 문을 닫는다.
(C) 손으로 쓴 메시지가 분명하지 않다.
(D) 물품의 재고가 없다.

어휘   handwritten 손으로 쓴   unclear 분명하지 않은   be in stock 재고가 있다

해설 세부 사항 관련 – 여자가 언급하는 문제
여자의 첫 번째 대사에서 약이 떨어졌다(we've just run out of that medication)고 말했으므로 정답은 (D)이다.

> ▸▸ Paraphrasing   대화의 **run out of that medication** → 정답의 **product is not in stock**

34

What does the woman recommend?

(A) Trying a direct shipping service
(B) Reading the back of a box
(C) Communicating by e-mail
(D) Taking another medication

여자는 무엇을 권하는가?

(A) 직배송 서비스를 이용할 것
(B) 상자 뒷면을 읽어볼 것
(C) 이메일로 연락할 것
(D) 다른 약을 복용할 것

어휘   direct 직행[직통]의   shipping 발송, 운송

해설 세부 사항 관련 – 여자가 권하는 것
여자의 두 번째 대사에서 약사 말로는 당분간 비슷한 약을 대신 복용할 수 있다(in the meantime, the pharmacist said that you can take a similar medication instead)고 말했고, 그렇게 하기를 권한다(I'd recommend that)고 말했으므로 정답은 (D)이다.

▸ Paraphrasing   대화의 take a similar medication
→ 정답의 taking another medication

35-37

M-Au **³⁵Ms. Lopez, can I talk to you for a minute?**

W-Am Oh hi, Phillip. What is it?

M-Au **³⁶Uh, since summer began, it's been really warm in the stadium snack bar.** I think it's because of the heat from the hot dog machines.

W-Am Yes, I'm sorry about that. I know it's uncomfortable.

M-Au **³⁷Well, I've been wondering if we could wear sandals instead of the usual close-toed shoes when we're back there.**

W-Am Unfortunately, the close-toed shoes aren't just for appearance—they're actually a safety precaution. But I'll set up an extra fan tomorrow. That should bring some cool air through.

남: 로페즈 씨, 잠시 얘기 좀 할 수 있을까요?
여: 안녕하세요, 필립. 무슨 일인가요?
남: 여름철이 되니 경기장 매점이 정말 더워요. 핫도그 기계에서 나오는 열기 때문인 것 같아요.
여: 네, 죄송해요. 불편하실 거라는 거 알아요.
남: 저, 판매대 뒤쪽에 있을 때는 평소에 신는 앞이 막힌 신발 말고 샌들을 신으면 안 될까요?
여: 아쉽지만 앞이 막힌 신발은 단지 외관 때문만은 아니에요. 사실 안전 조치죠. 하지만 내일 선풍기를 더 설치할게요. 그러면 시원한 공기가 좀 들어올 거예요.

어휘 snack bar 매점, 스낵바   machine 기계
uncomfortable 불편한 instead of ~ 대신에 close-toed shoe 앞이 막힌 신발, 발가락 부분에 트임이 없는 신발
appearance 겉모습, 모양 safety 안전 precaution 예방 조치[수단] set up 설치하다 extra 추가의 fan 선풍기

35

What does the woman imply when she says, "What is it"?

(A) She needs assistance with a task.
(B) She is curious about a machine.
(C) She has time to listen to the man.
(D) She thinks an error has been made.

여자가 "무슨 일인가요"라고 말할 때 암시하는 것은 무엇인가?
(A) 일하는 데 도움이 필요하다.
(B) 기계에 대해 궁금한 것이 있다.
(C) 남자의 말을 들을 시간이 있다.
(D) 오류가 있었다고 생각한다.

해설 화자의 의도 파악 – 무슨 일인지 물은 의도

남자의 첫 번째 대사에서 잠시 얘기 좀 할 수 있는지(can I talk to you for a minute) 묻자 여자가 무슨 일인지(What is it) 되묻고 있는 것으로 보아 남자의 이야기를 들어주겠다는 의도임을 알 수 있다. 따라서 정답은 (C)이다.

36

Where most likely does the conversation take place?

(A) At a clothing store
(B) At a stadium
(C) At an airport
(D) At a supermarket

대화가 일어난 장소는 어디이겠는가?
(A) 옷 가게
(B) 경기장
(C) 공항
(D) 슈퍼마켓

해설 전체 내용 관련 – 대화 장소

남자의 두 번째 대사에서 여름철이 되니 경기장 매점이 정말 덥다(since summer began, it's been really warm in the stadium snack bar)고 했으므로 정답은 (B)이다.

37

What does the man suggest changing?

(A) A dress code
(B) A heating method
(C) An inventory procedure
(D) A rest break policy

남자는 무엇을 바꾸자고 제안하는가?
(A) 복장 규정
(B) 난방 방식
(C) 재고 관리 절차
(D) 휴식 규정

어휘 dress code 복장 규정 heating 난방 method 방식
inventory 재고(품), 재고 목록 procedure 절차, 진행 break 휴식
policy 방침, 규정

해설 세부 사항 관련 – 남자의 제안 사항

남자의 세 번째 대사에서 판매대 뒤쪽에 있을 때는 평소에 신는 앞이 막힌 신발 대신에 샌들을 신어도 되는지(I've been wondering if we could wear sandals instead of the usual close-toed shoes when we're back there)를 묻고 있다. 즉 남자는 복장 규정을 바꾸자고 제안한 것이므로 정답은 (A)이다.

38-40

W-Br Hi, Mr. Ahn. **³⁸This is Haley from Ledward Furniture.** I'm calling to let you know that your new sofa is ready for pickup. Can you come by tomorrow?

M-Au **³⁹Oh, uh—I don't have a car.** Could you bring the sofa out to my house? I live on Bennett Street, just outside of town.

W-Br Sure, we can do that. **⁴⁰But since you're outside of the city limits, there'll be a ten-dollar delivery charge.**

M-Au **⁴⁰That's fine.**

W-Br Great. How does tomorrow at 10 A.M. sound?

여 안녕하세요, 안 씨. 저는 레드워드 퍼니처의 헤일리입니다. 새로 주문하신 소파가 준비되어 있으니 찾아가셔도 된다고 알려드리고자 전화 드립니다. 내일 들르실 수 있으세요?

남 아, 이런. 저는 차가 없어요. 소파를 저희 집으로 갖다 주실 수 있을까요? 저는 도시 바로 외곽에 있는 베네트가에 살아요.

여 물론입니다. 갖다 드릴 수 있어요. 하지만 시외 지역이므로 10달러의 배송비가 있습니다.

남 괜찮습니다.

여 좋습니다. 내일 오전 10시 어떠세요?

어휘 be ready to ~할 준비가 되다 pickup (상품 등의) 픽업, (물건을) 찾으러 감 come by 들르다 bring out 갖고 나가다 limit (경계선 안의) 범위, 구역 delivery charge 배송비

38

Where does the woman most likely work?

(A) At a car dealership
(B) At a moving company
(C) At an interior design firm
(D) At a furniture store

여자는 어디에서 일하겠는가?
(A) 자동차 영업소
(B) 이삿짐 센터
(C) 인테리어 디자인 회사
(D) 가구 매장

어휘 dealership 영업소, 판매 대리점 moving company 이삿짐 운송 회사, 이삿짐 센터

해설 전체 내용 관련 – 여자가 근무하는 곳
여자의 첫 번째 대사에서 레드워드 퍼니처의 헤일리(This is Haley from Ledward Furniture)라고 자신을 소개하고 있는 것으로 보아 여자는 가구 매장 직원임을 알 수 있으므로 정답은 (D)이다.

▸▸ Paraphrasing 대화의 Ledward Furniture
→ 정답의 a furniture store

39

What problem does the man have?

(A) He does not have a vehicle.
(B) He did not order an item.
(C) He is currently not at home.
(D) He did not receive an invoice.

남자의 문제는 무엇인가?
(A) 차가 없다.
(B) 상품을 주문하지 않았다.
(C) 지금 집에 없다.
(D) 송장을 받지 못했다.

어휘 vehicle 차, 탈 것 order 주문하다 item 물품 currently 지금, 현재 receive 받다 invoice 송장

해설 세부 사항 관련 – 남자의 문제
남자는 가구가 준비되어 있으니 찾아가라는 여자의 말에 차가 없다(I don't have a car)면서 집으로 갖다 줄 수 있는지(Could you bring the sofa out to my house) 물었으므로 정답은 (A)이다.

▸▸ Paraphrasing 대화의 don't have a car
→ 정답의 does not have a vehicle

40

What does the man agree to do?

(A) Give driving directions
(B) Wait for a few days
(C) Pay an extra fee
(D) Visit the woman's office

남자는 무엇을 하는 데 동의하는가?
(A) 차로 오는 길 알려주기
(B) 며칠 기다리기
(C) 추가 요금 지불하기
(D) 여자의 사무실 방문하기

어휘 give directions 길을 안내하다 extra fee 추가 요금

해설 세부 사항 관련 – 남자의 동의 사항
여자의 두 번째 대사에서 시외 지역이므로 10달러 배송비가 있다(since you're outside of the city limits, there'll be a ten-dollar delivery charge)고 하자 남자가 괜찮다(That's fine)고 대답했으므로 배송비 추가 지불에 동의했음을 알 수 있다. 따라서 정답은 (C)이다.

41-43

W-Am Hi, Todd, it's Abby. Uh, I'm not feeling well today either. **⁴¹It looks like I won't be able to drive you to the company fundraiser like we'd planned.** Will you still be able to get there?

M-Cn Oh, sure. I'll be fine. Since you told me yesterday that this might happen, I'm prepared. **⁴²But you might want to call one of the organizers and let them know you're not coming.**

W-Am **⁴²Don't worry, I did.**

M-Cn OK, then. I hope you feel better. **⁴³Oh, and I'll save one of the donor appreciation gifts for you, since you already signed up to make a contribution. I'll bring it to your office on Monday.**

여 안녕하세요, 토드. 애비예요. 어, 오늘도 몸이 좋지 않아요. 계획했던 대로 당신을 회사 모금 행사장까지 태워다 줄 수 없을 거 같아요. 그래도 거기에 갈 수 있겠어요?

남 오, 물론이죠. 괜찮아요. 어제 그럴 수도 있다고 얘기하셔서 대비하고 있었죠. 하지만 주최측에 전화해서 불참을 알리는 것이 좋을 것 같아요.

여 걱정 말아요, 연락했어요.

남: 좋아요. 쾌차하기 바라요. 오, 이미 기부를 신청하셨으니 제가 기부자 사은 선물을 하나 챙겨 둘게요. 월요일에 당신 사무실로 갖다 드리죠.

어휘 | fundraiser 모금 행사 prepared 준비[각오]가 되어 있는 might want to ~하는 게 좋을 것이다 organizer 주최자, 조직자 donor 기부자 appreciation gift 사은 선물 sign up 신청[등록]하다 make a contribution 기부하다

41

What is the purpose of the telephone call?

(A) To cancel a plan
(B) To correct a misunderstanding
(C) To ask the man to head a committee
(D) To suggest a type of transport

전화를 건 목적은 무엇인가?
(A) 계획을 취소하기 위해
(B) 오해를 바로잡기 위해
(C) 남자에게 위원회를 이끌어 달라고 요청하기 위해
(D) 교통편을 제안하기 위해

어휘 | cancel 취소하다 correct 수정하다, 바로잡다 misunderstanding 오해 head 이끌다 transport 차량, 이동 (방법) committee 위원회

해설 | 전체 내용 관련 – 전화를 건 목적
여자의 첫 번째 대사에서 몸이 좋지 않아서 계획했던 대로 남자를 회사 모금 행사장까지 태워다 줄 수 없을 것 같다(It looks like I won't be able to drive you to the company fundraiser like we'd planned)고 했으므로 정답은 (A)이다.

42

What does the woman say she has already done?

(A) Chosen an entertainer
(B) Checked a fuel level
(C) Notified an organizer
(D) Looked up a location

여자는 무엇을 이미 했다고 말하는가?
(A) 연예인 선정하기
(B) 잔류 연료 확인하기
(C) 주최측에 통지하기
(D) 장소 찾아보기하기

어휘 | choose 고르다 entertainer 예능인, 연예인 fuel 연료 level 양, 수준 notify 알리다, 통지하다 look up ~을 찾아보다 location 장소, 위치

해설 | 세부 사항 관련 – 여자가 이미 한 일
남자의 첫 번째 대사에서 주최측에 전화해서 불참을 알리는 것이 좋을 것 같다 (you might want to call one of the organizers and let them know you're not coming)고 제안하자 여자가 걱정 말라면서 연락했다(Don't worry, I did)고 대답했으므로 정답은 (C)이다.

▸▸ Paraphrasing | 대화의 call ~ and let them know
→ 정답의 Notified

43

What will the man bring to the woman?

(A) A guest list
(B) A sign-up sheet
(C) An expense report
(D) A thank-you gift

남자는 여자에게 무엇을 갖다 줄 것인가?
(A) 손님 목록
(B) 신청서
(C) 지출품의서
(D) 사은 선물

해설 | 세부 사항 관련 – 남자가 여자에게 줄 것
남자의 마지막 대사에서 이미 기부를 신청했으니 기부자 사은 선물 하나를 챙겨 두었다가(I'll save one of the donor appreciation gifts for you, since you already signed up to make a contribution) 월요일에 사무실로 갖다 주겠다(I'll bring it to your office on Monday)고 했으므로 정답은 (D)이다.

▸▸ Paraphrasing | 대화의 appreciation gifts
→ 정답의 thank-you gift

44-46 3인 대화

M-Cn OK, I'm glad we could talk about the Bellmont Plaza design project. **44Once again, I'd like to welcome Natalie on board Richard's design team...**

W-Am Thank you. I'm excited to help the team complete this project. **45I spent yesterday familiarizing myself with the plans.**

M-Cn Good. Richard, what would you like Natalie to work on first?

M-Au **46Well, I'd like help choosing some potted plants to add to the lobby.** We're starting to come close to our budget limit, so we need something inexpensive.

W-Am OK. I'll come up with a few options that would harmonize with the lobby's other design elements.

남1: 알겠습니다. 벨몬트 플라자 디자인 프로젝트에 관해 얘기 나누게 되어 기쁘군요. 리차드 씨가 이끄는 디자인 팀에 나탈리 씨가 합류한 것을 다시 한 번 환영합니다.
여: 감사합니다. 프로젝트를 완수할 수 있도록 팀을 돕게 되어 기쁩니다. 어제는 기획을 숙지하는 데 시간을 보냈어요.
남1: 잘했군요. 리차드 씨, 나탈리 씨가 먼저 어떤 일에 착수했으면 하세요?
남2: 음, 로비에 들여놓을 화분을 고르는 일을 도와 주셨으면 좋겠네요. 예산 한도에 거의 다다르고 있어서 저렴한 것이 필요해요.
여: 알겠습니다. 로비의 다른 디자인 요소들과 조화를 이룰 수 있는 몇 가지 안을 찾아보겠습니다.

44

What are the speakers mainly discussing?

(A) A problem with some landscaping
(B) A new team member starting work
(C) A strategy for a team-building seminar
(D) A delivery date for some furnishings

화자들은 주로 무엇에 대해 이야기하는가?

(A) 조경에 관한 문제
(B) **일을 시작한 신규 팀원**
(C) 팀워크 세미나를 위한 전략
(D) 가구 배송 일자

어휘 landscaping 조경 strategy 전략 team-building 팀의
결속력을 다져주는 furnishings 비품, 세간, 가구

해설 전체 내용 관련 – 대화의 주제

첫 번째 남자의 첫 번째 대사에서 리차드 씨가 이끄는 디자인 팀에 나탈리 씨가
합류한 것을 다시 한 번 환영한다(Once again I'd like to welcome Natalie
on board Richard's design team)고 했으므로 정답은 (B)이다.

> ▸ Paraphrasing 대화의 welcome Natalie on board
> Richard's design team
> → 정답의 new team member starting work

45

What does the woman say she did yesterday?

(A) Began preparing a slide show
(B) Completed some request forms
(C) Introduced herself to colleagues
(D) Studied some project materials

여자는 어제 무엇을 했다고 말하는가?

(A) 슬라이드 쇼를 준비하기 시작했다.
(B) 요청서를 작성했다.
(C) 동료들에게 자기 소개를 했다.
(D) **프로젝트 자료를 검토했다.**

어휘 prepare 준비하다 request 요청 form 양식 introduce
소개하다 colleague 동료 material 자료

해설 세부 사항 관련 – 여자가 어제 한 일

여자의 첫 번째 대사에서 어제는 기획을 숙지하는 데 시간을 보냈다(I spent
yesterday familiarizing myself with the plans)고 말했으므로 정답은 (D)
이다.

> ▸ Paraphrasing 대화의 familiarizing myself with the plans
> → 정답의 Studied some project materials

46

What does Richard ask for help with?

(A) Presenting a budget
(B) Selecting some plants
(C) Investigating flooring options
(D) Distributing a memo

리차드 씨는 어떤 일에 도움을 요청하는가?

(A) 예산 제출하기
(B) **식물 고르기**
(C) 바닥재 선택안 조사하기
(D) 메모 회람하기

어휘 present 제시[제출]하다 select 선정하다 investigate 조사하다
flooring 바닥재 memo 메모 distribute 회람하다

해설 세부 사항 관련 – 리차드 씨가 도움을 요청하는 일

두 번째 남자의 첫 번째 대사에서 로비에 들여놓을 화분을 고르는 일을 도와
줬으면 한다(I'd like help choosing some potted plants to add to the
lobby)고 했으므로 정답은 (B)이다.

> ▸ Paraphrasing 대화의 choosing some potted plants
> → 정답의 Selecting some plants

47-49

W-Br	Hello, this is Lynnette from online banking customer support.
M-Au	[47]Hi. I can't figure out how to send money electronically to my friend who lives in another state. I just keep getting a message that says "Error 2549".
W-Br	[48]Ah, that means that your friend's account is no longer active. You should verify the information with him or her.
M-Au	Oh, OK. That was so simple. Is there a way for me to find out the meaning of error messages by myself?
W-Br	[49]Well, I can give you a link to a page that explains them. But we're going to change to a more user-friendly system soon, so you might not need it.

여: 안녕하세요, 온라인 뱅킹 고객지원팀의 리네트입니다.

남: 안녕하세요, 다른 주에 살고 있는 친구에게 온라인으로 돈을 좀
보내려고 하는데 방법을 모르겠어요. 그냥 '오류 2549'라는 메시지만
계속 나와요.

여: 아, 그건 친구분의 계좌가 더 이상 활성 상태가 아니라는 의미입니다.
그분께 정보를 확인해 보셔야 합니다.

남: 오, 알겠습니다. 아주 간단한 거였군요. 저 혼자서 오류 메시지의
의미를 알아낼 방법이 있나요?

여: 음, 오류 코드에 대한 설명이 나와 있는 웹페이지 링크를 보내 드릴게요.
하지만 사용자가 더 쉽게 사용할 수 있는 시스템으로 곧 교체할
예정이라 필요 없으실 듯합니다.

47

What is the man unable to do?

(A) Join a rewards program
(B) Update an address
(C) View a balance
(D) Transfer some money

남자는 무엇을 할 수 없는가?

(A) 보상 프로그램에 가입하기
(B) 주소 업데이트하기
(C) 잔액 확인하기
(D) 송금하기

어휘 rewards program 보상[포상] 프로그램 update 최신 정보를
알려주다, 갱신하다 view 보다 balance 잔고, 잔액 transfer
이체하다

해설 세부 사항 관련 – 남자가 할 수 없는 것

남자의 첫 번째 대사에서 다른 주에 살고 있는 친구에게 온라인으로 돈을 좀
보내려고 하는데 방법을 모르겠다(I can't figure out how to send money
electronically to my friend who lives in another state)고 말하며 '오
류 2549'라는 메시지만 계속 나온다(I just keep getting a message that
says "Error 2549")고 했다. 따라서 송금이 안 된다는 의미이므로 정답은 (D)
이다.

▸▸ Paraphrasing 대화의 send money → 정답의 Transfer money

48

What does the woman say caused the problem?

(A) A promotional period has ended.
(B) An account has been closed.
(C) A message was deleted.
(D) A Web browser is out-of-date.

여자는 문제의 원인이 무엇이라고 말하는가?

(A) 홍보 기간이 끝났다.
(B) 계좌가 폐쇄되었다.
(C) 메시지가 삭제되었다.
(D) 웹브라우저가 오래된 것이다.

어휘 promotional 홍보의, 판촉용의 period 기간 delete 삭제하다
out-of-date 시대에 뒤떨어진, 구식의

해설 세부 사항 관련 – 문제의 원인

남자가 온라인 송금이 안 된다고 하자 여자는 친구의 계좌가 더 이상 활성 상태
가 아니라는 의미(that means that your friend's account is no longer
active)라고 알려주고 있다. 따라서 문제의 원인은 계좌가 폐쇄되어 있기 때문
이므로 정답은 (B)이다.

▸▸ Paraphrasing 대화의 account is no longer active
→ 정답의 An account has been closed.

49

What does the woman offer to do for the man?

(A) Provide a Web page link
(B) Explain a registration process
(C) Put his information into a system
(D) Reduce a service charge

여자는 남자에게 무엇을 해 주겠다고 하는가?

(A) 웹페이지 링크 제공하기
(B) 등록 절차 설명하기
(C) 남자의 정보를 시스템에 입력하기
(D) 서비스 비용 낮추기

어휘 registration 등록 process 절차 put into (글자를) 쓰다,
입력하다 reduce 줄이다 charge 요금

해설 세부 사항 관련 – 여자의 제안 사항

여자의 마지막 대사에서 오류 코드에 대한 설명이 나와 있는 웹페이지 링크를
보내겠다(I can give you a link to a page that explains them)고 했으므
로 정답은 (A)이다.

▸▸ Paraphrasing 대화의 give you a link to a page
→ Provide a Web page link

50-52

M-Cn Yoon-Jung, I'm glad I ran into you. **50I
just read your interview with that tennis
champion—it was fascinating!**

W-Br Thanks! It was fun to do. She's very
charming—and she picked a great
restaurant to meet in. I'm proud of the
piece.

M-Cn I'm sure it'll lead to more assignments in
the future too. **51Who are you going to talk
to next?**

W-Br Well, that's not decided yet. But yesterday
I had the opportunity to speak with Axel
Schneider, the classical musician.

M-Cn Wow, I'm a huge fan of his. **52I'd love to
sit down with you sometime and hear all
about it. Actually,** I saw a café around the
corner...

W-Br Sure, let's go!

남:	윤정 씨, 만나서 반갑네요. **테니스 선수권 대회 우승자 인터뷰 글을 방금 읽었어요. 흥미롭더군요!**
여:	고마워요! 인터뷰는 재미있었어요. 아주 매력적인 사람이더군요. 인터뷰 장소로 아주 멋진 식당을 골랐던데요. 저도 그 글을 쓰고 뿌듯했어요.
남:	덕분에 앞으로 더 많은 일을 맡게 될 기리 믿어요. **다음에는 누구를 인터뷰할 예정인가요?**
여:	음, 아직 결정되지 않았어요. 하지만 어제는 클래식 음악가인 악셀 슈나이더와 이야기할 기회가 있었죠.
남:	와, 제가 그분의 열혈 팬이에요. 언제 한번 자리 잡고 앉아서 그 이야기를 전부 듣고 싶네요. **실은 바로 앞에 카페가 있던데요…**
여:	좋아요, 가죠!

어휘	run into 우연히 만나다 fascinating 흥미로운 charming 매력적인 pick 고르다 be proud of ~를 자랑스러워하다 piece 기사 lead to ~로 이어지다 assignment 과제, 임무 decide 결정하다 opportunity 기회 classical 고전 음악의 huge 엄청난 around the corner 아주 가까운

50

What did the woman recently do?

(A) She built a recreational facility.
(B) She accepted a promotion.
(C) She conducted an interview.
(D) She played on a sports team.

여자는 최근에 무엇을 했는가?
(A) 위락 시설을 건설했다.
(B) 승진을 수락했다.
(C) 인터뷰를 진행했다.
(D) 스포츠 구단에서 뛰었다.

어휘 recreational 휴양의, 오락의 facility 시설 accept 수락하다 promotion 진급, 승진 conduct 수행하다, 실시하다

해설 세부 사항 관련 – 여자가 최근에 한 일
남자의 첫 번째 대사에서 당신이 쓴 테니스 선수권 대회 우승자 인터뷰 글을 방금 읽었는데 흥미로웠다(I just read your interview with that tennis champion—it was fascinating)고 말했으므로 정답은 (C)이다.

51

What does the man ask the woman about?

(A) Her other skills
(B) Her reading habits
(C) Her next assignment
(D) Her food preferences

남자는 여자에게 무엇에 대해 질문하는가?
(A) 다른 역량
(B) 독서 습관
(C) 다음 업무
(D) 선호하는 음식

어휘 skill 기술, 역량 habit 습관 preference 선호

해설 세부 사항 관련 – 여자가 질문한 것
남자의 두 번째 대사에서 다음에는 누구를 인터뷰할 예정인지(Who are you going to talk to next) 질문하며 다음 인터뷰 대상에 대해 물었으므로 정답은 (C)이다.

52

What does the man mean when he says, "I saw a café around the corner"?

(A) He hopes the woman can talk now.
(B) He would like to have a snack before an event.
(C) A photo needs a better background.
(D) It is too cold to wait outdoors.

남자가 "실은 바로 앞에 카페가 있던데요"라고 말하는 의미는 무엇인가?
(A) 여자가 지금 이야기해 주길 바란다.
(B) 행사에 앞서 간식을 먹고 싶어 한다.
(C) 사진에 더 좋은 배경이 필요하다.
(D) 밖에서 기다리기에는 너무 춥다.

어휘 background 배경 too ~ to 너무 ~해서 …할 수 없다 outdoors 옥외에서, 야외에서

해설 화자의 의도 파악 – 바로 앞에 카페가 있다고 말한 의도
인용문 바로 앞 문장에서 남자가 언제 한번 자리 잡고 앉아서 그 이야기를 전부 듣고 싶다(I'd love to sit down with you sometime and hear all about it)고 했으므로, 지금 당장 카페에 가서 이야기를 듣고 싶다는 의미임을 알 수 있다. 따라서 정답은 (A)이다.

53-55

W-Am	Bingwen, I saw you speaking with the sales representative from Fenstoke earlier. **[53]Do they have some tools that are worth investing in before we have the team break ground on the warehouse for Drexler Motors?**
M-Au	Yes, I think so. I'm especially impressed with their new hammer drill. You can see it in this brochure.
W-Am	Oh, OK. What do you like about it?
M-Au	**[54]Well, it has quite a lot of force, which would really speed up the concrete testing process.**
W-Am	Hmm… it looks like it's also relatively expensive. **[55]How about asking the sales representative for a price reduction in exchange for placing a large order?**
M-Au	That's a good idea.

여:	빙웬, 오전에 펜스톡 사 영업 사원과 이야기하는 것을 봤어요. **드렉슬러 모터스 창고 공사에 착수하라고 팀에 지시하기 전에 투자할 만한 가치가 있는 연장들이 있던가요?**
남:	네, 있는 것 같아요. 새로 나온 착암기가 특히 인상적이었어요. 이 소책자에서 볼 수 있어요.
여:	알겠어요. 어떤 점이 마음에 드나요?
남:	**음, 힘이 꽤 좋아요. 콘크리트 테스트 속도를 아주 높여 줄 겁니다.**
여:	음… 비교적 비싼 것 같군요. **대량 주문 조건으로 가격을 인하할 수 있는지 영업 사원에게 물어보는 게 어때요?**
남:	좋은 생각이네요.

Test 6

어휘 sales representative 판매 사원, 영업 사원 tool 연장, 공구 be worth -ing ~할 가치가 있다 invest in ~에 투자하다 break ground (건물) 공사를 시작하다, 착공[기공]하다 warehouse 창고 be impressed with ~에 감명 받다[깊은 인상을 받다] hammer drill 해머 드릴, 착암기 brochure 소책자 force 힘 speed up 속도를 높이다 concrete 콘크리트 testing process 시험 과정 relatively 비교적 price reduction 가격 인하[할인] in exchange for ~ 대신으로, ~와의 교환으로 place a large order 대량 주문하다

53

Who most likely are the speakers?

(A) Auto mechanics

(B) Electronics vendors

(C) Warehouse clerks

(D) Construction supervisors

화자들은 누구이겠는가?

(A) 자동차 정비공

(B) 전자 제품 판매자

(C) 창고 직원

(D) **공사 감독관**

어휘 auto 자동차 mechanic 정비공 electronics 전자 제품 vendor 판매[공급] 업체 clerk 점원 construction 공사 supervisor 감독관

해설 전체 내용 관련 – 화자들의 신분
여자의 첫 번째 대사에서 남자에게 드렉슬러 모터스 창고 공사에 착수하라고 팀에 지시하기 전에 투자할 만한 가치가 있는 연장이 있는지(Do they have some tools that are worth investing in before we have the team break ground on the warehouse for Drexler Motors)를 묻고 있다. 따라서 화자들이 공사 감독자임을 알 수 있으므로 정답은 (D)이다.

54

What does the man like about the product?

(A) It passed a special safety test.

(B) It uses energy efficiently.

(C) It is powerful.

(D) It is lightweight.

남자는 제품의 어떤 점을 마음에 들어 하는가?

(A) 특별 안전성 테스트를 통과했다.

(B) 연료를 효율적으로 사용한다.

(C) **강력하다.**

(D) 가볍다.

어휘 safety test 안전성 테스트[시험] efficiently 효율적으로 lightweight 가벼운

해설 세부 사항 관련 – 남자가 신제품에서 마음에 드는 점
남자의 두 번째 대사에서 신제품이 힘이 꽤 좋다면서 콘크리트 테스트 속도를 아주 높여 줄 것(it has quite a lot of force, which would really speed up the concrete testing process)이라고 했으므로 정답은 (C)이다.

▶ **Paraphrasing** 대화의 **has quite a lot of force**
→ 정답의 **is powerful**

55

What does the woman propose?

(A) Making a comparative chart

(B) Placing an advance order

(C) Negotiating a lower price

(D) Consulting a technical expert

여자는 무엇을 제안하는가?

(A) 대조표 만들기

(B) 예약 주문하기

(C) **더 저렴한 가격으로 협상하기**

(D) 기술 전문가와 상의하기

어휘 comparative 비교의 advance order 예약 주문 negotiate 협상하다 consult 상담하다, 상의하다 expert 전문가

해설 세부 사항 관련 – 여자의 제안 사항
대화 후반부에서 여자가 가격이 비싼 것 같다면서 대량 주문을 하면 가격을 인하할 수 있는지 영업 사원에게 물어보라(How about asking the sales representative for a price reduction in exchange for placing a large order)고 제안하고 있으므로 정답은 (C)이다.

▶ **Paraphrasing** 대화의 **a price reduction**
→ 정답의 **a lower price**

56-58 3인 대화

M-Cn	Hello, Ms. Gibson. **56I'm Eric Kawakami. So, what motivated you to apply for the position of accounting manager here?**
W-Br	**57I'd really like to help The Brunford Conservancy's cause. I feel strongly about the importance of protecting wild animals.**
M-Cn	I'm glad to hear that. Now, if you're hired, you'll be working with Ron here. Is there anything you'd like to ask, Ron?
M-Au	Yes, thank you. Ms. Gibson, what can you bring to the position that other candidates can't?
W-Br	**58Well, everyone in my field is very careful and thorough, but I think I have an advantage when it comes to adapting quickly to change. I enjoy the challenge of learning a new system.**

남1: 안녕하세요, 깁슨 씨. 에릭 카와카미입니다. 자, 저희 회사의 회계팀장직에 지원하신 동기가 무엇인가요?

여: 브런포드 보존위원회의 활동을 진심으로 돕고 싶기 때문입니다. 야생동물 보호의 중요성에 대해 확고한 신념이 있습니다.

남1: 그 말을 들으니 기쁘군요. 자, 만약 채용되신다면, 여기 론과 함께 일하게 되실 겁니다. 뭐 물어보고 싶은 것 있어요, 론?

남2: 네, 감사합니다. 깁슨 씨, 그 자리에 지원한 다른 지원자들과 어떤 점이 차별화된다고 생각하세요?

여: 글쎄요, 제 분야의 모든 분들이 아주 신중하고 철저하지만, 변화에 재빨리 적응하는 것이 제 강점이라고 생각합니다. 저는 새로운 시스템을 익히는 일을 즐깁니다.

어휘   motivate 동기를 부여하다   apply for ~에 지원하다, 신청하다   position (일)자리   conservancy 관리[보존] 위원회   cause (사회적인) 운동, 대의명분   protect 보호하다   wild animal 야생동물   hired 고용된   bring to ~로 가지고 오다   candidate 지원자, 후보자   field 분야   thorough 철저한, 완벽한   advantage 장점, 이점   when it comes to ~에 관해서는, ~의 문제라면   adapt to ~에 적응하다   challenge 난제, 도전

56

Who most likely is Mr. Kawakami?

(A) A hiring manager at an organization
(B) An admissions officer for a graduate program
(C) A reporter for a business journal
(D) A participant in an open forum

카와카미 씨는 누구이겠는가?

(A) 기관의 채용 관리자
(B) 대학원 과정 입학사정관
(C) 비즈니스 잡지 기자
(D) 공개 토론회 참가자

어휘   hiring manager 채용 관리자   organization 기관, 조직   admissions officer 입학사정관   graduate program 대학원 과정   reporter 기자   journal 신문, 잡지   participant 참가자   open forum 공개 토론회

해설   전체 내용 관련 - 카와카미 씨의 신분
대화 초반부에서 남자가 자신을 에릭 카와카미(I'm Eric Kawakami)라고 소개하며, 여자에게 회계팀장직에 지원한 동기가 무엇인지(what motivated you to apply for the position of accounting manager here)를 묻고 있으므로 채용 면접 상황임을 알 수 있다. 따라서 카와카미 씨는 채용 관리자이므로 정답은 (A)이다.

57

What does the woman say she hopes to do?

(A) Oversee a large group of people
(B) Take advantage of new technology
(C) Experience a casual office culture
(D) Work in service of a certain cause

여자는 무엇을 하기를 바란다고 말하는가?

(A) 많은 사람들을 감독하기
(B) 새로운 기술을 이용하기
(C) 자유분방한 사내 문화 경험하기
(D) 특정 명분을 위해 활동하는 곳에서 근무하기

어휘   oversee 감독하다   take advantage of ~을 이용하다   experience 경험하다   casual 격식을 차리지 않는   service 업무, 사업, 공헌

해설   세부 사항 관련 - 여자가 바라는 일
여자의 첫 번째 대사에서 야생동물 보호의 중요성에 대해 확고한 신념이 있으며, 브런포드 보존위원회의 활동을 돕고자 한다(I'd really like to help The Brunford Conservancy's cause. I feel strongly about the importance of protecting wild animals)고 했으므로 정답은 (D)이다.

▸▸ Paraphrasing   대화의 help The Brunford Conservancy's cause → 정답의 Work in service of a certain cause

58

What does the woman say is her strong point?

(A) Attention to detail
(B) Flexibility
(C) Creativity
(D) Trustworthiness

여자는 자신이 강점이 무엇이라고 말하는가?

(A) 세심한 주의력
(B) 적응성
(C) 창의력
(D) 신뢰감

어휘   attention to ~에 대한 주의   detail 세부 사항   flexibility 적응성, 유연성   trustworthiness 신뢰감

해설   세부 사항 관련 - 여자의 강점
대화 후반부에서 여자가 자신의 강점은 변화에 빨리 적응하는 것(I think I have an advantage when it comes to adapting quickly to change)이라고 했으므로 정답은 (B)이다.

▸▸ Paraphrasing   대화의 adapting quickly to change → 정답의 Flexibility

59-61

M-Cn	Hi, is this Noreen Ralpert? [59]**This is Hank Altman with Daisy Maps, the online map service. I'm calling because one of our users has claimed that the listing for your business is no longer correct.** [60]**Can you confirm that Ralpert Dry Cleaning has closed down?**
W-Am	[60]**Yes, that's right.** We went out of business last month. You can remove our listing from your site.
M-Cn	Actually, we like to leave them up for some time in this situation. Otherwise, users might think a business is still running but just not listed. [61]**So I'll insert some text into your listing explaining that you've closed.** The change should become visible tomorrow.

남: 안녕하세요. 노린 랠퍼트 씨인가요? 저는 온라인 지도 제공 서비스 업체인 데이지 맵스의 행크 알트먼이라고 합니다. 저희 사용자 중 한 분께서 귀사의 항목은 이제는 맞지 않다고 하셔서 전화 드립니다. 랠퍼트 드라이클리닝이 폐업했는지 확인해 주실 수 있나요?

여: 네. 맞습니다. 지난달에 폐업했어요. 사이트에서 저희 업체는 삭제하셔도 됩니다.

남: 사실 이런 경우에는 당분간 그대로 두는 게 좋겠군요. 그렇지 않으면 사용자들은 매장이 아직 영업 중인데 명부에서 누락됐다고 생각할 수 있거든요. 그러니 폐업했다는 설명을 귀사 항목에 넣겠습니다. 변경 사항은 내일부터 보일 겁니다.

어휘	claim 주장하다 listing 목록[명단] 상의 위치[항목] no longer 더 이상 ~ 아닌 correct 정확한 confirm 확인해 주다 close down 폐쇄하다 go out of business 폐업하다 remove 제거하다 situation 상황 otherwise 그렇지 않으면 run 계속하다 list 리스트[목록/명단]에 포함시키다 visible 눈에 보이는

59

What are the speakers discussing?

(A) The focus of an advertisement
(B) The cover of a pamphlet
(C) A claim in a blog post
(D) A listing on an online map

화자들은 무엇에 대해 이야기하는가?
(A) 광고의 주안점
(B) 팸플릿 표지
(C) 블로그 게시물에 나온 요구 사항
(D) **온라인 지도상의 명부**

어휘 focus 주안점 advertisement 광고 cover 표지 pamphlet
팸플릿, 책자 claim 요구, 주장 post 게시물

해설 전체 내용 관련 – 대화의 주제
남자의 첫 번째 대사에서 온라인 지도 제공 서비스 업체의 직원이라고 소개한
후(This is Hank Altman with Daisy Maps, the online map service) 사
용자 중 한 명이 귀사의 항목은 이제는 맞지 않다고 해서 전화했다(I'm calling
because one of our users has claimed that the listing for your
business is no longer correct)고 말했으므로 정답은 (D)이다.

60

What does the woman confirm has changed about a dry cleaner?

(A) Its operating status
(B) Its phone number
(C) Its specialty
(D) Its owner

드라이클리닝 업체에 대해 여자가 확인해 준 변경 사항은 무엇인가?
(A) **영업 상태**
(B) 전화번호
(C) 전문 분야
(D) 소유주

어휘 operating 경영상의 status 상태 specialty 전문 owner
소유주

해설 세부 사항 관련 – 여자가 확인해 준 변경 사항
남자의 첫 번째 대사에서 랠퍼트 드라이클리닝이 폐업했는지 확인해 줄 수 있
냐(Can you confirm that Ralpert Dry Cleaning has closed down)고
질문하자 여자가 그렇다(Yes, that's right)고 말했으므로 정답은 (A)이다.

▸▸ Paraphrasing 대화의 **has closed down**
→ 정답의 **operating status**

61

What does the man say he will do?

(A) Remove a section from a text
(B) Make the size of some words larger
(C) Add a note to some contents
(D) Rearrange the layout of a page

남자는 무엇을 하겠다고 말하는가?
(A) 글의 일부 삭제하기
(B) 일부 글자 크기 확대하기
(C) **일부 콘텐츠에 주석 추가하기**
(D) 페이지 배치 조정하기

어휘 remove 제거하다 section 부분 text 글 add to ~에 추가하다
content 내용 rearrange 재배열하다 layout 레이아웃[배치]

해설 세부 사항 관련 – 남자가 하겠다고 하는 것
남자의 두 번째 대사에서 폐업했다는 설명을 해당 항목에 넣겠다(I'll insert
some text into your listing explaining that you've closed)고 했으므로
정답은 (C)이다.

▸▸ Paraphrasing 대화의 **insert some text into your listing**
→ 정답의 **Add a note to some contents**

62-64 대화 + 공지

M-Au	Hi. I recently started working here at the Technology Complex, but the parking area is still under construction. **62And, uh... it's hard to find parking spots nearby...**
W-Br	Right. Because of the construction, the company provides a shuttle bus service connecting the head office with this complex. You know about that, right?
M-Au	**63Yes, the building where I work is linked by Route Three, but the first bus leaves at 6:30 A.M. It's too late for me.**
W-Br	**63Ah, here's a notice about service upgrades—that bus now starts operating at 6 A.M.**
M-Au	Oh, that works.
W-Br	Good. **64The buses are comfortable, and they have community newsletters on hand for riders to browse through.**

남:	안녕하세요, 최근에 테크놀로지 콤플렉스에 입사했는데, 주차장이 여전히 공사 중이네요. **그리고, 음, 근처에서 주차 공간을 찾기가 어려워요….**
여:	맞아요. 공사 때문에 회사에서 본사와 이 복합 단지를 연결하는 셔틀 버스 서비스를 제공하고 있어요. 그건 알죠, 그렇죠?
남:	네, 제가 근무하고 있는 건물은 3호선과 연결되는데, 첫 버스가 오전 6시 30분에 출발해요. 그런데 그건 너무 늦어서요.
여:	아, 여기 서비스 개선 사항에 관한 공고가 있네요. 그 버스가 지금은 오전 6시에 운행을 시작해요.
남:	오, 그럼 됐네요.
여:	잘됐네요. 버스는 편안한 데다, 지역 소식지가 구비돼 있어 탑승객들이 훑어볼 수 있거든요.

Test 6

어휘 complex 복합 건물, (건물) 단지 parking area 주차
공간(= parking spot) (under) construction 건축
(중인), 공사 (중인) connect 연결하다 head office
본사 link 연결하다 notice 안내, 공고 upgrade 개선
(사항) operate 운영하다, 운행하다 comfortable 편안한
community 커뮤니티, 지역사회 newsletter 뉴스레터,
소식지 on hand 수중에 (있는), 구할 수 있는 browse
through ~을 훑어보다

Notice
New earlier shuttle departures!

Route	Destination Building	First departure
One	Martell	6:30 A.M.
Two	Spinatak	6:45 A.M.
63Three	Bayareth	6:00 A.M.
Four	Rossmore	6:15 A.M.

공고
셔틀 버스가 더 일찍 출발합니다!

노선	목적지 빌딩	첫 출발 시간
1	마르텔	오전 6시 30분
2	스피내택	오전 6시 45분
3	바야레스	오전 6시
4	로스모어	오전 6시 15분

62
According to the man, what is difficult?

(A) Logging on to a staff e-mail program
(B) Obtaining an employee access card
(C) Finding nearby parking spaces
(D) Using a renovated office building

남자에 따르면, 어떤 점이 어려운가?
(A) 직원 이메일 프로그램에 접속하기
(B) 직원 출입 카드 얻기
(C) 근처에서 주차 공간 찾기
(D) 개조된 사무실 건물 이용하기

어휘 log on to ~에 접속하다 obtain 얻다 employee 직원 access
출입 renovate 개조하다

해설 세부 사항 관련 – 남자가 어려워하는 점
남자의 첫 번째 대사에서 근처에서 주차 공간을 찾기 어렵다(it's hard to find
parking spots nearby)고 했으므로 정답은 (C)이다.

▸▸ Paraphrasing 대화의 parking spots nearby
→ 정답의 nearby parking spaces

63
Look at the graphic. Which building does the man most
likely work in?

(A) Martell
(B) Spinatak
(C) Bayareth
(D) Rossmore

시각 정보에 의하면, 남자는 어느 건물에서 일하겠는가?
(A) 마르텔
(B) 스피내택
(C) 바야레스
(D) 로스모어

해설 시각 정보 연계 – 남자가 근무하는 건물
대화 중반부에서 남자는 자신이 근무하고 있는 건물은 3호선과 연결되는데,
첫 버스가 오전 6시 30분에 출발해서 늦다(the building where I work
is linked by Route Three, but the first bus leaves at 6:30 A.M. It's
too late for me)고 하자 여자는 서비스 개선 사항에 관한 공고가 있다며,
그 버스가 지금은 6시에 운행을 시작한다(here's a notice about service
upgrades—that bus now starts operating at 6 A.M.)고 했다. 시
각 정보에 따르면 6시에 출발하는 3호선의 목적지는 바야레스(Three
Bayareth 6:00 A.M.)이므로 정답은 (C)이다.

64
What does the woman say shuttle bus passengers can
do?

(A) Enjoy views of the city
(B) Connect to the Internet
(C) Charge electronic devices
(D) Read local newsletters

여자는 셔틀버스 승객들이 무엇을 할 수 있다고 말하는가?
(A) 시 경치 감상하기
(B) 인터넷에 접속하기
(C) 전자 장비 충전하기
(D) 지역 소식지 읽기

어휘 view 경치 connect to ~와 연결하다 charge 충전하다
electronic 전자의 device 장치 local 지역의, 지방의

해설 세부 사항 관련 – 버스 승객들이 할 수 있는 것
여자의 마지막 대사에서 버스는 편안한 데다, 지역 소식지가 구비돼 있어 탑
승객들이 훑어볼 수 있다(The buses are comfortable, and they have
community newsletters on hand for riders to browse through)고 했
으므로 정답은 (D)이다.

▸▸ Paraphrasing 대화의 community newsletters
→ 정답의 local newsletters
대화의 browse through → 정답의 Read

65-67 대화 + 표

W-Br Excuse me—do you sell vinegar for
cleaning purposes? 65I heard that it's a
good option if you want to clean without
releasing harsh chemicals into the
environment.

M-Cn Well, plain white vinegar will work for almost anything. We have a few different brands over here. What are you planning to clean?

W-Br **66Food storage jars.** Uh, do you know how strong of a solution I should use?

M-Cn I think glass requires a high vinegar concentration. Ah yes, there's a chart on the back label of this bottle.

W-Br OK, I'll take two. **67And I'd better get some scrubbing sponges too.** Where can I find those?

여: 실례합니다, 세척용 식초 파세요? 유독 화학물질을 환경에 배출하지 않고 세척하는 데 식초가 좋은 방법이라고 들었어요.

남: 글쎄요, 일반적인 흰 식초로도 거의 대부분 세척돼요. 여기 여러 가지 브랜드들이 있어요. 뭘 세척하시려고요?

여: **식품 저장 용기요.** 용액을 얼마큼의 농도로 사용해야 하는지 아세요?

남: 유리에는 고농도 식초가 필요할 거예요. 아, 네, 이 병 뒤쪽 라벨에 표가 있어요.

여: 두 개 주세요. **수세미도 좀 사야겠어요.** 수세미는 어디 있나요?

어휘 vinegar 식초 purpose 목적 option 선택지 release into ~를 배출하다 harsh 유독한 chemicals 화학 물질 environment 환경 plain 평범한 work 효과가 있다 storage jar 저장용 병 solution 용액 strong 진한, 강한 concentration (용액의) 농축 had better ~하는 편이 낫다 scrubbing sponge 수세미

Item to Be Cleaned	Vinegar to Use Per Gallon of Water
Solid Flooring	1/2 cup
Refrigerators	1 cup
Windows	2 cups
66Food Jars	1 gallon

용도	물 1갤런당 식초 사용량
단단한 바닥	1/2컵
냉장고	1컵
창문	2컵
음식 저장용 병	1갤런

65

Why does the woman want to clean with vinegar?

(A) It costs less than other products.
(B) It is environmentally-friendly.
(C) It is widely available.
(D) It can be used on various surfaces.

여자가 식초로 세척하고 싶어 하는 이유는 무엇인가?
(A) 다른 제품들보다 더 저렴하다.
(B) 환경 친화적이다.
(C) 어디서든 구하기 쉽다.
(D) 다양한 표면에 사용할 수 있다.

어휘 cost (비용이) 들다 product 제품 environmentally-friendly 환경 친화적인 widely 널리 available 구할 수 있는 various 다양한 surface 표면

해설 세부 사항 관련 – 여자가 식초로 세척하기 원하는 이유

여자의 첫 번째 대사에서 유독 화학물질을 환경에 배출하지 않고 세척하는 데 식초가 좋은 방법이라고 들었다(I heard that it's a good option if you want to clean without releasing harsh chemicals into the environment)고 했으므로 정답은 (B)이다.

▶ Paraphrasing 대화의 **without releasing harsh chemicals into the environment**
→ 정답의 **environmentally-friendly**

66

Look at the graphic. How much vinegar should the woman mix with a gallon of water?

(A) 1/2 cup
(B) 1 cup
(C) 2 cups
(D) 1 gallon

시각 정보에 의하면, 여자는 물 1갤런에 식초를 얼마큼 희석해야 하는가?
(A) 1/2컵
(B) 1컵
(C) 2컵
(D) 1갤런

해설 시각 정보 연계 – 물 1갤런에 희석시켜야 할 식초의 양

여자의 두 번째 대사에서 식초로 식품 저장 용기(Food storage jars)를 세척하고 싶어 한다는 것을 알 수 있으며, 시각 정보에 따르면 식품 저장 용기를 세척할 때는 식초 1갤런(Food Jars 1 gallon)을 섞어야 하므로 정답은 (D)이다.

67

What does the woman decide to buy in addition to vinegar?

(A) Some cleaning sponges
(B) Some rubber gloves
(C) A dishtowel
(D) A measuring cup

여자는 식초 외에 무엇을 구입하기로 결정하는가?
(A) 세척용 수세미
(B) 고무 장갑
(C) 마른 행주
(D) 계량컵

어휘 in addition to ~뿐만 아니라 rubber gloves 고무 장갑 dishtowel 마른 행주 measuring cup 계량컵

해설 세부 사항 관련 – 여자가 식초 외에 구입하고자 결정한 것

여자의 마지막 대사에서 수세미도 좀 사야겠다(I'd better get some scrubbing sponges too)고 했으므로 정답은 (A)이다.

▶ Paraphrasing 대화의 **scrubbing sponges**
→ 정답의 **cleaning sponges**

M-Au All right, we're almost there! **68It'll be exciting to have lunch at Rinaldi's Italian Kitchen again.** I've been looking forward to it all week. Do you know what you're going to order?

W-Am Definitely the pasta primavera. I had it on my first day as an intern at our company. **69I've really missed it since we moved across town. 70But, hey, the driver just announced Vornell Square. Shouldn't we press the "Stop" button?**

M-Au **70No, we want the next stop after that.** We'll have a long walk if we get off at Vornell Square.

W-Am OK, I'll trust you. I've never taken this bus before.

남: 좋아요, 거의 다 왔어요! 리날디 이탈리안 키친에서 다시 점심을 먹게 돼서 기대돼요. 이번 주 내내 기다려 왔어요. 뭘 주문할지 정했나요?

여: 물론 파스타 프리마베라죠. 우리 회사 인턴이 된 첫 날 먹어 봤는데요. 회사가 반대편으로 이전하고 나서 못 먹게 되니 정말 아쉽더라고요. 그런데 운전사가 방금 보넬 스퀘어라고 방송했어요. "정차" 버튼을 눌러야 하지 않나요?

남: 아니요, 그 다음 정거장이에요. 보넬 스퀘어에 내리면 한참 걸어야 할 거예요.

여: 네, 당신 말이 맞겠죠. 이 버스는 타 본 적이 없거든요.

어휘 order 주문하다 definitely 확실히, 분명히 miss 섭섭하게 생각하다 move 옮기다 announce (방송으로) 알리다 press 누르다 have a long walk 오래 걷다 get off 하차하다 trust 믿다

Bus Line Map

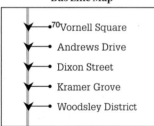

- 70Vornell Square
- Andrews Drive
- Dixon Street
- Kramer Grove
- Woodsley District

버스 노선도

- 보넬 스퀘어
- 앤드류스 드라이브
- 딕슨 스트리트
- 크래이머 그로브
- 우드슬리 디스트릭트

68

What will the speakers do at their destination?

(A) Eat a meal
(B) Shop for a party
(C) Hand out flyers
(D) Attend a workshop

화자들은 목적지에서 무엇을 할 것인가?

(A) 식사하기
(B) 파티를 위한 쇼핑하기
(C) 전단지 나눠 주기
(D) 워크숍 참석하기

어휘 hand out 나눠 주다 flyer 전단지 attend 참석하다

해설 세부 사항 관련 – 화자들이 목적지에서 할 일

남자의 첫 번째 대사에서 리날디 이탈리안 키친에서 다시 점심을 먹게 돼서 기대된다(It'll be exciting to have lunch at Rinaldi's Italian Kitchen again)고 했으므로 정답은 (A)이다.

▸▸ **Paraphrasing** 대화의 have lunch → 정답의 Eat a meal

69

According to the woman, what did the speakers' company do?

(A) Launched a publicity campaign
(B) Relocated to a different area
(C) Restructured its intern training course
(D) Announced a corporate merger

여자에 따르면, 화자들이 다니는 회사는 무엇을 했는가?

(A) 홍보 캠페인을 시작했다.
(B) 다른 장소로 이전했다.
(C) 인턴 교육 과정을 개편했다.
(D) 회사 합병을 발표했다.

어휘 launch 개시하다 publicity 홍보[광고] campaign 캠페인, 운동 relocate to ~로 이전하다 restructure 재구성하다 training course 교육 과정 corporate 기업의 merger 합병

해설 세부 사항 관련 – 화자들이 다니는 회사가 한 것

여자의 첫 번째 대사에서 회사가 반대편으로 이전하고 나서 못 먹게 되니 정말 아쉬웠다(I've really missed it since we moved across town)고 했으므로 정답은 (B)이다.

▸▸ **Paraphrasing** 대화의 we moved across town → 정답의 Relocated to a different area

---

70

Look at the graphic. Which stop will the speakers get off at?

(A) Vornell Square
(B) Andrews Drive
(C) Kramer Grove
(D) Woodsley District

시각 정보에 의하면, 화자들은 어느 정류장에서 내릴 것인가?

(A) 보넬 스퀘어
(B) 앤드류스 드라이브
(C) 크래이머 그로브
(D) 우드슬리 디스트릭트

해설 시각 정보 연계 - 화자들이 내릴 정류장
여자의 두 번째 대사에서 운전사가 방금 보넬 스퀘어라고 방송했으니(the driver just announced Vornell Square) "정차" 버튼을 눌러야 하지 않냐(Shouldn't we press the "Stop" button)고 물어보자 남자가 그 다음 정거장(we want the next stop after that)이라고 말했다. 시각 정보에 따르면 화자들이 내릴 정류장은 앤드류스 드라이브이므로 정답은 (B)이다.

PART 4

71-73 방송

> M-Cn I'm Cullen Nam, and you're listening to Norrisley Radio. **71In local sports news, the Norrisley High School girls' soccer team won its first playoff game last night thanks to clever strategizing by head coach Keeley Boyce.** The team will now move on to the second round of the tournament. **72All Wildcats fans should come down to Norrisley Field on Friday night to support them as they face their next opponent, the highly-ranked Lonsdale.** **73And speaking of Norrisley Field, a fallen tree is causing congestion on some nearby roads this morning. For the latest on this story, we go now to Heather Miles.**

저는 컬런 남이며, 여러분은 노리슬레이 라디오를 듣고 계십니다. **지역 스포츠 소식**을 전해드리겠습니다. 노리슬레이 고등학교 여자 축구팀이 킬리 보이스 감독의 기발한 전략 덕분에 지난밤 첫 결승전 경기에서 승리했습니다. 팀은 이제 토너먼트 2라운드에 진출하게 됩니다. **모든 와일드캐츠 팬들은 금요일 밤 노리슬레이 경기장으로 오셔서 팀을 응원해 주시기 바랍니다. 다음에 맞설 상대팀은 상위권의 론즈데일입니다.** 그리고 노리슬레이 경기장에 관해 말씀드리면, 오늘 아침 나무가 쓰러져 인근 도로의 교통이 혼잡합니다. 지금 헤더 마일즈를 연결해 현재 교통 상황을 알아보도록 하겠습니다.

어휘 local 지역의 playoff 결승전 thanks to ~ 덕분에 strategize 전략을 세우다 head coach 수석 코치, 감독 move on to ~로 넘어가다 round 한 차례 (시합) tournament 시합, 경기, 승자진출전 support 지지하다 face 직면하다, 맞서다 opponent (게임·대회·논쟁 등의) 상대 rank 등급을 매기다, 평가하다 speaking of ~에 관해서 말한다면, ~의 이야기라면 cause 초래하다 congestion 교통 혼잡 latest 최신 소식

71

Who most likely is Ms. Boyce?

(A) A soccer coach
(B) A sportswriter
(C) A school principal
(D) A city politician

보이스 씨는 누구이겠는가?

(A) 축구 감독
(B) 스포츠 담당 기자
(C) 학교 교장
(D) 시 정치인

어휘 sportswriter (신문의) 스포츠 담당 기자 principal 교장 politician 정치인

해설 전체 내용 관련 - 보이스 씨의 신분
지문 초반부에서 지역 스포츠 뉴스를 전하면서 노리슬레이 고등학교 여자 축구팀이 킬리 보이스 감독의 기발한 전략 덕분에 지난밤 첫 결승전 경기에서 승리했다(In local sports news, the Norrisley High School girls' soccer team won its first playoff game last night thanks to clever strategizing by head coach Keeley Boyce)고 했다. 즉 보이스 씨는 축구팀 감독임을 알 수 있으므로 정답은 (A)이다.

72

What are some listeners encouraged to do?

(A) Watch a sports competition
(B) Write letters to a newspaper
(C) Donate to a building project
(D) Vote on an educational initiative

청자들에게 무엇을 하라고 권하는가?

(A) 스포츠 경기 관람하기
(B) 신문사에 편지 쓰기
(C) 건축 프로젝트에 기부하기
(D) 교육 법안에 투표하기

어휘 competition 경기, 대회 donate to ~에 기부하다 vote on ~에 대하여 표결하다 initiative 주민 법안 발의, 발의권

해설 세부 사항 관련 - 청자들에 대한 권장 사항
지문 중반부에서 모든 와일드캐츠 팬들은 금요일 밤 노리슬레이 경기장으로 와서 팀을 응원해 주길 바라며, 다음에 맞설 상대팀은 상위권의 론즈데일(All Wildcats fans should come down to Norrisley Field on Friday night to support them as they face their next opponent, the highly-ranked Lonsdale)이라고 응원을 권하고 있으므로 정답은 (A)이다.

73

According to the speaker, what will be broadcast next?

(A) Some song rankings
(B) Some traffic updates
(C) A news debate
(D) An advertisement

화자에 따르면, 다음으로 무엇을 방송할 것인가?

(A) 노래 순위
(B) 교통 속보
(C) 뉴스 토론
(D) 광고

어휘 ranking 순위 traffic 교통(량) update 최신 소식 debate 토론 advertisement 광고

해설 세부 사항 관련 – 다음 방송 주제

지문 후반부에서 오늘 아침 나무가 쓰러져 노리슬레이 경기장 인근 도로가 혼잡하다면서, 헤더 마일즈를 연결해 최신 소식을 듣겠다(And speaking of Norrisley Field, a fallen tree is causing congestion on some nearby roads this morning. For the latest on this story, we go now to Heather Miles)고 했다. 따라서 다음으로 교통 뉴스가 방송될 것임을 알 수 있으므로 정답은 (B)이다.

74-76 담화

> W-Am **74Hello, everyone, and thank you again for agreeing to take part in this focus group on food packaging designs.** I'm Mia, and I'll be leading your session today. **75In just a moment, I'm going to give each of you a tablet computer.** Once you've logged in using your assigned number, I'll show you some designs on this big screen and ask you some questions. You'll be able to input your answers in the tablet. Does everyone understand so far? All right. **76And before we get started, I want to ask you to keep noise to a minimum during the session.** This will ensure that everyone can hear my questions.

> 안녕하세요, 여러분. 식품 포장 디자인에 관한 이번 포커스 그룹에 참여하는 데 동의해 주셔서 다시 한 번 감사드립니다. 저는 미아라고 하며, 오늘 포커스 그룹을 이끌 예정입니다. 잠시 후, 여러분께 각각 태블릿 컴퓨터를 드릴 겁니다. 할당된 번호로 로그인하시면 큰 화면으로 일부 디자인들을 보여드리고 질문을 할 것입니다. 태블릿에 답을 입력하실 수 있습니다. 여기까지 이해되셨나요? 좋습니다. 시작하기 전에 먼저 설문 조사 중에는 소음을 최소화해 주실 것을 요청드립니다. 그래야 모든 분들이 제 질문을 잘 들을 수 있습니다.

> **어휘** agree to ~하는 데 동의하다 take part in ~에 참가하다 focus group 포커스 그룹(시장조사나 여론조사를 위해 각 계층을 대표하도록 뽑은 소수의 사람들) packaging 포장 lead 이끌다 session (특정 활동을 위한) 시간 once ~하자마자 log in ~에 로그인하다 assigned 할당된 screen 화면 input 입력하다 so far 지금[여기]까지 get started 시작하다 noise 소음 to a minimum 최소한도로 ensure 보장하다

74

What are the listeners about to do?

(A) Take an employment exam
(B) Participate in a focus group
(C) Observe a graphic design class
(D) Attend a television show taping

청자들은 무엇을 하려고 하는가?

(A) 채용 시험 응시
(B) 포커스 그룹 참여
(C) 그래픽 디자인 수업 참관
(D) TV 프로그램 녹화 참여

어휘 employment 고용, 취업 participate in ~에 참여하다 observe 관찰하다 attend 참가하다

해설 전체 내용 관련 – 청자들이 하려고 하는 것

지문 초반부에서 식품 포장 디자인에 관한 이번 설문 조사에 참여하는 데 동의해 주셔서 다시 한 번 감사 드린다(thank you again for agreeing to take part in this focus group on food packaging designs)고 했으므로 정답은 (B)이다.

> ▶▶ **Paraphrasing** 지문의 agreeing to take part in this focus group → 정답의 Participate in a focus group

75

What will the speaker distribute?

(A) Pencils
(B) Headphones
(C) Tablet computers
(D) Survey forms

화자는 무엇을 나눠 줄 것인가?

(A) 연필
(B) 헤드폰
(C) 태블릿 컴퓨터
(D) 설문 조사 양식

어휘 survey 설문 조사 form 양식

해설 세부 사항 관련 – 화자가 나눠 줄 것

지문 중반부에서 청자들에게 각각 태블릿 컴퓨터를 나눠줄 것(I'm going to give each of you a tablet computer)이라고 했으므로 정답은 (C)이다.

76

What are the listeners instructed to do?

(A) Remain quiet
(B) Double-check their work
(C) Raise their hands to ask questions
(D) Turn off their mobile phones

청자들은 무엇을 하라는 지시를 받았는가?

(A) 정숙하기
(B) 작업 두 번 확인하기
(C) 손을 들어 질문하기
(D) 휴대전화 끄기

어휘 remain 여전히 ~이다 double-check 재확인하다 raise 들어올리다 turn off 끄다

해설 세부 사항 관련 – 청자들이 하도록 지시받은 일

지문 후반부에서 시작하기 전에 먼저 설문 조사 중에는 소음을 최소화해 주실 것을 요청한다(I want to ask you to keep noise to a minimum during the session)고 말했으므로 정답은 (A)이다.

▶ Paraphrasing   지문의 **keep noise to a minimum**
                   → 정답의 **Remain quiet**

77-79 전화 메시지

W-Br   Hi, this is Caroline in Administration. **⁷⁷I'm calling about the database program that you issued to me yesterday. ⁷⁸I just tried to get started with it, but I couldn't even install it. I looked more closely at the installation disk, and realized** the program was made for the Andeskie system. **⁷⁸Is there a version for the Leggett system?** If not, I'll need you to look into other options that will be compatible. **⁷⁹Please give me a call back when you are available.** It's extension 509, and I'll be in my office all afternoon. Thanks.

안녕하세요, 총무부의 캐롤라인입니다. **어제 주신 데이터베이스 프로그램 때문에 전화드립니다. 그걸 구동시키려고 했는데, 설치 못하겠네요.** 설치 디스크를 자세히 살펴보았는데, 그 프로그램은 안데스키 시스템용이었어요. **레깃 시스템용 버전이 있나요?** 없다면, 호환 가능한 다른 옵션을 조사해 주세요. **시간 나실 때 회신해 주시고요.** 내선 509번인데, 오후 내내 사무실에 있을 거예요. 고마워요.

어휘   administration 총무부   issue 배급[지급]하다   get started with ~을 시작하게 하다   install 설치하다   installation 설치   version (소프트웨어) 버전   look into ~을 조사하다   option 선택지   compatible 호환이 되는   available 시간이 있는   extension 내선 번호

77

What department does the listener most likely work for?

(A) Legal
(B) Administration
(C) Information Technology
(D) Public Relations

청자는 어느 부서에서 일하겠는가?
(A) 법률
(B) 총무
(C) IT
(D) 홍보

어휘   legal 법률의   information technology 정보 통신 기술   public relations 홍보

해설   세부 사항 관련 – 청자의 근무 부서

지문 초반부에서 청자가 준 데이터베이스 프로그램 때문에 전화한다(I'm calling about the database program that you issued to me yesterday)고 했다. 따라서 청자는 IT 부서에서 일한다는 것을 알 수 있으므로 정답은 (C)이다.

78

What does the speaker imply when she says, "the program was made for the Andeskie system"?

(A) She intends to uninstall a program.
(B) She is surprised that Andeskie created a program.
(C) She cannot answer a technical question.
(D) She uses a different operating system.

화자가 "그 프로그램은 안데스키 시스템용이었어요"라고 말한 의도는 무엇인가?
(A) 그녀는 프로그램을 삭제하려고 한다.
(B) 그녀는 안데스키가 프로그램을 만들었다는 사실에 놀랐다.
(C) 그녀는 기술적인 질문에 대답할 수 없다.
(D) 그녀는 다른 운영 체제를 사용한다.

어휘   intend to ~할 작정이다   uninstall 프로그램을 삭제하다   create 만들다   technical 기술적인   operating system 운영 체제

해설   화자의 의도 파악 – 안데스키 시스템용 프로그램이라는 말의 의도

지문 초반부에서 데이터베이스 프로그램을 구동하려고 했는데 설치도 못했다 (I just tried to get started with it, but I couldn't even install it)고 했으며, 살펴보니 그 프로그램은 안데스키 시스템용이라(I looked more closely at the installation disk, and realized the program was made for the Andeskie system) 레깃 시스템용 버전이 있는지(Is there a version for the Leggett system)를 묻고 있다. 즉 인용문은 화자가 안데스키 시스템이 아닌 다른 운영 체제를 사용한다는 뜻이므로 정답은 (D)이다.

79

What is the listener asked to do?

(A) Locate a software manual
(B) Move a project deadline
(C) Return a phone call
(D) Lead a training session

청자에게 무엇을 해 달라는 요청을 받는가?
(A) 소프트웨어 사용 설명서 찾기
(B) 프로젝트 마감일 옮기기
(C) 회신 전화하기
(D) 교육 과정 진행하기

어휘   locate 찾아내다   manual 매뉴얼, 사용 설명서   deadline 마감일   return 회답하다   lead 이끌다   training session 교육 (과정)

해설   세부 사항 관련 – 청자가 요청 받은 사항

지문 후반부에서 청자에게 시간 날 때 회신 전화를 달라(Please give me a call back when you are available)고 요청했으므로 정답은 (C)이다.

▶ Paraphrasing   지문의 **give me a call back**
                   → 정답의 **Return a phone call**

80-82 안내 방송

M-Au   **⁸⁰Everyone, thank you for joining us in the beautiful Lillard Murray Hotel for the seventh annual Lillard Mathematics Conference.** We are proud to have gathered such a distinguished group of mathematicians. **⁸¹Tonight's welcome reception is meant to kick off the conference in style, giving you a chance to greet old friends as well as make some new ones.** We'll have a professional photographer circulating to capture some of these magical moments. **⁸²Oh, and to facilitate networking, please wear your conference badge so that others can see your name and details.** OK, we hope you enjoy the evening.

여러분, 제7회 연례 릴라드 수학 회의 참석차 아름다운 릴라드 머레이 호텔에서 함께해 주셔서 감사합니다. 저명한 수학자들을 모시게 되어 영광입니다. 오늘 환영회는 새로운 벗을 사귀는 동시에 오랜 친구들과 인사를 나눌 기회를 드릴 수 있도록 멋지게 시작해 보려 합니다. 저희는 이 즐거운 순간을 필름에 담을 전문 사진작가도 모실 예정입니다. 오, 친분을 맺는 데 도움이 되도록 다른 사람들이 여러분의 이름과 상세 사항을 잘 볼 수 있게 회의 배지를 착용해 주세요.

어휘 annual 연례의 conference 컨퍼런스, 회의 be proud of ~를 자랑스럽게 여기다 gather 모으다 distinguished 유명한, 뛰어난 mathematician 수학자 be meant to ~하기로 되어 있다 kick off 시작하다 in style 아주 멋지게 chance 기회 greet 인사하다, 환영하다 as well as ~뿐만 아니라 circulate 순회하다, 돌아다니다 magical 마법 같은, 아주 즐거운 capture 포착하다 facilitate 촉진시키다, 가능하게 하다 networking 네트워킹, 인맥 쌓기 so that ~할 수 있도록 detail 세부 사항

80

Where is the announcement taking place?

(A) In a hotel
(B) At a museum
(C) On a boat
(D) In a restaurant

이 안내 방송은 어디에서 나오는가?

(A) 호텔
(B) 박물관
(C) 보트
(D) 레스토랑

해설 전체 내용 관련 – 안내 방송이 나오는 장소
지문 초반부에서 제7회 연례 릴라드 수학 회의 참석차 아름다운 릴라드 머레이 호텔에서 함께해 주신 여러분께 감사하다(Everyone, thank you for joining us in the beautiful Lillard Murray Hotel for the seventh annual Lillard Mathematics Conference)고 했다. 따라서 호텔에서 들을 수 있는 안내 방송임을 알 수 있으므로 정답은 (A)이다.

81

What is the purpose of the event?

(A) To present an award
(B) To open a conference
(C) To welcome a new director
(D) To raise money for a charity

행사의 목적은 무엇인가?

(A) 시상
(B) 회의 개회
(C) 신임 이사 환영
(D) 자선단체를 위한 모금

어휘 present 수여하다 award 상 director 이사, 책임자 raise money 모금하다 charity 자선단체

해설 세부 사항 관련 – 행사의 목적
지문 중반부에서 오늘 환영회는 새로운 벗을 사귀는 동시에 오랜 친구들과 인사를 나눌 기회를 제공할 수 있도록 멋지게 시작해 보려 한다(Tonight's welcome reception is meant to kick off the conference in style, giving you a chance to greet old friends as well as make some new ones)고 했다. 따라서 행사의 목적이 회의 개회임을 알 수 있으므로 정답은 (B)이다.

82

What are the listeners urged to do?

(A) Save a purchase receipt
(B) Put on an identification badge
(C) Examine an informative brochure
(D) Form an orderly line

청자들은 무엇을 하라는 권고를 받는가?

(A) 구입 영수증 보관하기
(B) 신분 확인 명찰 달기
(C) 유익한 소책자 살펴보기
(D) 질서 정연하게 줄 서기

어휘 purchase receipt 구매 영수증 put on 착용하다 identification badge 신분 확인 명찰 examine 검토하다 informative 유익한, 교육적인 brochure 소책자 orderly 정돈된 form a line 줄을 서다

해설 세부 사항 관련 – 청자들에게 권하는 사항
지문 후반부에서 친분을 맺는 데 도움이 되도록 다른 사람들이 여러분의 이름과 상세 사항을 잘 볼 수 있게 회의 배지를 착용하라(Oh, and to facilitate networking, please wear your conference badge so that others can see your name and details)고 권하고 있으므로 정답은 (B)이다.

▸▸ Paraphrasing 지문의 wear your conference badge → 정답의 Put on an identification badge

83-85 회의 발췌

M-Cn **⁸³Now, a couple of people in the department have asked about the range of menu options that will be available at the upcoming company banquet. I know you're worried about finding something that suits your dietary requirements. ⁸⁴So I passed your questions on to the event-planning committee last week, and they finally got back to me this morning.** They're really busy these days. Anyway,

I thought it would be best to give the information to all of you at once at this meeting. ⁸⁵**Uh, so I've summarized the details at the bottom of today's agenda.** I hope it puts your concerns to rest.

부서원 두 명이 곧 있을 회사 연회에 나올 음식에 대한 질문을 했습니다. 여러분이 요구하는 식단에 맞는 음식이 있을지 염려하신다는 걸 알고 있습니다. 그래서 지난주에 여러분의 문의 내용을 이벤트 기획위원회에 전달했고 오늘 아침 드디어 답을 받았습니다. 위원회가 요즘 정말 바쁘거든요. 아무튼 이 회의에서 여러분 모두에게 한꺼번에 정보를 제공하는 것이 가장 좋을 것이라고 생각했습니다. 아, 그래서 오늘 회의 안건 제일 밑에 세부 사항을 요약해 두었습니다. 여러분의 염려를 불식시킬 수 있기를 바랍니다.

어휘 a couple of 둘의 department 부서 range 범위 menu 요리, 음식 option 선택지 available 이용할 수 있는 upcoming 다가오는 banquet 연회 suit ~에 맞다 dietary 식이 요법의, 음식물의 requirement 요구 pass on to ~로 전하다 event-planning 이벤트 기획의 committee 위원회 get back to (회답하기 위해) ~에게 나중에 다시 연락하다 at once 한꺼번에 summarize 요약하다 at the bottom of ~의 제일 아래에 agenda 안건 put ~ to rest ~을 잠재우다 concern 우려

83

What have the listeners been concerned about?

(A) The range of some choices
(B) The elimination of some requirements
(C) The format of a document
(D) The distance to a venue

청자들은 무엇에 대해 염려하는가?

(A) 선택 사항의 범위
(B) 요구 사항의 배제
(C) 문서 형식
(D) 장소까지의 거리

어휘 choice 선택(권) elimination 제거, 배제 format 형식, 서식 document 문서, 서류 distance 거리 venue 장소, 개최지

해설 세부 사항 관련 – 청자들의 염려 사항

지문 초반부에서 부서원 두 명이 곧 있을 회사 연회에 나올 음식에 대한 질문을 했다(a couple of people in the department have asked about the range of menu options that will be available at the upcoming company banquet)고 말한 후, 여러분이 요구하는 식단에 맞는 음식이 있을지 염려한다는 걸 알고 있다(I know you're worried about finding something that suits your dietary requirements)고 했으므로 정답은 (A)이다.

> ▸ **Paraphrasing** 지문의 the range of menu options
> → 정답의 **The range of some choices**

84

Why does the speaker say, "They're really busy these days"?

(A) To encourage listeners to handle tasks by themselves
(B) To explain a delayed response to an inquiry
(C) To congratulate a team on an achievement
(D) To suggest offering support to a committee

화자가 "위원회가 요즘 정말 바쁘거든요"라고 말한 이유는 무엇인가?

(A) 청자들이 스스로 문제를 해결하도록 장려하려고
(B) **질문에 대한 답이 늦어진 이유를 설명하려고**
(C) 팀의 성과에 대해 축하하려고
(D) 위원회에 도움을 주자고 제안하려고

어휘 encourage to ~하라고 장려하다 handle 다루다 task 과제 explain 설명하다 delayed 연기된 response to ~에 대한 응답 inquiry 문의 사항 congratulate on ~에 대해 축하하다 achievement 성취, 업적 suggest 제안하다 offering 제공 support 지원, 지지

해설 화자의 의도 파악 – 위원회가 요즘 바쁘다고 말한 이유

지문의 중반부에서 지난주에 청자들의 문의 내용을 이벤트 기획위원회에 전달했고(I passed your questions on to the event-planning committee last week) 오늘 아침 드디어 답을 받았다(they finally got back to me this morning)고 말한 후 위원회가 요즘 정말 바쁘다고 말했다. 즉 너무 바빠서 회신이 늦었다는 이유를 밝히고 있으므로 정답은 (B)이다.

85

According to the speaker, where is some information available?

(A) In a meeting agenda
(B) On a projection screen
(C) In an event invitation
(D) On a posted notice

화자에 따르면, 정보는 어디서 볼 수 있는가?

(A) **회의 안건**
(B) 프로젝션 스크린
(C) 행사 초대장
(D) 게시된 공지

어휘 projection 영사기 screen 화면 posted 게시된 notice 공지

해설 세부 사항 관련 – 정보를 볼 수 있는 곳

지문 후반부에서 회의 안건 제일 밑에 세부 사항을 요약해 두었다(I've summarized the details at the bottom of today's agenda)고 했으므로 정답은 (A)이다.

86-88 광고

W-Am Looking to improve your medical practice's revenues? ⁸⁶**DRC Resources is a leading consulting firm that offers its services exclusively to medical clinics.** Our expert consultants show you how to deliver better health care solutions at the same operating costs. ⁸⁷**And we're especially skilled at helping clinics modify their offerings to reflect developments in the marketplace.** DRC Resources will put your business at the forefront of the medical industry. To learn more about our services, visit our Web site. ⁸⁸**Or, if you're attending the Northwest Health Trade Show in**

July, make sure to stop by our booth. We always welcome the opportunity to work with new clients.

진료 수익을 높이고자 하십니까? DRC 리소스는 병원 전용 서비스를 제공해 드리는 선도적인 컨설팅 업체입니다. 저희 전문 컨설턴트들이 동일한 운영비로 보다 나은 의료 솔루션을 제공하는 법을 알려드립니다. 저희는 시장의 변화에 발맞추어 병원에서 제공하는 서비스도 재정비하실 수 있도록 돕는 데 특화돼 있습니다. DRC 리소스는 귀사를 의료업계의 선두주자로 만들어 드립니다. 저희 서비스에 대해 더 자세한 내용을 알고 싶으시면 웹사이트를 방문하십시오. 또는 7월에 있을 노스웨스트 의료박람회에 참가하시는 경우 저희 부스에 꼭 들러 주십시오. 저희는 새로운 고객 여러분과 함께할 기회를 언제나 환영합니다.

어휘 look to 애쓰다 improve 개선하다 medical practice 의료 행위 revenue 수입, 수익 exclusively 독점적으로, 전문적으로 medical clinic 병원 expert 전문적인 consultant 상담가, 자문위원 deliver 전하다 health care 보건 solution 해결책 operating cost 운영비용 be skilled at ~에 능숙하다 modify 수정하다 offering 제공물 reflect 반영하다 development 진전된 새 단계, 발전 marketplace 시장 at the forefront of ~의 선두 industry 산업, 업계 trade show 박람회 make sure 반드시 ~하다 stop by 들르다 opportunity 기회 client 고객

86

What type of business does DRC Resources provide consulting services for?

(A) Savings banks
(B) Convenience stores
(C) Fitness centers
(D) Medical clinics

DRC 리소스는 어떤 업종을 위한 컨설팅 서비스를 제공하는가?

(A) 저축은행
(B) 편의점
(C) 피트니스 센터
(D) 병원

어휘 savings 예금 fitness 신체 단련

해설 세부 사항 관련 – DRC 리소스가 컨설팅 서비스를 제공하는 업종
지문 초반부에서 DRC 리소스는 병원 전용 서비스를 제공하는 선도적인 컨설팅 업체(DRC resources is a leading consulting firm that offers its services exclusively to medical clinics)라고 했으므로 정답은 (D)이다.

87

According to the speaker, what can DRC Resources help a business do?

(A) Adjust to market trends
(B) Enlarge its client base
(C) Improve employee morale
(D) Decrease its operating costs

화자에 따르면 DRC 리소스는 업체가 무엇을 하도록 돕는가?

(A) 시장 트렌드에 적응하기
(B) 고객층 확대하기
(C) 직원 사기 돋우기
(D) 운영비 절감하기

해설 세부 사항 관련 – DRC 리소스가 하도록 돕는 것
지문 중반부에서 시장의 변화에 발맞추어 병원에서 제공하는 서비스도 재정비할 수 있도록 돕는 데 특화돼 있다(we're especially skilled at helping clinics modify their offerings to reflect developments in the marketplace)고 했으므로 정답은 (A)이다.

▸▸ Paraphrasing 지문의 modify their offerings
→ 정답의 Adjust to market trends

88

What will happen in July?

(A) A new service will become available.
(B) A Web site will offer a discount.
(C) A discussion will be broadcast.
(D) A trade show will be held.

7월에 어떤 일이 있을 것인가?

(A) 신규 서비스가 나올 것이다.
(B) 웹사이트에서 할인을 할 것이다.
(C) 토론이 방영될 것이다.
(D) 박람회가 개최될 것이다.

어휘 discount 할인 broadcast 방송[방영]하다

해설 세부 사항 관련 – 7월에 있을 일
지문 후반부에서 7월에 노스웨스트 의료박람회에 참가하는 경우(if you're attending the Northwest Health Trade Show in July) 자사 부스에 꼭 들러 달라(make sure to stop by our booth)고 했으므로 정답은 (D)이다.

89-91 전화 메시지

W-Br Hi, Himari. **89I just received the proposal from the writer, Mr. Evans, where he outlined his ideas for a photography book titled *City Perspectives*. Of course, we've published two of his previous works in the past.** Now, for this new book, he wants to present a collection of black-and-white images of world cities shown alongside digitally-altered photos that look like cartoon illustrations. **90I don't think we've ever published something so innovative.** We've got to get back to him right away. Uh, I've forwarded the proposal to your e-mail account. **90, 91Let's meet later this afternoon and discuss what kind of offer we should make.** See you then.

안녕하세요, 히마리. 에반스 작가님한테서 〈시티 퍼스펙티브스〉라는 사진집에 관한 개요가 설명된 제안서를 받았어요. 물론, 저희는 이전에 작가님의 작품집을 두 권 출판했는데요. 이번 신간을 위해 작가님은 만화 삽화처럼 보이도록 컴퓨터로 수정한 사진과 전 세계 도시의 흑백 이미지를 나란히 보여주길 원하세요. 저희는 이렇게 혁신적인 작품은 한 번도 출간해 본 적이 없는 것 같아요. 당장 작가님께 다시 연락해야 해요. 어, 당신 이메일 계정으로 제안서를 전달했어요. 오늘 오후에 만나서 우리가 어떤 제의를 해야 할지 논의해 봐요. 이따 봬요.

어휘 receive 받다 proposal 제안(서) outline 개요를 서술하다 title 제목을 붙이다 publish 출간하다 previous 이전의 work 작품 in the past 과거에 present 제시하다 collection 모음 black-and-white 흑백의 alongside ~와 나란히 alter 변경하다, 바꾸다 cartoon 만화 illustration 삽화 innovative 혁신적인 get back to ~에게 다시 연락하다 forward 보내다, 전송하다 account 계정, 계좌 discuss 논의하다 make an offer 제의하다

89

Who most likely is the speaker?

(A) A film producer
(B) An event photographer
(C) A publishing executive
(D) A tourism official

화자는 누구이겠는가?
(A) 영화 제작자
(B) 행사 사진가
(C) 출판사 간부
(D) 관광청 공무원

어휘 film producer 영화 제작자 executive 고위 간부, 임원 official 공무원, 간부

해설 전체 내용 관련 – 화자의 신분
지문 초반부에서 에반스 작가한테서, 사진집에 관한 개요가 설명된 제안서를 받았으며(I just received the proposal from the writer, Mr. Evans, where he outlined his ideas for a photography book titled City Perspectives) 전에도 그의 작품집을 두 권 출판한 적이 있다(Of course, we've published two of his previous works in the past)고 했다. 화자는 출판사에서 근무한다는 것을 알 수 있으므로 정답은 (C)이다.

90

What does the speaker mean when she says, "We've got to get back to him right away"?

(A) A mistake must be fixed immediately.
(B) She is impressed with a résumé.
(C) She wants to accept a proposal.
(D) A company may choose another firm.

화자가 "당장 작가님께 다시 연락해야 해요"라고 말한 의미는 무엇인가?
(A) 당장 실수를 바로잡아야 한다.
(B) 이력서에 깊은 인상을 받았다.
(C) 제안서를 수락하고 싶어 한다.
(D) 회사는 다른 업체를 선택할 수도 있다.

어휘 mistake 실수 fix 고치다, 바로잡다 immediately 당장 be impressed with ~에 감명 받다, 깊은 인상을 받다 résumé 이력서 accept 수락하다 choose 선택하다 firm 업체, 회사

해설 화자의 의도 파악 – 당장 작가에게 연락해야 한다는 말의 의미
인용문 앞 문장에서 에반스 작가가 보내 온 제안 내용을 설명하며 이렇게 혁신적인 작품은 한 번도 출간한 적이 없다(I don't think we've ever published something so innovative)고 말했다. 뒤이어서 오늘 오후에 만나서 우리가 어떤 제의를 해야 할지 논의해 보자(Let's meet later this afternoon and discuss what kind of offer we should make)고 말하고 있다. 따라서 제안서가 마음에 드니 작가에 연락해 출간을 추진해 보자는 의미이므로 정답은 (C)이다.

91

What does the speaker ask the listener to do?

(A) Revise a production budget
(B) Meet with her later in the day
(C) Forward a confirmation e-mail
(D) Contact a branch office

화자는 청자에게 무엇을 해 달라고 요청하는가?
(A) 제작 비용 수정하기
(B) 오후 늦게 만나기
(C) 확인 이메일 전달하기
(D) 지점에 연락하기

어휘 production budget 제작 비용 confirmation 확인 contact 연락하다 branch office 지점

해설 세부 사항 관련 – 화자의 요청 사항
지문 후반부에서 작가의 제안서를 전달했으니 오늘 오후에 만나서 우리가 어떤 제의를 해야 할지 논의하자(Let's meet later this afternoon and discuss what kind of offer we should make)고 요청하고 있으므로 정답은 (B)이다.

92-94 뉴스 보도

M-Cn Now it's time for our Finance Corner. **92This week, we'd like to let our listeners know about *Counting Coins*, a great new book by financial planner Alice Fung.** It offers several tips that people with average incomes can use to save impressive amounts of money. **93For example, we urge listeners to take Ms. Fung's advice to be more patient when making major purchases.** She writes that waiting for a seasonal or yearly sale can result in huge savings. Pick up *Counting Coins* to learn more tips, or **94check out today's issue of the *Greenley Chronicle* newspaper for a glowing review that discusses the book's points in detail.**

자 〈파이낸스 코너〉 시간입니다. 이번 주에는 청취자 여러분에게 자산관리사 앨리스 펑의 훌륭한 신간인 〈동전 세기〉에 관해 알려드리고자 합니다. 이 책은 평균 임금을 받는 사람들이 상당한 액수의 돈을 절약할 수 있는 몇 가지 비결을 제시합니다. 예를 들어 비싼 물품을 구입할 때는 더 인내심을 발휘하라는 펑 씨의 조언을 청취자분들도 귀담아들으시기를 바랍니다. 펑 씨는 시즌 세일이나 연간 세일을 기다리면 막대한 비용을 절감할 수 있다고 전합니다. 〈동전 세기〉를 구입하셔서 더 많은 비법에 대해 알아보시거나 책의 요점을 상세히 다룬 생생한 후기를 보시려면 오늘자 〈그린레이 크로니클〉 신문을 확인해 보세요.

어휘 coin 동전 financial planner 재무설계사, 자산관리사 offer 제공하다 several 여러 가지의 tip 조언 average 평균(의) income 수입, 소득 save 절감하다 impressive 인상적인, 인상 깊은 urge to ~하도록 촉구하다 patient 참을성 있는 purchase 구매 seasonal 계절의, 제철의 yearly 매년의 result in ~을 낳다 huge 막대한 savings 절약된 금액 pick up ~을 사다 check out 살펴보다 glowing 격찬하는, 생생한 review 후기 in detail 자세하게, 상세하게

Test 6

TEST 6 **177**

92

What is being announced?

(A) A change to a tax law
(B) The release of a publication
(C) The expansion of a business
(D) A rise in an exchange rate

무엇이 방송되고 있는가?

(A) 세법 변경
(B) 출판물 발간
(C) 사업 확장
(D) 환율 상승

어휘 tax law 세법 release (책·영화 등의) 출시, 개봉 publication
출판물 expansion 확장 rise in ~의 증가 exchange rate 환율

해설 전체 내용 관련 – 방송되는 내용

지문 초반부에서 이번 주에 청취자 여러분에게 자산관리사 앨리스 펑의 훌륭한 신간인 〈동전 세기〉에 관해 알려 드리고자 한다(This week, we'd like to let our listeners know about *Counting Coins*, a great new book by financial planner Alice Fun)고 했으므로 정답은 (B)이다.

▸▸ Paraphrasing   지문의 book → 정답의 publication

93

What are listeners advised to do?

(A) Exercise more patience
(B) Look for digital coupons
(C) Invest in new industries
(D) Use a mobile app

청자들은 어떻게 하라는 조언을 받는가?

(A) 더 많은 인내심 발휘하기
(B) 디지털 쿠폰 찾아보기
(C) 새로운 산업에 투자하기
(D) 모바일 앱 사용하기

어휘 exercise 발휘하다 patience 인내심 invest in ~에 투자하다
industry 산업

해설 세부 사항 관련 – 청자에 전하는 조언

지문 중반부에서 비싼 물품을 구입할 때는 더 인내심을 발휘하라는 펑 씨의 조언을 청취자들이 귀담아들으라(we urge listeners to take Ms. Fung's advice to be more patient when making major purchases)고 했으므로 정답은 (A)이다.

▸▸ Paraphrasing   지문의 be more patient
→ 정답의 Exercise more patience

94

What does the speaker say can be found in a newspaper?

(A) A press interview
(B) A book review
(C) Some job descriptions
(D) Some editorials

화자는 신문에서 무엇을 찾을 수 있다고 말하는가?

(A) 언론 인터뷰
(B) 서평
(C) 직무 기술서
(D) 사설

어휘 press 언론 job description 직무 내용 설명서 editorial 사설

해설 세부 사항 관련 – 신문에 게재된 것

지문 후반부에서 책의 요점을 상세히 다룬 생생한 후기를 보려면 오늘자 〈그린레이 크로니클〉 신문을 확인하라(check out today's issue of the *Greenley Chronicle* newspaper for a glowing review that discusses the book's points in detail)고 했으므로 정답은 (B)이다.

▸▸ Paraphrasing   지문의 a glowing review that discusses the book's points in detail
→ 정답의 A book review

95-97 전화 메시지 + 일정표

M-Au Hi, Greg, it's David. 95**I'm calling about the meeting we're leading this afternoon on the changes to staff travel benefits.** I think that people are going to be confused by some of the details, so we'll want to take some time to address all of the questions they have. 96**I'm going to try to extend my room reservation until 3 P.M.** Otherwise, my preparations are on schedule. 97**I'll be sending out the final reminder notifications about an hour before everyone leaves for lunch.** Let me know if you need any help on your end.

안녕하세요, 그레그 씨. 데이비드입니다. **오늘 오후에 저희가 주재하는 직원 출장 수당 변경에 관한 회의 때문에 전화 드렸습니다.** 사람들이 세부 사항에 대해 혼란스러워할 것 같아서 질문할 수 있는 시간을 가졌으면 합니다. **오후 3시까지 회의실 예약 시간을 연장해 볼 겁니다.** 그 밖에는 예정대로 다 준비돼 있고요. **모두 점심을 먹으러 나가기 한 시간 전쯤 최종 공지를 보낼 예정입니다.** 도움이 필요하면 알려주세요.

어휘 lead 진행하다, 이끌다 travel 출장 benefits 수당, 보조금
be confused by ~에 혼란스러워하다 address a question
질문을 하다 extend 연장하다 reservation 예약 otherwise 그
외에는 preparation 준비 be on schedule 예정대로이다 send
out ~을 보내다 final 마지막의 reminder 상기시켜 주는 메모
notification 알림, 공지 end 몫

Room	1 P.M.–2 P.M.	2 P.M.–3 P.M.
Seminar Room A		Reserved (Bruce)
Seminar Room B		
Seminar Room C	Reserved (Elisha)	
96Seminar Room D	Reserved (David)	

회의실	오후 1시-오후 2시	오후 2시-오후 3시
세미나룸 A		예약됨 (브루스)
세미나룸 B		
세미나룸 C	예약됨 (엘리샤)	
세미나룸 D	예약됨 (데이비드)	

95

What will the speaker discuss at a meeting?

(A) A funding shortage
(B) Some software upgrades
(C) Some staff benefits
(D) A travel itinerary

화자는 회의에서 무엇을 논의할 것인가?
(A) 자금 부족
(B) 소프트웨어 업그레이드
(C) 직원 혜택
(D) 출장 일정

어휘 funding 자금 shortage 부족 itinerary 일정(표)

해설 세부 사항 관련 – 화자가 회의에서 논의할 것
지문 초반부에서 오늘 오후 주재하는 직원 출장 수당 변경에 관한 회의 때문에 전화 드렸다(I'm calling about the meeting we're leading this afternoon on the changes to staff travel benefits)고 했으므로 정답은 (C)이다.

▸▸ Paraphrasing 지문의 **staff travel benefits**
→ 정답의 **staff benefits**

96

Look at the graphic. Which room will the speaker try to reserve for a 2 P.M. meeting?

(A) Seminar Room A
(B) Seminar Room B
(C) Seminar Room C
(D) Seminar Room D

시각 정보에 의하면, 화자는 오후 2시 회의를 위해 어떤 회의실을 예약하려고 하겠는가?
(A) 세미나룸 A
(B) 세미나룸 B
(C) 세미나룸 C
(D) 세미나룸 D

해설 시각 정보 연계 – 회의를 위해 예약할 회의실
지문의 중반부에서 오후 3시까지 회의실 예약 시간을 연장해 볼 것(I'm going to try to extend my room reservation until 3 P.M.)이라고 말했다. 시각 정보에 따르면 3시까지 연장이 필요한 회의실은 세미나룸 D이므로 정답은 (D)이다.

97

What does the speaker say he will do before lunch?

(A) Photocopy some instructions
(B) Finalize an estimate
(C) Unpack a shipment
(D) Send some notifications

화자는 점심 식사 전에 무엇을 하겠다고 말하는가?
(A) 지시 사항 복사하기
(B) 견적서 마무리하기
(C) 배송 물품 풀기
(D) 공지 보내기

어휘 photocopy 복사하다 instruction 설명, 지시 finalize 마무리짓다 estimate 견적서 unpack 풀다 shipment 배송품

해설 세부 사항 관련 – 화자가 점심 식사 전에 할 일
지문 후반부에서 모두가 점심을 먹으러 나가기 한 시간 전쯤 최종 공지를 보낼 예정(I'll be sending out the final reminder notifications about an hour before everyone leaves for lunch)이라고 했으므로 정답은 (D)이다.

▸▸ Paraphrasing 지문의 **sending out the final reminder notifications**
→ 정답의 **Send some notifications**

98-100 담화 + 지도

W-Br **98Thank you all for volunteering for today's effort to tidy up Shoates Park.** We at the Ranger Station really appreciate your community spirit. Now, the plan is to split into two groups and start making our way around the grounds. **99We'll cover all of the park except for a portion around the stage, which is closed due to renovations.** It should take about four hours, so I hope you've all worn comfortable shoes and brought hats or sunglasses as suggested. **100Oh, and we're providing plastic gloves and trash grabbers at the table near the station entrance. Please take a set each before we get going.** That way, you'll be able to pick up sharp objects safely.

오늘 쇼아티스 공원 청소에 자원해 주신 여러분 모두에게 감사드립니다. 저희 관리소에서는 여러분의 공동체 의식에 대해 감사를 표하는 바입니다. 자, 두 그룹으로 나누어 부지 주변을 청소할 계획입니다. 보수 공사 때문에 폐쇄된 무대 주변 구역을 제외한 공원 전역을 청소할 겁니다. 4시간 정도 소요될 예정이므로 여러분 모두 말씀드린 대로 편안한 신발을 신고 모자와 안경을 가져오셨기를 바랍니다. 아, 그리고 관리소 정문 가까이에 있는 탁자에서 비닐 장갑과 쓰레기 집게를 제공해 드릴 예정입니다. 시작하기 전에 각자 한 세트씩 가져가십시오. 그래야 날카로운 물건을 안전하게 집을 수 있을 겁니다.

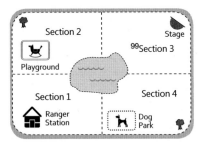

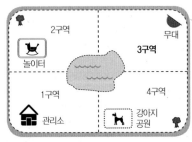

98

Why have the listeners come to the park?

(A) To assist with cleaning it
(B) To take part in a festival
(C) To decorate it for a holiday
(D) To go on a guided tour

청자들이 공원에 온 이유는 무엇인가?
(A) 공원 청소를 돕기 위해
(B) 축제에 참가하기 위해
(C) 휴일을 맞아 공원을 장식하기 위해
(D) 가이드가 인솔하는 관광을 하기 위해

어휘   assist with ~을 돕다 take part in ~에 참가하다 decorate
         장식하다 guided tour 가이드가 인솔하는 관광

해설   세부 사항 관련 – 청자들이 공원에 온 이유
지문 초반부에서 오늘 쇼아티스 공원 청소에 자원한 여러분 모두에게 감사한다
(Thank you all for volunteering for today's effort to tidy up Shoates
Park)고 했으므로 정답은 (A)이다.

> **Paraphrasing**   지문의 **tidy up** → 정답의 **clean**

99

Look at the graphic. Which section is partially closed?

(A) Section 1
(B) Section 2
(C) Section 3
(D) Section 4

시각 정보에 의하면, 어느 구역이 부분적으로 폐쇄되어 있는가?
(A) 1구역
(B) 2구역
(C) 3구역
(D) 4구역

어휘   partially 부분적으로

해설   시각 정보 연계 – 폐쇄 구역
지문 중반부에서 보수 공사 때문에 폐쇄된 무대 주변 구역을 제외한 공원 전역
을 청소할 계획(We'll cover all of the park except for a portion around
the stage, which is closed due to renovations)이라고 했다. 시각 정보에
따르면 무대 주변은 3구역이므로 정답은 (C)이다.

100

What can listeners do at a table?

(A) Look at a park map
(B) Enter a prize drawing
(C) Get some special gear
(D) Throw away some waste

청자들은 탁자에서 무엇을 할 수 있는가?
(A) 공원 약도 보기
(B) 경품 추첨에 응모하기
(C) 특정 도구 얻기
(D) 쓰레기 버리기

어휘   enter 참가 신청을 하다 prize drawing 경품 추첨 gear 도구, 장비
         throw away 버리다 waste 쓰레기

해설   세부 사항 관련 – 탁자에서 할 수 있는 것
지문 후반부에서 관리소 정문 가까이에 있는 탁자에서 비닐 장갑과 쓰레
기 집게를 제공할 예정이니(we're providing plastic gloves and trash
grabbers at the table near the station entrance) 시작하기 전에 각자
한 세트씩 가져가라(Please take a set each before we get going)고 했
으므로 정답은 (C)이다.

> **Paraphrasing**   지문의 **plastic gloves and trash grabbers**
>   → 정답의 **some special gear**

TEST 7

1 (D)	**2** (B)	**3** (B)	**4** (C)	**5** (A)
6 (A)	**7** (C)	**8** (A)	**9** (A)	**10** (C)
11 (C)	**12** (B)	**13** (A)	**14** (B)	**15** (C)
16 (A)	**17** (B)	**18** (B)	**19** (A)	**20** (C)
21 (A)	**22** (A)	**23** (C)	**24** (B)	**25** (C)
26 (A)	**27** (B)	**28** (A)	**29** (C)	**30** (C)
31 (B)	**32** (B)	**33** (A)	**34** (B)	**35** (D)
36 (D)	**37** (C)	**38** (B)	**39** (D)	**40** (B)
41 (B)	**42** (D)	**43** (B)	**44** (A)	**45** (A)
46 (B)	**47** (A)	**48** (D)	**49** (A)	**50** (A)
51 (B)	**52** (B)	**53** (A)	**54** (C)	**55** (B)
56 (B)	**57** (D)	**58** (B)	**59** (A)	**60** (B)
61 (C)	**62** (A)	**63** (D)	**64** (C)	**65** (D)
66 (B)	**67** (A)	**68** (B)	**69** (D)	**70** (A)
71 (A)	**72** (C)	**73** (D)	**74** (C)	**75** (D)
76 (A)	**77** (B)	**78** (C)	**79** (B)	**80** (A)
81 (C)	**82** (D)	**83** (C)	**84** (B)	**85** (A)
86 (C)	**87** (B)	**88** (D)	**89** (D)	**90** (C)
91 (C)	**92** (B)	**93** (C)	**94** (C)	**95** (C)
96 (B)	**97** (D)	**98** (D)	**99** (D)	**100** (A)

PART 1

1 W-Am

(A) He's picking up a jacket.
(B) He's driving a car by himself.
(C) He's stocking shelves at a store.
(D) He's placing an item into a cart.

(A) 남자가 상의를 집어 들고 있다.
(B) 남자가 혼자서 운전하고 있다.
(C) 남자가 상점에서 선반에 물건을 채우고 있다.
(D) 남자가 카트에 물건을 넣고 있다.

어휘 pick up 집어 들다 stock 채우다, 갖추다 place 놓다

해설 1인 등장 사진 – 인물의 동작 묘사

(A) 동사 오답. 남자가 상의를 집어 드는(is picking up a jacket) 모습이 아니므로 오답.

(B) 동사 오답. 남자가 운전을 하는(is driving a car) 모습이 아니므로 오답.

(C) 동사 오답. 남자가 선반에 물건을 채우는(is stocking shelves) 모습이 아니므로 오답.

(D) 정답. 남자가 카트에 물건을 넣는(is placing an item into a cart) 모습이므로 정답.

2 W-Br

(A) The women are washing some clothing items.
(B) One of the women is using a sewing machine.
(C) The women are folding some pieces of cloth.
(D) One of the women is cutting some thread.

(A) 여자들이 의류를 세탁하고 있다.
(B) 여자 중 한 명이 재봉틀을 사용하고 있다.
(C) 여자들이 천을 접고 있다.
(D) 여자 중 한 명이 실을 자르고 있다.

어휘 clothing items 의류품 sewing machine 재봉틀 fold 접다 cloth 옷감, 천 thread 실

해설 2인 이상 등장 사진 – 인물의 동작 묘사

(A) 동사 오답. 여자들이 의류를 세탁하는(are washing some clothing items) 모습이 아니므로 오답.

(B) 정답. 여자 중 한 명이 재봉틀을 사용하는(is using a sewing machine) 모습이므로 정답.

(C) 동사 오답. 여자들이 천을 접고 있는(are folding some pieces of cloth) 모습이 아니므로 오답.

(D) 동사 오답. 여자 중 한 명이 실을 자르는(is cutting some thread) 모습이 아니므로 오답.

3 M-Cn

(A) Some plants are being watered outdoors.
(B) Some people are planting items in the soil.
(C) Square bricks are being laid at a patio.
(D) Workers are gathering trash from the ground.

(A) 야외에서 식물에 물을 주고 있다.
(B) 사람들이 식물들을 땅에 심고 있다.
(C) 테라스에 사각 벽돌이 놓이고 있다.
(D) 인부들이 땅에 있는 쓰레기를 모으고 있다.

어휘 plant 식물; 심다 water 물을 주다 soil 토양 brick 벽돌 lay 놓다[두다] patio 테라스 gather 모으다 trash 쓰레기 ground 지면, 땅

해설 2인 이상 등장 사진 – 사람 또는 사물 중심 묘사

(A) 동사 오답. 식물에 물을 주는(are being watered) 모습이 아니므로 오답.

(B) 정답. 사람들이 식물들을 땅에 심고 있는(are planting items in the soil) 모습이므로 정답.

(C) 동사 오답. 테라스에 사각 벽돌이 놓이는(are being laid) 모습이 아니므로 오답.

(D) 동사 오답. 인부들이 땅에 있는 쓰레기를 모으는(are gathering trash from the ground) 모습이 아니므로 오답.

4 M-Au

(A) She's putting away a laptop.
(B) She's writing on a notepad.
(C) She's typing on a computer.
(D) She's tidying up her desk.

(A) 여자가 노트북을 치우고 있다.
(B) 여자가 메모지에 글을 쓰고 있다.
(C) 여자가 컴퓨터로 타자를 치고 있다.
(D) 여자가 책상을 정리하고 있다.

어휘 put away 치우다 laptop 노트북 컴퓨터 notepad 메모지 type 타자[입력]하다 tidy up 정리하다

해설 1인 등장 사진 – 인물의 동작 묘사

(A) 동사 오답. 여자가 노트북을 치우는(is putting away a laptop) 모습이 아니므로 오답.

(B) 동사 오답. 여자가 메모지에 글을 쓰는(is writing on a notepad) 모습이 아니므로 오답.

(C) 정답. 여자가 컴퓨터로 타자를 치는(is typing on a computer) 모습이므로 정답.

(D) 동사 오답. 여자가 책상을 정리하는(is tidying up her desk) 모습이 아니므로 오답.

5 W-Br

(A) Boxes are stacked on top of each other.
(B) The woman is operating a delivery truck.
(C) They are opening the door.
(D) The man is packing some containers.

(A) 상자들이 차곡차곡 쌓여 있다.
(B) 여자가 배달 트럭을 운전하고 있다.
(C) 사람들이 문을 열고 있다.
(D) 남자가 용기들을 싸고 있다.

어휘 stack 쌓다 on top of ~의 위에 operate 조작[가동]하다 pack 싸다, 포장하다 container 그릇, 용기

해설 2인 이상 등장 사진 – 사람 또는 사물 중심 묘사

(A) 정답. 상자들이 서로 차곡차곡 쌓여 있는(are stacked on top of each other) 모습이므로 정답.

(B) 동사 오답. 여자가 배달 트럭을 운전하는(is operating a delivery truck) 모습이 아니므로 오답.

(C) 동사 오답. 사람들이 문을 여는(are opening the door) 모습이 아니므로 오답.

(D) 동사 오답. 남자가 용기들을 싸는(is packing some containers) 모습이 아니므로 오답.

6 M-Cn

(A) Some bicycles have been left unattended.
(B) Some cyclists are heading toward the finish line.
(C) Some stools are being constructed.
(D) Some bicycles are on display in a shop.

(A) 자전거들이 방치되어 있다.
(B) 자전거를 탄 사람들이 결승선을 향하고 있다.
(C) 의자들이 조립되고 있다.
(D) 자전거들이 상점에 진열되어 있다.

어휘 unattended 지켜보는 사람이 없는, 방치된 head toward ~를 향하다 finish line 결승선 stool (등받이가 없는) 의자 construct 건설하다, 조립하다 on display 진열 중인

해설 사물/배경 사진 – 사람 또는 사물 중심 묘사

(A) 정답. 자전거들이 방치되어 있는(have been left unattended) 모습이므로 정답.

(B) 동사 오답. 자전거를 탄 사람들(cyclists)이 결승선을 향하고 있는(are heading toward the finish line) 모습이 아니므로 오답.

(C) 동사 오답. 의자들이 조립되고 있는(are being constructed) 모습이 아니므로 오답.

(D) 사진에 없는 명사를 이용한 오답. 사진에 상점의 모습이 보이지 않으므로 오답.

PART 2

7

W-Br Do you need more time to look over the options on the menu?

M-Cn (A) It's two fifteen, according to my watch.
(B) A new restaurant chef is working here.
(C) No, I'm ready for you to take my order.

메뉴의 선택 사항을 살펴볼 시간이 더 필요하십니까?
(A) 제 시계로는 2시 15분입니다.
(B) 식당의 새 요리사는 여기서 일합니다.
(C) 아니오, 주문할 준비가 됐습니다.

어휘 look over ~를 살펴보다 option 선택지 according to ~에 따르면 chef 주방장 take an order 주문을 받다

해설 시간이 더 필요한지 묻는 조동사 의문문

(A) 연상 단어 오답. 질문의 time에 대해 연상 가능한 two fifteen을 이용한 오답.

(B) 연상 단어 오답. 질문의 menu에 대해 연상 가능한 restaurant chef를 이용한 오답.

(C) 정답. 메뉴의 선택 사항을 살펴볼 시간이 더 필요한지 묻는 질문에 No라는 부정적인 응답을 한 후, 주문할 준비가 됐다고 말하고 있으므로 정답.

8

M-Au Who knows how to replace the toner in the copy machine?

W-Am (A) The receptionist usually handles that.

(B) The equipment is stored on my floor.

(C) Every few months or so.

복사기 토너 교체 방법을 누가 알고 있나요?

(A) 보통 접수 담당자가 처리합니다.
(B) 기기가 저희 층에 보관되어 있습니다.
(C) 몇 달마다요.

어휘 replace 교체하다 toner (복사기 등의) 토너 handle 다루다 receptionist 접수원, 접수 담당자 equipment 장비 store 보관하다, 저장하다

해설 복사기 토너 교체 방법을 누가 아는지 묻는 Who의문문

(A) 정답. 복사기 토너 교체 방법을 누가 아는지에 대한 질문에 보통 접수 담당자가 처리한다고 구체적인 사람을 명시하고 있으므로 정답.

(B) 연상 단어 오답. 질문의 copy machine에서 연상 가능한 equipment를 이용한 오답.

(C) 질문과 상관없는 오답. 빈도를 묻는 How often 의문문에 어울리는 응답이므로 오답.

9

M-Cn What time should I pick you up for the theater performance?

W-Br (A) As soon as you get off work.

(B) We enjoyed the show tremendously.

(C) I really appreciate that.

연극 관람을 위해 몇 시에 데리러 갈까요?

(A) 퇴근하시는 대로요.
(B) 저희는 공연을 아주 즐겁게 봤어요.
(C) 정말 감사합니다.

어휘 pick up ~를 (차에) 태우러 가다 performance 공연 as soon as ~하자마자 get off work 퇴근하다 tremendously 엄청나게 appreciate 고마워하다

해설 몇 시에 데리러 가야 하는지 묻는 What 의문문

(A) 정답. 연극 관람을 위해 데리러 갈 시간을 묻는 질문에 퇴근하시는 대로라고 답하고 있으므로 정답.

(B) 연상 단어 오답. 질문의 theater performance에 대해 연상 가능한 show를 이용한 오답.

(C) 질문과 상관없는 오답. 연극 관람을 위해 데리러 갈 시간을 묻는 질문에 감사하다는 대답은 문맥에 어울리지 않으므로 오답.

10

W-Am How long can I use the free trial of the software?

M-Au (A) The standard length is one meter.

(B) To track charges over time.

(C) For a maximum of thirty days.

소프트웨어 무료 체험은 얼마 동안 해 볼 수 있나요?

(A) 표준 길이는 1미터입니다.
(B) 시간에 따른 요금을 추적해 보려고요.
(C) 최대 30일 동안이요.

어휘 free trial 무료 체험 standard 표준의 track 추적하다 charge 요금 over time 시간이 지나면서 maximum 최대

해설 무료 체험 기간을 묻는 How 의문문

(A) 연상 단어 오답. 질문의 How long에 대해 기간이 아닌 길이 측면에서 연상 가능한 one meter를 이용한 오답.

(B) 연상 단어 오답. 질문의 free에 대해 연상 가능한 charge를 이용한 오답.

(C) 정답. 소프트웨어 무료 체험을 얼마 동안 해 볼 수 있냐는 질문에 최대 30일 동안이라고 구체적인 기간으로 응답하고 있으므로 정답.

11

W-Br Can you play the piano without using sheet music?

M-Cn (A) That's entirely up to you.

(B) It's another sheet.

(C) Only a few songs.

악보를 보지 않고 피아노를 연주할 수 있나요?

(A) 전적으로 당신에게 달렸어요.
(B) 그건 다른 종이에요.
(C) 몇 곡만이요.

어휘 sheet music 악보 entirely 전적으로 sheet (종이) 한 장

해설 악보를 보지 않고 피아노를 연주할 수 있는지를 묻는 조동사 의문문

(A) 질문과 상관없는 오답. 질문에 어울리지 않는 응답을 하고 있으므로 오답.

(B) 단어 반복 오답. 질문의 sheet을 반복한 오답.

(C) 정답. 악보를 보지 않고 피아노를 연주할 수 있는지 묻는 질문에 몇 곡은 가능하다고 응답하고 있으므로 정답.

12

W-Br Where can I donate my gently used clothing?

M-Au (A) It looks flattering on you.

(B) Try the community center.

(C) I've already donated fifty dollars.

깨끗이 입은 옷은 어디에 기부할 수 있을까요?

(A) 당신을 돋보이게 하는군요.
(B) 지역 센터에 해 보세요.
(C) 이미 50달러를 기부했어요.

어휘 donate 기부하다 flattering 돋보이게 하는

해설 기부할 장소를 묻는 Where 의문문

(A) 연상 단어 오답. 질문의 clothing에 대해 연상 가능한 looks flattering을 이용한 오답.

Test 7

(B) 정답. 깨끗이 입은 옷을 어디에 기부할 수 있는지를 묻는 질문에 지역 센터에 가 보라며 구체적인 장소로 응답하고 있으므로 정답.

(C) 단어 반복 오답. 질문의 donate를 과거형인 donated로 반복한 오답.

13

M-Au When does the author's new mystery novel come out?

M-Cn (A) The hardback or paperback version?

(B) It had a surprise ending.

(C) Sure, I'd like to come with you.

그 작가의 새 추리소설은 언제 나오나요?

(A) 양장본이요, 아니면 문고판이요?
(B) 결말이 뜻밖이었어요.
(C) 물론이죠. 제가 함께 가고 싶습니다.

어휘 mystery novel 추리소설 come out 출간되다 author 저자 hardback 양장본 surprise ending 뜻밖의 결말 paperback 문고판

해설 새 추리소설이 언제 나오는지 묻는 When 의문문

(A) 정답. 그 작가의 새 추리소설이 언제 나오는지를 묻는 질문에 양장본인지 문고판인지 되물음으로써 추가적인 정보를 요구하고 있으므로 정답.

(B) 연상 단어 오답. 질문의 novel에서 연상 가능한 surprise ending을 이용한 오답.

(C) 단어 반복 오답. 질문의 come을 반복한 오답.

14

W-Am How were the refreshments at the seminar?

W-Br (A) Please put the fresh ones here.

(B) Actually, I didn't sample any.

(C) We learned quite a lot about business.

세미나에서 다과는 어땠나요?

(A) 신선한 것들을 여기에 두십시오.
(B) 사실 하나도 시식하지 않았어요.
(C) 사업에 관해 꽤 많이 배웠습니다.

어휘 refreshment 다과 actually 사실 sample 시식하다, 시음하다

해설 세미나의 다과는 어땠는지 묻는 How 의문문

(A) 유사 발음 오답. 질문의 refreshments와 부분적으로 발음이 동일한 fresh를 이용한 오답.

(B) 정답. 세미나에서 다과는 어땠는지 묻는 질문에 사실 하나도 시식하지 않았다고 대답함으로써 모른다는 대답을 우회적으로 하고 있으므로 정답.

(C) 연상 단어 오답. 질문의 seminar에서 연상 가능한 learned quite a lot을 이용한 오답.

15

W-Am Does the campground offer a shower facility for those who stay there?

M-Au (A) We camped in tents for three nights.

(B) It's in a popular national park.

(C) No, only restrooms and outdoor sinks.

야영지에서 야영하는 사람들을 위해 샤워 시설을 제공하나요?

(A) 텐트에서 사흘밤을 야영했어요.
(B) 인기 있는 국립공원에 있어요.
(C) 아니오, 화장실과 실외 개수대만 있어요.

어휘 campground 야영지 facility 시설 camp 야영하다 outdoor 야외의 sink 개수대

해설 샤워 시설을 제공하는지 여부를 묻는 조동사 의문문

(A) 유사 발음 오답. 질문의 campground와 부분적으로 발음이 동일한 camped를 이용한 오답.

(B) 연상 단어 오답. 질문의 campground에서 연상 가능한 national park를 이용한 오답.

(C) 정답. 야영지에서 숙박하는 사람들을 위해 샤워 시설을 제공하는지 묻는 질문에 No라는 부정적인 응답을 한 후, 화장실과 실외 개수대만 있다며 부연 설명을 하고 있으므로 정답.

16

M-Cn Who locked a bicycle to the railing outside?

W-Am (A) I have no idea.

(B) Yes, it should remain locked.

(C) You can drive to work.

누가 자전거를 밖에 있는 철책에 고정해 뒀죠?

(A) 모르겠어요.
(B) 네, 자전거는 고정해 둬야 합니다.
(C) 운전해서 출근하셔도 됩니다.

어휘 lock 잠그다 railing 철책, 난간

해설 누가 자전거를 철책에 고정했는지를 묻는 Who 의문문

(A) 정답. 자전거를 누가 밖에 있는 철책에 고정해 뒀는지를 묻는 질문에 모르겠다고 답하므로 정답.

(B) Yes/No 불가 오답. Who 의문문에 Yes/No 응답이 불가능하므로 오답.

(C) 질문과 상관없는 오답. 누가 자전거를 철책에 고정했는지 묻는 질문에 운전해서 출근하라는 대답은 문맥에 맞지 않으므로 오답.

17

M-Au Could you pick up some souvenirs at the museum?

W-Br (A) To see a contemporary art exhibition.

(B) What did you have in mind?

(C) It's near my apartment building.

박물관에서 기념품을 사다 줄 수 있나요?

(A) 현대 미술 전시회를 보기 위해서요.
(B) 생각해 두신 게 뭔가요?
(C) 제 아파트 근처에 있습니다.

어휘 pick up ~을 사다 souvenir 기념품 contemporary 동시대의 exhibition 전시회 have in mind 염두에 두다, 생각하다

해설 기념품을 사다 줄 수 있는지 묻는 요청 의문문

(A) 질문과 상관없는 오답. 이유를 묻는 Why 의문문에 어울리는 응답이므로 오답.

(B) 정답. 박물관에서 기념품을 사다 줄 수 있느냐는 요청에 생각해 둔 게 뭔지 되물음으로써 추가적인 정보를 요구하고 있으므로 정답.

(C) 질문과 상관없는 오답. 장소를 묻는 Where 의문문에 어울리는 응답이므로 오답.

18

M-Cn What is the fee for getting a building permit?

W-Br (A) Yes, and a building expansion too.

(B) It depends on the type of project.

(C) Sure, that's fine with me.

건축 허가 수수료는 얼마입니까?
(A) 네, 건물 확장도 그렇고요.
(B) **프로젝트 유형에 따라 다릅니다.**
(C) 물론입니다. 저는 괜찮아요.

어휘 permit 허가 fee 수수료, 요금 expansion 확장 depend on ~에 달려 있다 type 유형

해설 건축 허가 수수료를 묻는 What 의문문
(A) 단어 반복 오답. 질문의 building을 반복한 오답.
(B) 정답. 건축 허가 수수료가 얼마냐는 질문에 프로젝트 유형에 따라 다르다는 우회적인 표현으로 응답하고 있으므로 정답.
(C) 질문과 상관없는 오답. 제안 의문문에 어울리는 응답이므로 오답.

19

M-Au Why is there cake and coffee in the break room?

W-Am (A) It's Ms. Garcia's birthday.

(B) I take mine with milk and sugar.

(C) Let's save a slice for later.

휴게실에 왜 케이크와 커피가 있죠?
(A) **가르시아 씨의 생일이거든요.**
(B) 저는 우유와 설탕을 넣어요.
(C) 나중을 위해 한 조각 남겨 둡시다.

어휘 break room 휴게실 take (음식물을) 먹다, 마시다 slice 조각

해설 휴게실에 케이크와 커피가 있는 이유를 묻는 Why 의문문
(A) 정답. 휴게실에 왜 케이크와 커피가 있느냐는 질문에 가르시아 씨의 생일이라는 이유로 답변하고 있으므로 정답.
(B) 연상 단어 오답. 질문의 coffee에서 연상 가능한 milk and sugar를 이용한 오답.
(C) 연상 단어 오답. 질문의 cake에서 연상 가능한 slice를 이용한 오답.

20

W-Am What's the balance due on the car loan?

M-Cn (A) Thanks, I could use a ride.

(B) I drive a two-door convertible.

(C) It's listed on the account statement.

자동차 대출 잔금이 얼마입니까?
(A) 감사합니다. 태워 주신다면 저야 좋죠.
(B) 투도어 컨버터블을 탑니다.
(C) **계좌 명세서에 나와 있습니다.**

어휘 balance due 미불액 loan 대출 could use ~을 얻을 수 있으면 좋겠다, 필요하다 two-door 문짝이 두 개인 convertible 오픈카 list 명단에 올리다 account statement 계좌 명세서

해설 지불해야 하는 잔액이 얼마인지 묻는 What 의문문
(A) 연상 단어 오답. 질문의 car에서 연상 가능한 ride를 이용한 오답.
(B) 연상 단어 오답. 질문의 car에서 연상 가능한 drive를 이용한 오답.
(C) 정답. 자동차 대출 잔금이 얼마인지 묻는 질문에 계좌 명세서에 나와 있다고 우회적으로 응답하고 있으므로 정답.

21

W-Br Would you like to pay for the merchandise by cash or credit card?

M-Au (A) I'll put it on my card this time.

(B) Yes, that's what we usually prefer.

(C) They get paid at the end of the month.

상품 결제를 현금 또는 신용카드 중 뭘로 하시겠습니까?
(A) **이번엔 신용카드로 하겠습니다.**
(B) 네, 그것이 저희가 보통 선호하는 것입니다.
(C) 그들은 월말에 급여를 받습니다.

어휘 merchandise 상품 put on ~에 (돈을) 부과하다 get paid 봉급을 받다

해설 구를 연결한 선택 의문문
(A) 정답. 상품 결제를 현금 또는 신용카드 중 뭘로 지불하겠냐는 질문에 신용카드로 지불하겠다고 응답하므로 정답.
(B) Yes/No 불가 오답. 선택 의문문 A or B에서 A, B가 구인 경우 Yes/No 응답이 불가능하므로 오답.
(C) 단어 반복 오답. 질문의 pay를 과거형인 paid로 반복한 오답.

22

W-Am You sell replacement components for the washing machine, don't you?

M-Cn (A) Only the most common ones.

(B) It has an extra rinse cycle.

(C) Yes, that's the best place for it.

세탁기 교체용 부품을 판매하시죠, 그렇죠?
(A) **가장 일반적인 부품만 팝니다.**
(B) 헹굼 추가 기능이 있습니다.
(C) 네, 가장 최적의 장소입니다.

어휘 replacement component 교체용 부품 common 흔한 extra 추가의 rinse cycle (세탁기) 헹굼 기능

해설 교체용 부품 판매 여부를 묻는 부가 의문문
(A) 정답. 세탁기 교체용 부품을 판매하느냐는 질문에 가장 일반적인 부품만 판다고 응답하고 있으므로 정답.
(B) 연상 단어 오답. 질문의 washing machine에서 연상 가능한 rinse cycle을 이용한 오답.
(C) 유사 발음 오답. 질문의 replacement와 부분적으로 발음이 동일한 place를 이용한 오답.

23

M-Cn When will the first issue of the magazine arrive?

W-Br (A) A lot of useful articles for subscribers.
(B) At the customer's residential address.
(C) In the middle of the month.

잡지 창간호가 언제 도착할 예정입니까?
(A) 구독자를 위한 유용한 기사가 많아요.
(B) 고객의 거주지 주소로요.
(C) 이번 달 중순이에요.

어휘 issue 호 article 기사 subscriber 구독자 residential 거주의
in the middle of ~의 중간에

해설 잡지가 언제 도착하는지를 묻는 When 의문문
(A) 연상 단어 오답. 질문의 magazine에서 연상 가능한 articles를 이용한
오답.
(B) 연상 단어 오답. 질문의 arrive에서 연상 가능한 residential address를
이용한 오답.
(C) 정답. 잡지 창간호가 언제 도착할 예정인지 묻는 질문에 이달 중순이라고
응답하므로 정답.

24

W-Am Should we rearrange the furniture in the waiting
room?

W-Br (A) Yes, I had to wait nearly an hour.
(B) But Mr. Blanton favors the current layout.
(C) The color of the sofa matches perfectly.

대기실 가구를 다시 배치해야 하나요?
(A) 네, 거의 한 시간을 기다려야 했습니다.
(B) 하지만 블랜턴 씨는 현재의 배치를 선호하는데요.
(C) 소파 색상이 완벽하게 어울립니다.

어휘 rearrange 재배열하다 waiting room 대기실 nearly 거의
favor 편애하다 current 현재의 layout 배치 match 어울리다

해설 가구 재배치 여부를 묻는 조동사 의문문
(A) 파생어 오답. 질문의 waiting과 파생 관계인 wait를 이용한 오답.
(B) 정답. 대기실 가구를 다시 배치해야 하는지를 묻는 질문에 블랜턴 씨가 현
재의 배치를 선호한다고 부정적으로 응답하고 있으므로 정답.
(C) 연상 단어 오답. 질문의 furniture에 대해 연상 가능한 sofa를 이용한 오답.

25

M-Cn Where is the best place to install this new device?

W-Br (A) In the evening, after everyone goes home.
(B) It will make a series of beeping noises.
(C) Maybe there's a recommendation in the
manual.

이 장치를 설치할 최적의 장소는 어디입니까?
(A) 오후요, 모두들 집에 간 후에요.
(B) 삐 소리가 연이어 날 거예요.
(C) 아마 설명서에 권고 사항이 있을 거예요.

어휘 install 설치하다 a series of 일련의 device 장치 beep 삐
소리를 내다 noise 소리, 소음 manual 설명서

해설 장치를 설치할 최적의 장소를 묻는 Where 의문문
(A) 질문과 상관없는 오답. 시간을 묻는 when의문문에 어울리는 응답이므로
오답.
(B) 연상 단어 오답. 질문의 device에 대해 연상 가능한 beeping noise를 이
용한 오답.
(C) 정답. 장치를 설치할 최적의 장소를 묻는 질문에 설명서에 권고 사항을 있
을 거라며 설명서를 확인해 볼 것을 권하고 있으므로 정답.

26

M-Au Some of the guests at the banquet are vegetarians.

W-Br (A) Has the chef been informed about this?
(B) We want to recognize the company's
achievements.
(C) Sorry, but I wasn't able to be in attendance.

연회 손님 일부는 채식주의자입니다.
(A) 주방장이 그 사실을 전달받았나요?
(B) 그 회사의 업적을 표창하고 싶습니다.
(C) 죄송합니다만 저는 참석할 수 없었어요.

어휘 banquet 연회 vegetarian 채식주의자 be informed 통지를
받다 recognize 공인하다, 표창하다 achievement 업적 be in
attendance 참석하다

해설 정보를 제공하는 평서문
(A) 정답. 연회 손님 일부는 채식주의자라는 말에 주방장이 그 사실을 전달받았
냐고 되묻고 있으므로 정답.
(B) 질문과 상관없는 오답. 연회 손님 일부는 채식주의자라는 말에 회사의 업적
을 표창하고 싶다고 문맥에 맞지 않는 응답을 하고 있으므로 오답.
(C) 연상 단어 오답. 질문의 banquet에 대해 연상 가능한 attendance를 이용
한 오답.

27

W-Am Will the picnic be canceled or postponed in case of
bad weather?

M-Cn (A) A major snowstorm is headed this way.
(B) We'll reschedule it for later.
(C) At the Kellerson Park picnic area.

날씨가 안 좋을 경우 소풍은 취소될까요, 아니면 연기될까요?
(A) 심한 눈보라가 이쪽을 향하고 있어요.
(B) 나중으로 일정을 다시 잡을 겁니다.
(C) 켈러슨 파크 소풍 구역에서요.

어휘 cancel 취소하다 postpone 연기하다 in case of ~의 경우
snowstorm 눈보라 head 향하다 reschedule 일정을 다시 잡다,
일정을 바꾸다

해설 구를 연결한 선택 의문문
(A) 연상 단어 오답. 질문의 bad weather에 대해 연상 가능한 snowstorm
을 이용한 오답.
(B) 정답. 날씨가 안 좋을 경우 소풍이 취소될지 아니면 연기될지 묻는 질문에
일정을 미룰 것이라고 응답하고 있으므로 정답.
(C) 단어 반복 오답. 질문의 picnic을 반복한 오답.

28

W-Am Why has the intermission been extended to twenty-five minutes?

M-Au (A) The theater manager would know.

(B) Between the first and second act of the play.

(C) No, you don't need permission to do so.

중간 휴식 시간이 왜 25분으로 연장됐나요?

(A) 극장 관리자가 알 겁니다.

(B) 연극 1막과 2막 중간이에요.

(C) 아니오, 그렇게 하는 데 허가는 필요 없습니다.

어휘 intermission 중간 휴식 시간 extend 연장하다 act 막 permission 허가

해설 휴식 시간이 늘어난 이유를 묻는 Why 의문문

(A) 정답. 휴식 시간이 25분으로 늘어난 이유를 묻는 질문에 극장 관리자가 알 것이라는 우회적인 표현을 통해 자신이 모른다는 것을 나타내고 있으므로 정답.

(B) 연상 단어 오답. 질문의 intermission에서 연상 가능한 the first and second act of play를 이용한 오답.

(C) Yes/No 불가 오답. Why 의문문에는 Yes/No 응답이 불가능하므로 오답.

29

M-Cn This medication won't make me sleepy, will it?

W-Am (A) Yes, you should expect that she will.

(B) I take it once in a while for backaches.

(C) It's designed specifically for daytime use.

이 약은 졸리게 하지 않죠, 그렇죠?

(A) 네, 그녀가 그럴 것이라고 예상해야 합니다.

(B) 요통 때문에 때때로 복용해요.

(C) 특별히 낮 시간용으로 제조되었습니다.

어휘 medication 약 expect 예상하다 take (약을) 복용하다 once in a while 때로, 가끔 backache 요통 design for ~을 목적으로 만들다 specifically 특별히 daytime 낮 (시간)

해설 약이 졸리게 하는지 여부를 묻는 선택 의문문

(A) 질문과 상관없는 오답. 이 약이 졸리게 하는지 여부에 대한 질문에 그녀가 그럴 것이라고 예상해야 한다며 문맥에 맞지 않는 응답을 하고 있으므로 오답.

(B) 연상 단어 오답. 질문의 medication에서 연상 가능한 take it과 backaches를 이용한 오답.

(C) 정답. 이 약이 졸리게 하지 않느냐는 질문에 특별히 낮 시간용으로 제조되었다고 응답해 졸리게 하지 않는다는 의미를 우회적으로 표현하고 있으므로 정답.

30

M-Au Do you need a transcript of the radio interview?

M-Cn (A) No, there wasn't a copy in the file I was given.

(B) Oh, I was invited to interview for a different job.

(C) The audio recording will be enough for my purposes.

라디오 인터뷰 대본이 필요하세요?

(A) 아니오, 제가 받은 파일에는 없었어요.

(B) 다른 일자리 면접에 오라고 요청받았어요.

(C) 제 용도로는 오디오 녹음으로 충분합니다.

어휘 transcript 글로 옮긴 기록 copy 부, 권

해설 인터뷰 대본이 필요한지 여부를 묻는 조동사 의문문

(A) 연상 단어 오답. 질문의 transcript에서 연상 가능한 copy와 file을 이용한 오답.

(B) 단어 반복 오답. 질문의 interview를 반복한 오답.

(C) 정답. 라디오 인터뷰 대본이 필요하냐는 질문에 오디오 녹음으로 충분하다고 응답해 필요 없음을 우회적으로 표현하고 있으므로 정답은 (C)이다.

31

M-Au There have been some surprising developments in the currency market.

W-Br (A) The prices are listed in Japanese yen and euros.

(B) We've got to keep a close eye on that.

(C) Wasn't it closed because of some road work?

통화시장에 놀라운 변화들이 있었습니다.

(A) 가격은 일본 엔화와 유로화로 나와 있습니다.

(B) 주의 깊게 지켜봐야겠군요.

(C) 그곳은 도로 작업 때문에 문을 닫지 않았나요?

어휘 development 새로이 전개된 국면 currency market 통화시장 keep a close eye on ~를 주의 깊게 지켜보다

해설 정보를 제공하는 평서문

(A) 연상 단어 오답. 질문의 currency에 대해 연상 가능한 yen and euros를 이용한 오답.

(B) 정답. 통화시장에 놀라운 변화들이 있었다는 말에 주의 깊게 지켜봐야 한다는 제안을 하고 있으므로 정답.

(C) 연상 단어 오답. 질문의 market을 일반적인 시장의 의미로 이해했을 때 문을 닫는다는 의미의 closed를 이용한 오답.

PART 3

32-34

W-Am [32]I'm sorry, sir, but this coupon cannot be used for your purchase. It's already past the expiration date.

M-Au I didn't realize that. [33]In that case, I don't want to get the electric drill. I was only buying it because of the discount. I'll just purchase the nails for today.

W-Am I've already rung up the items. [34]Since I'm not authorized to make changes myself, I need to call my manager. It'll just take a moment, though.

여:	죄송합니다만 이 쿠폰은 구매하신 물품에 사용하실 수 없습니다. 이미 만료일자가 지났거든요.
남:	몰랐습니다. 그렇다면 전동 드릴은 사고 싶지 않습니다. 할인 때문에 사려고 한 거예요. 오늘은 그냥 못만 사겠습니다.
여:	이미 금전등록기에 상품 가격을 입력했어요. 저는 변경할 권한이 없어서 관리자에게 전화해야 해요. 하지만 금방 될 겁니다.

어휘	purchase 구매품; 구매하다 past 지나서 expiration date 만료일자 electric 전기의 nail 못 ring up (금전등록기에 상품 가격을) 입력하다 be authorized to ~할 권한이 있다

32

What problem does the woman mention?

(A) A product has been discontinued.
(B) A coupon has expired.
(C) An item is out of stock.
(D) A sale period has ended.

여자는 어떤 문제를 언급하는가?

(A) 제품이 단종됐다.
(B) 쿠폰이 만료됐다.
(C) 상품의 재고가 없다.
(D) 할인 기간이 끝났다.

어휘 discontinue 중단하다 expire 만료되다 out of stock 재고가 없는, 품절 상태인

해설 전체 내용 관련 - 여자가 언급하는 문제

여자의 첫 번째 대사에서 쿠폰을 구매한 물품에 사용할 수 없다(this coupon cannot be used for your purchase)며 쿠폰이 이미 만료일자가 지났다(it's already past the expiration date)고 했으므로 정답은 (B)이다.

▸▸ Paraphrasing 대화의 **already past the expiration date** → 정답의 **has expired**

33

Where most likely are the speakers?

(A) At a hardware store
(B) At a pharmacy
(C) At a clothing shop
(D) At a bookstore

화자들은 어디에 있겠는가?

(A) 철물점
(B) 약국
(C) 옷가게
(D) 서점

어휘 hardware store 철물점 pharmacy 약국

해설 전체 내용 관련 - 화자들이 있는 장소

남자의 첫 번째 대사에서 쿠폰을 사용할 수 없으므로 전동 드릴은 사지 않겠다(I don't want to get the electric drill)며 할인 때문에 사려고 했던 것(I was only buying it because of the discount)이라고 말했다. 이어서 오늘은 못만 사겠다(I'll just purchase the nails for today)고 했으므로 정답은 (A)이다.

▸▸ Paraphrasing 대화의 **electric drill, nails** → 정답의 **hardware**

34

What will the woman most likely do next?

(A) Show the man some merchandise
(B) Contact a supervisor
(C) Give the man a receipt
(D) Authorize a discount

여자는 다음으로 무엇을 하겠는가?

(A) 남자에게 상품 보여 주기
(B) 상관에게 연락하기
(C) 남자에게 영수증 주기
(D) 할인 승인하기

어휘 merchandise 상품 supervisor 상사, 관리자 receipt 영수증 authorize 승인하다

해설 세부 사항 관련 - 여자의 계획

여자는 본인은 변경할 권한이 없어서 관리자에게 전화해야 한다(Since I'm not authorized to make changes myself, I need to call my manager)고 말했으므로 정답은 (B)이다.

▸▸ Paraphrasing 대화의 **call my manager** → 정답의 **Contact a supervisor**

35-37

M-Au	Polly, have you seen the latest sales report? **35The number of units sold has declined by nearly twenty percent compared to last quarter.**
W-Br	Yes, I was concerned to see those figures. I think we'd better set up a committee to examine the driving force behind the change. **36Lynnette Beck could head up that project since she's an expert in market research.**
M-Au	Good idea. We'll need about five or six people to join the committee.
W-Br	OK. **37I'll find some volunteers who are willing to take on this task.**

남:	폴리 씨, 최근 영업보고서 봤어요? 판매된 제품 수량이 지난 분기에 비해 거의 20퍼센트 하락했어요.
여:	네, 그 수치를 보니 우려가 됩니다. 위원회를 소집해 이러한 변화의 배후 요소를 조사하는 것이 좋을 듯합니다. 리네트 벡 씨가 시장조사 전문가이니 그 프로젝트를 이끌 수 있을 겁니다.
남:	좋은 생각이군요. 위원회에 참여할 사람이 대여섯 명 필요할 겁니다.
여:	알겠습니다. 이 일을 맡을 의향이 있는 지원자를 찾아볼게요.

어휘	sales report 영업보고서 unit (상품의) 한 개[단위] decline 하락하다 compared to ~와 비교하여 quarter 분기 be concerned 우려하다 figure 수치 had better ~하는 편이 낫다 set up 마련하다 committee 위원회 driving force 원동력, 추진력 head up 이끌다 expert 전문가 market research 시장조사 be willing to 기꺼이 ~하다 take on (일 등을) 맡다

35

What is the conversation mainly about?

(A) A company relocation
(B) A product launch
(C) A change in policy
(D) A decline in sales

대화는 주로 무엇에 관한 것인가?

(A) 회사 이전
(B) 제품 출시
(C) 정책 변경
(D) 매출 하락

어휘 relocation 이전 launch 출시 policy 방침 decline in ~의 하락

해설 전체 내용 관련 – 대화의 주제

남자의 첫 번째 대사에서 판매된 제품 수량이 지난 분기에 비해 거의 20퍼센트 하락했다(The number of units sold has declined by nearly twenty percent compared to last quarter)고 말했으므로 정답은 (D)이다.

▶▶ **Paraphrasing** 대화의 **The number of units sold has declined** → 정답의 **A decline in sales**

36

What does the woman mention about Ms. Beck?

(A) She completed a project quickly.
(B) She has compiled a report.
(C) She joined the team last quarter.
(D) She has expertise in the field.

여자가 벡 씨에 관해 언급한 것은 무엇인가?

(A) 프로젝트를 빠르게 완료했다.
(B) 보고서를 작성했다.
(C) 지난 분기에 팀에 합류했다.
(D) 해당 분야의 전문 지식을 갖고 있다.

어휘 compile 만들다 expertise 전문 지식, 전문 기술 field 분야

해설 세부 사항 관련 – 여자가 벡 씨에 관해 언급한 것

여자의 첫 번째 대사에서 리네트 벡 씨가 시장조사 전문가이므로 그 프로젝트를 이끌 수 있을 것(Lynnette Beck could head up that project since she's an expert in market research)이라고 말했으므로 정답은 (D)이다.

▶▶ **Paraphrasing** 대화의 **she's an expert in market research** → 정답의 **She has expertise in the field.**

37

What does the woman say she will do?

(A) Reserve a meeting space
(B) Update some figures
(C) Recruit group members
(D) Congratulate some volunteers

여자는 무엇을 하겠다고 말하는가?

(A) 회의 장소 예약하기
(B) 수치 업데이트하기
(C) 그룹 구성원 모집하기
(D) 지원자들을 축하하기

어휘 reserve 예약하다 recruit 모집하다, 뽑다

해설 세부 사항 관련 – 여자의 계획

여자의 두 번째 대사에서 이 일을 맡을 의향이 있는 지원자를 찾아보겠다(I'll find some volunteers who are willing to take on this task)고 했으므로 정답은 (C)이다.

▶▶ **Paraphrasing** 대화의 **find some volunteers** → 정답의 **Recruit group members**

38-40

M-Cn	Good morning. **38I registered for the conference online and was mailed the admission pass in the welcome packet but, unfortunately, I forgot to bring it with me.**
W-Am	I can check your ID and print you a new pass, but that'll take about fifteen minutes. The opening talk starts in just five minutes.
M-Cn	**39Am I allowed to go in after it begins so that I can at least see part of it?**
W-Am	**40I think that's all right as long as you sit in the back, but let me check that with my colleague just to be sure.** I wouldn't want you to have any trouble at the door.

남:	안녕하세요. 저는 온라인으로 회의에 등록했고 환영 패키지에 든 입장권을 우편으로 받았는데요. 안타깝게도 잊고 가져오지 못했어요.
여:	귀하의 신분증을 확인하고 새 입장권을 출력해 드릴 수 있습니다. 하지만 15분 정도 걸릴 겁니다. 개회사가 5분 후면 시작돼요.
남:	시작한 후에 들어가서 최소한 일부라도 볼 수 있나요?
여:	뒤쪽에 앉아 있는 한 괜찮을 것 같습니다. 하지만 혹시나 모르니 제 동료에게 물어 보겠습니다. 입구에서 문제가 생기지 않았으면 하거든요.

어휘 register for ~에 등록하다 conference 회의 mail (우편으로) 부치다 admission pass 입장권 welcome packet 환영 패키지(여러 정보가 담긴 꾸러미) opening talk 개회사 be allowed to ~하는 것이 허용되다 as long as ~ 하는 한 check with ~에게 문의하다 just to be sure 혹시나 해서 have trouble 곤란을 겪다 colleague 동료

38

What is the man's problem?

(A) He missed a registration deadline.
(B) He does not have an admission pass.
(C) He could not get a Web site to load.
(D) He lost his welcome packet.

남자에게 어떤 문제가 있는가?

(A) 등록 마감 기한을 놓쳤다.
(B) 입장권을 소지하고 있지 않다.
(C) 웹사이트가 로딩되지 않았다.
(D) 환영 패키지를 잃어버렸다.

어휘 miss 놓치다 registration 등록하다 load (데이터나 프로그램이) 로딩되다

해설 전체 내용 관련 – 남자의 문제

남자의 첫 번째 대사에서 온라인으로 회의에 등록했고(I registered for the conference online) 환영 패키지에 든 입장권을 우편으로 받았는데, 안타깝게도 잊고 가져오지 못했다(was mailed the admission pass in the welcome packet but, unfortunately, I forgot to bring it with me)고 말했으므로 정답은 (B)이다.

39

What does the man inquire about?

(A) Signing up for a different talk
(B) Getting a partial refund
(C) Making a last-minute payment
(D) Entering a session late

남자는 무엇에 대해 문의하는가?

(A) 다른 강연에 등록하기
(B) 일부 환불 받기
(C) 막바지에 지불하기
(D) 회의에 늦게 들어가기

어휘 sign up for ~을 신청하다 talk 연설, 강연 partial 부분적인
last-minute 막바지의 session 수업 (시간), 강습회

해설 세부 사항 관련 – 남자가 문의하는 것

남자의 두 번째 대사에서 시작한 후에 들어가서 최소한 일부라도 볼 수 있느냐(Am I allowed to go in after it begins so that I can at least see part of it)고 묻고 있으므로 정답은 (D)이다.

▸▸ Paraphrasing 대화의 go in after it begins
→ 정답의 Entering a session late

40

What will the woman most likely do next?

(A) Verify the man's address
(B) Confirm some details
(C) Reserve a seat near the back
(D) Print out a registration form

여자는 다음으로 무엇을 하겠는가?

(A) 남자의 주소 확인하기
(B) 세부 사항 확인하기
(C) 뒤쪽 좌석 예약하기
(D) 신청서 출력하기

어휘 verify 확인하다, 인증하다 print out 출력하다

해설 세부 사항 관련 – 여자가 할 일

여자의 두 번째 대사에서 혹시나 모르니 제 동료에게 물어보겠다(let me check that with my colleague just to be sure)고 했으므로 정답은 (B)이다.

▸▸ Paraphrasing 대화의 check that with my colleague just
to be sure → 정답의 Confirm some details

41-43

M-Au **41Cara, could you cover my shift at the restaurant on Friday?** I know you wanted to pick up extra shifts to save money for your vacation next month.

W-Br You're right about that, **41but there's a folk music festival on Friday.** It's one night only.

M-Au I understand. I'll try to get someone else to do it.

W-Br Why are you taking time off?

M-Au **42My friend is having a special dinner because he recently got a promotion, so I wanted to be there.**

W-Br You know, I think Gary wanted to work extra shifts too. **43I can give you his number if you want to try calling him.**

M-Au Thanks. I appreciate that.

남: 카라 씨, 금요일에 식당에서 저 대신 근무해 주실 수 있나요? 다음 달 휴가 자금 저축을 위해 초과 근무를 하고 싶어 하시는 걸로 아는데요.

여: 맞아요. 하지만 금요일에 포크 음악 축제가 있어요. 딱 하루만 하는 거라서요.

남: 그렇군요. 다른 사람을 구해 볼게요.

여: 왜 휴가를 내세요?

남: 제 친구가 최근 승진을 해서 특별히 저녁 식사를 하는데 거기에 가고 싶어요.

여: 개리 씨도 추가 근무를 하고 싶어 했던 것 같아요. 그에게 전화해 보고 싶으시면 번호를 드릴 수 있어요.

남: 그래주면 고맙겠어요.

어휘 cover one's shift ~ 대신 근무하다 pick up ~을 얻다
extra 추가의 take time off 휴가를 내다 get a
promotion 승진하다

41

What does the woman mean when she says, "It's one night only"?

(A) A deadline for a task is too short.
(B) She cannot work in the man's place.
(C) A payment will not be large enough.
(D) She plans to take a short vacation.

여자가 "딱 하루만 하는 거라서요"라고 말할 때, 그 의도는 무엇인가?

(A) 일의 마감 기한이 너무 짧다.
(B) 남자 대신 일할 수 없다.
(C) 급여가 충분치 않을 것이다.
(D) 짧은 휴가를 계획하고 있다.

어휘 task 과제, 일 in one's place ~ 대신에

해설 화자의 의도 파악 – 딱 하루만 한다는 말의 의미

남자가 첫 번째 대사에서 금요일에 식당에서 대신 근무할 수 있는지(could you cover my shift at the restaurant on Friday) 묻자 여자가 금요일에 포크 음악 축제가 있고(there's a folk music festival on Friday) 딱 하루만 한다(it's one night only)고 말했다. 따라서 축제에 가야 해서 남자 대신 일할 수 없다는 의미이므로 정답은 (B)이다.

42

Why does the man ask for the woman's help?

(A) He has tickets to a music festival.
(B) He would like to get training at an industry event.
(C) He is preparing himself for a job promotion.
(D) He wants to attend a celebratory event.

남자는 왜 여자의 도움을 요청하는가?

(A) 음악 축제 입장권을 갖고 있다.
(B) 업계 행사에서 교육을 받고 싶다.
(C) 승진을 준비 중이다.
(D) 축하 행사에 참석하고 싶다.

어휘 get training 훈련을 받다 industry 산업 prepare oneself for ~의 준비를 하다 celebratory 기념하는, 축하하는

해설 세부 사항 관련 – 남자가 도움을 요청하는 이유

남자의 세 번째 대사에서 친구가 최근 승진을 해서 특별히 저녁 식사를 하는데 거기에 가고 싶다(My friend is having a special dinner because he recently got a promotion, so I wanted to be there)고 했으므로 정답은 (D)이다.

▸▸ Paraphrasing 대화의 a special dinner
→ 정답의 a celebratory event

43

What does the woman offer to do?

(A) Give the man a confirmation number
(B) Provide some contact information
(C) Work more hours than usual
(D) Call Gary about the situation

여자는 무엇을 해 주겠다고 하는가?

(A) 남자에게 확인 번호 주기
(B) 연락처 제공하기
(C) 평소보다 오래 일하기
(D) 개리 씨에게 전화해 상황 이야기하기

어휘 confirmation 확인, 확정 than usual 평소보다 더 situation 상황

해설 세부 사항 관련 – 여자의 제안

여자의 세 번째 대사에서 개리 씨가 추가 근무를 하고 싶어 했던 것 같고, 그에게 전화하고 싶다면 번호를 줄 수 있다(I can give you his number if you want to try calling him)고 했으므로 정답은 (B)이다.

▸▸ Paraphrasing 대화의 I can give you his number
→ 정답의 Provide some contact information

44-46

M-Cn **⁴⁴The company's new CEO, Zhi Chan, plans to place a greater emphasis on professional development. ⁴⁵Consequently, employees can take a tax certification course next month. Are you going to do it?**

W-Br **My former company did the same thing.** You should definitely take it, though. It's well worth your time.

M-Cn It might not be exactly the same. **⁴⁶I'd be happy to show you the workbook, accompanying articles, and my notes if you're interested.**

W-Br Thanks! I think it'd be really helpful to brush up on the contents.

남: 회사의 신임 최고경영자인 치 찬 씨는 전문성 개발을 더욱 강조할 계획입니다. 이에 따라 직원들은 다음 달 세금 자격증 과정을 들을 수 있습니다. 들을 예정이신가요?

여: 이전 회사에서 같은 과정을 했어요. 그런데 꼭 들으셔야 해요. 시간을 들일 가치가 충분합니다.

남: 똑같지는 않을 겁니다. 관심이 있으시다면 워크북, 첨부 기사, 제 메모 등을 보여드리고 싶어요.

여: 감사합니다. 내용을 복습하는 데 아주 유용할 것 같아요.

어휘 CEO 최고경영자(= Chief Executive Officer) place an emphasis on ~를 강조하다 professional development 전문성 개발 consequently 그 결과, 따라서 tax 세금 certification 증명(서), 자격증 definitely 확실히, 분명히 well worth 가치가 충분한 accompanying 동봉[첨부]한 brush up on ~을 다시 공부하다, 복습하다 contents 내용

44

What has the speaker's company recently done?

(A) Hired a new executive
(B) Developed a unique product
(C) Undergone an inspection
(D) Obtained board certification

화자의 회사는 최근에 무엇을 했는가?

(A) 새 임원을 고용했다
(B) 독특한 제품을 개발했다
(C) 조사를 받았다
(D) 이사회 인증을 받았다

어휘 hire 채용하다 executive 임원 unique 독특한 undergo ~을 겪다[받다] inspection 점검 obtain 얻다 board 이사회

해설 세부 사항 관련 – 화자의 회사가 최근에 한 일

남자의 첫 번째 대사에서 회사의 신임 최고경영자인 치 찬 씨는 전문성 개발을 더욱 강조할 계획(The company's new CEO, Zhi Chan, plans to place a greater emphasis on professional development)이라고 말했으므로 정답은 (A)이다.

▸▸ Paraphrasing 대화의 new CEO → 정답의 new executive

45

What does the woman suggest when she says, "My former company did the same thing"?

(A) She is not planning to take part in a course.
(B) She wants the company to remain competitive.
(C) She thinks a proposal is a good idea.
(D) She will ask an old employer for information.

여자가 "이전 회사에서도 같은 과정을 했어요"라고 말할 때, 그 의도는 무엇인가?

(A) 과정에 참가할 계획이 없다.
(B) 회사가 경쟁력을 유지하기를 바란다.
(C) 제안이 좋은 생각이라고 여긴다.
(D) 이전 고용주에게 정보를 요청할 것이다.

어휘 take part in ~에 참여하다 competitive 경쟁력 있는 proposal
제안 ask for ~을 요청하다

해설 화자의 의도 파악 – 이전 회사에서도 같은 과정을 했다는 말의 의미
남자의 첫 번째 대사에서 직원들은 다음 달 세금 자격증 과정을 들을 수 있다면서(employees can take a tax certification course next month)면서 여자에게 들을 예정인지(Are you going to do it) 물었다. 이에 여자가 이전 회사에서 같은 과정을 했다(My former company did the same thing)고 말했다. 따라서 이전 회사에서 했기 때문에 들을 필요가 없다는 의미이므로 정답은 (A)이다.

46

What will the man show the woman?

(A) Some alternative suggestions
(B) Some instructional materials
(C) A training schedule
(D) A copy of a certificate

남자는 여자에게 무엇을 보여줄 것인가?

(A) 대안이 되는 제안
(B) 교육 자료
(C) 교육 일정
(D) 증명서 사본

어휘 alternative 대안의 instructional 교육의 material 자료
certificate 증서, 증명서

해설 세부 사항 관련 – 남자가 여자에게 보여줄 것
남자의 두 번째 대사에서 관심이 있다면 워크북, 첨부 기사, 메모를 보여주고 싶다(I'd be happy to show you the workbook, accompanying articles, and my notes if you're interested)고 했으므로 정답은 (B)이다.

> ▸ Paraphrasing   대화의 **workbook, accompanying articles, and my notes**
> → 정답의 **Some instructional materials**

47-49

W-Am Benjamin, our delivery of office supplies was left in the lobby. **⁴⁷We can't have boxes stacked up like that when the investors visit at three o'clock or they might have a negative opinion of our company.**

M-Cn Those must have arrived while I was on my lunch break. **⁴⁸Since Adam just started working here, I guess he was unsure about what to do with them when they were delivered.**

W-Am **⁴⁹OK, I'll go find him now and ask him to put the boxes in the storage room.** Meanwhile, please set up the projector and video screen in the conference room.

여: 벤자민 씨, 저희 사무용품이 배달되어 로비에 있어요. **투자자들이 3시에 방문할 때 상자들을 그렇게 쌓아둔 모습을 보여드릴 순 없습니다. 그렇지 않으면 우리 회사에 대해 부정적인 인식을 갖게 될 거예요.**

남: 제가 점심 먹으러 간 동안 도착했나 보네요. 애덤 씨가 여기서 일을 막 시작했기 때문에 배송되면 어떻게 해야 하는지 확실히 몰랐나 봅니다.

여: 알겠습니다. 그에게 가서 상자를 창고에 두라고 말할게요. 그동안 회의실에 프로젝터와 비디오 화면을 설치해 주세요.

어휘 delivery 배송 office supplies 사무용품 stack up 쌓다
investor 투자자 negative 부정적인 opinion of ~에 대한
판단[평가] be on lunch break 점심 시간을 갖다 unsure
확신하지 못하는 deliver 배달하다 storage room 창고,
보관실 meanwhile 한편, 그동안 set up 설치하다

47

What is the woman concerned about doing?

(A) Making a bad impression
(B) Delaying a delivery of supplies
(C) Completing repairs in a lobby
(D) Investing in the wrong company

여자는 무엇에 대해 염려하는가?

(A) 나쁜 인상을 주는 것
(B) 물품 배송이 지연되는 것
(C) 로비 보수를 완료하는 것
(D) 엉뚱한 회사에 투자하는 것

어휘 delay 지연시키다 repair 수리 invest in ~에 대한 투자

해설 세부 사항 관련 – 여자가 염려하는 것
여자의 첫 번째 대사에서 투자자들이 3시에 방문할 때 상자들을 그렇게 쌓아둔 모습을 보일 수 없다(We can't have boxes stacked up like that when the investors visit at three o'clock)고 말했고, 그들이 우리 회사에 대해 부정적인 인식을 갖게 될 것(they might have a negative opinion of our company)이라고 말했으므로 정답은 (A)이다.

> ▸ Paraphrasing   대화의 **have a negative opinion**
> → 정답의 **Making a bad impression**

48

What does the man say about Adam?

(A) He ordered the wrong supplies.
(B) He is taking a lunch break.
(C) He arrived to work late.
(D) He is a new employee.

남자는 애덤 씨에 대해 뭐라고 말하는가?

(A) 사무용품을 잘못 주문했다.
(B) 점심을 먹고 있다.
(C) 지각했다.
(D) 신입 직원이다.

어휘 take a lunch break 점심 시간을 갖다

해설 세부 사항 관련 – 남자가 애덤 씨에 대해 하는 말

남자의 첫 번째 대사에서 애덤 씨가 여기서 일을 막 시작했기 때문에(Since Adam just started working here) 배송되면 어떻게 해야 하는지 확실히 몰랐던 것 같다(I guess he was unsure about what to do with them when they were delivered)고 말했으므로 정답은 (D)이다.

▶▶ **Paraphrasing** 대화의 **Adam just started working here**
→ 정답의 **He is a new employee.**

49

What will Adam be asked to do?

(A) Move some containers
(B) Set up some equipment
(C) Clean a conference room
(D) Organize a storage room

애덤 씨는 무엇을 하라고 요청받을 것인가?

(A) 상자 옮기기
(B) 장비 설치하기
(C) 회의실 청소하기
(D) 창고 정리하기

어휘 container 용기 organize 정리하다, 준비하다

해설 세부 사항 관련 – 애덤 씨가 요청받는 것

여자의 두 번째 대사에서 지금 그에게 가서 상자를 창고에 둘 것을 요청하겠다(I'll go find him now and ask him to put the boxes in the storage room)고 했으므로 정답은 (A)이다.

▶▶ **Paraphrasing** 대화의 **put the boxes in the storage room**
→ 정답의 **Move some containers**

50-52 3인 대화

W-Am Good morning. I'd like to speak to Monica Volker, please. This is Lucille Shane.

M-Au I'm afraid Ms. Volker is out of the office. Is there something I can assist you with?

W-Am **50, 51Ms. Volker is organizing an anniversary party for my company, and there will be twenty more guests than originally planned.**

M-Au Let me transfer you to Mr. Irwin, Ms. Volker's assistant. Please hold for a moment.

W-Am All right.

M-Cn Hi, Ms. Shane? **52This is Curt Irwin.** My colleague explained your situation.

W-Am Will it be a problem?

M-Cn Not at all. **52I just need to know whether any of the new people have food allergies before I call the caterer with an update.**

여 안녕하세요. 모니카 볼커 씨와 통화하고 싶습니다. 저는 루실 세인입니다.

남1 죄송합니다만, 볼커 씨는 사무실에 안 계시는데요. 도와드릴 일이 있나요?

여 **볼커 씨가 저희 회사 기념 파티를 준비하고 있는데, 당초 계획보다 손님이 20명 더 많을 듯합니다.**

남1 볼커 씨의 비서인 어윈 씨에게 연결해 드릴게요. 잠시 기다리세요.

여 알겠습니다.

남2 안녕하세요, 세인 씨? **커트 어윈입니다.** 제 동료가 상황을 설명해 줬습니다.

여 문제가 될까요?

남2 전혀 아닙니다. 새 손님 중 음식 알레르기가 있는 분이 있는지만 알면 됩니다. 음식 공급업체에게 전화해서 새로운 정보를 줘야 하니까요.

어휘 assist with ~을 돕다 anniversary 기념일 originally 원래 transfer to ~에게 전화를 돌리다 assistant 조수 hold (수화기를 들고) 기다리다 colleague 동료 caterer 음식 공급사

50

Who most likely is Ms. Volker?

(A) An event planner
(B) A job applicant
(C) A venue owner
(D) A private caterer

볼커 씨는 누구이겠는가?

(A) 행사 기획자
(B) 구직자
(C) 장소 소유주
(D) 사설 음식 공급업체

어휘 planner 기획자 applicant 지원자 venue 장소 private 사설의, 개인의

해설 전체 내용 관련 – 볼커 씨의 직업

여자의 두 번째 대사에서 볼커 씨가 회사의 기념 파티를 준비하고 있다(Ms. Volker is organizing an anniversary party for my company)고 했으므로 정답은 (A)이다.

▶▶ **Paraphrasing** 대화의 **organizing an anniversary party**
→ 정답의 **An event planner**

51

What does the woman want to do?

(A) Move the deadline of a project
(B) Add people to a guest list
(C) Update information on an invitation
(D) Change the location of a party

여자는 무엇을 하고 싶어 하는가?

(A) 프로젝트 마감 기한 옮기기
(B) **손님 명단에 인원 추가하기**
(C) 초대 정보 업데이트하기
(D) 파티 장소 변경하기

어휘 add to ~에 추가하다 guest list 방명록, 손님 명부 location 장소, 위치

해설 세부 사항 관련 – 여자가 하고 싶어 하는 일

여자의 두 번째 대사에서 당초 계획보다 손님이 20명 더 늘어날 것(there will be twenty more guests than originally planned)이라고 했으므로 정답은 (B)이다.

> ▸▸ Paraphrasing   대화의 **twenty more guests than originally planned**
> → 정답의 **Add people to a guest list**

52

What does Mr. Irwin ask the woman to do?

(A) Call back when Ms. Volker is available
(B) Give information about dietary restrictions
(C) Wait on the phone line for a moment
(D) Select some entrées for a meal

어윈 씨는 여자에게 무엇을 하라고 요청하는가?
(A) 볼커 씨가 시간이 될 때 다시 전화하기
(B) 식단 제한 사항에 관한 정보 제공하기
(C) 잠시 끊지 않고 기다리기
(D) 식사를 위한 주요리 선택하기

어휘 available 시간이 있는 dietary 음식물의, 식사의 restriction 제한 select 선택하다 entrée 앙트레, 주요리

해설 세부 사항 관련 – 어윈 씨가 여자에게 요청하는 것

두 번째 남자의 두 번째 대사에서 새 손님 중 음식 알레르기가 있는 분이 있는지 여부를 알고 싶다(I just need to know whether any of the new people have food allergies)고 했으므로 정답은 (B)이다.

> ▸▸ Paraphrasing   대화의 **food allergies**
> → 정답의 **dietary restrictions**

53-55

> W-Br   Congratulations, Lawrence! **53I heard that you were able to get Mercado International to sign a contract to use our financial services. The volume of business they do is nearly double that of the majority of our other clients.**
>
> M-Cn   Yes, I'm very pleased with the outcome. **54With Mercado International on board, we'll finally surpass the market share of Haven Finance.** That'll help us to establish our reputation as experts.
>
> W-Br   Right. But you might have trouble handling a business of Mercado International's size on your own. **55Since there's plenty of room in the budget, we should hire another staff member.**

여: 축하합니다, 로렌스 씨! 메르카도 인터내셔널이 저희 금융서비스를 이용하는 계약을 체결하셨다고 들었습니다. 그들의 거래량이 다른 대다수 고객의 거의 두 배에 달합니다.

남: 네, 결과에 아주 만족합니다. 메르카도 인터내셔널이 합류해서 마침내 헤이븐 파이낸스의 시장 점유율을 앞지르게 될 겁니다. 전문가로서 우리의 명성을 다지는 데 도움이 되겠죠.

여: 맞습니다. 하지만 단독으로 메르카도 인터내셔널의 사업 규모를 감당하기에는 어려움을 겪을 수도 있습니다. 예산에 여유가 많으니 다른 직원을 채용해야 합니다.

어휘 sign a contract 계약을 체결하다 financial service 금융서비스 volume of business 거래량, 업무량 double 두 배의 majority 대다수 outcome 결과 on board 승선하여, 합류하여 surpass 능가하다, 뛰어넘다 market share 시장점유율 establish 수립하다 reputation 평판 have trouble -ing ~하는 데 애를 먹다 on one's own 혼자서, 단독으로 plenty of 많은 room 여지, 여유 budget 예산 hire 채용하다

53

Why does the woman congratulate the man?

(A) He secured a major client.
(B) He found an error in a contract.
(C) He was offered a promotion.
(D) He will transfer to an overseas office.

여자가 남자에게 축하를 건넨 이유는 무엇인가?
(A) 중요한 고객을 확보했다.
(B) 계약서에서 실수를 발견했다.
(C) 승진 제의를 받았다.
(D) 해외 지사로 전근할 것이다.

어휘 secure 확보하다 promotion 승진 transfer 옮기다, 전근하다 overseas 해외의

해설 세부 사항 관련 – 여자가 축하하는 이유

여자의 첫 번째 대사에서 메르카도 인터내셔널이 자사의 금융서비스를 이용하는 계약을 남자가 성사시켰다고 들었고(I heard that you were able to get Mercado International to sign a contract to use our financial services) 그들의 거래량이 다른 대다수 고객의 거의 두 배에 달한다(The volume of business they do is nearly double that of the majority of our other clients)고 했으므로 정답은 (A)이다.

> ▸▸ Paraphrasing   대화의 **sign a contract**
> → 정답의 **secured a client**

54

What does the man suggest about Haven Finance?

(A) It will be a useful corporate partner.
(B) It is currently expanding its workforce.
(C) It is his company's largest competitor.
(D) It recently changed its owner.

남자가 헤이븐 파이낸스에 대해 암시한 것은 무엇인가?
(A) 도움이 되는 협력 업체일 것이다.
(B) 현재 노동력을 확충하고 있다.
(C) 회사의 최대 경쟁업체이다.
(D) 최근 소유주가 바뀌었다.

어휘 currently 현재 expand 확장하다 workforce 인력
competitor 경쟁사 recently 최근에

해설 세부 사항 관련 – 헤이븐 파이낸스에 대해 암시하는 것

남자의 첫 번째 대사에서 메르카도 인터내셔널이 합류해서(with Mercado International on board) 우리가 마침내 헤이븐 파이낸스의 시장 점유율을 앞지르게 될 것(we'll finally surpass the market share of Haven Finance)이라고 했으므로 정답은 (C)이다.

55

What does the woman recommend doing?

(A) Reviewing budget details
(B) Hiring another employee
(C) Attending a board meeting
(D) Holding a staff celebration

여자는 무엇을 하라고 권하는가?

(A) 예산 세부 사항 검토
(B) 다른 직원 채용
(C) 이사회 참석
(D) 직원 축하연 개최

어휘 review 검토하다 budget 예산 hire 고용하다 attend 참석하다
board meeting 이사회 hold 개최하다 celebration 축하 행사

해설 세부 사항 관련 – 여자의 권유

여자의 두 번째 대사에서 예산에 여유가 많기 때문에 다른 직원을 채용해야 한다(Since there's plenty of room in the budget, we should hire another staff member)고 제안했으므로 정답은 (B)이다.

▸▸ **Paraphrasing** 대화의 **hire another staff member**
→ 정답의 **Hiring another employee**

56-58

> W-Am Hi. My name is Gail Henderson, and I registered for your Fun in the Sun cruise to the Caribbean. ⁵⁶**I just realized that my passport has expired, and there won't be time to get a new one. Can I travel with a driver's license instead?**
>
> M-Au Yes. Because our cruise itinerary begins and ends at the same U.S. location, any photo identification from the government is accepted for U.S. citizens. ⁵⁷**You should go over the list of approved forms from the registration packet we mailed you.**
>
> W-Am I never received a packet. I only got an e-mail confirmation.
>
> M-Au Sorry about that. I'll mail another one right away. ⁵⁸**Could you tell me the best place to send it?**

여: 안녕하세요. 저는 게일 헨더슨입니다. 카리브해로 가는 펀인더썬 유람선 여행을 신청했는데요. 제 여권이 만료된 것을 방금 알았는데, 새 여권을 받을 시간이 없을 것 같아요. 대신 운전면허증을 가지고 여행할 수 있을까요?

남: 네, 크루즈 일정이 미국 내 동일 장소에서 시작하고 끝나기 때문에 미국 시민은 사진이 부착된 정부 발급 신분증이면 어떤 것이나 받습니다. **저희가 우편으로 보낸 등록 안내서에서 공인 양식 목록을 살펴보세요.**

여: 안내서는 못 받았는데요. 확정 이메일만 받았어요.

남: 죄송합니다. 다시 바로 보내드리겠습니다. **보낼 곳을 말씀해 주시겠습니까?**

어휘 register for ~에 등록하다 cruise 유람선 여행 expire
만료되다 itinerary 여행 일정 location 위치, 장소 photo
identification 사진이 부착된 신분증 go over 검토하다
approved 공인된 registration 등록 packet (특정
목적용으로 제공되는 서류 등의) 뭉치, 자료집 confirmation
확정 right away 바로, 곧장

56

Why is the woman calling?

(A) To book a cruise
(B) To check ID requirements
(C) To update a reservation
(D) To renew a passport

여자가 전화를 건 이유는 무엇인가?

(A) 유람선 여행을 예약하려고
(B) 신분증 요건을 확인하려고
(C) 예약을 업데이트하려고
(D) 여권을 갱신하려고

어휘 book 예약하다 requirement 요건 reservation 예약 renew
갱신하다

해설 전체 내용 관련 – 여자의 전화 목적

여자의 첫 번째 대사에서 여권이 만료된 것을 방금 알았는데(I just realized that my passport has expired) 새 여권을 받을 시간이 없을 것 같다(there won't be time to get a new one)고 하며 대신 운전면허증을 가지고 여행할 수 있는지(Can I travel with a driver's license instead) 묻고 있으므로 정답은 (B)이다.

▸▸ **Paraphrasing** 대화의 **passport, a driver's license**
→ 정답의 **ID**

57

What does the man recommend doing?

(A) Saving a receipt
(B) Visiting a Web site
(C) Using an express service
(D) Reviewing a list

남자는 무엇을 하라고 권하는가?

(A) 영수증 보관하기
(B) 웹사이트 방문하기
(C) 속달 서비스 이용하기
(D) 목록 살펴보기

어휘 save 보관하다, 아끼다 receipt 영수증 express 급행의, 속달의

해설 세부 사항 관련 – 남자의 추천

남자의 첫 번째 대사에서 등록 안내서에서 공인 양식 목록을 살펴보라(You should go over the list of approved forms from the registration packet)고 했으므로 정답은 (D)이다.

Test 7

58

What information does the man ask for?

(A) A license number
(B) A mailing address
(C) A preferred date
(D) A confirmation code

남자는 어떤 정보를 요청하는가?

(A) 면허증 번호
(B) 우편 주소
(C) 선호하는 일자
(D) 확정 코드

──────────────

어휘   mailing (우편물) 발송   preferred 선호하는

해설   세부 사항 관련 – 남자가 요청하는 정보

여자가 안내서를 못 받았다고 하자 남자가 바로 보내주겠다고 하면서 보낼 곳을 물어보고(Could you tell me the best place to send it) 있으므로 정답은 (B)이다.

59-61 3인 대화

W-Am   Hi, Fumio and Oscar. **59We just got a nice e-mail from Deltray Bank, thanking us for the catering services we provided them last night.** Your team did a great job!

M-Cn   Good to hear. **60And I'd like to say that Oscar handled every task well, even though he just started with us.**

M-Au   Thank you for the compliment! Likewise, Fumio has been very helpful as a mentor.

W-Am   Terrific. Oscar, is there any area you need more training on?

M-Au   Just the paperwork—you know, for keeping track of supplies for the events.

W-Am   I see. **61Fumio, could you print out a copy of last night's inventory form?** Then Oscar can study it as a sample.

여: 안녕하세요, 후미오 씨, 오스카 씨. 델트레이 은행으로부터 지난밤 저희가 제공한 출장 뷔페 서비스에 감사하는 이메일을 받았습니다. 팀이 정말 잘 해냈군요!

남1:   반가운 소식이네요. 오스카 씨가 이제 막 저희와 일을 시작했는데도 모든 일을 잘 처리했다는 말씀을 드리고 싶군요.

남2:   칭찬 감사합니다. 후미오 씨도 멘토로서 굉장히 많은 도움이 됐습니다.

여: 좋아요. 오스카 씨, 교육을 더 받아야 하는 부분이 있습니까?

남2:   행사용 물품을 기록하는 서류 작업이 있습니다.

여: 알겠습니다. 후미오 씨, 어젯밤 재고 목록 양식 사본을 출력해 주시겠어요? 그러면 오스카 씨가 견본 삼아 살펴볼 수 있겠죠.

──────────────

어휘   catering service 음식 공급 서비스, 출장 뷔페 서비스   handle 다루다, 처리하다   task 업무, 과제   compliment 칭찬   likewise 마찬가지로, 비슷하게   mentor 조언자, 스승   paperwork 서류 작업   keep track of ~를 계속 기록[파악]하다   supplies 물품   print out 출력하다   inventory 재고   study 주의해[유심히] 보다

59

What kind of business do the speakers most likely work for?

(A) A catering company
(B) A commercial bank
(C) A package delivery service
(D) A job placement agency

화자들은 어떤 종류의 업체에서 일하겠는가?

(A) 음식 공급 업체
(B) 시중 은행
(C) 택배 서비스
(D) 직업소개소

──────────────

어휘   catering 음식 공급   commercial 상업의, 민간의   package delivery 택배   job placement 직업 소개[알선]

해설   전체 내용 관련 – 화자들이 일하는 회사의 종류

여자의 첫 번째 대사에서 델트레이 은행으로부터 지난밤 화자들의 회사가 제공한 출장 연회 서비스에 감사하는 이메일을 받았다(we just got a nice e-mail from Deltray Bank, thanking us for the catering services we provided them last night)고 했으므로 정답은 (A)이다.

60

What is mentioned about Oscar?

(A) He will help open a branch office.
(B) He is a newly hired employee.
(C) He received a gift from a customer.
(D) He is invited to speak at a conference.

오스카 씨에 대해 언급된 것은 무엇인가?

(A) 지사를 여는 데 도움을 줄 것이다.
(B) 새로 채용된 직원이다.
(C) 고객으로부터 선물을 받았다.
(D) 회의에서 연설해 달라고 초청받았다.

──────────────

어휘   branch office 지점   newly 최근에, 새로   hired 고용된

해설   세부 사항 관련 – 오스카 씨에 대해 언급된 것

남자의 첫 번째 대사에서 오스카 씨가 이제 막 같이 일을 시작했는데도 모든 일을 잘 처리했다(Oscar handled every task well, even though he just started with us)고 말했으므로 정답은 (B)이다.

61

What does the woman ask Fumio to do?

(A) Phone a client
(B) Clean out a storage area
(C) Print out a document
(D) Revise a training manual

여자는 후미오 씨에게 무엇을 하라고 요청하는가?

(A) 고객에게 전화하기
(B) 창고 청소하기
(C) 서류 출력하기
(D) 교육 안내서 수정하기

어휘 clean out 깨끗이 치우다 storage 보관, 저장 revise
수정[개정]하다 manual 설명서, 안내서

해설 세부 사항 관련 – 여자의 요청

여자의 세 번째 대사에서 후미오 씨에게 어젯밤 재고 목록 양식 사본을 출력
해 달라(Fumio, could you print out a copy of last night's inventory
form)고 요청했으므로 정답은 (C)이다.

▸▸ Paraphrasing 대화의 a copy of last night's inventory form
→ 정답의 a document

62-64 대화 + 가격표

M-Au	Hello, Ms. Phillips. This is Kevin from *Garden Solutions magazine*. ⁶²Your subscription will expire next month, so I'm calling to encourage you to renew it.
W-Br	⁶³I enjoy reading your magazine, but I'm moving to a different apartment in July, so my address will change.
M-Au	That's no problem. You can just inform us of any changes at that time, and your deliveries will continue as usual. I can renew your subscription and take payment over the phone right now if you'd like.
W-Br	Oh, all right. ⁶⁴In that case, I guess I want to sign up for one more year. Let me just get my credit card.

남:	안녕하세요, 필립스 씨. 저는 〈가든 솔루션즈〉 잡지의 케빈이라고 합니다. 귀하의 구독이 다음 달에 만료될 예정이어서 갱신을 권유하고자 전화했습니다.
여:	잡지를 재미있게 보고 있어요. 하지만 7월에 다른 아파트로 이사해서 주소가 바뀔 겁니다.
남:	상관 없습니다. 그때 변경 사항을 저희에게 알려주시기만 하면 평상시대로 계속 배송될 겁니다. 원하시면 지금 전화로 구독을 갱신하고 요금을 결제할 수 있습니다.
여:	아, 알겠습니다. 그렇다면 1년 더 신청하고 싶어요. 제 신용카드를 가져올게요.

어휘 subscription 구독 expire 만료되다 encourage
권장하다 inform of ~을 알리다 as usual 평상시대로
renew 갱신하다 payment 지불(금) sign up for ~을
신청하다

Subscription Fees	
3 Months	$22.99
6 Months	$41.99
⁶⁴1 Year	$79.99
2 Years	$139.99

구독료	
3개월	22.99달러
6개월	41.99달러
1년	79.99달러
2년	139.99달러

62

What is the purpose of the call?

(A) To promote a renewal
(B) To request a late payment
(C) To confirm contact details
(D) To sign up a new customer

전화를 건 목적은 무엇인가?

(A) 갱신을 유도하려고
(B) 체납분을 요청하려고
(C) 연락처를 확인하려고
(D) 신규 고객과 계약하려고

어휘 promote 홍보하다 renewal 갱신 late payment 체납 sign
up 계약하다

해설 전체 내용 관련 – 전화의 목적

남자의 첫 번째 대사에서 귀하의 구독이 다음 달에 만료될 예정(Your
subscription will expire next month)이어서 갱신을 권유하고자 전화했다
(I'm calling to encourage you to renew it)고 말했으므로 정답은 (A)이다.

▸▸ Paraphrasing 대화의 encourage you to renew it
→ 정답의 promote a renewal

63

What does the woman plan to do in July?

(A) Upgrade a service
(B) Start a new job
(C) Cancel her subscription
(D) Move to a new home

여자는 7월에 무엇을 하려고 계획하는가?

(A) 서비스 업그레이드
(B) 새로운 일 시작
(C) 구독 취소
(D) 새집으로 이사

어휘 cancel 취소하다

해설 세부 사항 관련 – 여자가 7월에 하려고 하는 일

여자의 첫 번째 대사에서 7월에 다른 아파트로 이사해서(I'm moving to a
different apartment in July) 주소가 바뀔 것(my address will change)
이라고 했으므로 정답은 (D)이다.

▸▸ Paraphrasing 대화의 moving to a different apartment
→ 정답의 Move to a new home

64

Look at the graphic. How much will the woman pay today?

(A) $22.99
(B) $41.99
(C) $79.99
(D) $139.99

시각 정보에 의하면, 여자는 오늘 얼마를 지불할 것인가?

(A) 22.99달러
(B) 41.99달러
(C) 79.99달러
(D) 139.99달러

해설 시각 정보 연계 – 여자가 지불할 금액

여자의 두 번째 대사에서 1년 더 신청하고 싶다(I want to sign up for one more year)고 했고 시각 정보에 나온 1년 구독료가 79.99달러이므로 정답은 (C)이다.

65-67 대화 + 차트

W-Am	Yoji, I've got some wonderful news. **65Milly Foster called me this morning. She's the literary agent for Ruby Ellis.**
M-Au	Oh, really? Ruby Ellis is one of the most popular authors right now.
W-Am	I know. And Ms. Foster said she's able to do a book signing event at our bookstore on May ninth.
M-Au	That's great, but we've already got someone booked for that day.
W-Am	I know, but we can't pass up this opportunity. **66I'll call the author scheduled for May ninth and ask her if she can come another day.** I think she had a flexible schedule.
M-Au	OK. **67Fortunately, I haven't uploaded the schedule to our Web site yet, so that's a relief.**

여	요지 씨, 아주 좋은 소식이 있어요. **밀리 포스터 씨가 오늘 아침에 전화했는데요. 루비 엘리스의 저작권 대리인이죠.**
남	아, 정말요? 루비 엘리스는 지금 가장 유명한 작가로 꼽히잖아요.
여	그래요. 포스터 씨가 말하길 엘리스 씨가 5월 9일에 저희 서점에서 도서 사인회를 할 수 있답니다.
남	잘됐네요. 하지만 그날은 이미 다른 사람이 예약되어 있는데요.
여	알지만 이 기회를 포기할 순 없어요. **제가 5월 9일에 예정된 작가에게 전화해서 다른 날 올 수 있는지 물어볼게요.** 그 작가는 일정에 여유가 있을 것 같아요.
남	알겠어요. 다행히 아직 웹사이트에 일정을 올리지 않았으니 안심이군요.

어휘	literary agent 저작권 대리인 author 작가 book 예약하다 pass up 거절하다, 포기하다 opportunity 기회 flexible 융통성 있는, 변경 가능한 upload (데이터를) 전송하다 relief 안심

Book Signing Events: Proposed Schedule	
Date	**Author**
May 2	Greta Tretiakov
66May 9	Linda Holmes
May 16	Cai Quan
May 23	Spencer Clarke

도서 사인회: 제안 일정	
날짜	**작가**
5월 2일	그레타 트레티아코프
5월 9일	린다 홈즈
5월 16일	카이 콴
5월 23일	스펜서 클라크

65

Who did the woman speak to in the morning?

(A) A prospective publisher
(B) A famous author
(C) A bookstore manager
(D) A literary agent

여자는 아침에 누구와 통화했는가?

(A) 전도유망한 출판사
(B) 유명 작가
(C) 서점 관리자
(D) 저작권 대리인

어휘 prospective 장래의, 유망한 publisher 출판사

해설 세부 사항 관련 – 여자가 통화한 사람

여자의 첫 번째 대사에서 밀리 포스터 씨가 오늘 아침에 전화했는데(Milly Foster called me this morning) 그녀가 루비 엘리스의 저작권 대리인 (She's the literary agent for Ruby Ellis)이라고 했으므로 정답은 (D)이다.

66

Look at the graphic. Who will the woman contact?

(A) Greta Tretiakov
(B) Linda Holmes
(C) Cai Quan
(D) Spencer Clarke

시각 정보에 의하면 여자는 누구에게 연락할 것인가?

(A) 그레타 트레티아코프
(B) 린다 홈즈
(C) 카이 콴
(D) 스펜서 클라크

해설 시각 정보 연계 – 여자가 연락할 사람

여자의 세 번째 대사에서 5월 9일에 예정된 작가에게 전화해서 다른 날에 올 수 있는지 물어보겠다(I'll call the author scheduled for May ninth and ask her if she can come another day)고 했다. 시각 정보를 보면 5월 9일에 예정된 작가는 린다 홈즈이므로 정답은 (B)이다.

67

Why is the man relieved?

(A) Some information has not been posted online.
(B) A schedule was approved by his boss.
(C) The turnout at an event was high.
(D) A book received a favorable review.

남자는 왜 안도하는가?
(A) 일부 정보가 온라인에 게시되지 않았다.
(B) 상관이 일정을 승인했다.
(C) 행사 참가자 수가 많았다.
(D) 책이 호평을 받았다.

어휘 post 게시하다 approve 승인하다 turnout 참가자 수
favorable 호의적인 review 평가

해설 세부 사항 관련 – 남자가 안도하는 이유
남자의 세 번째 대사에서 다행히 아직 웹사이트에 일정을 올리지 않았으니 안심(I haven't uploaded the schedule to our Web site yet, so that's a relief)이라고 말했으므로 정답은 (A)이다.

▸▸ Paraphrasing 대화의 I haven't uploaded the schedule to our Web site → 정답의 Some information has not been posted online.

68-70 대화 + 그림

W-Br	Hi. **68I ordered a standing lamp from your store last week.** I referred to the weekly catalog from your information desk, and made an online order. However, the one that was delivered today was the wrong size.
M-Cn	I'm sorry about that, ma'am. Could you tell me which brand it was?
W-Br	Yes, it was the Haynes brand. **69I ordered model R667, but I was sent a lamp that was one size larger.** Can I exchange it?
M-Cn	Of course. **70The online exchange process is quite slow, though, so it would be best to stop into one of our branches.**
W-Br	All right. What do I need to bring with me?
M-Cn	Just a printed copy of your order and the item you received. And, again, I'm very sorry for the inconvenience.

여: 안녕하세요. **지난주에 이 매장에서 스탠딩 램프를 주문했습니다.** 안내데스크에 있는 주간 카탈로그를 보고 온라인으로 주문했어요. 하지만 오늘 배송된 물건은 크기가 달라요.
남: 죄송합니다, 손님. 어떤 상표인지 말씀해 주시겠어요?
여: 네, 헤인즈라는 상표예요. **저는 R667 모델을 주문했는데 한 사이즈 큰 램프를 받았어요.** 교환할 수 있나요?
남: 물론입니다. 그런데 온라인 교환 절차가 꽤 느려서 저희 지점 중 한 군데로 들르시면 가장 좋을 것 같습니다.
여: 알겠어요. 제가 뭘 가져야 하나요?
남: 주문서 복사본과 받으신 물건만 가져오시면 됩니다. 다시 한 번 불편을 드려 대단히 죄송합니다.

어휘 refer to ~을 보다 make an order 주문하다 exchange 교환(하다) process 과정, 절차 stop 잠깐 들르다 branch 지점 item 품목 receive 받다 inconvenience 불편함

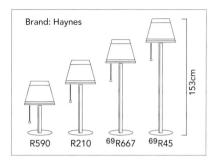

Brand: Haynes

R590   R210   69R667   69R45   153cm

상표: 헤인즈

R590   R210   R667   R45   153cm

68

What kind of business is the woman most likely calling?

(A) A delivery service
(B) A department store
(C) A Web design company
(D) A manufacturing facility

여자는 어떤 회사에 전화를 걸고 있겠는가?
(A) 배송 서비스 업체
(B) 백화점
(C) 웹디자인 회사
(D) 제조 시설

어휘 manufacturing 제조 facility 시설

해설 전체 내용 관련 – 여자가 전화한 업체
여자의 첫 번째 대사에서 지난주에 이 매장에서 스탠딩 램프를 주문했다(I ordered a standing lamp from your store last week)고 했으므로 램프를 파는 곳을 선택해야 한다. 따라서 정답은 (B)이다.

69

Look at the graphic. Which item was the woman sent?

(A) R590
(B) R210
(C) R667
(D) R45

시각 정보에 의하면, 여자는 어떤 물건을 받았는가?
(A) R590
(B) R210
(C) R667
(D) R45

해설 시각 정보 연계 – 여자가 받은 물건

여자의 두 번째 대사에서 R667 모델을 주문했는데 한 사이즈 큰 램프를 받았다(I ordered model R667, but I was sent a lamp that was one size larger)고 했다. 시각 정보를 보면 R667모델보다 한 사이즈 큰 램프는 R450이므로 정답은 (D)이다.

70

What does the man recommend doing?

(A) Visiting a business in person
(B) Waiting for the next delivery
(C) Calling back another day
(D) Checking an order's status online

남자는 무엇을 하라고 권하는가?

(A) 직접 업체 방문하기
(B) 다음 배송 기다리기
(C) 다른 날 다시 전화하기
(D) 주문 상태를 온라인으로 확인하기

어휘 in person 몸소, 직접 wait for ~을 기다리다 status 상태

해설 세부 사항 관련 – 남자의 제안

남자의 두 번째 대사에서 온라인 교환 절차가 꽤 느려서(The online exchange process is quite slow) 지점 한 군데로 들르는 게 가장 좋을 것 같다(it would be best to stop into one of our branches)고 말했으므로 정답은 (A)이다.

▸▸ Paraphrasing 대화의 **stop into one of our branches**
→ 정답의 **Visiting a business in person**

PART 4

71-73 전화 메시지

W-Br **71Hi, this is Stephanie calling from the 8th Avenue Gym.** As you're a new member of our gym, you are eligible for a free health consultation. Our records show that you booked an appointment for this for today at 3 P.M. **72Unfortunately, some of our equipment used to run the tests is not working. 73Therefore, so that you get the most information possible, it would be better to rebook the session. Please do so by Friday.** Thanks for your understanding!

안녕하세요, 저는 8th 애비뉴 짐의 스테파니입니다. 귀하는 저희 체육관의 신규 회원이시니 무료 건강 상담을 받으실 수 있는데요. 저희 기록에 따르면 오늘 오후 3시에 예약하셨는데요. 안타깝게도 테스트를 시행하기 위해 사용하던 저희 장비 일부가 작동되지 않습니다. 따라서 정보를 최대한 받으실 수 있도록 시간을 다시 예약하는 편이 나을 것 같습니다. 금요일까지 예약해 주십시오. 이해해 주셔서 감사합니다!

71

Where does the speaker work?

(A) At a fitness facility
(B) At a medical clinic
(C) At a pharmacy
(D) At a hair salon

화자는 어디에서 일하는가?

(A) 피트니스 시설
(B) 병원
(C) 약국
(D) 미용실

해설 전체 내용 관련 – 화자의 근무지

지문의 초반부에서 화자가 8th 애비뉴 짐에서 전화하는 스테파니(this is Stephanie calling from the 8th Avenue Gym)라고 말했으므로 정답은 (A)이다.

▸▸ Paraphrasing 지문의 **8th Avenue Gym**
→ 정답의 **a fitness facility**

72

According to the speaker, what has caused a problem?

(A) A double-booking
(B) An absent employee
(C) A technical issue
(D) A lost document

화자에 따르면, 무엇 때문에 문제가 생겼는가?

(A) 이중 예약
(B) 결근한 직원
(C) 기술적 문제
(D) 분실된 서류

어휘 double-book 이중으로 예약을 받다 absent 결석[결근]한 technical 기술적인 issue 문제 lost 분실된

해설 세부 사항 관련 – 발생된 문제

지문 중반부에서 안타깝게도 테스트에 사용하던 일부 장비가 작동되지 않는다(some of our equipment used to run the tests is not working)고 했으므로 정답은 (C)이다.

▸▸ Paraphrasing 지문의 **equipment ~ is not working**
→ 정답의 **A technical issue**

73

What should the listener do by Friday?

(A) Update contact information
(B) Renew a membership
(C) Make a payment
(D) Rebook an appointment

청자는 금요일까지 무엇을 해야 하는가?

(A) 연락처 업데이트하기
(B) 회원권 갱신하기
(C) 지불하기
(D) 다시 예약하기

해설 세부 사항 관련 – 청자가 금요일까지 해야 하는 것

지문 후반부에서 정보를 최대한 받을 수 있도록 시간을 다시 예약하는 편이 나을 것 같다(so that you get the most information possible, it would be better to rebook the session)고 말하며, 금요일까지 예약해 달라(Please do so by Friday)고 했으므로 정답은 (D)이다.

74-76 담화

> **W-Am** Good evening, and welcome to this session of the monthly lecture series at the Hanifan Art Museum. **⁷⁴It is my pleasure to introduce Ms. Helen Anderson, who has an impressive twenty-year career of taking photos all over the world.** She will talk about how she got into the business. **⁷⁵If you're interested in seeing examples of her work, I highly recommend buying her recently published autobiography,** *Through the Lens.* **⁷⁶Before we get to Ms. Anderson's talk, I'd like to show you a brief clip of an interview she did for a documentary.** I hope you enjoy it. Following her talk, Ms. Anderson will take questions from the audience.

안녕하세요. 하니판 미술관에서 열리는 월례 강좌에 오신 것을 환영합니다. 헬렌 앤더슨 씨를 소개하게 되어 기쁩니다. 전 세계에서 20년 동안 사진 촬영을 해 온 인상적인 경력을 갖고 계시죠. 어떻게 이 일에 종사하게 됐는지 이야기하실 겁니다. 앤더슨 씨의 대표적인 작품들을 보는 데 관심이 있으시다면 최근 출간된 자서전 〈렌즈를 통해〉 구매를 적극 추천합니다. 앤더슨 씨의 강의에 앞서 그녀가 다큐멘터리를 위해 응했던 인터뷰를 짤막하게 보여 드리고자 합니다. 즐겁게 감상하시기 바랍니다. 강의에 이어 앤더슨 씨가 청중으로부터 질문을 받으실 겁니다.

어휘 lecture 강의 series 연속 (강의), 시리즈(물) career 직업, 경력 get into ~을 (시작하게 되다 publish 출간하다 highly recommend 적극 추천하다 autobiography 자서전 get to ~을 시작하다 brief 짧은 clip 발췌 영상 audience 청중

74

Who most likely is Helen Anderson?

(A) A gallery owner
(B) A painting instructor
(C) A museum tour guide
(D) A professional photographer

헬렌 앤더슨 씨는 누구이겠는가?

(A) 화랑 소유주
(B) 그림 강사
(C) 박물관 안내원
(D) 전문 사진작가

어휘 gallery 화랑 owner 소유주 instructor 강사

해설 전체 내용 관련 – 헬렌 앤더슨 씨의 직업

지문 초반부에서 화자는 헬렌 앤더슨을 소개하며 전 세계에서 20년 동안 사진 촬영을 해 온 인상적인 경력을 갖고 있다(It is my pleasure to introduce Ms. Helen Anderson, who has an impressive twenty-year career of taking photos all over the world)고 했으므로 정답은 (D)이다.

> ▶▶ **Paraphrasing** 지문의 **twenty-year career of taking photos** → 정답의 **A professional photographer**

75

According to the speaker, what has Helen Anderson recently done?

(A) Launched a Web site
(B) Started a class
(C) Won an award
(D) Published a book

화자에 따르면, 헬렌 앤더슨 씨는 최근 무엇을 했는가?

(A) 웹사이트를 개설했다
(B) 강좌를 시작했다
(C) 수상했다
(D) 책을 출판했다

어휘 launch 출시하다 award 상

해설 세부 사항 관련 – 헬렌 앤더슨 씨가 최근에 한 것

지문 중반부에서 앤더슨 씨의 대표적인 작품들을 보는 데 관심이 있으면(If you're interested in seeing examples of her work) 최근 출간된 자서전 〈렌즈를 통해〉 구매를 적극 추천한다(I highly recommend buying her recently published autobiography, *Through the Lens*)고 했으므로 정답은 (D)이다.

> ▶▶ **Paraphrasing** 지문의 **her recently published autobiography** → 정답의 **Published a book**

76

What will most likely happen next?

(A) The listeners will watch a video.
(B) Ms. Anderson will respond to questions.
(C) The speaker will check the attendance.
(D) The listeners will take a break.

다음으로 어떤 일이 있겠는가?

(A) 청자들이 동영상을 볼 것이다.
(B) 앤더슨 씨가 질문에 답할 것이다.
(C) 화자가 출석을 확인할 것이다.
(D) 청자들이 휴식할 것이다.

어휘 respond to ~에 응답하다 attendance 출석, 참석 take a break 휴식하다

해설 세부 사항 관련 – 다음에 있을 일

지문 후반부에서 앤더슨 씨의 강의에 앞서 그녀가 다큐멘터리를 위해 응했던 인터뷰를 짤막하게 보여 주겠다(I'd like to show you a brief clip of an interview she did for a documentary)고 했으므로 정답은 (A)이다.

▶▶ Paraphrasing   지문의 **I'd like to show you a brief clip**
     → 정답의 **The listeners will watch a video.**

77-79 전화 메시지

> M-Au   Hello, Ms. Murphy? This is Ken calling from the Rosser Hotel. **77We received your online booking for two hotel rooms so that you and your colleagues could go to the National Technology Conference here in Atlanta. 78I know that you asked for rooms that are side by side, but I'm afraid that our last two rooms are on separate floors.** I'm very sorry about this. **79To make up for the inconvenience, I'll give you some vouchers for twenty percent off all food at the on-site restaurant.** You can pick them up when you check in.

> 안녕하세요, 머피 씨? 저는 로서 호텔의 켄입니다. 귀하와 동료분들이 이곳 애틀랜타에서 열리는 전국기술회의 참석 차 온라인으로 호텔 객실 두 개를 예약하신 내역을 접수했습니다. 나란히 있는 방으로 요청하신 것을 알고 있습니다만 유감스럽게도 저희에게 남은 마지막 객실 두 개는 서로 다른 층에 있습니다. 정말 죄송합니다. 불편함을 보상해 드리기 위해 호텔 레스토랑 20퍼센트 할인 쿠폰을 드리겠습니다. 체크인할 때 가져가시면 됩니다.

> 어휘   booking 예약   so that ~하도록   colleague 동료   side by side 나란히   separate 별개의, 떨어진   make up for ~를 보상하다[보전하다]   voucher 상품권, 쿠폰   off 할인하여   on-site 현장의   pick up ~을 찾아오다   check in 투숙 수속을 밟다

77

Why will the listener travel to Atlanta?

(A) To inspect a hotel
(B) To attend a conference
(C) To open a business
(D) To visit family members

청자가 애틀랜타로 가는 이유는 무엇인가?
(A) 호텔을 조사하려고
(B) 회의에 참석하려고
(C) 개업하려고
(D) 가족을 만나려고

어휘   inspect 조사하다, 점검하다

해설   세부 사항 관련 – 청자가 애틀랜타로 가는 이유
지문 초반부에서 귀하와 동료들이 애틀랜타에서 열리는 전국기술회의 참석 차 온라인으로 호텔 객실 두 개를 예약한 내역을 접수했다(We received your online booking for two hotel rooms so that you and your colleagues could go to the National Technology Conference here in Atlanta)고 했으므로 정답은 (B)이다.

▶▶ Paraphrasing   지문의 **go to the National Technology Conference** → 정답의 **attend a conference**

78

What problem does the speaker mention?

(A) The hotel is fully booked for the requested date.
(B) The listener was given an incorrect price quote.
(C) The reserved rooms are not next to each other.
(D) A reservation was canceled accidentally.

화자는 어떤 문제를 언급하는가?
(A) 요청한 일자에 호텔 예약이 다 찼다.
(B) 청자에게 잘못된 가격 견적서를 전달했다.
(C) 예약된 객실들이 나란히 있지 않다.
(D) 예약이 우연히 취소됐다.

어휘   fully booked 모두 예약된   incorrect 잘못된   price quote 견적서   reserved 예약된   next to each other 나란히   reservation 예약   cancel 취소하다   accidentally 우연히, 뜻하지 않게

해설   세부 사항 관련 – 언급한 문제
지문 중반부에서 나란히 있는 방으로 요청했지만(I know that you asked for rooms that are side by side) 유감스럽게도 남은 마지막 객실 두 개는 서로 다른 층에 있다(I'm afraid that our last two rooms are on separate floors)고 했으므로 정답은 (C)이다.

▶▶ Paraphrasing   지문의 **two rooms are on separate floors** → 정답의 **rooms are not next to each other**

79

What does the speaker say he will do?

(A) Contact another branch
(B) Provide discount vouchers
(C) Issue a refund of a deposit
(D) Offer a free room upgrade

화자는 무엇을 할 것이라고 말하는가?
(A) 다른 지점에 연락하기
(B) 할인 쿠폰 제공하기
(C) 보증금 환불해 주기
(D) 객실 무료 업그레이드 해주기

어휘   branch 지점   issue 발행하다   refund 환불(금)   deposit 보증금

해설   세부 사항 관련 – 화자의 계획
지문 후반부에서 불편함을 보상해 주기 위해 호텔 레스토랑 20퍼센트 할인 쿠폰을 주겠다(To make up for the inconvenience, I'll give you some vouchers for twenty percent off all food at the on-site restaurant)고 했으므로 정답은 (B)이다.

▶▶ Paraphrasing   지문의 **vouchers for twenty percent off** → 정답의 **discount vouchers**

80-82 방송

> M-Cn   I'm Brandon Mercer, here with the local news report. **80November twentieth has been selected as the date for this year's Founder's Day Parade.** It will be led by newly-elected

mayor Margaret Warren. The parade will start at Fredericks Elementary School and end at McLaughlin Park. **81To see a map of the route that parade officials have planned, visit the city's Web site. 82Following the parade, members of the Green City organization will be collecting donations for the maintenance of McLaughlin Park, which has suffered under recent budget cuts.**

저는 지역 뉴스의 브랜든 머서입니다. 11월 20일이 올해 창립자 기념일 퍼레이드를 하는 날로 선정됐습니다. 새로 선출된 마가렛 워렌 시장이 지휘할 예정입니다. 퍼레이드는 프레데릭스 초등학교에서 시작해 맥러플린 파크에서 끝납니다. 퍼레이드 관계자들이 계획한 노선도를 보시려면 시 웹사이트를 방문하십시오. 퍼레이드에 이어 그린시티 단체 회원들이 최근 예산 삭감으로 어려움을 겪는 맥러플린 파크 유지를 위해 기부금을 걷을 예정입니다.

어휘 local 지방의, 지역의 select 선정하다 founder 창립자 newly-elected 새로 선출된 · route 경로, 길 official 관계자 organization 기관, 단체 collect donation 기부금을 걷다 maintenance 유지, 보수 suffer 고통받다, 어려움을 겪다 recent 최근의 budget cut 예산 삭감

80
What will happen on November 20?
(A) A community parade
(B) A local election
(C) A food festival
(D) A musical performance

11월 20일에는 어떤 일이 있을 것인가?
(A) 지역 퍼레이드
(B) 지방선거
(C) 음식 축제
(D) 음악 공연

어휘 community 지역사회의

해설 세부 사항 관련 – 11월 20일에 있을 일
지문 초반부에서 11월 20일은 올해 창립자 기념일 퍼레이드를 하는 날로 선정됐다(November twentieth has been selected as the date for this year's Founder's Day Parade)고 했으므로 정답은 (A)이다.

▸▸ Paraphrasing 지문의 **Founder's Day Parade** → 정답의 **A community parade**

81
According to the speaker, what can listeners do on the Web site?
(A) Download a calendar
(B) Order some tickets
(C) View a planned route
(D) Share their opinions

화자에 따르면, 청자들은 웹사이트에서 무엇을 할 수 있는가?
(A) 달력 다운로드하기
(B) 입장권 주문하기
(C) 계획된 노선 보기
(D) 의견 공유하기

어휘 share 나누다, 공유하다

해설 세부 사항 관련 – 청자들이 웹사이트에서 할 수 있는 것
지문 중반부에서 퍼레이드 관계자들이 계획한 노선도를 보려면(To see a map of the route that parade officials have planned) 시 웹사이트를 방문하라(visit the city's Web site)고 했으므로 정답은 (C)이다.

▸▸ Paraphrasing 지문의 **see a map of the route that parade officials have planned** → 정답의 **View a planned route**

82
What project will be supported by the event?
(A) Improving an animal shelter
(B) Renovating a city building
(C) Running a future event
(D) Maintaining a public park

어떤 프로젝트가 행사에 의해 지원되는가?
(A) 동물 보호소 개선
(B) 시 건물 개조
(C) 향후 행사 운영
(D) 시민공원 유지

어휘 improve 개선하다 animal shelter 동물 보호소 renovate 개조하다 run 운영하다 maintain 유지하다

해설 세부 사항 관련 – 지원될 행사
지문 후반부에서 그린시티 단체 회원들이 최근 예산 삭감으로 어려움을 겪는 맥러플린 파크 유지를 위해 기부금을 걷을 예정(members of the Green City organization will be collecting donations for the maintenance of McLaughlin Park, which has suffered under recent budget cuts)이라고 했으므로 정답은 (D)이다.

▸▸ Paraphrasing 지문의 **the maintenance of McLaughlin Park** → 정답의 **Maintaining a public park**

83-85 회의 발췌

M-Au Next on the agenda, the company will be changing its compensation for employees. **83Your benefits—including vacation time, insurance, and retirement pay—will be adjusted starting from next month.** I've created folders with information about the changes. These are on the table by the entrance. **What you receive will depend on how long you've been working here, so I've listed the specific details for each of you. 84That's why the folders are labeled with** your names. Be sure to get the right one. **85If you have any questions, I'll be here at the front of the room following the meeting, so please feel free to ask me about anything.**

다음 회의 안건으로, 직원 보상 체계를 변경할 예정입니다. 휴가 시간, 보험, 퇴직금 등을 비롯해 여러분이 받는 혜택이 다음 달부터 조정될 것입니다. 제가 변경 정보를 담은 서류철을 만들었습니다. 입구 옆 탁자에 놓여 있습니다. 여러분이 받는 혜택은 근속 기간에 따라 다릅니다. 그래서 여러분 개개인을 위한 세부 사항을 열거했습니다. 서류철에 여러분의 이름이 붙어 있는 이유입니다. 반드시 본인 서류를 가져가십시오. 질문 있으시면 회의 후 제가 회의실 앞쪽에 있을 예정이니 자유롭게 물어보십시오.

어휘 agenda 회의 안건 compensation 보상 benefit 혜택, 복리후생 insurance 보험 retirement pay 퇴직금 adjust 조정하다 depend on ~에 달려 있다[좌우되다] specific 특정한, 구체적인 label 표[꼬리표]를 붙이다 feel free to 자유롭게 ~하다

83

What does the company plan to change?

(A) A dress code policy
(B) The hours of operation
(C) A benefits package
(D) The vacation request process

회사는 무엇을 변경하려고 계획하는가?
(A) 복장 규정 정책
(B) 업무 시간
(C) 복리후생 제도
(D) 휴가 요청 절차

어휘 dress code 복장 규정 operation 운영 benefits package 복리후생 process 절차

해설 세부 사항 관련 – 회사가 변경하려고 하는 것
지문 초반부에서 휴가 시간, 보험, 퇴직금 등을 비롯해 직원들이 받는 혜택이 다음 달부터 조정될 것(Your benefits — including vacation time, insurance, and retirement pay — will be adjusted starting from next month)이라고 했으므로 정답은 (C)이다.

▸▸ **Paraphrasing** 지문의 benefits — including vacation time, insurance, and retirement pay
→ 정답의 A benefits package

84

What does the speaker mean when he says, "Be sure to get the right one"?

(A) He wants listeners to make a decision.
(B) Listeners should know that the data is personalized.
(C) Each department has to use a different form.
(D) He is concerned about errors in a report.

화자가 "반드시 본인 폴더를 가져가십시오"라고 말할 때, 그 의도는 무엇인가?
(A) 청자들이 결정하기를 바란다.
(B) 청자들은 데이터가 개인별 맞춤형임을 알아야 한다.
(C) 각 부서는 서로 다른 양식을 사용해야 한다.
(D) 보고서의 오류를 염려한다.

어휘 make a decision 결정하다 personalize 개인의 필요에 맞추다 department 부서 be concerned about ~을 걱정하다

해설 화자의 의도 파악 – 반드시 본인 폴더를 가져가라는 말의 의미
지문 중반에서 직원들이 받는 혜택은 회사 근속 기간에 따라 다르고(What you receive will depend on how long you've been working here), 개개인을 위한 세부 사항을 열거했기(I've listed the specific details for each of you) 때문에 서류철에 직원의 이름이 붙어 있다(That's why the folders are labeled with your names)고 했다. 즉 반드시 본인 폴더를 가져가라는 말은 개개인의 세부 사항이 다르다는 의미이므로 정답은 (B)이다.

85

What should listeners do if they have questions?

(A) Stay after the meeting
(B) E-mail them to the speaker
(C) Complete a survey
(D) Meet with their team leader

청자들은 질문이 있을 경우 어떻게 해야 하는가?
(A) 회의 후 남아 있어야 한다.
(B) 화자에게 이메일로 질문을 보내야 한다.
(C) 설문 조사를 완료해야 한다.
(D) 팀장과 면담해야 한다.

어휘 survey 설문 조사 meet with (논의하기 위해) ~와 만나다

해설 세부 사항 관련 – 청자들이 질문이 있을 경우 해야 하는 일
지문 후반부에서 질문 있으면(If you have any questions) 회의 후 화자가 회의실 앞쪽에 있을 예정(I'll be here at the front of the room following the meeting)이니 자유롭게 물어보라(please feel free to ask me about anything)고 했으므로 정답은 (A)이다.

▸▸ **Paraphrasing** 지문의 be here ~ following the meeting
→ 정답의 Stay after the meeting

86-88 전화 메시지

W-Br Hi, Tadao. This is Sun-Jin. **86I'm here at the Sanford Center, doing the preliminary setup for the luncheon we're catering for Wilson Travel Agency.** I've got all of the serving trays and plates I need, **87but I'm wondering if you can drop off more electric warming trays.** I think four would be enough. **87Also, I'll need another drinks dispenser.** They've decided that they want two separate tables for the buffet. **88I'd come back and get them myself,** but I'm the only one here right now. Please call me back and let me know how soon this can be done. Thanks!

204

안녕하세요, 타다오 씨. 저는 선진입니다. **샌포드 샌터에서 윌슨 여행사 출장 뷔페 오찬 준비를 하고 있습니다.** 필요한 서빙 쟁반과 접시를 모두 받았습니다만 전기 보온쟁반을 좀 더 갖다 주실 수 있는지 알고 싶습니다. 네 개면 충분할 것 같습니다. **또한 음료 디스펜서가 하나 더 필요합니다.** 고객들이 두 개의 뷔페 테이블을 따로 놓기로 결정했거든요. 제가 가서 직접 가져오고 싶지만 지금 여기에 혼자 있습니다. 제게 전화 주셔서 언제쯤 갖다 줄 수 있는지 알려주세요. 감사합니다!

어휘 preliminary 예비의 setup 구성, 배치 luncheon 오찬 cater 음식을 공급하다 tray 쟁반 drop off 갖다 주다, 갖다 놓다 electric 전기의 warming 보온, 가온 drinks dispenser 음료 디스펜서[공급기] separate 분리된

86

Who most likely is the speaker?

(A) A deliveryperson
(B) A travel agent
(C) A caterer
(D) A hotel manager

화자는 누구이겠는가?
(A) 배송 직원
(B) 여행사 직원
(C) 음식 공급자
(D) 호텔 매니저

해설 전체 내용 관련 – 화자의 신분
지문의 초반부에 샌포드 센터에서 윌슨 여행사 출장 뷔페 오찬 준비를 하고 있다(I'm here at the Sanford Center, doing the preliminary setup for the luncheon we're catering for Wilson Travel Agency)고 했으므로 정답은 (C)이다.

▸▸ Paraphrasing 지문의 **doing the preliminary setup for the luncheon we're catering**
→ 정답의 **A caterer**

87

What is the listener asked to do?

(A) Bring some equipment
(B) Recruit more employees
(C) Contact a client
(D) Work an extra shift

청자는 무엇을 하라고 요청받았는가?
(A) 기기 가져오기
(B) 더 많은 직원 채용하기
(C) 고객에게 연락하기
(D) 추가 근무하기

해설 세부 사항 관련 – 청자가 요청받은 일
지문 중반부에서 전기 보온쟁반을 좀 더 갖다 줄 수 있는지 알고 싶다(I'm wondering if you can drop off more electric warming trays)고 했으므로 정답은 (A)이다.

▸▸ Paraphrasing 지문의 **drop off more electric warming trays** → 정답의 **Bring some equipment**

88

What does the speaker suggest when she says, "I'm the only one here right now"?

(A) She decided to work after hours.
(B) She made an error with the schedule.
(C) She is upset about a late employee.
(D) She does not want to leave a site.

화자가 "지금 여기에 혼자 있습니다"라고 말할 때, 그 의도는 무엇인가?
(A) 잔업을 하기로 결정했다.
(B) 일정 관련 실수를 했다.
(C) 지각한 직원 때문에 화가 났다.
(D) 현장을 떠나고 싶지 않다.

어휘 after hours 근무 시간 후에 site 현장

해설 화자의 의도 파악 – 지금 여기에 혼자 있다는 말의 의미
화자는 본인이 가서 직접 가져오고 싶지만(I'd come back and get them myself) 지금 혼자 있다(I'm the only one here right now)고 했다. 따라서 직접 가지러 가고 싶지만 혼자 있기 때문에 갈 수 없다는 의미이므로 정답은 (D)이다.

89-91 라디오 방송

W-Am Up next, Radio 104 will be airing its jazz music hour. But first, it's the local news update. **[89]Residents of Lakewood are pleased that the construction project to expand the Lakewood Public Library has now been completed.** The project added twenty-five hundred square feet of additional space. A section of the new wing houses a computer lab, and **[90]computer skills classes will start on September first for all ages.** **[91]Library Director Leo Cervantes was happy with the construction crew, as they finished the building work in just six weeks, two weeks ahead of the original deadline.** Residents are invited to tour the new wing during the library's hours of operation.

다음으로 라디오 104에서 재즈 음악을 방송할 예정입니다. 그에 앞서 지역 뉴스를 보내드립니다. 레이크우드 주민들은 레이크우드 공립 도서관 확장 공사가 완료되어 기뻐하고 있습니다. 이 프로젝트로 2천 5백 제곱피트의 추가 공간이 생겼습니다. 새 동에는 컴퓨터실이 있으며 모든 연령대를 위한 컴퓨터 강좌가 9월 1일에 시작됩니다. 도서관장 레오 세르반테스 씨는 건물 공사가 당초 기한보다 2주 앞당겨 단 6주만에 완료된 것에 대해 공사 담당자들에게 흡족해하고 있습니다. 주민들은 도서관 개관 시간 동안 새 동을 둘러볼 수 있습니다.

어휘 air 방송하다 resident 주민 construction 공사 expand 확장하다 add 추가하다 square feet 제곱피트 additional 추가의 section 구획, 구역 wing (건물의) 동 lab 실습실 crew (같은 일에 종사하는) 팀, 조 ahead of ~에 앞서 original 원래의, 애초의 hours of operation 운영 시간

89

What is the broadcast mainly about?

(A) A jazz festival
(B) A building permit
(C) A reading program
(D) A library expansion

방송은 주로 무엇에 관한 것인가?
(A) 재즈 축제
(B) 건축 허가
(C) 독서 프로그램
(D) 도서관 확장

어휘 building permit 건축 허가 expansion 확장

해설 전체 내용 관련 – 방송 주제
지문의 초반부에 레이크우드 주민들은 레이크우드 공립 도서관 확장 공사가 완료되어 기뻐하고 있다(Residents of Lakewood are pleased that the construction project to expand the Lakewood Public Library has now been completed)고 했으므로 정답은 (D)이다.

▸▸ **Paraphrasing** 지문의 **expand the Lakewood Public Library** → 정답의 **A library expansion**

90

What will begin from September 1?

(A) Some construction work
(B) A fundraising event
(C) Computer classes
(D) A recruitment drive

9월 1일에 무엇이 시작될 것인가?
(A) 공사 작업
(B) 모금 행사
(C) **컴퓨터 강좌**
(D) 모집 활동

어휘 fundraising 모금 recruitment 모집, 채용 drive 활동, 운동

해설 세부 사항 관련 – 9월 1일에 시작될 일
지문 중반부에서 모든 연령대를 위한 컴퓨터 강좌가 9월 1일에 시작된다(computer skills classes will start on September first for all ages)고 했으므로 정답은 (C)이다.

91

What was Mr. Cervantes pleased about?

(A) How popular a new program is
(B) How high some donations were
(C) How quickly a project was completed
(D) How inexpensive some work was

세르반테스 씨는 무엇에 만족하는가?
(A) 새 프로그램이 얼마나 인기 있는지
(B) 기부금이 얼마나 많은지
(C) **프로젝트가 얼마나 빨리 완료됐는지**
(D) 작업비가 얼마나 저렴했는지

어휘 popular 인기 있는 donation 기부(금), 기증 inexpensive 값싼

해설 세부 사항 관련 – 세르반테스 씨가 만족하는 점
지문 후반부에서 도서관장 레오 세르반테스 씨는 건물 공사가 당초 기한보다 2주 앞당겨 단 6주만에 완료된 것에 대해 공사 담당자들에 흡족해하고 있다(Library Director Leo Cervantes was happy with the construction crew, as they finished the building work in just six weeks, two weeks ahead of the original deadline)고 했으므로 정답은 (C)이다.

▸▸ **Paraphrasing** 지문의 **finished the building work ~ two weeks ahead of the original deadline** → 정답의 **How quickly a project was completed**

92-94 녹음 메시지

M-Cn **92Thank you for calling Nelson Energy.** All of our customer service agents are busy at the moment. If you are reporting a downed power line, please hang up and call 555-0177. **93For bill paying and account inquiries, stay on the line.** Alternatively, you may check your account and make a payment at www.nelson.com. If you're in a hurry, we recommend visiting the Web site. To leave a message and request a call back from one of our representatives, press one. **94To hear this message again, press the star key.**

넬슨 에너지에 전화해 주셔서 감사합니다. 저희 고객서비스 직원이 현재 모두 통화 중입니다. 내려앉은 송전선을 신고하시려면 전화를 끊고 555-0177로 전화해 주십시오. 요금 납부 및 계좌 문의는 끊지 말고 기다려 주십시오. 또는 www.nelson.com에서도 계좌 확인 및 납부가 가능합니다. 급하신 분은 웹사이트 방문을 권합니다. 메시지를 남기시고 저희 상담사가 전화하도록 요청하시려면 1번을 누르십시오. 메시지를 다시 들으시려면 별표를 눌러 주십시오.

어휘 down 떨어뜨리다 power line 송전선 hang up 끊다 bill paying 요금 납부 account inquiry 계좌 문의 stay on the line 전화를 끊지 않고 기다리다 alternatively 그 대신에, 그렇지 않으면 in a hurry 서둘러, 급히 request 요청하다 representative 직원 press 누르다

92

What kind of business is the listener most likely calling?

(A) A construction company
(B) A utility company
(C) An electronics store
(D) An Internet provider

청자는 어떤 종류의 업체에 전화를 걸고 있겠는가?
(A) 건설 회사
(B) **공익 기업**
(C) 전자제품 매장
(D) 인터넷 서비스 제공업체

어휘 utility company (전기, 가스, 수도 등) 공익기업 provider 제공업체, 공급업체

해설 전체 내용 관련 – 청자가 전화를 한 업체
지문의 초반부에서 넬슨 에너지에 전화해 주셔서 감사하다(Thank you for calling Nelson Energy)고 했으므로 정답은 (B)이다.

▸▸ **Paraphrasing** 지문의 **Nelson Energy**
→ 정답의 **A utility company**

93

What does the speaker suggest when he says, "we recommend visiting the Web site"?

(A) Online customers can get a discount.
(B) Some new information has been posted.
(C) A process will be faster online.
(D) There is a charge for phone inquiries.

화자가 "웹사이트 방문을 권합니다"라고 말할 때, 그 의도는 무엇인가?
(A) 온라인 고객은 할인을 받을 수 있다.
(B) 새로운 정보가 게시됐다.
(C) **온라인으로 하면 절차가 더 빠르다.**
(D) 전화 문의에는 비용이 든다.

어휘 post 게시하다 charge 요금 inquiry 문의

해설 화자의 의도 파악 – 웹사이트 방문을 권한다는 말의 의미
지문의 중반부에 요금 납부 및 계좌 문의를 하려면 전화를 끊지 말고 기다려 달라고 했고(For bill paying and account inquiries, stay on the line), 또는 www.nelson.com에서도 계좌 확인 및 납부가 가능하다(Alternatively, you may check your account and make a payment at www.nelson.com)고 말함으로써 두 가지 방법을 제시한다. 즉 급하다면(If you're in a hurry) 웹사이트 방문을 권한다는 말의 의미는 전화로 진행하는 것보다 온라인으로 하는 게 더 빠르다는 의미이므로 정답은 (C)이다.

94

Why should the listeners press the star key?

(A) To pay a bill
(B) To leave a message
(C) To repeat the recording
(D) To access a staff directory

청자들은 별표를 왜 눌러야 하는가?
(A) 요금을 납부하려고
(B) 메시지를 남기려고
(C) **녹음 내용을 반복하려고**
(D) 직원 명부에 접속하려고

어휘 access 접근하다 directory 명부

해설 세부 사항 관련 – 별표를 누르는 이유
지문 후반부에서 메시지를 다시 들으려면 별표를 눌러 달라(To hear this message again, press the star key)고 했으므로 정답은 (C)이다.

▸▸ **Paraphrasing** 지문의 **hear this message again**
→ 정답의 **repeat the recording**

95-97 회의 발췌 + 차트

W-Am I just got off the phone with Elite Consulting, who did some market research for our company. ⁹⁵**The good news is that our line of makeup and lotions is within the top four most popular brands.** ⁹⁶**Last year, we had about twenty percent of the market share, and that has grown to twenty-eight percent, which is great news.** ⁹⁷**To bring a larger number of young consumers into our customer base, we'll be creating new creams with sun protection that don't wear off during outdoor activities. Carol Foster will be leading that team, and we're looking forward to what they come up with.**

방금 저희 회사 시장조사를 담당한 엘리트 컨설팅과의 통화를 끝냈는데요. **좋은 소식은 저희 메이크업 및 로션 제품이 가장 인기 있는 브랜드 4위권에 진입했다는 겁니다. 작년에 시장점유율이 약 20퍼센트였는데 28퍼센트로 증가했습니다. 멋진 소식이죠. 다수의 젊은 소비자들을 저희 고객층으로 끌어들이기 위해 야외 활동 중에도 지워지지 않는 자외선 차단제가 든 새 크림을 만들 예정입니다. 캐롤 포스터 씨가 팀을 이끌 예정이며 팀에서 선보일 제품을 기대하고 있습니다.**

어휘 get off the phone with ~와의 전화 통화를 끝내다 market research 시장 조사 line 상품군 market share 시장점유율 consumer 소비자 bring into ~로 끌어들이다 customer base 고객층 sun protection 자외선 차단제 wear off 사라지다, 없어지다 outdoor 야외의 come up with ~을 내놓다

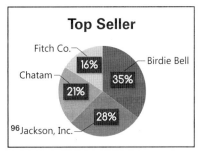

Top Seller

Fitch Co. 16%
Birdie Bell 35%
Chatam 21%
⁹⁶Jackson, Inc. 28%

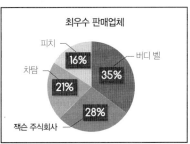

최우수 판매업체

피치 16%
버디 벨 35%
차탐 21%
잭슨 주식회사 28%

Test 7

95

What kind of goods does the speaker's company produce?

(A) Telephones
(B) Furniture
(C) Cosmetics
(D) Clothing

화자의 회사는 어떤 종류의 물품을 생산하는가?

(A) 전화기
(B) 가구
(C) 화장품
(D) 의류

해설 세부 사항 관련 – 회사가 생산하는 제품의 종류

지문 초반부에서 화자 회사의 메이크업 및 로션 제품이 가장 인기 있는 브랜드 4위권에 진입했다(our line of makeup and lotions is within the top four most popular brands)고 했으므로 정답은 (C)이다.

▸▸ **Paraphrasing** 지문의 **makeup and lotions**
→ 정답의 **Cosmetics**

96

Look at the graphic. Where do the listeners work?

(A) Birdie Bell
(B) Jackson, Inc.
(C) Chatam
(D) Fitch Co.

시각 정보에 의하면, 청자들은 어디에서 일하는가?

(A) 버디 벨
(B) 잭슨 주식회사
(C) 차탐
(D) 피치

해설 시각 정보 연계 – 청자들의 근무지

지문의 중반부에서 작년에 시장점유율이 약 20퍼센트였는데 28퍼센트로 증가했다(Last year, we had about twenty percent of the market share, and that has grown to twenty-eight percent)고 했다. 시각 정보를 보면 28퍼센트의 시장점유율을 보인 회사는 잭슨 주식회사이므로 정답은 (B)이다.

97

What will Ms. Foster's team be in charge of doing?

(A) Running an advertising campaign
(B) Planning an outdoor activity
(C) Finding new suppliers
(D) Developing some new products

포스터 씨의 팀은 어떤 일을 맡을 것인가?

(A) 광고 캠페인 운영하기
(B) 야외 활동 계획하기
(C) 신규 공급업체 찾기
(D) 신제품 개발하기

어휘 be in charge of ~를 담당하다 run 운영하다 supplier 공급업체, 납품업체 develop 개발하다 product 제품

해설 세부 사항 관련 – 포스터 씨의 팀이 맡을 일

지문 후반부에서 다수의 젊은 소비자들을 고객층으로 끌어들이기 위해(To bring a larger number of young consumers into our customer base) 야외 활동 중에도 지워지지 않는 자외선 차단제가 든 새 크림을 만들 예정(we'll be creating new creams with sun protection that don't wear off during outdoor activities)이라고 했고 캐롤 포스터 씨가 그 팀을 이끌 것(Carol Foster will be leading that team)이라고 했으므로 정답은 (D)이다.

▸▸ **Paraphrasing** 지문의 **creating new creams with sun protection**
→ 정답의 **Developing some new products**

98-100 공지 + 목록

M-Au Attention, all passengers with tickets for the 12:30 P.M. departure to Bennigan Station. **⁹⁸This train will depart approximately one hour late due to a mechanical issue. We're very sorry about this,** and we are doing everything we can to minimize the inconvenience. **⁹⁹To make your waiting time more enjoyable, the Station Café is offering thirty percent off all hot drinks and twenty-five percent off all sandwiches.** It's located near the northern end of Platform 3. **¹⁰⁰We'll be announcing updates regularly, so don't forget to listen out for these.** Thank you.

오후 12시 30분에 베니건 역으로 출발하는 탑승권을 가진 승객께서는 모두 주목해 주십시오. 열차가 기계상의 문제로 약 한 시간 늦게 출발할 예정입니다. 대단히 죄송합니다. 불편을 최소화할 수 있도록 최선을 다하고 있습니다. 대기 시간을 좀 더 즐겁게 보내시도록 스테이션 카페에서는 뜨거운 음료 일체를 30퍼센트, 샌드위치 일체를 25퍼센트 할인해 드리고 있습니다. 카페는 3번 플랫폼 북쪽 끝 근처에 위치해 있습니다. 새로운 소식을 자주 알려드릴 예정이니 잊지 말고 주의해서 들으시기 바랍니다. 감사합니다.

어휘 departure 출발 depart 출발하다 approximately 거의 (정확하게) due to ~ 때문에 mechanical 기계의 issue 문제 minimize 최소화하다 inconvenience 불편 off 할인하여 locate ~에 위치하다 announce 발표하다 regularly 자주, 정기적으로 listen out for ~을 들으려고 귀를 기울이다

Station Café	
⁹⁹Sandwich	£3.49
⁹⁹Hot coffee	£2.99
⁹⁹Hot tea	£2.59
Iced tea	£2.29

스테이션 카페	
샌드위치	3.49파운드
뜨거운 커피	2.99파운드
뜨거운 차	2.59파운드
차가운 차	2.29파운드

98

Why does the speaker apologize?

(A) A train car was overbooked.
(B) A journey has been canceled.
(C) A station will close early.
(D) A train has been delayed.

화자가 사과하는 이유는 무엇인가?

(A) 열차가 초과 예약됐다.
(B) 여정이 취소됐다.
(C) 역을 일찍 닫을 예정이다.
(D) 열차가 지연됐다.

어휘   overbook 초과 예약하다   journey 여정   cancel 취소하다   delay
지연하다

해설   세부 사항 관련 – 화자가 사과하는 이유

지문 초반부에서 열차가 기계상의 문제로 약 한 시간 늦게 출발할 예정(This
train will depart approximately one hour late due to a mechanical
issue)이기 때문에 미안하다(We're very sorry about this)고 했으므로 정답
은 (D)이다.

▸▸ Paraphrasing   지문의 **This train will depart approximately
one hour late**
→ 정답의 **A train has been delayed.**

99

Look at the graphic. Which price will not be changed?

(A) £3.49
(B) £2.99
(C) £2.59
(D) £2.29

시각 정보에 의하면, 변동이 없는 가격은 어느 것인가?

(A) 3.49파운드
(B) 2.99파운드
(C) 2.59파운드
(D) 2.29파운드

해설   시각 정보 연계 – 변동이 없는 가격

지문의 중반부에서 대기 시간을 좀 더 즐겁게 보낼 수 있도록(To make your
waiting time more enjoyable) 스테이션 카페에서는 뜨거운 음료 일체를
30퍼센트, 샌드위치 일체를 25퍼센트 할인해 주고 있다(the Station Café is
offering thirty percent off all hot drinks and twenty-five percent off
all sandwiches)고 했다. 시각 정보를 확인해 보면 차가운 차는 할인 대상이
아니므로 정답은 (D)이다.

100

What are the listeners reminded to do?

(A) Listen for announcements
(B) Wait at the platform
(C) Exchange their tickets
(D) Keep their luggage with them

청자들에게 무엇을 하라고 상기시키는가?

(A) 안내 방송 듣기
(B) 플랫폼에서 기다리기
(C) 탑승권 교환하기
(D) 짐을 가지고 있기

어휘   announcement 안내방송, 공지   exchange 교환하다
luggage 짐

해설   세부 사항 관련 – 청자들에게 상기시킨 점

지문 후반부에서 새로운 소식을 자주 알려 드릴 예정(We'll be announcing
updates regularly)이니 잊지 말고 주의해서 듣길 바란다(don't forget to
listen out for these)고 했으므로 정답은 (A)이다.

TEST 8

1 (A)	**2** (D)	**3** (C)	**4** (A)	**5** (C)
6 (B)	**7** (A)	**8** (C)	**9** (A)	**10** (C)
11 (A)	**12** (B)	**13** (C)	**14** (C)	**15** (A)
16 (B)	**17** (C)	**18** (A)	**19** (C)	**20** (A)
21 (A)	**22** (A)	**23** (B)	**24** (B)	**25** (C)
26 (C)	**27** (A)	**28** (C)	**29** (C)	**30** (A)
31 (A)	**32** (A)	**33** (C)	**34** (B)	**35** (D)
36 (A)	**37** (B)	**38** (A)	**39** (B)	**40** (D)
41 (A)	**42** (D)	**43** (B)	**44** (D)	**45** (D)
46 (D)	**47** (C)	**48** (C)	**49** (D)	**50** (C)
51 (D)	**52** (A)	**53** (B)	**54** (D)	**55** (A)
56 (B)	**57** (D)	**58** (C)	**59** (B)	**60** (A)
61 (D)	**62** (A)	**63** (B)	**64** (C)	**65** (C)
66 (A)	**67** (A)	**68** (C)	**69** (B)	**70** (D)
71 (B)	**72** (A)	**73** (B)	**74** (D)	**75** (A)
76 (C)	**77** (B)	**78** (C)	**79** (A)	**80** (A)
81 (A)	**82** (C)	**83** (A)	**84** (C)	**85** (B)
86 (D)	**87** (A)	**88** (C)	**89** (A)	**90** (B)
91 (B)	**92** (A)	**93** (D)	**94** (C)	**95** (D)
96 (B)	**97** (A)	**98** (C)	**99** (A)	**100** (C)

PART 1

01 M-Cn

(A) He's grasping a pipe.
(B) He's packing up some tools.
(C) He's fixing a water fountain.
(D) He's wiping some tiles.

(A) **남자가 파이프를 잡고 있다.**
(B) 남자가 공구들을 챙기고 있다.
(C) 남자가 식수대를 수리하고 있다.
(D) 남자가 타일을 닦고 있다.

어휘 grasp 잡다 pack up 짐을 싸다 tool 연장, 공구 fix 고치다
water fountain (분수식) 식수대 wipe 닦다

해설 1인 등장 사진 – 사람의 상태 묘사
(A) 정답. 남자가 파이프를 잡고 있는(is grasping a pipe) 모습이므로 정답.
(B) 동사 오답. 사진에 남자는 보이지만 도구를 챙기고 있지(is packing up some tools) 않으므로 오답.
(C) 사진에 없는 명사를 이용한 오답. 사진 속에 식수대(water fountain)가 보이지 않으므로 오답.
(D) 동사 오답. 사진에 남자는 보이지만 타일을 닦고 있지(is wiping some tiles) 않으므로 오답.

02 W-Am

(A) They're picking up notebook computers.
(B) They're turning the pages of magazines.
(C) One of the men is leaning against a wall.
(D) One of the men is wearing a suit jacket.

(A) 사람들이 노트북 컴퓨터를 집어 들고 있다.
(B) 사람들이 잡지 페이지를 넘기고 있다.
(C) 남자 중 한 명이 벽에 기대 있다.
(D) **남자 중 한 명이 정장 재킷을 입는 중이다.**

어휘 pick up 집어 들다 turn 넘기다 lean against ~에 기대다

해설 2인 이상 등장 사진 – 사람의 상태 묘사
(A) 동사 오답. 사진에 사람들은 보이지만 노트북 컴퓨터를 집어 드는 중(are picking up notebook computers)이 아니므로 오답.
(B) 동사 오답. 사진에 사람들은 보이지만 잡지 페이지를 넘기는 중(are turning the pages of magazines)이 아니므로 오답.
(C) 동사 오답. 사진에 남자는 보이지만 벽에 기대 있는 모습(is leaning against a wall)이 아니므로 오답.
(D) 정답. 남자 중 한 명이 정장 재킷을 입고 있는 상태(is wearing a suit jacket)이므로 정답.

03 M-Au

(A) Some doors are opening.
(B) A woman is looking in her purse.
(C) A train is stopped at a station.
(D) Benches line a platform.

(A) 문 몇 개가 열리고 있다.
(B) 여자가 핸드백 안을 들여다보고 있다.
(C) **열차가 역에 서 있다.**
(D) 벤치가 플랫폼을 따라 늘어서 있다.

어휘 purse 지갑, 핸드백 line ~을 따라 늘어서다

해설 1인 등장 사진 – 사람 또는 사물 중심 묘사
(A) 동사 오답. 사진에 문 몇 개는 있지만 열리고 있지(are opening) 않으므로 오답.
(B) 동사 오답. 사진에 여자는 있지만 핸드백 안을 들여다보고 있지(is looking in her purse) 않으므로 오답.
(C) 정답. 열차가 역에 서 있는 모습(is stopped at a station)이므로 정답.
(D) 사진에 없는 명사를 이용한 오답. 사진에 벤치(benches)가 보이지 않으므로 오답.

04 W-Br

(A) A shopper is examining a store display.
(B) Some boxes have been put in a van.
(C) Some clerks are operating cash registers.
(D) A buffet table has been loaded with fruit.

(A) 쇼핑객이 매장 진열대를 살펴보고 있다.
(B) 몇몇 상자들이 밴에 실려 있다.
(C) 몇몇 직원들이 금전 등록기를 조작하고 있다.
(D) 뷔페 테이블에 과일이 놓여 있다.

어휘 examine 조사하다 display 진열대 put 두다, 놓다 van 운반차
clerk 점원 operate 조작하다 cash register 금전 등록기 load
with ~을 싣다

해설 1인 등장 사진 – 사람 또는 사물 중심 묘사
(A) 정답. 쇼핑객이 매장 진열대를 살펴보고 있는(is examining a store
display) 모습이므로 정답.
(B) 사진에 없는 명사를 이용한 오답. 사진에 밴(van)이 보이지 않으므로 오답.
(C) 사진에 없는 명사를 이용한 오답. 사진에 금전 등록기(cash registers)가
보이지 않으므로 오답.
(D) 사진에 없는 명사를 이용한 오답. 사진에 뷔페 테이블(buffet table)이 보
이지 않으므로 오답.

05 M-Cn

(A) A stone street runs beside a river.
(B) Planters have been placed around a garden.
(C) Motorbikes have been parked by a building.
(D) A group of diners is sitting at outdoor tables.

(A) 강 옆으로 돌이 깔린 길이 뻗어 있다.
(B) 화분들이 정원 곳곳에 놓여 있다.
(C) 오토바이들이 건물 옆에 세워져 있다.
(D) 식사하는 사람들이 야외 테이블에 앉아 있다.

어휘 run 뻗다, 통하다 planter 화분 place 놓다 motorbike 오토바이
park 주차하다 diner 식사하는 사람

해설 사물/배경 사진 – 사물의 위치 묘사
(A) 사진에 없는 명사를 이용한 오답. 사진에 강(river)이 보이지 않으므로 오답.
(B) 사진에 없는 명사를 이용한 오답. 사진에 정원(garden)이 보이지 않으므로
오답.
(C) 정답. 오토바이들이 건물 옆에 세워져 있는 모습(have been parked by
a building)이므로 정답.

(D) 사진에 없는 명사를 이용한 오답. 사진에 식사하는 사람들(A group of
diners)이 보이지 않으므로 오답.

06 W-Br

(A) Some grass is being trimmed.
(B) Trees are reflected in some water.
(C) A small house is being painted.
(D) A hillside is covered with snow.

(A) 잔디가 다듬어지고 있다.
(B) 나무들이 물에 비친다.
(C) 작은 집이 페인트칠되고 있다.
(D) 비탈이 눈으로 덮여 있다.

어휘 trim 다듬다, 손질하다 reflect 비추다, 반사하다 hillside 비탈
be covered with ~로 덮여 있다

해설 사물/배경 사진 – 사물의 상태 묘사
(A) 동사 오답. 사진에 잔디(grass)는 보이지만 다듬어지고 있지(is being
trimmed) 않으므로 오답.
(B) 정답. 나무들이 물에 비치고 있는(are reflected in some water) 모습이
므로 정답.
(C) 동사 오답. 사진에 작은 집(small house)은 보이지만 페인트칠되고 있지
(is being painted) 않으므로 오답.
(D) 사진에 없는 명사를 이용한 오답. 사진에 비탈(hillside)과 눈(snow)이 보
이지 않으므로 오답.

PART 2

07

W-Br When did you hold the first session?
M-Cn (A) A month ago.
　　　(B) Not the first one.
　　　(C) Certainly.

첫 시간은 언제 진행했나요?
(A) 한 달 전이에요.
(B) 처음 것은 아니에요.
(C) 물론이죠.

어휘 session (특정 활동을 위한) 시간, 기간

해설 첫 시간을 언제 진행했는지를 묻는 When 의문문
(A) 정답. 첫 시간을 언제 진행했는지를 묻는 질문에 한 달 전이라는 구체적인
시점을 언급하고 있으므로 정답.
(B) 단어 반복 오답. 질문의 first를 반복한 오답.
(C) 질문과 상관없는 오답. 부탁/요청 의문문에 어울리는 응답이므로 오답.

08

M-Au Can I help you with your luggage?

W-Br (A) The suitcase is attractive.

(B) In the outer pocket.

(C) Thanks, it's very heavy.

제가 짐을 들어드릴까요?

(A) 여행 가방이 멋지네요.

(B) 바깥 주머니 안에요.

(C) 고마워요. 아주 무겁거든요.

어휘 luggage 짐, 수화물 attractive 멋진, 매력적인 outer 바깥의, 외부의

해설 제안/권유 의문문

(A) 연상 단어 오답. 질문의 luggage에 대해 연상 가능한 suitcase를 이용한 오답.

(B) 연상 단어 오답. 질문의 luggage에 대해 연상 가능한 outer pocket를 이용한 오답.

(C) 정답. 짐을 들어주겠다는 제안에 고맙다는 긍정적인 대답을 하고 있으므로 정답.

09

M-Cn The handle to the supply room door is loose.

W-Am (A) Talk to Jeff in maintenance about that.

(B) A drawer in my desk.

(C) Because they're easy to lose.

비품실 문 손잡이가 헐거워요.

(A) 관리실의 제프에게 이야기하세요.

(B) 제 책상 서랍이요.

(C) 그것들은 잃어버리기 쉽거든요.

어휘 handle 손잡이 supply room 비품실 loose 느슨한, 헐거운 maintenance 유지, 보수 drawer 서랍 lose 잃어버리다

해설 사실/정보 전달의 평서문

(A) 정답. 비품실 문 손잡이가 헐겁다는 말에 관리실의 제프에게 이야기하라는 우회적인 응답을 하고 있으므로 정답.

(B) 유사 발음 오답. 질문의 door와 발음이 비슷한 drawer를 이용한 오답.

(C) 유사 발음 오답. 질문의 loose와 부분적으로 발음이 동일한 lose를 이용한 오답.

10

W-Am Have they installed the software program?

M-Au (A) Near the computer lab.

(B) Temporary employees.

(C) No, not yet.

그들이 소프트웨어 프로그램을 설치했나요?

(A) 컴퓨터실 근처에요.

(B) 임시 직원들이요.

(C) 아뇨, 아직이요.

어휘 install 설치하다 lab 실습실 temporary 임시의, 일시적인 employee 직원

해설 소프트웨어 프로그램 설치 여부를 묻는 조동사(have) Yes/No의문문

(A) 연상 단어 오답. 질문의 software program에 대해 연상 가능한 computer lab을 이용한 오답.

(B) 질문과 상관없는 오답. Who 의문문에 어울리는 응답이므로 오답.

(C) 정답. 소프트웨어 프로그램 설치 여부에 대해 먼저 No로 부정적 응답을 한 후, 아직 안 했다고 응답하고 있으므로 정답.

11

M-Cn How can we make it to the train station on time?

W-Br (A) We'll need to hurry.

(B) Who's training them?

(C) He came to work late.

제시간에 기차역에 가려면 어떻게 해야 할까요?

(A) 서둘러야 할 거예요.

(B) 누가 그들을 훈련시킬 건가요?

(C) 그는 직장에 지각했어요.

어휘 on time 제시간에 hurry 서두르다 train 훈련시키다

해설 기차역에 제시간에 가는 방법을 묻는 How 의문문

(A) 정답. 제시간에 기차역에 가는 방법을 묻는 How 의문문에 서둘러야 한다는 직접적인 방법을 제시한 답변이므로 정답.

(B) 유사 발음 오답. 질문의 train과 부분적으로 발음이 동일한 training을 이용한 오답.

(C) 연상 단어 오답. 질문의 on time에 대해 연상 가능한 late를 이용한 오답.

12

W-Br When can we expect to receive your report?

M-Au (A) A few more pages.

(B) By the end of the month.

(C) Yes, I've received a copy.

보고서는 언제 받을 수 있나요?

(A) 몇 페이지 더요.

(B) 이달 말까지요.

(C) 네, 제가 한 부 받았어요.

어휘 expect 예상하다 receive 받다 copy 사본

해설 보고서 수령 시점을 묻는 When 의문문

(A) 연상 단어 오답. 질문의 report에 대해 연상 가능한 pages를 이용한 오답.

(B) 정답. 보고서를 언제 받을 수 있느냐는 질문에 이달 말이라는 직접적인 시점으로 응답하고 있으므로 정답.

(C) Yes/No 불가 오답. When 의문문에 Yes/No 응답은 불가능하므로 오답.

13

M-Cn Shall we talk about possible topics for the mayor's speech?

W-Am (A) It was about a city initiative.

(B) The audience loved it, I heard.

(C) Sure, I have a few ideas.

시장님 연설 주제로 뭐가 적당할지 얘기해 볼까요?
(A) 그건 도시 법안에 대한 것이었어요.
(B) 청중이 좋아했다고 들었어요.
(C) 물론이죠. 제게 몇 가지 아이디어가 있어요.

어휘 mayor 시장 speech 연설, 강연 initiative 법안 발의 audience 청중

해설 제안/권유의 의문문
(A) 연상 단어 오답. 질문의 topics에 대해 연상 가능한 city initiative를 이용한 오답.
(B) 연상 단어 오답. 질문의 speech에 대해 연상 가능한 audience를 이용한 오답.
(C) 정답. 시장님 연설 주제로 뭐가 적당할지 논의하자는 제안에 Sure라는 긍정적인 응답을 한 후 몇 가지 아이디어가 있다고 부연 설명하고 있으므로 정답.

14

W-Am Are you planning to apply for the new branch manager position?

W-Br (A) Didn't the crew trim those trees?

(B) That's what we thought too.

(C) I thought it had already been filled.

새로운 지점장 자리에 지원할 계획인가요?
(A) 작업반이 이 나무들을 다듬지 않았나요?
(B) 우리도 그렇게 생각했어요.
(C) 그 자리는 이미 충원된 줄 알았는데요.

어휘 plan to ~할 계획이다 apply for ~에 지원하다 branch 지사, 분점 position (일)자리 crew (함께 일하는) 팀, 반, 조 trim 손질하다, 다듬다 fill 메우다

해설 계획을 묻는 be동사 Yes/No 의문문
(A) 연상 단어 오답. 질문의 branch를 다른 의미로 잘못 이해했을 때 연상 가능한 trees를 이용한 오답.
(B) 질문과 상관없는 오답. we가 가리키는 대상이 없으므로 오답.
(C) 정답. 지점장 자리에 지원할 계획이냐는 질문에 자리가 이미 충원된 줄 알았다는 우회적인 응답을 하고 있으므로 정답.

15

W-Br What color of paint do you prefer for the lobby?

M-Au (A) I think the dark blue might work.

(B) No, behind the reception desk.

(C) I'd prefer to take a taxi.

로비에는 무슨 색 페인트가 좋을까요?
(A) 어두운 파란색이면 어울릴 것 같아요.
(B) 아뇨, 접수처 뒤에요.
(C) 저는 택시를 탈게요.

어휘 prefer 선호하다 work 효과가 있다 reception desk 접수처

해설 로비에 어울릴 색을 묻는 What color 의문문
(A) 정답. 페인트의 색을 묻는 질문에 어두운 파란색이라는 특정 색을 언급하고 있으므로 정답.
(B) Yes/No 불가 오답. Who 의문문에 Yes/No 응답은 불가능하므로 오답.
(C) 단어 반복 오답. 질문의 prefer를 반복한 오답.

16

M-Cn Who's responsible for ordering office supplies?

W-Am (A) The response was good.

(B) What do you need?

(C) It's a new supplier.

사무실 비품 주문은 누구 담당이죠?
(A) 대응이 좋았어요.
(B) 뭐가 필요하세요?
(C) 신규 공급업체예요.

어휘 be responsible for ~에 책임이 있다 office supplies 사무용품 response 대답, 대응 supplier 공급자

해설 비품 주문 책임자를 묻는 Who 의문문
(A) 유사 발음 오답. 질문의 responsible과 부분적으로 발음이 동일한 response를 이용한 오답.
(B) 정답. 비품 주문 책임자를 묻는 질문에 대해 무엇이 필요하냐는 우회적인 질문으로 응답을 하고 있으므로 정답.
(C) 파생어 오답. 질문의 supplies와 파생어 관계인 supplier를 이용한 오답.

17

M-Au You've revised all the budget figures, haven't you?

W-Br (A) The Human Resources Department.

(B) He's no longer our advisor.

(C) I finished that this morning.

예산 수치는 모두 변경하셨죠?
(A) 인사 부서요.
(B) 그는 이제 우리 고문이 아니에요.
(C) 오늘 아침에 마쳤어요.

어휘 revise 수정[변경]하다 budget 예산 figure 수치 human resources 인사 department 부서 no longer 더 이상 ~ 아닌 advisor 고문

해설 예산 수치 변경 여부를 확인하는 부가의문문
(A) 질문과 상관없는 오답. Who 의문문에 어울리는 응답이므로 오답.
(B) 질문과 상관없는 오답. He를 가리키는 대상이 질문에 없으므로 오답.
(C) 정답. 예산 수치 변경 여부를 확인하는 질문에 오늘 아침에 마쳤다는 직접적인 응답을 하고 있으므로 정답.

18

M-Cn Where should I leave my registration information?

W-Am (A) There are instructions on the form.

(B) Only for the online subscriptions.

(C) Anytime before March tenth.

제 등록 정보를 어디에 두어야 하나요?

(A) 양식에 설명이 있습니다.

(B) 온라인 구독에만요.

(C) 3월 10일 전이면 언제든 상관없어요.

어휘 registration 등록 instruction 설명, 지시 form 서식, 양식
subscription 구독

해설 등록 정보를 놓을 위치를 묻는 Where 의문문

(A) 정답. 등록 정보를 놓을 위치를 묻는 질문에 양식에 설명이 있다고 장소를 찾는 방법을 우회적으로 언급하고 있으므로 정답.

(B) 연상 단어 오답. 질문의 registration에 대해 연상 가능한 online subscriptions을 이용한 오답.

(C) 질문과 상관없는 오답. When 의문문에 어울리는 응답이므로 오답.

19

W-Am Why did you ask for the McKinney contract?

M-Au (A) In the filing cabinet by the door.

(B) Camilla signed them already.

(C) I meant the McKenzie contract.

맥키니 계약서는 왜 요청하셨죠?

(A) 문 옆의 서류 캐비닛 안이요.

(B) 카밀라가 이미 서명했어요.

(C) 맥켄지 계약서를 말한 건데요.

어휘 contract 계약(서) filing cabinet 서류 캐비닛 sign 서명하다

해설 계약서 요청 이유를 묻는 Why 의문문

(A) 질문과 상관없는 오답. Where 의문문에 어울리는 응답이므로 오답.

(B) 연상 단어 오답. 질문의 contract를 듣고 연상 가능한 signed를 이용한 오답.

(C) 정답. 맥키니 계약서를 요청한 이유를 묻는 질문에 맥켄지라는 다른 사람의 계약서를 말한 거였다고 우회적으로 응답하고 있으므로 정답.

20

M-Cn I have this room reserved for a focus group meeting.

W-Br (A) OK, I'll be out in a moment.

(B) By adjusting the focus control.

(C) How did they happen to meet?

제가 포커스 그룹 미팅 때문에 이 회의실을 예약했는데요.

(A) 알겠습니다. 금방 나갈게요.

(B) 초점 조정장치를 조절해서요.

(C) 그들이 어쩌다 마주쳤죠?

어휘 reserve 예약하다 focus group 포커스 그룹(시장·여론 조사를 위해 각 계층을 대표하는 소수 인원으로 이뤄진 그룹) adjust 조절하다 focus control 초점 조정장치 happen to 우연히 ~하다

해설 사실/정보 전달의 평서문

(A) 정답. 포커스 그룹 미팅 때문에 이 회의실을 예약했다는 말에 금방 나가겠다고 응답하고 있으므로 정답.

(B) 단어 반복 오답. 질문의 focus를 반복한 오답.

(C) 파생어 오답. 질문의 meeting과 파생어 관계인 meet을 이용한 오답.

21

W-Am Shouldn't we mail her a paper catalog?

M-Cn (A) No, Harrison already did that.

(B) Yes, her blog is very popular.

(C) In the morning edition.

그녀에게 종이 카탈로그를 우편으로 보내야 하지 않을까요?

(A) 아니에요, 해리슨이 이미 보냈어요.

(B) 맞아요, 그녀의 블로그는 아주 인기가 많으니까요.

(C) 조간 신문에요.

어휘 mail 우편물을 발송하다 morning edition 조간 신문

해설 카탈로그 우편 발송 여부를 묻는 부정의문문

(A) 정답. 그녀에게 종이 카탈로그를 우편으로 보내야 하는지에 대한 질문에 먼저 No라는 부정적인 응답을 한 후, 해리슨이 이미 보냈다고 응답하고 있으므로 정답.

(B) 단어 반복 오답. 질문의 her를 반복한 오답.

(C) 연상 단어 오답. 질문의 paper에 대해 연상 가능한 in the morning edition을 이용한 오답.

22

M-Au I'm sorry to say we'll need to shut down the assembly line.

W-Am (A) That's the fourth time this week.

(B) Did you make one too?

(C) On the conveyor belt.

안타깝지만 우리는 조립 라인을 중단해야 합니다.

(A) 이번 주에만 네 번째네요.

(B) 당신도 하나 만들었나요?

(C) 컨베이어 벨트 위에요.

어휘 shut down 문을 닫다, 정지시키다 assembly line 조립 라인
conveyor belt 컨베이어 벨트

해설 사실/정보 전달의 평서문

(A) 정답. 조립 라인을 중단해야 한다는 말에 이번 주에만 벌써 네 번째라고 우회적으로 부정적으로 응답하고 있으므로 정답.

(B) 질문과 상관없는 오답. 유감을 표하는 내용과는 무관한 질문이므로 오답.

(C) 연상 단어 오답. 질문의 assembly line에 대해 연상 가능한 conveyor belt를 이용한 오답.

23

M-Cn Didn't you pick up your dress shirts last night?

M-Au (A) Your claim ticket, please.

(B) The dry cleaner was closed.

(C) These fancy pie charts.

어젯밤에 정장 셔츠를 찾아오지 않았어요?
(A) 교환증을 보여 주세요.
(B) 드라이클리닝 전문점이 문을 닫았어요.
(C) 이 화려한 원 그래프요.

어휘 pick up ~을 찾아오다 dress shirt 정장용 셔츠 claim ticket 보관증 fancy 복잡한, 화려한 pie chart 원 그래프

해설 정장 셔츠를 찾아왔는지 여부를 묻는 부정의문문
(A) 질문과 상관없는 오답. 요청 의문문에 어울리는 응답이므로 오답.
(B) 정답. 정장 셔츠를 어젯밤에 찾아왔는지 여부를 묻는 질문에 드라이클리닝 전문점이 문을 닫았다고 우회적으로 부정적으로 응답하고 있으므로 정답.
(C) 질문과 상관없는 오답. Which 의문문에 어울리는 응답이므로 오답.

24

W-Br You told me the financial analysis would be done Tuesday, didn't you?

M-Cn (A) He led the discussion quite well.

(B) Yes, but I may need an extra day.

(C) No, they'll pay in cash.

재무 분석이 화요일에 있을 거라고 했죠?
(A) 그는 논의를 제법 잘 이끌었어요.
(B) 네, 하지만 하루 더 필요할지도 몰라요.
(C) 아뇨, 그들은 현금으로 지불할 거예요.

어휘 financial 금융[재정]의 analysis 분석 lead 이끌다 discussion 논의 extra 추가의 in cash 현금으로

해설 재무 분석이 화요일에 있을지 여부를 묻는 부정의문문
(A) 질문과 상관없는 오답. He가 가리키는 대상이 질문에 없으므로 오답.
(B) 정답. 재무 분석이 화요일에 있을지 확인을 하는 질문에 먼저 Yes라는 긍정적인 응답을 한 후 하루 더 필요할지도 모른다고 부연 설명하고 있으므로 정답.
(C) 연상 단어 오답. 질문의 financial analysis에 대해 연상 가능한 cash를 이용한 오답.

25

M-Au Which contractor did Ms. Winchester choose?

W-Br (A) A short-term lease.

(B) Her most comfortable shoes.

(C) I think she's still comparing quotes.

윈체스터 씨가 어느 도급업자를 선택했나요?
(A) 단기 임대요.
(B) 그녀의 가장 편한 신발이요.
(C) 아직 견적을 비교해 보고 있을 거예요.

어휘 contractor 도급업자 choose 고르다 short-term 단기의 lease 임대차 계약 comfortable 편안한 compare 비교하다 quote 견적

해설 어느 도급업자를 선택했는지 묻는 Which 의문문
(A) 연상 단어 오답. 질문의 contractor에 대해 연상 가능한 lease를 이용한 오답.
(B) 유사 발음 오답. 질문의 choose와 부분적으로 발음이 동일한 shoes를 이용한 오답.
(C) 정답. 어느 도급업자를 선택했는지 묻는 질문에 그녀가 아직 견적을 비교해 보고 있을 것이라고 우회적으로 응답하고 있으므로 정답.

26

M-Cn How did you get those booklets of coupons?

W-Am (A) About a twenty-percent discount.

(B) No, used books and magazines.

(C) I registered for them online.

그 쿠폰 소책자를 어떻게 얻었나요?
(A) 약 20퍼센트 할인이에요.
(B) 아뇨, 중고 서적과 잡지요.
(C) 온라인에서 신청했어요.

어휘 booklet 소책자 discount 할인 used 중고의 register for ~에 등록하다

해설 쿠폰 소책자를 얻은 방법을 묻는 How의문문
(A) 연상 단어 오답. 질문의 coupons에 대해 연상 가능한 discount를 이용한 오답.
(B) Yes/No 불가 오답. How 의문문에 Yes/No 응답은 불가능하므로 오답.
(C) 정답. 쿠폰 소책자를 어떻게 얻었는지를 묻는 질문에 온라인에서 신청했다는 구체적 방법을 알려주므로 정답.

27

W-Am Where did Floyd's Fresh Café open its first location?

M-Au (A) In downtown Hollisville.

(B) About ten years ago.

(C) Is there a table next to the window?

플로이드의 프레시 카페는 첫 지점을 어디에 열었죠?
(A) 홀리스빌 시내에요.
(B) 약 10년 전에요.
(C) 창가 테이블이 있나요?

어휘 location 장소, 위치

해설 카페 첫 지점의 장소를 묻는 Where 의문문
(A) 정답. 플로이드의 프레시 카페가 어디에 첫 지점을 열었는지를 묻는 질문에 구체적인 장소로 응답하고 있으므로 정답.
(B) 질문과 상관없는 오답. When 의문문에 어울리는 응답이므로 오답.
(C) 연상 단어 오답. 질문의 Café에 대해 연상 가능한 table을 이용한 오답.

28

M-Cn Have you considered hiring a cleaning service for the office?

W-Br (A) Some cream-colored curtains.

(B) That's considerate of him.

(C) Yes, but it's too expensive.

사무실 청소 용역업체 고용을 고려해 봤어요?
(A) 크림색 커튼이요.
(B) 그가 참 사려 깊네요.
(C) 네, 하지만 너무 비싸요.

어휘 consider 고려하다 hire 고용하다 considerate 사려 깊은, 배려하는

해설 청소 용역업체 고용을 고려해봤는지 묻는 조동사(have) Yes/No 의문문

(A) 유사 발음 오답. 질문의 cleaning와 부분적으로 발음이 동일한 cream을 이용한 오답.

(B) 질문과 상관없는 오답. him이 가리키는 대상이 질문에 없으므로 오답.

(C) 정답. 사무실에 청소 용역업체 고용을 고려해 봤냐는 질문에 먼저 Yes라는 긍정적인 응답을 한 후 그렇지만 너무 비싸다고 응답하고 있으므로 정답.

29

W-Br When will the recreation center close on New Year's Eve?

M-Au (A) It actually has two entrances.

(B) They're expanding the parking area.

(C) Six o'clock, like it does on weekends.

새해 전날에 레크리에이션 센터는 언제쯤 문을 닫나요?
(A) 사실 입구가 두 개 있어요.
(B) 그들은 주차 공간을 확장할 거예요.
(C) 주말이면 그렇듯 6시예요.

어휘 recreation 레크리에이션, 오락 actually 사실 entrance 입구 expand 확장하다 parking area 주차장

해설 레크리에이션 센터 폐관 시간을 묻는 When 의문문

(A) 연상 단어 오답. 질문의 recreation center에 대해 연상 가능한 entrances를 이용한 오답.

(B) 연상 단어 오답. 질문의 recreation center에 대해 연상 가능한 parking area를 이용한 오답.

(C) 정답. 새해 전날에 레크리에이션 센터가 언제쯤 문을 닫느냐는 질문에 6시라고 구체적인 시간으로 응답하므로 정답.

30

W-Am Are these receipts from several sales months or only one?

M-Cn (A) They're all from September.

(B) For credit card payments.

(C) So that we can get rid of them.

이 영수증들은 영업 수 개월 분인가요 아니면 1개월 분인가요?
(A) 모두 9월 분이에요.
(B) 신용카드 결제를 위해서요.
(C) 그걸 없앨 수 있게요.

어휘 receipt 영수증 payment 결제, 지불 get rid of ~을 없애다

해설 구를 연결한 선택의문문

(A) 정답. 영수증이 수 개월 분인지, 1개월 분인지 묻는 질문에 9월 분이라고 응답하고 있으므로 정답.

(B) 연상 단어 오답. 질문의 receipts에 대해 연상 가능한 credit card를 이용한 오답.

(C) 질문과 상관없는 오답. Why 의문문에 어울리는 응답이므로 오답.

31

M-Au Please shorten the legs of these trousers by three centimeters.

W-Br (A) OK, I'll get started right away.

(B) This fabric has a striped pattern.

(C) Yes, the table has three legs.

이 바지의 밑단을 3센티미터 줄여 주세요.
(A) 알겠습니다. 바로 시작할게요.
(B) 이 원단은 줄무늬예요.
(C) 네, 그 테이블은 다리가 세 개예요.

어휘 shorten 줄이다 leg 바짓가랑이 get started 시작하다 right away 당장 fabric 천, 원단 striped 줄무늬가 있는 pattern 패턴, 무늬

해설 부탁/요청 의문문

(A) 정답. 바지의 밑단을 3센티미터 줄여 달라는 요청에 먼저 OK라는 긍정적인 응답을 한 후 바로 시작하겠다고 응답하고 있으므로 정답.

(B) 연상 단어 오답. 질문의 trousers에 대해 연상 가능한 striped pattern을 이용한 오답.

(C) 단어 반복 오답. 질문의 legs를 반복한 오답.

PART 3

32-34

> **M-Cn** Thanks for coming in. **32I just wanted to make sure that you're settling in and feeling ready for the fall semester, as you are our newest addition to our Economics Department's faculty.**
>
> **W-Br** Yes, my class preparations are going well, and I look forward to meeting my students. **33Oh, but there is one thing I'd like to ask about—how do I get a permit to park in the faculty lot?** Is there an office on campus that handles that?

M-Cn **34There is, but I recommend using our portal site to apply for the permit from home.** When you're logged in with your faculty account, it's really easy to do.

남	와 주셔서 감사합니다. 잘 적응하시면서 가을 학기 준비를 하고 계신지 확인하고 싶었습니다. 우리 경제학과에 최근 합류하신 교수님이시니까요.
여	네, 수업 준비는 잘 진행되고 있고 학생들을 빨리 만나고 싶습니다. 아, 그런데 한 가지 여쭤 보고 싶은 것이 있습니다. 교수진 주차장 주차 허가증을 어떻게 받죠? 이를 처리하는 교내 사무실이 있나요?
남	있습니다. 하지만 저희 포털 사이트를 이용해 댁에서 허가증을 신청하실 것을 권합니다. 교수 계정으로 로그인하면 정말 쉽거든요.

어휘	settle in 적응하다 semester 학기 addition 증원 인력, 새 얼굴 faculty 교수단, 모든 교수들 permit 허가(증) lot 부지 handle 처리하다 apply for ~를 신청하다 account 계정

32

Where most likely do the speakers work?

(A) At a university
(B) At a rental car agency
(C) At a staffing service
(D) At a post office

화자들은 어디에서 일하겠는가?
(A) 대학교
(B) 차량 대여 업체
(C) 직원 채용 서비스 업체
(D) 우체국

어휘 rental 임대의 staffing 직원 채용

해설 전체 내용 관련 – 화자들이 일하는 곳

남자의 첫 번째 대사에서 경제학과에 합류한 새 교수로서(as you are our newest addition to our Economics Department's faculty) 잘 적응하며 가을 학기 준비를 하고 있는지 확인하고 싶었다(I just wanted to make sure that you're settling in and feeling ready for the fall semester)고 말했으므로 정답은 (A)이다.

33

What does the woman want to do?

(A) Correct a billing error
(B) Apply for a promotion
(C) Obtain a parking permit
(D) Remodel an office space

여자는 무엇을 하고 싶어 하는가?
(A) 청구서 오류 정정하기
(B) 진급 신청하기
(C) 주차 허가증 받기
(D) 사무 공간 개조하기

어휘 correct 바로잡다 obtain 얻다 remodel 개조[보수]하다

해설 세부 사항 관련 – 여자가 하기 원하는 것

여자의 첫 번째 대사에서 교수용 주차장 주차 허가증을 어떻게 받는지(how do I get a permit to park in the faculty lot) 물어봤으므로 정답은 (C)이다.

▸▸ Paraphrasing 대화의 **get a permit**
→ 정답의 **Obtain a parking permit**

34

What does the man recommend doing?

(A) Using an expense account
(B) Going through a process online
(C) Contacting a former coworker
(D) Scanning a set of documents

남자는 무엇을 하라고 권하는가?
(A) 비용 계정 사용하기
(B) 온라인으로 절차 처리하기
(C) 이전 동료에게 연락하기
(D) 문서 스캔하기

어휘 expense 경비 go through 거치다 process 절차 former 예전의

해설 세부 사항 관련 – 남자가 권하는 것

남자의 두 번째 대사에서 포털 사이트를 이용해 댁에서 허가증을 신청할 것을 권한다(I recommend using our portal site to apply for the permit from home)고 말했으므로 정답은 (B)이다.

▸▸ Paraphrasing 대화의 **using our portal site to apply for the permit**
→ 정답의 **Going through a process online**

35-37

W-Am Emmett, sorry I'm late for my shift. **35The lobby looks pretty quiet, but I heard there was a problem with one of the double rooms on the third floor.**

M-Cn Right, Housekeeping noticed it this morning. **36The door lock won't accept the keycard, so we can't get in.**

W-Am And Maintenance wasn't able to fix it?

M-Cn No, we had to call the manufacturer. They're sending someone now.

W-Am **37I hope it can be repaired fast. We're fully booked for the next two evenings, and it would be bad publicity to turn away anyone who wishes to stay at our accommodations.**

여	에멧, 교대 시간에 늦어서 미안해요. 로비는 꽤 조용해 보이는데, 3층 2인실에 문제가 있었다고 들었어요.
남	맞아요. 객실 관리 부서에서 오늘 아침에 발견했죠. 문 잠금 장치가 키카드를 인식하지 못해서 들어갈 수가 없어요.
여	관리실에서 고치지 못했나요?
남	네, 제조사에 전화를 해야 했어요. 거기서 지금 사람을 보내 줄 거예요.
여	빨리 고칠 수 있으면 좋겠네요. 앞으로 이틀 저녁 동안은 전 객실이 예약되어 있는데, 우리 숙소에 투숙하고자 하는 사람을 돌려보내면 평판이 나빠질 테니까요.

shift 교대 근무 (시간) housekeeping 시설 관리 부서 notice 알아채다 lock 자물쇠 maintenance 관리실 fix 고치다 manufacturer 제조사 repair 수리하다 fully booked 예약이 꽉 찬 publicity 평판, 홍보 turn away ~을 돌려보내다 accommodation 거처, 숙소

35

Where most likely are the speakers?

(A) At a fitness center
(B) At an art gallery
(C) At a pharmacy
(D) At a hotel

화자들은 어디에 있겠는가?

(A) 피트니스 센터
(B) 화랑
(C) 약국
(D) 호텔

어휘 pharmacy 약국, 조제실

해설 전체 내용 관련 – 대화의 장소

여자의 첫 번째 대사에서 로비는 꽤 조용해 보이는데(The lobby looks pretty quiet), 3층의 2인실에 문제가 있었다(there was a problem with one of the double rooms on the third floor)고 들었다고 했으므로 정답은 (D)이다.

▸▸ Paraphrasing   대화의 the double rooms → 정답의 a hotel

36

What is out of order?

(A) An electronic lock
(B) A water dispenser
(C) A desktop computer
(D) An elevator door

무엇이 고장 났는가?

(A) 전자 잠금 장치
(B) 식수통
(C) 데스크톱 컴퓨터
(D) 엘리베이터 문

어휘 dispenser (바로 뽑아 쓸 수 있는) 자동 지급기, 디스펜서

해설 세부 사항 관련 – 고장 난 것

남자의 첫 번째 대사에서 문 잠금 장치가 키카드를 인식하지 못해서 들어갈 수가 없다(The door lock won't accept the keycard so we can't get in)고 했으므로 정답은 (A)이다.

▸▸ Paraphrasing   대화의 the keycard
→ 정답의 An electronic lock

37

Why should the repair be done quickly?

(A) Some complaints were received.
(B) Many visitors are expected.
(C) A warranty will expire.
(D) A security issue may arise.

수리가 빨리 이루어져야 하는 이유는 무엇인가?

(A) 항의가 들어왔다.
(B) 많은 방문객이 예상된다.
(C) 보증이 만료될 것이다.
(D) 보안 문제가 생길 수 있다.

어휘 complaint 항의 warranty 보증 expire 만료되다 security 보안 issue 문제 arise 생기다

해설 세부 사항 관련 – 신속한 수리가 필요한 이유

여자의 세 번째 대사에서 빨리 고칠 수 있으면 좋겠다(I hope it can be repaired fast)고 한 후 앞으로 이틀 저녁 동안은 전 객실이 예약되어 있다(We're fully booked for the next two evenings)고 했으므로 정답은 (B)이다.

▸▸ Paraphrasing   대화의 fully booked
→ 정답의 Many visitors are expected.

38-40

M-Au	**38Wen-Ling, can I talk to you about the plans for the Berlin trade show?**
W-Am	Oh sure, Byron.
M-Au	Well, I like that we'll have staff hand out cheap pens with our logo on them, but I was thinking about a second giveaway item for booth visitors that we really want to impress.
W-Am	I just had the same idea, actually. **39Why don't I put in an order for branded USB chargers?** They're very useful for portable electronics like smartphones.
M-Au	Ah, that could work. **40But we'll need to check the product details of the chargers to make sure that they're of reasonably high quality.** Could you send that information to me before you buy them?

남: 웬링, 베를린 무역 박람회 계획에 관해 얘기 좀 할 수 있을까요?
여: 물론이죠, 바이런.
남: 음, 직원들을 시켜서 우리 로고가 찍힌 저렴한 펜을 나누어 준다는 건 마음에 드는데, 전 우리가 정말 좋은 인상을 주고 싶은 부스 방문객들에게 줄 두 번째 증정품을 생각하던 참이었어요.
여: 실은 저도 방금 같은 생각을 했어요. 브랜드가 찍힌 USB 충전기를 주문하면 어떨까요? 스마트폰 같은 휴대용 전자 기기에 매우 유용하거든요.
남: 아, 그러면 되겠네요. 하지만 충전기의 제품 상세 정보를 확인해서 적당히 품질이 좋은지 점검해야 해요. 충전기를 구매하기 전에 그 정보를 제게 보내 주시겠어요?

38

What is the conversation mainly about?

(A) A trade fair
(B) A staff uniform
(C) A prize drawing
(D) A company logo

대화의 주요 내용은 무엇인가?
(A) 무역 박람회
(B) 직원 유니폼
(C) 경품 추첨
(D) 회사 로고

어휘　drawing 제비 뽑기, 추첨

해설　전체 내용 관련 – 대화의 주제
남자의 첫 번째 대사에서 베를린 무역 박람회 계획에 관해 얘기 좀 할 수 있을
지(can I talk to you about the plans for the Berlin trade show) 물었
으므로 정답은 (A)이다.

▸▸ Paraphrasing　대화의 **the Berlin trade show**
　　　　　　　　→ 정답의 **A trade fair**

39

What does the woman offer to do?

(A) Arrange a brainstorming session
(B) Order some promotional items
(C) Collect some packing boxes
(D) Notify a graphic designer

여자는 무엇을 하겠다고 제안하는가?
(A) 브레인스토밍 회의 준비하기
(B) 판촉 물품 주문하기
(C) 포장 상자 수거하기
(D) 그래픽 디자이너에게 통보하기

어휘　arrange 마련하다　brainstorming 아이디어 개진
　　　promotional 홍보[판촉]의　collect 모으다　packing 포장
　　　notify 알리다

해설　세부 사항 관련 – 여자가 제안한 일
여자의 두 번째 대사에서 브랜드가 찍힌 USB 충전기를 주문하면 어떨지(Why
don't I put in an order for branded USB chargers) 물었으므로 정답은
(B)이다.

▸▸ Paraphrasing　대화의 **put in an order for branded USB**
　　　　　　　　chargers
　　　　　　　　→ 정답의 **Order some promotional items**

40

What does the man request?

(A) A purchase receipt
(B) A floor plan
(C) Contact details
(D) Product specifications

남자는 무엇을 요청하는가?
(A) 구매 영수증
(B) 평면도
(C) 연락처 정보
(D) 제품 사양

어휘　floor plan (건물의) 평면도　contact 연락처　specification 사양,
　　　명세서

해설　세부 사항 관련 – 남자가 요청하는 것
남자의 마지막 대사에서 충전기의 제품 상세 정보를 확인해서 적당히 품질이
좋은지 점검해야 한다(we'll need to check the product details of the
chargers to make sure that they're of reasonably high quality)고 했
으므로 정답은 (D)이다.

▸▸ Paraphrasing　대화의 **product details**
　　　　　　　　→ 정답의 **Product specifications**

41-43 3인 대화

M-Au	Brandon, is Lorna around? **⁴¹A client just called to tell me about a technical issue with our Web site.**
M-Cn	I don't think she's here today, Klaus. She isn't signed into the company messaging service.
M-Au	Hmm, that's not good. **⁴²I was hoping to have this problem taken care of right away. Wait**—Brandon, aren't you taking night classes in Web development?
M-Cn	Yeah, but I'd need special access to the site to be able to change anything. I think you'll have to ask Lorna.
M-Au	OK. Alice, do you know where Lorna is?
W-Br	**⁴³Oh, she's probably out sick. She said yesterday that she might be catching a cold.**

남1: 브랜든, 거기에 로나 있나요? **고객이 우리 웹사이트의 기술적 문제에**
　　관해 전화했어요.
남2: 오늘은 안 나올 것 같네요, 클라우스. 회사 메신저에도 로그인하지
　　않았네요.
남1: 흠, 곤란하게 됐네요. **당장 이 문제를 처리하고 싶었거든요. 잠깐만요.**
　　브랜든, 야간에 웹 개발 수업을 듣고 있지 않나요?
남2: 네, 하지만 변경 시 사이트에 대한 특수 접근 권한이 필요해요.
　　로나에게 부탁해야 할 거예요.
남1: 알겠어요. 앨리스, 로나가 어디 있는지 아세요?
여: 아마 병가를 냈을 거예요. 어제 감기에 걸린 것 같다고 했거든요.

어휘	issue 문제 sign into 로그인하다 take care of 처리하다
	development 개발 access 접근 be out sick 아파서
	결근하다 catch a cold 감기에 걸리다

41

What has a client done?

(A) Reported a problem

(B) Missed a deadline

(C) Arrived at a building

(D) Filled out an online form

고객은 무엇을 했는가?

(A) **문제를 신고했다**

(B) 기한을 어겼다

(C) 건물에 도착했다

(D) 온라인 양식을 작성했다

어휘 report 신고하다 miss 놓치다 fill out a form 양식을 작성하다

해설 세부 사항 관련 – 고객이 한 일

첫 번째 남자의 첫 번째 대사에서 고객이 방금 웹사이트의 기술적인 문제와 관련해서 전화했다(A client just called to tell me about a technical issue with our Web site)고 했으므로 정답은 (A)이다.

▸▸ Paraphrasing 대화의 **tell me about a technical issue**
→ 정답의 **Reported a problem**

42

What does Klaus mean when he says, "Brandon, aren't you taking night classes in Web development"?

(A) Brandon is probably not interested in an opportunity.

(B) Brandon can describe an educational program.

(C) Brandon will not be able to work overtime.

(D) Brandon might know how to fix a technical issue.

클라우스가 "브랜든, 야간에 웹 개발 수업을 듣고 있지 않나요"라고 말하는 의미는 무엇인가?

(A) 브랜든은 아마도 어떤 기회에 흥미가 없을 것이다.

(B) 브랜든은 교육 프로그램을 설명할 수 있다.

(C) 브랜든은 초과 근무를 할 수 없을 것이다.

(D) **브랜든은 기술적 문제를 고칠 방법을 알고 있을지도 모른다.**

어휘 opportunity 기회 describe 설명하다 work overtime 야근하다

해설 의도 파악 – 웹 개발 야간 수업을 듣는지 물은 의도

인용문 바로 앞 문장에서 당장 이 문제를 처리하고 싶었다(I was hoping to have this problem taken care of right away)고 한 뒤 무언가 떠오른 듯 이어서 질문하고 있으므로 브랜든이 고칠 방법을 알고 있을지도 모른다는 의미이다. 따라서 정답은 (D)이다.

43

What does the woman guess that Lorna is doing?

(A) Running some errands

(B) Attending to an illness

(C) Leading a technology workshop

(D) Playing a winter sport

여자는 로나가 무엇을 하고 있으리라 추측하는가?

(A) 심부름

(B) **질병 치료**

(C) 기술 워크숍 진행

(D) 겨울 스포츠

어휘 run errands 심부름을 하다 attend to ~을 돌보다[처리하다]

해설 세부 사항 관련 – 로나의 행동 추측

여자의 대사에서 아마 병가를 냈을 것(she's probably out sick)이라고 말했으므로 정답은 (B)이다.

▸▸ Paraphrasing 대화의 **is probably out sick**
→ 정답의 **Attending to an illness**

44-46

W-Am	Do you have a minute, Trent? I have some exciting news. **44I just negotiated an agreement with Jadley Publishing to carry their products in our bookstore.**
M-Cn	That's nice, but—don't we already have enough coloring books on sale? I'm not sure what the benefit of this deal could be.
W-Am	**45Jadley Publishing's coloring books are for senior citizens, a new market.** They've allowed the company to double its size just in the past year.
M-Cn	Oh, wow. Well, I guess that could work.
W-Am	You're still not convinced? Well, wait until their books arrive. They're really beautiful. **46I'm going to set them up in the store window.** You'll see what I mean.

여: 트렌트 씨, 잠깐 시간 있어요? 멋진 소식이 있습니다. **우리 서점에서 재들리 출판사 제품을 취급하기로 협상을 타결했습니다.**

남: 잘됐군요. 하지만 판매 중인 컬러링 북은 이미 충분하지 않나요? 이번 협상에 따른 혜택이 있을지 잘 모르겠군요.

여: **재들리 출판사의 컬러링 북은 어르신들을 위한 거예요. 새로운 시장이죠.** 이 책으로 작년 한 해에만 회사 규모를 두 배로 키웠어요.

남: 대단하네요. 잘될 수도 있겠군요.

여: 아직 수긍이 안 되나 보네요. 그럼 책이 도착할 때까지 기다리세요. 정말 훌륭해요. **진열창에 둘 겁니다.** 제 말이 무슨 뜻인지 알게 되실 거예요.

어휘 negotiate an agreement 협상을 타결하다, 합의를 도출하다 carry 취급하다 benefit 혜택 deal 거래 senior citizen 고령자 market 시장 allow 가능하게 하다 double the size 두 배가 되다 convinced 확신하는 set up 놓다

44

Why does the woman speak to the man?

(A) To suggest collaborating on a book
(B) To ask for his opinion on an advertisement
(C) To invite him to a negotiation meeting
(D) To inform him of a business deal

여자가 남자에게 이야기한 이유는 무엇인가?
(A) 책을 합작할 것을 제안하려고
(B) 광고에 대한 의견을 물으려고
(C) 협상 회의에 초청하려고
(D) 사업상의 거래에 대해 알려 주려고

어휘 collaborate on ~에 대해 협동하다 advertisement 광고
      negotiation 협상

해설 전체 내용 관련 – 대화의 목적
여자의 첫 번째 대사에서 우리 서점에서 재들리 출판사 제품을 취급하기로 협상을 타결했다(I just negotiated an agreement with Jadley Publishing to carry their products in our bookstore)고 했으므로 정답은 (D)이다.

▸▸ Paraphrasing   대화의 negotiated an agreement
                  → 정답의 a business deal

45

What does the woman say about Jadley Publishing?

(A) It won an industry award.
(B) Its headquarters are nearby.
(C) Some of its branches were founded a year ago.
(D) Some of its books are aimed at a certain age range.

재들리 출판사에 대해 여자가 언급한 것은 무엇인가?
(A) 업계에서 상을 받았다.
(B) 본사가 근처에 있다.
(C) 일부 지점들이 일 년 전에 설립됐다.
(D) 일부 서적은 특정 연령대를 겨냥한다.

어휘 win an award 수상하다 headquarters 본사 found 설립하다
      be aimed at ~을 목표로 하다 age range 연령대

해설 세부 사항 관련 – 여자가 재들리 출판사에 대해 언급한 것
여자의 두 번째 대사에서 재들리 출판사의 컬러링 북은 어르신들을 위한 것이니 새로운 시장(Jadley Publishing's coloring books are for senior citizens, a new market)이라고 말했으므로 정답은 (D)이다.

▸▸ Paraphrasing   대화의 for senior citizens
                  → 정답의 aimed at a certain age range

46

What does the woman say she will do?

(A) Set up a conference call
(B) Sign up for a newsletter
(C) Browse a catalog
(D) Create a display

여자는 무엇을 하겠다고 말하는가?
(A) 전화 회의 준비
(B) 소식지 신청
(C) 카탈로그 검색
(D) 진열

어휘 set up 마련하다 conference call 전화 회의 sign up for ~을
      신청하다 browse 검색하다 display 진열(대)

해설 세부 사항 관련 – 여자가 할 일
여자의 세 번째 대사에서 컬러링 북을 진열창에 둘 것(I'm going to set them up in the store window)이라고 했으므로 정답은 (D)이다.

▸▸ Paraphrasing   대화의 set them up in the store window
                  → 정답의 Create a display

47-49

W-Br	Hi, Joel. It's Sheila. **47I'm looking over the itinerary for the company retreat at Fridley Resort next month, and... how did you calculate the driving time to the resort?**
M-Au	**48I got it from a route-planning Web site that one of the editors recommended.** Why? Is something wrong?
W-Br	**49Well, it says that the bus ride there will only take an hour, but the resort is all the way out past Cashmore.** And since it's near the city, there'll be traffic too.
M-Au	Oh, I see. Thank you for pointing out this problem. I'll try to find a more accurate estimate.

여: 안녕하세요, 조엘. 셰일라예요. 다음 달 프라이들리 리조트에서 있을 회사 야유회 일정표를 검토하는 중이에요. 그런데… 리조트까지 운전하는 시간을 어떻게 계산하셨나요?
남: 편집자 중 한 사람이 추천해 준 경로 계획 웹사이트에서 알아냈어요. 왜요? 뭐가 잘못됐나요?
여: 거기까지 버스로 1시간밖에 안 걸릴 거라고 되어 있는데, 리조트는 캐시모어를 지나 한참 더 가야 해서요. 게다가 도시 근처에 있으니 차도 막히겠죠.
남: 아, 알겠어요. 이 문제를 지적해 줘서 고마워요. 더 정확한 추정치를 얻도록 해 볼게요.

어휘 itinerary 여행 일정표 retreat 야유회 calculate 계산하다
      route 경로 editor 편집자 ride (타고 가는) 길[여정]
      traffic 교통(량) point out 지적하다 accurate 정확한
      estimate 추정(치)

47

What are the speakers mainly discussing?

(A) A vacation policy
(B) A booking procedure
(C) A trip itinerary
(D) A workshop venue

화자들은 주로 무엇에 대해 이야기하고 있는가?
(A) 휴가 정책
(B) 예약 절차
(C) 여행 일정표
(D) 워크숍 장소

어휘 policy 정책 booking 예약 procedure 절차 venue 장소

해설 전체 내용 관련 – 대화의 주제
여자의 첫 번째 대사에서 다음 달 프라이들리 리조트에서 있을 회사 야유회 일정표를 검토하고 있다(I'm looking over the itinerary for the company retreat at Fridley Resort next month)고 한 뒤 리조트까지 운전하는 시간을 어떻게 계산했는지(how did you calculate the driving time to the resort) 묻고 있으므로 정답은 (C)다.

▸▸ Paraphrasing 대화의 the itinerary for the company
retreat → 정답의 A trip itinerary

48

What does the man say he did?

(A) Checked an account balance
(B) Listened to a traffic report
(C) Used a route-planning service
(D) Edited a travel brochure

남자는 무엇을 했다고 말하는가?
(A) 계좌 잔고를 확인했다
(B) 교통 방송을 들었다
(C) 경로 계획 서비스를 이용했다
(D) 여행 소책자를 편집했다

어휘 account 계좌, 계정 balance 잔고 traffic 교통 방송[정보] edit
편집하다

해설 세부 사항 관련 – 남자가 한 일
남자의 첫 번째 대사에서 편집자 중 한 사람이 추천해 준 경로 계획 웹사이트에서 운전 시간을 알아냈다(I got it from a route-planning Web site that one of the editors recommended)고 했으므로 정답은 (C)다.

▸▸ Paraphrasing 대화의 got it from a route-planning Web
site
→ 정답의 Used a route-planning service

49

What does the woman mention about a resort?

(A) It has many rooms.
(B) It received good reviews.
(C) It recently closed.
(D) It is far away.

여자는 리조트에 대해 뭐라고 말하는가?
(A) 객실이 많다.
(B) 좋은 평가를 받았다.
(C) 최근 문을 닫았다.
(D) 멀다.

어휘 review 후기, 평가 far away 멀리 떨어진

해설 세부 사항 관련 – 여자가 리조트에 대해 말하는 것
여자의 두 번째 대사에서 거기까지 버스로 1시간밖에 안 걸릴 거라고 되어 있는데, 리조트는 캐시모어를 지나 한참 더 가야 한다(it says that the bus ride there will only take an hour, but the resort is all the way out past Cashmore)고 말했으므로 정답은 (D)이다.

▸▸ Paraphrasing 대화의 all the way out past Cashmore
→ 정답의 far away

50-52

M-Cn	**50Now, can I interest you in buying this piece of equipment?** It's a sound level testing device. It can be used to make sure that the noise levels in your factory are safe for workers.
W-Am	Hmm… it looks like it would break easily. **51Does it come with a case or covering?**
M-Cn	Yes, it does. You won't need to worry about problems like that.
W-Am	How do I know if the levels are too high?
M-Cn	**52The product information booklet shows how the noise levels will appear on the electronic display.** It's pretty easy to figure out. Would you like to test it out?

남:	이 기기를 구매할 의향은 없으신가요? 소음 측정 기기인데요. 귀하의 공장 소음도가 작업자들에게 안전한지 확인하는 데 쓸 수 있습니다.
여:	음… 쉽게 망가질 것 같네요. 용기나 덮개도 있나요?
남:	네, 그렇습니다. 그런 문제는 걱정하지 않아도 됩니다.
여:	소음이 너무 큰지는 어떻게 알죠?
남:	제품 정보 소책자에 소음도가 전자 화면에 어떻게 나타나는지 나와 있습니다. 확인하기 아주 쉽습니다. 한번 시험해 보시겠어요?

어휘 interest (남)에게 관심을[흥미를] 갖게 하다 equipment 장비,
기기 device 장치 noise level 소음도 come with ~이
딸려 있다 case 용기 covering 덮개 booklet 소책자
appear 나타나다 display 화면 figure out 알아내다
test out 시험해 보다

50

What is the man doing?

(A) Training a technician
(B) Inspecting a factory
(C) Promoting a product
(D) Installing a machine

남자는 무엇을 하고 있는가?
(A) 기술자 교육
(B) 공장 시찰
(C) 제품 홍보
(D) 기계 설치

어휘 technician 기술자 inspect 시찰하다 promote 홍보하다
install 설치하다

해설 전체 내용 관련 - 남자가 하고 있는 일

남자의 첫 번째 대사에서 이 기기를 구매할 의향이 있는지(can I interest you in buying this piece of equipment) 묻고 있으므로 정답은 (C)이다.

▸▸ Paraphrasing   대화의 interest you in buying this piece of equipment → 정답의 Promoting a product

51

What does the woman ask about?

(A) Benefits for employees
(B) The cause of a loud noise
(C) The procedure for requesting a repair
(D) A protective covering for a device

여자는 무엇에 대해 질문하는가?

(A) 직원에게 주는 혜택
(B) 큰 소음의 원인
(C) 수리 요청 절차
(D) 기기 보호 덮개

어휘 benefit 혜택 cause 원인 procedure 절차 protective 보호용의

해설 세부 사항 관련 - 여자의 질문

여자의 첫 번째 대사에서 용기나 덮개도 있냐(Does it come with a case or covering)고 질문했으므로 정답은 (D)이다.

▸▸ Paraphrasing   대화의 a case or covering → 정답의 covering for a device

52

What does the man say is explained in a booklet?

(A) How to understand the information on a screen
(B) How often a test should be performed
(C) How to operate an electric vehicle
(D) How many levels a course has

남자는 소책자에 무엇이 설명되어 있다고 말하는가?

(A) 화면에서 정보 보는 법
(B) 시험해야 하는 주기
(C) 전기 차량 작동법
(D) 교육 강좌의 단계

어휘 perform 수행하다 operate 작동하다 electric 전기의 vehicle 차량

해설 세부 사항 관련 - 소책자에 설명되어 있는 것

남자의 세 번째 대사에서 제품 정보 소책자에 소음도가 전자 화면에 어떻게 나타나는지 나와 있다(The product information booklet shows how the noise levels will appear on the electronic display)고 말했으므로 정답은 (A)이다.

▸▸ Paraphrasing   대화의 show how the noise levels will appear on the electronic display → 정답의 How to understand the information on a screen

53-55 3인 대화

M-Au **53Soo-Hyun, can I pull you away from your experiment for a minute?**

W-Am Sure, Walter. What's up?

M-Au This is Felicia Green, another one of our accomplished scientists. **54I wanted to introduce you two because you both live in Migton Heights.** If you drive to work together, you'll be eligible for preferred parking under our company's new ride-share program.

W-Am Oh, I'm very interested in that. Felicia, it's great to meet you. I think I read your paper in *Biology Quarterly*. **55I need to concentrate on this experiment now, but let's talk later to see if our start and finish times match up.**

W-Br Sounds good. Here's my extension number.

남: 수현 씨, 실험 중이신데 잠시 짬을 내 줄 수 있나요?
여1: 물론이죠, 월터 씨. 무슨 일이죠?
남: 이 분은 뛰어난 우리 연구원 중 한 분인 펠리시아 그린 씨입니다. 두 분 모두 미그턴 하이츠에 사시니 서로 소개시켜 드리고 싶었어요. 함께 차를 타고 출근하시면 회사의 새로운 카풀 프로그램에 따라 우선 주차를 할 자격이 생깁니다.
여1: 오, 아주 솔깃한데요. 펠리시아 씨, 만나서 반갑습니다. 〈계간 생물학〉지에서 논문을 읽은 것 같습니다. 지금은 실험에 집중해야 하니 나중에 출퇴근 시간이 맞는지 얘기해 봐요.
여2: 좋습니다. 여기 제 내선번호예요.

어휘 pull away from ~에서 떼어 놓다 experiment 실험 accomplished 기량이 뛰어난 eligible 적격의, 자격이 있는 preferred 선순위의, 우선의 parking 주차 ride-share 차량 함께 타기, 카풀 paper 논문 concentrate on ~에 집중하다 match up 어울리다, 맞다 extension 내선

53

Who most likely are the women?

(A) Magazine editors
(B) Research scientists
(C) Medical care providers
(D) Academic librarians

여자들은 누구이겠는가?

(A) 잡지 편집자
(B) 연구원
(C) 의료 서비스 종사자
(D) 대학교 사서

어휘 medical care 보건, 의료 provider 제공자 academic 학교[대학]의

해설 전체 내용 관련 - 여자들의 신분

남자의 첫 번째 대사에서 실험 중인데 잠시 짬을 내 줄 수 있나(can I pull you away from your experiment for a minute)고 물어봤으므로 정답은 (B)이다.

▶▶ **Paraphrasing**   대화의 **your experiment**
　　　　　　　　　　→ 정답의 **Research scientists**

54

Why are the women being introduced?

(A) They will appear on television together.
(B) They will travel to a convention together.
(C) They went to the same school.
(D) They live in the same area.

여자들이 서로 소개받은 이유는 무엇인가?

(A) TV에 함께 출연할 예정이다.
(B) 함께 학회에 갈 예정이다.
(C) 같은 학교에 다닌다.
(D) 같은 지역에 살고 있다.

─────────────────────

어휘   appear 출연하다   convention 집회, 대회

해설   세부 사항 관련 – 여자들이 서로 소개받는 이유

남자의 두 번째 대사에서 두 사람 모두 미그턴 하이츠에 사니 서로 소개시켜 주고 싶었다(I wanted to introduce you two because you both live in Migton Heights)고 했으므로 정답은 (D)이다.

▶▶ **Paraphrasing**   대화의 **both live in Migton Heights**
　　　　　　　　　　→ 정답의 **live in the same area**

55

What will the women talk about later?

(A) Their typical work schedules
(B) Their preferred contact methods
(C) The topics they are interested in
(D) The places they want to visit

여자들은 나중에 무엇에 대해 이야기할 것인가?

(A) 일상 업무 스케줄
(B) 선호하는 연락 방식
(C) 관심 있는 주제
(D) 방문하고 싶은 장소

─────────────────────

어휘   typical 보통의, 일반적인   method 방법

해설   세부 사항 관련 – 여자들이 나중에 할 대화

첫 번째 여자의 두 번째 대사에서 나중에 출퇴근 시간이 맞는지 얘기해 보자(let's talk later to see if our start and finish times match up)고 말했으므로 정답은 (A)이다.

▶▶ **Paraphrasing**   대화의 **our start and finish times**
　　　　　　　　　　→ 정답의 **typical work schedules**

56-58

M-Cn   **56Nicole, you're the one in charge of sewing the main character's party costume, right?**

W-Br   **56Yes, that's me.** It's almost finished.

M-Cn   **57Will you need much more time? We need to begin filming the scene tomorrow morning.**

W-Br   It'll be fine. The basic version of the suit is ready, and my assistant is picking up the rare gold-colored fabric for the trim right now.

M-Cn   **58Oh, in that case, we can do a fitting with the actor, right? I'll tell Blake to come in and try it on.**

W-Br   That's a good idea. Thanks.

─────────────────────

남: 니콜, 당신이 주인공 파티 의상을 재봉하는 일을 맡고 있죠?
여: 네, 저예요. 거의 완성했어요.
남: 시간이 많이 필요할까요? 우린 내일 아침에 그 장면 촬영에 들어가야 해요.
여: 괜찮을 거예요. 정장의 기본 형태는 준비됐고 제 조수가 구하기 어려운 테두리 장식용 금색 원단을 지금 가져올 거거든요.
남: 아, 그렇다면 배우와 함께 가봉해 볼 수 있는 거죠? 블레이크에게 와서 입어 보라고 전할게요.
여: 좋은 생각이네요. 고마워요.

─────────────────────

어휘   in charge of ~을 맡은[담당한]   sew 바느질하다   main character 주인공   costume 의상   film 촬영하다   version 형태   assistant 조수   rare 드문, 희귀한   fabric 천, 원단   trim 가장자리 장식   fitting 가봉

56

What is the woman responsible for?

(A) Making a costume
(B) Choosing some lighting
(C) Decorating a ballroom
(D) Rewriting some scripts

여자는 어떤 일을 담당하고 있는가?

(A) 의상 제작
(B) 조명 선정
(C) 무도회장 장식
(D) 대본 수정

─────────────────────

어휘   lighting 조명   decorate 장식하다   rewrite 고쳐 쓰다   script 대본

해설   세부 사항 관련 – 여자가 담당하는 일

남자의 첫 번째 대사에서 여자에게 주인공 파티 의상을 재봉하는 일을 맡고 있는지(you're the one in charge of sewing the main character's party costume, right) 물었고 여자가 그렇다(Yes, that's me)고 대답했으므로 정답은 (A)이다.

▶▶ **Paraphrasing**   대화의 **in charge of**
　　　　　　　　　　→ 질문의 **be responsible for**
　　　　　　　　　　대화의 **sewing the main character's party costume** → 정답의 **Making a costume**

57

Why does the man say, "We need to begin filming the scene tomorrow morning"?

(A) To indicate that filming may take a long time
(B) To explain why he cannot provide help
(C) To remind the woman to arrive early
(D) To urge the woman to work quickly

남자가 "우리 내일 아침에 그 장면 촬영에 들어가야 해요"라고 말하는 이유는 무엇인가?

(A) 촬영 시간이 오래 걸린다는 것을 알리기 위해
(B) 도움을 줄 수 없는 이유를 설명하기 위해
(C) 여자에게 일찍 도착하라고 상기시키기 위해
(D) 여자에게 빨리 일하라고 재촉하기 위해

어휘 indicate 나타내다 filming 촬영 remind 상기시키다 urge 재촉하다

해설 의도 파악 – 내일 아침 촬영에 들어가야 한다는 말의 의도
인용문 앞 남자의 두 번째 대사에서 시간이 많이 필요한지(Will you need much more time) 물었으므로 여자에게 일을 재촉하기 위해 한 말임을 알 수 있다. 따라서 정답은 (D)이다.

58

What does the man decide to do?

(A) Speak with an actor
(B) Try out a camera filter
(C) Lend the woman his car
(D) Pack up an outfit

남자는 무엇을 하기로 결정하는가?

(A) 배우와 이야기하기
(B) 카메라 필터 시험해 보기
(C) 여자에게 자기 차를 빌려 주기
(D) 옷 싸기

어휘 try out 시험해 보다 pack up (짐을) 싸다 outfit 옷, 복장

해설 세부 사항 관련 – 남자가 하기로 결정한 일
남자의 세 번째 대사에서 배우와 함께 가봉해 볼 수 있는지(we can do a fitting with the actor, right) 물은 뒤 블레이크에게 와서 입어 보라고 전하겠다(I'll tell Blake to come in and try it on)고 했으므로 정답은 (A)이다.

▸▸ Paraphrasing 대화의 **tell Blake to come in**
→ 정답의 **Speak with an actor**

59-61

W-Am **59Daisuke, I saw our new self check-in machines being tested when I flew into Hendren Airport yesterday.** That's exciting.

M-Au Yes, the process is well under way. And so far, it seems that passengers like them. **60They appreciate that the kiosks will cut down on the time spent waiting in line for staffed check-in stations.** I think they'll be a big success.

W-Am Glad to hear it. **61Do you think they'll be installed in Terminal C before it begins operation?**

M-Au I'm not sure. **61We'd have to hurry to meet the February deadline.**

여: 다이스케 씨, 제가 어제 헨드렌 공항에 입국했을 때 자사 최신 셀프 체크인 기계가 테스트되고 있는 걸 봤어요. 흥미로웠어요.

남: 네, 절차가 순조롭게 진행되고 있어요. 그리고 지금까지는 승객들이 그 기계를 마음에 들어 하는 것 같아요. 승객들은 키오스크가 직원이 있는 체크인 구역에서 줄을 서서 기다리는 시간을 줄여 줄 것이라고 평가하고 있어요. 전 그 기계들이 큰 성공을 거두리라 생각합니다.

여: 잘됐네요. 터미널 C에도 운영을 개시하기 전에 설치될까요?

남: 잘 모르겠네요. 2월 기한을 맞추려면 서둘러야 할 겁니다.

어휘 check-in 탑승 수속 fly into 비행기를 타고 ~에 오다 be well under way 잘 진행되다 appreciate 평가하다 kiosk 무인 기계, 키오스크 cut down on ~을 줄이다 wait in line 줄을 서서 기다리다 staff 직원을 제공하다 install 설치하다 operation 영업, 운영 meet the deadline 마감에 맞추다

59

What is the topic of the conversation?

(A) Aircraft layouts
(B) Ticketing machines
(C) A baggage requirement
(D) A mileage program

대화의 주제는 무엇인가?

(A) 항공기 배치
(B) 탑승권 발급 기계
(C) 수화물 요건
(D) 마일리지 프로그램

어휘 layout 배치 baggage 짐, 수화물 requirement 요건

해설 전체 내용 관련 – 대화의 주제
여자의 첫 번째 대사에서 어제 헨드렌 공항에 입국했을 때 자사 최신 셀프 체크인 기계가 테스트되고 있는 걸 봤다(I saw our new self check-in machines being tested when I flew into Hendren Airport yesterday)고 했으므로 정답은 (B)이다.

▸▸ Paraphrasing 대화의 **self check-in machines**
→ 정답의 **Ticketing machines**

60

What does the man say is the benefit of a change?

(A) Reduced wait times for passengers
(B) Fairer distribution of staff workloads
(C) Better communication between staff
(D) More types of savings for passengers

남자는 변화의 이점이 무엇이라고 말하는가?

(A) 승객들의 대기 시간 축소
(B) 직원 업무량의 더 공평한 분배
(C) 직원 간 원활한 소통
(D) 승객들을 위한 절약 유형

어휘 reduce 줄이다 fair 공평한 distribution 분배 workload 업무량 saving 절약

해설 세부 사항 관련 – 변화의 이점

남자의 첫 번째 대사에서 승객들은 키오스크가 직원이 있는 체크인 구역에서 줄을 서서 기다리는 시간을 줄여 줄 것이라고 평가하고 있다(They appreciate that the kiosks will cut down on the time spent waiting in line for staffed check-in stations)고 했으므로 정답은 (A)이다.

▶ Paraphrasing 대화의 cut down on the time spent waiting in line
→ 정답의 Reduced wait times

61

What will most likely happen in February?

(A) A mobile app will be released.
(B) A decision will be announced.
(C) A law will go into effect.
(D) A new terminal will open.

2월에는 무슨 일이 있겠는가?

(A) 모바일 앱이 공개될 것이다.
(B) 결정 사항이 발표될 것이다.
(C) 법이 효력을 발휘할 것이다.
(D) 새로운 터미널이 개장할 것이다.

어휘 release 공개하다 announce 발표하다 go into effect 시행되다

해설 세부 사항 관련 – 2월에 벌어질 일

여자의 두 번째 대사에서 터미널 C에도 운영을 개시하기 전에 설치될 거라 생각하냐(Do you think they'll be installed in Terminal C before it begins operation)고 물어보자 2월 기한을 맞추려면 서둘러야 할 거라고 (We'd have to hurry to meet the February deadline) 말했으므로 정답은 (D)이다.

▶ Paraphrasing 대화의 before it begins operation
→ 정답의 A new terminal will open

62-64 대화 + 좌석표

W-Br Hello, Howie. I'm excited to see this play. Everyone is recommending it. **62Oh, before I forget—how much do I owe you for my ticket?**

M-Cn I think it's printed on the tickets... Yes, here it is. It's a little expensive, right? But we should have a great view. **63Our seats are right in the center of the balcony section.**

W-Br Well, then I'm sure it will be worth it. Let's head inside. Wow, they've decorated the whole lobby.

M-Cn Yeah. There are even life-sized figures of the cast over by the snack bar.

W-Br **64Why don't we take each other's picture with them?** Those would make great souvenirs.

M-Cn OK! Let's go.

여: 안녕하세요, 하위 씨. 이 연극을 보게 되어 설렙니다. 모두가 추천하더군요. 아, 잊어버리기 전에 여쭤볼게요. 제 입장권은 얼마인가요?

남: 입장권에 나와 있을 것 같은데요. 네, 여기 있군요. 좀 비싸네요, 그렇죠? 하지만 아주 잘 보이는 곳일 겁니다. 발코니 구역 정중앙에 있는 자리거든요.

여: 음, 그렇다면 분명 값어치를 할 겁니다. 안으로 들어가죠. 와, 로비 전체를 장식했군요.

남: 네. 매점 옆에는 실물 크기의 출연진 등신상도 있어요.

여: 출연진 등신상 옆에서 서로 사진을 찍어 주면 어때요? 멋진 기념품이 될 거예요.

남: 네, 그렇게 합시다.

어휘 play 연극 owe 빚지다 print 인쇄하다 view 조망 worth it 그만한 가치가 있는 head 향하다 decorate 장식하다 life-sized 실물 크기의 figure 조상 cast 출연진 snack bar 매점 souvenir 기념품

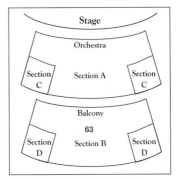

62

What does the woman want to know?

(A) The price of a ticket
(B) The size of a theater
(C) The length of a performance
(D) The popularity of a play

여자는 무엇을 알고 싶어하는가?

(A) 입장권 가격
(B) 극장 크기
(C) 상연 시간
(D) 연극의 인기도

어휘 length (소요) 시간 performance 공연

해설 세부 사항 관련 – 여자가 알고 싶어 하는 것

여자의 첫 번째 대사에서 입장권이 얼마인지(how much do I owe you for my ticket) 묻고 있으므로 정답은 (A)이다.

63

Look at the graphic. Which area will the speakers most likely sit in?

(A) Section A
(B) Section B
(C) Section C
(D) Section D

시각 정보에 의하면, 화자들은 어떤 구역에 앉겠는가?
(A) A 구역
(B) B 구역
(C) C 구역
(D) D 구역

해설 시각 정보 연계 – 화자들이 앉을 구역

남자의 첫 번째 대사에서 좌석이 발코니 구역 정중앙(Our seats are right in the center of the balcony section)이라고 했고, 시각 정보에 따르면 발코니 정중앙에 있는 자리는 Section B이므로 정답은 (B)이다.

64

What does the woman suggest doing?

(A) Checking a seating chart
(B) Visiting a souvenir shop
(C) Taking some pictures
(D) Buying some snacks

여자는 무엇을 하자고 제안하는가?
(A) 좌석표 확인
(B) 기념품 가게 방문
(C) 사진 촬영
(D) 간식 구입

해설 세부 사항 관련 – 여자의 제안

여자의 세 번째 대사에서 출연진 등신상 옆에서 서로 사진을 찍어 주면 어떠냐 (Why don't we take each other's picture with them)고 제안하고 있으므로 정답은 (C)이다.

65-67 대화 + 송장

M-Au Hahm's Home Market, this is Alvin. How can I help you?

W-Br Hi. There's a problem with the shipment I just got from your store. My order number was 36433. **65Two of the drinking glasses in the package have large cracks in them.** I think they weren't wrapped well enough.

M-Au I'm sorry. We'll replace them immediately. **66OK, I'm checking, and... oh, that brand of tableware has gone out of production.** And we don't have any more in stock.

W-Br That's disappointing. I'd like to return the other glasses, then.

M-Au Actually, you're welcome to keep them. **67And of course, I'll issue you a refund for their full price.**

W-Br All right. Thank you very much.

남: 함스 홈마켓의 앨빈입니다. 어떻게 도와드릴까요?

여: 안녕하세요. 매장에서 구입해 배송시킨 물품에 문제가 생겼어요. 제 주문번호는 36433입니다. **포장된 물컵 중 두 개에 크게 금이 갔어요.** 포장이 제대로 안 됐나 봐요.

남: 죄송합니다. 바로 바꿔 드리겠습니다. **네, 확인 중입니다... 아, 이 식기 브랜드는 생산이 중단됐군요.** 재고가 더 이상 없습니다.

여: 안타깝네요. 그럼 다른 컵들도 반품하고 싶어요.

남: 실은 그냥 가지셔도 됩니다. **물론 전액 환불해 드리겠습니다.**

여: 알겠습니다. 정말 감사합니다.

어휘 shipment 배송품 crack 금 wrap 포장하다 replace 교체하다 immediately 즉시 tableware 식기류 go out of production 생산이 중단되다 in stock 재고로 welcome to ~을 자유로이 할 수 있는 issue a refund 환불해 주다

Invoice		
		Order no. 36433
Item	**Quantity**	**Total price**
67Drinking glass	4	$24
Scented candle	8	$32
Toaster	1	$45
Small chair	2	$56

청구서		
		주문번호 36433
물품	**수량**	**총액**
물컵	4	24달러
향초	8	32달러
토스터	1	45달러
소형 의자	2	56달러

65

What is the problem with the woman's shipment?

(A) It was delayed in transit.
(B) It was not gift-wrapped.
(C) It contains damaged goods.
(D) It is missing a tracking number.

여자의 배송품에 어떤 문제가 있는가?
(A) 운송이 지연됐다.
(B) 선물 포장이 되어 있지 않다.
(C) 손상된 물품이 포함되어 있다.
(D) 추적 번호가 없다.

어휘 in transit 운송 중인 gift-wrap 선물용으로 포장하다 contain ~이 들어 있다 damaged 손상된 goods 상품 miss 빠뜨리다 tracking number 추적 번호

Test 8

해설 세부 사항 관련 – 여자의 배송에 대한 문제

여자의 첫 번째 대사에서 포장된 물컵 중 두 개에 크게 금이 갔다(Two of the drinking glasses in the package have large cracks in them)고 말했으므로 정답은 (C)이다.

▶▶ Paraphrasing 대화의 **have large cracks**
→ 정답의 **damaged goods**

66

What does the man say about some tableware?

(A) It is no longer manufactured.
(B) It has beautiful products.
(C) It is inexpensive.
(D) It is imported from overseas.

남자는 식기류에 대해 뭐라고 하는가?

(A) 더 이상 제조하지 않는다.
(B) 훌륭한 상품이다.
(C) 저렴하다.
(D) 해외에서 수입한다.

어휘 manufacture 제조[생산]하다 import from ~로부터 수입하다

해설 세부 사항 관련 – 남자가 식기류에 대해 말하는 것

남자의 두 번째 대사에서 이 식기 브랜드는 생산이 중단됐다(that brand of tableware has gone out of production)고 말했으므로 정답은 (A)이다.

▶▶ Paraphrasing 대화의 **gone out of production**
→ 정답의 **no longer manufactured**

67

Look at the graphic. What refund amount will the woman most likely receive?

(A) $24
(B) $32
(C) $45
(D) $56

시각 정보에 의하면, 여자는 얼마를 환불받겠는가?

(A) 24달러
(B) 32달러
(C) 45달러
(D) 56달러

해설 시각 정보 연계 – 여자가 환불받을 금액

남자의 세 번째 대사에서 전액 환불해 준다(I'll issue you a refund for their full price)고 했고, 시각 정보에 따르면 물컵 가격은 24달러이므로 정답은 (A)이다.

68-70 대화 + 평면도

W-Am Welcome to Bachman Language Academy. How can I help you?

M-Au Hi, my name is Spencer Rutlege. **68I'm scheduled to interview for the English instructor position at two.**

W-Am Let me see... ah, here you are. **69Uh, we'll have you give a teaching demonstration first, so you can start setting up in the small classroom behind my desk.** I'll just tell the staff director you're here.

M-Au Thank you. **70Oh, sorry—could you write down the password for your wireless Internet service for me?** I'd like to put my laptop on a desk and stream a video during my demonstration.

여: 바흐만 어학원에 오신 것을 환영합니다. 어떻게 도와드릴까요?
남: 안녕하세요. 제 이름은 스펜서 루틀리지입니다. 두 시에 영어 강사 면접이 잡혀 있습니다.
여: 확인해 볼게요... 아, 여기 있군요. 어, 우선 강의 시연을 하셔야 하니 제 책상 뒤에 있는 작은 교실에서 준비하시죠. 인사부장에게 여기 계시다고 얘기할게요.
남: 감사합니다. 아, 죄송하지만 무선 인터넷 서비스 비밀번호를 적어 주시겠어요? 노트북 컴퓨터를 책상 위에 놓고 시연 중에 동영상을 바로 재생하고 싶어서요.

어휘 be scheduled to ~할 예정이다 position (일)자리
instructor 강사 demonstration 시연 set up 마련하다
wireless 무선의 stream (동영상 등을) 인터넷에서 다운로드와 동시에 재생하다

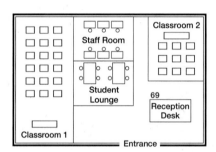

68

What is the purpose of the man's visit?

(A) To find a lost item
(B) To register for a course
(C) To attend a job interview
(D) To repair a piece of equipment

남자의 학원 방문 목적은 무엇인가?

(A) 잃어버린 물품을 찾으러
(B) 과정에 등록하러
(C) **구직 면접에 참석하러**
(D) 장비를 수리하러

어휘 register for ~에 등록하다 attend 참석하다 repair 수리하다
equipment 장비

해설 세부 사항 관련 – 남자가 학원을 방문한 목적
남자의 첫 번째 대사에서 두 시에 영어 강사 면접이 잡혀 있다(I'm scheduled to interview for the English instructor position at two)고 말했으므로 정답은 (C)이다.

▸▸ Paraphrasing 대화의 interview for the English instructor position → 정답의 a job interview

69

Look at the graphic. Which room does the woman direct the man to?

(A) Classroom 1
(B) Classroom 2
(C) The Student Lounge
(D) The Staff Room

시각 정보에 의하면 여자는 남자를 어느 방으로 안내하는가?

(A) 교실 1
(B) **교실 2**
(C) 학생 휴게실
(D) 직원 사무실

해설 시각 정보 연계 – 여자가 남자를 안내할 교실
여자의 두 번째 대사에서 우선 강의 시연을 해야 하니 책상 뒤에 있는 작은 교실에서 준비하라(we'll have you give a teaching demonstration first, so you can start setting up in the small classroom behind my desk)고 했고 시각 자료에 따르면 책상 뒤에 있는 작은 교실은 교실 2이므로 정답은 (B)이다.

70

What does the man ask for?

(A) A business card
(B) A writing tool
(C) A connecting cable
(D) A network password

남자는 무엇을 요청하는가?

(A) 명함
(B) 필기 도구
(C) 연결 케이블
(D) **네트워크 비밀번호**

어휘 tool 도구 connecting 연결하는 cable 전선, 케이블

해설 세부 사항 관련 – 남자의 요청 사항
남자의 마지막 대사에서 무선 인터넷 서비스 비밀번호를 적어 달라(could you write down the password for your wireless Internet service for me)고 부탁하므로 정답은 (D)이다.

▸▸ Paraphrasing 대화의 **the password for your wireless Internet service**
→ 정답의 **A network password**

PART 4

71-73 공지

W-Br Attention, all Healthy Organics Plus shoppers. **71As the region's oldest natural food grocery shop, we are proud to bring you the freshest locally-sourced products available. 72And we encourage customers to take advantage of our latest offering—hands-on cooking classes, held every month here at this store.** You'll discover great recipes and learn how to make delicious new dishes. Not sure if they're for you? **73Right now we're giving away free samples of the amazing healthy drinks that our instructors can teach you how to make.** Come to the front of the store and try some!

헬시 오거닉스 플러스 쇼핑객 여러분께 알려드립니다. 이 지역에서 가장 오래된 유기농 식품점으로서, 저희는 여러분께 가장 신선한 현지 재료로 만든 상품을 제공하는 데 자부심을 느낍니다. 또한 최근 들어 제공해 드리고 있는 요리 실습 강좌를 이곳 매장에서 매달 진행하고 있으니 이용해 주시기 바랍니다. 여러분은 훌륭한 요리법을 발견하고 맛있는 새 요리를 만드는 법을 배우시게 됩니다. 여러분께 필요한 강좌인지 잘 모르시겠다고요? 지금 무료 시음 행사를 통해 저희 강사들이 제조법을 알려 드릴 탁월한 건강 음료를 나눠 드리고 있습니다. 매장 앞으로 오셔서 시음해 보세요!

어휘 region 지역 locally-sourced 현지에서 생산된
encourage 권장하다 take advantage of ~를 이용하다
offering 제공하는 것 hands-on 직접 해 보는 recipe 요리법
dish 요리 give away 나누어 주다 instructor 강사

71

What does the store mainly sell?

(A) Children's toys
(B) Groceries
(C) Clothing
(D) Gardening supplies

매장에서 주로 파는 것은 무엇인가?

(A) 어린이 장난감
(B) **식료품**
(C) 의류
(D) 원예용품

지문의 초반부에서 이 지역에서 가장 오래된 유기농 식품점으로서(As the region's oldest natural food grocery shop), 가장 신선한 현지 재료로 만든 상품을 제공하는 데 자부심을 느낀다(we are proud to bring you the freshest locally-sourced products available)고 말했으므로 정답은 (B)이다.

72

According to the announcement, what is new at the store?

(A) Monthly classes
(B) Spaces for relaxation
(C) Discounts on large purchases
(D) Home delivery options

공지에 따르면 매장에서 새로운 것은 무엇인가?
(A) 매달 있는 수업
(B) 휴식 공간
(C) 대량 구입 시 할인
(D) 가정 배송 옵션

어휘 relaxation 휴식 discount on ~에 대한 할인

해설 세부 사항 관련 - 매장에서 새로운 것

지문의 초반부에서 최근 들어 제공하고 있는 요리 실습 강좌를 매달 매장에서 진행하고 있으니 이용해 달라(And we encourage customers to take advantage of our latest offering—hands-on cooking classes, held every month here at this store)고 했으므로 정답은 (A)이다.

▸▸ Paraphrasing   지문의 classes, held every month
→ 정답의 Monthly classes

73

What can customers do at the front of the store?

(A) Obtain a coupon
(B) Have refreshments
(C) See new merchandise
(D) Buy a gift certificate

고객들은 매장 앞에서 무엇을 할 수 있는가?
(A) 쿠폰 얻기
(B) 다과 먹기
(C) 신상품 보기
(D) 상품권 사기

어휘 obtain 얻다 refreshment 다과 merchandise 상품 gift certificate 상품권

해설 세부 사항 관련 - 매장 앞에서 고객들이 할 수 있는 것

지문의 후반부에서 지금 무료 시음 행사를 통해 강사들이 제조법을 알려 줄 탁월한 건강 음료를 나눠 준다(Right now we're giving away free samples of the amazing healthy drinks that our instructors can teach you how to make)고 말한 뒤 매장 앞으로 와서 마셔 보라(Come to the front of the store and try some)고 했으므로 정답은 (B)이다.

▸▸ Paraphrasing   지문의 the amazing healthy drinks
→ 정답의 refreshments

74-76 전화 메시지

> M-Cn Hi, Ming-Zhu. It's Gabe from the advertising association. [74]I'm calling about the panel discussion on digital advertising that you're hosting at our upcoming conference. [75]Uh, Nell Reed called this morning to say that she might not be able to take the time off to participate in the panel after all. Since that kind of change would affect your preparations, I wanted to make you aware of it. I'll call you again when we know for sure one way or the other. [76]Oh, and speaking of preparations, I'm almost finished with the set of suggested questions for your panel. It should give you some ideas about topics to cover.

안녕하세요, 밍즈 씨. 광고협회의 게이브입니다. 다가오는 학회에서 진행하실 디지털 광고 패널 토의에 관해 전화 드립니다. 어, 넬 리드가 오늘 아침 전화해서 결국 패널에 참석할 시간이 없을지도 모른다고 말했습니다. 이 변동 사항이 당신이 준비하는 데 영향을 미칠 수 있어서 알려 드리고 싶었습니다. 확실해지면 어떻게든 다시 전화 드리겠습니다. 오, 준비 얘기가 나와서 말인데 패널용 제안 질문은 거의 끝냈습니다. 그걸 보면 다룰 주제에 대한 감을 잡으실 수 있을 것입니다.

어휘 advertising 광고 association 협회 panel 패널(토론단) host 주최하다 upcoming 다가오는 conference 회의, 학회 take time off 시간을 내다 participate in ~에 참여하다 after all 결국 affect 영향을 미치다 preparation 준비 aware of ~을 아는 for sure 확실히 one way or the other 어떻게든 speaking of ~의 이야기라면 cover 다루다

74

What will the listener do for a conference?

(A) Write a news article
(B) Design an advertisement
(C) Provide housing for a visitor
(D) Lead a discussion

청자는 회의를 위해 무엇을 할 것인가?
(A) 뉴스 기사 쓰기
(B) 광고 디자인하기
(C) 방문객에게 숙소 제공하기
(D) 토의 진행하기

어휘 article 기사 housing 주거, 숙소

해설 세부 사항 관련 - 청자가 회의에서 할 일

지문의 초반부에서 다가오는 학회에서 진행할 디지털 광고 패널 토의에 관해 전화한다(I'm calling about the panel discussion on digital advertising that you're hosting at our upcoming conference)고 했으므로 정답은 (D)이다.

▸▸ Paraphrasing   지문의 hosting → 정답의 Lead

75

What does the speaker say Ms. Reed might do?

(A) Cancel an appearance
(B) Bring a colleague
(C) Take a later flight
(D) Call the listener

화자는 리드 씨가 무엇을 할 수도 있다고 말하는가?

(A) 출석 취소
(B) 동료 데려오기
(C) 더 늦은 비행기 타기
(D) 청자에게 전화하기

어휘 cancel 취소하다 appearance 출석, 출연

해설 세부 사항 관련 – 리드 씨가 할 수도 있는 일
지문의 초반부에서 넬 리드가 오늘 아침 전화해서 결국 패널에 참석할 시간이 없을지도 모른다(Nell Reed called this morning to say that she might not be able to take the time off to participate in the panel after all)고 했으므로 정답은 (A)이다.

▸▸ Paraphrasing 지문의 might not be able to take the time off to participate
→ 정답의 Cancel an appearance

76

What is the speaker preparing?

(A) A conference program
(B) A profile of a participant
(C) A set of questions
(D) An expense estimate

화자는 무엇을 준비하고 있는가?

(A) 회의 프로그램
(B) 참석자 소개
(C) 질문
(D) 비용 견적

어휘 profile 인물 소개 participant 참석자 expense 비용 estimate 견적

해설 세부 사항 관련 – 화자가 준비하고 있는 것
지문의 후반부에서 준비 얘기가 나와서 말인데 패널용 제안 질문은 거의 끝냈다(speaking of preparations, I'm almost finished with the set of suggested questions for your panel)고 했으므로 정답은 (C)이다.

77-79 회의 발췌

W-Am Finally, I'd like to remind you all that we'll have an important visitor on Friday. **⁷⁷Lou Bonnet, a high-ranking official in the French embassy, is coming to discuss the benefits of a possible trade agreement in our industry.** Now, we'll want to make a good impression on Mr. Bonnet and his associates. **⁷⁸Please take a few minutes on Friday morning to straighten up your desk and** **the space around it.** Just make sure everything looks neat when they come in at eleven. **⁷⁹I know this request is a little annoying when you're all so busy, but I'd really appreciate your cooperation.** And I won't forget it. Thanks.

마지막으로, 저는 여러분 모두에게 금요일에 중요한 손님이 오신다는 점을 다시 알려드리고 싶습니다. 프랑스 대사관의 고위 관리인 루 보네 씨가 우리 업계에서 가능한 무역 협정의 혜택에 대해 논의하러 오십니다. 자, 우리는 보네 씨와 그 동료들에게 좋은 인상을 남기고 싶습니다. 금요일 오전에 잠시 시간을 내서 책상과 주위 공간을 정리해 주십시오. 그분들이 11시에 오실 때 모든 것이 깔끔해 보이게만 해 주십시오. 여러분 모두 바쁘실 때라 좀 귀찮은 요청이라는 것을 알지만 협조해 주시면 정말 감사하겠습니다. 그리고 잊지 않겠습니다. 감사합니다.

어휘 remind 상기시키다 high-ranking 고위의 official 관리 embassy 대사관 benefit 혜택, 이점 trade 무역 agreement 계약, 협정 industry 산업, 업계 associate 동료 straighten up ~을 정돈하다 neat 깔끔한 request 요청 annoying 귀찮은, 성가신 appreciate 감사하다 cooperation 협조, 협력

77

Who will visit the speaker's workplace?

(A) An athlete
(B) A diplomat
(C) A musician
(D) A journalist

화자의 직장을 누가 방문할 것인가?

(A) 운동선수
(B) 외교관
(C) 음악가
(D) 기자

해설 세부 사항 관련 – 화자의 직장을 방문할 사람
지문 초반부에서 프랑스 대사관의 고위 관리인 루 보네 씨가 우리 업계에서 가능한 무역 협정의 혜택에 대해 논의하러 온다(Lou Bonnet, a high-ranking official in the French embassy, is coming to discuss the benefits of a possible trade agreement in our industry)고 했으므로 정답은 (B)이다.

▸▸ Paraphrasing 지문의 a high-ranking official in the French embassy → 정답의 A diplomat

78

What are listeners asked to do?

(A) Plan a lunch
(B) Read a notice
(C) Tidy a work area
(D) Put up decorations

청자들은 무엇을 하라고 요청받는가?

(A) 점심 식사 계획하기
(B) 공지 읽기
(C) 업무 공간 정리하기
(D) 장식물 걸기

해설 세부 사항 관련 – 청자에 대한 요청 사항

지문 중반부에서 금요일 오전에 잠시 시간을 내서 책상과 주위 공간을 정리해 달라(Please take a few minutes on Friday morning to straighten up your desk and the space around it)고 했으므로 정답은 (C)이다.

▸▸ Paraphrasing   지문의 **straighten up your desk and the space** → 정답의 **Tidy a work area**

다. 해당 대출 상품의 약관은 찾으시는 대출과 매우 유사합니다. 대출 신청서에 제공해 주신 주소로 이메일을 보냈습니다. **관심이 있으시다면 살펴봐 주십시오.** 감사합니다.

어휘 apply 신청[지원]하다 finance 자금을 대다 contracting business 도급업 loan 대출 (상품) qualify for ~의 자격을 얻다 financial institution 금융 기관 aware of ~을 아는 in case ~할 경우 terms (합의, 계약 등의) 조건, 약관 seek 찾다 application 지원[신청](서) look over 살펴보다

79

What does the speaker imply when she says, "I won't forget it"?

(A) The listeners will be rewarded for some work.
(B) The listeners do not need to handle a task.
(C) She was impressed by a previous event.
(D) She has memorized some information.

화자가 "잊지 않겠습니다"라고 말한 의도는 무엇인가?

(A) 청자들은 작업에 대해 보상을 받을 것이다.
(B) 청자들은 업무를 처리할 필요가 없다.
(C) 과거 행사에 감명받았다.
(D) 어떤 정보를 외웠다.

어휘 be rewarded for ~에 대한 보상을 받다 handle 처리하다 previous 이전의 memorize 외우다

해설 화자의 의도 파악 – 잊지 않겠다는 말의 의미

인용문 앞에서 모두 바쁠 때라 좀 귀찮은 요청이라는 것을 알지만 협조해 주면 정말 고맙겠다(I know this request is a little annoying when you're all so busy, but I'd really appreciate your cooperation)고 한 뒤 잊지 않겠다고 했다. 즉 잊지 않고 보답하겠다는 의미임을 알 수 있으므로 정답은 (A)이다.

80

Where most likely does the speaker work?

(A) At a bank
(B) At a real estate agency
(C) At a utility company
(D) At a law office

화자는 어디서 일하겠는가?

(A) 은행
(B) 부동산 중개 업체
(C) 공익 기업
(D) 법률 사무소

어휘 real estate 부동산 utility (가스·수도 등) 공익 사업

해설 전체 내용 관련 – 화자들이 일하는 곳

지문 초반부에서 몇 달 전 귀하가 도급업 자금 조달을 신청하셨을 때 뵀다(We met when you applied here for financing for your contracting business a few months ago)고 했으므로 정답은 (A)이다.

▸▸ Paraphrasing   지문의 **financing for your contracting business** → 정답의 **a bank**

80-82 전화 메시지

M-Au Ms. Hixon, this is Brian Laird from McGlanton. **80We met when you applied here for financing for your contracting business a few months ago.** While we weren't able to help you then, we have a new type of small business loan that you may qualify for. **81Now, I realize that you might have already received the money you needed from another financial institution, but I wanted to make you aware of this option in case you haven't.** The terms of this loan would be quite similar to what you are seeking. I sent an e-mail to the address you provided on your loan application. **82Please look over it to see if you would be interested.** Thanks.

힉슨 씨, 저는 맥글랜턴의 브라이언 레어드입니다. **몇 달 전 도급업 자금 조달을 신청하셨을 때 뵀습니다.** 그때는 도와드릴 수 없었지만 자격이 되실 만한 소기업 대상 대출 상품이 새로 나왔습니다. **필요한 금액을 다른 금융기관에서 이미 대출 받으셨으리라 생각하지만 그렇지 않은 경우 이 선택 사항도 알고 계셨으면 합니**

81

What potential problem does the speaker mention?

(A) The listener may not need a service.
(B) The listener may be charged extra.
(C) A contract may not be renewed.
(D) A government regulation may change.

화자가 언급한 잠재적인 문제점은 무엇인가?

(A) 청자에게 대출 서비스가 필요하지 않을 수 있다.
(B) 청자에게 추가 요금을 청구할 수 있다.
(C) 계약이 갱신되지 않을 수 있다.
(D) 정부 규제가 변경될 수 있다.

어휘 charge 요금을 부과하다 extra 추가분 renew 갱신하다 regulation 규제

해설 세부 사항 관련 – 화자가 언급한 잠재적 문제점

지문 중반부에서 필요한 금액을 다른 금융 기관에서 이미 대출 받았으리라 생각하지만(I realize that you might have already received the money you needed from another financial institution) 그렇지 않은 경우 이 선택 사항도 알고 있었으면 한다(I wanted to make you aware of this option in case you haven't)고 말했으므로 정답은 (A)이다.

▸▸ Paraphrasing   지문의 **you might have already received the money** → 정답의 **may not need a service**

82

What is the listener asked to do?

(A) Withdraw an application
(B) Confirm an account number
(C) Read an e-mail message
(D) Find a postal address

청자는 무엇을 하라고 요청받았는가?

(A) 신청 철회하기
(B) 계좌번호 확인하기
(C) **이메일 메시지 확인하기**
(D) 우편주소 확인하기

어휘 withdraw 철회하다 confirm 확인해 주다 postal 우편의

해설 세부 사항 관련 – 청자가 하도록 요청받은 일

지문 후반부에서 대출 신청서에 제공한 주소로 이메일을 보냈다(I sent an e-mail to the address you provided on your loan application)고 했고 관심이 있다면 살펴봐 달라(Please look over it to see if you would be interested)고 말했으므로 정답은 (C)이다.

▸▸ Paraphrasing   지문의 **look over it**
→ 정답의 **Read an e-mail message**

83-85 방송

> **W-Br** Hello, food fans. This is *Kathy's Kitchen Live*. **83Before we get started today, I want to emphasize that, all month, viewers who comment on our Web site have the chance to win special prizes.** What are you waiting for? **84Today we're going to talk about Huber Foods's new pre-packaged pasta meals.** They're a tasty option for days when you don't want to spend hours staring at a recipe. And I'm really excited to say that Isaiah Huber himself is about to join me. He founded Huber Foods last year after winning a cooking contest on this very network. **85He's going to tell us all about how these delicious meals are made.** Welcome, Mr. Huber!

안녕하세요, 음식 애호가 여러분. 〈캐시의 키친 라이브〉입니다. **오늘 시작하기 전에 이달 내내 웹사이트에 의견을 올리신 시청자 분들은 특별한 상품을 탈 기회가 있다는 점 강조하고 싶습니다.** 지금 당장 의견을 올려 주세요. **오늘 우리는 후버 식품의 신제품인 파스타 포장 식품에 대해 이야기하겠습니다.** 조리법을 들여다보느라 몇 시간씩 보내고 싶지 않은 날을 위한 맛있는 제품이죠. 아이제이아 후버 본인께서 곧 나오신다는 말씀을 드리게 되어 아주 기쁘군요. 후버 씨는 지난해 바로 이 방송국에서 진행한 요리 경연 대회에서 우승한 뒤 후버 식품을 설립했습니다. **후버 씨가 이 맛있는 식사가 어떻게 제조되는지 전부 알려 주실 겁니다.** 어서 오세요, 후버 씨.

어휘 emphasize 강조하다 viewer 시청자 comment 논평하다, 댓글을 달다 pre-packaged 사전 포장된, 미리 조리된 stare 빤히 보다 found 설립하다 contest 경연 대회 network 방송망

83

What are listeners encouraged to do on a Web site?

(A) Leave comments
(B) Watch instructional videos
(C) Vote in a contest
(D) Download recipes

청자들은 웹사이트에서 무엇을 하라고 권유받는가?

(A) **의견 남기기**
(B) 교육용 동영상 시청하기
(C) 대회에 투표하기
(D) 조리법 다운로드하기

어휘 instructional 교육용의 vote 투표하다

해설 세부 사항 관련 – 청자들이 웹사이트에서 하도록 권유받은 것

지문 초반부에서 오늘 시작하기 전에 이달 내내 웹사이트에 의견을 올리는 시청자들은 특별한 상품을 탈 기회가 있다는 점을 강조하고 싶다(Before we get started today, I want to emphasize that, all month, viewers who comment on our Web site have the chance to win special prizes)고 말했으므로 정답은 (A)이다.

▸▸ Paraphrasing   지문의 **comment on our Web site**
→ 정답의 **Leave comments**

84

What will be discussed on the broadcast?

(A) A cookbook
(B) Some restaurant locations
(C) Some packaged food
(D) A kitchen appliance

방송에서 논의될 것은 무엇인가?

(A) 요리책
(B) 식당 위치
(C) **포장 식품**
(D) 주방 가전 제품

어휘 location 장소, 위치 packaged 포장된 appliance 가전 제품

해설 전체 내용 관련 – 방송에서 논의될 것

지문 초반부에서 오늘 후버 식품의 신제품인 파스타 포장 식품에 대해 이야기하겠다(Today we're going to talk about Huber Foods's new pre-packaged pasta meals)고 말했으므로 정답은 (C)이다.

▸▸ Paraphrasing   지문의 **new pre-packaged pasta meals**
→ 정답의 **packaged food**

85

What does the speaker say Mr. Huber will do?

(A) Conduct a taste test
(B) Describe a manufacturing process
(C) Display a collection of accessories
(D) Announce a career change

화자는 후버 씨가 무엇을 할 것이라고 말하는가?

(A) 시식 진행하기
(B) **제조 공정 설명하기**
(C) 장신구 컬렉션 전시하기
(D) 진로 변경 발표하기

어휘 conduct 실시하다 describe 설명하다 manufacturing process 제조 공정

해설 세부 사항 관련 – 후버 씨가 할 일
지문 후반부에서 후버 씨가 이 맛있는 식사가 어떻게 제조되는지 전부 알려줄 것(He's going to tell us all about how these delicious meals are made)이라고 했으므로 정답은 (B)이다.

▸▸ Paraphrasing 지문의 tell us all about how these delicious meals are made → 정답의 Describe a manufacturing process

86-88 워크숍 발췌

M-Cn **86All right, the purpose of this workshop is to enhance the quality of your sales presentations.** Making a sale depends on your delivering an effective sales message, but buyers may not believe that your product fits their needs. So, today we'll go over some techniques to get potential customers to overcome their doubts and buy your products. **87We'll begin with a role play.** I'll distribute this handout that describes a common sales situation, and you'll act as salespeople and potential customers. **88Now, I'm sure many of you find this kind of activity embarrassing, and it might make you feel shy.** But in the sales field, there's no room for that. So let's get started.

자, 이번 워크숍의 목적은 제품 소개의 질을 높이는 것입니다. 판매를 성사시키는 것은 효과적인 영업 메시지를 전달하는 데 달려 있지만, 구매자들은 여러분의 제품이 그들의 필요에 맞는다는 점을 믿지 않을 수도 있습니다. 따라서, 오늘 우리는 잠재 고객이 의심을 버리고 여러분의 제품을 구매하도록 만들 기법들을 살펴보겠습니다. 역할극부터 시작하겠습니다. 제가 일반적인 영업 상황을 묘사하는 이 유인물을 나눠 드릴 텐데, 여러분은 영업자와 잠재 고객 역할을 하게 됩니다. 자, 이런 활동이 창피하다고 생각할 분도 많을 테고 쑥스럽기도 할 겁니다. 하지만 영업 분야는 그럴 여유가 없습니다. 그러니 시작하죠.

어휘 enhance 강화하다, 높이다 sales presentation 제품 소개 depend on ~에 의존하다 deliver 전하다 effective 효과적인 fit ~에 맞다 potential 잠재적인 overcome 극복하다 doubt 의심 role play 역할극 distribute 분배하다 handout 유인물 describe 설명하다, 묘사하다 act 역할을 하다 salespeople 영업사원 embarrassing 창피한, 당황스러운 field 분야 room 여지, 여유

86
What is the workshop about?
(A) Becoming a more effective manager
(B) Designing customer surveys
(C) Maintaining company Web sites
(D) Giving better sales presentations

워크숍은 무엇에 관한 것인가?
(A) 더 유능한 매니저 되기
(B) 고객 설문 조사 설계하기
(C) 회사 웹사이트 관리하기
(D) 더 나은 제품 소개하기

어휘 survey 설문 조사 maintain 유지[관리]하다

해설 전체 내용 관련 – 워크숍의 주제
지문 초반부에서 이번 워크숍의 목적은 제품 소개의 질을 높이는 것(the purpose of this workshop is to enhance the quality of your sales presentations)이라고 했으므로 정답은 (D)이다.

▸▸ Paraphrasing 지문의 enhance the quality of your sales presentations
→ 정답의 Giving better sales presentations

87
What will the workshop include?
(A) An acting task
(B) A painting exercise
(C) A question-and-answer period
(D) A physical competition

워크숍에는 무엇이 포함될 것인가?
(A) 연기 과제
(B) 그림 연습
(C) 질의응답 시간
(D) 체력 대결

어휘 period 시간 physical 육체의 competition 시합, 경쟁

해설 세부 사항 관련 – 워크숍에 포함될 것
지문 중반부에서 역할극부터 시작하겠다(We'll begin with a role play)고 했으므로 정답은 (A)이다.

▸▸ Paraphrasing 지문의 a role play → 정답의 An acting task

88
What does the speaker mean when he says, "there's no room for that"?
(A) An item must be moved to a storage area.
(B) It is important for listeners to avoid careless mistakes.
(C) The listeners must overcome their discomfort.
(D) A planned activity cannot take place.

화자가 "그럴 여유가 없습니다"라고 말하는 의미는 무엇인가?
(A) 상품을 창고로 옮겨야 한다.
(B) 청자들이 부주의한 실수를 피하는 것이 중요하다.
(C) 청자들은 불편함을 극복해야 한다.
(D) 계획된 활동을 할 수 없다.

어휘 storage 보관 avoid 피하다 careless 부주의한 discomfort 불편함

해설 화자의 의도 – 그럴 여유가 없다는 말의 의미
지문 중반부에서 역할극부터 시작한다고 한 뒤 인용문 바로 앞에서 이런 활동이 창피하다고 생각할 분도 많을 테고 쑥스럽기도 할 것('m sure many of you find this kind of activity embarrassing, and it might make you feel shy)이라고 했다. 즉 영업을 하려면 그런 감정을 떨쳐내야 한다는 의미임을 알 수 있으므로 정답은 (C)이다.

89-91 담화

W-Am Hi, everyone, and thank you for coming today. **89I know you're all experienced servers, but some training will still be necessary before our restaurant opens.** We want to be completely ready on opening night. **90Now, I was hoping to begin by showing you the facilities, but unfortunately, we can't go into the kitchen right now. The construction team is still replacing the flooring.** So, let's focus on getting to know each other for now. I'm Inga, the co-owner of this restaurant. **91Sharon, the other co-owner will join us in a minute. She's trying to keep everything organized as it comes in, and** the dishware was just delivered. Norma, why don't you introduce yourself next?

안녕하세요, 여러분. 오늘 와 주셔서 감사합니다. 여러분 모두 숙련된 웨이터라는 것을 알지만 식당을 개업하기 전에 아직 필요한 교육이 있습니다. 개업일 저녁에 완벽하게 준비되었으면 하니까요. 자, 시설을 보여 드리는 것으로 시작하고 싶었지만, 안타깝게도 지금은 주방에 들어갈 수 없습니다. 건축팀이 아직 바닥재를 교체하고 있거든요. 그러니까 지금으로서는 서로를 알아가는 데 초점을 맞춥시다. 저는 이 식당의 공동 소유주인 잉가예요. 또 다른 공동 소유주인 샤론이 곧 합류할 겁니다. 샤론은 모든 물품이 들어오는 대로 정돈하느라 애쓰고 있는데, 식기류가 방금 배송됐어요. 노마, 다음으로 자기소개를 해주시겠어요?

어휘 experienced 숙련된 necessary 필요한 facility 시설 unfortunately 불행히도 construction 공사 replace 교체하다 flooring 바닥(재), 마루 focus on ~에 집중하다 co-owner 공동 소유주 organize 준비하다, 정리하다 dishware 식기류

89

Who most likely are the listeners?
(A) Waitstaff
(B) Cooks
(C) Cashiers
(D) Dishwashers

청자들은 누구이겠는가?
(A) 서빙 담당 종업원들
(B) 요리사들
(C) 계산원들
(D) 설거지 담당 종업원들

해설 세부 사항 관련 - 청자들의 신분
지문 초반부에서 여러분 모두 숙련된 웨이터라는 것을 알지만 식당을 개업하기 전에 아직 필요한 교육이 있다(I know you're all experienced servers, but some training will still be necessary before our restaurant opens)고 했으므로 정답은 (A)이다.

▸▸ Paraphrasing 지문의 servers → 정답의 Waitstaff

90

Why does the speaker say they will not visit the kitchen?
(A) It is poorly lit.
(B) It is under renovation.
(C) Its doors are locked.
(D) Its flooring is being cleaned.

화자가 주방에 가지 않겠다고 말한 이유는 무엇인가?
(A) 조명 상태가 좋지 않다.
(B) 수리 중이다.
(C) 문이 잠겨 있다.
(D) 바닥을 청소하고 있다.

어휘 poorly 좋지 않게 light 비추다 renovation 개조 lock 잠그다

해설 세부 사항 관련 - 주방에 가지 않는 이유
지문 중반부에서 지금은 주방에 들어갈 수 없다(we can't go into the kitchen right now)고 한 뒤 건축팀이 아직 바닥재를 교체하고 있다(The construction team is still replacing the flooring)고 했으므로 정답은 (B)이다.

▸▸ Paraphrasing 지문의 is still replacing the flooring → 정답의 under renovation

91

Why does the speaker say, "the dishware was just delivered"?
(A) To assign a responsibility
(B) To make an excuse
(C) To show relief
(D) To emphasize a policy

화자가 "식기류가 방금 배송됐어요"라고 말하는 이유는 무엇인가?
(A) 직무를 배정하려고
(B) 변명을 하려고
(C) 안도감을 표현하려고
(D) 규정을 강조하려고

어휘 assign 배정하다, 할당하다 make an excuse 변명하다 relief 안도감 emphasize 강조하다 regulation 규칙, 규정

해설 화자의 의도 파악 - 식기류가 방금 배송됐다는 말의 의도
인용문 바로 앞 문장에서 공동 소유주인 샤론이 곧 합류할 텐데(Sharon, the other co-owner will join us in a minute) 들어오는 대로 모두 정돈하느라 애쓰고 있다(She's trying to keep everything organized as it comes in)고 한 후 식기류가 방금 배송됐다고 말했다. 즉 식기류가 방금 도착해서 정돈하느라 오지 못했다는 변명의 의미임을 알 수 있으므로 정답은 (B)이다.

92-94 광고

M-Au **92If you're tired of taking your trash and recyclables all the way to a drop-off center, it's time to give Siskin Disposal a call. Our curbside pickup subscription makes getting rid of your trash simple.** Just choose the container sizes and pickup frequency that suit you, fill the

Test 8

containers as necessary, and let us do the rest. 93**As of this year, we've even become licensed to haul potentially harmful items, like batteries or pesticides, to the appropriate center.** Siskin Disposal is the best around. 94**But don't just take our word for it—visit our Web site to see glowing evaluations from our current customers.** When you're ready to sign up, our operators will be standing by.

쓰레기와 재활용 쓰레기를 수집 센터까지 가져가는 일에 지치셨다면 시스킨 폐기 회사로 전화하세요. 저희의 차로변 수거 정기 서비스는 쓰레기 폐기를 간편하게 만들어 드립니다. 여러분에게 맞는 용기 크기와 수거 빈도를 선택한 다음 필요에 따라 용기를 채우기만 하시고, 나머지는 저희에게 맡기세요. 올해부터 저희는 배터리나 살충제 등 잠재적으로 유해한 물질도 적절한 센터까지 수송하는 허가를 받았습니다. 시스킨 폐기 회사는 지역 최고입니다. 하지만 저희 말을 그냥 믿지는 마십시오. 저희 웹사이트를 방문해서 현재 고객들이 남긴 극찬을 확인하십시오. 등록할 준비가 되면 저희 상담원이 대기하고 있습니다.

어휘 be tired of ~에 싫증나다 trash 쓰레기 recyclable 재활용 쓰레기 drop-off center 쓰레기 수집 센터 disposal 처리 curbside (연석이 있는) 차도 가장자리 subscription 구독, 정기 사용 get rid of ~을 없애다 container 용기, 컨테이너 frequency 빈도 as necessary 필요에 따라 rest 나머지 as of ~부터 licensed 허가를 받은 haul 운반하다 potentially 잠재적으로 harmful 해로운 pesticide 살충제 appropriate 적절한 take one's word for it ~의 말을 곧이 듣다 glowing 열광적인, 극찬하는 evaluation 평가 sign up 신청[등록]하다 operator 교환원, 운영자 stand by 대기하다

92

What kind of business is being advertised?

(A) A disposal service
(B) A moving company
(C) A groundskeeping company
(D) An environmental advising firm

어떤 업종이 광고되고 있는가?
(A) 폐기 서비스
(B) 이삿짐 운송 회사
(C) 토지 관리 업체
(D) 환경 자문 회사

어휘 groundskeeping 토지 관리 advising 자문

해설 전체 내용 관련 – 광고되는 업종
지문 초반부에서 쓰레기와 재활용 쓰레기를 수집 센터까지 가져가는 일에 지쳤다면 시스킨 폐기 회사에 전화하라(If you're tired of taking your trash and recyclables all the way to a drop-off center, it's time to give Siskin Disposal a call)고 한 뒤 차로변 수거 정기 서비스로 쓰레기 폐기가 간편해진다(Our curbside pickup subscription makes getting rid of your trash simple)고 했으므로 정답은 (A)이다.

▸▸ **Paraphrasing** 지문의 **getting rid of your trash**
→ 정답의 **A disposal service**

93

What does the speaker mention is now offered?

(A) A free consultation session
(B) An extra-large container
(C) Landscaping machinery rentals
(D) Transport of dangerous materials

화자는 이제 무엇이 제공된다고 말하는가?
(A) 무료 상담 시간
(B) 초대형 용기
(C) 조경 기계 대여
(D) 위험 물질 수송

어휘 consultation 상담 landscaping 조경 rental 대여 transport 운송 material 물질

해설 세부 사항 관련 – 제공되는 것
지문 중반부에서 올해부터 배터리나 살충제 등 잠재적으로 유해한 물질도 적절한 센터까지 수송하는 허가를 받았다(As of this year, we've even become licensed to haul potentially harmful items, like batteries or pesticides, to the appropriate center)고 했으므로 정답은 (D)이다.

▸▸ **Paraphrasing** 지문의 **haul potentially harmful items**
→ 정답의 **Transport of dangerous materials**

94

What are listeners encouraged to do?

(A) Sign up on a Web site
(B) Visit a local branch
(C) Look at some reviews
(D) Compare some offers

청자들은 무엇을 하라고 권유받는가?
(A) 웹사이트에 등록하기
(B) 근처 지점 방문하기
(C) 평가 보기
(D) 상품 비교해 보기

어휘 sign up on ~을 신청하다 local 지역의 branch 지점 offer 제공(품)

해설 세부 사항 관련 – 청자들이 권유받은 것
지문 후반부에서 우리 말을 그냥 믿지는 말고 웹사이트를 방문해서 현재 고객들이 남긴 극찬을 확인해 보라(don't just take our word for it—visit our Web site to see glowing evaluations from our current customers)고 했으므로 정답은 (C)이다.

▸▸ **Paraphrasing** 지문의 **see glowing evaluations**
→ 정답의 **Look at some reviews**

95-97 전화 메시지 + 쿠폰

W-Br 95**Liz, I wanted to touch base about the outing to celebrate our big sales increase last quarter.** We're still holding it at Arden's Amusement Complex on July fifteenth, from one to eight that evening. 96**Most invited people are from your sales team, so we'll have no more**

than twenty people attending. Uh, we have that coupon for the park, but we can't use it. We'll need to pay full price for our entrance. But it's all right—we have the budget for it. **⁹⁷Oh, and the director gave me permission to rent a bus to take us all there together.** I'll be sending around a memo soon with all the details.

리즈 씨, 지난 분기 매출 급신장을 축하하기 위한 야유회 건으로 다시 연락 드립니다. 7월 15일 1시부터 저녁 8시까지 아덴 놀이공원에서 개최하는데요. 초청한 분들 중 대다수가 리즈 씨의 영업팀 직원이라서 참석자가 20명밖에 안 됩니다. 음, 공원 쿠폰이 있지만 사용할 수 없어요. 입장료 전액을 지불해야 합니다. 하지만 예산이 있어서 괜찮습니다. 아, 임원께서 모두 함께 이동할 수 있는 버스를 대절하도록 허가해 주셨어요. 모든 세부 사항이 적힌 회람을 곧 돌리겠습니다.

어휘 touch base 다시 연락하다 outing 야유회 sales 매출 quarter 분기 hold 개최하다 no more than 단지 ~에 지나지 않다 attend 참석하다 pay full price 전액 지불하다 entrance 입장 budget 예산 give permission 허가하다 rent 대여하다 memo 회람

Arden's Amusement Complex

20% Off

entrance to the main park

– Valid July 1 to July 31
⁹⁶– For groups of 30 or more people

아덴 놀이공원

주 공원 입장권 20퍼센트 할인

— 7월 1일부터 7월 31일까지 유효함
— 30인 이상 단체에 해당

어휘 valid 유효한

95

What most likely is being celebrated?

(A) A company's anniversary
(B) The end of a business year
(C) The completion of a project
(D) Improved sales results

무엇을 축하하겠는가?
(A) 회사 기념일
(B) 사업연도 마감
(C) 프로젝트 완료
(D) 매출 실적 향상

어휘 anniversary 기념일 business year 사업 연도 completion 완료 improved 개선된

해설 세부 사항 관련 – 축하될 일

지문 초반부에서 지난 분기 매출 급신장을 축하하기 위한 야유회 건으로 다시 연락 드린다(I wanted to touch base about the outing to celebrate our big sales increase last quarter)고 했으므로 정답은 (D)이다.

▸▸ Paraphrasing 지문의 big sales increase
→ 정답의 Improved sales results

96

Look at the graphic. What will prevent the speaker from using the coupon?

(A) The time of the group's arrival
(B) The number of attendees
(C) The date of the outing
(D) The location of the venue

시각 정보에 의하면, 화자가 쿠폰을 사용할 수 없는 이유는 무엇인가?
(A) 단체 도착 시간
(B) 참석자 수
(C) 야유회 날짜
(D) 장소 위치

어휘 attendee 참석자 location 위치 venue 장소, 개최지

해설 시각 정보 연계 – 쿠폰을 사용할 수 없는 이유

지문 중반부에서 초청한 분들 중 대다수가 리즈 씨의 영업팀 직원이라서 참석자가 20명밖에 안 된다(Most invited people are from your sales team, so we'll have no more than twenty people attending)고 했고, 시각 정보에 따르면 할인은 30명 이상의 단체에게 제공되므로 정답은 (B)이다.

97

What does the speaker say about the outing?

(A) The participants will share transportation.
(B) It will include an overnight stay.
(C) Employees' family members are welcome.
(D) A supervisor's permission is required to attend.

화자는 야유회에 대해 무엇을 언급하는가?
(A) 참석자들이 같은 교통편을 이용할 것이다.
(B) 1박이 포함될 것이다.
(C) 직원 가족들도 올 수 있다.
(D) 참석하는 데 상사의 허가가 필요하다.

어휘 participant 참석자 transportation 교통편 overnight stay 일박 supervisor 감독관 be required to ~하도록 요구되다

해설 세부 사항 관련 – 야유회에 대해 언급하는 것

지문 후반부에서 임원께서 모두 함께 이동할 수 있는 버스를 대절하도록 허가해 주셨다(the director gave me permission to rent a bus to take us all there together)고 했으므로 정답은 (A)이다.

▸▸ Paraphrasing 지문의 rent a bus to take us all there together → 정답의 share transportation

M-Au Everyone, let's get started with today's seminar. Uh, first, I need to draw attention to a change to our calendar. **98Our March seminar has been postponed until further notice because of a scheduling conflict.** So far, nothing has been mentioned about April. Anyway, despite this change, I want to emphasize that these seminars are important. **99The ideas you come up with today, for example, will be used to update our training manual next week.** So please make an effort to participate. **100Now, I'd like you to divide yourselves into groups of three to four people.** Don't forget to bring your handouts with you. Go ahead.

여러분, 오늘 세미나를 시작하죠. 어, 우선 우리 일정표 변동 사항에 주목해 주시기 바랍니다. 일정이 겹치는 바람에 3월 세미나는 추가 공지가 있을 때까지 연기되었습니다. 지금까지 4월 일정에 대해서는 별 얘기가 없습니다. 어쨌든 이 변경에도 불구하고, 저는 이들 세미나가 중요하다는 점을 강조하고 싶습니다. 예를 들어, 여러분이 오늘 내는 아이디어들은 다음 주 교육 지침서를 개정하는 데 활용될 예정입니다. 그러니 참여에 성의를 다해 주십시오. 자, 서너 명씩 그룹별로 나누시기 바랍니다. 유인물 가져오는 것 잊지 마시고요. 시작하세요.

어휘 draw attention to ~에 주의를 집중시키다 postpone 연기하다 further notice 추후 통보 scheduling conflict 일정 충돌 emphasize 강조하다 come up with 찾아내다, 내놓다 update 갱신[개정]하다 manual 지침서 make an effort 애쓰다 participate 참가하다 divide into ~으로 나누다 handout 유인물

Date	Seminar Name
January 8	Our Brand Identity
February 5	Dealing with Customer Objections
98March 4	Sharing Success Stories
April 9	Voicemail Practices

일자	세미나명
1월 8일	자사 브랜드 정체성
2월 5일	고객 항의에 대처하기
3월 4일	**성공담 공유하기**
4월 9일	음성 메시지 관행

어휘 identity 정체성 deal with 처리하다 objection 반대, 항의 voicemail 음성 메시지

98

Look at the graphic. Which seminar has been postponed?

(A) Our Brand Identity
(B) Dealing with Customer Objections
(C) Sharing Success Stories
(D) Voicemail Practices

시각 정보에 의하면, 어느 세미나가 연기되었는가?
(A) 자사 브랜드 정체성
(B) 고객 항의에 대처하기
(C) 성공담 공유하기
(D) 음성 메시지 관행

해설 시각 정보 연계 – 연기된 세미나 시간
지문 초반부에서 일정이 겹치는 바람에 3월 세미나는 추가 공지가 있을 때까지 연기되었다(Our March seminar has been postponed until further notice because of a scheduling conflict)고 했다. 시각 정보에 따르면 3월에 있을 워크숍은 '성공담 공유하기'(Sharing Success Stories)이므로 정답은 (C)이다.

99

What will the speaker's company do next week?

(A) Revise a manual
(B) Release new software
(C) Determine a seminar date
(D) Request feedback from the listeners

화자의 회사는 다음 주에 무엇을 할 것인가?
(A) 지침서 개정하기　　(B) 새 소프트웨어 출시하기
(C) 세미나 일자 결정하기　(D) 청자들에게 의견 요청하기

어휘 revise 수정하다 release 출시하다 determine 결정하다 feedback 의견

해설 세부 사항 관련 – 다음 주에 회사가 할 일
지문 후반부에서 오늘 내는 아이디어들은 다음 주 교육 지침서를 개정하는 데 활용될 것(The ideas you come up with today, for example, will be used to update our training manual next week)이라고 했으므로 정답은 (A)이다.

▸▸ **Paraphrasing** 지문의 **update our training manual** → 정답의 **Revise a manual**

100

What will the listeners most likely do next?

(A) View a television commercial
(B) Read over a handout
(C) Form some small groups
(D) Count some product samples

청자들은 다음으로 무엇을 하겠는가?
(A) 텔레비전 광고 보기　　(B) 유인물 재독하기
(C) 소그룹으로 모이기　　(D) 제품 샘플 세기

어휘 commercial 광고 read over 다시 읽다 form 구성하다 count 세다

해설 세부 사항 관련 – 청자들이 다음으로 할 일
지문 후반부에서 서너 명씩 그룹별로 나누라(Now, I'd like you to divide yourselves into groups of three to four people)고 했으므로 정답은 (C)이다.

▸▸ **Paraphrasing** 지문의 **divide yourselves into groups of three to four people** → 정답의 **Form some small groups**

TEST 9

1 (D)	**2** (B)	**3** (C)	**4** (C)	**5** (A)
6 (D)	**7** (C)	**8** (B)	**9** (C)	**10** (B)
11 (C)	**12** (C)	**13** (A)	**14** (B)	**15** (A)
16 (C)	**17** (C)	**18** (C)	**19** (B)	**20** (A)
21 (C)	**22** (C)	**23** (B)	**24** (A)	**25** (B)
26 (C)	**27** (C)	**28** (B)	**29** (A)	**30** (B)
31 (A)	**32** (C)	**33** (D)	**34** (D)	**35** (C)
36 (B)	**37** (B)	**38** (A)	**39** (D)	**40** (D)
41 (A)	**42** (C)	**43** (D)	**44** (D)	**45** (C)
46 (D)	**47** (B)	**48** (A)	**49** (A)	**50** (C)
51 (B)	**52** (B)	**53** (A)	**54** (C)	**55** (D)
56 (B)	**57** (A)	**58** (B)	**59** (B)	**60** (A)
61 (C)	**62** (D)	**63** (B)	**64** (C)	**65** (B)
66 (B)	**67** (C)	**68** (C)	**69** (D)	**70** (D)
71 (C)	**72** (B)	**73** (B)	**74** (D)	**75** (C)
76 (A)	**77** (C)	**78** (B)	**79** (B)	**80** (D)
81 (A)	**82** (C)	**83** (B)	**84** (C)	**85** (C)
86 (B)	**87** (C)	**88** (C)	**89** (C)	**90** (B)
91 (D)	**92** (B)	**93** (A)	**94** (D)	**95** (A)
96 (D)	**97** (C)	**98** (D)	**99** (D)	**100** (D)

PART 1

1　W-Am

(A) One of the men is adjusting his tie.
(B) The woman is giving a presentation.
(C) One of the men is setting up a display board.
(D) Some people are having a meeting.

(A) 남자들 중 한 명이 넥타이를 고쳐 매고 있다.
(B) 여자가 발표를 하고 있다.
(C) 남자들 중 한 명이 게시판을 설치하고 있다.
(D) **몇 사람이 회의를 하고 있다.**

어휘　adjust 조정하다　set up 세우다, 설치하다　display board 게시판

해설　2인 이상 등장 사진 – 인물의 상태 묘사
(A) 동사 오답. 남자가 넥타이를 고쳐 매는(is adjusting his tie) 모습이 아니므로 오답.
(B) 동사 오답. 여자가 발표를 하는(is giving a presentation) 모습이 아니므로 오답.
(C) 사진에 없는 명사를 이용한 오답. 사진에 게시판(display board)이 보이지 않으므로 오답.
(D) 정답. 사람들이 회의를 하고 있는(are having a meeting) 모습이므로 정답.

2　M-Au

(A) She's sweeping a kitchen.
(B) She's wiping off a counter.
(C) She's putting on some gloves.
(D) She's emptying a sink.

(A) 여자가 주방을 쓸고 있다.
(B) **여자가 조리대를 닦고 있다.**
(C) 여자가 장갑을 끼고 있다.
(D) 여자가 싱크대를 비우고 있다.

어휘　sweep 쓸다　wipe off 닦아 내다　counter (주방의) 조리대　put on 착용하다　empty 비우다　sink 싱크대[개수대]

해설　1인 등장 사진 – 인물의 동작 묘사
(A) 동사 오답. 여자가 주방을 쓸고 있는(is sweeping a kitchen) 모습이 아니므로 오답.
(B) 정답. 여자가 싱크대를 닦고 있는(is wiping off a counter) 모습이므로 정답.
(C) 동사 오답. 여자가 장갑을 끼는 동작(is putting on some gloves)을 하는 모습이 아니므로 오답.
(D) 동사 오답. 여자가 싱크대를 비우는(is emptying a sink) 모습이 아니므로 오답.

3　W-Br

(A) They're washing a car.
(B) They're changing a tire.
(C) They're facing a vehicle.
(D) They're exchanging business cards.

(A) 사람들이 세차를 하고 있다.
(B) 사람들이 타이어를 교체하고 있다.
(C) **사람들이 차를 마주보고 있다.**
(D) 사람들이 명함을 교환하고 있다.

어휘　face 마주보다　exchange 교환하다　business card 명함

해설　2인 이상 등장 사진 – 인물의 상태 묘사
(A) 동사 오답. 사람들이 세차를 하는(are washing a car) 모습이 아니므로 오답.
(B) 동사 오답. 사람들이 타이어를 교체하는(are changing a tire) 모습이 아니므로 오답.
(C) 정답. 사람들이 차를 마주보고 있는(are facing a vehicle) 모습이므로 정답.
(B) 동사 오답. 사람들이 명함을 교환하는(are exchanging business cards) 모습이 아니므로 오답.

4 M-Cn

(A) He's stirring some food.
(B) He's placing items on a shelf.
(C) He's looking at a vegetable.
(D) He's holding some plates.

(A) 남자가 음식을 젓고 있다.
(B) 남자가 선반에 물건을 놓고 있다.
(C) 남자가 채소를 보고 있다.
(D) 남자가 접시를 들고 있다.

어휘 stir 젓다 place 놓다 shelf 선반 hold (손에) 들다 plate 접시

해설 1인 등장 사진 – 인물의 상태 묘사
(A) 동사 오답. 남자가 음식을 젓고 있는(is stirring some food) 모습이 아니므로 오답.
(B) 동사 오답. 남자가 선반에 물건을 놓는(is placing items on a shelf) 모습이 아니므로 오답.
(C) 정답. 남자가 채소를 보는(is looking at a vegetable) 모습이므로 정답.
(D) 동사 오답. 남자가 접시를 들고 있는(is holding some plates) 모습이 아니므로 오답.

5 W-Am

(A) Railings have been built along a dock.
(B) A boat has been pulled onto the shore.
(C) Some plants are growing near a waterfall.
(D) Mountains overlook a crowded pier.

(A) 선창을 따라 난간이 세워져 있다.
(B) 보트 한 대가 뭍에 올라와 있다.
(C) 폭포 근처에 식물들이 자라고 있다.
(D) 산에서 붐비는 부두가 내려다보인다.

어휘 railing 난간, 울타리 dock 부두, 선창 pull onto ~로 끌어올리다 shore 해안, 뭍 waterfall 폭포 overlook 내려다보다 crowded 붐비는 pier 부두

해설 사물/배경 사진 – 사물의 상태 묘사
(A) 정답. 선창을 따라 난간이 세워져 있는(Railings have been built) 모습이므로 정답.
(B) 동사 오답. 보트가 뭍에 올라와 있는(has been pulled onto the shore) 모습이 아니므로 오답.
(C) 사진에 없는 명사를 이용한 오답. 사진에 폭포(waterfall)가 보이지 않으므로 오답.
(D) 사진에 없는 명사를 이용한 오답. 사진에 붐비는 부두(crowded pier)가 보이지 않으므로 오답.

6 M-Au

(A) Workers are repairing an engine.
(B) An airplane has taken off.
(C) Passengers are boarding a plane.
(D) An aircraft is being directed.

(A) 인부들이 엔진을 고치고 있다.
(B) 비행기가 이륙했다.
(C) 승객들이 비행기에 탑승하고 있다.
(D) 비행기가 방향 지시를 받고 있다.

어휘 repair 수리하다 take off 이륙하다 board (비행기·배 등에) 탑승하다 aircraft 비행기 direct 인도하다, 이끌다

해설 2인 이상 등장 사진 – 사람 또는 사물 중심 묘사
(A) 동사 오답. 인부들이 엔진을 고치고 있는(are repairing an engine) 모습이 아니므로 오답.
(B) 동사 오답. 비행기가 이륙한(has taken off) 모습이 아니므로 오답.
(C) 사진에 없는 명사를 이용한 오답. 사진에 승객들(passengers)이 보이지 않으므로 오답.
(D) 정답. 비행기(aircraft)가 방향 지시를 받고 있는(is being directed) 모습이므로 정답.

PART 2

7

W-Br Who can answer my questions about vacation time?
M-Cn (A) Two weeks every year.
(B) I hope you have a great time.
(C) Ms. Pacheco can help you.

휴가 기간에 대한 문의에 누가 답해 줄 수 있을까요?
(A) 일년에 2주입니다.
(B) 즐겁게 보내시기 바랍니다.
(C) 파체코 씨가 도와드릴 수 있을 거예요.

해설 문의에 답할 사람을 묻는 Who 의문문
(A) 질문과 상관없는 오답. 기간을 묻는 How much time에 어울리는 응답이므로 오답.
(B) 단어 반복 오답. 질문의 time을 반복한 오답.
(C) 정답. 휴가 기간 문의에 답해줄 사람을 묻는 질문에 파체코 씨가 도와드릴 수 있다고 구체적인 사람의 이름을 언급하고 있으므로 정답.

8

W-Am How long will my dental appointment last?
M-Au (A) Sorry, it's the last one.
(B) Forty minutes at most.
(C) Yes, at the Shine Clinic.

제 치과 진료는 얼마나 걸릴까요?

(A) 죄송합니다. 이게 마지막입니다.

(B) 길어야 40분입니다.

(C) 네, 사인 진료소에서요.

어휘 dental 치과의 appointment (진료) 예약 last 지속되다; 마지막의 at most 많아 봐야, 기껏해야

해설 치과 진료 시간을 묻는 How 의문문

(A) 단어 반복 오답. 질문의 last를 다른 의미의 last로 반복한 오답.

(B) 정답. 진료가 얼마나 걸릴지 묻는 질문에 40분이라고 구체적인 시간을 말해 주고 있으므로 정답.

(C) Yes/No 불가 오답. How 의문문에는 Yes/No 응답이 불가능하므로 오답.

9

M-Cn Is this shelving unit easy to assemble?

W-Br (A) I'll assemble the rest of the staff.

(B) It holds up to fifty books.

(C) Yes, you don't even need instructions.

이 선반은 조립하기 쉬운가요?

(A) 제가 나머지 직원들을 불러 모을게요.

(B) 최대 50권까지 올릴 수 있습니다.

(C) 네, 설명서도 필요 없어요.

어휘 shelving unit 선반 assemble 조립하다: 모으다 hold 담다, 수용하다 up to ~까지 instructions (사용) 설명서

해설 선반이 조립하기 쉬운지 묻는 be동사 Yes/No 의문문

(A) 단어 반복 오답. 질문의 assemble을 다른 의미의 assemble로 반복한 오답.

(B) 연상 단어 오답. 질문의 shelving unit에서 연상 가능한 books를 이용한 오답.

(C) 정답. 선반이 조립하기 쉬운지를 묻는 질문에 그렇다고 대답하고 나서 설명서도 필요 없다고 부연 설명을 하고 있으므로 정답.

10

M-Au Could we finish some of these files tomorrow?

W-Am (A) The file cabinet will be delivered.

(B) I don't have a problem with that.

(C) They're customer information forms.

우리 이 파일들 중 일부는 내일 끝낼까요?

(A) 파일 캐비닛이 배달될 겁니다.

(B) 그렇게 하지요.

(C) 그것들은 고객정보 양식입니다.

어휘 deliver 배달하다 have a problem with ~에 동의하지 않다 customer 고객 form 양식, 서식

해설 제안/권유의 의문문

(A) 단어 반복 오답. 질문의 files를 반복한 오답.

(B) 정답. 파일들 중 일부를 내일 끝내자는 제안에 그렇게 해도 문제 없다고 긍정적인 응답을 하고 있으므로 정답.

(C) 연상 단어 오답. 질문의 files에서 연상 가능한 forms를 이용한 오답.

11

M-Cn When should I make my first payment?

W-Br (A) For a new home.

(B) Directly to the bank.

(C) On July twentieth.

제 첫 상환은 언제 해야 합니까?

(A) 새 집에 대해서요.

(B) 은행으로 직접이요.

(C) 7월 20일이요.

어휘 make payment 지불하다 directly 직접적으로

해설 담보 대출 상환을 언제 해야 하는지 묻는 When 의문문

(A) 질문과 상관없는 오답. 이유를 묻는 why 의문문에 적절한 응답이므로 오답.

(B) 연상 단어 오답. 질문의 payment에서 연상 가능한 bank를 이용한 오답.

(C) 정답. 첫 담보 대출 상환이 언제냐는 질문에 7월 20일이라는 구체적인 시점을 알려주고 있으므로 정답.

12

M-Au We need to bring a microphone to the event, don't we?

W-Am (A) Please use my mobile phone number.

(B) By turning up the volume manually.

(C) Well, the venue will provide one.

행사에 마이크를 가지고 가야 되죠, 그렇지 않나요?

(A) 제 휴대전화 번호를 이용해 주세요.

(B) 손으로 볼륨을 높여서요.

(C) 행사장 측에서 제공할 거예요.

어휘 turn up 소리를 높이다 manually 수동으로 venue (행사 등의) 장소 provide 제공하다

해설 마이크를 가지고 가야 하는지 여부를 확인하는 부가의문문

(A) 유사 발음 오답. 질문의 microphone과 부분적으로 발음이 동일한 mobile phone을 이용한 오답.

(B) 연상 단어 오답. 질문의 microphone에서 연상 가능한 turning up the volume을 이용한 오답.

(C) 정답. 마이크를 가지고 가야 되는지 여부를 묻는 질문에 행사장 측에서 제공한다는 말로 필요 없다는 것을 우회적으로 표현하고 있으므로 정답.

13

W-Br What time does the laboratory open?

M-Au (A) It's different every day.

(B) No, you need an access code.

(C) To get the sample tested.

실험실은 몇 시에 열죠?

(A) 매일 달라요.

(B) 아니요, 비밀번호를 아셔야 합니다.

(C) 샘플을 테스트하기 위해서요.

어휘 laboratory 실험실, 연구실 access code 접근 부호, 비밀번호 test 시험[테스트]하다

Test 9

해설 실험실이 몇 시에 열리는지 묻는 What 의문문

(A) 정답. 실험실이 몇 시에 여는지 묻는 질문에 매일 다르다고 답하고 있으므로 정답.

(B) Yes/No 불가 오답. What 의문문에는 Yes/No 응답이 불가능하므로 오답.

(C) 연상 단어 오답. 질문의 laboratory에서 연상 가능한 tested를 이용한 오답.

14

W-Am How was your shopping trip to the mall?

M-Cn (A) That sounds like fun.

(B) I found some bargains.

(C) The one in Southfield.

몰로 쇼핑간 건 어땠어요?

(A) 재미있을 것 같네요.

(B) 몇 가지 싸게 샀어요.

(C) 사우스필드에 있는 거요.

어휘 bargain 싸게 사는 물건

해설 쇼핑이 어땠는지 묻는 How 의문문

(A) 연상 단어 오답. 질문의 shopping에서 연상 가능한 fun을 이용한 오답.

(B) 정답. 쇼핑이 어땠는지 묻는 질문에 몇 가지 싸게 샀다고 답하고 있으므로 정답.

(C) 질문과 상관없는 오답. 어느 것인지를 묻는 which 의문문에 어울리는 응답이므로 오답.

15

W-Am Whose keys are these?

M-Au (A) Probably the building manager's.

(B) Libby has enough.

(C) The main conference room.

이 열쇠들 누구 거죠?

(A) 아마도 건물 관리인 거 같은데요.

(B) 리비는 충분히 있어요.

(C) 주 회의실이요.

어휘 conference room 회의실

해설 열쇠의 주인이 누구인지 묻는 Whose 의문문

(A) 정답. 열쇠의 주인이 누구인지 묻는 질문에 아마도 건물 관리인의 것 같다고 답하고 있으므로 정답.

(B) 연상 단어 오답. 질문의 whose에서 연상 가능한 사람 이름(Libby)을 이용한 오답.

(C) 질문과 상관없는 오답. 장소를 묻는 Where 의문문에 어울리는 응답이므로 오답.

16

M-Cn Where's a good place to park in this neighborhood?

M-Au (A) Yes, I've lived here a while.

(B) A playground and some picnic tables.

(C) On the next street over.

이 근처에 주차하기 좋은 곳은 어디입니까?

(A) 네, 전 여기서 좀 살았습니다.

(B) 놀이터와 피크닉 테이블이요.

(C) 저기 다음 도로요.

어휘 park 주차하다 neighborhood 동네, 인근 playground 놀이터 over 저쪽으로

해설 적절한 주차 공간이 어디 있는지 묻는 Where 의문문

(A) Yes/No 불가 오답. Where 의문문에는 Yes/No 응답이 불가능하므로 오답.

(B) 연상 단어 오답. 질문의 park를 공원의 의미로 잘못 이해했을 때 연상 가능한 playground와 picnic tables를 이용한 오답.

(C) 정답. 주차하기 좋은 곳이 어디냐는 질문에 다음 도로라고 응답하고 있으므로 정답.

17

W-Br Why did we get paid a day early?

W-Am (A) Is six A.M. early enough?

(B) I asked for a raise.

(C) Because tomorrow is a holiday.

왜 우리 급여를 하루 일찍 받은 거죠?

(A) 아침 6시면 충분히 이른 건가요?

(B) 제가 월급을 올려 달라고 했어요.

(C) 내일이 휴일이라서요.

어휘 get paid 보수[급여]를 받다 raise 임금 인상

해설 급여를 하루 더 빨리 받은 이유를 묻는 Why 의문문

(A) 단어 반복 오답. 질문의 early를 반복한 오답.

(B) 연상 단어 오답. 질문의 get paid에서 연상 가능한 raise를 이용한 오답.

(C) 정답. 급여를 하루 일찍 받은 이유를 묻는 질문에 내일이 휴일이기 때문이라는 구체적인 이유로 답하고 있으므로 정답.

18

W-Br Does this perfume come in another size?

M-Cn (A) It's on sale today.

(B) I wear a medium.

(C) No, it doesn't.

이 향수 다른 사이즈도 있습니까?

(A) 그건 오늘 할인 중입니다.

(B) 전 중간 사이즈 입어요.

(C) 아니요, 없습니다.

어휘 perfume 향수 come in (상품이) 들어오다 be on sale 할인 중이다

해설 향수의 다른 사이즈도 있는지 묻는 일반동사 의문문

(A) 연상 단어 오답. 질문의 perfume에서 연상 가능한 sale을 이용한 오답.

(B) 연상 단어 오답. 질문의 another size에서 연상 가능한 medium을 이용한 오답.

(C) 정답. 다른 사이즈의 향수가 있는지 묻는 질문에 없다고 응답하고 있으므로 정답.

19

W-Am Could you put labels on these crates?

M-Au (A) She was late again.

(B) I'll take care of that now.

(C) Supplies from overseas.

이 나무 상자들에 라벨 좀 붙여 주시겠습니까?

(A) 그녀는 또 지각했어요.

(B) 지금 제가 처리하죠.

(C) 해외에서 온 물품입니다.

어휘 put on ~을 붙이다 label 라벨, 딱지 crate 나무 상자 take care of ~을 처리하다 supplies 물품, 비품

해설 부탁/요청의 의문문

(A) 유사 발음 오답. 질문의 labels와 부분적으로 발음이 유사한 late를 이용한 오답.

(B) 정답. 나무 상자에 라벨을 붙여 주겠냐는 요청에 지금 하겠다고 응답하므로 정답.

(C) 연상 단어 오답. 질문의 labels 및 crates에서 연상 가능한 supplies를 이용한 오답.

20

W-Br What did you like most about Mr. Branson's speech?

M-Cn (A) His enthusiastic attitude.

(B) At the staff banquet.

(C) Usually a guest speaker.

브랜슨 씨의 강연에서 가장 좋았던 점이 무엇입니까?

(A) 그의 열정적인 태도요.

(B) 직원 연회에서요.

(C) 대개 초청 연사요.

어휘 speech 연설, 강연 enthusiastic 열정적인, 열광적인 banquet 연회, 축하연

해설 브랜슨 씨의 연설에서 가장 좋았던 것이 무엇인지 묻는 What 의문문

(A) 정답. 브랜슨 씨의 강연에서 가장 좋았던 점이 무엇이었냐는 질문에 그의 열정적인 태도였다고 응답하므로 정답.

(B) 질문과 상관없는 오답. 장소를 묻는 Where 의문문에 어울리는 응답이므로 오답.

(C) 연상 단어 오답. 질문의 speech에서 연상 가능한 a guest speaker를 이용한 오답.

21

W-Am Where do I turn in my questionnaire?

M-Au (A) No, not yet.

(B) With a blue or black pen.

(C) You have to mail it to the address listed.

제 설문지는 어디에 제출하는 건가요?

(A) 아뇨, 아직이요.

(B) 파란펜이나 검정펜으로요.

(C) 등재된 주소로 발송해야 합니다.

어휘 turn in 제출하다, 내다 questionnaire 설문지 mail to ~에 우편으로 보내다 list 명단에 올리다

해설 설문지를 어디에 제출하는지를 묻는 Where 의문문

(A) Yes/No 불가 오답. Where 의문문에는 Yes/No 응답이 불가능하므로 오답.

(B) 연상 단어 오답. 설문지 작성 측면에서 질문의 questionnaire에서 연상 가능한 blue or black pen을 이용한 오답.

(C) 정답. 설문지를 어디에 제출해야 하느냐는 질문에 등재된 주소로 발송해야 한다고 장소와 방법을 알려주고 있으므로 정답.

22

W-Br Should we hold the fundraiser in the spring or in the fall?

M-Au (A) To fund the charity.

(B) Fortunately, no one was hurt.

(C) We always do it in March.

모금 행사를 봄에 열어야 할까요, 아니면 가을에 열어야 할까요?

(A) 자선단체에 자금을 지원하기 위해서요.

(B) 다행히도 아무도 다치지 않았습니다.

(C) 저희는 늘 3월에 합니다.

어휘 hold 열다 fundraiser 모금 행사 fund 자금을 charity 자선 단체

해설 자선 행사를 언제 할 것인지를 묻는 선택의문문

(A) 질문과 상관없는 오답. 이유를 묻는 Why 의문문에 어울리는 응답이므로 오답.

(B) 유사 발음 오답. 질문의 fundraiser와 부분적으로 발음이 동일한 fund를 이용한 오답.

(C) 정답. 모금 행사를 봄에 열지 가을에 열지 묻는 선택 의문문에 3월이라는 말로 봄을 선택했으므로 정답.

23

W-Br Photography is forbidden at this museum, right?

M-Cn (A) Let's take a group photo.

(B) Yes, except in the main lobby.

(C) The exhibit was fantastic.

이 박물관에서는 사진 촬영 금지죠, 그렇죠?

(A) 단체 사진 찍읍시다.

(B) 네, 중앙 로비만 빼고요.

(C) 전시가 환상적이었습니다.

어휘 forbid 금지하다, 금하다 except ~을 제외하고 exhibit 전시(물)

해설 사진 촬영 금지 여부를 묻는 부가의문문

(A) 유사 발음 오답. 질문의 photography과 부분적으로 발음이 동일한 photo를 이용한 오답.

(B) 정답. 이 박물관에서 사진 촬영이 금지인지 묻는 질문에 중앙 로비만 제외하고 금지라고 응답하므로 정답.

(C) 연상 단어 오답. 질문의 museum에서 연상 가능한 exhibit을 이용한 오답.

24

M-Au When did you reserve a table for our dinner with the investors?

W-Am (A) Actually, I haven't called yet.

(B) They're considering our experience.

(C) At the Martinville Steakhouse.

우리 투자자들과의 저녁 식사 예약을 언제 했습니까?
(A) 실은 아직 전화하지 않았어요.
(B) 그들은 우리의 경력을 고려하고 있어요.
(C) 마틴빌 스테이크하우스에서요.

어휘 reserve 예약하다 investor 투자자 consider 참작하다, 고려하다

해설 투자자들과의 저녁 식사 예약을 언제 했는지 묻는 When 의문문
(A) 정답. 투자자들과의 저녁 식사 예약을 언제 했는지 묻는 질문에 아직 전화를 안 했다고 응답하므로 정답.
(B) 질문과 상관없는 오답. 투자자들과의 저녁 식사 예약을 언제 했냐는 질문에 그들이 우리의 경력을 고려하고 있다는 응답은 문맥과 어울리지 않으므로 오답.
(C) 연상 단어 오답. 질문의 dinner에서 연상 가능한 Martinville Steakhouse를 이용한 오답.

25

M-Cn Should we announce who got the promotion?
W-Br (A) To fill the assistant manager position.
      (B) We'd better wait for Shawn.
      (C) You truly deserve it.

누가 승진했는지 발표해야 할까요?
(A) 부매니저 자리를 충원하려고요.
(B) 션을 기다리는 게 좋겠어요.
(C) 당신은 정말 자격이 있어요.

어휘 announce 발표하다 promotion 승진 fill a position 자리를 채우다, 직무를 맡다 assistant 보조의 had better ~하는 편이 낫다 truly 진심으로 deserve ~을 받을 만하다, ~해야 마땅하다

해설 승진자 발표 여부를 묻는 조동사 의문문
(A) 질문과 상관없는 오답. 이유를 묻는 Why 의문문에 어울리는 응답이므로 오답.
(B) 정답. 승진자를 발표해야 할지를 묻는 질문에 션이 올 때까지 기다리는 것이 낫다고 응답하므로 정답.
(C) 연상 단어 오답. 질문의 promotion에서 연상 가능한 deserve를 이용한 오답.

26

M-Au Is it better to post our job notice online or print it in the newspaper?
W-Br (A) Nobody seemed to notice.
      (B) I read it every morning.
      (C) The budget allows both.

우리 채용 공고를 온라인에 올리는 게 나을까요, 아니면 신문에 내는 게 나을까요?
(A) 아무도 눈치 못 챈 것 같던데요.
(B) 저는 그걸 매일 아침 읽습니다.
(C) 둘 다 하기에 예산이 충분합니다.

어휘 post 게시하다 print 싣다, 게재하다 notice 공지; 알아채다 budget 예산 allow ~을 고려하다[계산에 넣다]

해설 채용 공고를 어디에 올릴지를 묻는 선택의문문
(A) 단어 반복 오답. 질문의 notice를 반복한 오답
(B) 연상 단어 오답. 질문의 newspaper에서 연상 가능한 read를 이용한 오답.
(C) 정답. 채용 공고를 온라인에 올리는 게 나을지 신문에 내는 게 나을지 묻는 질문에 예산이 넉넉해 둘 다 가능하다고 응답하므로 정답.

27

W-Am I don't think all of the employees know how to clean up spills properly.
M-Cn (A) Yes, the lab is looking very clean.
      (B) Please find out what was in the container.
      (C) Then we'd better hold a training session.

엎지른 액체를 제대로 치우는 방법을 모르는 직원도 있는 것 같아요.
(A) 네, 실험실이 아주 깨끗해 보여요.
(B) 용기 안에 무엇이 있었는지 알아보세요.
(C) 그렇다면 교육을 실시하는 게 좋겠네요.

어휘 spill 흘린 액체, 엎지름 properly 제대로 lab 실험실(= laboratory) find out 알아보다 container 용기 hold 열다 training session 교육

해설 의견 제시의 평서문
(A) 단어 반복 오답. 질문의 clean을 반복한 오답.
(B) 연상 단어 오답. 질문의 clean up spills에서 연상 가능한 container를 이용한 오답.
(C) 정답. 엎지른 액체를 치우는 방법을 모르는 직원도 있다는 말에 대해 교육을 실시하자고 제안하고 있으므로 정답.

28

W-Br This dress would be perfect for the awards ceremony.
M-Au (A) Everyone had a great time.
      (B) Isn't it too formal?
      (C) I'll send you the mailing list.

이 드레스는 시상식 용으로 완벽할 것 같은데요.
(A) 모두들 즐거운 시간을 보냈습니다.
(B) 너무 격식을 차린 것 같지 않나요?
(C) 수취인 명부를 보내드리겠습니다.

어휘 awards ceremony 시상식 formal 격식을 차린 mailng list 우편물[이메일] 수신자 명단

해설 의견 제시의 평서문
(A) 연상 단어 오답. 질문의 ceremony에서 연상 가능한 great time을 이용한 오답.
(B) 정답. 이 드레스가 시상식 용으로 완벽할 것 같다는 의견에 너무 격식을 차려 입은 것 아니냐고 되물으며 부정적으로 응답하므로 정답.
(C) 질문과 상관없는 오답. 이 드레스가 수상식 용으로 완벽할 것 같다는 의견에 수취인 명부를 보내 주겠다는 대답은 문맥에 어울리지 않으므로 오답.

29

W-Br Would you like to attend a free yoga session on Saturday?
M-Cn (A) Sure, I'll give it a try.
      (B) To get in shape.
      (C) I prefer plain yogurt.

토요일에 무료 요가 강좌에 참석해 보실래요?

(A) **물론이죠. 한번 해 보죠.**
(B) 몸매를 유지하기 위해서요.
(C) 플레인 요거트가 더 좋아요.

어휘 attend 참석하다　session 수업 (시간), 강습회　give ~ a try ~를 한번 해 보다　get in shape 좋은 몸(매) 상태를 유지하다

해설 제안을 나타내는 의문문
(A) 정답. 무료 요가 강좌에 참석해 보라는 제안에 한번 해 보겠다고 응답하므로 정답.
(B) 질문과 상관없는 오답. 이유를 묻는 Why 의문문에 어울리는 응답이므로 오답.
(C) 유사 발음 오답. 질문의 yoga와 부분적으로 발음이 유사한 yogurt를 이용한 오답.

30

W-Am Why is the hallway window broken?
M-Cn (A) It's the first door on the left.
(B) Check with Tina about that.
(C) Joon-Hae, the head of Maintenance.

복도 창문이 왜 깨졌죠?
(A) 왼쪽 첫 번째 문입니다.
(B) 티나에게 확인해 보세요.
(C) 관리부 팀장인 준해 씨요.

어휘 hallway 복도　broken 깨진, 고장 난　check with ~에게 문의하다　head 장(長), 우두머리　maintenance 보수, 관리

해설 복도 창문에 금이 간 이유를 묻는 Why 의문문
(A) 연상 단어 오답. 질문의 hallway에서 연상 가능한 first door를 이용한 오답.
(B) 정답. 복도 창문이 깨진 이유를 묻는 질문에 티나에게 확인해 보라는 우회적인 응답을 통해 본인은 모른다는 사실을 나타내고 있으므로 정답.
(C) 질문과 상관없는 오답. 누구인지를 묻는 who 의문문에 어울리는 응답이므로 오답.

31

M-Au What's the password for getting into the database?
W-Am (A) Oh, I was going to ask you.
(B) Yes, that's the most recent one.
(C) For gathering company information.

데이터베이스 접속 비밀번호가 어떻게 되나요?
(A) 아, 제가 여쭤 보려던 건데요.
(B) 네. 그게 가장 최근 거예요.
(C) 기업 정보를 수집하기 위해서요.

어휘 get into ~에 들어가다　recent 최근의　gather 수집하다

해설 데이터베이스 접속 비밀번호를 묻는 What 의문문
(A) 정답. 데이터베이스 접속 비밀번호를 묻는 질문에 당신에게 물어보려고 했다고 답해 본인도 모른다는 사실을 우회적으로 나타내고 있으므로 정답.
(B) Yes/No 불가 오답. What 의문문에는 Yes/No 응답이 불가능하므로 오답.
(C) 유사 발음 오답. 질문의 getting과 부분적으로 발음이 유사한 gathering을 이용한 오답.

PART 3

32-34

W-Br Excuse me. **32I'm here to have an interview with Danielle Monroe at ten.** I noticed that your elevators are out of order. Are those the only ones in the building? **33Her office is on the top floor.**

M-Cn Don't worry, ma'am. You can take the service elevators, which are usually used for large deliveries. They're on the west side of the building. **34If you look at the map in the lobby, you'll see exactly how to get to them.**

W-Br That's very helpful. Thanks a lot. There's no way I could have walked up all those stairs.

여 실례합니다. 전 대니엘 먼로 씨와 10시에 면접이 있어 왔는데요. 근데 엘리베이터가 고장 나 있더군요. 건물에 그 엘리베이터들이 다인가요? 먼로 씨 사무실이 꼭대기 층에 있어요.

남 걱정하지 마세요. 보통 부피가 큰 배달물을 운반할 때 쓰는 업무용 엘리베이터를 이용하시면 됩니다. 건물 서쪽에 있습니다. 로비에 있는 약도를 보시면 정확히 가는 길을 확인할 수 있습니다.

여 유용한 정보네요. 정말 고맙습니다. 아무래도 제가 저 많은 계단을 다 올라가진 못했을 거예요.

어휘 notice 알아채다, 인지하다　out of order 고장 난　top 꼭대기의　service elevator 업무용[직원용] 엘리베이터　delivery 배달물　exactly 정확히　(There is) no way 절대로 아니다[안 되다]　walk up the stairs 계단을 오르다

32

Why did the woman visit the building?

(A) To conduct a survey
(B) To deliver some goods
(C) To attend an interview
(D) To perform an inspection

여자는 왜 그 건물에 갔는가?
(A) 설문 조사를 하기 위해
(B) 물건들을 배달하기 위해
(C) 면접에 참석하기 위해
(D) 점검하기 위해

어휘 conduct 실시하다　survey 설문 조사　goods 상품　attend 참석하다　perform 수행하다　inspection 점검, 시찰

해설 세부 사항 관련 – 여자가 빌딩에 방문한 이유

여자의 첫 번째 대사에서 대니엘 먼로 씨와 10시에 면접이 있어 왔다(I'm here to have an interview with Danielle Monroe at ten)고 했으므로 정답은 (C) 이다

▸▸ Paraphrasing　대화의 **I'm here to have an interview** → 정답의 **To attend an interview**

33

What does the woman say about Ms. Monroe's office?

(A) It is difficult to find.
(B) It is near the elevators.
(C) It is being renovated.
(D) It is on the highest floor.

여자는 먼로 씨 사무실에 대해 뭐라고 말하는가?
(A) 찾기 힘들다.
(B) 엘리베이터 근처다.
(C) 보수 중이다.
(D) 가장 높은 층에 있다.

어휘 renovate (건물, 가구 등을) 개조하다, 보수하다

해설 세부 사항 관련 – 여자가 사무실에 대해 말하는 것
여자의 첫 번째 대사에서 그녀의 사무실이 꼭대기 층에 있다(Her office is on the top floor)고 했으므로 정답은 (D)이다.

▶▶ Paraphrasing 대화의 the top floor
→ 정답의 the highest floor

34

What does the man recommend doing?

(A) Coming back later
(B) Waiting in the lobby
(C) Calling Ms. Monroe directly
(D) Checking a building map

남자는 무엇을 하라고 권하는가?
(A) 나중에 오기
(B) 로비에서 기다리기
(C) 먼로 씨에게 직접 전화하기
(D) 건물 약도 확인하기

어휘 directly 직접

해설 세부 사항 관련 – 남자가 하라고 권하는 것
남자의 첫 번째 대사에서 로비에 있는 약도를 보면(If you look at the map in the lobby) 정확히 가는 길을 알 수 있다(you'll see exactly how to get to them)고 했으므로 정답은 (D)이다.

▶▶ Paraphrasing 대화의 look at the map
→ 정답의 Checking a building map

35-37

W-Am Good afternoon. ³⁵I got a flyer in the mail promoting the opening of your business. It's perfect timing because I need to buy new cabinets for my kitchen.

M-Au Wonderful! These cabinets are currently on sale for thirty percent off. These are just for the standard sizes, though. ³⁶If you need custom cabinets, they would be full price.

W-Am ³⁶Oh, no! Really? I need custom ones because my kitchen is irregularly shaped. That's going to cost me a fortune.

M-Au Well, you don't have to pay the total all at once. ³⁷You can spread the cost over six monthly payments.

여 안녕하세요. 우편물로 개업을 알리는 전단지를 받았는데요. 타이밍이 딱 맞네요. 제가 주방에 새 수납장을 들여야 하거든요.

남 잘됐네요! 이 수납장들은 현재 30퍼센트 할인 중입니다. 근데 표준 사이즈들만 할인해요. 맞춤형 수납장이 필요하시다면 정가를 주셔야 합니다.

여 저런, 그래요? 저희 주방이 불규칙한 모양이라 맞춤형이 필요해요. 그건 돈이 많이 들 텐데요.

남 음, 총액을 한꺼번에 내지 않아도 됩니다. 6개월 할부로 액수를 나눠서 낼 수 있습니다.

어휘 flyer 전단지 promote 판촉하다 on sale 세일 중인 currently 현재 off 할인하여 standard 보통의 custom 맞춤의 full price 정가 irregularly shaped 모양이 불규칙적인 cost a fortune 엄청나게 비싸다 total 총액 (all) at once 한꺼번에 spread over ~에 걸쳐 나누다, 분산하다 monthly payment 할부

35

How did the woman find out about the business?

(A) By watching a commercial
(B) By visiting a Web site
(C) By receiving an advertising leaflet
(D) By talking to a friend

여자는 업체를 어떻게 알게 되었는가?
(A) 방송 광고를 보고
(B) 웹사이트를 방문해서
(C) 광고 전단지를 받고
(D) 친구에게 들어서

어휘 find out 알아내다 commercial (방송) 광고 leaflet (광고) 전단

해설 세부 사항 관련 – 여자가 업체를 알게 된 경로
여자의 첫 번째 대사에서 우편물로 개업을 알리는 전단지를 받았다(I got a flyer in the mail promoting the opening of your business)고 했으므로 정답은 (C)이다.

▶▶ Paraphrasing 대화의 got a flyer ~ promoting
→ 정답의 receiving an advertising leaflet

36

Why is the woman disappointed?

(A) The store is out of stock on some products.
(B) The discount does not apply to the item she wants.
(C) The delivery fee is higher than she expected.
(D) The store's promotional sale has ended.

여자가 실망한 이유는 무엇인가?
(A) 상점에 일부 제품들이 품절되어서
(B) 그녀가 원하는 제품에 할인이 적용되지 않아서
(C) 배송료가 예상보다 비싸서
(D) 상점 판촉행사가 끝나서

어휘 out of stock 품절[매진]이 되어 apply to ~에 적용되다 delivery fee 배송료 promotional 판촉의, 홍보의

해설 세부 사항 관련 – 여자가 실망하는 이유

남자의 첫 번째 대사에서 맞춤형 수납장은 정가를 지불해야 한다(If you need custom cabinets, they would be full price)고 했고 여자의 두 번째 대사에서 주방이 불규칙한 모양이라 맞춤형이 필요하다(I need custom ones because my kitchen is irregularly shaped)고 했으므로 정답은 (B)이다.

▸▸ Paraphrasing   대화의 full price
→ 정답의 The discount does not apply

37

What does the man tell the woman about?

(A) A product catalog
(B) A payment option
(C) A membership program
(D) A monthly sale

남자는 여자에게 무엇에 대해 말하는가?

(A) 상품 카탈로그
(B) 결제 방식
(C) 회원제 프로그램
(D) 월례 세일

어휘 monthly 매달의, 월례의

해설 세부 사항 관련 – 남자가 여자에게 말하는 것

남자의 두 번째 대사에서 6개월 할부로 액수를 나눠서 낼 수 있다(You can spread the cost over six monthly payments)고 했으므로 정답은 (B)이다.

38-40

M-Cn	Stacey, have you tried Florenti yet? It's the new Italian restaurant downtown.
W-Am	Not yet, but I'd like to. 38**Critics have been admiring it ever since it opened.** But I heard it's difficult to get a reservation.
M-Cn	39**Well, you're in luck. I have one for Friday at seven for five people**, but someone dropped out.
W-Am	Thanks! I'd love to join you!
M-Cn	I'm glad to hear that. I think you'll really enjoy it.
W-Am	I think so too. Should I just meet you there?
M-Cn	Actually, it's all people from the office and we're leaving from here. 40**So, I can take you with me in my car.**

남	스테이시, 플로렌티 아직 안 가 봤어? 시내에 새로 생긴 이탈리아 레스토랑 말이야.
여	아니, 아직. 근데 가고 싶어. **개점한 이후 평들이 아주 좋더라고.** 근데 예약하기 힘들다고 들었어.
남	아, 너 운 좋다. 내가 금요일 7시에 다섯 명 예약을 했는데, 누가 안 간대.

여	고마워! 나 같이 가고 싶어!
남	그렇다니 다행이네. 네가 정말 좋아할 거야.
여	나도 그럴 것 같아. 거기서 만나면 되는 거지?
남	실은 모두 사무실 사람들이고 여기서 출발할 거야. **그러니까 내가 차로 너를 태워 갈 수 있어.**

어휘 try 시험 삼아 해 보다 critics 평론가, 비평가 admire 감탄하다, 찬사를 보내다 get a reservation 예약하다 in luck 운이 좋아서, 운 좋게 drop out 빠지다, 떨어져 나가다

38

What does the woman mention about Florenti?

(A) It received excellent reviews.
(B) It is near the speakers' office.
(C) It takes phone reservations.
(D) It serves a variety of dishes.

여자가 플로렌티에 대해 언급하는 것은 무엇인가?

(A) 훌륭한 평을 받았다.
(B) 화자의 사무실 근처다.
(C) 전화 예약을 받는다.
(D) 다양한 요리를 제공한다.

어휘 review 평, 후기 serve (음식을) 제공하다 a variety of 다양한 ~

해설 세부 사항 관련 – 여자가 플로렌티에 대해 언급하는 것

여자의 첫 번째 대사에서 개점한 이후 평들이 아주 좋다(Critics have been admiring it ever since it opened)고 했으므로 정답은 (A)이다.

▸▸ Paraphrasing   대화의 Critics have been admiring it
→ 정답의 excellent reviews

39

Why does the man say, "someone dropped out"?

(A) To show disappointment
(B) To request some assistance
(C) To explain an error
(D) To extend an invitation

남자가 "누가 안 간대"라고 말하는 이유는 무엇인가?

(A) 실망감을 표하기 위해
(B) 도움을 요청하기 위해
(C) 오류를 설명하기 위해
(D) 초대하기 위해

어휘 disappointment 실망 request 요청하다 assistance 도움 explain 설명[해명]하다 extend an invitation 초대하다

해설 화자의 의도 파악 – 누가 안 간다는 말의 의미

여자의 첫 번째 대사에서 예약하기 힘들다고 들었다(I heard it's difficult to get a reservation)고 했고 남자의 두 번째 대사에서 여자가 운이 좋다(you're in luck)고 말하며 금요일 7시에 다섯 명 예약을 했는데(I have one for Friday at seven for five people), 누가 안 간다(someone dropped out)고 말했다. 즉 안 온다고 한 사람 대신 여자가 오면 된다는 의미이므로 정답은 (D)이다.

Test 9

40

What does the man offer to do on Friday?

(A) Introduce the woman to his colleagues
(B) Let the woman leave early
(C) Make a menu recommendation
(D) Give the woman a ride

남자는 금요일에 무엇을 해 주겠다고 하는가?

(A) 여자를 동료들에게 소개하기
(B) 여자를 일찍 퇴근시키기
(C) 메뉴 추천하기
(D) **여자를 차에 태워 주기**

어휘 colleague 동료 give a ride 태워 주다

해설 세부 사항 관련 – 남자가 금요일에 해 주겠다고 하는 것

남자의 네 번째 대사에서 차로 여자를 태워 갈 수 있다(I can take you with me in my car)고 말했으므로 정답은 (D)이다.

▸▸ **Paraphrasing** 대화의 **take you with me in my car** → 정답의 **Give the woman a ride**

41

What is the purpose of the man's call?

(A) To inquire about a tour
(B) To schedule a newspaper interview
(C) To purchase a ticket
(D) To check the museum's hours

남자가 전화한 목적은 무엇인가?

(A) **견학에 대해 문의하기 위해**
(B) 신문사 인터뷰 일정을 잡기 위해
(C) 티켓을 구매하기 위해
(D) 박물관 관람 시간을 확인하기 위해

어휘 inquire about ~에 대해 문의하다 purchase 구입하다

해설 전체 내용 관련 – 남자가 전화한 목적

남자의 첫 번째 대사에서 박물관에서 단체 견학을 제공한다고 신문에서 봤다(I recently read in the newspaper that you offer group tours of the museum)고 했고, 그것에 대해 좀 더 알고 싶다(I'd like to find out more about them)고 말했으므로 정답은 (A)이다.

▸▸ **Paraphrasing** 대화의 **find out more about it** → 정답의 **inquire about a tour**

41-43

M-Cn	Hello. **⁴¹I recently read in the newspaper that you offer group tours of the museum. I'd like to find out more about them.**
W-Br	Certainly. Our guide leads a group of up to twenty people on a private tour of the artwork. This is scheduled daily except for holidays.
M-Cn	**⁴²That's too bad. I'm planning to visit with just four people, so I guess that wouldn't be enough, would it?**
W-Br	Don't worry. That's no problem. We can combine your party with others. **⁴³How about I e-mail you a pamphlet regarding the activity so you can get all the details?**

남	여보세요. 요전에 신문에서 읽었는데요. 거기서 박물관 단체 견학을 해 주신다고요. 좀 더 자세하게 알고 싶어서요.
여	물론이죠. 저희 가이드는 최대 20명의 인원을 인솔해 맞춤형 작품 관람을 안내하고 있습니다. 공휴일을 제외하고 매일 견학 일정이 잡혀 있습니다.
남	너무 아쉽네요. 저는 4명이랑 가려고 하거든요. 그러면 인원이 충분치 않은 거죠, 그렇죠?
여	걱정하지 마세요. 괜찮습니다. 다른 일행과 합류하면 됩니다. 내용을 상세히 살펴보실 수 있도록 견학 안내 책자를 제가 이메일로 보내드리면 어떨까요?

어휘 find out 알아내다, 찾아내다 private (개인·집단) 전용의 artwork 예술 작품 daily 매일 except for ~을 제외하고는 combine A with B A를 B와 합하다 party 일행 pamphlet 팸플릿 regarding ~에 관한

42

What is the man concerned about?

(A) A security issue
(B) An increase in price
(C) A minimum group size
(D) An upcoming holiday closure

남자가 우려하는 것은 무엇인가?

(A) 보안 문제 (B) 가격 인상
(C) **단체 최소 인원** (D) 다가오는 공휴일 휴관

어휘 be concerned about ~에 대해 우려하다 security 보안, 치안 minimum 최소한의 upcoming 다가오는 closure 폐점

해설 세부 사항 관련 – 남자가 우려하는 것

남자의 두 번째 대사에서 4명이랑 가려고 하는데(I'm planning to visit with just four people), 그러면 인원이 충분치 않겠다(so I guess that wouldn't be enough)고 말했으므로 최소 인원에 못 미쳐 우려하고 있음을 알 수 있다. 따라서 정답은 (C)이다.

43

What does the woman offer to do?

(A) Book an appointment
(B) Offer a discount voucher
(C) Speak to a manager
(D) Provide additional information

여자는 무엇을 해 주겠다고 하는가?

(A) 예약하기 (B) 할인권 제공하기
(C) 매니저에게 말하기 (D) **추가 정보 제공하기**

어휘 book 예약하다 discount voucher 할인권, 할인 쿠폰 additional 추가의

해설 세부 사항 관련 – 여자가 제안하는 것

여자의 두 번째 대사에서 견학 안내 책자를 이메일로 보내드리면 어떨지(How about I e-mail you a pamphlet regarding the activity) 제안하고 있으므로 정답은 (D)이다.

▸▸ Paraphrasing 대화의 e-mail you a pamphlet
→ 정답의 Provide additional information

44-46

M-Au	Ms. Carson, is everything set up in the main conference room? **44Representatives from Estell International will arrive at two for the contract negotiations.**
W-Am	It's not quite ready yet. We didn't have enough chairs, so I brought in some metal folding chairs from the storage room. **45But those don't have any padding at all, and I'm worried that people who use them won't feel comfortable after sitting in them for hours.**
M-Au	How about we move some of the chairs from the employee lounge? **46Ask Mr. Aguilar to help you.** I know his team has carts they use for moving heavy objects when they're fixing things.
W-Am	Good idea. I'll do that right now.

남	카슨 씨, 주회의실 준비 다 됐나요? 에스텔 인터내셔널 직원들이 계약 협상을 위해 2시에 도착할 거예요.
여	아직 준비가 되지 않았습니다. 의자가 충분치 않아서 창고에서 접이식 철제 의자들을 좀 가지고 왔어요. 그런데 이 의자들에는 충전재가 전혀 없어서 이 의자를 사용하는 사람들이 몇 시간 앉아 있다 보면 불편할 것 같아 걱정입니다.
남	직원 휴게실에 있는 의자를 좀 옮겨 오는 게 어떨까요? 애귈라 씨에게 좀 도와달라고 하세요. 애귈라 씨 팀은 수리 작업용으로 무거운 물건 옮길 때 사용하는 카트가 있는 것으로 알아요.
여	좋은 생각이네요. 당장 그렇게 할게요.

어휘	set up 설치하다, 마련하다 representative 직원 contract 계약 negotiation 협상 metal 금속 folding chair 접이식 의자 storage room 창고 padding (푹신하게 하거나 형체를 잡기 위해 안에 대는) 충전재 not ~ at all 전혀 ~가 없는 comfortable 편안한 object 물건, 물체 fix 수리하다

44

What is the purpose of the meeting?

(A) To explain a policy
(B) To demonstrate a product
(C) To negotiate a contract
(D) To welcome new employees

회의의 목적은 무엇인가?

(A) 정책 설명하기
(B) 제품 시연하기
(C) 계약 협상하기
(D) 신입 직원 환영하기

어휘 policy 방침 demonstrate 시연하다, 보여주다 negotiate 협상하다

해설 전체 내용 관련 – 회의의 목적

남자의 첫 번째 대사에서 에스텔 인터내셔널 직원들이 계약 협상을 위해 2시에 도착한다(Representatives from Estell International will arrive at two for the contract negotiations)고 했으므로 정답은 (C)이다.

45

Why is the woman concerned about the meeting?

(A) Some attendees will be late.
(B) The agenda is not ready yet.
(C) Some guests might be uncomfortable.
(D) A conference room is too small.

여자가 회의에 대해 우려하는 이유는 무엇인가?

(A) 일부 참석자가 늦을 것이다.
(B) 의제가 아직 준비되지 않았다.
(C) 일부 손님들이 불편할 수도 있다.
(D) 회의실이 너무 작다.

어휘 attendee 참석자 agenda 의제 uncomfortable 불편한

해설 세부 사항 관련 – 여자가 우려하는 것

여자의 첫 번째 대사에서 의자들에는 충전재가 전혀 없어서(those don't have any padding at all) 이 의자를 사용하는 사람들이 몇 시간 앉아 있다 보면 불편하지 않을까 걱정이 된다(I'm worried that people who use them won't feel comfortable after sitting in them for hours)고 했으므로 정답은 (C)이다.

▸▸ Paraphrasing 대화의 won't feel comfortable
→ 정답의 uncomfortable

46

Who most likely is Mr. Aguilar?

(A) A furniture designer
(B) A potential client
(C) A moving company owner
(D) A maintenance worker

애귈라 씨는 누구이겠는가?

(A) 가구 디자이너
(B) 잠재 고객
(C) 이삿짐 센터 업주
(D) 시설 보수 직원

어휘 potential 잠재적인 client 고객 moving company 이삿짐 센터 maintenance 유지 보수

해설 세부 사항 관련 – 애귈라 씨의 신분

남자의 두 번째 대사에서 애귈라 씨에게 도움을 요청하라(Ask Mr. Aguilar to help you)면서 애귈라 씨 팀은 수리 작업용으로 무거운 물건을 옮길 때 사용하는 카트가 있는 것으로 안다(I know his team has carts they use for moving heavy objects when they're fixing things)고 했으므로 정답은 (D)이다.

▸▸ Paraphrasing 대화의 fixing things → 정답의 maintenance

47-49

> W-Br Good morning, Halim. Will you be around this afternoon? **47A representative from HT Electronics is going to demonstrate the features of the company's new 3D printer.**
>
> M-Cn I read about that on the company intranet. Yes, I'm planning on going. I think it's going to be really interesting. The activity will be held on site in our conference room, right?
>
> W-Br Actually, no. **48Since so many people wanted to come, our on-site facility just isn't large enough.** It'll be held at the Lakeland Convention Center instead. **49If you need a pass to park your car for free, just stop by my office.**
>
> M-Cn Thanks, but in that case, I think I'll just take the subway.

> 여 안녕하세요, 할림, 오늘 오후에 회사에 있죠? HT전자의 영업 직원이 신제품 3D 프린터의 기능들을 시연할 예정이에요.
>
> 남 회사 인트라넷에서 읽었어요. 네, 갈 거예요. 아주 재미있을 것 같아요. 우리 회의실에서 현장 시연 열리는 거 맞죠?
>
> 여 아뇨. 많은 사람들이 참석하고 싶어 하는데 회사 현장 설비는 그만큼 넓지 않아요. 대신 레이크랜드 컨벤션 센터에서 열릴 거예요. 무료 주차권이 필요하면 내 사무실에 들르세요.
>
> 남 고마워요. 하지만 거기서 열리는 거라면 그냥 지하철을 탈게요.

> 어휘 representative 외판원, 영업 직원 demonstrate 시연하다 feature 특징, 기능 on-site 현장에서[의] pass 출입증, 통행증 park 주차하다 for free 무료로 stop by 들르다

47

What are the speakers mainly discussing?

(A) A job interview
(B) A product demonstration
(C) A national conference
(D) A company policy

화자들은 주로 무엇에 대해 이야기하는가?
(A) 취업 면접
(B) 제품 시연
(C) 전국 회의
(D) 회사 정책

해설 전체 내용 관련 – 대화의 주제
여자의 첫 번째 대사에서 HT전자의 영업 직원이 신제품 3D 프린터의 기능들을 시연할 것(A representative from HT Electronics is going to demonstrate the features of the company's new 3D printer)이라고 말했으므로 정답은 (B)이다.

▸▸ Paraphrasing 대화의 **demonstrate the features of the company's new 3D printer**
→ 정답의 **A product demonstration**

48

What problem does the woman mention?

(A) A room is too small.
(B) Some guests have canceled.
(C) An activity is expensive.
(D) The wrong copies were made.

여자가 언급하는 문제는 무엇인가?
(A) 공간이 너무 협소하다.   (B) 취소한 손님들이 있다.
(C) 활동이 비싸다.   (D) 복사가 잘못되었다.

어휘 cancel 취소하다 expensive 비싼 make a copy 복사하다

해설 세부 사항 관련 – 여자가 언급하는 문제
여자의 두 번째 대사에서 많은 사람들이 참석하고 싶어 하는데 회사 현장 설비는 그만큼 넓지 않다(Since so many people wanted to come, our on-site facility just isn't large enough)고 말했으므로 정답은 (A)이다.

▸▸ Paraphrasing 대화의 **isn't large enough** → 정답의 **too small**

49

Why does the woman suggest that the man visit her office?

(A) To obtain a parking pass
(B) To sign up for a carpool
(C) To pick up a subway map
(D) To ask for driving directions

여자는 왜 남자에게 그녀의 사무실에 들르라고 하는가?
(A) 주차권을 얻기 위해
(B) 카풀을 신청하기 위해
(C) 지하철 노선도를 챙기기 위해
(D) 운전자용 약도를 요청하기 위해

어휘 obtain 획득하다, 얻다 parking pass 주차권 sign up for ~을 신청하다 directions 길 안내

해설 세부 사항 관련 – 남자가 여자의 사무실에 들러야 하는 이유
여자의 두 번째 대사에서 무료 주차권이 필요하면 사무실에 들르라(If you need a pass to park your car for free, just stop by my office)고 했으므로 정답은 (A)이다.

▸▸ Paraphrasing 대화의 **a pass to park your car**
→ 정답의 **a parking pass**

50-52 3인 대화

> M-Cn Hello. **50I just received my monthly invoice, and I noticed that I was charged eighty dollars instead of my usual rate of forty-five dollars.**
>
> W-Am **51I'm sorry, but this line is for reporting problems with a loss of Internet service.**
>
> M-Cn I didn't realize that. What's the number I need to call?
>
> W-Am I'll transfer you to our billing department.
>
> M-Cn All right, thanks.

W-Br	Good afternoon, how may I help you?
M-Cn	I'm calling about a problem with my September bill.
W-Br	I'm very sorry about that. Due to a computer error, the billing for all residential customers was incorrect. **⁵²We're issuing new invoices this week, so we'd appreciate your patience in waiting until you get the new one.**

남	안녕하세요. **이번 달 청구서를 받았는데요. 평소 내던 요금인 45달러가 아니고 80달러가 청구됐어요.**
여	**죄송합니다만 이 회선은 인터넷 서비스 불통 문제 신고 전용입니다.**
남	몰랐어요. 몇 번으로 걸어야 하나요?
여1	제가 청구서 발송과로 연결해 드리죠.
남	네, 고마워요.
여2	안녕하세요. 무엇을 도와드릴까요?
남	9월달 청구서 문제로 전화드립니다.
여2	정말 죄송합니다. 컴퓨터 오류로 가정용 인터넷 고객분들께 전부 잘못된 청구서가 나갔습니다. **저희가 이번 주에 새로 청구서를 발행하니 새 청구서를 수령하실 때까지 기다려 주시면 감사하겠습니다.**

어휘	invoice 송장, 청구서 charge 청구하다 rate 요금 report 신고하다 loss 상실, 손실 transfer (전화를) 바꿔 주다 billing 청구서 발부 residential 거주의, 주거의 incorrect 부정확한 issue 발행하다 appreciate 고마워하다 patience 인내

50
Why is the man calling?

(A) He had a loss of service.
(B) He wants to sign up as a customer.
(C) He was overcharged on his bill.
(D) He intends to cancel a contract.

남자가 전화한 이유는 무엇인가?
(A) 서비스가 끊겼다.
(B) 고객으로 등록하고 싶어한다.
(C) **청구서에 요금이 과다 청구되었다.**
(D) 약정을 해지하고자 한다.

어휘 sign up 가입[등록]하다 overcharge 과다 청구하다 intend to ~할 작정이다 cancel 취소하다 contract 계약

해설 전체 내용 관련 - 남자가 전화한 이유
남자의 첫 번째 대사에서 평소 내던 요금인 45달러가 아니고 80달러가 청구됐다(I was charged eighty dollars instead of my usual rate of forty-five dollars)고 했으므로 정답은 (C)이다.

▸▸ Paraphrasing 대화의 **charged eighty dollars instead of my usual rate of forty-five dollars** → 정답의 **overcharged**

51
Where do the women most likely work?

(A) At a power company
(B) At an Internet provider
(C) At a telephone company
(D) At a courier company

여자들은 어디에서 일하겠는가?
(A) 전력 회사
(B) **인터넷 서비스 업체**
(C) 전화 회사
(D) 택배 회사

어휘 provider (인터넷 접속) 서비스 업체 courier 운반원, 택배 기사

해설 전체 내용 관련 - 여자들의 근무지
첫 번째 여자의 첫 번째 대사에서 이 회선은 인터넷 서비스 불통 문제 신고 전용(this line is for reporting problems with a loss of Internet service)이라고 했으므로 정답은 (B)이다.

▸▸ Paraphrasing 대화의 **Internet service** → 정답의 **Internet provider**

52
What is the man asked to do?

(A) Provide a customer number
(B) Wait for a new document
(C) Hold the line
(D) Verify his residential address

남자는 무엇을 해 달라는 요청을 받는가?
(A) 고객 번호 제공하기
(B) **새 서류 기다리기**
(C) 전화 끊지 않고 기다리기
(D) 집 주소 확인해 주기

해설 세부 사항 관련 - 남자가 요청 받는 것
두 번째 여자의 두 번째 대사에서 이번 주에 새로 청구서를 발행하니(We're issuing new invoices this week) 새 청구서를 수령할 때까지 기다려 달라(we'd appreciate your patience in waiting until you get the new one)고 했으므로 정답은 (B)이다.

53-55

W-Am	**⁵³Here's the final draft of our company's guide for employees. I've added a section about computer usage and changed the dress code to our most recent regulations.**
M-Au	This looks fantastic, Melissa. **⁵⁴I like how you added photos to each section.** It's a helpful way of summarizing the information.
W-Am	Thanks. I'm going to send the file to the printer and use the express service so that we have them done by Wednesday.
M-Au	All right. **⁵⁵Just make sure to request durable paper because we're going to be using these for a long time.**

여	여기 우리 회사의 직원 지침 최종안입니다. 제가 컴퓨터 사용에 대한 절을 추가했고 복장 규정도 최신 규정대로 수정했습니다.
남	훌륭해 보이네요, 멜리사. 각 절에 사진을 추가한 거 좋아요. 정보를 요약해서 유용하겠어요.
여	감사합니다. 인쇄소로 파일을 보내고 속달 서비스를 이용해서 수요일까지 완료될 수 있게 하겠습니다.
남	좋아요. 꼭 튼튼한 종이로 해 달라고 하세요. 오래 사용할 거니까요.

53

What does the woman say she has done?

(A) Updated an employee handbook
(B) Posted informational signs
(C) Trained some new employees
(D) Worked as a guide for guests

여자는 무엇을 했다고 말하는가?

(A) 직원 안내서를 개정했다
(B) 정보 표지판들을 게시했다
(C) 신입 사원들을 교육했다
(D) 내빈을 위한 가이드를 담당했다

어휘 update 갱신하다, 개정하다 post 게재하다, 게시하다

해설 세부 사항 관련 - 여자가 한 일
여자의 첫 번째 대사에서 회사의 직원 지침 최종안을 제출한다(Here's the final draft of our company's guide for employees)고 했고, 컴퓨터 사용에 대한 절을 추가했으며 복장 규정도 최신 규정대로 수정했다(I've added a section about computer usage and changed the dress code to our most recent regulations)고 했으므로 정답은 (A)이다.

▸▸ Paraphrasing 대화의 our company's guide for
employees
→ 정답의 an employee handbook

54

Why does the man praise the woman?

(A) She saved the company money.
(B) She completed a task early.
(C) She provided useful graphics.
(D) She worked extra hours.

남자는 왜 여자를 칭찬하는가?

(A) 회사 경비를 아꼈다.
(B) 과제를 조기 완료했다.
(C) 유용한 시각 자료를 제공했다.
(D) 초과 근무를 했다.

어휘 complete 완료하다 task 직무, 과업 graphic (그림, 사진 등) 시각
자료 extra 추가의

해설 세부 사항 관련 - 남자가 여자를 칭찬하는 이유
남자의 첫 번째 대사에서 각 절에 사진을 추가한 게 좋다(I like how you added photos to each section)고 했으므로 정답은 (C)이다.

▸▸ Paraphrasing 대화의 added photos
→ 정답의 provided useful graphics

55

What does the man suggest doing?

(A) Printing a document in color
(B) Requesting an express service
(C) Asking for a bulk discount
(D) Using long-lasting materials

남자가 무엇을 하라고 제안하는가?

(A) 컬러로 서류 출력하기
(B) 속달 서비스 요청하기
(C) 대량 구매 할인 요청하기
(D) 오래 가는 재질 사용하기

어휘 bulk (큰) 규모[양] long-lasting 오래 가는 material 재료, 소재

해설 세부 사항 관련 - 남자의 제안
남자의 두 번째 대사에서 꼭 튼튼한 종이로 해 달라고 하라(Just make sure to request durable paper)고 했으므로 정답은 (D)이다.

▸▸ Paraphrasing 대화의 durable paper
→ 정답의 long-lasting materials

56-58

M-Au	Hey, Yoon-Hee. **56, 57Is the application period still going for the open position on our bank's business loan team?**
W-Br	The last day was Friday. **57We've already started reviewing the applications.**
M-Au	That's a shame. A friend of mine just heard about the job and was interested in it. He has a lot of experience working in this field.
W-Br	Hmm… we could make an exception if he's highly qualified. **58Please give him my name and e-mail address so he can send me his résumé.**

남	저기, 윤희 씨. 우리 은행 기업대출팀 결원 충원은 아직 진행 중인가요?
여	금요일이 마감이었어요. 벌써 지원서를 검토하기 시작했어요.
남	아쉽네요. 내 친구가 그 구인 건에 대해 방금 듣고 관심을 보였거든요. 이 분야에 경험이 아주 많은 친구죠.
여	음… 자격이 충분하다면 예외로 할 수 있어요. 나한테 이력서 보낼 수 있도록 그 사람한테 내 이름과 이메일을 알려 줘요.

어휘 application 지원 period 기간 open 공석의 position
(일자리, 직위 loan 대출 review 검토하다 a shame
애석한[아쉬운] 일 field 분야 make an exception 예외로
하다, 특별 취급하다 qualified 자격을 갖춘 résumé 이력서

56

Where do the speakers work?

(A) At an accounting firm
(B) At a financial institution
(C) At a recruitment agency
(D) At a job training center

화자들은 어디에서 일하는가?

(A) 회계사무소
(B) 금융 기관
(C) 채용정보회사
(D) 직업교육 센터

어휘 accounting 회계 financial 금융의 recruitment 신규 모집, 채용 agency 대행사

해설 전체 내용 관련 – 화자들이 일하는 장소

남자의 첫 번째 대사에서 은행 기업대출팀 결원 충원은 아직 진행 중인지(Is the application period still going for the open position on our bank's business loan team)를 묻고 있으므로 정답은 (B)이다.

> ▸▸ Paraphrasing 대화의 **our bank's business loan team**
> → 정답의 **financial institution**

57

What does the woman mean when she says, "The last day was Friday"?

(A) A deadline has passed.
(B) A decision has been made.
(C) A meeting was held.
(D) A position has been filled.

여자가 "금요일이 마감이었어요"라고 말한 의미는 무엇인가?

(A) 기한이 지났다.
(B) 결정이 내려졌다.
(C) 회의가 열렸다.
(D) 그 직책이 충원됐다.

어휘 deadline 기한 pass 지나가다 fill 메우다

해설 화자의 의도 파악 – 금요일이 마감이었다는 말의 의미

인용문 앞에 나온 문장인 남자의 첫 번째 대사에서 은행 기업대출팀 결원 충원은 아직 진행 중인지(Is the application period still going for the open position on our bank's business loan team) 묻고 있고, 인용문 뒤에 나온 여자의 대사에서 벌써 지원서를 검토하기 시작했다(We've already started reviewing the applications)고 말했다. 따라서 금요일이 마지막 날이었다는 말은 금요일에 이미 지원서 접수가 마감되었다는 의미이므로 정답은 (A)이다.

> ▸▸ Paraphrasing 대화의 **The last day was Friday.**
> → 정답의 **A deadline has passed.**

58

What does the woman tell the man to do?

(A) Check a résumé for errors
(B) Share her contact details with a friend
(C) E-mail her a job description
(D) Provide a list of job candidates

여자는 남자에게 무엇을 하라고 하는가?

(A) 오류가 없는지 이력서 검토하기
(B) 자신의 연락처를 친구에게 제공하기
(C) 자신에게 이메일로 직무 설명 보내기
(D) 입사 지원자 명단 제공하기

어휘 share 공유하다 description 묘사, 기술 job description 직무 설명 job candidate 입사 지원자

해설 세부 사항 관련 – 여자의 요청

여자의 두 번째 대사에서 남자에게 자신의 이름과 이메일 주소를 친구에게 알려 주라(Please give him my name and e-mail address)고 했으므로 정답은 (B)이다.

> ▸▸ Paraphrasing 대화의 give him my name and e-mail address → 정답의 Share her contact details with a friend

59-61

W-Am	[59]Thank you for all your hard work in preparing for the safety inspection, Tony. We received the highest score ever—ninety-eight out of one hundred.
M-Au	I'm glad to hear that! But I can't really take the credit. [60]Junichi McCroy has been leading workshops so employees have ongoing practice with the equipment. I think the habits they've developed really helped us in the various categories of the inspection.
W-Am	Well, that just shows that the changes we've made around here are working. If you've got a minute now, could you gather the staff? [61]I'd like to tell them the good news.

여	안전 점검 준비하느라 애 쓰신 거 감사드려요, 토니. 저희는 100점 만점에 역대 최고점인 98점을 받았습니다.
남	반가운 소식이네요! 하지만 제게 공을 돌리면 안 됩니다. 직원들이 장비로 계속 실습할 수 있도록 주니치 맥크로이 씨가 워크숍을 이끌어 왔죠. 여기서 기른 습관들이 여러 검사 항목에서 큰 도움이 됐습니다.
여	바로 저희가 만들어 낸 변화가 효과를 거두고 있다는 증거죠. 잠깐 시간되면 직원들을 좀 모아 주시겠어요? 직원들에게 이 좋은 소식을 전하고 싶습니다.

어휘 prepare for ~을 준비하다 safety inspection 안전 점검 score 점수 take the credit 공(훈)을 인정 받다, 칭찬 받다 ongoing 지속적인 equipment 장비 develop a habit 습관을 들이다 various 다양한 category 범주 work (효과를) 낳다 gather 모으다 staff 직원

59

What is the conversation mainly about?

(A) An industry award
(B) An inspection result
(C) A business proposal
(D) A workforce expansion

대화의 주요 내용은 무엇인가?

(A) 업계 상
(B) 점검 결과
(C) 사업 제안
(D) 인력 확충

어휘 industry 산업 proposal 제안 workforce (한 조직 등의 전체) 직원, 인력 expansion 확장

Test 9

해설 　전체 내용 관련 – 대화의 주제

여자의 첫 번째 대사에서 안전 점검을 위한 준비를 열심히 해 줘서 감사하다(Thank you for all your hard work in preparing for the safety inspection)고 했고, 검사 결과가 좋았음(We received the highest score ever)을 알리고 있으므로 정답은 (B)이다.

60

According to the man, what did Mr. McCroy do?

(A) Held training sessions
(B) Issued a line of credit
(C) Purchased new equipment
(D) Hired some experts

남자에 따르면 맥크로이 씨는 무엇을 했는가?

(A) 직원 연수를 실시했다
(B) 융자를 제공했다
(C) 새 장비를 구입했다
(D) 전문가를 고용했다

어휘 　line of credit 융자 (상품)　expert 전문가

해설 　세부 사항 관련 – 맥크로이 씨가 한 일

남자의 첫 번째 대사에서 직원들이 장비로 계속 실습할 수 있도록 주니치 맥크로이 씨가 워크숍을 이끌었다(Junichi McCroy has been leading workshops so employees have ongoing practice with the equipment)고 했으므로 정답은 (A)이다.

61

What will the woman most likely do next?

(A) Contact a news agency
(B) Post information online
(C) Make an announcement
(D) Review some applications

여자는 다음으로 무엇을 하겠는가?

(A) 언론사에 연락하기
(B) 정보를 온라인에 올리기
(C) 발표하기
(D) 지원서 검토하기

어휘 　news agency 통신사, 언론사　post 게시하다　make an announcement 발표하다

해설 　세부 사항 관련 – 여자의 계획

여자의 두 번째 대사에서 직원들에게 이 좋은 소식을 전하고 싶다(I'd like to tell them the good news)고 했으므로 정답은 (C)이다.

> ▸▸ Paraphrasing 　대화의 tell them the good news
> → 정답의 Make an announcement

62-64 대화 + 표지판

W-Br　Welcome to DLT Bike Rentals. How can I help you?

M-Au　Hi. It's my first time here, and I'd like to rent a bike. But, uh, do I need any kind of reservation?

W-Br　No. **62In fact, no reservations are ever taken here.** We rent bikes on a first-come, first-served basis—and we have some available today. Our rates are listed on that sign there.

M-Au　Oh, terrific. Hmm... Well, it's a great day for cycling. **63So the six-hour rental would be best.** I'll pay cash.

W-Br　Great. I'll show you to the bike—it's out in the parking area. **64Also, here's a free map that shows the city's bike trails in detail.**

여 　DLT 자전거 대여점에 오신 걸 환영합니다. 무엇을 도와드릴까요?
남 　안녕하세요. 여기 처음 와 보는데요. 자전거를 대여하고 싶어요. 예약이라도 해야 하나요?
여 　아니오. 사실, 저희는 예약을 받지 않습니다. 저희는 선착순으로 자전거를 대여하거든요. 오늘 몇 대 남아 있네요. 이용 요금은 저기 표지판에 나와 있습니다.
남 　아, 좋네요. 음, 오늘은 자전거 타기 좋은 날이라서요. 6시간 대여가 제일 좋을 것 같네요. 저 현금으로 계산할게요.
여 　좋습니다. 제가 자전거까지 안내해 드릴게요. 바깥 주차장에 있거든요. 그리고 이건 시내 자전거 도로를 상세하게 알려 주는 무료 지도예요.

어휘 　reservation 예약　on a first-come-first-served basis 선착순으로　available 이용할 수 있는　rate 요금　list 목록에 올리다　sign 표지판　rental 대여　parking area 주차장　bike trail 자전거 도로　in detail 상세하게

DLT Bike Rentals

Our rental rates are:	
3 hours	$12
636 hours	$20
1 day	$30
2 days	$45

DLT 자전거 대여점

대여 요금:	
3시간	12달러
6시간	20달러
1일	30달러
2일	45달러

어휘 　rental rate 대여료

62

What does the woman say about DLT Bike Rentals?

(A) It has more than one rental office.
(B) It is in its first month of business.
(C) It also purchases used bicycles.
(D) It does not accept reservations.

여자가 DLT 자전거 대여점에 대해 언급한 것은 무엇인가?

(A) 대여소가 하나 이상 있다.
(B) 영업한 지 한 달이 안됐다.
(C) 중고 자전거도 구매한다.
(D) 예약을 받지 않는다.

어휘 　business 영업　purchase 구매하다　used 중고의　accept 받다, 수용하다

해설 세부 사항 관련 – 여자가 DLT 자전거 대여점에 대해 말하는 것

여자의 두 번째 대사에서 여기선 예약을 받지 않는다(no reservations are ever taken here)고 했으므로 정답은 (D)이다.

> ▸▸ Paraphrasing 대화의 **no reservations are ever taken**
> → 정답의 **does not accept reservations**

63

Look at the graphic. How much will the man probably pay for a rental?

(A) $12
(B) $20
(C) $30
(D) $45

시각 정보에 의하면, 남자는 대여 요금으로 얼마를 낼 것인가?

(A) 12달러   (B) 20달러
(C) 30달러   (D) 45달러

해설 시각 정보 연계 – 대여 요금으로 남자가 낼 돈

남자의 두 번째 대사에서 6시간 대여가 제일 좋을 것 같다(the six-hour rental would be best)고 말했다. 시각 정보에 따르면 6시간 대여는 20달러 이므로 정답은 (B)이다.

64

What does the woman give the man?

(A) A bicycle lock
(B) A loyalty card
(C) A guide map
(D) A parking voucher

여자는 남자에게 무엇을 주는가?

(A) 자전거 자물쇠   (B) 고객 카드
(C) 안내 지도   (D) 주차권

어휘 lock 자물쇠 loyalty card 고객 카드 parking 주차 voucher 이용권, 쿠폰

해설 세부 사항 관련 – 여자가 남자에게 주는 것

여자의 세 번째 대사에서 시내 자전거 도로를 자세하게 알려 주는 무료 지도를 주겠다(here's a free map that shows the city's bike trails in detail)고 했으므로 정답은 (C)이다.

> ▸▸ Paraphrasing 대화의 **a free map that shows the city's bike trails** → 정답의 **A guide map**

65-67 대화 + 그림

W-Am Hello. I ordered a coffee maker from your online store about two weeks ago. ⁶⁵**The courier dropped it off yesterday, but when I opened the box this morning, I noticed a problem.**

M-Cn I'm sorry for the inconvenience, ma'am. Could you tell me what happened?

W-Am It looks like it wasn't handled very carefully while in transit. ⁶⁶**There's a big crack in the brew basket.**

M-Cn ⁶⁷**Well, unfortunately, we can't send you just one component, so we'll replace the whole machine for you.** I'll send a new one by express mail today.

W-Am Oh, thank you! What should I do with the damaged device?

M-Cn You can send it back in the box that will be provided.

여 안녕하세요. 한 2주 전에 귀사 온라인몰에서 커피메이커를 주문했는데요. 택배 기사가 어제 배달을 했는데 오늘 아침 박스를 열어 보니 문제가 있더라고요.

남 불편을 끼쳐드려 죄송합니다. 무슨 문제인지 말씀해 주시겠어요?

여 배송 중 취급에 주의하지 않은 것 같아요. 추출 용기에 큰 금이 나 있습니다.

남 아쉽지만 저희는 부품 하나만 보내 드리진 못하고요. 기기 전체를 교환해 드릴게요. 오늘 속달로 신품을 보내드리겠습니다.

여 감사합니다. 그럼 이 손상된 기기는 어떻게 할까요?

남 보내 드리는 상자에 넣어서 보내 주시면 됩니다.

어휘 courier 택배기사 drop off 배달하다 notice 알아차리다 inconvenience 불편 handle 다루다, 취급하다 in transit 배송 중, 이동 중 crack (갈라져 생긴) 금 brew (커피나 차를) 만들다, 우려내다 component 구성요소, 부품 replace 교체하다 by express mail 속달로 damaged 손상된 device 기기

어휘 protective 보호하는 lid 뚜껑 pitcher 주전자 base 바닥

65

When was the device delivered to the woman?

(A) This morning
(B) Yesterday
(C) A few days ago
(D) Two weeks ago

기기는 언제 여자에게 배달되었는가?

(A) 오늘 아침   (B) 어제
(C) 며칠 전   (D) 2주 전

해설   세부 사항 관련 - 기기가 여자에게 배달된 때

여자의 첫 번째 대사에서 택배 기사가 어제 배달했다(The courier dropped it off yesterday)고 했으므로 정답은 (B)이다.

66

Look at the graphic. What component did the woman have a problem with?

(A) B314
(B) E984
(C) R586
(D) C520

시각 정보에 의하면, 여자가 문제 삼은 부품은 무엇인가?

(A) B314   **(B) E984**
(C) R586   (D) C520

해설   시각 정보 연계 - 여자가 문제 삼은 부품

여자의 두 번째 대사에서 추출 용기에 큰 금이 나 있다(There's a big crack in the brew basket)고 했고, 시각 정보에 따르면 추출 용기는 Brew Basket Item #E984이므로 정답은 (B)이다.

67

What does the man say he will do?

(A) Send a replacement part
(B) Give the woman a refund
(C) Exchange the entire item
(D) Contact a local store

남자는 무엇을 하겠다고 말하는가?

(A) 대체 부품 보내기   (B) 여자에게 환불해 주기
(C) 물품 전체를 교환해 주기   (D) 지역 매장에 연락하기

어휘   replacement 대체, 교체   part 부품   give a refund 환불하다   exchange 교환하다   entire 전체의   local 지역의

해설   세부 사항 관련 - 남자의 계획

남자의 두 번째 대사에서 부품 하나만 보낼 수 없으므로(we can't send you just one component) 기기 전체를 교환해 주겠다(we'll replace the whole machine for you)고 했으므로 정답은 (C)이다.

> ▶▶ Paraphrasing   대화의 replace the whole machine
> → 정답의 Exchange the entire item

68-70 대화 + 차트

M-Au   Hi, Keesha. **68Could you cover the International Summit on the Environment on March 10 in Berlin?** Jerry Mitchell was supposed to do it, but he can't go now.

W-Br   Sure. I'm almost done with my transportation safety article. But... uh... the summit seems like a two-person job, don't you think?

M-Au   Yes. **69That's why I've asked Pavit Chanda to join you. We've decided to cancel the other article he was assigned.**

W-Br   All right, then I'll set up a meeting with Pavit for sometime next week.

M-Au   Perfect. **70And could you please e-mail me a scanned image of your passport so I can book the ticket?**

W-Br   Sure. **70I'll do that tomorrow morning.**

남   안녕하세요, 키샤. 3월 10일 베를린에서 열리는 국제환경정상회담을 취재해 줄 수 있나요? 제리 미첼이 하기로 했는데 지금 갈 수가 없어요.

여   네, 제 교통 안전 기사를 거의 끝냈어요. 그런데 어 … 정상회담은 두 사람이 해야 할 것 같은데, 그렇게 생각하지 않으세요?

남   맞아요. 그래서 패빗 챈다에게 합류하라고 부탁했답니다. 그한테 배정했던 다른 기사는 취소하기로 결정했어요.

여   좋습니다. 그럼 다음 주 중으로 패빗과 회의를 잡죠.

남   아주 좋습니다. 그리고 항공권을 예매하려고 하니 여권을 스캔해서 이메일로 저한테 보내 주실래요?

여   네, 내일 아침에 해 드리겠습니다.

어휘   cover 취재하다   summit 정상회담   be supposed to ~하기로 되어 있다, ~해야 한다   be done with ~을 다 처리하다   transportation 교통, 운송   article 기사   assign 할당하다, 배정하다   book 예약하다

Current Writing Assignments

Jerry Mitchell	"Fashion Trends for Professionals"
Misa Kure	"Proposed Immigration Changes"
Keesha Gibbs	"Domestic Transportation Safety"
69Pavit Chanda	"The Power of Manners"

현재 배당 기사

제리 미첼	"전문직을 위한 패션 동향"
미사 큐어	"이민법 개정안"
키샤 깁스	"국내 교통 안전"
패빗 챈다	**"매너의 힘"**

어휘   assignment 배정, 배당   trend 동향, 추세   professional 전문 직업인, 전문직 종사자   proposed 제안된   immigration 이민   domestic 국내의   manners 매너, 예의

68

What kind of event is taking place in March?

(A) A company's grand opening
(B) A political debate
(C) An environmental conference
(D) A career fair

3월에 어떤 종류의 행사가 열리는가?

(A) 회사의 개업   (B) 정치 토론
(C) 환경 회의   (D) 취업 박람회

어휘 grand opening 개업, 개점 political 정치의 debate 토론
environmental 환경의 career fair 취업 박람회

해설 세부 사항 관련 – 3월에 열릴 행사의 종류
남자의 첫 번째 대사에서 3월 10일 베를린에서 열리는 국제환경정상회담을 취재해 줄 수 있는지(Could you cover the International Summit on the Environment on March 10 in Berlin) 물었으므로 정답은 (C)이다.

▸▸ Paraphrasing 대화의 International Summit on the Environment
→ 정답의 An environmental conference

69
Look at the graphic. Which article has been canceled?

(A) "Fashion Trends for Professionals"
(B) "Proposed Immigration Changes"
(C) "Domestic Transportation Safety"
(D) "The Power of Manners"

시각 정보에 의하면, 어떤 기사가 취소되었는가?
(A) 전문직을 위한 패션 동향
(B) 이민법 개정안
(C) 국내 교통 안전
(D) 매너의 힘

해설 시각 정보 연계 – 취소된 기사
남자의 두 번째 대사에서 패빗 챈다에게 합류하라고 부탁했고(I've asked Pavit Chanda to join you) 그한테 배정했던 다른 기사는 취소하기로 결정했다(we've decided to cancel the other article he was assigned)고 했다. 시각 정보에 따르면 패빗 챈다에게 배정됐던 기사는 "매너의 힘"이므로 정답은 (D)이다.

70
What will the woman do tomorrow morning?

(A) Meet with a colleague
(B) Scan an itinerary
(C) Book a flight
(D) Send a file

여자는 내일 아침에 무엇을 할 것인가?
(A) 동료와 회의하기
(B) 여행 일정 스캔하기
(C) 비행기 예약하기
(D) 파일 보내기

어휘 itinerary 여행 일정표

해설 세부 사항 관련 – 여자가 내일 아침에 할 일
남자의 세 번째 대사에서 항공권을 예매하려고 하니 여자에게 여권을 스캔해서 이메일로 보내 달라고(could you please e-mail me a scanned image of your passport so I can book the ticket) 하자 여자는 내일 아침에 하겠다(I'll do that tomorrow morning)고 말했으므로 정답은 (D)이다.

▸▸ Paraphrasing 대화의 e-mail me a scanned image
→ 정답의 Send a file

PART 4

71-73 전화 메시지

> W-Br Hi, 71**this message is for Marilyn Walpole. This is Cindy from the Ace Clinic. 71I'm calling about your dog, let's see, um… a five-year-old bulldog.** You said it seemed to be very low on energy. 72**Well, I'm afraid we won't be able to keep the appointment we made for tomorrow.** The veterinarian has to go out of town unexpectedly. 73**The issue seems rather urgent, so I think you should go to our other branch on Seneca Street, right across from Robinson University.** It should be easy to get a booking there.

> 안녕하세요. 메릴린 월폴 씨에게 전하는 메시지입니다. 저는 에이스 클리닉의 신디라고 합니다. 고객님의 개, 어… 5살 불독 때문에 전화드렸습니다. 개가 기운이 많이 없어 보인다고 말씀하셨는데요. 죄송하지만 내일로 잡힌 진료는 어려울 것 같습니다. 수의사 선생님이 갑자기 출장을 가셔야 해서요. 문제가 상당히 위급한 것 같으니 세네카 가에 있는 다른 지점으로 가셔야 할 것 같습니다. 로빈슨대학 바로 건너편에 있어요. 거기 예약 잡기는 쉬울 거예요.

> 어휘 appointment (진료) 예약 veterinarian 수의사 go out of town (출장 등으로) 도시를 떠나다 unexpectedly 뜻밖에, 갑자기 rather 꽤 urgent 위급한 branch 지점 booking 예약

71
Who most likely is Ms. Walpole?

(A) A professor
(B) A medical patient
(C) A pet owner
(D) A veterinarian

월폴 씨는 누구이겠는가?
(A) 교수
(B) 환자
(C) 반려동물 주인
(D) 수의사

어휘 medical 의료의 patient 환자 pet 반려동물

해설 전체 내용 관련 – 월폴 씨의 신분
지문 초반부에서 월폴 씨에게 메시지를 남긴다(this message is for Marilyn Walpole)고 하며 당신의 개 때문에 전화했다(I'm calling about your dog)고 말했으므로 정답은 (C)이다.

72
What does the speaker tell Ms. Walpole about?

(A) An increase in fees
(B) An appointment cancellation
(C) A change in policy
(D) A business relocation

Test 9

화자는 월풀 씨에게 무엇에 대해 이야기하는가?

(A) 수수료 인상 　　　　　(B) 예약 취소
(C) 정책 변경 　　　　　　(D) 회사 이전

어휘　increase in ~의 인상, 증가　fee 수수료　cancellation 취소
　　　policy 방침　relocation 이주, 이전

해설　세부 사항 관련 – 월풀 씨에게 말한 것

지문 중반부에서 죄송하지만 내일로 잡힌 진료는 어려울 것 같다(I'm afraid we won't be able to keep the appointment we made for tomorrow)고 했으므로 정답은 (B)이다.

> ▸▸ Paraphrasing　지문의 won't be able to keep the appointment
> 　　　　　　　　　→ 정답의 An appointment cancellation

73

What does the speaker suggest doing?

(A) Calling back another day
(B) Visiting a different site
(C) Using a side entrance
(D) Checking information online

화자는 무엇을 하라고 제안하는가?

(A) 다른 날 다시 전화하기
(B) 다른 곳 방문하기
(C) 옆문 이용하기
(D) 온라인으로 정보 확인하기

어휘　site 장소, 위치　entrance 입구

해설　세부 사항 관련 – 화자의 제안

지문 후반부에서 문제가 상당히 급한 것 같으니(the issue seems rather urgent) 로빈슨대학 바로 건너편에 있는 세네카 가에 있는 다른 지점으로 가야 할 것 같다(I think you should go to our other branch on Seneca Street, right across from Robinson University)고 했으므로 정답은 (B)이다.

> ▸▸ Paraphrasing　지문의 go to our other branch
> 　　　　　　　　　→ 정답의 Visiting a different site

74-76 방송

> M-Cn You're listening to Flash Radio, the station that brings you news on the local stories that matter to you most. **74This week, the city announced plans to bring the historic Ingram Cathedral back to its original condition.** Crumbling walls will be replaced, and windows and other fixtures will be fixed. Improvements will also be made to its extensive gardens. **75Community members can help support the work by visiting www.ingramcathedral.org and making a financial contribution. 76To tell us more about the project, I've got Mayor Katrina Thomas here in the studio today. Welcome, Ms. Thomas.**

여러분께서는 지금 플래시 라디오를 듣고 계십니다. 여러분께 가장 중요한 지역 이야기를 담은 소식을 전해드리는 채널입니다. **이번 주 시 당국은 역사적으로 중요한 잉그램 성당을 본래 상태로 복원한다는 계획을 발표했습니다.** 허물어지는 벽들은 교체되고 창문과 기타 설비들도 수리될 것입니다. 넓은 정원들도 개선될 것입니다. **지역사회 구성원은 www.ingramcathedral.org를 방문해 성금을 기부함으로써 복원 작업을 지원할 수 있습니다. 프로젝트에 대한 더 자세한 이야기를 해 주시기 위해 오늘 카트리나 토마스 시장님을 스튜디오에 모셨습니다. 토마스 시장님, 어서 오세요.**

어휘　local 지역의　matter 중요하다, 문제가 되다　announce 발표하다　historic 역사적으로 중요한, 역사적인　bring back to ~으로 회복시키다　original 원래의　condition 상태　crumble 부서지다, 무너지다　replace 교체하다　fixture 설치물, 설비　fix 고치다　make improvements 개선하다　extensive 넓은, 광대한　support 지원하다　financial 재정의　contribution 기부, 기증　mayor 시장

74

What is the broadcast about?

(A) A community picnic
(B) A garden festival
(C) A local election
(D) A building repair project

무엇에 대한 방송인가?

(A) 지역 공동체 야유회
(B) 가든 축제
(C) 지역 선거
(D) 건물 보수 프로젝트

해설　전체 내용 관련 – 방송의 주제

지문 초반부에서 시 당국이 역사적으로 중요한 잉그램 성당을 본래의 상태로 복원한다는 계획을 발표했다(the city announced plans to bring the historic Ingram Cathedral back to its original condition)고 했으므로 정답은 (D)이다.

> ▸▸ Paraphrasing　지문의 bring the historic Ingram Cathedral back to its original condition
> 　　　　　　　　　→ 정답의 A building repair project

75

According to the speaker, what can listeners do on the Web site?

(A) Check a schedule
(B) Purchase a ticket
(C) Make a donation
(D) View some photos

화자에 따르면 청취자들은 웹사이트에서 무엇을 할 수 있는가?

(A) 일정 확인
(B) 티켓 구매
(C) 기부하기
(D) 사진 보기

어휘　purchase 구매하다　donation 기부　view 보다

해설　세부 사항 관련 – 청취자들이 웹사이트에서 할 수 있는 것

지문 중반부에서 지역 사회 구성원들이 www.ingramcathedral.org를 방문해 성금을 기부함으로써 복원 작업을 지원할 수 있다(Community members can help support the work by visiting www.ingramcathedral.org and making a financial contribution)고 했으므로 정답은 (C)이다.

> ▸▸ Paraphrasing　지문의 making a financial contribution
> → 정답의 Make a donation

76

Who will the speaker interview next?

(A) A city official
(B) A landscape architect
(C) A financial expert
(D) An award winner

화자는 다음으로 누구를 인터뷰하는가?

(A) 시 당국자
(B) 조경사
(C) 재무 전문가
(D) 수상자

어휘　official 관리, 공무원　landscape 풍경, 조경　architect 설계자, 건축가　expert 전문가

해설　세부 사항 관련 – 화자가 다음으로 인터뷰할 사람

지문 후반부에서 프로젝트에 대한 더 자세한 이야기를 위해(To tell us more about the project) 오늘 카트리나 토마스 시장님을 스튜디오에 모셨다(I've got Mayor Katrina Thomas here in the studio today)고 했고, 환영한다(Welcome, Ms. Thomas)고 했으므로 정답은 (A)이다.

> ▸▸ Paraphrasing　지문의 Mayor Katrina Thomas
> → 정답의 A city official

77-79 전화 메시지

> W-Am　Hi, this message is for Dustin Choo. This is Laura from Swanson's. **⁷⁷You requested that we call you when we got more of our Deka brand washing machines back in stock.** Well, they've just been delivered this morning. We can't hold one for you, so you'll have to visit the store in person. **⁷⁸We're open from 9 A.M. to 8 P.M. on weekends and 10 A.M. to 7 P.M. on weekends. ⁷⁹I highly recommend that you stop by tomorrow, as it's the first day of our anniversary sale and we're sure to still have this item in stock.**

안녕하세요. 더스틴 추 씨에게 남기는 메시지입니다. 스완슨에서 일하는 로라입니다. 저희 데카 브랜드 세탁기들이 더 입고되면 전화 달라고 요청하셨는데요. 오늘 아침에 막 배송됐습니다. 밀러 씨를 위해 하나를 따로 남겨 둘 수 없으니 직접 매장에 나오셔야 합니다. 저희는 평일 오전 9시에서 오후 8시, 주말에는 오전 10시부터 오후 7시까지 영업합니다. 내일 방문하시기를 적극 권해드려요. 저희 기념일 할인 첫날이라서 그때까지는 분명 제품이 남아 있을 겁니다.

어휘　washing machine 세탁기　in stock 재고가 있는, 비축되어 in person 몸소, 직접　stop by 들르다　anniversary 기념일　be sure to 반드시 ~하다

77

Where does the speaker most likely work?

(A) At a repair shop
(B) At a courier service
(C) At an appliance store
(D) At a clothing shop

화자는 어디에서 일하겠는가?

(A) 수리점　　　　　　　(B) 택배 회사
(C) 가전 매장　　　　　(D) 의류 매장

어휘　repair 수리　courier 택배　appliance (가정용) 기기

해설　전체 내용 관련 – 화자가 일하는 장소

지문 초반부에서 청자는 데카 브랜드 세탁기들이 더 입고되면 전화 달라고 요청했다(You requested that we call you when we got more of our Deka brand washing machines back in stock)고 말했으므로 정답은 (C)이다.

> ▸▸ Paraphrasing　지문의 washing machines
> → 정답의 appliance

78

When does the business close on weekdays?

(A) At 7 P.M.
(B) At 8 P.M.
(C) At 9 P.M.
(D) At 10 P.M.

평일 폐점 시간은 언제인가?

(A) 오후 7시　　　　　　**(B) 오후 8시**
(C) 오후 9시　　　　　　(D) 오후 10시

해설　세부 사항 관련 – 평일 폐점 시간

지문 중반부에서 평일에는 오전 9시에서 오후 8시까지 영업한다(We're open from 9 A.M. to 8 P.M. on weekdays)고 했으므로 정답은 (B)이다.

79

According to the speaker, what will happen tomorrow?

(A) A service will be free.
(B) A discount promotion will begin.
(C) A delivery will be made.
(D) A new brand will be introduced.

화자에 따르면 내일은 어떤 일이 있는가?

(A) 서비스가 무료이다.　　**(B) 할인 행사가 시작된다.**
(C) 배송이 된다.　　　　　(D) 신규 브랜드가 출시된다.

어휘　discount 할인　promotion 판촉, 홍보 (활동)　introduce 소개하다

해설　세부 사항 관련 – 내일 있을 일

마지막 문장에서 내일 방문할 것을 적극 권하며(I highly recommend that you stop by tomorrow) 기념일 할인 첫날이라 그때까지는 분명 제품이 남아 있을 것(as it's the first day of our anniversary sale and we're sure to still have this item in stock)이라고 말했으므로 정답은 (B)이다.

> ▸▸ Paraphrasing　지문의 the first day of our anniversary sale
> → 정답의 A discount promotion will begin.

Test 9

80-82 담화

M-Au Ladies and gentlemen, we're glad you could be here tonight so that we could show our appreciation for your hard work. **80Without unpaid workers like you, we would never be able to complete so many worthwhile projects for our town.** You truly help Marysville reach its full potential. **81Don't forget to provide your address on the sign-up sheets that are coming around so that we may mail you a thank-you gift.** **82And now, it's my pleasure to announce the winner of this year's Gold Star Award, which is given to someone who has gone the extra mile to help others.** Let's give a big round of applause for Eric Ortega!

신사 숙녀 여러분, 저희가 여러분의 노고에 감사를 표할 수 있도록 오늘 저녁 함께해 주셔서 매우 기쁩니다. 여러분처럼 무보수로 일하시는 분들이 없다면 저희는 우리 고장을 위한 그토록 많은 소중한 프로젝트들을 완수할 수 없을 것입니다. 여러분들은 메리스빌이 잠재력을 최대한으로 실현할 수 있도록 돕고 계십니다. 지금 돌고 있는 서명지에 잊지 마시고 주소를 꼭 기입해 주세요. 그래야 저희가 감사 선물을 보내드릴 수 있습니다. 자, 이제 남을 돕기 위해 남다른 노고를 기울이신 분에 돌아가는 올해 골드스타상 수상자를 발표하겠습니다. 에릭 오르테가 씨에게 큰 박수 부탁드립니다!

어휘 so that ~하도록 appreciation 감사, 존중 unpaid 보수를 받지 않는 complete 완수하다, 완결하다 worthwhile 가치 있는 truly 진정으로 reach one's full potential 잠재력을 최대한 발휘하다 sign-up 등록, 가입 sheet (종이) 한 장 mail (우편으로) 부치다 thank-you gift 감사의 선물 go the extra mile 특별히 애쓰다 a round of applause 한 차례의 박수(갈채)

80

Who most likely are the listeners?

(A) Potential clients
(B) New employees
(C) Medical professionals
(D) Community volunteers

청자들은 누구이겠는가?

(A) 잠재 고객
(B) 신입 직원
(C) 의료계 종사자
(D) **지역사회 자원봉사자**

어휘 potential 잠재적인 client 고객 medical 의료의 volunteer 자원봉사자

해설 전체 내용 관련 - 청자들의 신분
지문 초반부에서 여러분처럼 무보수로 일해주는 분들이 없다면 우리 고장을 위한 그토록 많은 소중한 프로젝트들을 완수할 수 없을 것(Without unpaid workers like you, we would never be able to complete so many worthwhile projects for our town)이라고 했으므로 정답은 (D)이다.

▸▸ Paraphrasing   지문의 unpaid workers like you
→ 정답의 volunteers

81

What are the listeners reminded to do?

(A) Provide their mailing information
(B) Sign up for a seminar
(C) Greet some special guests
(D) Vote for a prize winner

청자들은 무엇을 하라고 당부 받는가?

(A) **우편 정보 제공하기**
(B) 세미나 참가 신청하기
(C) 특별 손님 환영하기
(D) 수상자 선정 투표하기

어휘 mailing (우편물) 발송 sign up for ~에 신청[등록]하다 greet 맞이하다 vote for ~에 투표하다 winner 우승자

해설 세부 사항 관련 - 청자들이 당부받은 일
지문 중반부에 지금 돌고 있는 서명지에 잊지 말고 주소를 꼭 기입해 달라(Don't forget to provide your address on the sign-up sheets that are coming around)고 했으므로 정답은 (A)이다.

▸▸ Paraphrasing   지문의 your address
→ 정답의 mailing information

82

What will the speaker do next?

(A) Introduce a company
(B) Show a video
(C) Present an award
(D) Answer audience questions

화자는 다음으로 무엇을 할 것인가?

(A) 회사 소개하기
(B) 비디오 상영하기
(C) **시상하기**
(D) 관객 질문에 답하기

어휘 present 수여하다 audience 청중

해설 세부 사항 관련 - 화자가 다음에 할 일
지문 후반부에 남을 돕기 위해 남다른 노고를 기울인 분에게 돌아가는 올해 골드스타상 수상자를 발표하겠다(it's my pleasure to announce the winner of this year's Gold Star Award)고 말하고 있으므로 정답은 (C)이다.

▸▸ Paraphrasing   지문의 announce the winner of this year's Gold Star Award
→ 정답의 Present an award

83-85 전화 메시지

M-Cn Hi, this is Roy Baxter from office 203. **84I'm afraid I haven't moved my desk out of my office for the carpet cleaning tomorrow.** I only heard about it just now from one of my coworkers. **83You see, the problem is that I never saw the memo because I was out of town for an important conference all of last week.** **84I'm leaving the** office now for another meeting, so I hope you can take care of it for me. There will be no time tomorrow because, as you know, they'll be here first thing in the morning. 85I won't lock my office when I leave so that you can get in here. Thanks for the help. I owe you!

안녕하세요. 203호실 로이 백스터입니다. **죄송하지만 내일 있을 카펫 청소를 위해 책상을 사무실 밖으로 내놓질 못했어요.** 동료에게 지금 막 이야기를 들었어요. 문제는 제가 공지를 못 봤다는 거죠. 지난주 내내 중요한 회의 때문에 출장 중이었거든요. 또 회의가 있어서 지금 사무실을 나서는 참인데 이 일을 대신 좀 처리해 주셨으면 합니다. 내일도 시간이 없어요. 알다시피 **청소하시는 분들이 내일 아침 일찍 여기 올 테니까요.** 제 사무실에 들어오실 수 있도록 퇴근 시 사무실을 잠그지 않을게요. 도와주셔서 감사해요. 큰 신세 지네요!

어휘 coworker 동료 be out of town (출장 등으로) 도시를 떠나 있다 conference 회의 take care of (업무 등을) 처리하다, 돌보다 first thing in the morning 무엇보다도 먼저, 아침에 맨 먼저 lock 잠그다 so that ~하도록 get in 들어가다 owe 빚지다, 신세를 지다

83

According to the man, why didn't he read a memo?

(A) His assistant lost it.
(B) He was away on business.
(C) He had a busy month.
(D) His computer malfunctioned.

남자에 따르면 남자는 왜 공지를 읽지 않았는가?
(A) 비서가 분실해서 **(B) 출장을 가서**
(C) 한 달 동안 바빠서 (D) 컴퓨터가 고장 나서

어휘 assistant 비서, 보조 be away 부재 중이다 on business 업무차 malfunction 오작동하다

해설 세부 사항 관련 – 남자가 공지를 읽지 않은 이유
지문 초반부에서 화자가 공지를 못 봤고(I never saw the memo) 그 이유가 지난주 내내 중요한 회의로 출장 중이었기 때문(because I was out of town for an important conference all of last week)이라고 했으므로 정답은 (B)이다.

▸ Paraphrasing 지문의 out of town for an important conference → 정답의 away on business

84

What does the man mean when he says, "they'll be here first thing in the morning"?

(A) He will come to work earlier than usual.
(B) A meeting time should be changed.
(C) He is unable to move some furniture.
(D) A delivery will be made to the office.

남자가 "청소하시는 분들이 내일 아침 일찍 여기 올 테니까요"라고 할 때 의도하는 바는 무엇인가?
(A) 그가 평소보다 일찍 출근할 것이다.
(B) 회의 시간이 변경되어야 한다.
(C) 그는 가구를 옮길 수 없다.
(D) 사무실로 배달될 것이다.

어휘 earlier than usual 평소보다 일찍 be unable to ~를 할 수 없다

해설 화자의 의도 파악 – 청소하시는 분들이 내일 아침 일찍 여기 온다는 말의 의미
지문 초반에서 메모를 받지 못해서 내일 있을 카펫 청소를 위해 책상을 사무실 밖으로 내놓지 못했다(I'm afraid I haven't moved my desk out of my office for the carpet cleaning tomorrow)고 말했고, 지문 중반부에서 내일도 시간이 없다며(there will be no time tomorrow) 그 이유로 청소하시는 분들이 내일 아침 일찍 여기 와서 그렇다(they'll be here first thing in the morning)고 말하고 있다. 따라서 가구를 옮길 시간이 없다는 의미이므로 정답은 (C)이다.

85

What does the man plan to do?

(A) Approve overtime work
(B) Call one of his coworkers
(C) Leave a room unlocked
(D) Make a formal complaint

남자는 무엇을 할 계획인가?
(A) 초과 근무 승인하기
(B) 동료 중 한 명에게 전화하기
(C) 사무실을 잠그지 않고 퇴근하기
(D) 정식으로 불만 제기하기

어휘 approve 승인하다 overtime 초과 근무의, 시간 외의 unlock 자물쇠를 열다 make a complaint 불만을 제기하다 formal 정식의

해설 세부 사항 관련 – 남자의 계획
지문 후반부에서 사무실에 들어올 수 있게 퇴근 시 사무실 문을 잠그지 않을 것(I won't lock my office when I leave so that you can get in here)이라고 말했으므로 정답은 (C)이다.

▸ Paraphrasing 지문의 won't lock my office → 정답의 Leave a room unlocked

86-88 회의 발췌

W-Br Good afternoon, everyone. Before we open the store today, I just wanted to let you know how we did on our customer survey. 86As the people who assist customers when they're shopping at our computer store, your contributions are very important. The entire management team is pleased with the results. 87We had eight hundred forty-two positive comments for our store on this year's survey. You know what? The Forestlane location had about a hundred. You should all be very proud. 88At five o'clock this afternoon, we'll have donuts, coffee, and juice in the break room, so be sure to stop by.

안녕하세요. 여러분. 오늘 개점하기 전에 저희 매장 고객 설문조사 결과가 어떻게 나왔는지 알려드리고 싶습니다. **고객들이 우리 컴퓨터 매장에서 쇼핑을 할 때 도와주는 역할로서의 공헌은 매우 중요합니다.** 전 경영진은 결과에 만족하고 있습니다. 올해 설문조사에서 저희 매장에 대한 긍정적 의견이 842개에 달했습니다. 그런데 말이죠. **포레스트레인 매장은 100개 정도였습니다.** 모두들 자부심을 가지셔야 합니다. 오늘 오후 다섯 시에 휴게실에서 도넛, 커피, 주스가 제공되니 꼭 들러 주세요.

어휘 customer survey 고객 설문조사 assist 돕다
contribution 기여, 공헌 entire 전체의 management team 경영진 be pleased with ~에 기뻐하다 positive 긍정적인
comment 의견 location 위치, 장소 break room 휴게실 be sure to 꼭 ~하다 stop by 들르다

86
Who most likely is the speaker addressing?

(A) Computer programmers
(B) Sales clerks
(C) Accountants
(D) Department managers

화자는 누구를 대상으로 말하겠는가?

(A) 컴퓨터 프로그래머
(B) 판매 점원
(C) 회계사
(D) 부서장

어휘 address (누구에게 직접) 말을 하다 sales 판매의 clerk 점원
accountant 회계사 department 부서

해설 전체 내용 관련 – 청자의 신분
지문 초반부에서 청자들은 고객들이 매장에서 컴퓨터 쇼핑을 할 때 도움을 주는 사람(As the people who assist customers when they're shopping at our computer store)이라고 말했으므로 정답은 (B)이다.

▸▸ Paraphrasing 지문의 the people who assist customers when they're shopping
→ 정답의 sales clerks

87
Why does the woman say, "The Forestlane location had about a hundred"?

(A) To update an inventory list
(B) To correct a misunderstanding
(C) To emphasize an achievement
(D) To compare recruitment drives

여자가 "포레스트레인 매장은 100개 정도였습니다"라고 말한 이유는 무엇인가?

(A) 재고 목록을 갱신하기 위해
(B) 오해를 바로잡기 위해
(C) 업적을 강조하기 위해
(D) 모집 활동을 비교하기 위해

어휘 update 갱신하다 inventory 재고 correct 바로잡다
misunderstanding 오해 emphasize 강조하다
achievement 업적, 성취 compare 비교하다 recruitment
신규 모집, 채용 drive (조직적) 운동

해설 화자의 의도 파악 – 포레스트레인 매장은 100개 정도였다는 말의 의미
지문 중반부에서 올해 설문조사에서 우리 매장에 대한 긍정적 의견이 842개에 달했다(we had eight hundred forty-two positive comments for our store on this year's survey)고 말한 후 포레스트레인 매장은 100개 정도였다(The Forestlane location had about a hundred)고 말했다. 즉 포레스트레인 매장과 비교해서 긍정적 의견이 훨씬 많았다는 의미이므로 정답은 (C)이다.

88
What can the listeners do at 5 P.M.?

(A) Collect a bonus check
(B) Leave work early
(C) Have some refreshments
(D) Visit the speaker's office

청자들은 오후 5시에 무엇을 할 수 있는가?

(A) 상여금 수령하기
(B) 일찍 퇴근하기
(C) 다과 즐기기
(D) 화자 사무실 들르기

어휘 collect 수금하다 bonus 상여금 check 수표 refreshments
다과

해설 세부 사항 관련 – 청자들이 5시에 할 수 있는 것
지문 후반부에서 오후 다섯 시에 휴게실에서 도넛, 커피, 주스가 제공될 예정(At five o'clock this afternoon, we'll have donuts, coffee, and juice in the break room)이니 꼭 들러 달라(be sure to stop by)고 요청하고 있으므로 정답은 (C)이다.

▸▸ Paraphrasing 지문의 donuts, coffee, and juice
→ 정답의 some refreshments

89-91 라디오 방송

M-Au **89This past weekend, Romano Valley welcomed a new addition to the city's skyline with the opening of Centennial Stadium.** The building is the perfect complement to the nearby Valley Vacation Amusement Park. The structure has seating for twenty thousand people. **89It will mainly be used as a baseball field, but during the off-season, concerts will be held there as well. 90Many people are pleased about the stadium, as it will increase tax revenues for Romano Valley.** On the other hand, opponents are concerned that it will cause traffic and pollution problems. **91We'd like to hear what you think. Call us at 555-0188.**

지난 주말, 센테니얼 스타디움의 개장으로 로마노 밸리의 스카이라인에는 새 건물이 들어섰습니다. 이 건물은 근처 밸리 베케이션 놀이공원을 완벽히 보완해 줍니다. 이 구조물은 2만 명을 수용할 수 있습니다. 이 경기장은 주로 야구장으로 쓰일 예정이며 비시즌에는 콘서트도 개최됩니다. 스타디움이 로마노 밸리의 세수

를 늘려 줄 것이기 때문에 많은 이들이 스타디움을 반기고 있습니다. 반면 반대하는 사람들은 스타디움이 교통 및 공해 문제를 일으킬 것이라 우려합니다. 여러분의 의견을 듣고 싶습니다. 555-0188로 전화해 주세요.

어휘 addition 추가(물) skyline (건물이) 하늘과 맞닿은 윤곽선 opening 개장 complement to ~에 대한 보완물 nearby 근처의 amusement park 놀이 공원 structure 건축물 seating 수용(력) mainly 주로 off-season 비수기, 비시즌 hold 개최하다 as well 또한 increase 증가하다, 올리다 tax revenue 세수 opponent 반대자 cause 야기하다 traffic 차량들, 교통(량) pollution 오염 concerned 우려하는

89

What has recently been opened in Romano Valley?

(A) An art museum
(B) An amusement park
(C) A sports facility
(D) A music institute

로마노 밸리에서 최근에 개장한 것은 무엇인가?

(A) 미술관
(B) 놀이공원
(C) 스포츠 시설
(D) 음악원

해설 세부 사항 관련 – 최근에 로마노 밸리에서 개장한 것

지문 초반부에서 지난 주말, 센테니얼 스타디움의 개장으로 로마노 밸리의 스카이라인에는 새 건물이 들어섰다(This past weekend, Romano Valley welcomed a new addition to the city's skyline with the opening of Centennial Stadium)고 말했고 지문 중반부에서 이 경기장이 주로 야구장으로 쓰일 것(It will mainly be used as a baseball field)이라고 말했으므로 정답은 (C)이다.

▸▸ Paraphrasing   지문의 **a baseball field**
→ 정답의 **A sports facility**

90

What benefit of the site does the speaker mention?

(A) It will offer educational opportunities.
(B) It will increase public funds.
(C) It will attract out-of-town tourists.
(D) It will improve the city's image.

화자가 언급하는 장소의 장점은 무엇인가?

(A) 교육 기회를 제공한다.
(B) 공공 자금을 늘려 줄 것이다.
(C) 외지 관광객들을 끌어들일 것이다.
(D) 시의 이미지를 개선해 줄 것이다.

어휘 opportunity 기회 public fund 공적 자금 attract 끌어들이다, 끌어모으다 out-of-town 다른 도시의 tourist 관광객 improve 개선시키다

해설 세부 사항 관련 – 화자가 장소에 대해 언급하는 장점

지문 중반에서 스타디움이 로마노 밸리의 세수를 늘려 줄 것(It will increase tax revenues for Romano Valley)이기 때문에 많은 이들이 스타디움을 반기고 있다(Many people are pleased about the stadium)고 했으므로 정답은 (B)이다.

▸▸ Paraphrasing   지문의 **increase tax revenues**
→ 정답의 **increase public funds**

91

What are the listeners encouraged to do?

(A) E-mail the speaker
(B) Attend a special event
(C) Call their supervisor
(D) Share their opinions

청자들이 권유받는 일은 무엇인가?

(A) 화자에게 이메일 보내기
(B) 특별 행사에 참석하기
(C) 관리자에게 전화하기
(D) 의견 공유하기

어휘 attend 참석하다 supervisor 감독관, 관리자 share 나누다, 공유하다

해설 세부 사항 관련 – 청자들에게 권하는 일

지문 후반부에 여러분의 의견을 듣고 싶으니 555-0188로 전화하라(We'd like to hear what you think. Call us at 555-0188)고 말했으므로 정답은 (D)이다.

▸▸ Paraphrasing   지문의 **We'd like to hear what you think**
→ 정답의 **Share their opinions**

92-94 워크숍 발췌

W-Am Welcome, all, to the Introduction to Painting workshop. **92This two-hour class is designed for complete novices who have never picked up a paintbrush before.** We'll learn the basics of watercolor painting, and you'll leave here today with your very own artwork. **93Our future workshops will cover the finer points of painting, and they do fill up quickly. So, just a reminder... Please make sure to sign up ahead of time to avoid missing out.** Now, uh... another group used this room before us. **94It'll take a moment to make sure everything we need is where it belongs.** Then I'll pass out the paper and brushes and we'll get to work.

회화 입문 워크숍에 오신 여러분 모두 환영합니다. **이 두 시간짜리 수업은 이전에 붓을 한 번도 잡아 보지 않은 완전 초보자들을 위한 것입니다.** 이 수업에서는 수채화의 기초를 배우는데요. 오늘 이곳을 나갈 때는 자신의 예술 작품 하나씩을 들고 가실 겁니다. **향후 워크숍에서는 회화의 더 상세한 부분을 다루게 되는데 수강 인원이 빨리 찹니다. 그러니까 기억하세요. 기회를 놓치지 않으려면 꼭 미리 등록하세요.** 자, 어... 앞서 다른 그룹이 이 교실을 사용했는데요. **필요한 것들이 모두 제자리에 있는지 확인하는 데 잠깐 시간이 걸립니다.** 그런 다음 종이와 붓을 나누어 드리고 작업을 시작하죠.

92

What is mentioned about the workshop?

(A) It is sponsored by an art gallery.
(B) It is designed for beginners.
(C) It is being offered free of charge.
(D) It was rescheduled from a previous date.

워크숍에 대해 언급된 것은 무엇인가?
(A) 화랑에서 후원한다.
(B) 초보자를 위한 것이다.
(C) 무료로 제공되고 있다.
(D) 이전 날짜에서 일정이 바뀌었다.

어휘 sponsor 후원하다 art gallery 화랑 beginner 초보자 free of
charge 무료로 reschedule 일정을 다시 잡다 previous 이전의

해설 세부 사항 관련 – 워크숍에 대해 언급된 것
지문 초반부에 이 두 시간짜리 수업은 이전에 붓을 한 번도 잡아 보지 않은 완
전 초보자들을 위한 것(This two-hour class is designed for complete
novices who have never picked up a paintbrush before)이라고 했으므
로 정답은 (B)이다.

▸▸ **Paraphrasing**   지문의 **complete novices** → 정답의 **beginners**

93

What does the speaker remind the listeners to do?

(A) Register for upcoming classes
(B) Pick up parking vouchers
(C) Display their name tags
(D) Post feedback on a Web site

화자는 청자들에게 무엇을 하라고 상기시키는가?
(A) 다가올 수업에 등록하기
(B) 주차권 수령하기
(C) 이름표 보여 주기
(D) 웹사이트에 의견 게시하기

어휘 register for ~을 신청[등록]하다 pick up 찾아오다 voucher
할인권 display 내보이다 name tag 명찰 post 게시하다
feedback 의견

해설 세부 사항 관련 – 청자들에게 하라고 상기시키는 것
지문 중반부에서 향후 워크숍에서는 회화의 더 상세한 부분을 다루게 되는
데 수강 인원이 빨리 차므로 기회를 놓치지 않으려면 꼭 미리 등록하라(Our
future workshops will cover the finer points of painting, and they
do fill up quickly. So, just a reminder… Please make sure to sign
up ahead of time to avoid missing out)고 했으므로 정답은 (A)이다.

▸▸ **Paraphrasing**   지문의 **sign up** → 정답의 **Register**

94

What does the speaker imply when she says, "another group used this room before us"?

(A) She is disappointed by the number of participants.
(B) A facility does not have many rooms.
(C) A room schedule was incorrect.
(D) Some supplies are unorganized.

화자가 말한 "앞서 다른 그룹이 이 교실을 사용했는데요"가 암시하는 것은 무엇인가?
(A) 그녀는 참석자 수에 실망했다.
(B) 시설에는 교실이 많지 않다.
(C) 교실 사용 시간표가 잘못되었다.
(D) 몇몇 물건들이 어질러져 있다.

어휘 be disappointed by ~에 실망하다 the number of
~의 수 participant 참석자 facility 시설 supplies 비품
unorganized (방 등이) 어질러진

해설 화자의 의도 파악 – 앞서 다른 그룹이 이 방을 사용했다는 말의 의미
지문 후반부에 앞서 다른 그룹이 이 교실을 사용했다(another group used
this room before us)고 말한 후, 우리가 필요한 것들이 모두 제자리에 있
는지 확인하는 데 잠깐 시간이 걸린다(It'll take a moment to make sure
everything we need is where it belongs)고 했다. 즉 앞서 방을 사용한 사
람들이 물건을 어질러 놓았을 수도 있다는 의미이므로 정답은 (D)이다.

95-97 공지 + 목록

M-Cn Attention, all Carolina Hardware shoppers.
Thank you for your patronage, and we hope
you find everything you need. **95We have the
region's largest variety of goods,** and we also
rent out equipment at the customer service
desk. The rental options are posted around
the store, **96but please note that we no longer
rent out paint sprayers.** And to make the most
of your shopping trip, **97don't forget to pick up
a coupon book from your cashier as you make
your purchase.** If there's anything we can do to
help, just let one of our customer representatives
know.

캐롤라이나 하드웨어 고객 여러분께 알려드립니다. 애용해 주셔서 감사드리며
원하시는 모든 상품을 찾으시길 바랍니다. 우리는 이 지역에서 가장 다양한 상품
을 갖추고 있고 또한 고객서비스 데스크에서 장비도 대여하고 있습니다. 대여 품
목들은 매장 곳곳에 게시되어 있습니다. 단, 페인트 분무기는 더 이상 대여하지
않음을 양지해 주십시오. 여러분이 오늘 쇼핑 나들이를 최대한 활용하시도록 구
매 시 계산대에서 쿠폰북을 꼭 챙기시기 바랍니다. 저희가 도와드릴 수 있는 일
이라면 무엇이든 고객 상담원에게 알려주세요.

Carolina Hardware: Equipment Rental	
Device	**Brand**
Circular Saw	Scharf
Floor Sander	Tikko
Nail Gun	Ashford
96Paint Sprayer	Viera

캐롤라이나 하드웨어: 장비 대여	
장비	**브랜드**
회전톱	샤프
바닥사포기	티코
못 박는 기계	애쉬포드
페인트 분무기	비에라

어휘 device 장비 circular 원형의, 나선 모양의 saw 톱 sander 사포로 닦는 기계 nail gun 못 박는 기계, 네일 건

95

What does the speaker say about Carolina Hardware?

(A) It has the area's widest selection.
(B) It has recently introduced a new brand.
(C) It has been open for a long time.
(D) It has regular demonstrations for customers.

화자가 캐롤라이나 하드웨어에 대해서 말하는 것은 무엇인가?
(A) 지역 내에서 가장 다양한 상품들이 있다.
(B) 최근 새로운 브랜드를 들여왔다.
(C) 문을 연 지 오래 됐다.
(D) 고객들을 위해 정기적으로 시연한다.

어휘 selection 정선품 regular 정기적인 demonstration 시범, 시연

해설 세부 사항 관련 – 캐롤라이나 하드웨어에 대해서 말하는 것
지문 초반부에서 가게가 이 지역에서 가장 다양한 상품들을 갖추고 있다(We have the region's largest variety of goods)고 했으므로 정답은 (A)이다.

▸▸ Paraphrasing 지문의 **the region's largest variety of goods** → **the area's widest selection**

96

Look at the graphic. Which brand is not available for rental?

(A) Scharf
(B) Tikko
(C) Ashford
(D) Viera

시각 정보에 의하면 대여할 수 없는 브랜드는 무엇인가?
(A) 샤프
(B) 티코
(C) 애쉬포드
(D) 비에라

해설 시각 정보 연계 – 대여할 수 없는 브랜드
지문의 중반부에서 페인트 분무기는 더 이상 대여하지 않음을 양지해 달라(please note that we no longer rent out paint sprayers)고 했고, 시각 자료에 따르면 페인트 분무기 브랜드는 비에라이므로 정답은 (D)이다.

97

According to the speaker, where can shoppers get discount coupons?

(A) From a Web site
(B) From the customer service desk
(C) From the checkout area
(D) From a display stand

화자에 따르면 고객들은 어디에서 할인 쿠폰을 얻을 수 있는가?
(A) 웹사이트에서
(B) 고객서비스 데스크에서
(C) 계산대에서
(D) 진열대에서

어휘 checkout (슈퍼마켓 등의) 계산대 display 전시, 진열 stand …대

해설 세부 사항 관련 – 고객들이 할인 쿠폰을 받는 장소
지문 후반부에서 구매 시 계산대에서 쿠폰북을 꼭 챙기라(don't forget to pick up a coupon book from your cashier as you make your purchase)고 했으므로 정답은 (C)이다.

▸▸ Paraphrasing 지문의 **from your cashier** → 정답의 **From the checkout area**

98-100 공지 + 티켓

W-Br Attention, all passengers. We are now departing for Manchester. During today's journey, sandwiches and hot drinks will be available from our dining car, which is near the front of the train, right before the first-class car. 98**For those of you in car D, the restroom will remain locked due to a mechanical problem. We're very sorry for the inconvenience.** Facilities are available in car C and E. Now that we're on our way, 99**please take a moment to review the safety information posted on the wall near your seat.** 100**This is an on-time departure, and our journey will take approximately three hours.** Thank you for traveling with us, and have a pleasant journey.

승객 여러분께 알려드립니다. 우리 열차는 지금 맨체스터로 출발합니다. 오늘 여행 동안 샌드위치와 따뜻한 음료들은 식당칸에서 이용하실 수 있습니다. 식당칸은 열차 앞쪽 일등석 바로 앞 칸입니다. D 객차 탑승객을 위한 화장실은 기계 결함으로 잠겨 있습니다. 불편을 끼쳐드려 대단히 죄송합니다. 화장실은 C와 E객차에서 사용하실 수 있습니다. 이제 출발했으니 잠깐 시간을 내시어 좌석 근처 벽에 게시된 안전 수칙 정보를 살펴보시기 바랍니다. 저희는 정시에 출발하였으며 행선지까지 약 3시간이 소요될 예정입니다. 저희 열차를 이용해 주셔서 감사합니다. 즐거운 여행 되시기 바랍니다.

Grand Isle Railways

One-Way Ticket
Adult: 1
Destination: Manchester
100 Departure Time: 1 P.M.

그랜드 아일 레일웨이스

편도 티켓
성인: 1명
목적지: 맨체스터
출발 시간: 오후 1시

어휘 one-way 편도의 destination 목적지

98

Why does the speaker apologize?

(A) Seats cannot be reserved.
(B) Beverages are not available.
(C) A train departed late.
(D) A restroom is off limits.

화자는 왜 사과하는가?
(A) 좌석을 예약할 수 없어서
(B) 음료수를 팔지 않아서
(C) 열차가 늦게 출발해서
(D) 화장실이 사용 불가여서

어휘 reserve 예약하다 beverage 음료 off-limits 출입금지의

해설 세부 사항 관련 – 화자가 사과하는 이유
지문의 초반부에 D 객차 탑승객을 위한 화장실은 기계 결함으로 잠겨 있다
(For those of you in car D, the restroom will remain locked due to
a mechanical problem)고 말했고, 불편을 끼쳐 대단히 죄송하다(We're
very sorry for the inconvenience)고 했으므로 정답은 (D)이다.

▸▸ Paraphrasing   지문의 **the restroom will remain locked**
→ 정답의 **A restroom is off limits.**

99

What does the speaker encourage listeners to do?

(A) Stay seated during the journey
(B) Keep their personal belongings with them
(C) Have their tickets ready to present
(D) Read some safety information

화자는 청자들에게 무엇을 하라고 권하는가?
(A) 운행 중 자리에 앉아 있기
(B) 휴대품 소지하기
(C) 티켓을 보여줄 수 있도록 준비해 놓기
(D) 안전 수칙 정보 읽기

어휘 stay 그대로 있다 seated (자리에) 앉은 personal 개인적인
belongings 소유물 have ~ ready ~을 준비해 두다 present
제시하다, 보여주다

해설 세부 사항 관련 – 청자들에게 권하는 것
지문 중반부에 잠깐 시간을 내어 좌석 근처 벽에 게시된 안전 수칙 정보를 살펴
보기 바란다(please take a moment to review the safety information
posted on the wall near your seat)고 했으므로 정답은 (D)이다.

▸▸ Paraphrasing   지문의 **review the safety information**
→ 정답의 **Read some safety information**

100

Look at the graphic. What time is the train expected to
arrive at Manchester?

(A) At around one o'clock
(B) At around two o'clock
(C) At around three o'clock
(D) At around four o'clock

시각 정보에 의하면 열차는 몇 시에 맨체스터에 도착할 예정인가?
(A) 1시경
(B) 2시경
(C) 3시경
(D) 4시경

해설 시각 정보 연계 – 열차 도착 시간
지문의 후반부에서 기차가 정시에 출발하였으며 행선지까지 약 3시간이 소
요될 것(This is an on-time departure, and our journey will take
approximately three hours)이라고 했고, 시각 정보를 보면 기차가 1시에
출발했으므로 정답은 (D)이다.

TEST 10

1 (C)	2 (A)	3 (D)	4 (C)	5 (C)
6 (D)	7 (A)	8 (B)	9 (A)	10 (C)
11 (C)	12 (B)	13 (A)	14 (B)	15 (C)
16 (B)	17 (C)	18 (C)	19 (B)	20 (C)
21 (C)	22 (B)	23 (A)	24 (A)	25 (B)
26 (A)	27 (B)	28 (A)	29 (C)	30 (A)
31 (A)	32 (A)	33 (A)	34 (B)	35 (A)
36 (C)	37 (A)	38 (D)	39 (B)	40 (B)
41 (B)	42 (D)	43 (C)	44 (C)	45 (C)
46 (A)	47 (A)	48 (C)	49 (A)	50 (C)
51 (D)	52 (B)	53 (A)	54 (B)	55 (B)
56 (C)	57 (B)	58 (B)	59 (A)	60 (D)
61 (B)	62 (A)	63 (C)	64 (A)	65 (B)
66 (A)	67 (C)	68 (B)	69 (A)	70 (C)
71 (C)	72 (A)	73 (D)	74 (B)	75 (A)
76 (C)	77 (D)	78 (B)	79 (A)	80 (A)
81 (C)	82 (A)	83 (A)	84 (D)	85 (B)
86 (D)	87 (D)	88 (B)	89 (C)	90 (B)
91 (C)	92 (D)	93 (B)	94 (C)	95 (A)
96 (D)	97 (B)	98 (D)	99 (C)	100 (C)

PART 1

1 W-Br

(A) The woman is handing some documents to the man.
(B) The woman is writing on some paper.
(C) The man is cutting paper with scissors.
(D) The man is removing equipment from a desk.
(A) 여자가 남자에게 문서들을 건네고 있다.
(B) 여자가 종이에 쓰고 있다.
(C) **남자가 가위로 종이를 자르고 있다.**
(D) 남자가 책상 위의 장비를 치우고 있다.

어휘 hand 건네 주다 scissors 가위 remove 제거하다, 없애다
equipment 장비, 설비

해설 2인 이상 등장 사진 – 인물의 동작 묘사

(A) 동사 오답. 여자가 남자에게 문서들을 건네는(is handing some documents) 모습이 아니므로 오답.

(B) 동사 오답. 여자가 종이에 쓰고 있는(is writing on some paper) 모습이 아니므로 오답.

(C) 정답. 남자가 가위로 종이를 자르는(is cutting paper with scissors) 동작을 하고 있으므로 정답.

(D) 동사 오답. 남자가 책상 위의 장비를 치우는(is removing equipment from a desk) 모습이 아니므로 오답.

2 M-Cn

(A) The woman is examining merchandise on a shelf.
(B) The woman is putting on a pair of glasses.
(C) The woman is tying a scarf around her neck.
(D) The woman is pushing a shopping cart in an aisle.
(A) 여자가 선반 위의 상품을 살펴보고 있다.
(B) 여자가 안경을 쓰고 있다.
(C) 여자가 목에 스카프를 둘러매고 있다.
(D) 여자가 통로에서 쇼핑 카트를 밀고 있다.

어휘 merchandise 상품 put on ~을 입다 shelf 선반 tie around
~에 두르다 aisle 통로, 복도

해설 1인 등장 사진 – 인물의 동작 묘사

(A) 정답. 여자가 선반 위의 상품을 살펴보는(is examining merchandise on a shelf) 모습이므로 정답.

(B) 동사 오답. 여자가 안경을 쓴 상태이지 안경을 쓰는(is putting on a pair of glasses) 동작을 하는 모습이 아니므로 오답.

(C) 동사 오답. 여자가 목에 스카프를 둘러맨 상태이지 둘러매는(is tying a scarf around her neck) 동작을 하는 모습이 아니므로 오답.

(D) 동사 오답. 여자가 통로에서(in an aisle) 쇼핑 카트를 미는(is pushing a shopping cart) 모습이 아니므로 오답.

3 W-Am

(A) Boxes are being moved with a motorized cart.
(B) One man is helping the other install floor tiles.
(C) One of the men is holding a ladder against a shelf.
(D) One of the men has raised some boxes off the ground.
(A) 상자들이 전동카트로 옮겨지고 있다.
(B) 한 남자가 다른 남자가 바닥 타일 까는 것을 돕고 있다.
(C) 남자들 중 한 명이 선반에 사다리를 받치고 있다.
(D) **남자들 중 한 명이 바닥에서 상자들을 들어 올리고 있다.**

어휘 motorized 엔진[동력]이 달린 install 설치하다 ladder 사다리
against ~에 기대어 raise (위로) 들어 올리다

해설 2인 이상 등장 사진 – 인물의 동작 묘사

(A) 사진에 없는 명사를 이용한 오답. 사진에 전동카트(a motorized cart)가 보이지 않으므로 오답.

(B) 동사 오답. 한 남자가 다른 남자가 바닥 타일 까는 것을 돕는(is helping the other install floor tiles) 모습이 아니므로 오답.

(C) 사진에 없는 명사를 이용한 오답. 사진에 사다리(a ladder)가 보이지 않으므로 오답.

Test 10

(D) 정답. 남자 중 한 명이 상자들을 들어 올리고 있는(has raised some boxes off the ground) 모습이므로 정답.

4 M-Au

(A) House plants are being watered.
(B) Curtains are being pulled together.
(C) Light is shining through a window.
(D) Beds have been arranged side by side.

(A) 실내 화초들에 물을 주고 있다.
(B) 커튼들을 치고 있다.
(C) 창문으로 빛이 비치고 있다.
(D) 침대가 나란히 배치되어 있다.

어휘 plant 식물, 화초 water 물을 주다 shine through ~을 통하여 비치다 arrange 배치하다, 배열하다 side by side 나란히

해설 사물/배경 사진 – 사물의 상태 묘사
(A) 동사 오답. 실내 화초들(plants)에 물을 주고 있는(are being watered) 동작을 하는 사람이 보이지 않으므로 오답.
(B) 동사 오답. 커튼들(curtains)을 치고 있는(are being pulled together) 동작을 하는 사람이 보이지 않으므로 오답.
(C) 정답. 빛(light)이 창문으로 비치고 있는(is shining through a window) 모습이므로 정답.
(D) 사진에 없는 명사를 이용한 오답. 사진에 침대(beds)가 보이지 않으므로 오답.

5 W-Br

(A) Snow is being swept off some chairs.
(B) The surface of a stream is covered with ice.
(C) A walking path is lined with benches.
(D) A worker is trimming some trees.

(A) 의자에서 눈이 치워지고 있다.
(B) 개울의 표면이 얼음으로 덮여 있다.
(C) 보도를 따라 벤치들이 줄지어 있다.
(D) 일꾼이 나뭇가지를 치고 있다.

어휘 sweep off 쓸다, 청소하다 surface 표면 stream 개울, 시내 be covered with ~로 덮여 있다 walking path 산책로 line ~을 따라 줄지어 서다 trim 다듬다, 잘라내다

해설 사물/배경 사진 – 사람 또는 사물 중심 묘사
(A) 동사 오답. 의자(chairs)에서 눈을 치우는(snow is being swept off) 동작을 하는 사람이 보이지 않으므로 오답.

(B) 사진에 없는 명사를 이용한 오답. 사진에 개울(a stream)이 보이지 않으므로 오답.
(C) 정답. 보도(a walking path)를 따라 벤치들이 줄지어 있는(is lined with benches) 모습이므로 정답.
(D) 사진에 없는 명사를 이용한 오답. 사진에 일꾼(a worker)이 보이지 않으므로 오답.

6 M-Cn

(A) The people are signing some paperwork.
(B) One of the men is holding a clipboard.
(C) The people are seated around a meeting table.
(D) Two of the men are shaking hands.

(A) 사람들이 서류에 서명하고 있다.
(B) 남자들 중 한 명이 클립보드를 들고 있다.
(C) 사람들이 회의 테이블 주위에 앉아 있다.
(D) 남자들 중 두 명이 악수하고 있다.

어휘 sign 서명하다 paperwork 서류 be seated 앉아 있다 shake hands 악수하다

해설 2인 이상 등장 사진 – 인물의 동작 묘사
(A) 동사 오답. 사람들(people)이 서류에 서명하는(are signing some paperwork) 모습이 아니므로 오답.
(B) 동사 오답. 남자 중 한 명이 클립보드를 들고 있는(is holding a clipboard) 모습이 아니므로 오답.
(C) 동사 오답. 사람들이 회의 테이블 주위에 앉아 있는(are seated around a meeting table) 모습이 아니므로 오답.
(D) 정답. 남자들 중 두 명이 악수를 하고 있는(are shaking hands) 모습이므로 정답.

PART 2

7

W-Am What time is the press conference about the merger?
M-Au (A) About an hour from now.
      (B) We learned a great deal.
      (C) Yes, I have plenty of time.

몇 시에 합병에 대한 기자회견이 있습니까?
(A) 약 1시간 후입니다.
(B) 우리는 많이 배웠습니다.
(C) 네, 전 시간 많아요.

어휘 press conference 기자회견 merger 합병 a great deal 다량, 많이

해설 기자회견 시작 시간을 묻는 What 의문문

(A) 정답. 기자회견이 몇 시인지를 묻는 질문에 1시간 후라고 답하고 있으므로 정답.

(B) 연상 단어 오답. 질문의 merger에 대해 연상 가능한 a great deal을 이용한 오답.

(C) Yes/No 불가 오답. What 의문문에 Yes/No 응답이 불가능하므로 오답.

8

W-Br Where can I find the luggage I checked for this flight?

M-Cn (A) To a European destination.

(B) It's at carousel five.

(C) Two suitcases and a laptop bag.

이 비행기에 제가 위탁한 수하물을 어디서 찾을 수 있나요?
(A) 행선지는 유럽입니다.
(B) 5번 수취대입니다.
(C) 여행 가방 2개와 노트북 가방 하나입니다.

어휘 luggage (여행용) 짐, 수하물 check 물표를 받고 맡기다[부치다] destination 행선지 carousel (공항의) 수하물 수취대

해설 수하물의 위치를 묻는 Where 의문문

(A) 연상 단어 오답. 질문의 where에 대해 연상 가능한 destination을 이용한 오답.

(B) 정답. 수하물을 어디서 찾을 수 있는지 묻는 질문에 5번 수취대라고 구체적인 장소로 대답하므로 정답.

(C) 연상 단어 오답. 질문의 luggage에 대해 연상 가능한 suitcases, bag을 이용한 오답.

9

M-Cn Would you like me to unpack these bags?

W-Am (A) Sure, that would be helpful.

(B) Look on the back side.

(C) They were delivered yesterday.

제가 이 가방을 풀어 드릴까요?
(A) 네, 그래 주시면 도움이 되죠.
(B) 뒷면을 보세요.
(C) 그것들은 어제 배달됐어요.

어휘 unpack (짐 등을) 풀다, 가방의 짐을 꺼내다 on the back side 뒷면에

해설 제안/권유의 의문문

(A) 정답. 가방을 풀어 드리겠다는 제안에 그래 주면 도움이 된다고 응답하고 있으므로 정답.

(B) 유사 발음 오답. 질문의 bags와 발음이 유사한 back을 이용한 오답.

(C) 질문과 상관없는 오답. 시간을 묻는 When 의문문에 어울리는 응답이므로 오답.

10

M-Au Should we rearrange the waiting room furniture or leave it as it is?

W-Br (A) Everyone liked the flower arrangement.

(B) I think he left the building already.

(C) Let's see what Ms. Thompson thinks.

대기실 가구를 재배치해야 할까요, 아니면 그대로 둘까요?
(A) 모두들 그 꽃꽂이를 좋아했어요.
(B) 그 사람은 이미 건물을 떠난 것 같아요.
(C) 톰슨 씨 생각은 어떤지 봅시다.

어휘 rearrange 재배치하다 as it is 있는 그대로 flower arrangement 꽃꽂이

해설 대기실의 가구 재배치 의견을 묻는 선택의문문

(A) 유사 발음 오답. 질문의 rearrange와 부분적으로 발음이 동일한 arrangement를 이용한 오답.

(B) 단어 반복 오답. 질문의 leave를 과거형인 left로 반복한 오답.

(C) 정답. 대기실 가구를 재배치할지에 대한 질문에 톰슨 씨의 생각이 어떤지 보자는 우회적인 응답을 통해 불확실함을 나타내고 있으므로 정답.

11

M-Cn Who discovered the error with the tax payment?

M-Au (A) It's due in two weeks.

(B) That's a relief.

(C) One of the accountants.

누가 세금 납부 오류를 발견했나요?
(A) 2주 후에 마감이에요.
(B) 다행이네요.
(C) 회계사 중 한 명이요.

어휘 discover 발견하다 error 오류 tax payment 세금 납부 due 예정된 relief 안도, 안심 accountant 회계사

해설 세금 납부 오류를 발견한 사람이 누구인지 묻는 Who 의문문

(A) 질문과 상관없는 오답. 시점을 묻는 When 의문문에 어울리는 응답이므로 오답.

(B) 질문과 상관없는 오답. 세금 납부 오류를 발견한 사람이 누구인지 묻는 질문에 다행이라는 응답은 문맥에 맞지 않으므로 오답.

(C) 정답. 세금 납부 오류를 발견한 사람이 누구인지 묻는 질문에 회계사들 중 한 명이라고 구체적인 사람으로 대답하고 있으므로 정답.

12

M-Cn Which road do I need to take for the airport?

W-Am (A) I live on Berkeley Avenue.

(B) Just follow the signs.

(C) They're adding another lane.

공항에 가려면 어느 도로를 타야 하나요?
(A) 전 버클리 가에 살아요.
(B) 표지판만 따라가세요.
(C) 차선 하나를 추가하고 있어요.

어휘 sign 표지판 add 추가하다 lane 차선, 차로

해설 어느 도로로 가야 하는지 묻는 Which 의문문

(A) 연상 단어 오답. 질문의 road에서 연상 가능한 Berkeley Avenue를 이용한 오답.

(B) 정답. 어느 도로를 타야 하는지 묻는 질문에 표지판만 따라가면 된다는 구체적인 방법을 제시하고 있으므로 정답.

(C) 연상 단어 오답. 질문의 road에서 연상 가능한 lane을 이용한 오답.

13

W-Br When should we take down the posters?

M-Au (A) After the concert is finished.

(B) The ones on that wall.

(C) At the Liverpool Convention Center.

언제 포스터를 떼야 할까요?

(A) 콘서트가 끝나고 난 후예요.

(B) 저 벽에 있는 거요.

(C) 리버풀 컨벤션 센터요.

어휘 take down 치우다

해설 홍보 포스터를 언제 떼야 하는지를 묻는 When 의문문

(A) 정답. 포스터를 언제 떼야 할지 묻는 질문에 콘서트가 끝나고 난 후라는 구체적인 시점으로 답하고 있으므로 정답.

(B) 질문과 상관없는 오답. Which 의문문에 어울리는 응답이므로 오답.

(C) 질문과 상관없는 오답. 장소를 묻는 Where 의문문에 어울리는 응답이므로 오답.

14

W-Am Is Kirk participating in the marathon race this weekend?

M-Cn (A) We had an overwhelming response.

(B) Yes, he's been training for months.

(C) Sorry, but I have to work on Saturday.

이번 주말에 커크가 마라톤 경주에 참가하나요?

(A) 우리는 큰 호응을 얻었어요.

(B) 네, 그는 수개월간 훈련해 왔습니다.

(C) 미안하지만 토요일에 일해야 해요.

어휘 participate in ~에 참가하다, 참여하다 overwhelming 압도적인, 엄청난

해설 커크의 마라톤 경주 참가 여부를 묻는 Be동사 의문문

(A) 질문과 상관없는 오답. 주말에 커크가 마라톤 경주에 참가하는지 묻는 질문에 우리가 큰 호응을 얻었다는 응답은 문맥에 맞지 않으므로 오답.

(B) 정답. 주말에 커크가 마라톤 경주에 참가하는지 묻는 질문에 Yes라는 긍정적인 응답을 한 후, 그가 수개월 동안 훈련을 해왔다는 부연 설명을 하고 있으므로 정답.

(C) 연상 단어 오답. 질문의 weekend에서 연상 가능한 Saturday를 이용한 오답.

15

W-Br Who brought the final blueprints to Ms. Anderson's office?

W-Am (A) I don't think she bought them.

(B) Jason said that red would be better.

(C) A courier from a nearby firm.

최종 청사진들을 앤더슨 씨 사무실에 가져다 준 사람이 누구죠?

(A) 그녀가 사진 않은 것 같아요.

(B) 제이슨은 빨강이 더 나을 것 같다고 했어요.

(C) 근처 회사에서 보낸 택배 기사가요.

어휘 blueprint 청사진 courier 택배 기사 firm 회사

해설 최종 청사진을 누가 가져다 줬는지 묻는 Who 의문문

(A) 유사 발음 오답. 질문의 brought와 발음이 유사한 bought를 이용한 오답.

(B) 연상 단어 오답. 질문의 blueprints의 blue에서 연상 가능한 색깔(red)을 이용한 오답.

(C) 정답. 최종 청사진을 누가 가져다 줬는지 묻는 질문에 근처 회사에서 보낸 택배 기사라는 구체적인 사람으로 응답하고 있으므로 정답.

16

W-Br Why are some sections of the museum closed off?

M-Cn (A) I prefer contemporary art to traditional pieces.

(B) That wasn't explained in our tour.

(C) You can turn them back on using this switch.

왜 박물관 일부 구역들이 차단되었나요?

(A) 저는 전통 작품보다는 현대 미술 작품이 더 좋습니다.

(B) 우리 투어에서는 거기에 대한 설명이 없었어요.

(C) 이 스위치를 이용해서 다시 켜면 돼요.

어휘 section 구역 close off 차단하다 contemporary 현대의, 당대의 turn on 켜다

해설 박물관 일부 구역이 왜 출입 금지인지 이유를 묻는 Why 의문문

(A) 연상 단어 오답. 질문의 museum에서 연상 가능한 contemporary art를 이용한 오답.

(B) 정답. 왜 박물관 일부 구역들이 차단됐는지 묻는 질문에 투어에서는 거기에 대한 설명이 없었다는 응답을 통해 잘 모른다는 것을 우회적으로 나타내고 있으므로 정답.

(C) 연상 단어 오답. 질문의 close off에서 연상 가능한 turn on, switch를 이용한 오답.

17

M-Au Do you think we should hold another safety drill?

W-Br (A) The storage area won't hold it.

(B) Maybe the hardware store sells them.

(C) Didn't we just have one?

안전 훈련을 한 번 더 해야 한다고 생각해요?

(A) 창고에 다 들어가지 않을 거예요.

(B) 아마도 철물점에서 그것들을 팔 거예요.

(C) 얼마 전에 하지 않았나요?

어휘 hold 개최하다 safety drill 안전 훈련 storage 저장(고) hardware store 철물점

해설 대피 훈련을 한 번 더 하는 것에 대한 의견을 묻는 조동사 의문문

(A) 단어 반복 오답. 질문의 hold를 다른 의미의 hold로 반복한 오답.

(B) 연상 단어 오답. 질문의 drill을 장비인 드릴로 잘못 이해했을 때 연상 가능한 hardware store를 이용한 오답.

(C) 정답. 안전 훈련을 한 번 더 하는 것에 대한 의견을 묻는 질문에 얼마 전에 하지 않았냐고 반문하고 있으므로 정답.

18

W-Am Wouldn't you prefer to send the invitations by e-mail?

M-Cn (A) I haven't read it yet.

(B) The manager's retirement dinner.

(C) That would be faster.

초대장을 이메일로 보내는 게 더 낫지 않겠어요?
(A) 전 아직 읽지 않았어요.
(B) 부장의 퇴임 기념 만찬이요.
(C) 그게 더 빠르겠네요.

어휘 retirement 은퇴, 퇴임

해설 초대장을 이메일로 보내는 게 어떤지 묻는 부정의문문

(A) 연상 단어 오답. 질문의 invitations에서 연상 가능한 read를 이용한 오답.

(B) 연상 단어 오답. 질문의 invitations에서 연상 가능한 retirement dinner를 이용한 오답.

(C) 정답. 초대장을 이메일로 보내는 게 어떤지 묻는 질문에 그게 더 빠르겠다고 부연 설명을 하고 있으므로 정답.

19

M-Cn Let's ask for a transcript of the radio interview.

W-Br (A) There were several promising candidates.

(B) The station already sent a copy.

(C) I usually listen while I'm driving.

라디오 인터뷰 대본을 요청해 봅시다.
(A) 유망한 후보들이 몇 명 있었습니다.
(B) 방송국에서 이미 한 부 보냈습니다.
(C) 전 보통 운전 중에 들어요.

어휘 transcript (말로 된 것을) 글로 옮긴 것, 기록 ask for ~을 요청하다 promising 유망한 candidate 후보자 station 방송국

해설 라디오 인터뷰 대본을 요청하자고 제안하는 평서문

(A) 연상 단어 오답. 질문의 radio interview에서 연상 가능한 candidates를 이용한 오답.

(B) 정답. 라디오 인터뷰 대본을 요청하자는 제안에 방송국에서 이미 한 부 보냈다는 대답으로 그럴 필요 없다는 말을 우회적으로 하고 있으므로 정답.

(C) 연상 단어 오답. 질문의 radio에서 연상 가능한 listen while I'm driving을 이용한 오답.

20

M-Au The rate of employee absences has gone up.

W-Am (A) I can cover your shift for you.

(B) Most staff members like the policy.

(C) Let's try to figure out why.

직원 결근률이 증가했습니다.
(A) 제가 대신 교대 근무를 할 수 있습니다.
(B) 대다수 직원들은 그 정책을 마음에 들어 합니다.
(C) 왜 그런지 한번 알아봅시다.

어휘 rate 비율 absence 결석, 결근 go up 오르다 cover 떠맡다, 담당하다 shift 교대조 policy 방침 figure out 알아내다

해설 정보를 제공하는 평서문

(A) 연상 단어 오답. 질문의 employee absences에서 연상 가능한 cover your shift를 이용한 오답.

(B) 연상 단어 오답. 질문의 employee에서 연상 가능한 staff members를 이용한 오답.

(C) 정답. 직원 결근률이 증가했다는 말에 왜 그런지 이유를 파악해 보자고 답하고 있으므로 정답.

21

W-Br Doesn't Ms. Murphy have a degree in journalism?

M-Cn (A) Let's turn the temperature down a few degrees.

(B) I write in my journal every evening.

(C) No, but she has a lot of experience.

머피 씨는 언론학 학위가 있지 않나요?
(A) 온도를 몇 도만 낮춥시다.
(B) 저는 매일 저녁 일기를 써요.
(C) 아니요. 하지만 그녀는 경험이 많아요.

어휘 degree 학위, (온도 단위) 도 journalism 언론 turn down 낮추다 temperature 온도 journal 일기, 정기 간행물

해설 머피 씨가 언론학 학위가 있는지를 묻는 부정의문문

(A) 연상 단어 오답. 질문의 degree를 온도 단위로 잘못 이해했을 때 연상 가능한 temperature, a few degrees를 이용한 오답.

(B) 유사 발음 오답. 질문의 journalism과 일부 발음이 동일한 journal을 이용한 오답.

(C) 정답. 머피 씨가 언론학 학위가 있는지 묻는 질문에 아니라고 대답한 후 그렇지만 경험이 많다고 부연 설명을 하고 있으므로 정답.

22

W-Am Can I say a few words before the ceremony begins?

W-Br (A) To present awards to team leaders.

(B) I'm not sure there will be time.

(C) But we have so few left.

식전에 제가 몇 마디 해도 될까요?
(A) 팀장들에게 상을 시상하기 위해서요.
(B) 시간이 될지 모르겠네요.
(C) 하지만 남은 게 거의 없어요.

어휘 ceremony 식, 의식 present 주다, 수여하다

해설 자신이 몇 마디 해도 되는지 묻는 요청 의문문

(A) 연상 단어 오답. 질문의 ceremony에서 연상 가능한 awards를 이용한 오답.

(B) 정답. 식전에 몇 마디 해도 되는지 요청하는 질문에 시간이 있을지 모르겠다는 말로 부정적으로 대답하고 있으므로 정답.

(C) 단어 반복 오답. 질문의 few를 반복한 오답.

23

M-Au Why do these containers have more labels than the others?

W-Br (A) They are filled with harmful chemicals.
(B) Please print clearly on the label.
(C) I'd be happy to give you another one.

이 용기들은 다른 것들보다 왜 라벨이 더 많이 붙어 있죠?
(A) 거기에는 유해 화학물질들이 가득 차 있어요.
(B) 라벨에 정자로 또렷하게 기입하세요.
(C) 기꺼이 하나 더 드리죠.

어휘 container 용기 label 표, 라벨 be filled with ~로 가득 차다
harmful 유해한 print 정자로 쓰다 clearly 또렷하게

해설 다른 용기보다 라벨이 더 많이 붙어 있는 이유를 묻는 Why 의문문
(A) 정답. 이 용기들에 왜 라벨이 더 많이 붙어 있느냐는 질문에 유해한 화학물질이 가득 차 있다고 이유를 설명하고 있으므로 정답.
(B) 단어 반복 오답. 질문의 labels를 반복한 오답.
(C) 유사 발음 오답. 질문의 others와 부분적으로 발음이 동일한 another를 이용한 오답.

24

W-Am How do I assemble this file cabinet?

M-Cn (A) Weren't some instructions included?
(B) He resembles someone I know.
(C) To keep confidential files secure.

이 파일 캐비닛은 어떻게 조립하는 겁니까?
(A) 설명서에 포함되어 있지 않던가요?
(B) 그는 내가 아는 사람을 닮았어요.
(C) 기밀 문서들을 안전하게 보관하기 위해서요.

어휘 assemble 조립하다 instructions (사용) 설명서 include 포함하다 resemble 닮다 confidential 기밀의 secure 안전하게 보관된

해설 캐비닛 조립 방법을 묻는 How 의문문
(A) 정답. 캐비닛 조립 방법을 묻는 질문에 설명서가 포함되어 있지 않느냐고 되물어 봄으로써 본인은 모른다는 걸 간접적으로 전달하고 있으므로 정답.
(B) 유사 발음 오답. 질문의 assemble과 부분적으로 발음이 동일한 resembles를 이용한 오답.
(C) 연상 단어 오답. 질문의 file cabinet에서 연상 가능한 keep confidential files secure를 이용한 오답.

25

M-Au Should we use the same supplier as last time or search for a new one?

W-Br (A) She used the Search function on her computer.
(B) I think we can find a better deal.
(C) Yes, the supplies are running low.

지난번과 같은 공급업체를 이용해야 하나요, 아니면 새 업체를 찾아야 하나요?
(A) 그녀는 컴퓨터에서 검색 기능을 사용했어요.
(B) 더 조건이 좋은 업체를 찾을 수 있을 거예요.
(C) 네, 비품들이 떨어져 가고 있습니다.

어휘 supplier 공급업체 search for ~을 찾다 function 기능 deal 거래, (사업 상) 합의 run low 고갈되다, 떨어져 가다

해설 업체 변경 여부를 묻는 선택의문문
(A) 단어 반복 오답. 질문의 use, search를 반복한 오답.
(B) 정답. 지난번과 같은 공급업체를 이용할지 새 업체를 찾을지 묻는 질문에 더 조건이 좋은 업체를 찾을 수 있을 거라고 응답해 새 업체를 찾아보자는 의견을 밝혔으므로 정답.
(C) 파생어 오답. 질문의 supplier와 파생어 관계인 supplies를 이용한 오답.

26

M-Cn Where can I find the train headed for Manila?

M-Au (A) Check the departures board.
(B) Every fifteen minutes or so.
(C) Yes, I'm the head of the department.

마닐라행 열차를 타려면 어디로 가야 하나요?
(A) 출발 시각 게시판을 확인하세요.
(B) 대략 15분마다 있어요.
(C) 네, 제가 부서장입니다.

어휘 be headed for ~로 향하다 departures board (역·공항의) 출발 시각 게시판 head 장(長) department 부서

해설 기차의 위치를 묻는 Where의문문
(A) 정답. 마닐라행 열차를 타려면 어디로 가야 하는지에 대한 질문에 출발 게시판을 확인해 보라며 우회적으로 모른다는 것을 표현하고 있으므로 정답.
(B) 질문과 상관없는 오답. 빈도를 물어보는 How often 의문문에 어울리는 응답이므로 오답.
(C) Yes/No 불가 오답. Where 의문문에는 Yes/No 응답이 불가능하므로 오답.

27

M-Au She is aware of the safety regulations, isn't she?

W-Am (A) Her gloves and shoes.
(B) As far as I know.
(C) Attending a safety workshop.

그녀가 안전 규정을 잘 알고 있죠, 그렇죠?
(A) 그녀의 장갑과 신발이요.
(B) 제가 아는 한 그렇습니다.
(C) 안전 워크숍 참석이요.

어휘 be aware of ~을 알다 safety regulation 안전 규정 as far as ~하는 한 attend 참석하다

해설 안전 규정을 아는지 여부를 묻는 부가의문문
(A) 연상 단어 오답. 질문의 safety regulations에서 연상 가능한 gloves and shoes를 이용한 오답.
(B) 정답. 그녀가 안전 규정을 아는지 묻는 질문에 본인이 아는 한 그렇다고 응답하므로 정답.
(C) 단어 반복 오답. 질문의 safety를 반복한 오답.

28

W-Br Where can I exchange foreign currency for the bills used locally?

M-Cn (A) It depends on what you have.

　　　(B) We had a wonderful trip abroad.

　　　(C) Change your ticket at the station.

현지 사용 지폐로 바꾸기 위한 환전은 어디서 할 수 있죠?

(A) 어떤 돈이냐에 따라 다릅니다.

(B) 저희는 멋진 해외여행을 했습니다.

(C) 역에서 승차권을 교환하세요.

어휘 exchange 환전하다 foreign currency 외화 bill 지폐 locally 지역[현지]에서 depend on ~에 달려 있다

해설 환전 장소를 묻는 Where 의문문

(A) 정답. 현지 사용 지폐로 바꾸기 위한 환전을 어디서 할 수 있느냐는 질문에 갖고 있는 돈에 따라 장소가 다르다고 답하고 있으므로 정답.

(B) 연상 단어 오답. 질문의 foreign에서 연상 가능한 abroad를 이용한 오답.

(C) 유사 발음 오답. 질문의 exchange와 부분적으로 발음이 동일한 change를 이용한 오답.

29

W-Am We should paint the house to make it more attractive to potential buyers.

M-Au (A) Actually, I'm living in an apartment.

　　　(B) Each one has a protective coating.

　　　(C) I'm not sure that would be worth it.

집을 새로 칠해서 잠재 구매자들에게 더 멋지게 보이도록 해야 합니다.

(A) 사실은 전 아파트에서 살아요.

(B) 각각 보호막 코팅이 되어 있어요.

(C) 그럴 만한 가치가 있을지 잘 모르겠네요.

어휘 attractive 멋진, 매력적인 potential 가능성이 있는, 잠재적인 protective 보호용의 coating 겉칠, 도료 worth ~의 가치가 있는

해설 페인트칠을 새로 해야 한다는 제안의 평서문

(A) 연상 단어 오답. 질문의 house에서 연상 가능한 apartment를 이용한 오답.

(B) 연상 단어 오답. 질문의 paint에서 연상 가능한 coating을 이용한 오답.

(C) 정답. 잠재 구매자들에게 더 멋지게 보이기 위해 집을 새로 칠해야 한다는 제안에 그럴 만한 가치가 있을지 모르겠다고 부정적으로 응답하고 있으므로 정답.

30

M-Cn Is the company going to reimburse my travel expenses?

W-Am (A) Only those related to business.

　　　(B) It's becoming more expensive.

　　　(C) I had a wonderful trip.

제 출장 경비를 회사에서 환급해 주나요?

(A) 업무 관련 경비만요.

(B) 더 비싸지고 있어요.

(C) 즐거운 여행이었어요.

어휘 reimburse 환급하다 expense 경비, 비용 related to ~에 관련된

해설 출장 경비 환급 여부를 묻는 의문문

(A) 정답. 출장 경비 환급 여부를 묻는 질문에 업무 관련 경비만 환급된다고 부연 설명을 하고 있으므로 정답.

(B) 유사 발음 오답. 질문의 expenses와 부분적으로 발음이 동일한 expensive를 이용한 오답.

(C) 연상 단어 오답. 질문의 travel에서 연상 가능한 trip을 이용한 오답.

31

M-Au The prototype doesn't require any more changes, does it?

W-Br (A) We're ready to go public with it.

　　　(B) I don't know when I'll retire.

　　　(C) A modern design.

시제품은 이제 더 이상 변경할 필요가 없는 거죠, 그렇죠?

(A) 일반에게 공개할 준비가 됐습니다.

(B) 제가 언제 은퇴할지 저도 모릅니다.

(C) 현대적 디자인이요.

어휘 prototype 시제품, 원형 require 필요로 하다 go public 공개하다 retire 은퇴하다 modern 현대의

해설 추가 변경이 필요한지 여부를 확인하는 부가 의문문

(A) 정답. 시제품은 더 이상 변경이 필요 없느냐는 질문에 일반에게 공개할 준비가 됐다는 말로 변경이 필요 없다는 응답을 하고 있으므로 정답.

(B) 유사 발음 오답. 질문의 require과 부분적으로 발음이 유사한 retire를 이용한 오답.

(C) 연상 단어 오답. 질문의 prototype에서 연상 가능한 design을 이용한 오답.

PART 3

32-34

W-Am Hello. **32I'm calling because I need to get my passport renewed, and I'm wondering how long the renewal process takes. 33I have to go to Singapore on July twelfth for a factory inspection.**

M-Au Our regular service takes four to six weeks. **34But since you don't have much time, you could pay an additional eighty dollars for our fast-track service.** Then you'll receive your passport in just one week.

W-Am **34OK, I'll do that.** I don't want to have to postpone my trip.

여 여보세요. 여권 갱신을 해야 해서 전화 드립니다. 갱신 절차가 얼마나 걸리는지 궁금한데요. 7월 12일에 공장을 시찰하러 싱가포르에 가야 합니다.

남 저희 일반 서비스는 4주에서 6주가 소요됩니다. **하지만 시간이 얼마 없으시니 80달러를 추가로 내시고 신속 서비스를 이용하실 수 있습니다.** 그러면 1주일 만에 여권을 수령하실 수 있습니다.

여 **네, 그렇게 하죠.** 출장을 연기하고 싶지 않아서요.

어휘 renew 갱신하다 process 절차 renewal 갱신
inspection 검사, 조사 regular 일반적인 additional
추가의 fast-track 신속한, 급행의 postpone 연기하다

32

Why is the woman calling?

(A) To inquire about a procedure
(B) To pay a late fee
(C) To book some plane tickets
(D) To report a lost passport

여자는 왜 전화하는가?

(A) 어떤 절차에 대해 문의하려고
(B) 연체료를 지불하려고
(C) 항공권을 예매하려고
(D) 여권 분실을 신고하려고

어휘 inquire about ~에 대해 문의하다 procedure 절차 late fee
연체료 book 예약하다 report 신고하다 lost 분실된

해설 전체 내용 관련 – 여자가 전화한 이유

여자의 첫 번째 대사에서 여권 갱신을 해야 해서 전화했고(I'm calling because I need to get my passport renewed), 갱신 절차가 얼마나 걸리는지 궁금하다(I'm wondering how long the renewal process takes)고 했으므로 정답은 (A)이다.

▸ Paraphrasing 대화의 **the renewal process**
→ 정답의 **a procedure**

33

Why will the woman travel to Singapore?

(A) To inspect a facility
(B) To receive an award
(C) To sign a contract
(D) To take a vacation

여자는 왜 싱가포르로 가는가?

(A) 시설을 시찰하기 위해
(B) 상을 수상하기 위해
(C) 계약을 체결하기 위해
(D) 휴가를 가기 위해

어휘 inspect 점검하다, 시찰하다 facility 시설 award 상 sign a
contract 계약을 맺다, 계약서에 서명하다

해설 세부 사항 관련 – 여자가 싱가포르로 가는 이유

여자의 첫 번째 대사에서 7월 20일에 공장을 시찰하러 싱가포르에 가야 한다 (I have to go to Singapore on July twelfth for a factory inspection)고 했으므로 정답은 (A)이다.

▸ Paraphrasing 대화의 **factory inspection**
→ 정답의 **inspect a facility**

34

What does the woman plan to do?

(A) Call back later
(B) Use an express service
(C) Postpone her trip
(D) Search for information online

여자는 무엇을 할 계획인가?

(A) 나중에 다시 전화하기
(B) 신속 서비스 이용하기
(C) 출장 연기하기
(D) 온라인에서 정보 검색하기

어휘 express 신속한 postpone 연기하다 search for ~을 찾다

해설 세부 사항 관련 – 여자의 계획

남자의 첫 번째 대사에서 시간이 얼마 없으니 80달러를 추가로 내고 신속 서비스를 이용할 수 있다(since you don't have much time, you could pay an additional eighty dollars for our fast-track service)고 했고 그 다음 대사에서 여자가 그렇게 하겠다(I'll do that)고 했으므로 정답은 (B)이다.

▸ Paraphrasing 대화의 **our fast-track service**
→ 정답의 **an express service**

35-37

M-Cn Good afternoon. One of your salespeople called. **35He said the air conditioner isn't running.**

W-Br **35We appreciate your coming so quickly.** You need to go to the third floor. **36Unfortunately, the section of our building with the elevators is being painted, so no one's allowed in there.** You'll have to take the stairs.

M-Cn That's no problem. I'll just grab my equipment from my truck parked outside. **36And when I'm finished, do I give the itemized bill to you or someone upstairs?**

W-Br You should talk to the department head, Sherry Jackson. Just ask for her when you get to the third floor.

M-Cn OK, thanks.

남 안녕하세요. 판매원 중 한 분이 전화하셨어요. **에어컨이 작동이 안 된다고 하던데요.**

여 **이렇게 빨리 와 주셔서 고맙습니다.** 3층으로 가셔야 해요. **어쩌죠, 건물 엘리베이터가 있는 구역에서 지금 페인트칠을 하고 있어요. 그래서 아무도 그쪽으로 갈 수 없거든요.** 계단을 이용하셔야 합니다.

남 괜찮습니다. 밖에 주차해 놓은 트럭에서 장비를 가지고 올게요. **그리고 제가 일을 마치면 청구명세서를 그쪽에게 드릴까요, 아니면 위층에 있는 분에게 드릴까요?**

여 부서장인 쉐리 잭슨 씨와 이야기하세요. 3층에 가셔서 잭슨 씨를 찾으시면 됩니다.

남 네, 감사합니다.

어휘 salespeople 판매원 run (기계 등이) 작동하다
appreciate 고마워하다 section 구역 allow 허용하다
stairs 계단 grab (급히) 잡다 equipment 장비 itemize
항목별로 정리하다, ~의 명세를 적다 bill 청구서 department
부서 head 장(長)

35

Who most likely is the man?

(A) A technician
(B) A security guard
(C) A salesperson
(D) A new client

남자는 누구이겠는가?

(A) 기술자
(B) 경비
(C) 판매원
(D) 신규 고객

해설 전체 내용 관련 – 남자의 신분

남자의 첫 번째 대사에서 판매원 한 명이 전화로 에어컨이 작동이 안 된다(the air conditioner isn't running)고 했고, 이에 여자가 빨리 와 주어서 감사하다(We appreciate your coming so quickly)고 했으므로 정답은 (A)이다.

36

What problem does the woman mention?

(A) A door is locked shut.
(B) A business has closed.
(C) An area is off limits.
(D) An employee is absent.

여자가 언급한 문제는 무엇인가?

(A) 문이 잠겼다.
(B) 영업이 끝났다.
(C) 어떤 구역이 출입 금지다.
(D) 직원 한 명이 결근했다.

어휘 lock 잠그다 shut 닫다 off limits 출입 금지의 absent 결석한, 결근한

해설 세부 사항 관련 – 여자가 언급한 문제

여자의 첫 번째 대사에서 건물 엘리베이터가 있는 구역에서 지금 페인트칠을 하고 있어(the section of our building with the elevators is being painted) 아무도 그쪽으로 갈 수 없다(so no one's allowed in there)고 했으므로 정답은 (C)이다.

▸▸ Paraphrasing 대화의 no one's allowed in there
→ 정답의 An area is off limits.

37

What does the man ask about?

(A) Where to submit an invoice
(B) When some equipment will arrive
(C) Where to park his truck
(D) When the work will be completed

남자는 무엇에 대해 문의하는가?

(A) 청구서를 어디에 내는지
(B) 언제 장비가 도착하는지
(C) 자신의 트럭을 어디에 주차해야 하는지
(D) 언제 업무가 끝날지

어휘 submit 제출하다 invoice 청구서, 송장 park 주차하다
complete 완료하다

해설 세부 사항 관련 – 남자가 문의하는 것

남자의 두 번째 대사에서 일을 마치면 청구명세서를 여자에게 줘야 하는지 아니면 위층에 있는 사람에게 줘야 하는지(when I'm finished, do I give the itemized bill to you or someone upstairs)를 묻고 있으므로 정답은 (A)이다.

▸▸ Paraphrasing 대화의 the itemized bill → 정답의 an invoice

38-40

M-Cn **38Hello, I'm moving to a new apartment, and my friend recommended your company. Could you tell me how much it would cost to move everything in a two-bedroom apartment?**

W-Am For two-bedroom apartments, we have a flat fee for moves within the city limits. It's five hundred dollars for weekend days. **39But if your schedule is flexible, you should book a time slot for Monday through Friday because it's twenty percent cheaper.**

M-Cn Hmm… the last day of my lease is a Saturday, but I might be able to change it. **40Let me call my landlord and see what he has to say.** Then I'll call you back.

W-Am All right. I hope it works out.

남 여보세요, 제가 새 아파트로 이사 가는데요. 제 친구가 이 회사를 추천해 줬어요. 방 두 개짜리 아파트의 짐 전부를 옮기는 데 비용이 얼마나 들까요?

여 방 두 개짜리 아파트는 시내 이사인 경우 정액제를 적용합니다. 주말에는 500달러입니다. 그러나 일정 조정이 가능하면 월요일에서 금요일 사이의 시간대를 예약하세요. 20퍼센트 더 싸거든요.

남 음, 임대 계약 마지막 날이 토요일입니다. 하지만 변경할 수 있을 거예요. 집주인한테 전화로 얘기해 볼게요. 그런 다음 다시 전화 드릴게요.

여 좋아요. 잘되길 바라요.

어휘 cost 비용이 들다 flat fee 정액 요금 within the city limits 시내에 flexible 유연한, 융통성 있는 book 예약하다 time slot 시간대 lease 임대차 계약 landlord 집주인, 임대주 work out (일이) 잘되다, 풀리다

38

What is the conversation mainly about?

(A) A real estate contract
(B) An apartment renovation
(C) A government regulation
(D) A moving service

대화의 주요 내용은 무엇인가?

(A) 부동산 계약
(B) 아파트 개조
(C) 정부 규정
(D) 이삿짐 운송 서비스

어휘 real estate 부동산 contract 계약 renovation 개조
regulation 규정

해설 전체 내용 관련 – 대화의 주제

남자의 첫 번째 대사에서 새 아파트로 이사 가는데(I'm moving to a new apartment), 방 두 개짜리 아파트의 짐 전부를 옮기는 데 비용이 얼마나 (Could you tell me how much it would cost to move everything in a two-bedroom apartment)고 질문하고 있으므로 정답은 (D)이다.

> ▸▸ Paraphrasing 대화의 **move everything in a two-bedroom apartment** → 정답의 **A moving service**

39

What does the woman suggest doing?

(A) Taking a citywide tour
(B) Booking a weekday appointment
(C) Reading a company brochure
(D) Making a payment in advance

여자는 무엇을 하라고 제안하는가?

(A) 시 관광하기
(B) 평일 예약하기
(C) 회사 안내 책자 읽기
(D) 미리 지불하기

어휘 take a tour 관광하다 citywide 시 전체에 book 예약하다
weekday 평일 brochure (광고, 안내) 소책자 make a payment 지불하다 in advance 사전에, 미리

해설 세부 사항 관련 – 여자의 제안

여자의 첫 번째 대사에서 일정 조정이 가능하면 월요일에서 금요일 사이의 시간대를 예약하는 게 좋고(if your schedule is flexible, you should book a time slot for Monday through Friday), 그것이 20퍼센트 더 싸다(it's twenty percent cheaper)고 했으므로 정답은 (B)이다.

> ▸▸ Paraphrasing 대화의 **book a time slot for Monday through Friday** → 정답의 **Booking a weekday appointment**

40

What will the man most likely do next?

(A) Confirm a deposit
(B) Make another phone call
(C) Give the woman his address
(D) E-mail his landlord

남자는 다음으로 무엇을 하겠는가?

(A) 입금 확인하기
(B) 또 다른 통화하기
(C) 여자에게 자신의 주소 제공하기
(D) 집주인에게 이메일 보내기

어휘 confirm 확인하다 deposit 예금, 입금

해설 세부 사항 관련 – 남자가 다음으로 할 일

남자의 두 번째 대사에서 집주인한테 전화로 얘기해 보고(Let me call my landlord and see what he has to say) 다시 전화하겠다고 했으므로 정답은 (B)이다.

> ▸▸ Paraphrasing 대화의 **call my landlord** → 정답의 **Make another phone call**

41-43 3인 대화

W-Am	**41Have you read the monthly report that came out this morning?** How is the Oak City branch already finished with their inventory assessments?
W-Br	They hired an outside company that sends in about fifty people to do all of the inventory work in one night.
M-Au	That sounds great, **42but... um... I'm not sure we could afford that. We've only budgeted a certain amount for this task.**
W-Br	Actually, since we have to pay our employees overtime to stay late, the cost is about the same. **43I'll get you the company's phone number so you can find out more.**
M-Au	Thanks. I'll check it out.

여1 오늘 아침에 나온 월례 보고서 읽어 보셨나요? 어떻게 오크 시티 지점은 벌써 재고 평가를 완료한 거죠?

여2 거기는 외부 회사를 고용했어요. 약 50명의 인원을 보내서 하룻밤에 모든 재고 관련 업무를 완수한대요.

남 좋네요. 그런데 우리도 그렇게 할 형편이 되는지 모르겠어요. 우리는 이 업무를 위해 일정 금액만 예산으로 책정해 놓았어요.

여2 사실 야근하는 직원들에게 초과 업무 수당을 지급해야 하기 때문에 비용은 거의 같습니다. 제가 그 회사 전화번호를 알려 드릴 테니 더 자세한 내용을 알아보세요.

남 고마워요. 제가 알아보죠.

어휘 monthly 월례의 come out 출간되다 branch 지점
inventory 재고 assessment 평가 outside 외부의
send in ~을 파견하다 afford 여유가 되다, 형편이 되다
budget 예산을 세우다, 예산으로 책정하다 amount 금액
task 과업, 업무 overtime 초과 근무 stay late 늦게까지
있다 find out 알아내다 check out ~을 확인[조사]하다

41

What happened this morning?

(A) A new branch was opened.
(B) A report was released.
(C) A delivery was made.
(D) A meeting was held.

오늘 아침에 무슨 일이 있었는가?

(A) 새 지점이 개점했다.
(B) 보고서가 나왔다.
(C) 배송품이 도착했다.
(D) 회의가 열렸다.

어휘 release 발표하다

해설 세부 사항 관련 – 오늘 아침에 있었던 일
여자의 첫 번째 대사에서 오늘 아침에 나온 월례 보고서를 읽어 보았는지
(Have you read the monthly report that came out this morning) 질
문했으므로 정답은 (B)이다.

▸▸ Paraphrasing 대화의 **the monthly report that came out this morning**
→ 정답의 **A report was released.**

42

What is the man concerned about?

(A) Losing a document
(B) Damaging some equipment
(C) Upsetting senior employees
(D) Exceeding a budget

남자는 무엇을 우려하는가?
(A) 문서 분실
(B) 장비 손상
(C) 상급 직원을 당황하게 만드는 것
(D) 예산 초과

어휘 damage 훼손하다 equipment 장비 upset 당황하게 하다
senior 상급의 exceed 초과하다, 능가하다 budget 예산

해설 세부 사항 관련 – 남자가 우려하는 것
남자의 첫 번째 대사에서 그렇게 할 형편이 되는지 모르겠다(I'm not sure we
could afford that)고 했고, 이 업무를 위해 일정 금액만 예산으로 책정해 놓
았다(We've only budgeted a certain amount for this task)고 했으므로
정답은 (D)이다.

43

What will the man receive from one of the women?

(A) Some discount coupons
(B) An updated contract
(C) Some contact details
(D) An overtime payment

남자는 여자 중 한 명에게 무엇을 받을 것인가?
(A) 할인 쿠폰
(B) 갱신된 계약서
(C) 연락처 정보
(D) 초과 근무 수당

어휘 discount 할인 updated 갱신된 detail 세부 사항

해설 세부 사항 관련 – 남자가 여자에게 받을 것
두 번째 여자의 두 번째 대사에서 그 회사의 전화번호를 알려 드릴 테니 더 자
세한 내용을 알아보라(I'll get you the company's phone number so you
can find out more)고 했으므로 정답은 (C)이다.

▸▸ Paraphrasing 대화의 **the company's phone number**
→ 정답의 **Some contact details**

44-46

M-Cn Corrine, **44I'm supposed to pick up Ms.
Balderas, one of our VIP clients, at the
train station this afternoon. What's the
best way to get there?**

W-Br Normally, I'd take Vanderburg Street all
the way to Portland Boulevard, but I heard
on the radio that there was a big traffic
jam on Vanderburg. **45You might want to
check the Department of Transportation's
traffic report on their Web site to see if
it's been cleared.**

M-Cn All right, I'll do that. Her train arrives at
two o'clock, so I want to make sure I'm
there on time.

W-Br **46If you need me to cover your company
phone while you're gone, just let me
know.** I can take down any important
messages.

남 코린, 제가 오후에 우리 VIP 고객 중 한 명인 발데라스 씨를 기차역에서
차로 태워 와야 하는데요. 거기로 가는 가장 좋은 경로가 어떻게
됩니까?

여 보통 저는 밴더버그를 타서 포트랜드 대로까지 갑니다만 라디오에서
밴더버그에 교통 체증이 심했다고 하던데요. 교통부 웹사이트에서
정체가 풀렸는지 교통 정보를 확인하시는 게 좋을 듯 합니다.

남 네, 그렇게 하죠. 고객이 타고 오는 기차가 2시에 도착하니 제시간에
거기에 가 있어야죠.

여 출타 중에 업무 전화를 대신 받아 줄 사람 필요하면 저한테 말씀하세요.
제가 중요한 전화 메시지를 받아 놓을게요.

어휘 be supposed to ~하기로 되어 있다 client 고객 all the
way 내내 traffic jam 교통 체증 might want to ~해
두면 좋을 것이다 department 부, 국 transportation
수송, 교통 traffic report 교통 정보[안내 정보] clear 치우다,
정리하다 make sure 반드시 ~하다 on time 정각에, 제때에
cover 떠맡다, 책임지다 be gone 부재[외출] 중이다 take
down 적어 두다

44

What does the man ask the woman to do?

(A) Pick up an important client
(B) Reserve a meeting space
(C) Give him driving directions
(D) Book some train tickets

남자는 여자에게 무엇을 해 달라고 부탁하는가?
(A) 중요 고객을 차로 모셔 오기
(B) 회의 장소 예약하기
(C) 운전 경로 설명하기
(D) 열차표 예약하기

Test 10

어휘 pick up 태우러 가다 reserve 예약하다 meeting space 회의
장소 driving directions 운전 경로 book 예약하다

해설 세부 사항 관련 - 남자가 여자에게 부탁한 일
남자의 첫 번째 대사에서 오후에 VIP 고객 중 한 명인 발데라스 씨를 기차역에
서 차로 태우고 와야 하는데(I'm supposed to pick up Ms. Balderas, one
of our VIP clients, at the train station this afternoon), 거기로 가는 가
장 좋은 경로가 어떻게 되는지(What's the best way to get there)를 묻고
있으므로 정답은 (C)이다.

▸▸ Paraphrasing   대화의 **the best way to get there**
                  → 정답의 **directions**

45

What does the woman recommend doing?

(A) Postponing an activity
(B) Borrowing a company car
(C) Checking a report online
(D) Using public transportation

여자는 무엇을 하라고 권하는가?
(A) 어떤 활동 연기하기
(B) 회사 차 빌리기
(C) 정보를 온라인으로 확인하기
(D) 대중교통 이용하기

어휘 postpone 연기하다 public transportation 대중교통

해설 세부 사항 관련 - 여자가 추천하는 것
여자의 첫 번째 대사에서 교통부 웹사이트에서 교통 정체가 풀렸는지 교통 정
보를 확인하는 게 좋겠다(You might want to check the Department of
Transportation's traffic report on their Web site to see if it's been
cleared)고 했으므로 정답은 (C)이다.

▸▸ Paraphrasing   대화의 **check the ~ traffic report on their
                  Web site** → 정답의 **Checking a report
                  online**

46

What does the woman offer to do?

(A) Answer the man's phone
(B) Send a reminder
(C) Copy some documents
(D) Accompany the man

여자는 무엇을 해 주겠다고 하는가?
(A) 남자의 전화 받아 주기
(B) 독촉장 보내기
(C) 문서 복사하기
(D) 남자와 동행하기

어휘 reminder (메모·전화 등) 상기시켜 주는 것, 독촉장 accompany
동행하다, 함께 가다

해설 세부 사항 관련 - 여자의 제안
여자의 두 번째 대사에서 출장 중에 업무 전화를 대신 받아 줄 사람이 필요하
면 말하라(If you need me to cover your company phone while you're
gone, just let me know)고 했으므로 정답은 (A)이다.

▸▸ Paraphrasing   대화의 **cover your company phone**
                  → 정답의 **Answer the man's phone**

47-49

M-Au	Hi, Ms. Dunford, this is Sean Goodman. **47There's a house for sale in the Pineview neighborhood that I want to show you.** It's within the price range of the loan that your bank has pre-approved.
W-Br	That neighborhood is near my office, so that'd be nice. **48Does it have four bedrooms as I requested?**
M-Au	**48Just three, actually,** but I think that you'll find that the rest of this property's amenities will more than make up for that.
W-Br	I'm sorry, but that point is nonnegotiable.
M-Au	I understand. **49In that case, I'll go through our database one more time to see if I can find the perfect match.**
W-Br	Thanks, I appreciate it.

남	안녕하세요, 던포드 씨. 전 숀 굿맨입니다. 파인뷰 지역에 보여 드리고 싶은 집이 매물로 나왔어요. 은행에서 사전 승인한 대출 금액에 맞는 가격대입니다.
여	그 동네는 제 사무실 근처예요. 좋네요. 제가 요청한 대로 침실 4개짜리인가요?
남	실은 3개뿐이에요. 하지만 이 집이 갖춘 다른 편의 시설들을 보시면 그것을 벌충하고도 남을 겁니다.
여	죄송해요. 그 조건은 양보할 수 없어요.
남	알겠습니다. 그러시다면 완벽히 일치하는 매물이 있는지 저희 데이터베이스를 다시 한 번 찾아보겠습니다.
여	고마워요. 그렇게 해 주시니 감사합니다.

어휘 for sale 팔려고 내놓은 neighborhood 동네, 지역 price
range 가격대 loan 대출 pre-approve 사전 승인하다
request 요청하다 property 부동산 amenities 편의 시설
make up for ~을 벌충하다 nonnegotiable 협상의 여지가
없는, 양보할 수 없는 go through ~을 살펴보다 perfect
match 안성맞춤

47

What most likely is the man's occupation?

(A) Real estate agent
(B) Construction worker
(C) Bank teller
(D) Interior designer

남자의 직업은 무엇이겠는가?
(A) 부동산 중개인
(B) 공사장 인부
(C) 은행 창구 직원
(D) 인테리어 디자이너

해설　전체 내용 관련 – 남자의 직업

남자의 첫 번째 대사에서 파인뷰 지역에 보여 드리고 싶은 집이 매물로 나왔다 (There's a house for sale in the Pineview neighborhood that I want to show you)고 했으므로 정답은 (A)이다.

48

What does the woman mean when she says, "that point is nonnegotiable"?

(A) She refuses to delete some contract terms.
(B) She will not agree to pay a higher price.
(C) She wants a certain number of rooms.
(D) She needs to live close to her office.

여자가 "그 조건은 양보할 수 없어요"라고 말할 때 의도하는 바는 무엇인가?

(A) 일부 계약 조건의 삭제를 거부한다.
(B) 돈을 더 많이 지불하는 것에 동의하지 않을 것이다.
(C) 특정 개수의 방을 원한다.
(D) 자신의 사무실 가까이 살아야 한다.

어휘　refuse 거부하다　delete 삭제하다　contract term 계약 조건

해설　화자의 의도 파악 – 양보할 수 없는 조건이라는 말의 의미

여자의 첫 번째 대사에서 요청한 대로 침실이 4개짜리인지를 묻자(Does it have four bedrooms as I requested) 남자가 방이 3개뿐(Just three, actually)이라고 말했다. 그러자 여자가 그 조건은 양보할 수 없다(that point is nonnegotiable)고 했으므로 정답은 (C)이다.

49

What does the man say he will do?

(A) Perform some research
(B) Refund a payment
(C) E-mail some information
(D) Visit the woman in person

남자가 무엇을 할 것이라고 말하는가?

(A) 조사하기
(B) 환불하기
(C) 정보를 이메일로 발송하기
(D) 여자를 직접 찾아가기

어휘　perform 실시하다　research 조사　refund 환불하다　payment 지불(금)　in person 직접

해설　세부 사항 관련 – 남자가 할 일

남자의 세 번째 대사에서 그렇다면 완벽히 일치하는 매물이 있는지 데이터베이스에서 다시 한 번 찾아보겠다(In that case, I'll go through our database one more time to see if I can find the perfect match)고 했으므로 정답은 (A)이다.

▸▸ Paraphrasing　대화의 go through our database
　　　　　　　　 → 정답의 Perform some research

50-52

W-Am　50OK, Kozo, you and I are supposed to clear out the stockroom and arrange everything we're keeping in an orderly fashion.

M-Cn　It's quite a big job. 51To make it go more smoothly, could you print some tags that we can attach to the boxes? Then people can know exactly what's inside without opening them.

W-Am　That would work great. I can borrow a printer and laptop from IT so we don't have to keep going back and forth.

M-Cn　Good idea. 52While you're doing that, I'll get a ladder from the maintenance department. I want to see what's on these top shelves.

여　자, 코조. 오늘 저하고 창고 청소하고 보관하고 있는 물건들 전부 정리정돈해야 돼요.

남　일이 많네요. 좀 더 순조롭게 진행하기 위해 상자들에 붙일 표를 출력해 줄래요? 그러면 상자를 열지 않아도 무엇이 들어 있는지 정확히 알 수 있을 거예요.

여　좋은 방법이네요. IT 부서에서 프린터와 노트북을 빌리면 계속 왔다 갔다 할 필요가 없을 것 같아요.

남　좋은 생각이네요. 그렇게 하시는 동안, 전 시설관리 부서에서 사다리를 가지고 올게요. 꼭대기 선반에 뭐가 있는지 보게요.

어휘　be supposed to ~하기로 되어 있다　clear out 치우다 stockroom (상점, 사무실 등의) 창고, 보관소　arrange 정리하다　orderly 정돈된, 규칙적인　fashion 방식 smoothly 순조롭게　print 출력하다　tag 꼬리표　attach to ~에 붙이다　work 효과가 있다　go back and forth 왔다 갔다 하다　ladder 사다리　maintenance 유지, 시설관리 top 꼭대기의　shelf 선반

50

What task have the speakers been assigned?

(A) Collecting some purchase orders
(B) Stocking the checkout aisle shelves
(C) Organizing a storage area
(D) Finding a new supplier

화자들은 어떤 업무를 맡았는가?

(A) 구입 주문서 수거하기
(B) 계산대 매대 상품 채우기
(C) 창고 정리하기
(D) 새 공급업체 찾기

어휘　collect 모으다, 수거하다　stock 채우다, 갖추다　supplier 공급업체, 납품업체

해설　세부 사항 관련 – 화자들이 맡은 업무

여자의 첫 번째 대사에서 오늘 나하고 사무실 창고를 청소하고 보관하고 있는 물건들 전부 정리정돈 해야 된다고(you and I are supposed to clear out the stockroom and arrange everything we're keeping in an orderly fashion) 했으므로 정답은 (C)이다.

51

What does the man ask the woman to do?

(A) Get detailed instructions
(B) Print a contract
(C) Change the opening hours
(D) Prepare some labels

남자는 여자에게 무엇을 해 달라고 부탁하는가?

(A) 상세한 사용설명서 구하기
(B) 계약서 출력하기
(C) 개점 시간 변경하기
(D) 라벨 준비하기

어휘   detailed 상세한   instructions (사용) 설명(서)   contract 계약서
prepare 준비하다, 마련하다

해설   세부 사항 관련 – 남자가 여자에게 부탁한 것

남자의 첫 번째 대사에서 좀 더 순조롭게 진행하기 위해 상자들에 붙일 표를 출력하라(To make it go more smoothly, could you print some tags that we can attach to the boxes)고 요청했으므로 정답은 (D)이다.

52

Where will the man go next?

(A) To the front entrance
(B) To the maintenance department
(C) To the break room
(D) To the IT department

남자는 다음으로 어디에 갈 것인가?

(A) 현관
(B) 시설관리 부서
(C) 휴게실
(D) IT 부서

해설   세부 사항 관련 – 남자가 다음으로 갈 장소

남자의 두 번째 대사에서 그렇게 하는 동안 시설관리 부서에서 사다리를 가지고 오겠다(While you're doing that, I'll get a ladder from the maintenance department)고 했으므로 정답은 (B)이다.

53-55 3인 대화

M-Au   **53Rachel, Christopher, we still have some planning to do for the outdoor orchestra concert at Ramsey Park.**

W-Am   Right. I'm really concerned about attendance. **54Tickets have been on sale for three weeks, and we still have eighty percent of them left.**

M-Cn   We're depending on that ticket revenue to cover the cost of the event. What can we do?

M-Au   **55Well, so far, we've mainly been advertising the event in the newspaper. How about getting some posters made and putting them up around town instead?**

M-Cn   That should help.

W-Am   Yeah, and I'll volunteer to prepare the design.

남1	레이첼, 크리스토퍼, 램지 파크 야외 오케스트라 콘서트를 위해 계획할 것들이 아직 남았어요.
여	맞아요. 난 관객 수가 정말 걱정돼요. 티켓 판매가 시작된 지 3주가 됐는데 아직 80퍼센트가 팔리지 않았어요.
남2	티켓 수익으로 공연 비용을 충당하고 있잖아요. 어떻게 하죠?
남1	음, 지금까지 주로 신문에 행사를 광고해 왔잖아요. 대신에 포스터를 만들어 시내 곳곳에 붙여 보는 게 어떨까요?
남2	그러면 도움이 되겠어요.
여	맞아요. 제가 디자인을 준비해 볼게요.

어휘   outdoor 야외의   be concerned about ~에 대해 우려하다
attendance 참석자 수, 참석률   on sale 판매되는   depend
on ~에 의존하다   revenue 수익, 수입   cover 충당하다   so
far 지금까지   mainly 주로   advertise 광고하다   put up
게시하다   volunteer 자진하여 하다, 자원하다   prepare
준비하다

53

What are the speakers planning?

(A) A musical performance
(B) A park tour
(C) A sports competition
(D) A volunteer recruitment drive

화자들이 계획하는 것은 무엇인가?

(A) 음악 공연
(B) 공원 관광
(C) 스포츠 대회
(D) 자원봉사자 모집 운동

어휘   performance 공연   competition 대회, 시합   recruitment
모집, 채용   drive 운동, 캠페인

해설   세부 사항 관련 – 화자들이 계획하고 있는 것

첫 번째 남자의 첫 번째 대사에서 램지 파크 야외 오케스트라 콘서트를 위해 계획할 것들이 아직 남아 있다(we still have some planning to do for the outdoor orchestra concert at Ramsey Park)고 말했으므로 정답은 (A)이다.

54

What problem does the woman mention?

(A) Prices have gone up sharply.
(B) Ticket sales have been slow.
(C) Bad weather is expected.
(D) A site has been double-booked.

여자가 언급하는 문제는 무엇인가?

(A) 가격이 급등했다.
(B) 티켓 판매가 저조하다.
(C) 궂은 날씨가 예상된다.
(D) 장소가 이중 예약 돼 있다.

어휘 go up 오르다 sharply 급격하게 sales 판매 expect 예상하다 site 장소 double-book 예약을 이중으로 받다

해설 세부 사항 관련 – 여자가 언급하는 문제
여자의 첫 번째 대사에서 티켓 판매가 시작된 지 3주가 됐지만 아직 80퍼센트가 팔리지 않았다(Tickets have been on sale for three weeks, and we still have eighty percent of them left)고 했으므로 정답은 (B)이다.

▸▸ Paraphrasing 대화의 We still have eighty percent of them left → 정답의 sales have been slow

55

What do the speakers decide to do?

(A) Schedule a newspaper interview
(B) Change an advertising method
(C) Ask for additional funding
(D) Postpone the event

화자들은 무엇을 하기로 결정하는가?

(A) 신문사 인터뷰 일정 잡기
(B) 광고 방법 바꾸기
(C) 추가 자금 요청하기
(D) 행사 연기하기

어휘 advertising 광고 method 방법 additional 추가의 funding 자금 제공, 재정 지원 postpone 연기하다

해설 세부 사항 관련 – 화자들이 하기로 결정한 것
첫 번째 남자의 두 번째 대사에서 지금까지 우리는 주로 신문에 행사를 광고해 왔으니(so far, we've mainly been advertising the event in the newspaper) 포스터를 만들어 시내 곳곳에 붙여 보는 게 어떨지(How about getting some posters made and putting them up around town instead) 제안하고 있으므로 정답은 (B)이다.

56-58

W-Br	Hi, Maki. ⁵⁶Did you hear that the Indian restaurant in the Hannigan neighborhood finally had its grand opening last weekend?
M-Au	⁵⁷Yes, I read a food critic's review on a Web site that has a dining out guide. The writer simply loved the food.

W-Br	My friend said they have the best Indian dishes he's ever eaten. We should check it out.
M-Au	Definitely. How about tomorrow night?
W-Br	⁵⁸Sorry, but I'm afraid I'm busy tomorrow. I've got to give a talk the following day about how the new trade deal will affect our business, so I'll be getting ready for that. Are you free next Monday at seven?
M-Au	Sure. I'll call and make a reservation.

여	안녕하세요, 마키. 해니건 지역에 인도 식당이 드디어 지난주에 개점했다는 소식 들었어요?
남	네, 외식 가이드를 제공하는 웹사이트에서 음식 평론가의 후기를 읽었어요. 글 쓴 사람은 거기 음식을 정말 좋아했어요.
여	제 친구는 자기가 먹어 본 인도 음식 중 최고라고 했어요. 우리 직접 가 봐요.
남	당연하죠. 내일 저녁 어때요?
여	미안하지만 내일은 바쁠 것 같아요. 그 다음날 새 무역 협정이 우리 회사에 어떤 영향을 미칠지에 대해 발표해야 해서 준비해야 하거든요. 다음 주 월요일 7시 시간 되나요?
남	그럼요. 제가 전화해서 예약할게요.

어휘 grand opening 개장, 개점 neighborhood 인근, 지역 finally 마침내 critic 비평가, 비판가 review 평, 후기 dining out 외식 guide 안내(서) simply 정말로 check out 살펴보다 definitely 그렇고 말고, 물론 give a talk 강연하다 following 그 다음의 trade deal 무역 협정 affect 영향을 미치다 get ready for ~에 대비하다 make a reservation 예약하다

56

What is the conversation mainly about?

(A) A company restructuring
(B) A neighborhood festival
(C) A new restaurant
(D) A cooking class

대화의 주요 내용은 무엇인가?

(A) 회사 구조조정
(B) 지역 축제
(C) 새로 문을 연 식당
(D) 요리 수업

어휘 restructuring 구조조정

해설 전체 내용 관련 – 대화의 주제
여자의 첫 번째 대사에서 해니건 지역에 인도 식당이 드디어 지난주에 개점했다는 소식을 들었냐(Did you hear that the Indian restaurant in the Hannigan neighborhood finally had its grand opening last weekend)고 묻고 있으므로 정답은 (C)이다.

▸▸ Paraphrasing 대화의 the Indian restaurant ~ had its grand opening → 정답의 A new restaurant

Test 10

57

Where did the man get some information?

(A) From a magazine advertisement
(B) From an online review
(C) From a friend's recommendation
(D) From a promotional poster

남자는 어디에서 정보를 얻었는가?

(A) 잡지 광고에서
(B) 온라인 후기에서
(C) 친구 추천으로
(D) 홍보 포스터에서

어휘 magazine 잡지 advertisement 광고 recommendation
추천 promotional 홍보의, 광고의

해설 세부 사항 관련 – 남자가 정보를 얻은 경로

남자의 첫 번째 대사에서 외식 가이드를 제공하는 웹사이트에서 음식 평론가
의 후기를 읽었다(I read a food critic's review on a Web site that has a
dining out guide)고 했으므로 정답은 (B)이다.

▸▸ Paraphrasing 대화의 **a food critic's review on a Web site**
→ 정답의 **an online review**

58

Why is the woman unavailable tomorrow?

(A) She is attending an industry trade show.
(B) She needs to prepare for a presentation.
(C) She is holding a meeting with a client.
(D) She has plans to go out of town.

여자가 내일 시간이 안 되는 이유는 무엇인가?

(A) 업계 무역 박람회에 참석한다.
(B) 발표를 준비해야 한다.
(C) 고객과 회의가 있다.
(D) 타지에 갈 계획이다.

어휘 unavailable 만날 수 없는 industry 산업 trade show 무역
박람회 prepare for ~를 준비하다 client 고객 go out of town
(출장 등으로) 도시를 떠나다

해설 세부 사항 관련 – 여자가 내일 시간이 안 되는 이유

여자의 세 번째 대사에서 그 다음날 새 무역 협정이 우리 회사에 어떤 영향
을 미칠지에 대해 발표해야 해서 준비해야 한다(I've got to give a talk
the following day about how the new trade deal will affect our
business, so I'll be getting ready for that)고 했으므로 정답은 (B)이다.

▸▸ Paraphrasing 대화의 **I'll be getting ready for that** → 정답의
needs to prepare for a presentation

59-61

M-Au Hello, Ms. Wheaton. My name is Seth
Mundy, and I'm a reporter for the *Upland
Tribune*. ⁵⁹**Would you be willing to meet
with me to discuss the particulars of the
hospital's expansion plan?**

W-Am Sure. ⁶⁰**We're looking for ways to
generate publicity for our fundraising
campaign, which starts next month.**
We hope it will cover a portion of the
construction expenses.

M-Au I can come to your office anytime this
week. ⁶¹**Or if you're busy, I could just
share my inquiries over the phone.**

W-Am How about now? ⁶¹**You caught me at a rare
moment of down time.**

남 여보세요. 휘턴 씨. 제 이름은 세스 먼디입니다. 〈업랜드 트리뷴〉
기자입니다. 만나서 병원 확장 계획에 관한 자세한 내용을 들려 주실 수
있는지요?

여 그럼요. 저희는 다음 달에 시작되는 기금 마련 캠페인에 대한 대중의
관심을 불러일으킬 방법을 찾고 있습니다. 그렇게 해서 건설 비용의
일부를 충당할 수 있길 바랍니다.

남 저는 이번 주 아무 때나 휘턴 씨 사무실로 찾아 뵐 수 있는데요. 혹
바쁘시면 문의 사항들을 전화로 나눌 수도 있고요.

여 지금은 어떠세요? 마침 제가 짬이 나거든요.

어휘 reporter 기자 be willing to 기꺼이 ~하다 discuss
논의하다 particulars 상세한 사실[사항] expansion
확장, 확대 look for ~을 찾다 way 방법 generate
낳다, 일으키다 publicity 대중[언론]의 관심 fundraising
자금 조달, 모금 cover 충당하다 portion 부분, 일부
construction 공사 expense 경비 inquiry 문의 rare
드문 down time (장비 등의) 가동 휴지 시간, (사람의) 한가한
시간

59

What is the purpose of the man's call?

(A) To set up an interview
(B) To make a medical appointment
(C) To promote a newspaper
(D) To respond to a request

남자가 전화한 목적은 무엇인가?

(A) 인터뷰 약속을 잡기 위해
(B) 병원 진료 예약을 위해
(C) 신문 판촉을 위해
(D) 요청에 답하기 위해

어휘 set up 마련하다 make an appointment (진료) 예약을 하다
promote 홍보하다 respond to ~에 응답하다 request 요청

해설 전체 내용 관련 – 전화의 목적

남자의 첫 번째 대사에서 만나서 병원 확장 계획에 관한 자세한 내용을 들려
줄 수 있는지(Would you be willing to meet with me to discuss the
particulars of the hospital's expansion plan) 묻고 있으므로 정답은 (A)
이다.

▸▸ Paraphrasing 대화의 **meet with me to discuss**
→ 정답의 **an interview**

60

According to the woman, what will happen next month?

(A) Workers will start a building expansion.
(B) The ownership of a hospital will change.
(C) An advertising campaign will begin.
(D) The hospital will raise money for a project.

여자에 따르면 다음 달에 무슨 일이 있는가?

(A) 인부들이 건물 확장 공사를 시작할 것이다.
(B) 병원 주인이 바뀔 것이다.
(C) 광고 캠페인이 시작될 것이다.
(D) **병원이 프로젝트를 위해 모금을 할 것이다.**

어휘 expansion 확장 ownership 소유(권) raise 모으다

해설 세부 사항 관련 – 다음 달에 일어날 일
여자의 첫 번째 대사에서 다음 달에 시작되는 기금 마련 캠페인에 대한 대중의 관심을 불러 일으킬 방법을 찾고 있다(We're looking for ways to generate publicity for our fundraising campaign, which starts next month)고 했으므로 정답은 (D)이다.

▶ **Paraphrasing** 대화의 **fundraising campaign**
→ 정답의 **raise money for a project**

61

Why does the woman say, "How about now"?

(A) To get the man's opinion about a change
(B) To suggest completing a task by phone
(C) To find out if an improvement was made
(D) To check that the phone volume is loud enough

여자가 "지금은 어때세요"라고 말한 이유는 무엇인가?

(A) 변화에 대한 남자의 의견을 듣기 위해
(B) **용무를 전화로 하자고 제안하기 위해**
(C) 개선이 이루어졌는지 알아보기 위해
(D) 전화 볼륨이 충분히 큰지 확인하기 위해

어휘 opinion 의견 suggest 제안하다 complete 수행하다, 완수하다 task 일, 과업 improvement 개선 enough 충분히

해설 화자의 의도 파악 – 지금은 어떤지 묻는 말의 의미
남자의 두 번째 대사에서 혹시 바쁘면 문의 사항들을 전화로 나눌 수도 있다(Or if you're busy, I could just share my inquiries over the phone)고 하자 여자가 지금은 어떠냐(How about now)고 물으며 마침 짬이 난다(You caught me at a rare moment of down time)고 했다. 즉 지금 전화로 질문하라는 의미이므로 정답은 (B)이다.

62-64 대화 + 가격표

W-Br Hello. I'm looking for some curtains for my bedroom. What's the best brand?

M-Cn **62You can't go wrong with curtains from Callaghan. Light can't penetrate through them because of their thick lining.**

W-Br That sounds perfect, as sometimes I work the night shift and sleep during the day. I'll take these charcoal gray ones.

M-Cn Do you know how long you need the curtains to be?

W-Br **63Yes, I've measured the space, and I'd need the seventy-two-inch curtains.**

M-Cn Wonderful. I can ring you up here. **64And you'll notice a code on your receipt. It's for a questionnaire on our Web site. If you complete it, you'll be entered into a prize drawing, so don't miss your chance.**

여 안녕하세요. 제 침실에 쓸 커튼을 찾는데요. 제일 좋은 브랜드가 뭐죠?
남 캘러건 커튼이라면 실패가 없어요. 두꺼운 안감 때문에 빛이 투과되지 않죠.
여 완벽하네요. 가끔 밤 근무를 하면 낮에 자는 경우가 있거든요. 이 진회색 커튼으로 할게요.
남 커튼 길이가 어느 정도여야 하는지 아시나요?
여 네. 제가 치수를 재 왔어요. 72인치 커튼이 필요해요.
남 좋습니다. 여기서 계산해 드릴게요. 영수증에 코드가 있을 거예요. 그건 우리 웹사이트 설문조사용이에요. 작성을 완료하시면 경품 추첨에 자동 참여가 되니 기회를 놓치지 마세요.

어휘 You can't go wrong with ~는 잘못되는 법이 없다[늘 괜찮은 해결책이다] penetrate 관통하다, 뚫다 thick 두꺼운 lining 안감 night shift 밤 근무조 charcoal gray 짙은 회색 measure 측정하다, 재다 space 공간 ring ~ up (상품 가격을 금전등록기에) 입력하다 notice 알아차리다 code 암호, 부호 questionnaire 설문 complete 완료하다 prize drawing 경품 추첨 enter into ~에 참여하다 miss 놓치다

Product Type: Curtains Brand: Callaghan / Width: 52 inches	
Length	Price (includes 2 panels)
54 inches	$79.99
63 inches	$84.99
63 72 inches	$109.99
84 inches	$129.99

제품 유형: 커튼 상표: 캘러건 / 폭: 52인치	
길이	가격 (패널 2개 포함)
54 인치	79.99달러
63 인치	84.99달러
72 인치	109.99달러
84 인치	129.99달러

어휘 product 제품 type 유형 width 폭, 너비 length 길이 include 포함하다

Test 10

62

What does the man mention about the Callaghan brand of curtains?

(A) They are good at blocking light.
(B) They are available in a variety of fabrics.
(C) They come with a money-back guarantee.
(D) They have been manufactured domestically.

남자가 캘러건표 커튼에 대해 언급한 것은 무엇인가?

(A) 빛 차단 기능이 좋다.
(B) 다양한 직물 제품들이 있다.
(C) 환불을 보장한다.
(D) 국내에서 생산됐다.

어휘 block 차단하다 available 구입[이용]할 수 있는 a variety of 다양한 ~ fabric 직물, 천 money-back 환불이 가능한 guarantee 보증 manufacture 생산하다 domestically 국내에(서)

해설 세부 사항 관련 - 남자가 커튼에 대해 언급한 것

남자의 첫 번째 대사에서 캘러건 커튼이라면 실패가 없다(You can't go wrong with curtains from Callaghan)면서 두꺼운 안감 때문에 빛이 투과되지 않는다(Light can't penetrate through them because of their thick lining)고 말했으므로 정답은 (A)이다.

▸▸ Paraphrasing   대화의 Light can't penetrate through them → 정답의 They are good at blocking light.

63

Look at the graphic. How much will the woman pay for her purchase?

(A) $79.99
(B) $84.99
(C) $109.99
(D) $129.99

시각 정보에 의하면, 여자는 얼마를 내야 하는가?

(A) 79.99달러
(B) 84.99달러
(C) 109.99달러
(D) 129.99달러

해설 시각 정보 연계 - 여자가 내야 할 금액

여자의 세 번째 대사에서 72인치 커튼이 필요하다(I'd need the seventy-two-inch curtains)고 말했고, 시각 정보에 따르면 72인치 커튼은 109.99달러이므로 정답은 (C)이다.

64

What does the man encourage the woman to do?

(A) Take a survey
(B) Use a gift-wrap service
(C) Copy the receipt
(D) Pick up a catalog

남자는 여자에게 무엇을 하라고 권하는가?

(A) 설문지 작성하기
(B) 선물 포장 서비스 이용하기
(C) 영수증 복사하기
(D) 카탈로그 챙기기

어휘 survey 설문 조사 gift-wrap 선물 포장

해설 세부 사항 관련 - 남자가 여자에게 제안하는 것

남자의 세 번째 대사에서 영수증에 코드가 있는데(You'll notice a code on your receipt) 설문조사용(It's for a questionnaire on our Web site)이라고 했다. 또한 작성을 완료하면 경품 추첨에 자동 참여가 되니 기회를 놓치지 말라(If you complete it, you'll be entered into a prize drawing, so don't miss your chance)고 했으므로 정답은 (A)이다.

▸▸ Paraphrasing   대화의 a questionnaire → 정답의 a survey

65-67 대화 + 티켓

M-Au Scarlett, just so you know, I'm leaving work early today. ⁶⁶I'm going to an event tonight, and I want to get there one hour before it starts.

W-Br No problem. Where are you going? An art exhibition?

M-Au ⁶⁵No, it's a talk by scientist George Russell about climate change.

W-Br That sounds interesting. I read his most recent book, and I was impressed with how he explained complex topics in a way that everyone can understand. Is he doing any other talks in town? I'd love to see him live.

M-Au Unfortunately, this is the only one, and it's sold out. ⁶⁷But I'd be happy to pick up a handout for you so you can see what was covered.

남 스칼렛, 혹시나 해서 말해 두는데요. 저 오늘 일찍 퇴근합니다. 오늘 밤 행사에 가는데 1시간 전에는 도착하고 싶어요.

여 그러세요. 어디 가세요? 미술 전시회?

남 아니요. 과학자 조지 러셀의 기후 변화에 대한 강연이에요.

여 재미있겠네요. 그의 최신 서적을 읽어봤는데 복잡한 주제들을 누구나 이해할 수 있도록 설명한 것이 인상적이었어요. 시내에서 또 강연 안 하나요? 강연을 실제로 보고 싶어요.

남 아쉽지만 이번 한 번만 하는 거고 표도 매진됐어요. 하지만 무슨 내용을 다뤘는지 볼 수 있게 제가 유인물을 챙겨다 줄게요.

어휘 leave work 퇴근하다 art exhibition 미술 전시회 talk 강연 climate change 기후 변화 recent 최신의 be impressed with ~에 깊은 인상을 받다 explain 설명하다 complex 복잡한 topic 주제 sold out 매진된 handout 유인물 cover 다루다

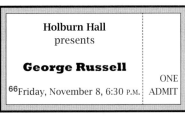

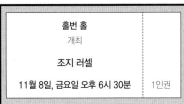

어휘 present 상연하다, 출연시키다 admit 입장을 허가하다

65

What is the conversation mainly about?

(A) An art exhibition
(B) An academic lecture
(C) A rock concert
(D) A comedy show

대화의 주요 내용은 무엇인가?
(A) 미술 전시회
(B) 학술 강연
(C) 록 콘서트
(D) 코미디 쇼

해설 전체 내용 관련 – 대화의 주제
남자의 두 번째 대사에서 기후 변화에 대한 과학자 조지 러셀의 강연(it's a talk by scientist George Russell about climate change)이라고 했으므로 정답은 (B)이다.

▸▸ Paraphrasing 대화의 **a talk by scientist**
→ 정답의 **An academic lecture**

66

Look at the graphic. When does the man plan to arrive at the venue?

(A) At 5:30 P.M.
(B) At 6:00 P.M.
(C) At 7:00 P.M.
(D) At 7:30 P.M.

시각 정보에 의하면, 남자는 행사 장소에 언제 도착할 계획인가?
(A) 오후 5:30
(B) 오후 6:00
(C) 오후 7:00
(D) 오후 7:30

해설 시각 정보 연계 – 남자가 행사에 도착할 시간
남자의 첫 번째 대사에서 오늘 밤 어떤 행사에 가는데 1시간 전에는 도착하고 싶다(I'm going to an event tonight, and I want to get there one hour before it starts)고 했고 시각 정보에 따르면 남자가 가는 행사는 저녁 6시 30분에 시작하므로 정답은 (A)이다.

67

What does the man offer to do for the woman?

(A) Save her a seat
(B) Purchase a ticket
(C) Bring her a document
(D) Record an event

남자는 여자에게 무엇을 해 주겠다고 하는가?
(A) 좌석 잡아 주기
(B) 티켓 구매하기
(C) 문서 가져다 주기
(D) 행사 녹음하기

어휘 save 챙겨 두다, 확보해 두다 purchase 구매하다 bring 가져다 주다 record 녹화[녹음]하다

해설 세부 사항 관련 – 남자의 제안
남자의 세 번째 대사에서 무슨 내용을 다뤘는지 볼 수 있게 유인물을 챙겨다 주겠다(I'd be happy to pick up a handout for you so you can see what was covered)고 했으므로 정답은 (C)이다.

▸▸ Paraphrasing 대화의 **pick up a handout for you**
→ 정답의 **Bring her a document**

68-70 대화 + 일정표

M-Cn	**68Maria, we've got a major problem with the show scheduled for September ninth next week.**
W-Am	Oh, no! What's happened?
M-Cn	**69Toshan Galloway had to be taken to the hospital due to a sudden illness.** He's OK, but since he's the lead actor, the show can't go on without him.
W-Am	I'm glad he's all right, but the fans will be disappointed about the cancellation.
M-Cn	Right, especially since it's on such short notice. We need to get the word out about this change.
W-Am	**70If you give me the username and password for the back end of the Web site, I'll update the schedule and put up a notice for patrons.**

남	마리아, 다음 주 9월 9일 공연에 큰 차질이 생겼어요.
여	맙소사, 무슨 일이에요?
남	토샨 갤러웨이 씨가 갑자기 병이 나서 병원에 실려 갔어요. 지금은 괜찮대요. 하지만 그가 주인공이니 그가 없으면 공연을 할 수가 없잖아요.
여	괜찮다니 다행이에요. 하지만 공연이 취소되면 팬들이 실망하겠어요.
남	맞아요. 특히나 갑자기 그렇게 됐으니 말입니다. 변동 사항에 대해 알려야 해요.
여	저한테 웹사이트 관리자용 사용자명과 비밀번호를 주시면, 제가 일정을 갱신하고 고객들을 위한 공지도 올릴게요.

어휘 major 심각한 scheduled for ~로 예정된 be taken to the hospital 병원에 실려가다 due to ~ 때문에 sudden 갑작스런 lead actor 주인공, 주연배우 disappointed 실망한 cancellation 취소 on short notice 갑자기, 충분한 예고 없이 get the word out 말을 퍼뜨리다 username 사용자 이름 back end (컴퓨터) 사용자가 눈으로 볼 수 없고 관리자만 접근할 수 있는 서버단 update 최신 정보를 추가하다 put up 게시하다 notice 공지 patron 후원자, 고객

Holbrook Theater Schedule
Week of September 5

Sept. 5 [Sun]	Belgium Dance Troupe
68 Sept. 9 [Thurs]	Comedy Showcase
Sept. 10 [Fri]	The McKenzie Brothers
Sept. 11 [Sat]	Jazz Extravaganza

홀브룩 극장 일정
9월 5일 – 9월 11일

9월 5일 [일]	벨기에 무용단
9월 9일 [목]	**코미디 쇼케이스**
9월 10일 [금]	맥켄지 형제
9월 11일 [토]	재즈쇼

어휘 troupe 공연단, 극단 showcase 공개 행사 extravaganza 화려한 쇼

68

Look at the graphic. Which show is affected by the cancellation?

(A) Belgium Dance Troupe
(B) Comedy Showcase
(C) The McKenzie Brothers
(D) Jazz Extravaganza

시각 정보에 의하면, 어떤 공연이 취소로 영향을 받는가?

(A) 벨기에 무용단
(B) 코미디 쇼케이스
(C) 맥켄지 형제
(D) 재즈쇼

해설 시각 정보 연계 – 취소로 영향을 받는 공연

남자의 첫 번째 대사에서 다음 주 9월 9일 공연에 큰 차질이 생겼다(we've got a major problem with the show scheduled for September ninth next week)고 했고, 시각 정보에 따르면 9월 9일 공연은 코미디 쇼케이스이므로 정답은 (B)이다.

69

Why will a show be canceled?

(A) A performer had a medical emergency.
(B) Not enough tickets have been sold.
(C) The venue was double-booked for that date.
(D) Some essential equipment is malfunctioning.

공연이 취소되는 이유는 무엇인가?

(A) 공연자에게 의료 응급 상황이 발생했다.
(B) 티켓이 충분히 팔리지 않았다.
(C) 장소가 같은 날짜에 이중 예약됐다.
(D) 필수 장비가 고장 났다.

어휘 performer 공연자 medical 의료의 emergency 응급 상황 enough 충분한 venue (공연 등의) 장소 double-book 이중으로 예약을 받다 essential 필수적인 malfunction 오작동하다, 고장 나다

해설 세부 사항 관련 – 공연이 취소된 이유

남자의 두 번째 대사에서 토산 갤러웨이 씨가 갑자기 병이 나서 병원에 실려 갔고(Toshan Galloway had to be taken to the hospital due to a sudden illness) 그가 주 공연자(he's the lead act)라고 말했으므로 정답은 (A)이다.

> ▸▸ Paraphrasing 대화의 taken to the hospital due to a sudden illness
> → 정답의 a medical emergency

70

What does the woman ask for?

(A) Some entertainers' names
(B) A Web site address
(C) Some login information
(D) An area code

여자는 무엇을 요청하는가?

(A) 연예인 명단
(B) 웹사이트 주소
(C) 로그인 정보
(D) 지역 번호

어휘 entertainer 연예인 login 접속, 로그인

해설 세부 사항 관련 – 여자의 요청 사항

여자의 세 번째 대사에서 웹사이트 관리자용 사용자명과 비밀번호를 주면(If you give me the username and password for the back end of the Web site) 일정을 갱신하고 고객들을 위한 공지도 올릴 것(I'll update the schedule and put up a notice for patrons)이라고 말했으므로 정답은 (C)이다.

> ▸▸ Paraphrasing 대화의 the username and password
> → 정답의 Some login information

PART 4

71-73 공지

> W-Am Good morning, everyone. I'd like to inform you that we have analyzed the results from last week's customer survey. One of the most frequent complaints was that shoppers cannot identify workers. ⁷¹**So, starting from next month, instead of just wearing nametags, all employees must wear a Vivi Electronics polo shirt and khaki trousers during their shift.** ⁷²**You can choose between navy blue and forest green, so talk to Joseph Burke to let him know which one you want.** ⁷³**If you'd like to see what the polo shirts will look like, feel free to come up to the front entrance area to see the photos I've hung up.**

> 안녕하세요, 여러분. 지난주 고객 설문 분석 결과가 나왔음을 알려드려요. 가장 많이 나온 불만 중 하나가 고객들이 누가 직원인지 구분을 못한다는 것이었습니다. 그래서 다음 달부터 전 직원은 단순히 명찰만 차는 대신 근무 시 비비 전자 폴로 셔츠와 카키색 바지를 착용해야 합니다. 여러분은 진한 감색과 진한 황록색 중에서 고를 수 있으니 조셉 버크 씨에게 원하는 색을 알려 주십시오. 폴로 셔츠가 어떤 모양인지 보고 싶으시면 정문 쪽으로 와서 제가 걸어 놓은 사진들을 보세요.

> 어휘 inform 알리다 analyze 분석하다 customer survey 고객 설문조사 frequent 빈번한 complaint 불만, 불평 identify (신원을) 확인하다, 알아보다 starting from ~부터 instead of ~ 대신에 name tag 명찰 employee 직원 trousers 바지 shift 근무 시간 choose 고르다 feel free to 마음대로 ~하다 come up to ~까지 오다 front entrance 정문 hang up 걸다

71

According to the speaker, what will happen at the business next month?

(A) The hours of operation will change.
(B) A customer survey will be conducted.
(C) The employees will start wearing uniforms.
(D) A new manager will be hired for the store.

화자에 따르면 다음 달 업체에서 무슨 일이 있을 것인가?
(A) 영업시간이 변경된다.
(B) 고객 설문이 실시된다.
(C) **직원들이 유니폼을 착용한다.**
(D) 새로운 지배인이 고용된다.

어휘 conduct 실시하다

해설 세부 사항 관련 – 다음 달에 업체에서 생길 일
지문 초반부에서 다음 달부터 모든 직원은 단순히 명찰만 차는 대신 비비 전자 폴로 셔츠와 카키색 팬츠를 착용해야 한다(starting from next month, instead of just wearing nametags, all employees must wear a Vivi Electronics polo shirt and khaki trousers during their shift)고 했으므로 정답은 (C)이다.

▶▶ Paraphrasing 지문의 a Vivi Electronics polo shirt and khaki trousers → 정답의 uniforms

72

Why should the listeners talk to Mr. Burke?

(A) To express a preference
(B) To request a work shift
(C) To volunteer for a task
(D) To get their questions answered

청자들은 왜 버크 씨에게 연락해야 하나?
(A) **선호하는 것을 알려 주려고**
(B) 근무조를 요청하려고
(C) 업무에 자원하려고
(D) 질문에 대한 답을 얻으려고

어휘 express 표현하다 preference 선호(하는 것) request 요청하다 work shift 근무 교대 volunteer for ~에 지원하다 task 과업, 업무

해설 세부 사항 관련 – 버크 씨에게 연락해야 하는 이유
지문의 중반부에서 직원들은 진한 감색과 진한 황록색 중 고를 수 있고 조셉 버크 씨에게 원하는 색을 알려 주라(You can choose between navy blue and forest green, so talk to Joseph Burke to let him know which one you want)고 했으므로 정답은 (A)이다.

▶▶ Paraphrasing 지문의 let him know which one you want → 정답의 express a preference

73

What does the speaker invite the listeners to do?

(A) Take a group photo
(B) Stop by her office
(C) Make some suggestions
(D) Look at some pictures

화자는 청자들에게 무엇을 하라고 권하는가?
(A) 단체 사진 찍기
(B) 그녀의 사무실에 들르기
(C) 제안하기
(D) **사진 보기**

어휘 stop by 들르다 make a suggestion 제안하다

해설 세부 사항 관련 – 화자가 청자에게 제안하는 것
지문의 후반부에서 폴로 셔츠가 어떤 모양인지 보려면 가까이 와서 걸어 놓은 사진들을 보라(If you'd like to see what the polo shirts will look like, feel free to come up to the front entrance area to see the photos I've hung up)고 했으므로 정답은 (D)이다.

▶▶ Paraphrasing 지문의 see the photos → 정답의 Look at some pictures

M-Au This is Radio 103 with your local news update. **⁷⁴This Saturday, residents of Kennerburg can enjoy one of the most popular events of the year, the town's annual Founder's Day Parade.** Event planners are pleased to announce that the number of floats and musical groups has nearly doubled, **⁷⁵so the procession will take about two hours, compared to just one hour last year. ⁷⁶There are many great places to see the action, so check out the map of the route on the city's Web site to make sure you get a good viewing spot.**

최신 지역 뉴스를 보내 드리는 라디오 103입니다. 오는 토요일, 케너버그 주민들은 연중 가장 인기 있는 행사 중 하나인 연례 창건자의 날 퍼레이드를 즐길 수 있습니다. 행사 기획자들은 참여하는 장식 차량과 악단의 수가 거의 배로 늘었다고 발표했는데요. 따라서 지난해에는 1시간만에 끝났지만 이번 행렬은 약 2시간이 소요될 예정입니다. 행렬을 볼 수 있는 좋은 장소들이 많습니다. 시 웹사이트에서 행진 노선을 확인해 좋은 관람 자리를 확보하시기 바랍니다.

어휘 resident 주민, 거주자 annual 연례의 be pleased to ~하게 되어 기쁘다 announce 발표하다 float (퍼레이드의) 장식 차량, 꽃 수레 double 배가 되다 procession 행렬, 행진 compared to ~에 비교하면 action 재미있는 일 check out ~을 확인하다 route 경로, 루트 make sure 반드시 ~하다 viewing spot 조망[관람] 지점

74

What is scheduled to happen on Saturday?
(A) A music contest
(B) A community parade
(C) A food festival
(D) A fireworks show

토요일에 무슨 일이 있을 예정인가?
(A) 음악 경연
(B) **지역 퍼레이드**
(C) 음식 축제
(D) 불꽃놀이 쇼

해설 세부 사항 관련 – 토요일에 생길 일
지문의 초반부에서 오는 토요일에 케너버그의 주민들은 연중 가장 인기 있는 행사 중 하나인 연례 창건자의 날 퍼레이드를 즐길 수 있다(This Saturday, residents of Kennerburg can enjoy one of the most popular events of the year, the town's annual Founder's Day Parade)고 했으므로 정답은 (B)이다.

> ▸▸ Paraphrasing　지문의 the town's annual Founder's Day Parade → 정답의 A community parade

75

According to the speaker, how is this year's event different from last year's?
(A) It will last for a longer period of time.
(B) It will take place earlier in the day.
(C) It will be held at a different location.
(D) It will charge a higher admission fee.

화자에 따르면 올해 행사는 작년과 어떻게 다른가?
(A) **더 오래 진행될 것이다.**
(B) 아침 일찍 개최될 것이다.
(C) 다른 장소에서 개최될 것이다.
(D) 입장료가 더 비싸질 것이다.

어휘 last 지속되다 period of time 기간, 시일 take place 일어나다, 개최되다 location 장소 charge 청구하다 admission fee 입장료

해설 세부 사항 관련 – 올해 행사와 작년 행사의 다른 점
지문의 중반부에서 지난해에는 1시간만에 끝났지만 이번 행렬은 약 2시간이 소요될 예정(the procession will take about two hours, compared to just one hour last year)이라고 했으므로 정답은 (A)이다.

> ▸▸ Paraphrasing　지문의 two hours, compared to just one hour last year → 정답의 last for a longer period of time

76

What does the speaker recommend doing?
(A) Using a public parking lot
(B) Arriving at a site early
(C) Consulting a map online
(D) Purchasing group tickets

화자는 무엇을 하라고 권하는가?
(A) 공영 주차장 이용하기
(B) 장소에 일찍 도착하기
(C) **온라인 지도 참고하기**
(D) 단체 티켓 구입하기

어휘 public 공공의 parking lot 주차장 site 현장, 장소 consult 참고하다 purchase 구매하다

해설 세부 사항 관련 – 화자가 추천하는 것
지문의 후반부에서 시 웹사이트에서 행진 노선을 확인해 좋은 관람 자리를 확보하기 바란다(check out the map of the route on the city's Web site to make sure you get a good viewing spot)고 했으므로 정답은 (C)이다.

> ▸▸ Paraphrasing　지문의 check out the map of the route on the city's Web site → 정답의 Consulting a map online

M-Cn Hi, this is Zack Vitella. I'm the office manager at Capitol Incorporated. **⁷⁷I just received our monthly bill for Internet services,** and it looks like we've been **overcharged.** We have downsized to the Standard Package, but we're still being charged for the Executive Package. **78Could you please e-mail me a new bill with the correct fees?** If you have any questions, you can call me at 555-0122. **79However, please note that I'll be away from my desk all afternoon, as I'm going to an in-house workshop.** Thanks.

안녕하세요. 저는 잭 비텔라라고 합니다. 캐피탈 인코퍼레이티드의 사무장입니다. 지금 막 인터넷 서비스 월별 청구서를 받았는데요. 보니까 과다 청구된 것 같아요. 저희는 일반 패키지 요금제로 줄였는데 아직도 고급 패키지로 청구되고 있네요. 정확한 요금이 적힌 새 청구서를 이메일로 보내 주시겠어요? 문의할 게 있으면 555-0122로 제게 전화주세요. 그런데 전 사내 워크숍에 가야 해서 오후 내내 자리를 비웁니다. 이 점 감안해 주시고요. 감사합니다.

어휘 receive 받다 monthly 월례의 bill 청구서 overcharge 과잉 청구하다 downsize 축소하다, 줄이다 standard 일반의, 표준의 charge for ~에 대한 요금으로 청구하다 executive 고급의 correct 정확한 note 주의하다, 유념하다 be away from 부재 중이다 in-house 사내의

77
What is the speaker calling about?
(A) An address change
(B) A promotional offer
(C) A loss of service
(D) A billing error

화자는 무엇에 대해 전화를 하는가?
(A) 주소 변경
(B) 판촉 할인
(C) 서비스 중단
(D) 청구서 오류

어휘 promotional 홍보의 offer 할인 loss 손실 billing 청구서 발부

해설 전체 내용 관련 – 통화의 주제
지문의 초반부에서 인터넷 서비스 월별 청구서를 받았는데(I just received our monthly bill for Internet services) 과다 청구된 것 같다(it looks like we've been overcharged)고 했으므로 정답은 (D)이다.

▸▸ Paraphrasing   지문의 we've been overcharged
→ 정답의 billing error

78
What is the listener asked to do?
(A) Return a software package
(B) Send a new document
(C) Contact the listener's manager
(D) E-mail an updated contract

청자는 무엇을 해 달라고 요청받는가?
(A) 소프트웨어 패키지를 반환하라고
(B) 새 서류를 보내라고
(C) 청자의 상사에게 연락하라고
(D) 갱신된 계약서를 이메일로 보내라고

해설 세부 사항 관련 – 요청 사항
지문의 중반부에서 화자가 정확한 요금이 적힌 새 청구서를 이메일로 보내 달라(Could you please e-mail me a new bill with the correct fees)고 요청했으므로 정답은 (B)이다.

▸▸ Paraphrasing   지문의 e-mail me a new bill
→ 정답의 Send a new document

79
Why is the speaker unavailable this afternoon?
(A) He will attend a training session.
(B) He will take a trip out of town.
(C) He will visit an important client.
(D) He will shop for some merchandise.

화자는 오후에 왜 연락이 안 되는가?
(A) 그는 연수에 참석할 것이다.
(B) 그는 외지로 여행을 갈 것이다.
(C) 그는 중요한 고객을 방문할 것이다.
(D) 그는 제품을 사러 갈 것이다.

어휘 unavailable (사람이) 없는, 부재의 attend 참석하다 training session 교육 take a trip 여행하다 out of town 도시를 떠나 client 고객 merchandise 상품, 제품

해설 세부 사항 관련 – 화자가 연락이 안 되는 이유
지문의 후반부에서 화자가 사내 워크숍에 가야 해서 오후 내내 자리를 비운다(I'll be away from my desk all afternoon, as I'm going to an in-house workshop)고 했으므로 정답은 (A)이다.

▸▸ Paraphrasing   지문의 going to an in-house workshop
→ 정답의 attend a training session

80-82 회의 발췌

W-Am **80Finally on the agenda, I'd like to talk about the new property on Renner Street. We're supposed to be moving our legal firm's operations there on March thirtieth. 81However, I just found out this morning that the company we were planning on using, Seltice Solutions, doesn't do corporate moves anymore.** That's unfortunate because they came highly recommended from a colleague of mine. **82In light of this, I think we should meet again on Thursday after I've had more time to look into this, and find a replacement.** I don't want to rush this decision.

오늘 마지막 의제로 레너가의 새 건물에 대해 이야기하고 싶은데요. 3월 30일에 우리 법무 사업을 그쪽으로 이전하기로 되어 있습니다. 하지만 오늘 아침에 우리가 이용하기로 했던 회사인 셀티스 솔루션즈가 더 이상 기업 이사는 하지 않는다는 것을 알게 됐습니다. 제 동료가 강력 추천한 회사라서 아쉽네요. 이 점을 고려해 제가 좀 더 살펴보고 대체 회사를 찾은 후 목요일에 다시 회의를 했으면 합니다. 급하게 결정하고 싶지 않아서요.

Test 10

어휘 finally 마지막으로 agenda (회의) 의제 property
재물, 부동산, 건물 be supposed to ~하기로 되어 있다 move
이전[이사](하다) legal firm 법률 회사 operation 영업, 운영 not
~ anymore 더 이상 ~ 않다 corporate 기업의 unfortunate
유감스러운, 아쉬운 colleague 동료 in light of ~에 비추어, ~을
고려하여 look into ~을 조사하다 replacement 대체자, 대체물
rush 서둘러 하다 decision 결정, 판단

80

What is the speaker mainly discussing?

(A) A business relocation
(B) Some property damage
(C) A legal fee
(D) Some regulation changes

화자가 이야기하는 주요 내용은 무엇인가?

(A) 회사 이전
(B) 재물 손괴
(C) 수임료
(D) 변경된 규정들

어휘 relocation 이전, 이주 damage 손상, 피해 legal fee 법적
수수료, 수임료 regulation 규정, 법규

해설 전체 내용 관련 – 이야기의 주제

지문의 초반부에서 오늘 마지막 의제로 레너가의 새 건물에 대해 이야기하고
싶고(I'd like to talk about the new property on Renner Street), 3월
30일에 법무 사업을 그 쪽으로 이전하기로 되어 있다(We're supposed to
be moving our legal firm's operations there on March thirtieth)고
했으므로 정답은 (A)이다.

▶▶ Paraphrasing 지문의 moving our legal firm's operations
there → 정답의 A business relocation

81

What problem is mentioned?

(A) A new employee is not qualified.
(B) A computer system is not working.
(C) A service is no longer available.
(D) A contract's terms were rejected.

어떤 문제가 언급되는가?

(A) 새 직원이 자격을 갖추지 못했다.
(B) 컴퓨터 시스템이 작동하지 않는다.
(C) 서비스를 더 이상 이용할 수 없다.
(D) 계약 조건들이 거부되었다.

어휘 qualified 자격을 갖춘 work 작동하다 no longer 더 이상 ~ 아닌
available 이용할 수 있는 contract 계약 term 조건 reject
거절하다, 거부하다

해설 세부 사항 관련 – 언급되고 있는 문제

지문의 중반부에서 이용하기로 했던 회사인 셀티스 솔루션즈가 더 이상 기
업 이사는 하지 않는다는 것을 오늘 아침에 알게 됐다(I just found out this
morning that the company we were planning on using, Seltice
Solutions, doesn't do corporate moves anymore)고 했으므로 정답은
(C)이다.

▶▶ Paraphrasing 지문의 the company ~ doesn't do
corporate moves anymore
→ 정답의 A service is no longer available.

82

What does the speaker suggest doing?

(A) Holding another meeting
(B) Voting on an issue
(C) Hiring a professional consultant
(D) Announcing a decision

화자는 무엇을 하자고 제안하는가?

(A) 회의 다시 하기
(B) 쟁점에 대해 투표하기
(C) 전문 컨설턴트 고용하기
(D) 결정 발표하기

어휘 vote 투표하다 issue 문제, 쟁점 hire 고용하다 professional
전문의 consultant 컨설턴트, 상담가, 자문역 announce 발표하다

해설 세부 사항 관련 – 화자의 제안

지문의 후반부에서 목요일에 다시 회의를 했으면 한다(I think we should
meet again on Thursday)고 했으므로 정답은 (A)이다.

▶▶ Paraphrasing 지문의 meet again on Thursday
→ 정답의 Holding another meeting

83-85 담화

M-Au All right, everyone. **83Thank you for being
here today for this food safety certification
class. You need to have a valid certificate to
work in a commercial kitchen or to serve food
to customers.** The certificate is valid for five
years, and you have to get a passing grade on
the exam at the end of this class. **84But don't
worry, it's very rare for someone to fail the test.**
In all my years of training, it only happened
once. **85We'll begin in fifteen minutes, starting off
with a brief instructional film.** Feel free to take
notes on the handout I gave you.

자, 여러분. 이번 식품안전인증 수업에 와 주셔서 감사드립니다. 영리 목적의 주
방에서 일하거나 고객에게 음식을 제공하는 일을 하려면 공인 자격증이 필요합니
다. 자격증은 5년간 유효하며 수업 말미에 있을 시험에서 합격점을 취득해야 합
니다. 하지만 걱정하지 마세요. 시험에 떨어지는 일은 아주 드뭅니다. 제가 교육
에 몸담은 기간 동안, 딱 한 번 봤습니다. 15분 후에 시작할 거예요. 먼저 짧은
교육용 영화를 볼 텐데요. 나눠 드린 유인물에 자유롭게 필기하세요.

어휘 safety 안전 certification 인증, 검증 valid 유효한
certificate 면허증, 자격증 commercial 상업의, 영리의 serve
(음식을) 제공하다 passing grade 합격점 rare 드문

start off with ~로 시작하다 brief 간결한, 짧은 instructional 교육의 feel free to 자유롭게 ~해도 좋다 take notes 기록하다, 메모하다 handout 인쇄물[수업 자료]

83

Who most likely are the listeners?

(A) Restaurant workers
(B) Delivery personnel
(C) Construction workers
(D) Appliance salespeople

청자들은 누구이겠는가?

(A) 식당 종사자
(B) 배송 기사
(C) 공사장 인부
(D) 가전제품 판매원

어휘 delivery 배송, 배달 personnel 직원들 construction 공사 appliance (가정용) 기구, 전기 제품 salespeople 판매원

해설 전체 내용 관련 – 청자들의 신분

지문의 초반부에서 식품 안전 인증 수업에 온 것을 환영한다(Thank you for being here today for this food safety certification class)며 영리 목적의 주방에서 일하거나 고객에게 음식을 제공하는 일을 하려면 공인 자격증이 필요하다(You need to have a valid certificate to work in a commercial kitchen or to serve food to customers)고 했으므로 정답은 (A)이다.

▸▸ Paraphrasing   지문의 **work in a commercial kitchen or to serve food to customers**
→ 정답의 **Restaurant workers**

84

What does the speaker suggest when he says, "it only happened once"?

(A) A class will take one day.
(B) A course will not be repeated.
(C) A problem has been resolved.
(D) A test will be easy to pass.

화자가 "딱 한 번 봤습니다"라고 말할 때 의미하는 바는 무엇인가?

(A) 수업이 하루 걸린다.
(B) 강좌는 반복되지 않는다.
(C) 문제가 해결되었다.
(D) 시험이 합격하기 쉽다.

어휘 repeat 반복되다 resolve 해결하다 pass 통과하다, 합격하다

해설 화자의 의도 파악 – 딱 한 번 있었다는 말의 의미

지문의 중반부에서 걱정하지 말라고 말하면서 시험에 떨어지는 일은 아주 드물다(But don't worry, it's very rare for someone to fail the test)고 했다. 그리고 교육에 몸담은 기간 동안 불합격한 경우는 딱 한 번 봤다(In all my years of training, it only happened once)고 했다. 따라서 시험 합격이 쉽다는 의미이므로 정답은 (D)이다.

85

What will the speaker do in fifteen minutes?

(A) Check attendance
(B) Show a video
(C) Answer some questions
(D) Distribute a handout

화자는 15분 후에 무엇을 할 것인가?

(A) 출석 체크하기
(B) 비디오 상영하기
(C) 질의에 응답하기
(D) 유인물 배포하기

어휘 attendance 출석 distribute 배포하다

해설 세부 사항 관련 – 15분 뒤에 화자가 할 일

지문의 후반부에서 15분 후에 짧은 교육용 영화를 보면서 시작하겠다(We'll begin in fifteen minutes, starting off with a brief instructional film)고 말했으므로 정답은 (B)이다.

▸▸ Paraphrasing   지문의 **a brief instructional film**
→ 정답의 **a video**

86-88 방송

M-Cn You're listening to *Inside Science*, the show that explores a wide variety of scientific fields. **86Today, my guest is Dr. Brandon Clark, a renowned linguist who has been studying how people acquire language skills. He'll be talking about this topic as well as giving you tips based on his research. 87Dr. Clark just got back from traveling abroad to explore the verbal patterns of the ethnic groups in South America.** He's going to start working on a book using his findings. **88If you'd like to pose a question to Dr. Clark, log on to the Radio 3 Web site and post it there.** We'll try to respond to as many as possible.

여러분은 지금 다양한 과학 분야를 탐사하는 프로그램인 〈인사이드 사이언스〉를 듣고 계십니다. 오늘 모실 게스트는 브랜든 클라크 박사님입니다. 사람들이 어떻게 언어 능력을 습득하는지 연구해 온 저명한 언어학자이십니다. 클라크 박사는 오늘 이 주제에 대해 말씀하실 예정이며 본인의 연구를 바탕으로 조언도 전해 주실 겁니다. 클라크 박사는 남미 소수 민족들의 언어 패턴을 연구하고 막 돌아오셨습니다. 이 연구 결과를 바탕으로 책 집필을 시작하실 예정이고요. 클라크 박사님께 질문하고 싶은 청취자들은 라디오 3 웹사이트에 로그인해서 질문을 올려 주세요. 최대한 많은 질문에 답변해 드리도록 하겠습니다.

어휘 explore 탐험하다, 탐사하다 a wide variety of 매우 다양한 renowned 저명한 linguist 언어학자 acquire 습득하다 skill 기술 topic 주제 as well as ~뿐만 아니라 tip 조언, 팁 based on ~을 바탕으로 한 research 연구 (조사) verbal 언어[말]의

pattern (정형화된) 양식, 패턴 ethnic (소수) 민족의 work on ~에 착수하다 finding 조사[연구] 결과 pose a question 질문을 제기하다 log on to ~에 접속하다 post 게시하다 respond to ~에 대답하다, 반응하다

86

What topic will Dr. Clark discuss with the speaker?

(A) Technological advancements
(B) Sleeping habits
(C) New medicines
(D) Learning languages

클라크 박사는 화자와 무슨 주제로 논의할 것인가?

(A) 기술 진보
(B) 수면 습관
(C) 신약
(D) 언어 학습

어휘 technological 기술적인 advancement 진보, 발달 habit 습관 medicine 약품

해설 전체 내용 관련 – 논의의 주제

지문의 초반부에서 오늘 모실 게스트는 브랜든 클라크 박사님이고 그는 사람들이 어떻게 언어 능력을 습득하는지를 연구해 온 저명한 언어학자(Today, my guest is Dr. Brandon Clark, a renowned linguist who has been studying how people acquire language skills)라고 소개했고, 이것에 대해 오늘 이야기하겠다(He'll be talking about this topic)고 했으므로 정답은 (D)이다.

▸▸ Paraphrasing 지문의 acquire language skills
→ 정답의 Learning languages

87

What has Dr. Clark recently done?

(A) Opened an institute
(B) Published his first book
(C) Received an award
(D) Returned from a trip abroad

클라크 박사가 최근에 한 일은 무엇인가?

(A) 연구소를 개소했다
(B) 첫 저서를 출간했다
(C) 수상했다
(D) 해외 여행을 마치고 귀국했다

어휘 institute 기관, 협회, 연구소 publish 출간하다 receive 받다 award 상 return from ~에서 돌아오다

해설 세부 사항 관련 – 클라크 박사가 최근에 한 일

지문의 중반부에서 클라크 박사는 남미 소수 민족의 언어 패턴을 연구하고 막 돌아왔다(Mr. Clark just got back from traveling abroad to explore the verbal patterns of the ethnic groups in South America)고 했으므로 정답은 (D)이다.

▸▸ Paraphrasing 대화의 got back from traveling abroad
→ 정답의 Returned from a trip abroad

88

According to the speaker, what can listeners do on the Web site?

(A) Sign up for an upcoming research study
(B) Submit questions for the guest
(C) Browse the findings of a study
(D) Download an interview schedule

화자에 따르면 청취자들은 웹사이트에서 무엇을 할 수 있는가?

(A) 다가올 연구에 참여 신청하기
(B) 게스트를 위한 질문 제출하기
(C) 연구 결과 둘러보기
(D) 인터뷰 일정 내려 받기

어휘 sign up for ~에 신청[등록]하다 upcoming 다가오는 research study 조사 연구 submit 제출하다 browse 둘러보다, 훑어보다 finding (조사·연구 등의) 결과

해설 세부 사항 관련 – 청자가 웹사이트에서 할 수 있는 것

지문의 후반부에서 클라크 박사님께 질문하고 싶은 청취자들은(If you'd like to pose a question to Dr. Clark) 라디오 3 웹사이트에 로그인해서 질문을 올려 달라(log on to the Radio 3 Web site and post it there)고 했으므로 정답은 (B)이다.

89-91 연설

W-Br **⁸⁹Thank you all for coming to this reception to greet our counterparts from the Toronto branch, who are here for a few days to observe us in action.** We'll have some live music later, and there will be time for networking and maybe even a little dancing. **⁹⁰I'd like to say a few words, but I won't go into too much detail about how the company has changed since its opening.** It's not the first time you've heard it. But it's important to remember where we've been. **⁹¹And I can't express how grateful I am for the staff's tireless efforts to keep working to get the job done.**

며칠간 우리 업무 현장을 시찰하러 오신 토론토 지사 동료 여러분들을 맞이하는 이 환영 리셉션에 와 주셔서 감사드립니다. 조금 뒤에 라이브 공연도 있고, 친교 시간과 함께 짤막한 댄스 타임도 가질 예정입니다. 몇 마디 드리고 싶은데요. 저희 회사가 시작부터 지금까지 어떻게 변화해 왔는지를 자세히 얘기하지는 않겠습니다. 처음 듣는 얘기는 아닐 테니까요. 하지만 우리가 어떤 과정을 거쳐왔는지 되짚는 것은 중요합니다. 그리고 업무 수행을 위해 지칠 줄 모르는 노고를 아끼지 않은 직원들에게 감사의 마음을 어떻게 전해야 할지 모르겠습니다.

어휘 reception 환영 파티, 리셉션 greet 맞다, 환영하다 counterpart (동일한 지위나 기능을 갖는) 상대 branch 지사 observe 관찰하다 networking 인맥 쌓기, 인적 네트워킹 형성 go into detail 상세히 설명하다 opening 개점 express 표현하다 grateful 고마워하는, 감사하는 staff 직원 tireless 지칠 줄 모르는 effort 노고, 노력 get the job done 일을 끝내다[해내다]

89

What is the purpose of the event?

(A) To observe a national holiday
(B) To celebrate an anniversary
(C) To welcome some visitors
(D) To present some awards

행사의 목적은 무엇인가?

(A) 국경일 기념
(B) 기념일 축하
(C) 방문객 환영
(D) 시상

어휘 observe (축제·생일 등을) 기념하다, 축하하다 national holiday
국경일 celebrate 축하하다 anniversary 기념일 welcome
환영하다 present 주다

해설 전체 내용 관련 – 행사의 목적

지문의 초반부에서 토론토 지사 동료 여러분들을 맞이하는 이 환영 리셉션에 오신 모든 분들께 감사한다(Thank you all for coming to this reception to greet our counterparts from the Toronto branch)고 했으므로 정답은 (C)이다.

▸▸ **Paraphrasing** 지문의 **reception to greet our counterparts**
→ 정답의 **welcome some visitors**

90

What does the speaker suggest when she says, "It's not the first time you've heard it"?

(A) Some well-known songs will be played for the listeners.
(B) The listeners are familiar with the company's history.
(C) Some items were accidentally repeated in the program.
(D) The speaker thinks a discussion topic should not be covered again.

화자가 말한 "처음 듣는 얘기는 아닐 테니까요"가 암시하는 것은 무엇인가?

(A) 잘 알려진 곡들이 청자들을 위해 연주될 것이다.
(B) 청자들은 회사의 역사에 대해 잘 알고 있다.
(C) 프로그램의 일부 코너가 뜻하지 않게 반복됐다.
(D) 화자는 논의 주제가 다시 거론되지 말아야 한다고 생각한다.

어휘 well-known 잘 알려진 be familiar with ~에 친숙하다 item
상연물 accidentally 우연히, 뜻하지 않게 repeat 반복하다
discussion 논의 cover 다루다

해설 화자의 의도 파악 – 처음 듣는 얘기는 아닐 것이라는 말의 의미

지문의 중반부에서 회사가 시작부터 지금까지 어떻게 변화해 왔는지를 자세히 말하지는 않겠다(I won't go into too much detail about how the company has changed since its opening)고 하면서 그 이유로 처음 듣는 이야기는 아닐 것(It's not the first time you've heard it)이라고 했다. 즉 청자들은 회사의 역사에 대해 잘 알고 있다는 의미이므로 정답은 (B)이다.

91

What does the speaker say she appreciates about the listeners?

(A) Their prompt response
(B) Their creative ideas
(C) Their hard work
(D) Their teamwork skills

화자는 청자들에게 무엇이 감사하다고 말하는가?

(A) 신속한 응대
(B) 창의적인 아이디어
(C) 노고
(D) 팀워크 역량

어휘 appreciate 고마워하다 prompt 신속한, 지체 없는 response
반응 creative 창의적인 skill 기술, 역량

해설 세부 사항 관련 – 화자가 청자에게 감사한 부분

지문의 후반부에서 업무 수행을 위해 지칠 줄 모르는 노고를 아끼지 않은 직원들에게 감사의 마음을 어떻게 전해야 할지 모르겠다(I can't express how grateful I am for the staff's tireless efforts to keep working to get the job done)고 했으므로 정답은 (C)이다.

▸▸ **Paraphrasing** 지문의 **staff's tireless efforts**
→ 정답의 **Their hard work**

92-94 전화 메시지

M-Au Hi, Ms. Schofield. This is Josh Wilkins. **92I know you're working on the arrangements for the special event on May seventh to recognize Arthur Hurst's long career as he retires from Jesmond Incorporated. 93I was looking at the catering order you placed, and it says you requested just two fruit and vegetable platters. Each one is supposed to serve about twenty guests, but... um... we'll have at least eighty people.** Please call the caterer to make the necessary changes. **94But you'd better hurry. Today's the last day to place the order, and they close in twenty minutes.**

안녕하세요, 쇼필드 씨. 저는 조쉬 윌킨스입니다. 5월 7일에 열리는 특별 행사를 준비하고 계신 걸로 알고 있는데요. 제스몬드 인코퍼레이티드에서 퇴직하시는 아서 허스트 씨의 오랜 경력을 기리는 행사 말이에요. 주문하신 출장 요리를 살펴보고 있는데, 과일, 채소 모듬 요리 두 개만 주문하셨네요. 모듬 요리 하나가 대략 20인분인데, 어… 최소 80명이 참석하잖아요. 출장요리 업체에 전화해서 필요한 변경 사항을 전해 주세요. 서두르시는 게 좋겠어요. 오늘이 주문할 수 있는 마지막 날인데다 업체가 20분 후에 영업 종료예요.

어휘 work on ~에 공들이다 arrangement 준비, 마련
recognize 인정하다, 표창하다 career 경력 retire 퇴직하다,
은퇴하다 catering (행사 등을 위한) 음식 공급 place an order
주문하다 request 요청하다 platter 플래터, 여러 음식을 차려 놓은
요리 be supposed to ~하기로 되어 있다 serve (음식을) 제공하다
caterer 음식 공급사 necessary 필요한 hurry 서두르다

92

What kind of event is the listener planning?

(A) A career fair
(B) A training session
(C) A product launch
(D) A retirement party

청자는 어떤 종류의 행사를 계획하고 있는가?

(A) 취업 박람회
(B) 연수
(C) 제품 출시
(D) 퇴직 파티

어휘 fair 박람회 training 교육 session 수업 (시간), 강습회 product
제품 launch (상품) 출시 retirement 퇴직

해설 세부 사항 관련 – 청자가 계획하고 있는 행사
지문의 초반부에서 5월 7일에 열리는 특별 행사를 준비하고 있는 걸로 아는
데 제스몬드 인코퍼레이티드에서 퇴직하는 아서 허스트 씨의 오랜 경력을 기리
는 행사(I know you're working on the arrangements for the special
event on May seventh to recognize Arthur Hurst's long career as
he retires from Jesmond Incorporated)라고 했으므로 정답은 (D)이다.

▸▸ Paraphrasing   지문의 recognize Arthur Hurst's long
career as he retires
→ 정답의 A retirement party

93

What does the speaker suggest when he says, "we'll
have at least eighty people"?

(A) He is not accepting more volunteers.
(B) More food will be needed.
(C) He is pleased with the turnout.
(D) A larger room should be reserved.

화자가 말한 "최소 80명이 참석하잖아요"이 암시하는 것은 무엇인가?

(A) 그는 지원자를 더 이상 받지 않는다.
(B) 음식이 더 필요하다.
(C) 그는 참석자 수에 만족한다.
(D) 더 큰 방을 예약해야 한다.

어휘 accept 받아들이다 volunteer 지원자, 자원봉사자 turnout
참가자[참석자] 수 reserve 예약하다

해설 화자의 의도 파악 – 최소 80명이 참석한다는 말의 의미
지문의 중반부에서 주문한 출장 요리를 살펴보고 있는데 과일, 채소 모듬 요리
두 개만 주문되어 있다(I was looking at the catering order you placed,
and it says you requested just two fruit and vegetable platters)고 했
고, 모듬 요리 하나가 대략 20인분(Each one is supposed to serve about
twenty guests)이라고 했다. 따라서 최소 80명이 참석한다는 말은 음식이 더
필요하다는 의미이므로 정답은 (B)이다.

94

What problem does the speaker mention?

(A) A deadline has already passed.
(B) An unexpected charge was imposed.
(C) A business is closing soon.
(D) A guest is missing an invitation.

화자가 언급한 문제는 무엇인가?

(A) 기한이 이미 지났다.
(B) 예상하지 못한 요금이 부과됐다.
(C) 업체가 곧 영업을 마감한다.
(D) 게스트 한 명이 초대장이 없다.

어휘 deadline 기한, 마감 unexpected 예상치 못한 impose 부과하다
miss ~이 없음을 깨닫다

해설 세부 사항 관련 – 화자가 언급한 문제
지문의 후반부에서 오늘이 주문을 할 수 있는 마지막 날인데다 업체가 20분 후
에 영업을 종료한다(Today's the last day to place the order, and they
close in twenty minutes)고 말했으므로 정답은 (C)이다.

▸▸ Paraphrasing   지문의 they close in twenty minutes
→ 정답의 A business is closing soon.

95-97 담화 + 표시

> W-Am Good afternoon. **95My name is Gina, and
> today I'm going to be demonstrating the newest
> coffee makers offered by Kirby Department
> Store, manufactured by Home Styles.** As savvy
> shoppers, you'll love this brand's sleek design
> and durable components. **96I'll start off with the
> most popular model, which makes two cups of
> coffee at a time and has a built-in milk warmer.**
> This really is the way to start the morning off
> right. **97For those of you standing in the back,
> there are some empty seats up front, so feel free
> to come and get a better view.**

안녕하세요. 제 이름은 지나입니다. 오늘 저는 홈 스타일즈에서 제조하고 커비 백
화점이 판매하는 최신 커피메이커들을 시연할 텐데요. 현명한 쇼핑객인 여러분
은 이 브랜드의 세련된 디자인과 튼튼한 구성품들이 마음에 드실 겁니다. 우선
가장 인기 있는 모델부터 시작할게요. 한 번에 커피 2잔을 만들 수 있고 우유 데
우기 기능이 내장된 모델입니다. 이것만 있으면 아침을 제대로 시작할 수 있죠.
뒤에 서 계신 분들은 여기 앞에 빈 자리가 몇 개 있으니 더 잘 보이는 이쪽으로 오
세요.

어휘 demonstrate 시연하다, 보여주다 manufacture 제조하다,
생산하다 savvy 현명한, 요령 있는 sleek 매끈한, 세련된 durable
내구성이 있는 component 요소, 부품 start off with ~로 시작하다
built-in 붙박이의, 내장의 warmer 데우는 기기 empty 빈 up
front 앞쪽에 feel free to 자유롭게 ~해도 좋다 get a view ~을
보다

Home Styles Coffee Maker

Model	Number of Cups Brewed	Milk Warmer
B-300	1	No
B-450	1	Yes
L-600	2	No
96L-780	2	Yes

홈 스타일스 커피메이커

모델	추출 컵 수	우유 데우기 기능
B-300	1	없음
B-450	1	있음
L-600	2	없음
L-780	2	있음

95

What is the purpose of the talk?

(A) To show how to operate a device
(B) To demonstrate a sales technique
(C) To explain a store's discount prices
(D) To gather feedback about a product

담화의 목적은 무엇인가?

(A) 기기 작동법 보여 주기
(B) 판매 기술 보여 주기
(C) 상점의 할인가 설명하기
(D) 제품에 대한 의견 수집하기

어휘 operate 작동하다 device 장치 sales 판매의 technique 기술, 기법 explain 설명하다 gather 모으다, 수집하다 feedback 의견 product 제품

해설 전체 내용 관련 – 담화의 목적
지문의 초반부에서 오늘 홈 스타일즈에서 제조하고 커비 백화점이 판매하는 최신 커피메이커들을 시연할 것(I'm going to be demonstrating the newest coffee makers offered by Kirby Department Store, manufactured by Home Styles)이라고 했으므로 정답은 (A)이다.

▸▸ Paraphrasing 지문의 demonstrating the newest coffee makers
→ 정답의 show how to operate a device

96

Look at the graphic. Which model is the speaker talking about?

(A) B-300
(B) B-450
(C) L-600
(D) L-780

시각 정보에 의하면, 화자가 이야기하고 있는 모델은 무엇인가?

(A) B-300
(B) B-450
(C) L-600
(D) L-780

해설 시각 정보 연계 – 화자가 언급하고 있는 모델
지문의 중반부에서 우선 가장 인기 있는 모델부터 시작한다(I'll start off with the most popular model)고 했고 그 제품은 한 번에 커피 2잔을 만들 수 있고 우유 데우기 기능이 내장된 모델(which makes two cups of coffee at a time and has a built-in milk warmer)이라고 했다. 시각 정보에 따르면 추출 컵 수가 2개이고 우유 데우기 기능이 있는 제품은 L-780이므로 정답은 (D)이다.

97

What will some of the listeners most likely do next?

(A) Watch a video
(B) Sit down
(C) Read a handout
(D) Ask questions

일부 청자들은 다음으로 무엇을 할 것인가?

(A) 비디오 감상하기
(B) 착석하기
(C) 유인물 읽기
(D) 질문하기

해설 세부 사항 관련 – 청자들이 다음으로 할 일
지문의 후반부에서 뒤에 서 계신 분들은 앞에 빈 자리 몇 개가 있으니 더 잘 보이는 이쪽으로 오라(For those of you standing in the back, there are some empty seats up front, so feel free to come and get a better view)고 했으므로 정답은 (B)이다.

98-100 회의 발췌 + 그래프

W-Br Good morning, everyone. 98**I've called this meeting today because we need to make decisions with our Fresh Face line of cosmetics. Since we're adding in some new items, we need to choose which ones to remove.** 99**We're also going to start offering our second-best seller in a two-ounce and four-ounce size, which I think customers will like.** You can see on the graph of last month's sales that there's still room for improvement. 100**To promote the changes, we've secured Sophie Fitzgerald as a spokesperson for our commercials. With her popular films and strong name recognition, her involvement could give a major boost to our company.**

안녕하세요, 여러분. 우리 프레시 페이스 화장품과 관련해 결정해야 할 사항들이 있어 오늘 회의를 소집했습니다. 새로 추가하는 품목들이 있으니 어떤 품목들을 빼야 할지 정해야 합니다. 그리고 우리 제품 중 두 번째로 많이 팔리는 제품을 앞으로 2온스와 4온스 두 용량으로 판매하게 됩니다. 고객들이 좋아할 거예요. 지난달 매출 그래프를 보시면 여전히 개선의 여지가 있음을 알 수 있습니다. 변화에 박차를 가하기 위해 소피 피츠제럴드 씨를 우리 광고의 얼굴로 영입했습니다. 그녀가 출연한 영화의 인기와 높은 인지도로 그녀의 참여는 우리 회사에 큰 힘을 실어줄 것입니다.

Monthly Sales

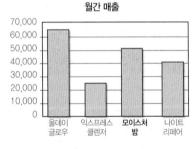

월간 매출

98

What is the purpose of the meeting?

(A) To introduce a new employee
(B) To assign some projects
(C) To explain a company policy
(D) To adjust a product line

회의의 목적은 무엇인가?
(A) 신입 직원 소개
(B) 프로젝트 배정
(C) 회사 정책 설명
(D) 제품군 조정

어휘 introduce 소개하다 employee 직원 assign 배정하다, 배치하다 policy 방침 adjust 조정하다, 조절하다

해설 전체 내용 관련 – 회의의 목적

지문의 초반부에서 프레시 페이스 화장품과 관련해 결정해야 할 사항들이 있어 오늘 회의를 소집했다(I've called this meeting today because we need to make decisions with our Fresh Face line of cosmetics)고 한 뒤 새로 추가하는 품목들이 있으니 어떤 품목들을 빼야 할지 정해야 한다(Since we're adding in some new items, we need to choose which ones to remove)고 했다. 따라서 제품군을 조정하기 위해 회의를 소집한 것임을 알 수 있으므로 정답은 (D)이다.

▸▸ **Paraphrasing** 지문의 Since we're adding in some new items, we need to choose which ones to remove. → 정답의 adjust a product line

99

Look at the graphic. Which item will be available in two sizes?

(A) All-Day Glow
(B) Express Cleanser
(C) Moisture Bomb
(D) Night Repair

시각 정보에 의하면, 어떤 품목이 두 가지 용량으로 판매될 것인가?
(A) 올데이 글로우
(B) 익스프레스 클렌저
(C) 모이스처 밤
(D) 나이트 리페어

해설 시각 정보 연계 – 두 가지 용량으로 판매될 품목

지문의 중반부에서 제품 중 두 번째로 많이 팔리는 제품을 앞으로 2온스와 4온스의 두 용량으로 판매할 것(We're also going to start offering our second-best seller in a two-ounce and four-ounce size)이라고 말했고 시각 정보에 따르면 두 번째로 많이 팔리는 제품은 Moisture Bomb이므로 정답은 (C)이다.

100

What most likely is Ms. Fitzgerald's occupation?

(A) Researcher
(B) Market analyst
(C) Actress
(D) Photographer

피츠제럴드 씨의 직업은 무엇이겠는가?
(A) 연구원
(B) 시장 분석가
(C) 여배우
(D) 사진작가

어휘 occupation 직업 market 시장 analyst 분석가

해설 세부 사항 관련 – 피츠제럴드 씨의 직업

지문의 후반부에서 변화에 박차를 가하기 위해 소피 피츠제럴드 씨를 우리 광고의 얼굴로 영입했고(To promote the changes, we've secured Sophie Fitzgerald as a spokesperson for our commercials) 영화의 인기와 높은 인지도로(With her popular films and strong name recognition) 그녀의 참여는 우리 회사에 큰 힘을 실어줄 것(her involvement could give a major boost to our company)이라고 말했으므로 정답은 (C)이다.

▸▸ **Paraphrasing** 지문의 her popular films → 정답의 Actress